*i*performance
series

MACROMEDIA®
DREAMWEAVER
DESIGN & APPLICATION
MX 2004

John Marshall Baker

EMCParadigm
PUBLISHING

Senior Editor	Christine Hurney
Cover and Text Designer	Leslie Anderson
Desktop Production	John Valo, Desktop Solutions
Copy Editor	Julie McNamee
Proofreading	Sharon O'Donnell
Indexer	Larry Harrison

Publishing Management Team

George Provol, Publisher; Janice Johnson, Director of Product Development; Tony Galvin, Acquisitions Editor; Lori Landwer, Marketing Manager; Shelley Clubb, Electronic Design and Production Manager

Acknowledgments

The author and publisher wish to thank the following reviewers for their technical and academic assistance in testing exercises and assessing instruction:
- Janet Blum, Fanshawe College, London, Ontario
- Susan Lynn Bowen, Valdosta Technical College, Valdosta, GA
- Stoney Gaddy, Independence Community College, Independence, KS
- Denise Seguin, Fanshawe College, London, Ontario
- Jon Storslee, Ph.D., Paradise Valley Community College, Phoenix, AZ

Library of Congress Cataloging-in-Publication Data

Baker, John Marshall, 1954-
   Macromedia ® Dreamweaver MX 2004 : design and application / John Marshall Baker.
            p. cm. – (iperformance series)
      ISBN 0-7638-1985-9
      1. Dreamweaver (Computer file) 2. Web sites—Design. I. Title. II. Series.

   TK5105.8885.D74B33 2005
   005.7'2—dc21

                                          2003051441

ISBN: 0-7638-1985-9
CN: 05609

© 2005 by Paradigm Publishing Inc.
      Published by **EMC**Paradigm
      875 Montreal Way
      St. Paul, MN 55102

      (800) 535-6865
      E-mail: educate@emcp.com
      Web site: www.emcp.com

CONTENTS

Preface   vii

Chapter 1
Dreamweaver MX 2004 Fundamentals 1

Advantages and Key Features of
Dreamweaver MX 2004 2
Starting Dreamweaver MX 2004 3
Dreamweaver MX 2004 Hands-On
Demonstration 4
The Dreamweaver MX 2004 Workspace 6
The Dreamweaver MX 2004 Environment 9
   Start Page 9
   Document Window 10
   Menu Bar 10
     Using the Site Menu Bar Command to
      Create a Dreamweaver Site 11
     Using the File Menu Bar Command to
      Create and Save a New Document 14
     Using the File Menu Bar Command to
      Open and Work with Design Files 16
   Title Bar 18
   Status Bar 18
     Tag Selector 19
     Window Size Indicator 21
     Document Size/Estimated Download
      Time Indicator 21
   Document Toolbar 21
   Insert Bar 24
   Standard Toolbar 27
   Vertical and Horizontal Panels 28
Using the Integrated File Browser to Locate and
Work with Files 32
Using the Help System 34
   Using Dreamweaver (Dreamweaver Help) 35
   Dreamweaver Tutorials 37
   Dreamweaver Support Center 37
   Macromedia Online Forums 37
   Context-Sensitive Help 41
Chapter Summary *42*
Key Terms *43*
Commands Review *46*
Concepts Check *46*
Skills Check *47*

Chapter 2
Creating a Basic Web Page 51

Previewing Pages in a Browser 52
   Browser Preview Preferences 52
   Temporary Files 53
Checking Browser Compatibility 54
Ensuring Accessibility 57
Entering Text 58
   Typing Text 58
   Opening Documents Directly 58
   Copying and Pasting 60
   Copying and Pasting Microsoft Word and
     Excel Document Content 63
   Importing Documents 65
Changing Text Properties with the Property
   Inspector 65
   Format 66
   Font 66
   Style 68
   Size 68
   Text Color 68
   Text Alignment 69
Setting Background and Text Color Defaults 70
Using the Assets Panel 74
Inserting Links 76
   Using the Property Inspector to Insert
     Links 78
   Using the Menu Bar to Insert Links 79
   Using the Insert Bar to Insert Links 79
   Using the Context-Sensitive Menu to
     Insert Links 80
     Internal (Anchor) Links 82
     E-mail Links 84
     Checking and Repairing Links 86
     Changing Link Colors 88
     Editing and Removing Links 88
Creating Lists 89
Finding and Replacing Text and Code 91
Checking Spelling 93
Using the History Panel 95
Inserting Comments 98
Using Meta Tags 99
Chapter Summary *101*
Key Terms *103*
Commands Review *106*
Concepts Check *106*
Skills Check *107*

Chapter 3
Working with Tables · 111

Understanding Tables	112
Table Components	112
Table Dimensions	113
Table Code	114
Using Tables to Control Page Layout	115
Creating Tables	117
Selecting Table Elements	122
Tables	122
Cells	123
Rows and Columns	124
Nonadjacent Cells	124
Navigating in Tables	125
Tab Keys	125
Arrow Keys	126
Using the Property Inspector to Format Tables and Table Cells	127
Table Property Inspector	127
Table Cell Property Inspector	129
Adding and Deleting Rows and Columns	131
Creating Nested Tables	134
Using the Format Table Command to Format Tables	137
Creating Tables in Layout Mode	139
Drawing Tables and Cells	140
Selecting, Moving, and Resizing Layout Tables and Cells	141
Using Autostretch	142
Adding Spacer Images	142
Using a Grid	146
Sorting Table Content	148
Chapter Summary	*150*
Key Terms	*153*
Commands Review	*155*
Concepts Check	*156*
Skills Check	*157*

Chapter 4
Working with Images · 161

Understanding Images	162
Inserting Images	164
Ensuring Image Accessibility	167
Inserting Image Placeholders	170
Defining Image Properties	172
Width and Height	173
Image Path	174
Alternate Text	174
CSS Class Style	174
Image Link	175
Horizontal and Vertical Space	175
Target Browser Window	175
Image Border	175
Image Alignment	176
Low Source Image	177
Image Maps and Hotspot Buttons	178
Image Name	179
Image Property Inspector Image Editing Buttons	183
Edit Button	183
Optimize in Fireworks Button	185
Crop Button	187
Resample Button	188
Brightness and Contrast Button	188
Sharpen Button	188
Creating a Page Background Image	190
Creating Table and Table Cell Background Images	192
Applying Behaviors to Images	194
Creating a Web Photo Album	196
Using Tracing Images	200
Using the Assets Panel to Manage Images	203
Favorites List	204
Favorites List Folders	204
Chapter Summary	*207*
Key Terms	*210*
Commands Review	*212*
Concepts Check	*213*
Skills Check	*213*

Chapter 5
Working with Frames · 217

Understanding Frames	218
Creating Framesets and Frames	220
New Framesets	221
Adding Frames to a Frameset	222
Opening Documents in a Frame	223
Changing Frame Document Background Color	224
Saving Framesets and Frames	224
Deleting Framesets and Frames	224
Predefined Framesets	227
Selecting Framesets and Frames	231
Framesets	231
Frames	232
Using the Frameset Property Inspector to Change Frameset Properties	234
Using the Frame Property Inspector to Change Frame Properties	237
Using Links to Change Frame Content	241
Creating Navigation Bars	243
Creating Accessible Frames with Frame Titles and Noframes Content	247
Chapter Summary	*250*
Key Terms	*254*
Commands Review	*255*
Concepts Check	*255*
Skills Check	*256*

Chapter 6
Using Cascading Style Sheets (CSS)   259

Setting the Dreamweaver MX 2004 CSS
   Formatting Default   260
Understanding CSS   260
   CSS Styles   261
   Cascading and Hierarchy   262
Creating a New External Style Sheet   263
   Redefining HTML Tags   264
   Using the CSS Style Definition
     Dialog Box   266
   Attaching an External Style Sheet to a
     Document   267
Grouping Selectors   271
Creating Contextual Selectors   274
Creating Class Styles   275
Modifying Hyperlinks with Pseudo Classes   278
Using Predefined Style Sheets   280
Creating an Internal or Embedded Style Sheet   283
Exporting Styles   285
Editing CSS Styles   287
Removing Styles and Style Sheets   291
Chapter Summary   *294*
Key Terms   *296*
Commands Review   *297*
Concepts Check   *297*
Skills Check   *298*

Chapter 7
Working with Layers   301

Understanding Layers   302
Setting Default Layer Preferences   303
Creating Layers   304
Creating Nested Layers   306
Selecting Layers   308
Moving Layers   309
Resizing Layers   310
Aligning Layers   310
Inserting Content into Layers   312
Using the Layer Property Inspector to Specify
   Layer Properties   314
Adding Behaviors to Layers   317
   Draggable Layers   318
   Pop-up Message Windows   320
   Show-Hide Layers   321
   Go To URL   323
Converting Layers to Tables   325
Chapter Summary   *326*
Key Terms   *328*
Commands Review   *329*
Concepts Check   *329*
Skills Check   *330*

Chapter 8
Using Templates and Library Items   333

Understanding Templates   334
Creating Templates   335
Creating Editable Regions   338
   Editable Regions   338
   Repeating Regions   342
   Repeating Tables   343
Attaching a New Document to a Template   345
Attaching a Template to an Existing Document   348
Creating Editable Tag Attributes   352
Creating Nested Templates   355
Updating Template-Based Documents and
   Detaching Templates from Documents   360
Creating Links in Templates   362
Setting Template Preferences   363
Understanding Library Items   363
   Creating Library Items   364
   Adding Library Items to Documents   364
   Editing Library Items   365
Chapter Summary   *369*
Key Terms   *372*
Commands Review   *373*
Concepts Check   *373*
Skills Check   *374*

Chapter 9
Adding Media Elements   379

Understanding Media Elements   380
   JavaScript   380
   Java Applets   381
   Helper Applications   381
   Plugins and ActiveX Controls   382
Playing Media within Dreamweaver MX 2004   384
Using the Insert Bar Media Button   384
   Flash Media   385
   Flash Buttons   389
   Flash Text   392
   Shockwave   395
   Applets   399
   Parameters   402
   Plugins   404
Adding (Audio) Sound to Web Pages   408
Chapter Summary   *410*
Key Terms   *414*
Commands Review   *415*
Concepts Check   *415*
Skills Check   *416*

Chapter 10
Creating Forms   419

Understanding Forms   420
Planning Forms   421
Creating Forms   422
Creating Text Fields   426
Creating Hidden Fields   431
Creating Check Boxes   432
Creating Radio Buttons   434
Creating Menus and Lists   436
Creating Jump Menus   440
Creating Image Fields   442
Creating File Fields for File Uploads   444
Creating Buttons   445
Applying Labels to Form Objects   446
Understanding the Fieldset Button   446
Attaching the Validate Form Behavior to Forms   447
Chapter Summary   *450*
Key Terms   *453*
Commands Review   *454*
Concepts Check   *454*
Skills Check   *455*

Appendix
Defining a Remote Site and Using
FTP to Upload Web Pages   459

Defining a Remote Site   459
Putting (Uploading) Files   462
Deleting or Removing Files from a Remote Site   463
Changing Files Panel Viewing Preferences   463
Using the Files Panel Site Map   464
Cloaking Folders or File Types   466
Key Terms   *468*
Concepts Check   *468*

Index   469

PREFACE

Macromedia® Dreamweaver MX 2004: Design and Application teaches the essential skills and creative applications made possible using Dreamweaver MX 2004. After completing this book, you will be proficient in creating functional, well-designed Web pages and Web sites. If you are familiar with earlier versions of Dreamweaver, you can use this text to improve your skills and become familiar with the latest features of this software.

This text provides hands-on experience with Dreamweaver MX 2004 as used in a typical Web design environment. After familiarizing yourself with the Dreamweaver MX 2004 environment and mastering the basics of Web page creation, you will learn more advanced skills that allow you quickly to produce professional-looking Web pages.

Design principles and best practices are demonstrated through comprehensive, hands-on practice. A variety of exercise types teach Dreamweaver MX 2004 skills using authentic context and guided practice techniques. Step-by-step exercises are rich with illustrative screen captures and detailed instructions. You will learn the importance of creating accessible pages; accessibility features are explained throughout the book and are included in the step-by-step exercises.

Organization of the Text

Chapter 1, *Dreamweaver MX 2004 Fundamentals,* and Chapter 2, *Creating a Basic Web Page,* introduce you to the Dreamweaver MX 2004 environment and teach the fundamentals of creating a basic HMTL document. Chapter 3, *Working with Tables,* shows you how to use tables for data display and page layout. Chapter 4, *Working with Images,* teaches the skills necessary to add images to HTML documents. In Chapter 5, *Working with Frames*, you learn how to create framesets and frames. Chapter 6, *Using Cascading Style Sheets (CSS),* introduces Cascading Style Sheets (CSS) and shows how to use CSS to exert greater control over page appearance. Chapter 7, *Working with Layers,* covers the use of layers. Chapter 8, *Using Templates and Library Items,* provides instruction on using templates and library items to streamline the Web page creation process. Chapter 9, *Adding Media Elements,* covers media objects, and teaches you how to insert and work with Flash objects, Shockwave movies, Java applets, plugins, ActiveX controls, and sound files. In Chapter 10, *Creating Forms,* you learn about forms, form elements, and form design basics. The Appendix, *Defining a Remote Site and Using FTP to Upload Web Pages,* shows you how to use Dreamweaver MX 2004 to upload files to a server.

To reinforce instruction, each chapter includes an end-of-chapter summary, a list of key terms and definitions, a review of commands, and a short quiz to review important concepts. Skills Check performance assessments at the end of each chapter provide opportunities for you to be creative while designing novel solutions to problems. Using a wide range of project cases, the assessments require you to demonstrate your proficiency with the skills required in the chapter. In these assessments, you create Web pages from scratch and also work with student files provided at this book's Internet Resource Center (IRC). In each chapter, the final performance assessment is a Design Portfolio project. This project is a comprehensive, cumulative experience that showcases your technical and creative abilities.

Student Resources

Extensive exercises provide you with a rich and imaginative learning environment by simulating different Web page design applications. Download student files and exercises model answers for each chapter from this book's Internet Resource Center (IRC) at the EMC/Paradigm Publishing Web site at www.emcp.com. Click College Division, and then click the Internet Resource Centers link in the sidebar.

The student files and intra-chapter exercises model answer files are available for download as ZIP-formatted files. If you do not have software capable of expanding ZIP files installed on your computer, the following programs can be downloaded from the Web:

- WinZip at www.winzip.com (shareware)
- Stuffit Expander at www.stuffit.com/expander (freeware)

For additional links to file-compression utilities you can download and use, visit this book's IRC at www.emcp.com or the Tucows site at www.tucows.com.

See this book's IRC for more pointers and tips on how to download the student files. Ask your instructor for additional help if you still have trouble successfully downloading and expanding them.

Instructor Resources

Instructor resources include teaching hints, model answers, PowerPoint teaching slides, and chapter quizzes. All instructor resources are furnished on both the password-protected instructor pages of the IRC and on the Instructor Resources CD. Copies of the student files are also available on the Instructor Resources CD.

Acknowledgments

This book could not have been written without the assistance of Christine Hurney, Senior Editor at EMC/Paradigm Publishing, and Janet Blum of Fanshawe College in London, Ontario. Ms. Hurney provided valuable editorial skills and management support throughout the project. Ms. Blum tested and retested the exercises until thoroughly fine tuned and proven for classroom success. To both a heartfelt thank you!

CHAPTER 1

DREAMWEAVER MX 2004 FUNDAMENTALS

PERFORMANCE OBJECTIVES

➤ List the advantages of using Dreamweaver MX 2004 for building Web pages and rich Internet applications.

➤ Identify the two Dreamweaver MX 2004 workspace options, differentiate between them, and indicate recommendations for their use.

➤ Identify the key components of the Dreamweaver MX 2004 environment.

➤ Define, edit, and remove Dreamweaver sites.

➤ Use the Dreamweaver MX 2004 Start Page.

➤ Create, open, and save documents.

➤ Open, modify, and save design files.

➤ Use the Tag selector and Quick Tag Editor to modify document content.

➤ Use the Window Size indicator to resize the Document window.

➤ Change the Download Time indicator default connection speed.

➤ Select and work in different Document views.

➤ Use the Insert bar to insert elements and objects into documents.

➤ Open, expand, collapse, undock, dock, and close panels.

➤ Open panel Options menus.

➤ Close and open the panel group interface.

➤ Use the integrated file browser to access and copy desktop and local network files and folders.

➤ Use Dreamweaver help, the Dreamweaver Support Center Web site, and Dreamweaver forums.

➤ Access and use context-sensitive menus and help resource information.

The student files for this chapter are available for download from the Internet Resource Center at www.emcp.com.

Dreamweaver MX 2004 is a powerful, yet easy-to-use, HTML editor for building professional, HTML-based Web sites and rich Internet applications. Dreamweaver MX 2004 features a full range of application tools that allows users to transform their ideas and goals into Web-based reality. Dreamweaver MX 2004 users can hand code, work in a visual editing environment, or combine both methods.

Dreamweaver MX 2004 enhances the user's ability to create and maintain attractive, functional, and professional-looking Web sites.

Advantages and Key Features of Dreamweaver MX 2004

Dreamweaver MX 2004 is an extremely flexible program, allowing users to accomplish tasks in a number of different ways to suit their needs and preferences. Although there are too many Dreamweaver MX 2004 features to list in their entirety, some of the most important are described in the following list.

- **Integrated Environment** Dreamweaver MX 2004 features a fully integrated workspace (Windows version only), with all of the tools needed to build Web pages only a mouse click away. Dreamweaver MX 2004 also allows users to customize many features, including toolbars and panel groups.

- **Dreamweaver MX 2004 Start Page** The Start Page furnishes a convenient method for opening recently used files and creating new files. It also offers users access to a quick tour of Dreamweaver MX 2004 as well as Dreamweaver MX 2004 tutorials.

- **Flexible Visual Environment** Dreamweaver MX 2004 offers a Code view mode, a split Code view/Design view mode, or a WYSIWYG (What You See Is What You Get) Design view mode. This flexibility allows users to develop Web pages in their preferred visual environment.

- **Site Definition Dialog Box** The Site Definition dialog box makes it easy to set up a Dreamweaver site by taking users through all of the necessary steps in creating a site. The Site Definition dialog box has basic and advanced modes to suit user experience levels.

- **Target Browser Checking** The default Dreamweaver MX 2004 setup automatically checks documents for any elements or objects that are not supported by specified target browsers. Browser checking can also be accomplished manually using the Document toolbar Check Target Browsers button.

- **Design Files** Design files are page layout and design element files that allow users to replace placeholder content with their own content, or use the files as starting points for further modification.

- **Templates** Dreamweaver MX 2004 templates speed up the design process and allow the creation of Web pages that let other users input content while preventing them from altering the Web page design. Editable regions can be created to let users input content and make design modifications in specified areas of documents created from templates if desired.

- **Image Placeholders** Image placeholders reserve space for images that can be inserted later. This greatly speeds up the construction process, allowing users to see how a layout will look even before the final images are in place. After the images are ready, users can click image placeholders to open the Select Image Source dialog box that handles all of the steps necessary for inserting images.

- **Automatic Link Updating** Dreamweaver MX 2004 automatically updates links for any files that have been renamed or moved as long as a document is saved in a Dreamweaver site. Developers can choose between having Dreamweaver MX 2004 prompt them when a link needs updating or having Dreamweaver MX 2004 update links automatically.

- **Integrated Image Editing Toolbar** Built-in Fireworks technology allows users to perform basic image editing without the need to open an external image editor.

- **Enhanced CSS Features** Enhanced Cascading Style Sheets (CSS) features such as the CSS Properties tab, CSS layout visualization, and a CSS-based Property inspector facilitate working with CSS.

- **Panels** Tools, menus, and libraries are contained in graphic interfaces known as panels. Panels are bundled together in panel groups that can be arranged to suit user preferences and collapsed so they are out of the way when not needed. Panels and panel groups also can be undocked so they float freely on the page wherever users prefer.

- **Insert Bar** The Insert bar functions as a convenient toolbar for adding elements and objects to a document at the click of a button. Elements and objects are categorized conveniently, and button categories can be configured as menu items or tabs. Clicking a category menu item or tab changes the buttons displayed on the Insert bar.

- **Context-Sensitive Menus** One of the most convenient Dreamweaver MX 2004 features is the ability to bring up context-sensitive menus by right-clicking an object or window in Code, Code and Design, and Design views. Context-sensitive menus display only commands that are relevant to the item selected.

- **Integrated File Browser** The Files panel contains an integrated file browser, allowing users to browse for assets and files without having to exit Dreamweaver MX 2004 to use a stand-alone browser. Using the file browser is easy because it functions like other popular file browsers, such as Windows Explorer.

- **Secure FTP** This feature allows users to use encryption to protect transmitted files from unauthorized access.

- **Help Features** Dreamweaver MX 2004 contains a full range of features to assist users, including online support from the Macromedia Support Center, reference material, help topics, tutorials, and access to online Dreamweaver forums, where Dreamweaver MX 2004 users of all levels can seek assistance and discuss issues with other users.

Starting Dreamweaver MX 2004

To start Dreamweaver MX 2004 in Windows XP:

1. Click Start.
2. Point to Programs.
3. Point to Macromedia.
4. Click Macromedia Dreamweaver MX 2004.

Alternatively, if a shortcut exists on the desktop, double-click the shortcut to launch Dreamweaver MX 2004. To create a desktop shortcut, follow the instructions above, but at Step 4 right-click Macromedia Dreamweaver MX 2004, point to Send To, and then click Desktop (create shortcut). Depending on your system configuration, the steps to start Dreamweaver MX 2004 on the computer you are using might differ. Check with your instructor if necessary.

To exit Dreamweaver MX 2004, click File on the Menu bar and then Exit.

Dreamweaver MX 2004 Hands-On Demonstration

The following demonstration exercise gives you a small taste of some of the many things that Dreamweaver MX 2004 can do. Once you are familiar with Dreamweaver MX 2004 tools and their functions, you will find it easy to create professional-looking Web pages.

exercise 1

CREATING AND WORKING WITH A DREAMWEAVER MX 2004 DOCUMENT

1. Create and edit an HTML document to get an idea of what Dreamweaver MX 2004 can do by completing the following steps:
   a. Use the Windows Explorer file-management program to create and save a folder named Chapter One. *Note: Ask your instructor where the folder should be saved on your computer's hard drive or local network you are using.*
   b. Follow the instructions in the preface of this book to download the ch_01_student_files folder from this book's IRC to the Chapter One folder you created in Step 1a.
   c. Expand the compressed ch_01_student_files folder and save it to the Chapter One folder. Delete the compressed folder when you are finished.
   d. Start Dreamweaver MX 2004.
   e. Look for the Create New column in the center of the Start Page and click *HTML* to create a new HTML document in the Document window. *Note: If the Start Page is not visible, close all open documents until it appears.*

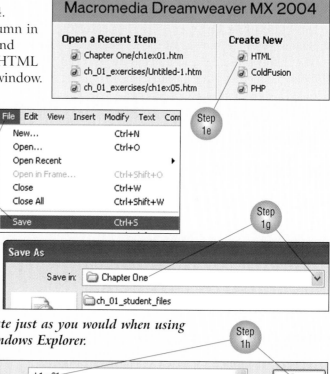

   f. Click File on the Menu bar and then click Save to open the Save As dialog box.
   g. Click the down-pointing arrow to the right of the *Save in* list box and navigate to the Chapter One folder you created in Step 1a. The Chapter One folder should appear in the *Save in* list box. *Hint: You can navigate just as you would when using most file browsers such as Windows Explorer.*

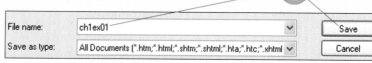

   h. Type ch1ex01 in the *File name* text box and then click the Save button to

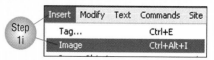

   name and save the document in the Chapter One folder as **ch1ex01.htm**. *Note: Dreamweaver MX 2004 will automatically add the .htm extension to the document name.*
   i. Click Insert on the Menu bar and then Image to open the Select Image Source dialog box.

j. Click the down-pointing arrow to the right of the *Look in* list box and navigate to the ch_01_student_files folder you placed in the Chapter One folder. When you are finished, the ch_01_student_files folder should appear in the *Look in* list box, and the **emcp** file will appear in the large white space just below the *Look in* list box.

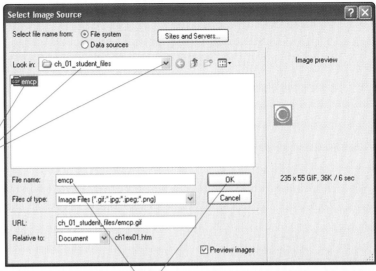

k. Click *emcp* so that the file name appears in the Select Image Source dialog box *File name* text box, and then click the OK button to insert the image into **ch1ex01.htm**.

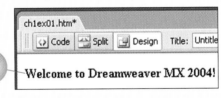

l. Position the mouse pointer to the left of the image and then click to place the insertion point in that location.

m. Press Enter four times to move the image down to the center of the Document window.

n. Click the image to select it, and then click the Align Center button in the Property inspector to align the image in the center of the document.

o. Place the insertion point in the upper-left corner of the document and type Welcome to Dreamweaver MX 2004!

p. Click the Property inspector Align Center button to align the text in the center of the document.

q. Click the Insert bar down-pointing arrow and select Text from the menu that appears to display the Insert bar text buttons.

r. Click the Insert bar h1 button to change the text into larger heading text. *Note: The insertion point must be on the same line as the text.*

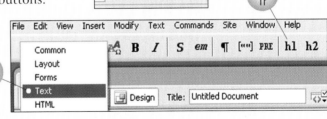

s. Click Modify on the Menu bar and then Page Properties to open the Page Properties dialog box.

t. Locate the *Background color* color box and click it to open the Color Picker. Use the eyedropper that appears to hover over the Color Picker colors. Note that hexadecimal values for the colors appear at the top of the Color Picker (for example, #00FF00). Move the eyedropper over the yellow color boxes in the Color Picker until you see #FFFF66 at the top of the Color Picker. Click the mouse button when you have located it. Click the OK button to close the Page Properties dialog box and apply the background color you just selected.

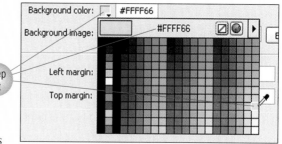

u. Place the insertion point in the *Title* text box on the Document toolbar and drag it over the *Untitled Document* text to select it.

v. Type **Dreamweaver MX 2004 Hands-On Demonstration** in the *Title* text box.

w. Click File on the Menu bar and then Save to save the changes to the document that you have made.

x. Click the Preview/Debug in browser button on the Document toolbar and then click Preview in iexplore to preview your document in a browser. Internet Explorer will open and display the document you just created. The image will be animated because it is an animated GIF (Graphics Interchange Format) file. Note that the blue Title bar at the very top of the browser window displays the title of the document. ***Note: You do not have to be connected to the Internet to view the page.***

y. Click File and then Close to close the browser.

z. Click File and then Close to close **ch1ex01.htm**.

The Dreamweaver MX 2004 Workspace

The first time Dreamweaver MX is opened, the Workspace Setup dialog box appears as shown in Figure 1.1. This dialog box allows users to choose between the Designer and Coder workspaces.

- **Dreamweaver MX 2004 Designer Workspace** The *Dreamweaver MX 2004 Designer workspace* contains all Document windows and panels integrated in a single application window as shown in Figure 1.2. Panel groups are located on the right side of the window. This workspace is recommended unless users plan to frequently work in code.

- **Dreamweaver MX 2004 Coder Workspace** The *Dreamweaver MX 2004 Coder workspace* also features an integrated workspace, but in the layout style used by Macromedia HomeSite and Macromedia ColdFusion Studio as shown in Figure 1.3. This workspace opens in Code view by default and is recommended for those who prefer to do their own coding.

The exercises in this book assume that the user is using the Designer workspace unless indicated by instructions to the contrary. To use the Designer workspace, make sure that the Workspace Setup dialog box *Designer* radio button is selected, and then click the OK button. Once a workspace has been selected, it can be changed using the Preferences dialog box.

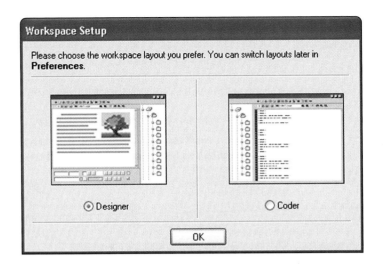

Figure 1.1
Dreamweaver MX 2004
Workspace Setup Dialog Box

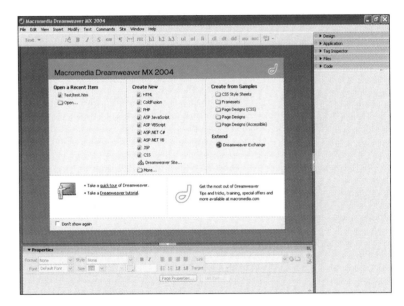

Figure 1.2
Dreamweaver MX 2004
Designer Workspace

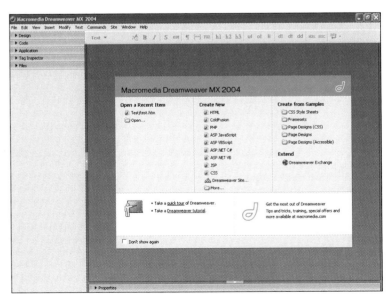

Figure 1.3
Dreamweaver MX 2004
Coder Workspace

1. Set Dreamweaver MX 2004 workspace preferences by completing the following steps:
   a. If necessary, start Dreamweaver MX 2004.
   b. At a clear document screen, click Edit on the Menu bar. *Note: A clear document screen means that no documents are open in the Document window. This does not refer to the Start Page, which will automatically close when a document is opened in the Document window.*
   c. Click Preferences on the drop-down menu. The Preferences dialog box appears.
   d. Select *General* (selecting an item highlights it) in the *Category* list box on the left side of the Preferences dialog box, if it is not already selected.

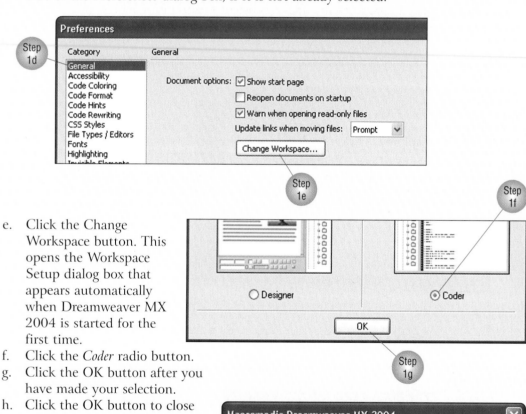

   e. Click the Change Workspace button. This opens the Workspace Setup dialog box that appears automatically when Dreamweaver MX 2004 is started for the first time.
   f. Click the *Coder* radio button.
   g. Click the OK button after you have made your selection.
   h. Click the OK button to close the dialog box advising that Dreamweaver MX 2004 will have to be restarted for the change to take place.
   i. Click the OK button to close the Preferences dialog box.
   j. Close and reopen Dreamweaver MX 2004 to view the Coder workspace.
2. Repeat Steps 1b–1j to reselect the Dreamweaver MX 2004 *Designer* workspace option. *Note: Do not skip this step as the exercises in this book were created using the Dreamweaver MX 2004 Designer workspace.*

The Dreamweaver MX 2004 Environment

The first time you see the Dreamweaver MX 2004 Designer workspace, it will probably seem like a complicated mix of panels, toolbars, and menu bars, as well as some other items you might not be familiar with. Identifying and understanding the different workspace features is one of the first steps in making sense of the Dreamweaver MX 2004 workspace. Figure 1.4 identifies the key components of the Dreamweaver MX 2004 workspace. You can always identify a button by moving the mouse pointer over it, which causes a small identification box *(tooltip)* to pop up as shown in Figure 1.5.

Start Page

The **Start Page** shown in Figure 1.4 provides a shortcut method for opening previously used documents or for creating new documents. The Start Page also contains hyperlinks that can be clicked to provide a quick tour of Dreamweaver MX 2004 or easy access to Dreamweaver MX 2004 tutorials. Users must be connected to the Internet in order to take the tour. The Start Page appears in the Document window area when Dreamweaver MX 2004 is first started, or when there are no documents open in the Document window.

A list of recently used documents will appear in the Start Page under the Open a Recent Item column. Clicking a document title opens it in the Document window. New documents can be created by clicking the desired document type under the Create New column. Documents can be created from sample documents by clicking the desired sample type under the Create from Samples column.

The Start Page is an alternative to using Menu bar commands to open or create documents, as will be described later in this chapter. It can be disabled by clicking the *Don't show again* check box in the lower-left corner of the Start Page. To reenable the Start Page, click Edit on the Menu bar and then Preferences to

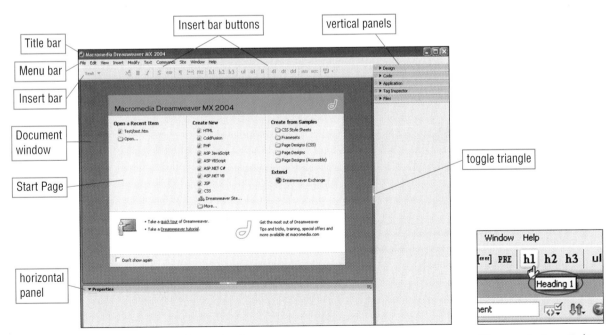

Figure 1.4 • Workspace Identification

Figure 1.5 • Tooltip

open the Preferences dialog box. Select *General* from the *Category* list box and then at the top of the *Document options* list, click the *Show Start Page* check box so that a check mark appears in the check box.

Document Window

The **Document window** is the workspace area where Dreamweaver MX 2004 documents appear on the screen. Documents appear in maximized form by default. When documents are maximized, only one document is visible in the Document window, but each open document will be indicated by a **document tab** appearing at the top of a document as shown in Figure 1.6. Document tabs for unsaved documents will display the word *untitled,* followed by a number reflecting the order in which the untitled document was created. Once a document has been named and saved, its document tab will display the document name and extension, such as index.htm, or arial.css. The document tab for the document appearing in the window (the current document) has a light gray background with black text, whereas the document tabs for documents that are open but not visible in the window have a dark gray background with white text, as shown in Figure 1.6. Clicking a document tab displays the document in the window.

Maximized documents cannot be moved in the Document window, but clicking the unnamed button located between the Minimize and Close buttons on a document's toolbar as shown in Figure 1.7 reduces the size of the document in the Document window. The document then can be moved around the Document window by clicking and holding down the mouse button inside the document's blue Title bar area to drag the document, and the document's borders can be resized by placing the insertion point on any border or corner until a diagonal, vertical, or horizontal *resize arrow* appears, as shown in Figure 1.8. A more precise method of adjustment can be made using the Window Size indicator as described in the "Status Bar" section of this chapter. A document can be restored to its former dimensions by clicking the same button again, which the tooltip now identifies as the **Restore button**.

Menu Bar

The **Menu bar** functions like a standard Windows Menu bar, with drop-down menus appearing when you click a Menu bar command. Dreamweaver MX 2004 contains Menu bar command categories for File, Edit, View, Insert, Modify, Text, Commands, Site, Window, and Help as shown in Figure 1.9.

Figure 1.6 • Document Tabs

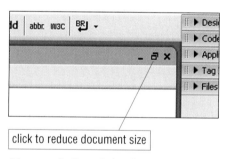

click to reduce document size

Figure 1.7 • Reduce Document Size Button

Figure 1.8
Horizontal Resize Arrow

Figure 1.9
Menu Bar

DREAMWEAVER MX 2004

Using the Site Menu Bar Command to Create a Dreamweaver Site

You should define (create) a local *Dreamweaver site* before you create and save your first document. A Dreamweaver site is a name used within Dreamweaver MX 2004 to identify a root folder on a computer or local network used for storing and organizing all of the documents associated with a Web site. Although it is possible to create Web pages without defining a Dreamweaver site, creating a Dreamweaver site allows you to take advantage of features such as automatic link updating, file management, and file sharing.

You should locate all Dreamweaver sites in one location on a computer or local network. For example, different root folders for different Web sites might be located under a folder named Sites, such as C:\Sites\root_folder1, C:\Sites\root_folder2, and so on.

You also should give lowercase names for all Web site files, including the root folder. Although Windows does not distinguish between uppercase and lowercase names for files, many servers do. Consistently using lowercase when naming files avoids any potential recognition problems when files are uploaded. File names should not contain any spaces; however, a hyphen (-) or an underscore (_) can be used to connect words in a file name.

There are two types of sites: local and remote. A *local site* is where users work on and test their Web site before placing it on a server. At a later point, a *remote site* can be defined. A remote site is a copy of the local site that has been placed on a server so that it can be viewed by others.

Clicking Site on the Menu bar and then clicking Manage Sites on the drop-down menu opens the Manage Sites dialog box. Clicking New and then Site in the Manage Sites dialog box opens the *Site Definition dialog box* as shown in Figure 1.10. The Site Definition dialog box takes you through all of the steps involved in defining a Dreamweaver site. You can use the Site Definition dialog

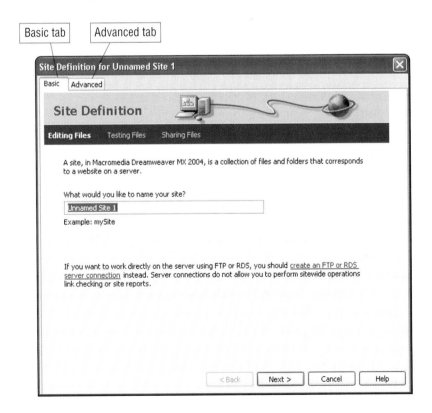

Figure 1.10
Site Definition Dialog Box

box in either Basic or Advanced modes by clicking the appropriate tab as shown in Figure 1.10. You also can switch back and forth between Basic and Advanced modes to define or edit a site when using the Site Definition dialog box.

    After a site has been created, you can edit or remove it by clicking Site on the Menu bar and then clicking Manage Sites. The Manage Sites dialog box will display all of the sites that have been defined. Clicking a site name and then clicking the Edit button opens the Site Definition dialog box, which can be used to edit the selected site.

exercise 3

USING THE SITE DEFINITION DIALOG BOX TO CREATE A DREAMWEAVER SITE

1. Create a Dreamweaver site by completing the following steps:

   a. At a clear document screen, click Site on the Menu bar.

   b. Click Manage Sites on the drop-down menu.

   c. Click the New button at the top of the Manage Sites dialog box and then click Site from the menu that appears. The Site Definition dialog box will open.

   d. Type **CH 01 Exercises** in the *What would you like to name your site?* text box, and then click the Next button. **Note: Site names are not viewed by browsers or Web servers, so they can be in uppercase, contain spaces, and use special characters (/, | , and so on). However, because all of the documents contained in your site will eventually be viewed by browsers and Web servers, names for root folders, subfolders, and files should be in lowercase and not contain any special characters. To separate words in file names, use an underscore (_) instead of a space.**

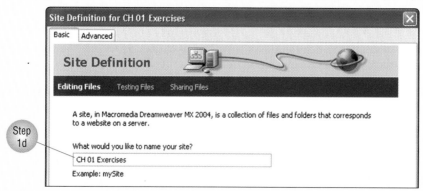

   e. Select the *No, I do not want to use a server technology.* radio button and then click the Next button. **Note: Server technologies are used when creating dynamic pages that work with databases.**

DREAMWEAVER MX 2004

f. Select the *Edit local copies on my machine, then upload to server when ready (recommended)* radio button unless your instructor specifies otherwise. Move down to the lower portion of the dialog box, and click the Browse for File button located next to the text box. This opens the Choose local root folder for site dialog box.

> How do you want to work with your files during development?
>
> ⊙ Edit local copies on my machine, then upload to server when ready (recommended)
> ○ Edit directly on server using local network
>
> **Step 1f**
>
> Where on your computer do you want to store your files?
>
> C:\Documents and Settings\ed\My Documents\CH 01 Exercises \

g. Create a folder named Sites that you will use to store your Dreamweaver site root folders by clicking the *Select* list box down-pointing arrow to browse to the location on your computer where you want to keep the folder (for example, on your hard drive C),

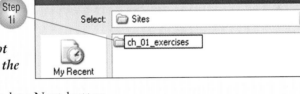

and then clicking the Create New Folder button to create a new folder. Click inside the highlighted text inside the folder name box and type **Sites** to rename the folder. ***Hint: If the folder name is not highlighted, right-click the folder and then click Rename from the context-sensitive menu that appears.***

h. Double-click the Sites folder to place it in the *Select* list box.

i. Click the Create New Folder button again, and create a root folder by typing **ch_01_exercises** in the folder name box. Double-click the folder name to place it in the *Select* list box and then click the Select button to close the dialog box. ***Hint: Root folder names do not have to be the same as site names.***

> **Step 1i**
>
> Choose local root folder for site CH 01 Exercises :
>
> Select: ☐ Sites
>
> ☐ ch_01_exercises
>
> My Recent

j. Click the Site Definition dialog box Next button.

k. Click the down-pointing arrow next to the *How do you connect to your remote server?* list box and then click *None* from the connection method list. Click the Next button. ***Note: When you are ready to publish your site, you can return to the Site Definition dialog box to specify remote server details as described in the appendix.***

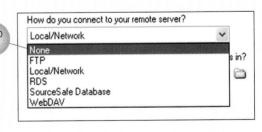

> How do you connect to your remote server?
>
> Local/Network
>
> **Step 1k**
>
> None
> FTP
> Local/Network
> RDS
> SourceSafe Database
> WebDAV

l. Click the Done button if the summary detailing all of the settings you selected is correct. If not, click the Back button until you come to the settings that need to be changed. You can make any changes necessary and proceed as you did previously. Click the Done button when you are finished.

m. Click the Manage Sites dialog box Done button to close the dialog box.

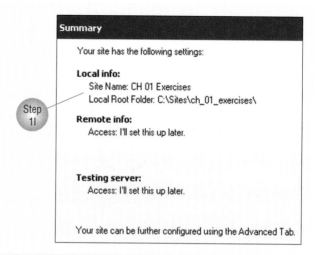

Using the File Menu Bar Command to Create and Save a New Document After a Dreamweaver site has been defined, you are ready to create and work with documents. Clicking File on the Menu bar and then clicking New on the drop-down menu brings up the New Document dialog box shown in Figure 1.11. Clicking a category type from the dialog box *Category* list box changes the content of the list box on the right to show the different document types available under that category. The *Preview* box provides a sample view of the document selected, and below that, a *Description* box provides further details about the document type. You choose a document type by selecting it. Clicking the Create button creates the document in the Document window. New documents can be saved using the Save or Save As commands.

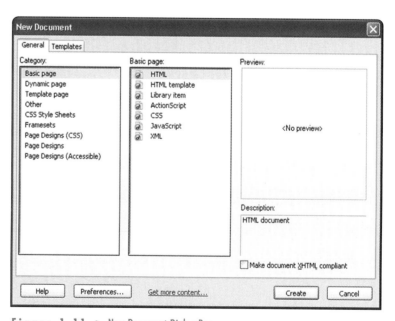

Figure 1.11 • New Document Dialog Box

DREAMWEAVER MX 2004

1. Create a new HTML document by completing the following steps:
   a. At a clear document screen, click File on the Menu bar and then click New on the drop-down menu. The New Document dialog box appears.
   b. Select *Basic page* in the *Category* list box if it is not already selected. ***Note: Make sure the General tab is selected***.

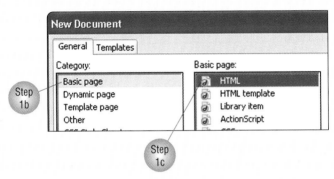

c. Select *HTML* in the *Basic page* list box on the right side of the dialog box if it is not already selected.
   d. Click the dialog box Create button to create the document in the Document window.
2. Save a new document by completing the following steps:
   a. Click File on the Menu bar and then click Save on the drop-down menu. Because you are saving a new document, the Save As dialog box appears.
   b. Click the *Save in* list box down-pointing arrow to browse and locate the site where you want to save your new document. ***Note: Save this document and future exercise documents created for this chapter in the ch_01_exercises root folder you created in Exercise 3.***

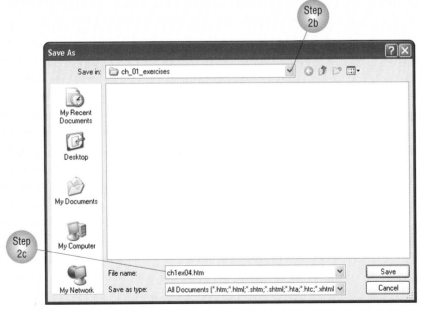

c. Type **ch1ex04.htm** in the *File name* text box. The .htm extension is added automatically, even if you type over the .htm extension in the *File name* text box. *Note: You might notice that some Web page documents have .htm extensions while others have .html extensions. With one exception, the only difference between the two is the "l" in .html—otherwise they function identically. The one exception is that some servers are set to recognize index documents with only .html extensions.*

d. Click the Save button when you are finished. *Hint: After a document has been saved, clicking Save on the Menu bar will save the document without bringing up the Save As dialog box. Save documents frequently to avoid losing your work.*

e. Click File on the Menu bar and then click Close to close the document.

Using the File Menu Bar Command to Open and Work with Design Files Dreamweaver MX 2004 offers a number of different document types (HTML, CSS, XML, and so on), sorted by category. You can start with the default HTML page, or start by working with another type of document, including *design files* with predefined *placeholder content* that can be modified to suit your preferences. Table 1.1 summarizes the different kinds of documents to choose from. The first time Dreamweaver MX 2004 is started, the *Basic page* category is selected in the New Document dialog box by default. The next time Dreamweaver MX 2004 is started, the default category and page will be the last one you selected.

Table 1.1 • New Document Dialog Box Document Types

Category	Examples	Description
Basic page	HTML, CSS, JavaScript	The most commonly used document types
Dynamic page	ASP JavaScript, ColdFusion, PHP	Web pages for use with server-side scripting in databases
Template page	ASP JavaScript Template, ColdFusion Template, PHP Template	Templates that protect page design in a number of different languages
Other	ActionScript communicator, Text, XML	Text-based documents
CSS Style Sheets	Basic: Arial; Forms: Arial; Full Design: Accessible	A variety of preformatted style sheets that can be linked to any number of Web pages to control page formatting
Framesets	Fixed Bottom, Fixed Top, Split Horizontal	Predefined framesets; each frameset containing two or more individual documents
Page Designs (CSS)	Halo Left Nav, Halo Right Nav, Three-column Left Nav	Predesigned, customizable, CSS-linked page layouts
Page Designs	Commerce: Product Catalog A; Image: Slide Show; Data: Figures List	Predesigned, customizable page layouts
Page Designs (Accessible)	Commerce: Product Catalog A; Image: Slide Show; Data: Figures List	Same as *Page Designs* document type, but including accessibility features for those with disabilities

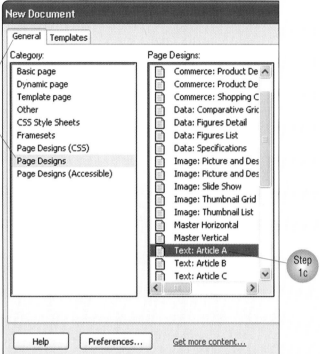

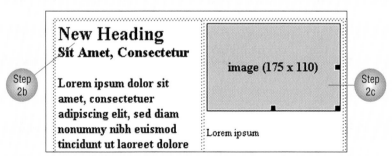

1. Create a design file by completing the following steps:

   a. At a clear document screen, click File on the Menu bar and then click New on the drop-down menu. The New Document dialog box appears.

   Step 1b

   b. Select *Page Designs* from the *Category* list box. ***Note: Make sure the General tab is selected.***

   c. Select *Text: Article A* from the *Page Designs* list box.

   Step 1c

   d. Click the Create button to create the **Text: Article A** document in the Document window. The predesigned page contains an image placeholder and Latin placeholder text in a three-column layout.

   e. Maximize the Document window by clicking the Restore button on the document Title bar if it is not maximized. ***Note: Dreamweaver MX 2004 remembers your preferences, so the next time you start Dreamweaver MX 2004, the Document window will be maximized***.

   Step 1e

2. Modify a design file by completing the following steps:

   a. Open the **Text: Article A** document in the Document window if it is not already open.

   b. Select the heading text at the top of the left column *(Lorem Ipsum Dolor)* and type New Heading. ***Note: You can select words easily by double-clicking inside the word or select multiple words by clicking and dragging across the words.***

   Step 2b

   c. Select the image placeholder.

   Step 2c

   d. Right-click in the image placeholder and select Copy from the context-sensitive menu.

   e. Scroll down the center column and position the insertion point just after the period following the word *volutpat* at the end of the text.

f.   Press Enter once to move the insertion point down two lines. *Note: When the Enter key is pressed, Dreamweaver MX 2004 creates a paragraph HTML tag (<p>), which automatically creates a space between the preceding paragraph and the next one. Holding down the Shift key while pressing the Enter key instructs Dreamweaver MX 2004 to use a line break tag (<br>) instead, which moves the insertion point down one line only.*

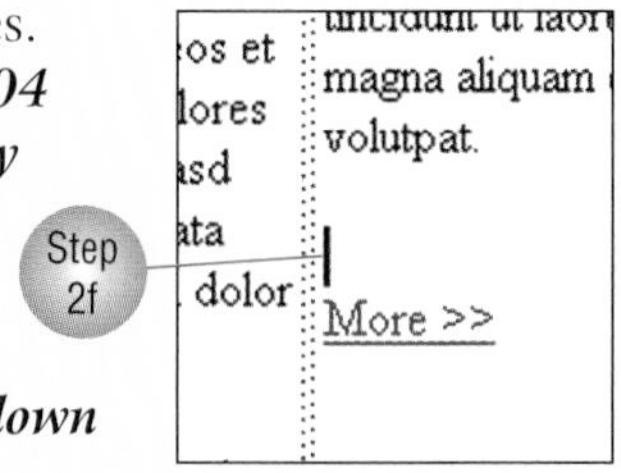

g.   Right-click and select Paste from the context-sensitive menu to insert a duplicate of the image placeholder at the insertion point location.

3.   Use the Save As command to name the file **ch1ex05.htm** and save it. Do not close the document.

Title Bar

The *Title bar* displays a document's title, folder location, and file name. Figure 1.12 shows the Title bar from a newly created document. The document number would be higher than 1 if other new documents had been opened during the current Dreamweaver MX 2004 session. "Untitled Document" means that the document has not been given a title, while "Untitled-1" means that the document has not been named. The document's folder location is not displayed because the document has not been saved. After a document is given a title and a file name and is saved, the Title bar will display the title of the document, its root folder, and its file name as shown in Figure 1.13.

Status Bar

The *Status bar* is located at the bottom of the workspace and contains the Tag selector, Window Size indicator, and Document Size/Estimated Download Time indicator as shown in Figure 1.14.

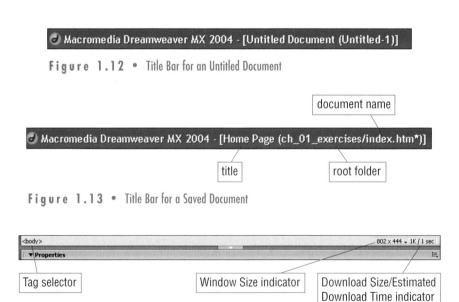

Figure 1.12 • Title Bar for an Untitled Document

Figure 1.13 • Title Bar for a Saved Document

Figure 1.14 • Status Bar

DREAMWEAVER MX 2004

Tag Selector The tags displayed in the *Tag selector* are the HTML tags related to the content at the location of the insertion point (cursor location) in the Document window. Clicking a tag selects the page elements or objects it controls on the document page, either by highlighting or outlining them in black. The Tag selector can be used the other way around as well—selecting a page element, object, or page in the Document window will display the tags controlling those items in the Tag selector.

In addition to helping you understand the relationship between tags and the visual elements of a document when working on complicated bits of code such as nested tables, the Tag selector also serves several other functions as described in the following paragraphs.

Deleting a tag in the Tag selector deletes any page content controlled by that tag. For example, deleting a body or table tag deletes any content appearing between those paired tags.

The Tag selector also allows users to use the **Quick Tag Editor** to edit code without leaving Design view. Right-clicking a tag in the Tag selector area brings up a context-sensitive menu with several functions, including Remove Tag and Edit Tag. Clicking Edit Tag allows users to edit a tag using the Quick Tag Editor as pictured in Figure 1.15. You can press the Tab key to move between the different tag attributes and values, which can then be changed.

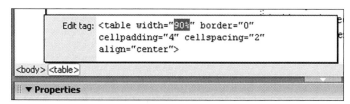

Figure 1.15 • Quick Tag Editor

WORKING WITH THE TAG SELECTOR AND QUICK TAG EDITOR

1. Use the Tag selector to observe the relationship between a tag and the content it controls by completing the following steps:
   a. With **ch1ex05.htm** open in the Document window, use the Save As command to rename the document **ch1ex06.htm** and then save it.
   b. Position the insertion point in the white space area between the two boxes titled *News* in the third column.
   c. Click <table> in the Tag selector. The entire document will be outlined in black. This reveals that this table tag controls the table used to contain the page content of this document.

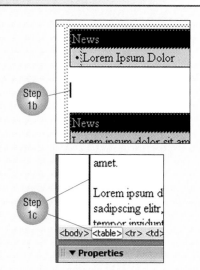

d. Click <td> in the Tag selector. The third column will now be outlined in black, indicating that this tag controls the third column.

2. Use the Quick Tag Editor to change a column width by completing the following steps:

   a. Right-click <td> in the Tag selector and select Edit Tag from the context-sensitive menu that appears.

   b. Change the width value from 30% to 20% in the Quick Tag Editor appearing at the bottom of the screen by selecting and typing over the previous value. Click inside the document when you are finished. The right column now appears reduced in width.

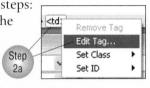

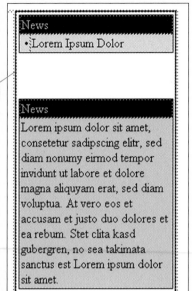

Edit tag: `<td width="20%" valign="top">`

Step 2b

3. Use the Quick Tag Editor to change the dimensions of an image placeholder by completing the following steps:

   a. Click the image placeholder located at the top of the second column.

   b. Right-click <img> in the Tag selector and select Edit Tag.

   c. Change the image width from 175 to 150. Click inside the document when you are finished. The image placeholder is now reduced in width and the new dimensions are indicated inside the image placeholder.

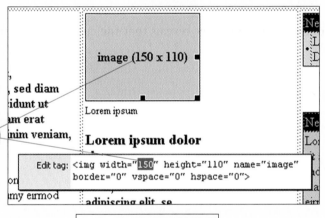

Edit tag: `<img width="150" height="110" name="image" border="0" vspace="0" hspace="0">`

4. Use the Tag selector to delete a column by completing the following steps:

   a. Position the insertion point to the right of the words *Lorem ipsum* located just below the uppermost image placeholder in the middle column.

   b. Click <td> in the Tag selector.

   c. Press the Delete or Backspace keys to delete the column. The second column disappears, leaving a two-column document. ***Note: If you delete something in a document and then change your mind, click Edit on the Menu bar and then click Undo Delete.***

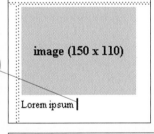

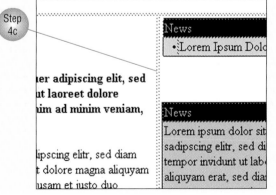

5. Save **ch1ex06.htm** but do not close it.

Window Size Indicator The **Window Size indicator** (not available in Code view) displays the Document window's dimensions in pixels. The window size dimensions can be changed so you can see how a page will look with different window size settings, but the dimension settings do not control the size of a document.

Window size dimensions can be changed by clicking the down-pointing arrow. This opens a drop-down menu with a number of different monitor dimensions. The first set of pixel dimensions are the inside dimensions of the browser window, while the second set in parentheses describes the monitor size. Clicking the desired dimension will resize the Document window. If the Document window is maximized, you must click the unnamed middle button on the document Title bar before you can use the Window Size indicator to change its dimensions. You can customize window dimensions by selecting Edit Sizes from the drop-down menu and then entering new values and a description for the new dimensions you enter.

Document Size/Estimated Download Time Indicator The **Document Size/Estimated Download Time indicator** is located on the Status bar to the right of the Window Size indicator. This indicator estimates the size of the current document as well as the time needed to load it and all linked objects, such as images and plug-ins. For example, a Document Size/Estimated Download Time indicator of 4 KB/2 sec reveals that the current document is 4 kilobytes in size and would take an estimated 2 seconds to download at the connection speed specified under Preferences.

The Download Time indicator default setting is set at 56.0 Kbps (Kilobits per second). Change the default connection speed by completing the following steps:

1. Click Edit on the Menu bar.
2. Click Preferences on the drop-down menu. The Preferences dialog box appears.
3. Select *Status Bar* in the *Category* list box.
4. Locate and select the connection speed you want in the *Connection Speed* drop-down list.
5. Click the OK button to close the Preferences dialog box.

Document Toolbar

The **Document toolbar** contains buttons and drop-down menus for different document-viewing options as well as other common functions, as shown in Figure 1.16. The Document toolbar also contains a text box for the current document title. The document title in Figure 1.16 is *Home Page*. If a title has not been specified for a document, the title will be *Untitled Document*.

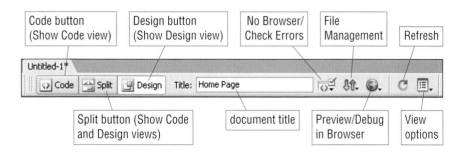

Figure 1.16
Document Toolbar

Three different *Document views* are available on the Document toolbar: Code view, Code and Design views, and Design view. Document views can be changed by clicking the desired document view button. Some document types can appear only in Code view, such as CSS pages, while others, such as HTML pages, can appear in all three views. If a Document view is not available for a document type, its button will be faded.

Dreamweaver MX 2004 automatically opens documents in either Code view or Design view depending on the type of document. Dreamweaver MX 2004 also remembers user choices. For example, the first time you open a new HTML document, it will appear in Design view. If Code view is later selected, the next time an HTML document is opened, it will appear in Code view.

Code view allows you to work as if you were using a text editor to input code. Not all features are available in Code view, such as behaviors. Code view is for users who prefer coding directly in HTML. Figure 1.17 shows what ch1ex05.htm looks like in Code view.

Design view approximates how a page will appear in a browser. Documents are still fully editable even though their code is hidden. Design view allows you to build complex Web pages without having to be an expert HTML coder.

Code and Design view offers a Document window split horizontally, with Code view visible in the top screen and Design view on the lower screen. If you are comfortable coding in HTML, you might prefer to use this view because you can instantly see how your code will appear in a browser. Even if you have only a basic knowledge of HTML code, you might find this view helpful in some circumstances as a useful way of troubleshooting problems. For example, if something is not working as expected in Design view, switching to Code and Design view allows you to view the underlying code for the problem area. This often provides clues to solving difficulties. Figure 1.18 shows how ch1ex05.htm looks in Code and Design view.

The Document toolbar can be undocked by clicking it and dragging it to the desired location. Double-clicking its Title bar returns the toolbar to its former location.

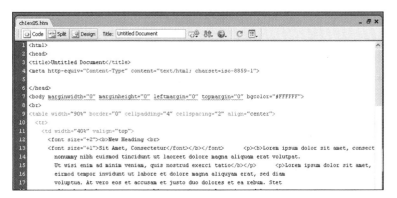

Figure 1.17 • Code View

DREAMWEAVER MX 2004

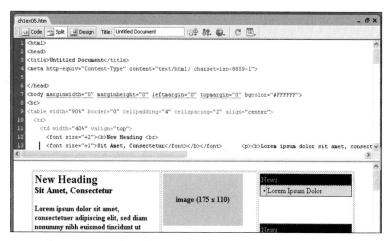

Figure 1.18 • Code and Design View

1. Work in Code view by completing the following steps:
   a. With **ch1ex06.htm** open in the Document window, use the Save As command to rename the document **ch1ex07.htm** and then save it.
   b. Click the Code button on the Document toolbar.

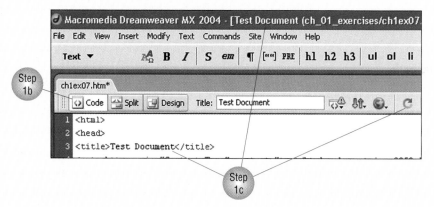

   c. Select *Untitled Document* between the two title tags (**<title>Untitled Document</title>**) and type Test Document over the text. Click the Refresh button on the Document toolbar (or press F5). *Note: The title you just typed now appears in the* Title *text box on the Document toolbar and on the Title bar at the top of the Document window. When the document is viewed in a browser, the title will appear on the browser's Title bar as well. Hint: You might need to scroll up to the top of the screen to see the title tags in Code view.*

2. Work in Code and Design view by completing the following steps:
   a. Click the Split button.
   b. Select the *New Heading* text in the upper portion of the left column in the Design view part of the screen. The corresponding text in the Code view window is now highlighted.
   c. Type Replacement Heading over the selected *New Heading* text while still in the Design view portion of the Document window. You will see the new text appear in the Code view portion of the Document window as you type the text.

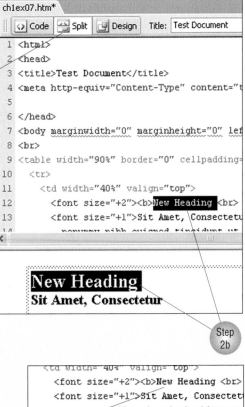

Step 2a

Step 2b

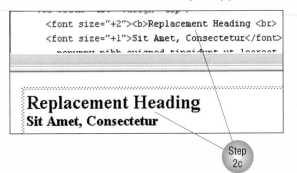

Step 2c

   d. Select *Replacement Heading* in the Code view portion of the Document window and type New Heading (the former heading) over the highlighted text. ***Note: The heading text does not change in the Design view portion of the Document window.***

Step 2d

   e. Click the Refresh button on the Document toolbar to see the changes you just made, or click inside the Design view portion of the Document window.
3. Save **ch1ex07.htm** and then close it.

Insert Bar

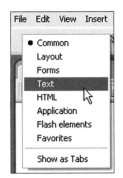

The ***Insert bar*** contains buttons for inserting various elements and objects into a document. Related buttons are grouped into categories, such as Common, Layout, Text, and so on. The Insert bar will be faded and inoperable if no documents are open in the Document window. The different Insert bar categories can be selected by clicking the down-pointing arrow to the left of the Insert bar buttons in the default Dreamweaver MX 2004 setup. This opens a menu as shown in Figure 1.19. Selecting a category changes the buttons that will be displayed to the right of the Insert bar menu. Users can opt to display Insert bar categories as a horizontal series of tabs by clicking Show as Tabs from the Insert bar menu. Clicking a tab changes the buttons displayed on the Insert bar below the tab. Right-clicking a menu item and then clicking Show as Menu from the context-sensitive menu that appears will return the Insert bar categories to their menu form as shown in Figure 1.20. When an object or element that calls for attributes is inserted, users

DREAMWEAVER MX 2004

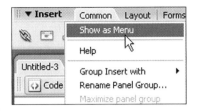

Figure 1.20
Reverting to Insert Bar
Category Menu Display

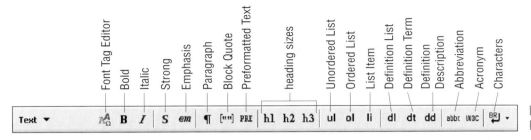

Figure 1.21
Insert Bar Text Buttons

will be prompted to enter the desired attributes. For example, clicking the Table button (Common menu item or tab) brings up a Table dialog box, which can be used to specify the attributes for the table, such as the number of rows and columns. Figure 1.21 shows the different text buttons that are available when the Text menu item or tab is selected. Some Insert bar buttons, such as the Table button, can be activated by clicking and dragging the button to a document. Although referred to as a bar, the Insert bar is actually a horizontal panel, and in tab display mode it can be docked and undocked just like other panels.

Users can save frequently used Insert bar buttons to an Insert bar Favorites category by right-clicking in the button area of any Insert bar category. This opens a context-sensitive menu. Clicking Customize Favorites opens up the Customize Favorite Objects dialog box which can be used to select the buttons that will appear under the Favorites Insert bar category.

exercise 8

USING THE INSERT BAR

1. Use the Insert bar to insert and format text by completing the following steps:
   a. Open **ch1ex04.htm**. Use the Save As command to rename the document **ch1ex08.htm** and then save it.
   b. Click the Design button on the Document toolbar if the document is not in Design view.
   c. Select the Insert bar Text menu item to display the text buttons.

d. Type the following text in the document: The Insert bar is a convenient way of inserting HTML elements and objects into documents.

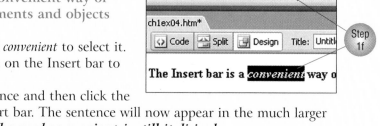

Step 1f

e. Double-click the word *convenient* to select it.
f. Click the Italic button on the Insert bar to italicize *convenient*.
g. Select the entire sentence and then click the h1 button on the Insert bar. The sentence will now appear in the much larger heading style. ***Note: The word*** convenient ***is still italicized.***

Step 1g

2. Add frequently used Insert bar buttons to the Favorites Insert bar category by completing the following steps:
   a. Right-click in the button area of the Insert bar.
   b. Click Customize Favorites from the context-sensitive menu that appears to open the Customize Favorite Objects dialog box.
   c. Click *Hyperlink* from the list box to select it.

Step 2b

Step 2c

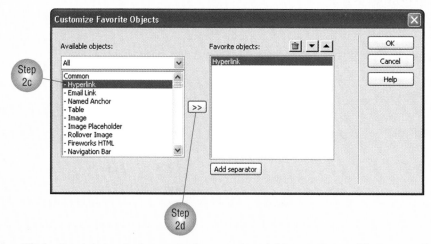

Step 2d

d. Click the right-pointing paired arrow (>>) button located between the *Available objects* and *Favorite objects* list boxes to place *Hyperlink* in the *Favorite objects* list box.
e. Click the OK button to close the dialog box. The Favorites category will now be selected and the Hyperlink button displayed.

Step 2e

DREAMWEAVER MX 2004

f. Follow Steps 2a and 2b to open the Customize Favorite Objects dialog box.

g. Click the Trash Can button to remove *Hyperlink* from the *Favorite objects* list box and then click the OK button to close the dialog box. ***Note: The up- and down-pointing arrow buttons can be used to change the order in which favorites buttons appear if there is more than one button in the* Favorite objects *list box and thus the Favorites Insert bar category.***

3. Save **ch1ex08.htm** and then close it.

Standard Toolbar

The ***Standard toolbar*** as shown in Figure 1.22 contains buttons for creating new files; opening existing files; saving files; saving all files; cutting, copying, and pasting; and undoing and redoing steps. The Standard toolbar is not displayed in the default Dreamweaver MX 2004 workspace. Display the Standard toolbar by completing the following steps:

1. Make sure a document is open in the Document window. If a document is not open you will be unable to activate the Standard toolbar.

2. Click View on the Menu bar.

3. Point to Toolbars on the drop-down menu.

4. A menu appears containing the words *Insert, Document,* and *Standard*. Click *Standard* and then release the mouse button to place a check next to *Standard,* indicating that the Standard toolbar will now be displayed in the workspace. To remove the Insert, Standard, or Document toolbars, repeat these same steps. Clicking *Insert, Document,* or *Standard* will remove the check mark and remove the toolbar from the workspace. ***Note: The exercises in this book assume that the Standard toolbar has been activated and is displayed.***

The Standard toolbar can be undocked (moved from its fixed position) by clicking on its far left side and ***dragging*** it to the desired location. Double-clicking the Standard toolbar Title bar returns the toolbar to its former location.

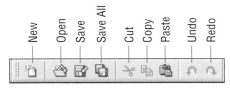

Figure 1.22 • Standard Toolbar

Vertical and Horizontal Panels

Panels provide a graphical interface for many Dreamweaver MX 2004 functions. In the Dreamweaver MX 2004 integrated workspace, most panels are grouped together in *panel groups* positioned vertically on the right side of the workspace. Panels located in panel groups are indicated by panel tabs as shown in Figure 1.23. The Property inspector and Results panel group are positioned horizontally at the bottom of the workspace. As noted earlier, the Insert bar (when in tab display mode) is actually a panel and can be docked and undocked just like any other panel.

The vertical Design, Code, Application, Tag Inspector, and Files panel groups appear in the Dreamweaver MX 2004 layout by default, as does the horizontal Property inspector panel. Other panels and panel groups can be displayed by clicking Window on the Menu bar and then the desired panel or panel group. Clicking a panel will open the panel or the panel group containing the panel.

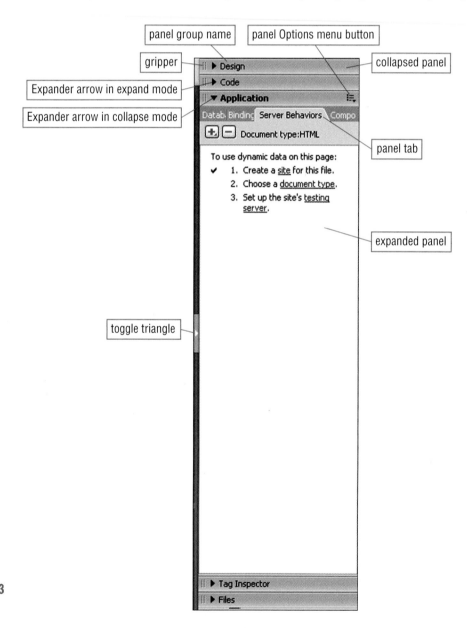

Figure 1.23
Panel Features

Panel groups can be expanded or collapsed, docked or undocked, as well as customized to suit user preferences. You can remove panels from panel groups so that they stand alone, move panels from one panel group to another, or even rename panel groups. Refer to Figure 1.23 when reading the following instructions:

- **Expanding and Collapsing Panel Groups** To expand a collapsed panel group, click the ***Expander arrow*** on the left side of a panel group's Title bar, or double-click the panel group's title. To collapse an expanded panel group, click the down-pointing arrow on an expanded panel group's Title bar.

- **Closing the Entire Panel Group Interface** To close the panel group interface and create more room for documents, click the ***toggle triangle*** located on the vertical bar to the left of the panel groups. To restore the panel groups, click the toggle triangle again.

- **Docking and Undocking Panel Groups** To ***undock*** a panel group, select and drag its ***gripper*** away from the docked position until an outline shows that it is no longer docked. To ***dock*** a panel group, select and move its gripper back into the docking area until the outline appears in the docking area. Panels that have been undocked are referred to as ***floating panels***.

- **Dragging Floating Panels** Undocked panels and panel groups (floating panels) can be moved around the workspace by selecting the blue bar above the panel group's Title bar and dragging the panel to the desired location.

- **Opening the Options Menu** A panel group's Options menu button is visible only when the panel is expanded. Clicking an Options menu button brings up its Options menu as shown in Figure 1.24. Right-clicking a collapsed panel group also brings up a panel group's ***Options menu***.

- **Maximizing a Panel** Maximize a panel group by selecting Maximize panel group from a panel group's Options menu.

- **Selecting (Displaying) a Panel in a Panel Group** Select a panel located within a panel group by clicking the panel's tab.

- **Moving Panels to Another Panel Group** Open the Options menu by clicking the Options menu button, or by right-clicking a panel tab, and selecting Group [name of panel] with. A drop-down menu listing all of the other panel groups appears. Select and click the panel group you want to move the panel to.

- **Moving a Panel to Its Own Panel Group** Open the Options menu by clicking the Options menu button or by right-clicking a panel tab and selecting Group [name of panel] with. Select and click New Panel Group from the drop-down menu that appears. The panel will now appear in its own panel group.

Figure 1.24
Panel Group Options Menu

Dreamweaver MX 2004 Fundamentals

29

- **Closing and Opening a Panel Group** To close a panel group, open the Options menu by clicking the Options menu button or by right-clicking a panel tab and selecting Close panel group. To open a panel group, click Window on the Menu bar, and then click the name of the desired panel or panel group.

- **Grouping a Panel Group with Another Panel Group** Open the Options menu by clicking the Options menu button, or by right-clicking a panel tab, and selecting Group [name of panel group] with. Select and click the name of the panel group you want to group it with from the drop-down menu that appears.

- **Renaming a Panel Group** Open the Options menu by clicking the Options menu button, or by right-clicking a panel tab, and then clicking Rename Panel Group. Type a name for the new panel group in the dialog box, and click the OK button.

exercise 9

WORKING WITH PANELS

1. Open a panel group not displayed in the default Dreamweaver MX 2004 workspace by completing the following steps:
   a. At a clear document screen, click Window on the Menu bar.
   b. Click Frames on the drop-down menu to display the Frames panel. *Note: Some panel group names do not appear on the Window drop-down menu. If you want to open a panel group that does not appear on the Window drop-down menu, you need to click one of the panels that comprise part of the panel group you want to open. For example, clicking CSS Styles or Layers will open the Design panel group that contains both panels.*

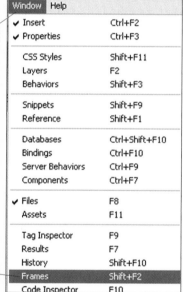
Step 1a
Step 1b

2. Collapse and expand a panel group by completing the following steps:
   a. Click the down-pointing arrow on the Frames panel Title bar to collapse the panel group.

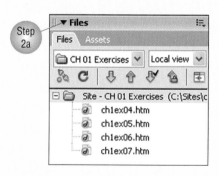
Step 2a

   b. Expand a panel group by clicking the right-pointing Expander arrow on the left side of the Files panel Title bar, or by double-clicking the panel group's Title bar. Contract the expanded panel group by clicking the Expander arrow again.

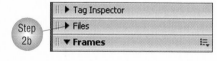
Step 2b

DREAMWEAVER MX 2004

3. Undock and dock the Files panel group by completing the following steps:

a. Hover the mouse pointer over the Files panel group's gripper, and when the Move pointer appears, click and drag the panel group toward the center of the Document window. Release the gripper when you have positioned the panel group where you want it.

Step 3a

b. Move the Files panel group to another location in the Document window by clicking and holding down the mouse button in the empty blue bar above the panel group's Title bar while dragging. *Note: If you move a panel or panel group all of the way to the left of the Document window in the integrated workspace, it will dock. To move the panel or panel group again, you need to click the gripper.*

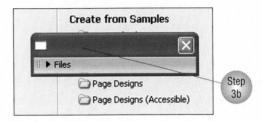

Step 3b

c. Redock the Files panel group by clicking its gripper and holding down the mouse button while sliding it to the right side of the workspace. Release the gripper when an outline of the panel group appears. *Hint: Slide the Move pointer to the right until it disappears over the right side of the screen.*

4. Access a panel's Options menu by completing the following steps:

a. If necessary, expand the Files panel group by clicking the arrow on the left side of its Title bar, or by double-clicking its title.

b. Click the Options menu button and view the Files panel Options menu. Click the Document window to close the Options menu.

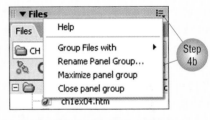

Step 4b

c. Click the Files panel group's Assets tab, and then click its Options menu button to view the Options menu. Click outside the Files panel group to close the Options menu. *Note: Panel Options menu contents will differ because they are context-sensitive.*

5. Close and reopen the Files panel group by completing the following steps:

a. Click the Files panel's Options menu button to view its Options menu.

b. Click Close panel group on the Options menu.

c. Restore the Files panel group by clicking Window on the Menu bar and then clicking Files from the drop-down menu.

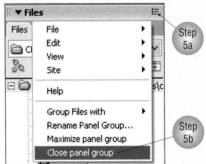

Step 5a

Step 5b

Using the Integrated File Browser to Locate and Work with Files

The Files panel pictured in Figure 1.25 contains an ***integrated file browser*** that provides a convenient way to locate and work with documents. The file browser functions like most popular file browsers, such as Windows Explorer, allowing users to create, copy, rename, move, and delete files and folders.

Files and folders can be managed by right-clicking the desired file or folder, pointing to Edit, and then clicking Cut, Copy, Paste, Delete, Duplicate, or Rename as shown in Figure 1.26. Clicking the down-pointing arrow next to the list box at the top of the Files panel provides access to other locations on your computer or local network, as well as your Dreamweaver sites as shown in Figure 1.27.

The Files panel integrated browser splits into two File view panes when expanded by clicking the Expand/Collapse button shown in Figure 1.28. The right pane displays the contents of the local site and the left pane displays the contents of the remote site or testing server. Clicking the Expand/Collapse button when in expanded view returns the Files panel to its previous size.

In File view, clicking the Minus (–) button located next to a folder closes the folder to hide its contents. The Minus (–) button then changes to a Plus (+) button. Clicking the Plus (+) button displays the folder contents and changes the button back to a Minus (–) button. Files can be deleted by selecting a file or folder and then pressing the Delete key.

Figure 1.25 • Files Panel Integrated File Browser

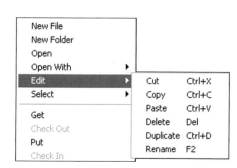

Figure 1.26 • Files Panel Integrated Browser Context-Sensitive Menu Edit Commands

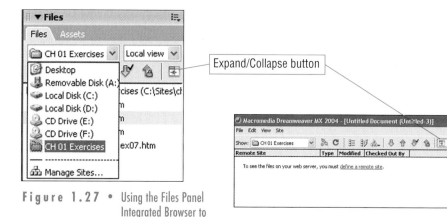

Figure 1.27 • Using the Files Panel Integrated Browser to Access Files and Folders

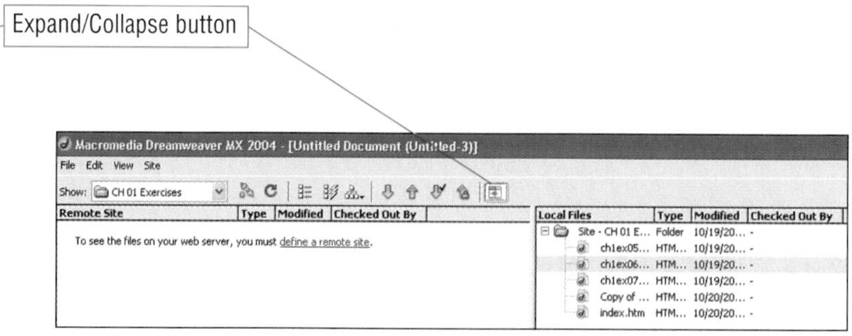

Figure 1.28 • Expanded Files Panel Integrated Browser

DREAMWEAVER MX 2004

1. Display and navigate the integrated file browser by completing the following steps:
   a. Expand the Files panel group if it is not already expanded and make sure the Files panel is displayed by clicking its tab.
   b. Click the down-pointing arrow next to the Files panel list box and locate the drive or network location where the Chapter One folder that you created in Exercise 1 is located. If folders or drive icons are in contracted mode (–), click the Plus (+) button to expand them and display their contents. Locate and expand the Chapter One folder and then the ch_01_student_files folder until you can see the **emcp.gif** file. *Hint: To make it easier to view your files, you can click the vertical bar separating the Document window from the panel groups and drag it to the left to enlarge the panel groups.*

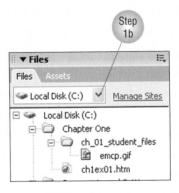

   c. Click and drag *emcp.gif* to the ch_01_exercises root folder located under the Sites folder. Release the file to place it in the root folder. *Note: If these folders are not expanded, you will need to expand them before you move the file.*

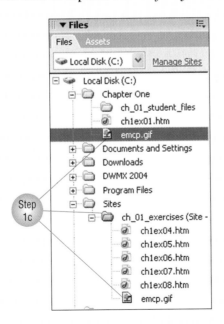

2. Copy and paste a file using the context-sensitive menu by completing the following steps:

   a. Right-click *ch1ex01.htm* in the Chapter One folder to open the context-sensitive menu. Point to Edit and then click Copy to copy the file.

   b. Navigate to the ch_01_exercises root folder and right-click. Point to Edit and then click Paste from the context-sensitive menu to paste a copy of the file into the root folder.

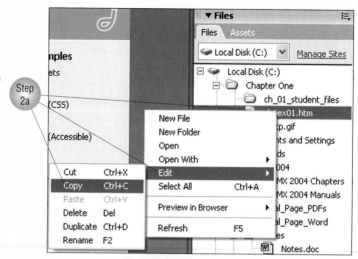

3. Use the Files panel integrated browser to open files in the Document window by completing the following steps:

   a. Close any files that are open in the Document window.

   b. Locate the **ch1ex01.htm** file using the Files panel integrated file browser. Double-click it to open it in the Document window. *Note: Notice that the image does not appear in the document. Because ch1ex01.htm was not created in a Dreamweaver site, the link between the file and the image was broken when it was moved to your root folder. If this file had been created in a Dreamweaver site, it could be moved around within the site and the link would be updated automatically. This is an example of why is it always a good idea to create and save your documents within a Dreamweaver site.*

   c. Close **ch1ex01.htm** without saving it.

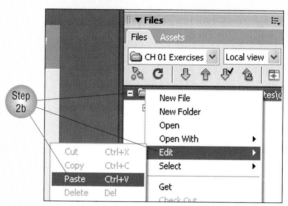

4. Click the down-pointing arrow next to the Files panel list box to locate and select the CH 01 Exercises site so that its contents are once again displayed in the Files panel integrated browser.

Using the Help System

You are not alone when working with Dreamweaver MX 2004. Clicking the Help command on the Menu bar or clicking context-sensitive Help buttons provide a variety of different methods you can use to learn more about Dreamweaver MX 2004. Dreamweaver MX 2004 assistance goes far beyond merely providing an index of help topics and includes tutorials, an online support center, online discussion forums, and much more.

Using Dreamweaver (Dreamweaver Help)

You can access help by clicking **Using Dreamweaver** from the Help command drop-down menu, or by pressing the F1 key. As shown in Figure 1.29, the Index tab lets you scroll down a list of help topics. Double-clicking a topic title opens it, and the topic can be searched by typing keywords in the *Type in the keyword to find* text box at the top of the Using Dreamweaver dialog box. The Contents tab displays a table of contents with information categorized by subject. The Search tab lets you search the entire text of the help system for any character string. Clicking the Print button at the top of the page prints a topic for later reference. The Favorites tab can be used to store help material so that it can be accessed again quickly when needed. Add or remove items to the Favorites list by completing the following steps:

1. Press F1 to open the Using Dreamweaver dialog box.
2. Select and display a help topic from the Using Dreamweaver dialog box.
3. Click the Favorites tab. The title or keywords from the topic appear in the *Current topic* text box at the bottom of the Favorites box.
4. You can change or edit the name of the topic by typing in the *Current topic* text box.
5. Add a topic to your favorites list by clicking the Add button in the lower-right corner of the Favorites box.
6. A topic title can be changed after it has been added to your favorites list by selecting the topic, right-clicking, choosing Rename, and typing the changes you want.
7. After you have added a topic to your favorites list, you can remove it by selecting the topic and then clicking the Remove button.
8. To display a topic from your favorites list, select the topic and then click the Display button or double-click a topic.

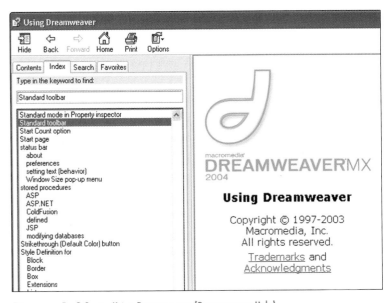

Figure 1.29 • Using Dreamweaver (Dreamweaver Help)

1. Press F1 or click Help on the Menu bar and then click Using Dreamweaver to open the Using Dreamweaver dialog box.
2. Search for information on a topic by completing the following steps:
   a. Click the Index tab if it is not already selected.
   b. Type **panel groups** in the *Type in the keyword to find* text box.
   c. Double-click *panel groups* in the search results list or click the Display button to display the topic.
   d. Read the *panel groups* topic and then click a hyperlink to move to another topic. ***Note: Hyperlinks appear in blue text and are underlined.***

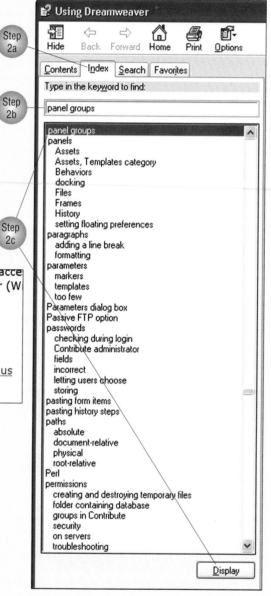

   e. Click one of the Previous arrows at the top or bottom of the page when you are finished reading the new topic to return to the *panel groups* topic.

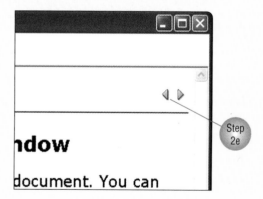

3. Search for a keyword appearing in any of the help topics by completing the following steps:

   a. Click the Search tab.

   b. Type **Style Sheets** in the *Type in the keyword to find* text box. Press Enter or click the List Topics button to display the search results.

   c. Scroll down to highlight and select a topic from the results list and then double-click it or click the Display button to display the topic. The search terms are highlighted on the page.

   d. Print the topic you selected by clicking the Print button on the Using Dreamweaver toolbar. *Note: Check with your instructor to obtain printing instructions.*

4. Close the Using Dreamweaver dialog box.

Dreamweaver Tutorials

Dreamweaver tutorials provide step-by-step lessons on different topics to walk you through Dreamweaver basics. Clicking Getting Started and Tutorials from the Help drop-down menu opens the Getting Started page, which contains a number of Dreamweaver MX 2004 tutorials. These tutorials can also be accessed from the Start Page by clicking the Dreamweaver Tutorial link located in the lower-left corner of the Start Page. Using tutorials is an excellent way to become familiar with some of the basic Dreamweaver MX 2004 functions.

Dreamweaver Support Center

Clicking *Dreamweaver Support Center* from the Help drop-down menu opens the Support Center Web page if you are online. The Support Center contains a variety of information useful to Dreamweaver MX 2004 users, whatever their experience level. There are too many tools available to list here, but among the items that new Dreamweaver MX 2004 users will find helpful are *FAQs* (Frequently Asked Questions), information on installing and getting started with Dreamweaver MX 2004, troubleshooting tips, tutorials and articles, and technical and release notes. A search function makes it easy to locate topics.

Macromedia Online Forums

Clicking *Macromedia Online Forums* from the Help drop-down menu opens the Macromedia Online Forums Web page if you are online. Macromedia sponsors a number of different discussion forums in which people can discuss technical issues and seek answers to questions online. The Forums home page contains instructions on how to use the forums, as well as descriptions and links to other Macromedia forums.

The forum of principle interest to those new to Dreamweaver MX 2004 is the ***Dreamweaver General Discussion forum*** illustrated in Figure 1.30. You can scroll down the list of topics to determine whether there is a ***thread*** (chain of topic postings) on the topic you are interested in, or you can use the forum search engine to search for information using keywords. You can post questions or reply to questions from other forum users. There is a Help button for accessing help, and a link to the Overview document that describes how to get started using the forums. Before using any of the forums, you should read the FAQ on forum use that is available under the "About the Product" forum heading and on the individual forum pages.

You do not have to log in to a forum to read the posted topics, but before you can post a question or reply, you must obtain a membership. After your membership has been accepted, you can log in and post new topics or create replies to existing threads. You will be notified by e-mail when someone replies to something you posted.

Figure 1.30 • Dreamweaver General Discussion Forum

exercise

12

USING THE DREAMWEAVER GENERAL DISCUSSION ONLINE FORUM

Web sites change in appearance and functionality. If links in this exercise do not appear as described, look elsewhere on the site or substitute using other instructions as provided by your instructor.

1. Connect to the Macromedia Online Forums Web page by completing the following steps:
   a. Connect to the Internet. ***Note: You must be connected to the Internet in order to access Macromedia forums.***

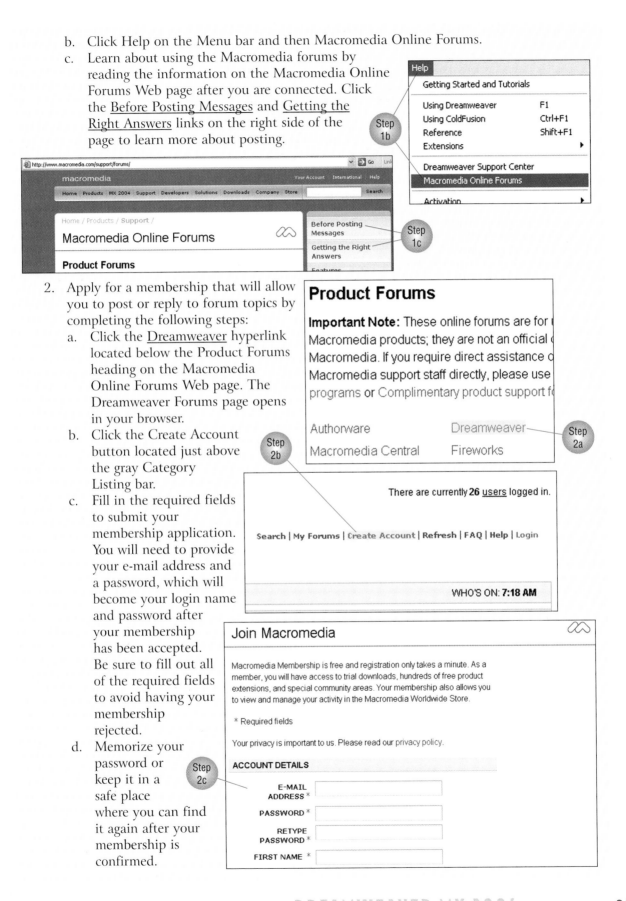

b. Click Help on the Menu bar and then Macromedia Online Forums.

c. Learn about using the Macromedia forums by reading the information on the Macromedia Online Forums Web page after you are connected. Click the <u>Before Posting Messages</u> and <u>Getting the Right Answers</u> links on the right side of the page to learn more about posting.

2. Apply for a membership that will allow you to post or reply to forum topics by completing the following steps:

a. Click the <u>Dreamweaver</u> hyperlink located below the Product Forums heading on the Macromedia Online Forums Web page. The Dreamweaver Forums page opens in your browser.

b. Click the Create Account button located just above the gray Category Listing bar.

c. Fill in the required fields to submit your membership application. You will need to provide your e-mail address and a password, which will become your login name and password after your membership has been accepted. Be sure to fill out all of the required fields to avoid having your membership rejected.

d. Memorize your password or keep it in a safe place where you can find it again after your membership is confirmed.

3. Log in to a Dreamweaver forum by completing the following steps:
    a. Open the Dreamweaver Forums page.
    b. Click the Login button. ***Note: You do not need to log in right away if you just want to browse postings. If you later decide that you want to post a new topic, you will be prompted to log in when you click the new topic button.***

There are currently **31** users logged in.

Step 3b

count | Refresh | **FAQ** | **Help** | Login

    c. Enter your e-mail account name and password on the new page when prompted for this information.

Step 3c

Home /

Sign In

For security reasons, we need to reverify your Macromedia Membership ID. Please re-enter your user name and password.

E-MAIL ADDRESS   jmbaker@emcp.net

Do you have a Macromedia password?

◉ **Yes**   ☑ **Remember me**

Did you forget your password?

○ **No, I will create one now.**

    After you are logged in, you are returned to the Dreamweaver Forums page.
4. Post a new topic on the Dreamweaver General Discussion forum by completing the following steps:
    a. Open the Dreamweaver Forums page.
    b. Click the FAQ button located just above the gray Category Listing bar to read and learn more about using Macromedia forums.
    c. Click the Dreamweaver General Discussion link to open the page in your browser. ***Note: Bookmark the page on your browser so that you can go directly to the forum in the future.***

There are currently **29** users logged in.

mize | Refresh | **FAQ** | **Help** | **Logout**

Step 4c

Step 4b

    d. Click the New Topic button just below the Navigation menu. A new message dialog box will open in your browser.

📁   Dreamweaver General Discussion

Topics: 77347   Last Post: Tuesday October 21, 2003 | 7:37 PM | by Digital Prophets

Message Title:

Dreamweaver Forums

Step 4e

Message Text:

| **B** | *I* | <u>U</u> | http |

Yesterday I experienced a pro
need to know if it can be fixe

Customize | Profile | New Topic | FAQ | Help |

Step 4d

REFERRING URLS

Referring URL 1 :
Referring URL 2 :
Referring URL 3 :
Referring URL 4 :
Referring URL 5 :

Step 4g

    e. Type a title for your topic in the *Message Title* text box.
    f. Type your question in the *Message Text* text box.
    g. Enter URLs or add attachments to your post if necessary using the buttons at the bottom of the dialog box.

DREAMWEAVER MX 2004

h. Click the Preview button to see how your post will appear when you have completed your new topic or click the Post Message button to send your message to the forum. With the default setup, you will receive an e-mail message notifying you every time someone replies to your topic.

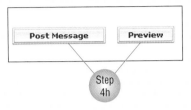

5. Reply to a thread by completing the following steps:
   a. Click the <u>Reply</u> link located below each thread.

   b. Post a reply in the Reply dialog box by following Steps 4f–4h. The Reply dialog box is almost identical to a new message dialog box except that the thread topic has automatically been entered in the *Message Title* text box.
6. Close the browser and disconnect from the Internet when you are finished.

Context-Sensitive Help

Context-sensitive help is also available in most dialog boxes, panels, and inspectors. As shown in Figure 1.31, you can access context-sensitive help by clicking the Help button in a dialog box, clicking the question mark button found in inspectors and some windows, or by choosing Help from the Options menu in a panel group Title bar.

Figure 1.31 • Context-Sensitive Help

CHAPTER summary

➤ Click Start, point to Programs (Windows XP), point to Macromedia, and then click Macromedia Dreamweaver MX 2004; or click the *Macromedia Dreamweaver MX 2004* icon on the desktop (if installed) to start Dreamweaver.

➤ There are two Dreamweaver MX 2004 workspace interfaces to choose from: Designer and Coder.

➤ Documents are displayed in the Document window portion of the Dreamweaver MX 2004 workspace.

➤ The Start Page allows users to open recently used documents, create new documents, access a tour of Dreamweaver MX 2004, or use Dreamweaver MX 2004 tutorials.

➤ The Document window can be resized.

➤ When the Document window is maximized, open documents are indicated by document tabs at the top of the window.

➤ The Preferences dialog box is used to change the default settings for many Dreamweaver MX 2004 tools.

➤ A Dreamweaver site is the location on a computer or network where the files that make up a Web site are stored.

➤ The Site Definition dialog box takes users through all of the steps necessary to define (create) a Dreamweaver site.

➤ Click File and then click New to create a new Dreamweaver MX 2004 document.

➤ Click Save or Save As to save a Dreamweaver MX 2004 document.

➤ Design files are files with layouts and placeholder elements and objects in place and ready for users to customize.

➤ The Title bar displays a document's title, folder location, and file name.

➤ The Status bar contains the Tag selector, Window Size indicator, and Document Size/Estimated Download Time indicator.

➤ The Tag selector is used to identify and work with HTML tags.

➤ The Quick Tag Editor allows the quick and easy modification of tag attributes.

➤ The Window Size indicator displays the current document's window dimensions in pixels.

➤ The Document Size/Estimated Download Time indicator displays the size of the current document in bytes and the estimated time it will take to download.

➤ Right-clicking an element or object opens a context-sensitive menu displaying commands relevant to the item selected.

➤ The Standard toolbar contains buttons for common activities such as creating, opening, and saving files; copying, cutting, and pasting; and undoing and redoing operations.

➤ There are three document views: Code view, Code and Design view, and Design view.

➤ The Insert bar contains buttons for inserting elements and objects into documents.

➤ Clicking an Insert bar menu item or tab changes the buttons displayed on the bar.

DREAMWEAVER MX 2004

➤ Panels provide a graphical interface for many Dreamweaver MX 2004 functions.

➤ Panels are grouped in panel groups and can be undocked from their standard location for placement anywhere in the Dreamweaver MX 2004 workspace.

➤ Grippers are used to undock and redock panel groups.

➤ The panel group interface can be resized or closed to create more Document window space.

➤ The Files panel contains an integrated file browser that can be used to manage files.

➤ The Files panel can be expanded so that it displays both local and remote site File views.

➤ The Help Menu bar command provides access to Dreamweaver help (Using Dreamweaver), tutorials, the Dreamweaver Online Support Center, online discussion forums, and much more.

➤ Pressing F1 opens the Using Dreamweaver dialog box (Dreamweaver help).

➤ Context-sensitive help is available in most dialog boxes, panels, and inspectors.

KEY terms

Code and Design view A horizontally split Document window view, with Code view displayed in the top window and Design view in the lower window.

Code view A Document window view used for viewing and working with HTML code.

context-sensitive help Help that is accessible in most dialog boxes, panels, and inspectors by clicking a Help button.

design files Files containing predesigned layouts, elements, and objects ready for customization.

Design view A Document view that approximates how a page will appear in a browser.

dock Refers to the attachment of panels and panel groups to the left, right, top, or bottom of the Document window.

Document Size/Estimated Download Time indicator An indicator located on the Status bar that estimates the size of a document as well as the time needed to load it and any other files linked to it.

document tab Open documents are indicated by a document tab appearing at the top of a maximized document. The document tab contains a document's name and extension.

Document toolbar A toolbar containing buttons and drop-down menus for different document-viewing options, as well as other functions, such as the No Browser Check Errors, Preview/Debug in Browser, and Refresh buttons.

Document views Refers to the different modes for viewing and working with documents. There are three Document views to choose from: Code view, Code and Design view, and Design view.

Document window The window where open documents appear in Dreamweaver MX 2004.

dragging The act of clicking a folder, file, or screen object and moving it (dragging) while holding down the mouse button.

Dreamweaver General Discussion forum A Dreamweaver online forum for general topics related to Dreamweaver.

Dreamweaver MX 2004 Coder workspace An integrated workspace in the layout style used by Macromedia HomeSite and Macromedia ColdFusion Studio. It opens in Code view by default and is recommended for those who prefer to do their own coding.

Dreamweaver MX 2004 Designer workspace This workspace contains all document windows and panels integrated in a single application window, with panel groups located on the right side of the window. This workspace is recommended unless users plan to frequently work in code.

Dreamweaver site The local site (root folder) on a computer or network where documents related to a Web site can be worked on and tested before uploading to a remote server. Also called *site*.

Dreamweaver Support Center A Dreamweaver Web site with the latest Dreamweaver information, including technical releases, tutorials, articles, product downloads, support programs, and much more.

Dreamweaver tutorials Tutorials provide step-by-step lessons on different topics and are available by clicking Tutorials from the Help drop-down menu, or by clicking the Start Page Dreamweaver Tutorial link. Additional tutorials are available on the Dreamweaver Support Center Web site.

Expander arrow The small arrow on a panel group Title bar used to expand it.

FAQs (Frequently Asked Questions) Lists containing questions that are frequently asked about a topic, along with answers to those questions.

floating panels Panels that have been undocked and relocated.

gripper The dotted area on the left side of a panel or panel group's Title bar used for docking and undocking.

Insert bar A toolbar containing buttons that allow users to insert various elements and objects into a document.

integrated file browser The Files panel contains an integrated file browser that provides access to the files and folders located on a computer or local network.

local site A local site is where users work on and test their Web site before placing it on a server so that others can view it. See *Dreamweaver site*.

Macromedia Online Forums Online forums where Dreamweaver MX 2004 users can post questions and discuss issues related to Dreamweaver MX 2004 and other Macromedia products.

Menu bar A bar containing different commands (such as File, Edit, and so on). Clicking a command opens a drop-down menu with a list of options associated with that command.

Options menu A context-sensitive drop-down menu that can be accessed from an expanded panel or panel group.

panel groups Panels grouped together under one heading. For example, the Files panel group contains the Files and Assets panels.

panels A graphical interface for almost all Dreamweaver MX 2004 functions. Most panels are grouped together with other panels in panel groups.

placeholder content Latin text used in design files to give users an idea of how a finished document will appear.

Quick Tag Editor A tool providing quick and easy editing of HTML tags.

remote site A copy of the local site that has been placed on a server so that it can be viewed by others.

resize arrow A double-headed arrow that can be used to resize the Document window.

Restore button A button located in the upper-right corner of a document's Title bar that can be used to restore the document to its maximum size.

site See *Dreamweaver site*.

Site Definition dialog box A dialog box that assists users with all of the tasks associated with setting up Dreamweaver sites.

Standard toolbar Contains buttons for creating new files; opening existing files; saving files; saving all files; cutting; copying, and pasting; and undoing and redoing steps.

Start Page A page in the Document window that allows users to open recently used documents, create new documents, access a tour of Dreamweaver MX 2004, or use Dreamweaver MX 2004 tutorials.

Status bar The bar at the bottom of the workspace containing the Tag selector, Window Size indicator, and Document Size/Estimated Download Time indicator.

Tag selector A tool used to select, edit, or remove tags while in Design view.

thread A series of postings on a topic in an online forum or discussion group.

Title bar The bar at the top of a window containing a description of the window's content. The workspace Title bar displays a document's title, location, and file name.

toggle triangle A switch located on the vertical bar separating the panel group interface from the Document window. Clicking the toggle triangle displays or hides the panel group interface.

tooltip A small identification box that appears when the mouse pointer hovers over Menu bar and panel buttons. Tooltip text is an accessibility feature and is read by screen readers.

undock To move a panel or panel group from its usual location in the Document window.

Using Dreamweaver The name of the Dreamweaver help function located on the Help command drop-down menu. Pressing F1 is a convenient shortcut for opening the Using Dreamweaver dialog box.

Window Size indicator Displays the Document window's dimensions in pixels when in Design view.

COMMANDS review

Change workspace preferences	Edit, Preferences, *General* category, Change Workspace
Close a file	File, Close
Create a Dreamweaver site	Site, Manage Sites, New, Site
Create a new file	File, New
Display panels	Window, click panel name
Display Standard toolbar	View, Toolbars, Standard
Dreamweaver Multimedia Forums	Help, Macromedia Online Forums
Edit a Dreamweaver site	Site, Manage Sites, select site, Edit
Exit Dreamweaver MX 2004	File, Exit
Help	Help, Using Dreamweaver
Redo	Edit, Redo
Save a Dreamweaver MX 2004 document	File, Save; or File, Save As to assign a file name
Cut, copy, or paste	Edit, and Cut, Copy, or Paste
Undo	Edit, Undo

CONCEPTS check

Indicate the correct term or command for each item.

1. This is the name of the workspace area where documents are displayed.
2. This accessibility feature causes an identification box to display alternate text in a browser window when the mouse pointer is rolled over a page element containing an alternate text description.
3. Press this key to access Dreamweaver help (the Using Dreamweaver dialog box).
4. Use this tool to estimate how long a document will take to download.
5. The Tag selector is located on this bar.
6. These files contain predefined layouts and elements.
7. This tool can be used to edit tags without leaving Design view.
8. This dialog box assists users in creating a Dreamweaver site.
9. Use this indicator to change the size of the Document window.
10. Use this Document view to approximate how your page will look in a browser.
11. Clicking this button on an expanded panel's Title bar accesses a menu specific to the panel.
12. This is the term for the area on a panel used to undock and dock panels.
13. This is the term for the switch used to hide or display the panel group interface.
14. This Files panel feature provides access to desktop and local network files and folders.

15. The Files panel is located in this panel group.
16. This is the term used to describe clicking and holding down the mouse button to move a file, folder, or object.
17. This button next to a folder in the integrated file browser indicates that the folder contents are hidden.
18. These two items are needed to log in to online Dreamweaver forums.
19. This is the term for the type of menu that appears when elements or objects are right-clicked.
20. This is the folder in a Dreamweaver site where all of the files for a Web site are saved.

SKILLS check

Use the Site Definition dialog box to create a separate Dreamweaver site named CH 01 Assessments to keep your assessment work for this chapter. Save the files for the site in a new root folder named ch_01_assessments under the Sites folder you created in Chapter 1, Exercise 3.

Assessment 1 • Create a Basic HTML Document

1. Create a new HTML Basic Page document in the Document window.
2. Save the document to the ch_01_assessments root folder, using the Save As command to save it as **ch1sa1.htm**.
3. Type the following title in the *Title* text box on the Document toolbar: Assessment 1 Exercise.
4. Type My First Dreamweaver MX 2004 Web Page in the Document window.
5. Use the Insert bar to change the text you just typed to h1 heading size.
6. At the end of the heading, press Enter twice to create blank space, and type This is my first Dreamweaver MX 2004 Web page. I look forward to learning more about the program and using it to create professional-looking Web pages. ***Note: Don't forget to proofread your typing and correct your spelling errors.***
7. Use the Insert bar to bold the word *first*.
8. Use Menu bar commands or right-click to copy the text you just typed.
9. Press Enter once to create a space, and paste the copied text to create a second paragraph.
10. Save and then close **ch1sa1.htm**.

Assessment 2 • Use the Files Panel to Work with Documents

1. Expand the Files panel if it is not already expanded.
2. Select *ch1sa1.htm* in the file browser and right-click. Point to Edit and then click Copy in the context-sensitive menu.
3. Right-click, point to Edit, and then click Paste in the context-sensitive menu.
4. Select *Copy of ch1sa1.htm,* right-click, point to Edit, and then click Rename in the context-sensitive menu.
5. Rename the copied file **ch1sa2.htm**. Be careful not to delete the file's .htm extension.

6. Use the integrated file browser to open **ch1sa2.htm** in the Document window.
7. Click the Split button on the Document toolbar.
8. Locate the document title in the Code view window and change it to **Assessment 2 Exercise**.
9. Write down on a piece of paper the tags enclosing the bold word *first*, the words *My First Dreamweaver MX 2004 Web Page*, and the two paragraphs.
10. Click the Design button to return to Design view.
11. Save and then close **ch1sa2.htm**.

Assessment 3 • Understand Panel Groups

1. Use the Window command to display all of the default panel groups in the workspace if they are not already displayed.
2. Use the Files panel group's Options menu to rename the panel group **Files-Assessment 3**. *Hint: Make sure you rename the panel group, not a file or folder.*
3. Move the Files-Assessment 3 panel group to the center of the Document window.
4. Expand the Files-Assessment 3 panel group.
5. Dock the Design and Application panel groups on the left side of the workspace.
6. Expand the Design and Application panel groups.
7. Group the Layers panel with the Files-Assessment 3 panel group using the Group Layers with command from the Layers panel Options menu.
8. Collapse the panels remaining on the right side of the workspace.
9. Press the Print Screen key to capture the screen.
10. Use a graphics program such as Paint or Photoshop to print the screen capture to demonstrate your panel knowledge.
11. Before closing Dreamweaver MX 2004, restore the name of the Files panel group, group the Layers panel back with the Design panel group, move all of the panels back to the right side of the workspace, and collapse all of the panels. *Hint: When the Layers panel was moved from the Design panel group to the Files panel group, the Design panel group name changed to CSS Styles because that was the name of the only panel remaining in what was formerly the Design panel group. Recreate the Design panel group by grouping the Layers panel with the CSS Styles panel, and then use the Rename Panel Group command to change the name of the CSS Styles panel group to the Design panel group.*

Assessment 4 • Create and Edit a Page Design Document

1. Create a new Dreamweaver MX 2004 document using the *Text: Article D* Page Design.
2. Save the file as **ch1sa4.htm**.
3. Position the insertion point in the *Lorem Ipsum Dolor* heading text and use the Quick Tag Editor to change the font size from +2 to +5. *Hint: Locate the font tag (<font>) in the Tag selector and right-click to open the Quick Tag Editor.*
4. Position the insertion point in the bold text of the first paragraph and use the Quick Tag Editor to unbold the paragraph. *Hint: The bold tag (<b>) controls the bold text.*

5. Use the Insert bar to bold the text in the second paragraph.
6. Use the Tag selector to remove the horizontal line between the first and second paragraphs. *Hint: The horizontal line is controlled by the horizontal line tag (<hr>).*
7. Save and then close **ch1sa4.htm**.

Assessment 5 • Research Web Site Planning and Design

1. Go online and open the Dreamweaver Support Center in your Web browser.
2. Click the <u>Tutorial and Article Index</u> link.
3. Click <u>Planning and Setting Up a Site</u> link located under the *Site Planning and Publishing* heading.
4. Click the blue links under the Tutorials and Articles heading to read each topic.
5. Print each topic for later reference. *Hint: Do not print the TechNotes.*
6. Close your Web browser.
7. Press F1 to open the Using Dreamweaver dialog box. Click the Contents tab and locate the <u>Dreamweaver Basics</u> link. Click the link, and then read the linked topics that are displayed. Read the information and print it for later reference.
8. Close the help dialog box.
9. Use the information you gathered to create a document in a word processing program summarizing the most important considerations when planning a Web site design. You may supplement your information by conducting additional research on the Web.
10. Save the document and name it **ch1sa5**. *Note: The file extension will vary depending on the word processing program used.*
11. Print and then close **ch1sa5**. Exit the word processing program.

Assessment 6 • Use the Dreamweaver General Discussion Forum

1. Log in to the Dreamweaver General Discussion forum. *Hint: You will need your e-mail address and password from Exercise 12.*
2. Use the Search function to find threads related to any one of the following topics: Insert bar, panels, or Quick Tag Editor.
3. Open one of the topic threads when the search results appear.
4. Locate and click the View thread in raw text format button in the thread page. *Hint: The button looks similar to the **Print** button icon.*
5. Click the <u>Print this thread</u> link to print the thread.
6. Think of a question you have about a Dreamweaver feature. Conduct a search to determine whether any previous threads deal with your question.
7. Create a new topic and post a question that you do not see answered in any previous threads. *Note: Before posting, be sure that you have read and understood the Dreamweaver forums FAQ and the other information about using forums.*
8. Look for your topic after you have posted it. Repeat Steps 4 and 5 to print the thread.
9. Check back later to see if there were any replies to your question. Follow up with a reply if necessary.
10. After you have received a reply or replies to your question, print the thread again.

Assessment 7 • Plan a Design Portfolio

Over the course of subsequent chapters, you will work on creating your own Web site that you can use as a design portfolio to showcase the skills you have learned. Use the information you learned in Assessment 5 to:

1. Write down your goals for your Web site.
2. Sketch a folder hierarchy for your site.
3. Create a mock-up page showing the basic "look" of the Web pages you plan for your site.

CREATING A BASIC WEB PAGE

PERFORMANCE OBJECTIVES

➤ Select browser preview preferences and preview documents in a browser.
➤ Use the Check Target Browsers tool.
➤ Ensure that the Web pages you create are accessible to those with disabilities.
➤ Type text directly.
➤ Copy and paste content, including Microsoft Word and Excel file content.
➤ Use the Property inspector to format text properties.
➤ Change default background and text colors.
➤ Use the Assets panel.
➤ Create and edit links to other pages.
➤ Create and edit internal links (anchor links).
➤ Create and edit e-mail links and attributes.
➤ Check and repair broken links.
➤ Edit and remove links.
➤ Create unordered, ordered, definition, and nested lists.
➤ Change list properties.
➤ Find and replace text and code.
➤ Check for spelling errors.
➤ Use the History panel to undo and redo steps and to save steps as commands.
➤ Add, edit, and remove comments.

The student files for this chapter are available for download from the Internet Resource Center at www.emcp.com.

In Chapter 1, you learned to identify and understand the basic components of the Dreamweaver MX 2004 workspace. In this chapter, you will use this knowledge to create Web pages, insert and format text, change color properties, use the Assets panel, insert links, create lists, undo and redo steps, search for items, check for spelling errors, and do other related tasks. You will find that there is almost always more than one way to do something in Dreamweaver MX 2004. Although it is important to become familiar with the different methods available, you are free to use only the tools you are comfortable with.

Previewing Pages in a Browser

Although Design view approximates how a page will look when displayed in a Web browser, the only way to be certain that pages will appear as intended is to preview them in a real browser. Dreamweaver MX 2004 simplifies this task by featuring a ***Preview/Debug in browser button*** on the Document toolbar as shown in Figure 2.1. Clicking the button and then clicking one of the browser preview commands from the drop-down menu opens the current document in a browser. In the default Dreamweaver MX 2004 setup, unsaved documents cannot be previewed, but the Preferences dialog box can be used to undo the default setting and enable the previewing of unsaved documents as described in Exercise 1.

Browser Preview Preferences

When previewing Web pages, it is a good idea to make sure they will perform as intended in the most commonly used browsers. Although Internet Explorer is used by the vast majority of Web users, significant numbers of people are using other browsers such as Netscape, Mozilla, and Opera. In addition, constant browser improvements mean that a number of different versions are in use for each browser type. Dreamweaver MX 2004 lets you specify up to 20 different browsers or browser versions for previewing. To ensure that pages are accessible to viewers with disabilities, at least one text-based browser should be selected. Browser preview preferences can be specified using the *Preview in Browser* selection from the *Category* list box in the Preferences dialog box as shown in Figure 2.2. One browser can be designated as a ***primary browser*** and another as a ***secondary browser***, allowing them to be conveniently opened by pressing the F12 key (primary browser), or by pressing the F12 key while holding down the Ctrl key (secondary browser).

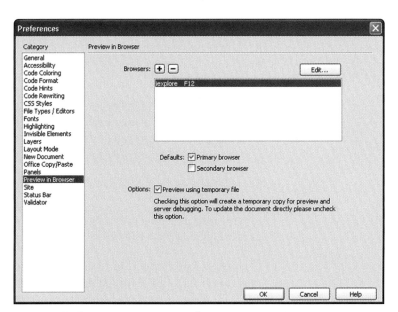

Figure 2.1 • Preview/Debug in Browser Button

Figure 2.2 • Preview in Browser Preferences

Temporary Files

When an unsaved page is previewed in Dreamweaver MX 2004, the program creates a temporary copy of the file and opens it in the specified browser, allowing you to preview a page without having to save it first. The Preview/Debug in browser button will need to be clicked again if changes are made to a page after previewing, because the temporary file will not be refreshed automatically.

exercise 1

Work in Design view unless a step instructs you to work in another document view. Check with your instructor before completing this exercise to see which browser you will add to and remove from the Preferences dialog box.

1. Enable previewing of unsaved documents by completing the following steps:
   a. If necessary, start Dreamweaver MX 2004.
   b. Click Edit on the Menu bar and then Preferences to open the Preferences dialog box.
   c. Click the *Preview in Browser* selection from the *Category* list box in the Preferences dialog box.
   d. Click to place a check mark in the *Preview using temporary file* check box. **Note: The exercises in this book assume that the Preview Using Temporary File feature has been enabled.**

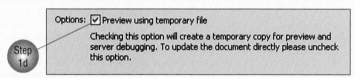

   e. Click the OK button to close the Preferences dialog box.
2. Preview a document in a browser by completing the following steps:
   a. At a clear document screen, open **ch1ex05.htm** in the Document window.
   b. Click the Preview/Debug in browser button on the Document toolbar.
   c. Click Preview in iexplore (Internet Explorer) on the drop-down menu. The browser opens and displays the current document. **Note: Choose a different browser if the computer you are using does not have Internet Explorer installed.**
   d. Close the browser window when you are finished previewing. If you make a change to the document after previewing it, repeat Steps 2b and 2c to preview it again.
3. Add browsers to or remove browsers from the browser list by completing the following steps:
   a. Click the Preview/Debug in browser button on the Document toolbar.
   b. Click Edit Browser List on the drop-down menu. The Preferences dialog box will display the browsers available when using the Preview/Debug in browser option.

c. Add a browser to the preferences list by clicking the Plus (+) button next to *Browsers* to open the Add Browser dialog box.

d. Click the Browse button to locate the browser program file. ***Hint: Browser programs are usually located in your computer's Program Files folder and have .exe extensions such as Netscp.exe or IEXPLORE.exe.***

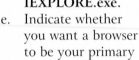 Step 3c

 Step 3d

Step 3e

e. Indicate whether you want a browser to be your primary or secondary choice by clicking to place a check mark in the check box next to *Primary browser* or *Secondary browser*.

f. Click OK to close the Add Browser dialog box.

g. Click OK to close the Preferences dialog box.

4. Remove a browser as a preview choice by completing the following steps:

a. Follow Steps 3a–3b, click the browser you want to remove from the browser list, and then click the Minus (–) button.

b. Click OK to close the Preferences dialog box.

c. Close **ch1ex05.htm** without saving it.

Checking Browser Compatibility

The Dreamweaver MX 2004 ***Check Target Browsers*** tool checks documents for any code that is not supported by browsers your target viewers are likely to be using, and is useful for determining the nature of problems, which may have been noticed when previewing a page. Notification can take the form of errors, warnings, and messages. Errors are serious and will cause a problem that will prevent the offending code from displaying. Warnings indicate a problem that will cause something to display incorrectly, while messages indicate that code is unsupported by a browser but will not have any effect. The Check Target Browsers tool does not correct errors, and once an error has been identified, it is up to you to take steps to repair or remove the unsupported code. In the default Dreamweaver MX 2004 setup, a target browser compatibility check is performed every time a document is opened. This automatic feature can be disabled by clicking the Document toolbar Check Target Browsers button and then clicking to remove the check mark next to Auto-check on Open as shown in Figure 2.3. Target browser compatibility checks can also be performed manually by clicking the Check Target Browsers button and then clicking Check Browser Support.

Check Target Browsers button

Figure 2.3
Check Target Browsers
Button and Drop-Down Menu

 **exercise** **2**

CHECKING TARGET BROWSER COMPATIBILITY

1. Specify target browsers by completing the following steps:
   a. At a clear document screen, click the Document toolbar Check Target Browsers button down-pointing arrow.
   b. Click Settings to open the Target Browsers dialog box.
   c. If necessary, place a check mark in the check box next to *Microsoft Internet Explorer*. Click the down-pointing arrow to the right of the list box next to *Microsoft Internet Explorer* and click *6.0* to select it.

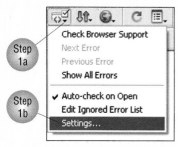

Step 1a

Step 1b

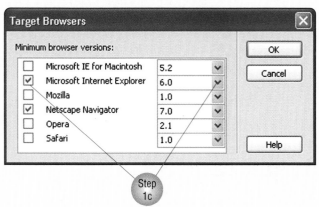

Step 1c

   d. Repeat Step 1c to select *Netscape Navigator* version *7.0*.
   e. Click the OK button to close the dialog box.
2. Review target browser compatibility check results by completing the following steps:
   a. Open **ch1ex05.htm**.
   b. A tooltip will appear below the Check Target Browsers button indicating the number of errors that were found. ***Note: If you click inside the document, the tooltip will disappear. Hover the mouse pointer over the Check Target Browsers button to view it again. If there are no errors in a document, the tooltip will read*** **No Browser Check Errors.**
   c. Click the Document toolbar Code button to view the document in Code view.

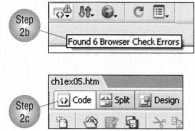

Step 2b

Step 2c

d. Hover the mouse pointer over any code underlined with a wavy red line. A tooltip will appear indicating which browsers do not support the item of code highlighted by the wavy red line.

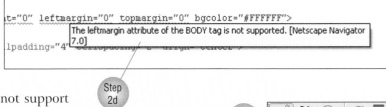

Step 2d

e. Click the Check Target Browsers button and then click Show All Errors.

Step 2e

f. The horizontal Results panel group will open at the bottom of the Document window displaying a list of all errors, warnings, and messages. Click the Browse Report button at the lower-left portion of the Results panel.

Step 2f

g. A Dreamweaver Target Browser Check report will open in a browser window. Click File and then Print to print a copy of the report. Close the browser window when you are finished. *Note: Reports can be saved by clicking the Save Report button located just above the Browse Report button in the Results panel. This opens a Save As dialog box that can be used to specify a location where the report will be saved.*

Dreamweaver Target Browser Check

27-October-2003 at 10:13:26 AM SE Asia Standard Time.

This report covered 1 file.

Target Browser	Errors	Warnings
Microsoft Internet Explorer 6.0	0	2
Netscape Navigator 7.0	6	0
Total	6	2

Files containing errors:

C:\Sites\ch_01_exercises\

Step 2g

h. Click Window and then Results to close the Results panel group.
i. Click the Design button to restore the Document window to Design view.

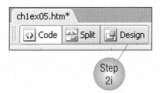

Step 2i

3. Close **ch1ex05.htm** without saving it.

Ensuring Accessibility

Millions of people have visual, hearing, physical, or neurological disabilities that might impair their ability to access Web page content. In recent years, there has been growing recognition that Web designers should not ignore this significant portion of the population when designing Web pages. Efforts to improve accessibility gained more exposure in 1997 when the World Wide Web Consortium (W3C), the main standards body for the Web, launched the Web Accessibility Initiative (www.w3.org/WAI). *Accessibility* is also a requirement of U.S. legislation, such as Section 508 of the Rehabilitation Act, which requires federal agencies to make their electronic and information technology accessible to people with disabilities.

Providing Web page accessibility is not difficult. Creating an alternative text description for images lets those with visual impairments understand them. Creating captions for audio material will do the same for people with hearing impairments, and creating keyboard shortcuts for mouse actions makes Web pages accessible to those with physical impairments. Dreamweaver MX 2004 can simplify the task of ensuring Web page accessibility by prompting users whenever an accessibility-related option is available. For example, a dialog box, as shown in Figure 2.4, prompts you to create an alternative text description when images are inserted if the accessibility option for images has been selected.

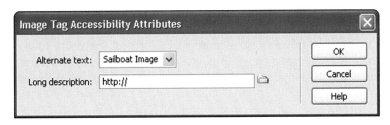

F i g u r e 2 . 4 • Image Tag Accessibility Attributes Dialog Box

F i g u r e 2 . 5 • Accessibility Preferences

Accessibility features can be activated by completing the following steps:

1. Click Edit on the Menu bar and then click Preferences to open the Preferences dialog box.
2. Click *Accessibility* in the *Category* list box.
3. Click the check boxes as shown in Figure 2.5 to place a check mark next to each option (*Form objects, Frames, Media,* and *Images*).
4. Click the OK button to close the Preferences dialog box.

Note: The exercises in this book assume that the Form objects, Frames, Media, *and* Images *accessibility options have been selected using the Accessibility page in the Preferences dialog box.*

Entering Text

Text can be entered into an HTML document by any of four different methods: typing text, opening documents directly, copying and pasting text, or importing text from other programs.

Typing Text

Text can be typed in Dreamweaver MX 2004 just as with any word processor. However, formatting text in Dreamweaver MX 2004 is somewhat different from formatting text in a word processor because a Dreamweaver MX 2004 document must follow HTML rules. For example, Dreamweaver MX 2004 inserts paragraph tags (<p>) when the Enter or Return keys are pressed, instructing browsers to display paragraph spacing at that point. Menu bar commands, Insert bar buttons, the Property inspector, and the Page Properties dialog box can all be used to format text.

Opening Documents Directly

Text documents (documents with .txt extensions) can be opened directly in Dreamweaver MX 2004 by clicking the File Menu bar command and then Open. The Open dialog box can then be used to locate and open the desired file. The Save As command can be used to save text documents as HTML documents, and then they can be formatted just like any other Dreamweaver MX 2004 HTML document. Other HTML documents can also be opened in Dreamweaver MX 2004, such as Word documents that have been saved as HTML files. HTML code created in other HTML editors often contains code that is not absolutely necessary. Dreamweaver MX 2004 features Clean Up HTML and Clean UP Word HTML commands as shown in Figure 2.6 that can be used to remove any extraneous code from documents. After the desired clean-up options have been selected, Dreamweaver MX 2004 removes any unnecessary HTML code and displays a log showing what was removed.

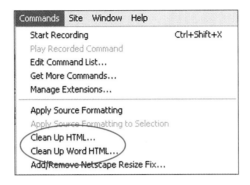

Commands Site Window Help

Start Recording   Ctrl+Shift+X
Play Recorded Command
Edit Command List...
Get More Commands...
Manage Extensions...

Apply Source Formatting
Apply Source Formatting to Selection

Clean Up HTML...
Clean Up Word HTML...
Add/Remove Netscape Resize Fix...

Figure 2.6
Clean Up HTML and Clean
UP Word HTML Commands

exercise 3

CLEANING UP A WORD HTML DOCUMENT

1. At a clear document screen, create a new site named CH 02 Exercises to store the exercises you create in this chapter. Name the root folder ch_02_exercises and save it under the Sites folder you created in Chapter 1, Exercise 3. Download the ch_02_student_files folder from the IRC to the CH 02 Exercises site root folder (ch_02_exercises) and expand it. Delete the compressed folder when you are finished. *Note: Refer to Chapter 1 for instructions on navigating with the Files panel integrated file browser.*

2. Clean up a Word Web page document by completing the following steps:
   a. Start Microsoft Word. *Note: Do not close Dreamweaver MX 2004.*
   b. Click File and then Open to locate and open the **ozymandius** student file. *Hint: The file path will be Sites/ch_02_exercises/ch_02_student files/ozymandius.*
   c. Click File and then Save As to open the Save As dialog box.
   d. Click the *Save in* list box down-pointing arrow to locate and select *ch_02_exercises* as the folder location where the file will be saved to. Rename the file **ch2ex03**, click the down-pointing arrow next to the *Save as type* list box, and click *Web Page* to save the document as a Word Web page document (an HTML file). Click the Save button to save the document. Close Word when you are finished.

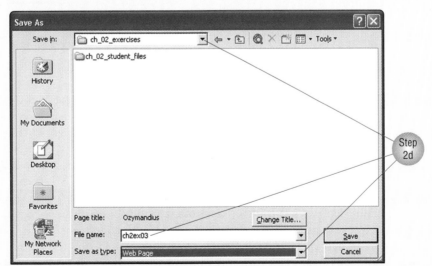

   e. Return to Dreamweaver MX 2004. Click File and then Open to locate and open the **ch2ex03.htm** Word Web page file.

f.   Click Commands on the Menu bar and then Clean Up Word HTML to open the Clean Up Word HTML dialog box as shown below.

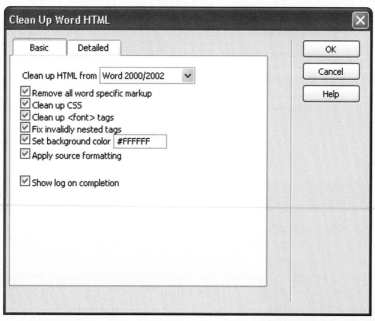

g.   Click the dialog box OK button to clean up the document and display a report documenting the extraneous code that has been removed from the document. Click the OK button to close the report when you are finished reading it.

3.   Save **ch2ex03.htm** and then close it.

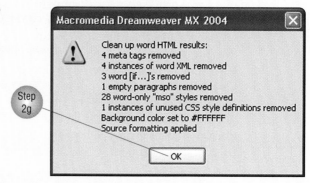

Step 2g

Copying and Pasting

The drop-down menu under the Edit command on the Menu bar contains Copy, Paste, Copy HTML, Paste HTML, and Paste Text commands as shown in Figure 2.7. The Copy and Paste commands are also accessible by right-clicking. Using the Copy and Paste commands will paste an exact duplicate of the copied material into a document with its HTML formatting intact. Sometimes, you might want to copy text from another document without copying its HTML formatting. This can be done in Design view by copying the selected material using the Copy command, and then pasting it into a document using the Paste Text command. You also can copy and paste material so that the HTML code is visible in the document when in Design view by copying the selected material using the Copy HTML command, and then pasting it into a document using the Paste or Paste Text commands. Copying material using the Copy HTML command and pasting it using the Paste HTML command produces the same result as using the Copy and Paste commands—an exact duplicate of the copied material.

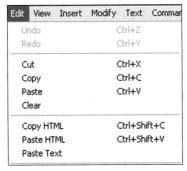

Figure 2.7 • Copy and Paste Commands

exercise 4

COPYING AND PASTING DOCUMENT CONTENT

1. Copy and paste an exact duplicate of selected content from one document to another by completing the following steps:

    a. At a clear document screen, click File on the Menu bar and then New to open the New Document dialog box.

    b. Click *Page Designs* in the *Category* list box and then click *Text: Article D* in the *Page Designs* list box. Click Create to open the document.

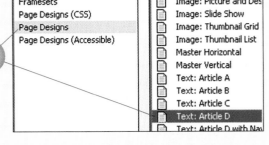

    c. Click File on the Menu bar and then Save or Save As.

    d. Type **ch2ex04-a.htm** in the *File name* text box in the Save As dialog box.

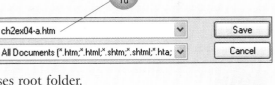

    e. Click the Save button to save the document in the ch_02_exercises root folder.

    f. Click <body> in the Tag selector (located just above the Properties panel) to select the page content.

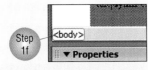

    g. Click Edit on the Menu bar and then Copy to copy the selected material.

    h. Create a new HTML document (HTML Basic page) by clicking File on the Menu bar and then New. Make sure *Basic page* and *HTML* are selected in the New Document dialog box *Category* and *Basic page* list boxes, and then click the Create button to place the document in the Document window.

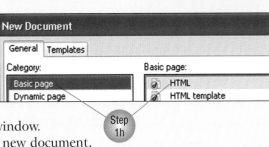

    i. With the insertion point located in the new document, click Edit on the Menu bar and then Paste. An exact duplicate of **Text: Article D** will appear in the new document.

    j. Use the Save or Save As commands to name the document **ch2ex04-b.htm**. Save the document and then close it.

2. Paste unformatted text into a document by completing the following steps:

   a. Select the first paragraph in **ch2ex04-a.htm**.

   b. Click Edit on the Menu bar and then Copy to copy the selected text.

   c. Create a new HTML document.

   d. Click Edit on the Menu bar and then Paste Text to paste the copied text. The copied text will appear in the document, but because the HTML formatting has been removed, it will not appear in bold.

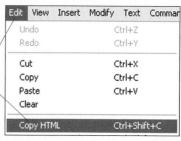

   e. Click File on the Menu bar and then Save or Save As to name the document **ch2ex04-c.htm**. Save the document and then close it.

3. Copy material from a document and paste it into another document so its HTML code is displayed by completing the following steps:

   a. Select the first paragraph in **ch2ex04-a.htm**.

   b. Click Edit on the Menu bar and then Copy HTML.

   c. Create a new HTML document.

   d. Click Edit on the Menu bar and then click Paste to paste the copied material. The text will appear in the document with starting and ending bold tags displayed at the beginning and end of the paragraph.

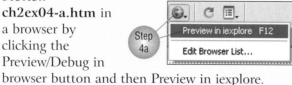

   e. Use the Save or Save As commands to name the document **ch2ex04-d.htm**. Save the Document and then close it.

4. Copy the code controlling a Web page and recreate the page in the Document window by completing the following steps:

   a. Preview **ch2ex04-a.htm** in a browser by clicking the Preview/Debug in browser button and then Preview in iexplore.

   b. Position the pointer over any of the text in the document, right-click, and then click View Source.

DREAMWEAVER MX 2004

c.   The source code for the document will appear in a text editor such as Notepad. Click Edit on the text editor's Menu bar and then Select All. Click Edit again and then Copy to copy the HTML code. Close the text editor and browser when you are finished. ***Note: Check with your instructor if a text editor other than Notepad opens.***

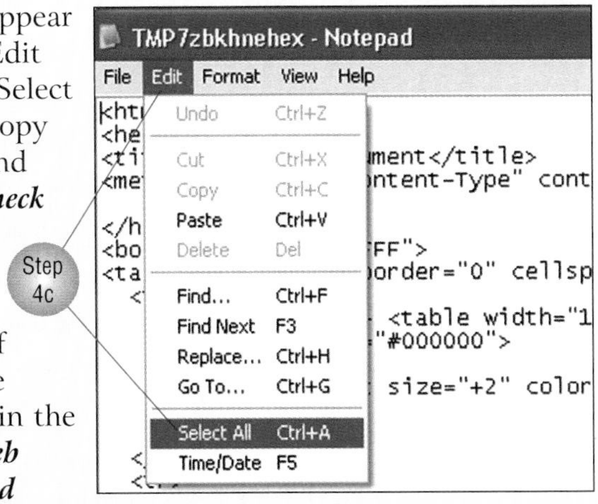

d.   Create a new HTML document.

e.   Position the insertion point at the top of the document. Click Edit and then Paste HTML. The Web page contents appear in the Document window. ***Note: If a copied Web page contains images and other associated files, they will not be copied. When the pasted HTML is viewed in the Document window, missing content will be indicated by placeholders.***

f.   Use the Save or Save As commands to name the document **ch2ex04-e.htm**. Save the document and then close it.

5.   Close **ch2ex04-a.htm**.

Copying and Pasting Microsoft Word and Excel Document Content

The contents of the latest versions of Microsoft Word and Excel documents can be copied and pasted into a Dreamweaver MX 2004 document with all or most of their formatting intact by using the Paste Formatted command. The Paste Formatted command as shown in Figure 2.8 will appear on the Edit drop-down menu after material has been copied from a Word or Excel document. During the pasting process, Dreamweaver MX 2004 automatically converts the document into HTML and copies it into the document open in the Document window. The original Microsoft document will remain unchanged. Using the Paste command will create an unformatted copy of the material.

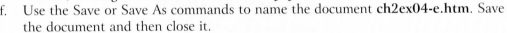

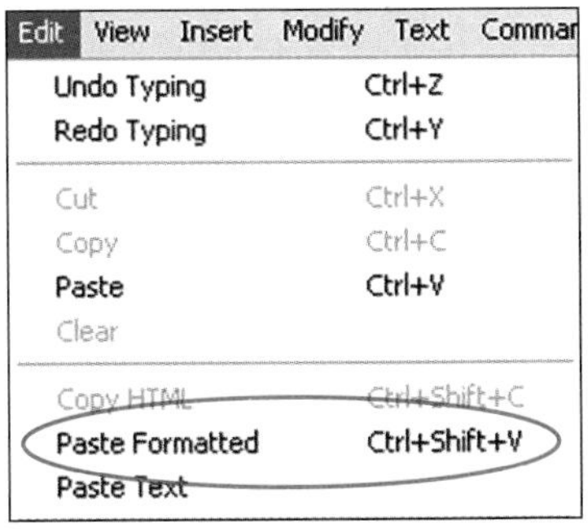

Figure 2.8 • Paste Formatted Command

1. Copy content from Word and Excel documents and paste it into a Dreamweaver HTML document by completing the following steps:

   a. At a clear document screen, create a new HTML document and use the Save or Save As commands to name and save it to the ch_02_exercises root folder as **ch2ex05.htm**.

   b. Start Microsoft Word. ***Note: Do not close Dreamweaver MX 2004.***

   c. Click File and then Open to locate and open the **ozymandius** student file. ***Hint: The file path will be Sites/ch_02_exercises/ch_02_student files/ozymandius.***

   d. Select the contents of **ozymandius**.

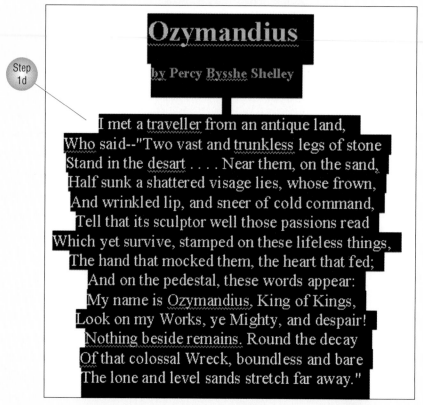

   e. Click Edit on the Word Menu bar and then Copy to copy the selected material. Close Word when you are finished copying the contents.

   f. Return to Dreamweaver MX 2004. Click Edit on the Menu bar and then Paste Formatted to paste a formatted copy of the selected Word document content into **ch2ex05.htm**.

   g. Press Enter two times to move the insertion point below the content you just pasted.

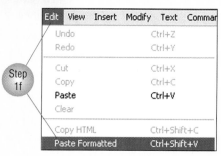

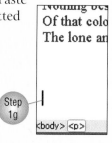

h. Start Microsoft Excel. *Note: Do not close Dreamweaver MX 2004.*

i. Click File and then Open to locate and open the **sales** student file. *Hint: The file path will be Sites/ch_02_exercises/ch_02_student files/sales.*

j. Select the Excel table.

k. Click Edit and then Copy to copy the selected table. Close Excel when you are finished copying the table.

l. Return to Dreamweaver MX 2004. Click Edit on the Menu bar and then Paste Formatted to paste a formatted copy of the selected Excel content into **ch2ex05.htm**.

m. Click Preview/Debug in Browser and then Preview in iexplore to view the document in a browser. Close the browser when you are finished.

2. Save **ch2ex05.htm** and then close it.

Importing Documents

It is possible to import Microsoft Word and Excel documents by clicking File on the Menu bar, Import, and then using the Open dialog box to locate and open the desired file in Dreamweaver MX 2004. In most cases it is better to copy and paste content from a Word or Excel file as that method preserves most or all of the formatting. However, if the file size is over 300 kilobytes (KB), the Word or Excel file should be imported.

Tabular data can be imported in Dreamweaver MX 2004 if first saved as a *delimited text file*. After a file has been saved as a delimited text file, it can be imported by clicking File on the Menu bar, Import, and then Tabular Data. An Import Tabular Data dialog box appears. The dialog box contains a Browse button to locate and open the file.

Changing Text Properties with the Property Inspector

In the default Dreamweaver MX 2004 setup, the Property inspector uses Cascading Style Sheet (CSS) rules to change text properties. While it is possible to specify that the Property inspector use HTML font tags to change text properties (click Edit, Preferences, select the *General* category, and remove the check mark next to *Use CSS instead of HTML tags*), the use of the font tag has been deprecated (discouraged) by the World Wide Web Consortium (W3C) in favor of using CSS to control the way page content is displayed. Using CSS to control text properties

DREAMWEAVER MX 2004   65

Creating a Basic Web Page

Figure 2.9
Property Inspector
Expander Arrow

has many advantages over marking up text with font tags; these advantages are described in Chapter 6, *Cascading Style Sheets (CSS)*. The exercises in this book assume that the *Use CSS instead of HTML tags* option has been enabled.

Most formatting options can be accessed as Menu bar commands, but the Property inspector offers a quicker and more convenient way of formatting in most circumstances. The **Property inspector** is located in the horizontal **Properties panel** and can be undocked and redocked like any other panel. The Property inspector can be expanded or contracted by clicking its Expander arrow as shown in Figure 2.9.

The various components of the Property inspector related to text properties are identified in Figure 2.10. The Property inspector also can be used to perform other functions not related to text formatting, which are described in subsequent chapters of this book.

Format

The *Format* list box drop-down list shown in Figure 2.11 lets you format selected text as a paragraph, choose from six different heading sizes, or mark the text as **preformatted text**. Sometimes, it is important to retain text formatting that HTML might ignore or override, such as for verse or HTML code. In situations like that, selecting *Preformatted* instructs browsers to display the text with its original formatting intact. When preformatted text is displayed in most browsers, it appears in a different font style to distinguish it from regularly formatted text.

Font

The *Font* text box drop-down list illustrated in Figure 2.12 lets you select the **font style** (also known as font face or typeface) for selected text and any text subsequently entered on the page. Each font style option on the list contains three related styles from the same font family. A selection of three styles is offered because not all computers have the same fonts installed. Selecting a font that is not available on a computer will cause a browser to display the affected text in a

Figure 2.10
Property Inspector

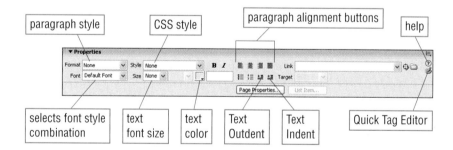

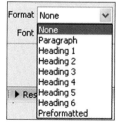

Figure 2.11 • *Format* List Box Drop-Down List

Figure 2.12 • *Font* Text Box Drop-Down List

default font that might be very different in appearance from the style intended. Specifying a list of three font styles increases the chances that a computer will have at least one of the three styles installed. The styles are listed by preference, and a computer will check to determine whether a style is installed beginning with the first style in the list.

You can create you own combinations of font styles using the font styles available on your computer. Font style combinations can be added or removed by completing the following steps:

1. Click the Property inspector *Font* text box down-pointing arrow.

2. Click *Edit Font List* at the bottom of the drop-down list to open the Edit Font List dialog box.

3. Check to see that *(Add fonts in list below)* is selected in the Edit Font List dialog box as shown in Figure 2.13. If it is not selected, click to select it.

4. The *Available fonts* list box in the lower-right corner of the dialog box contains the list of fonts available. Select a font for the combination you want to create, and then click the left-pointing paired arrow (<<) button to add it to the *Chosen fonts* list box. When you are finished adding fonts, click the Plus (+) button at the top of the dialog box to create your new font combination. You can continue creating new combinations by clicking the Plus (+) button to add each combination.

5. Font combinations can be removed by clicking the Minus (–) button after they have been selected.

6. Fonts can be removed from a font combination by selecting a font combination, selecting the font to be removed in the *Chosen fonts* list box, and then clicking the right-pointing paired arrow (>>) button to remove the font.

7. Fonts can be added to an existing font combination by selecting a font combination, selecting the font to be added in the *Available fonts* list box, and then clicking the left-pointing paired arrow button to add the font.

8. Click OK to close the Edit Font List dialog box.

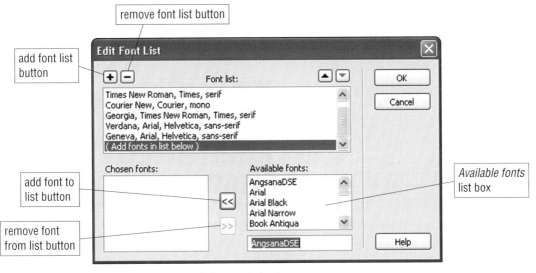

Figure 2.13 • Edit Font List Dialog Box

Style

The *Style* list box displays the CSS class style that is applied to selected text. This list box will be described more fully in Chapter 6, *Cascading Style Sheets (CSS)*.

Size

The *Size* drop-down list shown in Figure 2.14 controls font size. In the default Dreamweaver MX 2004 setup, font sizes specified in pixels are listed *(9, 10, 12, 14, 16, 18, 24, 36)*, as well as relative sizes (*xx-small, x-small, small*, etc.). When a number is selected, the list box located to the right of the *Size* text box displays additional units of measurement such as points, picas, cm, and so forth.

Text Color

Text colors can be changed by clicking the Property inspector's **text color box**, the small, unlabeled gray square to the right of the *Size* text box. Clicking the text color box opens a Web-safe color palette known as the **Color Picker** as shown in Figure 2.15. **Web-safe colors** refers to colors that will appear the same in both Netscape or Explorer browsers running on either Windows or Macintosh systems operating in 256-color mode.

The **Eyedropper** pictured in Figure 2.15 can be used to change the color of selected text by clicking a color anywhere in the Color Picker or on the screen, even outside of Dreamweaver MX 2004. All text entered subsequently will be in this color unless you click the Color Picker **Strikethrough button** to restore the default text color setting. Clicking the black arrow in the top-right corner of the Color Picker opens a drop-down menu with additional color palettes, and clicking the **Color Wheel button** opens the Windows Color Selection palette containing 48 basic colors. Not all of these palettes are Web-safe. If a color is chosen from a palette that is not Web-safe, it is important to preview the page in several browsers to check the results.

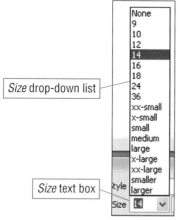

Figure 2.14 • Property Inspector *Size* Text Box Drop-Down List (CSS Mode)

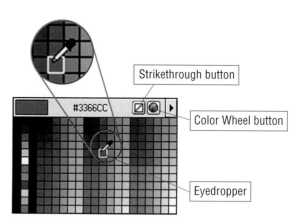

Figure 2.15 • Color Picker

When a color is selected using the Color Picker or a color palette, its hexadecimal code is displayed in the text color text box. If you are familiar with the *hexadecimal color values* used in HTML, you can enter the desired code directly in the text box. You also can type a recognized color by name, such as red, blue, green, and so on into the text color text box.

Text Alignment

Selected text can be aligned by clicking one of the Property inspector alignment buttons for left, center, right, or justify. Text justification is not supported by all browsers, so if this option is chosen, be sure to preview the page in several different browsers. The **Text Indent button** inserts **blockquote tags** (<blockquote>) to indent text. Each time the Text Indent button is clicked, it indents selected text even further. The **Text Outdent button** undoes text indenting.

USING THE PROPERTY INSPECTOR TO FORMAT TEXT

1. Add heading formatting to text by completing the following steps:
   a. At a clear document screen, open **ch2ex04-a.htm** and select the first paragraph of the document.
   b. Click Edit on the Menu bar and then Copy to copy the paragraph. Close **ch2ex04-a.htm** when you are finished.

   Step 1a

   Lorem Ipsum Dolor

   Lorem ipsum dolor sit amet, consetetur sadipscing elitr, sed diam nonumy eirmod tempor invidunt ut labore et dolore magna aliquyam erat, sed diam voluptua. Lorem ipsum dolor sit amet, consetetur sadipscing elitr

   c. Create a new HTML document. Click File and then Save or Save As to name and save the document as **ch2ex06.htm**.
   d. Click Edit and then Paste Text to paste the copied paragraph into **ch2ex06.htm** without any formatting.
   e. Position the insertion point just before the first word in the paragraph *(Lorem),* and then press Enter to move the paragraph down.
   f. Position the insertion point at the top-left corner of the document and then type **This Is a Heading**. *Note: Do not type a period.*
   g. Position the insertion point anywhere in the *This Is a Heading* text.
   h. Click the *Format* list box down-pointing arrow in the Property inspector, scroll down the list, and then click *Heading 2.* The heading text you typed appears in a larger font. *Note: The smaller the heading size number the larger it appears.* **Heading 1** *produces the largest heading text and* **Heading 6** *the smallest.*

   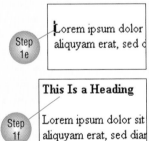

   Step 1e

   Lorem ipsum dolor aliquyam erat, sed d

   Step 1f

   This Is a Heading

   Lorem ipsum dolor sit aliquyam erat, sed dia

   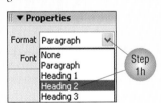

   Step 1h

2. Change a font style by completing the following steps:
   a. Select the heading text in **ch2ex06.htm**.

b. Click the *Font* text box down-pointing arrow in the Properties panel and then click *Arial, Helvetica, sans-serif* from the drop-down list. The heading appears in the font style you selected.

c. Position the insertion point just after the heading and press Enter. Type New Text. Note that this new text appears in the same font style as the heading but in a smaller default font size. ***Note: After a font style is changed, any subsequently entered text appears in that style until a new style is selected.***

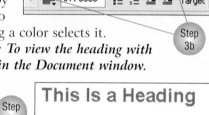

3. Change text color by completing the following steps:

   a. Select the heading text in **ch2ex06.htm**.

   b. Open the Color Picker in the Property inspector by clicking the Text Color box. Use the Eyedropper to pick a shade of red from the Color Picker. Clicking a color selects it. The heading appears in the color you select. ***Note: To view the heading with the new color, deselect the heading text by clicking in the Document window.***

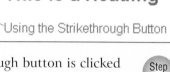

   c. Position the insertion point at the end of the heading text and press Enter. Type Using the Strikethrough Button. The text appears in the same text color you selected for the heading. Whenever text color is changed, all subsequently entered text will appear in that color until the Strikethrough button is clicked or another color is selected.

   d. Select the *Using the Strikethrough Button* text.

   e. Click the Property inspector text color box and then click the Strikethrough button on the Color Picker to restore the default color (black) to the selected text.

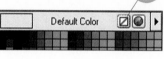

   f. Position the insertion point at the end of the text and press Enter to create a new line. Type Default Text. This text will appear in black, the default text color.

4. Change alignment by completing the following steps:

   a. Position the insertion point anywhere on the same line as the heading.

   b. Click the Align Center button in the Property inspector to align the heading in the center of the page.

   c. Position the insertion point anywhere in the paragraph text. Click the Justify button to justify (flush-left and flush-right margins) the paragraph margins.

   d. Save **ch2ex06.htm** but do not close it.

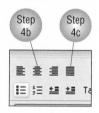

Setting Background and Text Color Defaults

The Page Properties dialog box Appearance page as shown in Figure 2.16 is used to specify default background and text colors. Clicking Modify on the Menu bar and then Page Properties, or clicking the Property inspector Page Properties button opens the Page Properties dialog box. Clicking *Appearance* in the *Category* list box displays the Page Properties dialog box Appearance page. Right-clicking in the Document window and then clicking Page Properties is another method that can be used to open the dialog box.

Page background color can be changed by clicking the *Background color* color box and using the Eyedropper to choose a new color from the Color Picker. Clicking the Apply button applies the color to the page background so that you can see how it looks. After you choose a color, click OK to confirm the choice and close the dialog box.

Default text color can be changed by clicking the *Text color* color box and following the same procedure used to specify a default background color. Using the text color box in the Property inspector to choose a text color overrides the default text color. Clicking the Color Picker Strikethrough button restores the default text color for selected text.

Dreamweaver MX 2004 also features a number of predefined Web-safe background and text color combinations as shown in Figure 2.17. The **Set Color Scheme Command dialog box** can be accessed by clicking Commands on the Menu bar and then Set Color Scheme. Clicking the Apply button shows how a color scheme will appear on a page, and clicking OK confirms a choice and closes the dialog box.

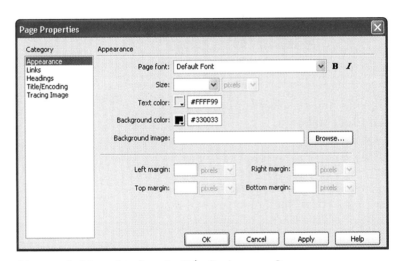

Figure 2.16 • Page Properties Dialog Box Appearance Page

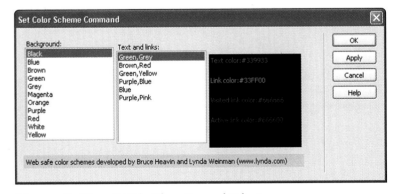

Figure 2.17 • Set Color Scheme Command Dialog Box

1. Change background and text default color settings by completing the following steps:
   a. With **ch2ex06.htm** open, click File on the Menu bar and then Save As to rename and save it as **ch2ex07-a.htm**.
   b. Click Modify on the Menu bar and then Page Properties.
   c. Click the *Background color* color box and use the Eyedropper to click and select a light yellow background color from the Color Picker. After you have selected the color, click the Apply button to see how it will look.

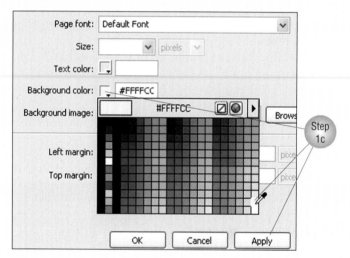

   d. Click the *Text color* color box to select a brown text color. Click Apply to see how the text will look in that color.
   e. Click OK to close the Page Properties dialog box and implement the changes. Because the Property inspector was used to override the text color for the heading, it will not appear in the default text color you selected.
   f. Select the heading and the *Using the Strikethrough Button* text, click the text color box in the Property inspector, and then click the Color Picker Strikethrough button. The selected text now appears in the default text color you chose in the Page Properties dialog box.

   g. Save **ch2ex07-a.htm** but do not close it.
2. Select a color in a non-Dreamweaver MX 2004 document by completing the following steps:
   a. Click File on the Menu bar and then Save As to rename and save **ch2ex07-a.htm** as **ch2ex07-b.htm**.
   b. Go online and search for a Web page with a background color you like.
   c. Click the *Dreamweaver MX 2004* icon on the Windows Taskbar to display Dreamweaver MX 2004 again.

d. Click the Dreamweaver MX 2004 Restore Down button located on the far right side of the blue Title bar at the top of the Dreamweaver MX 2004 workspace. The Dreamweaver MX 2004 workspace will shrink in size. If it does not you can use the resize arrows on the workspace borders to shrink the workspace until it fills about one quarter of the screen. *Hint: It may be necessary to drag down the Dreamweaver MX 2004 Title bar slightly to access the resize arrows.*

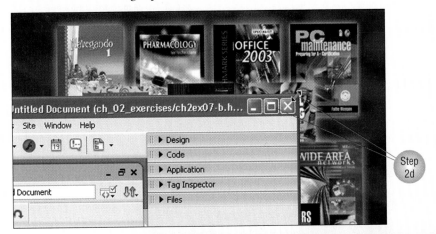

Step 2d

e. Click Modify on the Menu bar and then Page Properties.

f. Open the *Background color* color box, click the Eyedropper anywhere in the Color Picker, and without releasing the mouse button, move to the background color of the Web page with the color you want to select. *Hint: If you release the mouse button, the Eyedropper will not appear after you move out of the Page Properties dialog box. If Dreamweaver MX 2004 is blocking the color you want, close the dialog box, drag Dreamweaver MX 2004 to uncover the color by clicking in its Title bar, and then reopen the dialog box to start the color-selection process again.* Release the mouse button when you see the background color in the color box.

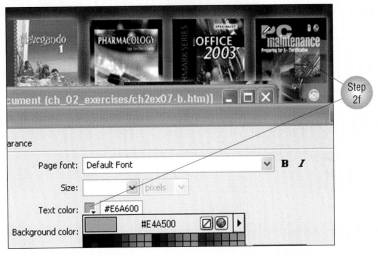

Step 2f

g. Click OK to close the Page Properties dialog box.

h. Click the Dreamweaver MX 2004 Maximize button to restore the Dreamweaver MX 2004 workspace to a full-size display. The background color you selected now appears in **ch2ex07-b.htm**. *Note: Depending on your background color selection, the text may be difficult to read. Change the default text color to a color that is legible with your background color selection.*

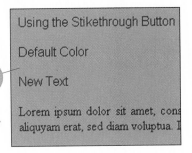

Step 2h

i. Save **ch2ex07-b.htm** and then close it.
3. Use a Dreamweaver MX 2004 predefined color scheme by completing the following steps:
a. Click File on the Menu bar and then New.
b. Click *Page Designs* in the New Document dialog box *Category* list box, *Text: Article A* in the *Page Designs* list box, and then Create to open the document.
c. Click File and then Save As to name and save the document as **ch2ex07-c.htm**.
d. Click Commands on the Menu bar and then Set Color Scheme.
e. Click *Yellow* in the *Background* list box, and *Green,Red,Orange* in the *Text and links* list box in the Set Color Scheme Command dialog box.

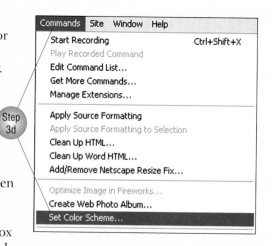

Step 3d

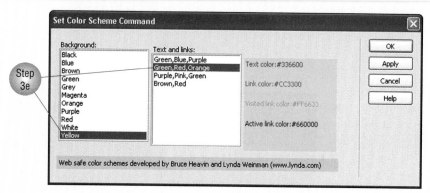

Step 3e

f. Click Apply to see how the color scheme will look on the page.
g. Click OK to apply the color scheme and close the dialog box.
4. Save **ch2ex07-c.htm** and then close it.

Using the Assets Panel

The *Assets panel* (in the Files panel group) maintains lists of all of the assets used in a site including images, colors, and URLs (external links including e-mail addresses). Assets can be used in a document by selecting the asset and clicking the Assets panel Apply button. Site assets can be viewed in the Assets panel by expanding the Files panel group, clicking the Assets tab, clicking the *Site* radio button, and then clicking the desired Asset button as shown in Figure 2.18. You also can select favorite assets and save them in the Assets panel's favorites list. Asset favorites can be inserted in documents in the same manner as normal assets, and can be viewed by clicking the Assets panel *Favorites* radio button. Exercise 8 deals with color assets, but the methods described are applicable to working with other asset types in the Assets panel as well.

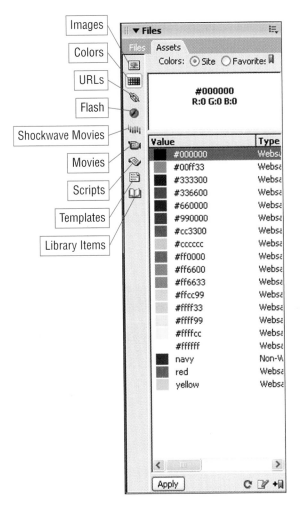

Images

Colors

URLs

Flash

Shockwave Movies

Movies

Scripts

Templates

Library Items

Figure 2.18
Assets Panel

SAVING AND USING COLOR FAVORITES

1. Create and save color favorites by completing the following steps:
   a. At a clear document screen, open **ch2ex04-a.htm**. Use the Save As command to rename and save it as **ch2ex08-a.htm**.
   b. Select the heading text in the first column and use the Property inspector to change the text color to green by clicking the text color box and using the Color Picker Eyedropper to click a shade of green. *Note: Because the text in ch2ex08-a.htm is contained in a table, the Property inspector now displays some table formatting properties. You will learn more about these in Chapter 3,* Working with Tables.

Step 1b

c. Right-click the selected heading text and then click Add to Color Favorites.

d. Expand the Files panel group and then click the Assets panel tab.

e. If necessary, click the *Favorites* radio button. The heading color appears in the *Favorites* color list.

f. Save **ch2ex08-a.htm** but do not close it.

2. Apply a color from the Assets panel *Favorites* list by completing the following steps:

a. Use the Save As command to rename and save **ch2ex08-a.htm** as **ch2ex08-b.htm**.

b. Select the text in the first paragraph.

c. Click the color you added to the Assets panel *Favorites* list and then click the Apply button. The text you just selected appears in the color chosen from the Assets panel.

3. Save a favorite color with the Asset panel's New Color button by completing the following steps:

a. With the Assets panel open and the *Favorites* radio button selected, click the New Color button located at the bottom right of the panel near the Apply button.

b. Use the Eyedropper to select a dark shade of red. Clicking the color saves it in the *Favorites* list.

c. Select the text in the second paragraph.

d. Click the red you just created and saved, and click the Apply button to apply the new color.

4. Save **ch2ex08-b.htm** and then close it.

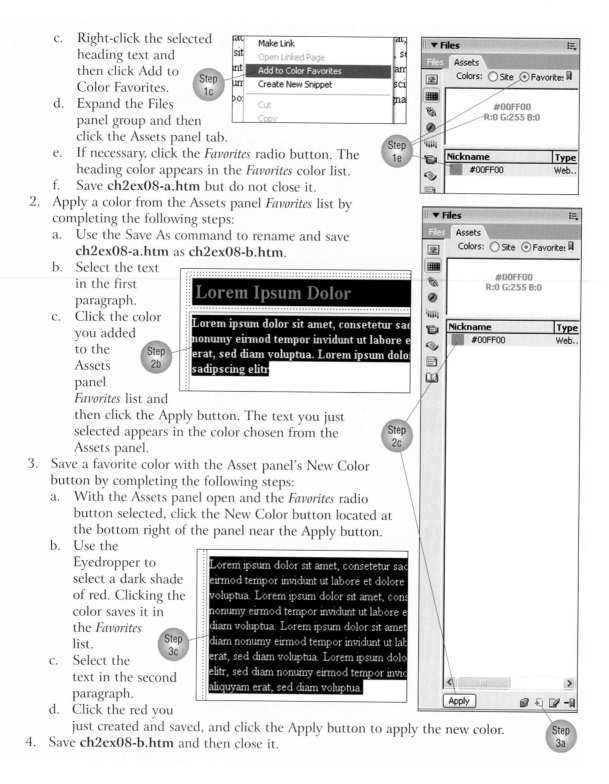

Inserting Links

Clicking a **hyperlink (link)** in a Web page can take you to another location on the same page or to a document on a server located thousands of miles away. The ability to create **hypertext documents** (documents containing links) is the

DREAMWEAVER MX 2004

basis of the **World Wide Web (WWW or "The Web")**. Dreamweaver MX 2004 makes creating and managing links easy by offering you a variety of different tools for working with links. Before creating links, you should have a basic understanding of how they work.

In HTML, a link consists of starting and ending **anchor tags** and an **href attribute** as shown in Figure 2.19. The anchor tags surround the text or object that will become a link. The **href** attribute directs a browser to the **link target** by specifying a **path** to the link target's location. For example, **<a href="page_2.htm">Page Two</a>** makes a link out of the enclosed Page Two text. Clicking the Page Two link directs a browser to find and open the link target, in this case, a document named page_2.htm.

When creating Web pages, you should be aware of two types of paths—absolute paths and document relative paths. **Absolute paths** include the complete **URL (Uniform Resource Locator)** for a linked document, including the protocol used. The protocol for Web pages is usually HTTP (Hypertext Transfer Protocol), so a typical Web page URL begins with *http://www*. The protocol is followed by the domain name of the server hosting the link target and then the link target document name and file extension. If the target document is located within a folder or subfolder, the folders are indicated by a forward slash. For example, http://www.domain_name.com/articles/holiday_spots.htm would instruct a browser to use HTTP to locate a domain, find a folder named articles on that server, and then find and display a document named holiday_spots.htm located in the articles folder as shown in Figure 2.20. An absolute path must be used whenever a link is

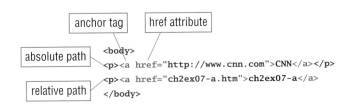

Figure 2.19
Absolute and Relative Paths

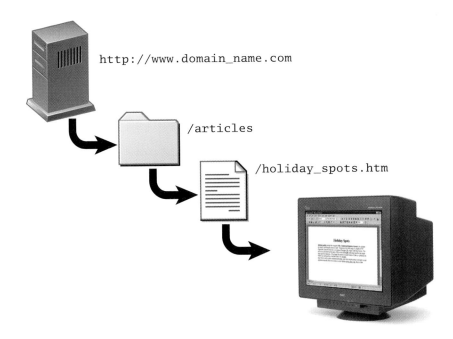

Figure 2.20
A Document Path

made to a document located on another server. Absolute paths also can be used to link to documents within the same site, but this is not recommended because links based on absolute paths might be broken if a document is moved.

Document relative paths are used to link documents that are located in the same folder or site. Document relative paths do not contain a protocol and also omit any portion of a path that is the same for the linking document and the target document. For example, a document in a folder could be linked to another document in the same folder using a relative path consisting only of the target document's file name, such as report.htm. If a document is located in another folder or subfolder, two dots and a forward slash (../) are used to indicate a parent folder, and a forward slash (/) is used to indicate a subfolder. Using document relative paths for all of the documents located in a Dreamweaver site allows Dreamweaver MX 2004 to update them automatically if their location is changed within the site.

By default, links appear in blue underlined text to differentiate them from ordinary text. After a link has been clicked, its color changes. (Some browsers also support changing the color of a link when the pointer hovers over it.) With Dreamweaver MX 2004, you can change link colors using the Page Properties dialog box Links page.

Links do not work when viewed in any of the workspace views because Dreamweaver MX 2004 is a text editor and not a browser. To check a link, the Preview/Debug in browser button and then the Preview in iexplore button should be clicked to preview the page in a browser. Any links to documents on the user's computer or local network will be active in the browser. If a link is to a document located on another server, the computer must be connected to the Internet to test it.

Using the Property Inspector to Insert Links

You can select the text or image that will become a link and then click the Property inspector's Browse for File button shown in Figure 2.21 to browse and locate the desired link target. After the link target is selected, its path appears in the *URL* text box of the Select File dialog box. *Document* should be selected in the *Relative to* list box unless you are working on a large Web site that uses several servers, or a server that hosts several different sites. All future links will be created using the path type specified in the *Relative to* list box, so this choice does not have to be made every time a link is created.

Links also can be created with the Property inspector using the ***Point to File button*** shown in Figure 2.21. Select a link and click the Point to File button while holding down the mouse button without releasing it so you can drag the arrow that appears to the link target location in the Files panel integrated file browser. Folders will expand when the arrow head is held over the expand/hide box. After the target link has been selected, its URL appears in the *Link* text box. Releasing the mouse button creates the link. If the Document window is not expanded, this same method can be used to link to any open document by dragging the arrow to the desired link target document.

Figure 2.21
Point to File and Browse for File Buttons

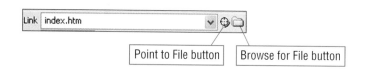

Another way that the Property inspector can be used to create a link is by selecting a link and typing a path in the *Link* text box. This method is used for creating links to documents located on other servers because they cannot be located using the Point to File or Browse for File buttons. This method is also used to create links to documents that have not yet been created. Be very careful when typing a path, because a single mistake will cause a link to fail. Documents from the Files panel also can be dragged into the *Link* text box to create a link to the dragged document, but only if the document is not open.

The *Target* list box drop-down list shown in Figure 2.22 lets you choose where the target link document will open. The default setting *_self* opens a target link document in the same browser window as the sending link, while *_blank* opens the target link document in a new window. The other target options are used with frames and are described in Chapter 5, *Working with Frames*.

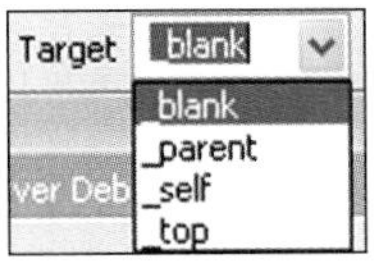

Figure 2.22
Target List Box Drop-Down List

Using the Menu Bar to Insert Links

Clicking Insert on the Menu bar and then Hyperlink opens the Hyperlink dialog box shown in Figure 2.23. The Hyperlink dialog box works differently from the Property inspector when creating links because the text that will become a link must be typed in the empty *Text* text box in the dialog box. The link target is located by clicking the Browse for File button. The *Title* and *Access key* text boxes are accessibility features. Providing a title for a link lets those using screen readers understand the purpose of the link. In newer browsers, a link title appears in a tooltip when the pointer hovers over the link as shown in Figure 2.24. Typing a single letter in the *Access key* text box allows users without a mouse to select a link by pressing the Alt key and the assigned access control letter (such as Alt+E), and then open the link by pressing Enter.

The *Tab index* text box lets you determine the order in which the link will be selected if the Tab key is pressed. For example, imagine three links named A, B, and C on a page. If the *Tab index* text box for link C was set as *1,* the *Tab index* for link A as *2,* and the *Tab index* for link B as *3,* successively pressing the Tab key would select link C first, followed by link A, and finally link B.

Using the Insert Bar to Insert Links

Clicking the Hyperlink button on the Insert bar (Common menu item or tab), as shown in Figure 2.25, is another method of opening the Hyperlink dialog box. The dialog box functions exactly the same as when opened using the Menu bar.

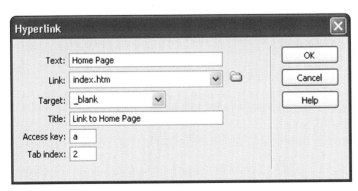

Figure 2.23 • Hyperlink Dialog Box

Figure 2.24 • Link Title Tooltip

Figure 2.25 • Insert Bar Hyperlink Button

Using the Context-Sensitive Menu to Insert Links

Selecting text, right-clicking, and then clicking Make Link opens the Select File dialog box, which can be used to browse for the link target file. After a file has been selected, its path is indicated in the *Link* text box in the Property inspector. Clicking OK closes the dialog box and creates the link.

exercise

9

1. Use the Property inspector to insert links by completing the following steps:
   a. Create two new HTML documents. Name one document **ch2ex09-a.htm** and the other **ch2ex09-b.htm**.
   b. With **ch2ex09-a.htm** open in the Document window, type Link One, Link Two, Link Three, and then save the document. ***Hint: Click the document tab for*** ch2ex09-a.htm ***to make it the current document.***

   Step 1b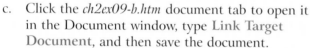

   c. Click the *ch2ex09-b.htm* document tab to open it in the Document window, type Link Target Document, and then save the document.

   Step 1c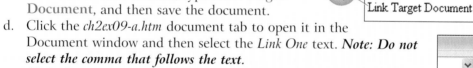

   Step 1e

   d. Click the *ch2ex09-a.htm* document tab to open it in the Document window and then select the *Link One* text. ***Note: Do not select the comma that follows the text.***
   e. Click the Browse for File button in the Property inspector to open the Select File dialog box.
   f. Use the file browser to locate **ch2ex09-b.htm**. To create the link, double-click the file, or select it and then click the OK button. Note that the file name also appears in the *URL* text box because you are creating a link.

   Step 1f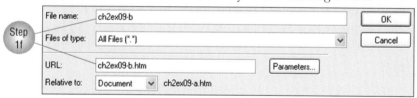

   g. Link One now appears in blue, underlined text to indicate that it is a link.

   Step 1g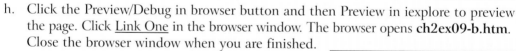

   h. Click the Preview/Debug in browser button and then Preview in iexplore to preview the page. Click Link One in the browser window. The browser opens **ch2ex09-b.htm**. Close the browser window when you are finished.

2. Use the Point to File button to insert a link by completing the following steps:
   a. With **ch2ex09-a.htm** as the current document, select the *Link Two* text.
   b. Make sure the Files panel is open. Click the Point to File button in the Property inspector and, without releasing the mouse button, drag the arrow line to *ch2ex09-b.htm* in the Files panel. Release the mouse button after you have verified that its path appears in the Property inspector *Link* text box. Link Two now links to **ch2ex09-b.htm**.

   Step 2b

c.   Click the Preview/Debug in browser button, click Preview in iexplore, and then check that the link works. Close the browser when you are finished.

3.   Drag a target link to the Property inspector to create a link by completing the following steps:

a.   Close **ch2ex09-b.htm**. *Note: If a document is open, it cannot be linked by dragging its file name from the Files panel to the* **Link** *text box.*

b.   With **ch2ex09-a.htm** as the current document, select the *Link Three* text.

c.   Position the pointer over *ch2ex09-b.htm* in the Files panel. Click and drag the mouse to the *Link* text box in the Property inspector. Release the mouse button to create the link. The path is displayed in the *Link* text box. *Note: The link formatting will not appear until you click in the document.*

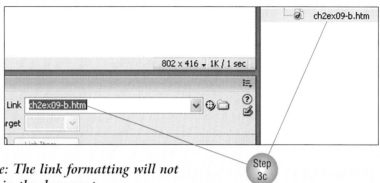

d.   Click the Preview/Debug in browser button and then click Preview in iexplore to check that the link works. Close the browser when you are finished.

4.   Insert links using the Insert bar or Menu bar by completing the following steps:

a.   With **ch2ex09-a.htm** as the current document, position the insertion point to the right of <u>Link Three</u> and press Enter to create a new line.

b.   Open the Hyperlink dialog box by clicking Insert on the Menu bar and then Hyperlink, or by clicking the Hyperlink button on the Insert bar (Common menu item or tab).

c.   Type Accessible Link in the *Text* text box.

d.   Click the Browse for File button to browse and locate **ch2ex09-b.htm**.

e.   Select *_blank* from the *Target* list box drop-down list.

f.   Type Link to ch2ex09-b.htm in the *Title* text box.

g.   Type a in the *Access key* text box.

h.   Type 1 in the *Tab index* text box.

i.   Click OK to create the link and close the dialog box.

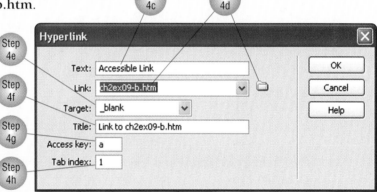

j.   Click the Preview/Debug in browser button and then click Preview in iexplore to preview the page.

k.   While holding down the Alt key, press the A key. If your browser supports this function, a dotted line appears around the link to indicate that it has been selected.

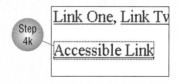

l.   Press Enter to open the link to **ch2ex09-b.htm**. Because you selected *_blank*, the document opens in a new browser window. Close both browser windows when you are finished. *Note: If your browser does not support this function (a dotted line does not appear around the link), simply click the link to open the link target.*

m. Click the Preview/Debug in browser button and then click Preview in iexplore to preview **ch2ex09-a.htm** again. Press the Tab key to select the links.

n. Hover the pointer over <u>Accessible Link</u>. If you have a recent browser version, the title you created for the link appears in a tooltip next to the link. Close the browser when you are finished.

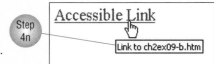

Step 4n

5. Save **ch2ex09-a.htm** and then close it.

Internal (Anchor) Links

Figure 2.26
Insert Bar Named Anchor Button

Anchor links are used to create links to locations within a document. Before creating an anchor link, the link target *(named anchor)* must be identified by placing the insertion point just before the desired target location within the document. The Named Anchor dialog box is opened by clicking Insert on the Menu bar and then Named Anchor. Another way to access the Named Anchor dialog box is by clicking the Named Anchor button on the Insert bar (Common menu item or tab) as shown in Figure 2.26. A *Named Anchor marker* appears at the named anchor location as shown in Figure 2.27 if the visibility option for *Named anchors* has been selected using the Preferences dialog box. To select this option, complete the following steps:

Figure 2.27
Named Anchor Marker

1. Click Edit on the Menu bar and then Preferences to open the Preferences dialog box.
2. Click *Invisible Elements* from the *Category* list box.
3. Click the *Named anchors* check box if it does not contain a check mark.
4. Click OK to close the dialog box.

After an anchor has been named, you can create a link to it by typing the pound sign (#) and the name of the anchor in the Property inspector *Link* text box, or by using the Point to File method.

exercise 10 — INSERTING ANCHOR LINKS

1. Create and insert a named anchor by completing the following steps:
    a. Open **ch2ex04-a.htm** and use the Save As command to rename and save it as **ch2ex10.htm**.
    b. Scroll down and click the insertion point immediately after the period following the word *voluptua* at the end of the document.

Step 1b

c. Click Insert on the Menu bar and then Named Anchor.

DREAMWEAVER MX 2004

d. Type endofpage in the *Anchor name* text box in the Named Anchor dialog box. Click OK to close the dialog box. A Named Anchor marker appears where you inserted the named anchor if you used the Preferences dialog box to select *Invisible Elements* in the *Category* list box and then selected the *Named anchor* check box. ***Note: Named anchors cannot begin with a number, and there should be no spaces in the anchor name. The Named Anchor marker can be deleted by right-clicking and then clicking Cut.***

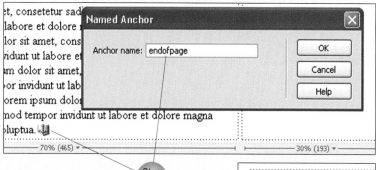

e. Scroll to the top of the page and select the first word of the first paragraph *(Lorem)*.

f. Type #endofpage in the Property inspector's *Link* text box. ***Note: The pound sign (#) lets browsers know that this is an internal link.***

g. Click the Preview/Debug in browser button and then click Preview in iexplore to preview the page.

h. Click the <u>Lorem</u> link. The screen jumps to the bottom of the page where the named anchor is located. Close the browser window when you are finished.

2. Create and insert a named anchor using the Point to File method by completing the following steps:

a. Select *Lorem* at the beginning of the paragraph text located in the second column of **ch2ex10.htm**.

b. Click the Property inspector Point to File button, and drag the arrow line to the very bottom of the document page that is visible

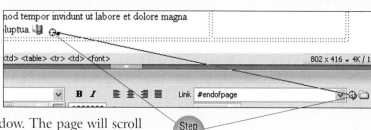

in the Document window. The page will scroll down. When you see the Named Anchor marker, point the arrow line to it and then release the mouse button to create the anchor link. ***Hint: If the page doesn't scroll down, try moving the arrow line to the area close to the bottom of the document and the top of the Property inspector. When the arrow line pointer is over the Named Anchor marker, the anchor path appears in the* Link *text box.***

c. Click the Preview/Debug in browser button, click Preview in iexplore, and then check the link. Close the browser window when you are finished.

3. Save **ch2ex10.htm** and then close it.

E-mail Links

Clicking an *e-mail link* opens a new blank message window, provided that a mail program has been associated with the browser. E-mail links are created using the Email Link dialog box as shown in Figure 2.28. You can open this dialog box by clicking the Email Link button on the Insert Bar (Common menu item or tab) shown in Figure 2.29 or by clicking Insert on the Menu bar and then Email Link. E-mail links also can be created by selecting the link text or image and entering *mailto:* followed by an e-mail address in the Property inspector *Link* text box. Note that there should not be a space between the colon following *mailto* and the e-mail address.

The *To* text box in the e-mail message window automatically contains the e-mail address specified in the e-mail link. You can specify additional recipients by separating them with a comma and a single space (for example, joe@emcp.net, mary@emcp.net, and so on).

You also can send carbon copy (CC) and blind carbon copy (BCC) messages to other addresses, and enter text for the *Subject* text box and body of the message as shown in Table 2.1.

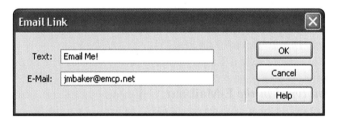

Figure 2.28 • Email Link Dialog Box

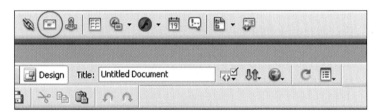

Figure 2.29 • Insert Bar Email Link Button

Table 2.1 • E-mail Message Attributes

Attribute	Action	Usage Example
CC	Copies message to other recipients.	mailto:(e-mail address)?CC=(e-mail address)
BCC	Copies message to other recipients and hides their addresses.	mailto:(e-mail address)?BCC=(e-mail address)
Subject	Enters text in the message *Subject* text box.	mailto:(e-mail address)?subject=(subject text)
Body	Enters text in the body of the message.	mailto:(e-mail address)?body=(body text)

Note: The first attribute must be separated from the e-mail recipient address using a question mark (?). Each subsequent attribute is indicated by an ampersand (&) without any spaces. For example: mailto:joesmith@emcp.net, caroljones@emcp.net?CC=laura@emcp.net&subject=Hello&body=I am testing out this e-mail link feature. Let me know if it works.

DREAMWEAVER MX 2004

Check with your instructor before completing this exercise. In Step 2, you will be adding two e-mail addresses to an e-mail link. If necessary, type fictitious e-mail addresses.

1. Create an e-mail link by completing the following steps:
   a. Create a new HTML document. Use the Save or Save As commands to name and save the document **ch2ex11.htm**.
   b. Position the insertion point at the top of the Document window and type **E-Mail Me!** Select the text when you are finished.
   c. Click Insert on the Menu bar and Email Link, or click the Email Link button on the Insert bar (Common menu item or tab) to open the Email Link dialog box.

   d. Type your e-mail address in the *E-Mail* text box. **Note: Text selected to create an e-mail link will appear in the Text** *text box of the Email Link dialog box. If no text or object was selected and you do not type anything in the* **Text** *text box, the e-mail address you typed in the* **E-Mail** *text box will appear on the page as the e-mail link.*

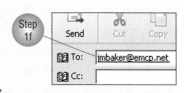

   e. Click OK to close the Email Link dialog box.
   f. Click the Preview/Debug in browser button and then click Preview in iexplore. Click the e-mail link. A preaddressed e-mail message form appears on your screen. Close the e-mail message form and the browser window when you are finished. **Note: If your browser has not been configured to work with an e-mail program, an e-mail message form will not appear.**

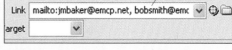

2. Add attributes to an e-mail link by completing the following steps:
   a. Position the insertion point in the e-mail link you created in Step 1.
   b. The Property inspector's *Link* text box displays *mailto:* followed by the e-mail address you typed in the Email Link dialog box. Position the insertion point after the last character of the e-mail address. Type a comma (,), press the spacebar to create a space, and then type another e-mail address.
   c. Type **?CC=** just after the last character of the second e-mail address. Type another e-mail address that will be copied on the message after the equal sign. **Note: Be sure that CC is in uppercase letters, and that there is no space between the equal sign and the e-mail address.**
   d. Type **&subject=Adding E-mail Attributes** immediately after the last character of the CC e-mail address.
   e. Type **&body=Adding attributes is an easy way to boost the functionality of e-mail links.**

f. Click the Preview/Debug in browser button and then click Preview in iexplore to preview the page.

g. Click the e-mail link you created. A pre-addressed e-mail message form with subject and body text should be displayed on your screen. Close the browser window when you are finished.

3. Save **ch2ex11.htm** and then close it.

Step 2g

Checking and Repairing Links

Broken links are links containing an invalid path, or a path leading to a document that no longer exists. In a large Web site, checking and repairing links one-by-one can be time consuming, but Dreamweaver MX 2004 makes this easy with the *Link Checker panel* shown in Figure 2.30. The Link Checker panel is located in the *Results panel group,* and can be used to prepare a report that lists any broken links within a document, portion of a local site, or an entire site. It also checks for any unlinked files in a site, known as *orphan files*. The Link Checker cannot check links to documents located outside a site, but will list all external links in its report. The Link Checker also can be used to repair broken links by clicking on the broken link in the Link Checker panel. A Browse for File button then appears. Clicking the button opens the Select File dialog box, which can be used to browse and locate the correct link.

document   broken link

Figure 2.30 • Link Checker Panel

1. Use the Link Checker panel to check links by completing the following steps:
   a. At a clear document screen, create a new HTML document and use the Save or Save As commands to name and save it to the ch_02_exercises root folder as **ch2ex12.htm**.
   b. Type ch2ex08-a in the upper left-hand corner of the document. Press Enter and then type ch2ex08-b.
   c. Select the *ch2ex08-a* text and use the Property inspector *Link* text box Browse for File button to create a link to **ch2ex08-a.htm**. Repeat this step to create a link from *ch2ex08-b* to **ch2ex08-b.htm**.
   d. Select the ch2ex08-a link and then delete *.htm* in the Property inspector *Link* text box to create an incomplete link. Repeat this step to delete *.htm* for the ch2ex08-b link.
   e. Click Window and then Results to open the Results panel group.
   f. Click the Link Checker panel tab. If necessary, click the *Show* list box down-pointing arrow and then click *Broken Links* from the drop-down list.

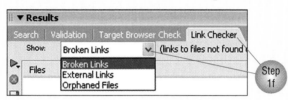

   g. Click the green Check Links button to open the drop-down menu and then click *Check Links In Current Document*. A report appears listing *ch2ex08-a* and *ch2ex08-b* as broken links. ***Note: The links are broken because their file extensions (.htm) are missing.***

2. Repair the broken links using the Link Checker panel by completing the following steps:
   a. Click *ch2ex08-a* in the *Broken Links* column of the broken links report. A Browse for File button appears.
   b. Click the Browse for File button and use the file browser to locate **ch2ex08-a.htm**. Select it and then click OK to restore the link and close the Select File dialog box.

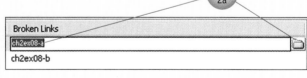

   c. Repeat Steps 2a–2b to repair the link for *ch2ex08-b*.
   d. Click the Preview/Debug in browser button and then click Preview in iexplore to preview the page and test the repairs you just made. Close the browser when you are finished.
4. Save **ch2ex12.htm** and then close it. Close the Results panel group by clicking its Options menu and then clicking Close panel group.

Changing Link Colors

Default link colors can be changed by clicking Modify on the Menu bar and then Page Properties to open the Page Properties dialog box. Clicking *Links* in the *Category* list box displays the Page Properties dialog box Links page as shown in Figure 2.31. The down-pointing arrow next to the *Link font* text box can be used to open a list of available font groups for links. The Bold and Italic buttons can be used to format links in bold or italic. The color boxes next to the different link types in the dialog box can be used to change their default colors. *Link color* controls the color of a link that has not yet been clicked, *Rollover links* controls the color of a link as the mouse pointer is rolled over it, *Visited links* controls the color of a link once it has been clicked, and *Active links* controls the color of a link at the moment it is clicked. *Underline style* is used to control the underline style for links, and includes *Always underline, Never underline, Show underline only on rollover,* and *Hide underline on rollover* options.

Editing and Removing Links

The Property inspector can be used to change an existing link path or target window. Selecting a link makes its path appear in the *Link* text box, where you can use the Point to File or Browse for File buttons to locate a new target document or type a new path.

You also can right-click a link in the Document window and click Change Link or Target Frame to change a path or target window. A link's title, access key, and tab order can be changed by selecting a link and then shifting to Code view. The link will be highlighted, and the title, access key, and tab order variables can be changed by deleting them and typing new values. The link path and target window also can be changed in this view, but it is probably easier to accomplish this using the Property inspector or by right-clicking to access the context-sensitive menu.

Right-clicking a link and selecting Remove Link or Remove Tag <a> removes the anchor tag from a link so that the link reverts to its previous state. You also can click the link and then delete its URL in the Property inspector *Link* text box.

To delete a link entirely (the text or object along with the anchor tags and **href** attribute), select the link and press the Delete or Backspace keys. You also can click a link, select its anchor tag (<a>) in the Tag selector, and press the Delete key to remove a link.

Figure 2.31
Page Properties Dialog Box
Links Page

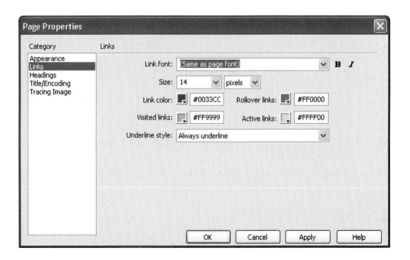

DREAMWEAVER MX 2004

EDITING AND REMOVING LINKS

1. Edit links by completing the following steps:
   a. Open **ch2ex12.htm** and use the Save As command to rename and save it as **ch2ex13.htm**.
   b. Position the insertion point inside the <u>ch2ex08-a</u> link.
   c. The path for the link *(ch2ex08-a.htm)* appears in the Property inspector's *Link* text box. Click the Browse for File button and use the file browser to locate **ch2ex04-a.htm**. Double-click the file or select the file and then click the OK button to change the link. The new path *ch2ex04-a.htm* appears in the *Link* text box.
   d. Select the link and type ch2ex04-a to rename it to reflect the new link.
   e. Click the Preview/Debug in browser button and then click Preview in iexplore to check that the link now connects to **ch2ex04-a.htm**. Close the browser window when you are finished.

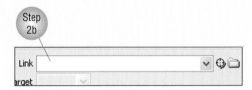

2. Remove a link by completing the following steps:
   a. Position the insertion point inside the <u>ch2ex04-a</u> link.
   b. Delete its path in the Property inspector's *Link* text box.
   c. Click in the document. The link formatting disappears, indicating that the text is no longer a link.

3. Delete links and link text by completing the following steps:
   a. Select the <u>ch2ex08-b</u> link.
   b. Press the Delete key or the Backspace key to delete the link along with the link text, or position the insertion point within the text, select the anchor tag (<a>) in the Tag selector, and then press the Delete or Backspace keys.

4. Save **ch2ex13.htm** and then close it.

Creating Lists

Three different types of lists can be created using Dreamweaver MX 2004. As shown in Figure 2.32, an *unordered list* places a bullet before each list item, an *ordered list* numbers each list item, and a *definition list* contains indented text that can be used to describe each list item. The portion of a list containing a sublist is called a *nested list*.

Unordered List (Bulleted)	Ordered List (Numbered)	Definition List
• List Item	1. List Item	Item
• List Item	2. List Item	Descriptive Text
• List Item	3. List Item	Item
o Nested List Item		Descriptive Text
o Nested List Item		

Figure 2.32
List Types

Lists can be created using the List buttons on the Insert bar (Text menu item or tab) or the List buttons in the Property inspector. Another method that can be used to create lists is to click Text on the Menu bar and then point to List. You can choose the type of list you want from the drop-down menu that appears. After a list option has been selected, a list number or bullet appears in the document and a list item can be typed. To create another item in a list, press Enter and type the next list item. To end the list, press Enter twice. Selecting list items and then clicking the Indent button in the Property inspector creates a nested list.

These same methods can be used to create a list from existing text. The text to be formatted as a list must be selected, and then you follow the same steps to start a list by using the Property inspector, Menu bar, or Insert bar.

To change list preferences, use the List Properties dialog box by clicking Text on the Menu bar, pointing to List, and then clicking Properties.

exercise 14 | CREATING LISTS AND CHANGING LIST PROPERTIES

1. Create a new list by completing the following steps:
   a. Create a new HTML document and use the Save or Save As commands to name and save it as **ch2ex14-a.htm**.
   b. Click in the Document window and then click the Unordered List (ul) button on the Insert bar (Text menu item or tab).

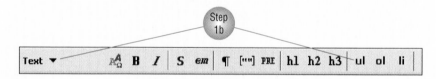

   c. Type **List Item**, and then press Enter. Repeat this step two more times. Each list item will be preceded by a bullet.
   d. Press Enter twice to stop the unordered list formatting.
2. Change an existing list type by completing the following steps:
   a. Select the list items you created in Step 1c. *Hint: Do not select any blank lines.*
   b. Click the Ordered List (ol) button on the Insert bar. The list will change to a numbered list.
3. Create a nested list by completing the following steps:
   a. Select the last two list items.
   b. Click the Text Indent button in the Property inspector, or click Text on the Menu bar and then Indent. The last two items will be indented and renumbered as items 1 and 2 of the nested list. *Note: In bulleted lists, the bullet type changes in nested lists.*

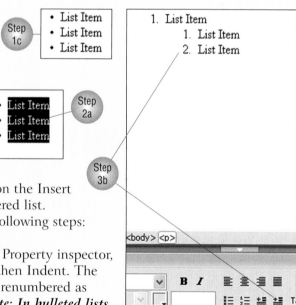

DREAMWEAVER MX 2004

4. Change list properties by completing the following steps:

   a. Position the insertion point in the nested list. *Note: **Do not select the list or the List Properties dialog box will be inaccessible.***

   b. Click Text on the Menu bar, point to List, and then click Properties to open the List Properties dialog box.

   c. Click *Roman Small (i, ii, iii...)* in the *Style* list box drop-down list and then click the OK button to close the dialog box. The nested list's numbers now

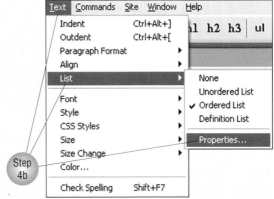

appear in small Roman numerals. ***Note: The parent list style does not change because the List Properties dialog box affects only the properties of the list where the insertion point was placed.***

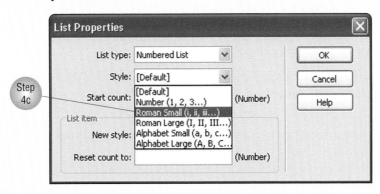

   d. Save **ch2ex14-a.htm** but do not close it.

5. Remove list formatting by completing the following steps:

   a. Select the list.

   b. Click the same button that was used to create or format the list. Because this is an ordered (numbered) list, click the Ordered List (ol) button on the Insert bar or in the Property inspector to remove the list formatting. ***Note: Nested items will still be indented.***

   c. Select the nested items and then click the Text Outdent button in the Property inspector to move the items back to the left margin.

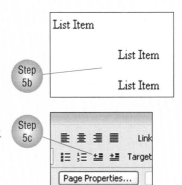

6. Use the Save As command to rename the document **ch2ex14-b.htm**, and then close it.

Finding and Replacing Text and Code

The Dreamweaver MX 2004 ***Find and Replace dialog box*** allows you to search and replace text, code, and combinations of text and code in current documents, documents in folders, or an entire site. You also can specify text or code to replace items after they are found. In Design view, click Edit on the Menu bar and then

Find and Replace to open the Find and Replace dialog box as shown in Figure 2.33. In Code view, right-click and then click Find and Replace to open the dialog box. You can select the following options from the *Find in* drop-down list:

- **Current Document** Confines the search to the current document and is available only when the Find and Replace dialog box is used with the Document window or activated using the Code view context-sensitive menu.
- **Selected Text** Searches any selected text in the current document.
- **Open documents** Searches all documents open in the Document window.
- **Folder** If this option is selected, a blank text box and a Browse for File button appear in the dialog box. Click the Browse for File button to browse and select the desired folder.
- **Selected Files in Site** The Files panel must be open and the desired files selected for this option to work. More than one file can be selected at a time by holding down the Ctrl key when clicking files.
- **Entire Current Local Site** Searches all HTML documents, library items, and text documents in the current site.

The *Search* list box allows you to select from the following options to specify how the search is conducted:

- **Source Code** Searches for text strings in the HTML source code. A Code inspector window opens when the search is conducted.
- **Text** Searches for text strings in the current document in Design view.
- **Text (Advanced)** Searches for text strings located inside or outside a specified tag or pair of tags. For example, searching for *Montana* within

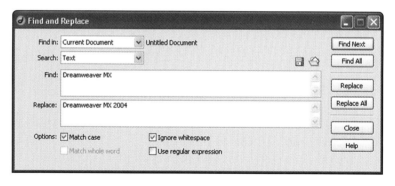

Figure 2.33
Find and Replace Dialog Box

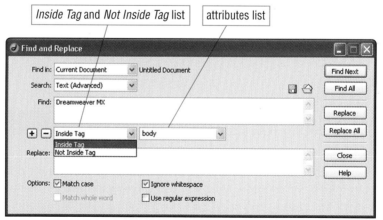

Figure 2.34
Advanced Text Search Options

DREAMWEAVER MX 2004

emphasis tags in the following code would locate and highlight the first occurrence of *Montana,* but ignore all other occurrences:

```
<em>Montana</em> Montana is home to Glacier National
Park. Montana is also home to…
```

When the *Text (Advanced)* option is selected, additional option fields appear that allow you to choose whether to search inside or outside a specified tag and to specify various tag attributes and values, as shown in Figure 2.34.

- **Specific Tag** Searches for specific tags, attributes, and values, such as all image tags with alignment set to "middle."

At the bottom of the dialog box, there are four check boxes. When selected, *Match case* looks for only exact case matches (*Layout* would not match *layout*), *Ignore whitespace* treats all white space as a single space (*tag editor* would match *tag editor,* but not *tageditor*), *Match whole word* limits a search to one or more complete words, and *Use regular expression* lets certain characters be interpreted as regular expression operators, such as ?, *, /w, and so on. A table listing regular expressions and their function can be viewed by clicking the Find and Replace dialog box Help button and then clicking the <u>Regular expressions</u> link.

Checking Spelling

The **Check Spelling dialog box** allows you to check the spelling in a document while ignoring HTML tags and attributes. Clicking Text on the Menu bar and then Check Spelling instructs Dreamweaver MX 2004 to begin checking the spelling in the current document. If no errors are encountered, a message box appears to let you know that the spelling check is complete. Clicking OK closes the box.

If Dreamweaver MX 2004 encounters a spelling error, the Check Spelling dialog box shown in Figure 2.35 opens. Any word not found in the Check Spelling dictionary appears at the top of the dialog box, and is highlighted in the document. If the dialog box is obstructing the page, you can move it out of the way by dragging the Title bar of the dialog box. Suggestions for alternative spellings appear in the *Suggestions* list box, and the most likely possibility appears in the *Change to* text box. Click the Change button to accept the proposed change. Click the Change All button to change all occurrences of the misspelled word. Click the Ignore or Ignore All buttons to skip any changes to the misspelled word or any other

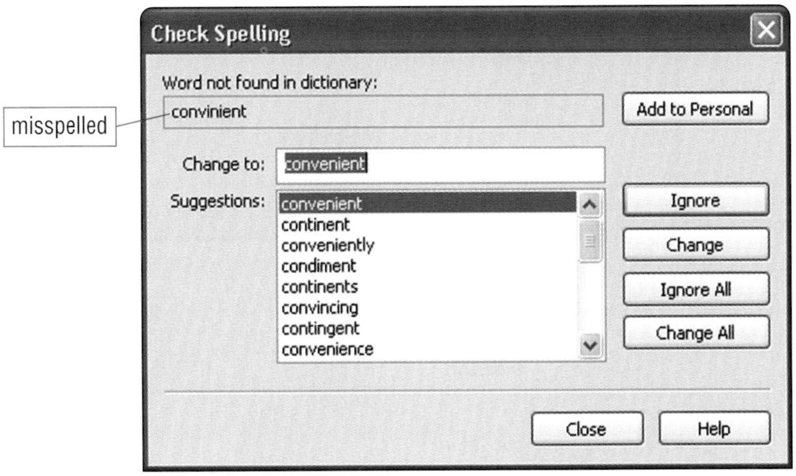

Figure 2.35
Check Spelling Dialog Box

Figure 2.36 • Preferences Dialog Box Spelling Dictionary List

occurrences of the word in the document. If you feel a spelling is correct, you can add that word to a personal dictionary by clicking the Add to Personal button. The next time Check Spelling is used, it will recognize the word as an accepted spelling and ignore it.

The default spelling dictionary for this feature is set to *English (American),* but other dictionaries can be specified by clicking Edit on the Menu bar, Preferences, and then *General* in the Preferences dialog box *Category* list box. At the bottom of the dialog box is a drop-down list with a number of different spelling dictionaries to choose from as shown in Figure 2.36. Select the desired dictionary and then click OK to confirm the change and close the dialog box.

exercise 15

CHECKING SPELLING AND USING FIND AND REPLACE

1. Check spelling by completing the following steps:
    a. Open the student file named **spelling.htm** and use the Save As command to rename and save it to the ch_02_exercises root folder as **ch2ex15.htm**. *Note: If a message box appears asking you if you want to update links, click the Yes button.*
    b. Click Text on the Menu bar and then Check Spelling to open the Check Spelling dialog box.
    c. Accept the recommended spelling for *spller.* by clicking the Change button to implement the correct spelling *(speller.).*
    d. When *Dream weaver* appears in the *Change to* text box, click the Ignore All button to make sure that *Dreamweaver* is not changed to *Dream weaver*.
2. Add a word to the Check Spelling dictionary by completing the following steps:
    a. Click the Add to Personal button to add the word *blockquote* to the Check Spelling dictionary when it appears in the *Change to* text box. After the button is clicked, a message appears to let you know that the spelling check has been completed.
    b. Click the OK button to close the message box. *Note: There is a second instance of* **blockquote** *in the last line of the second paragraph but it will not be flagged as a*

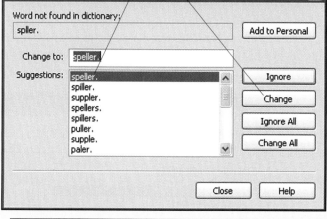

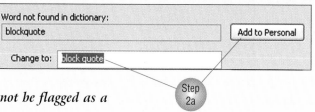

DREAMWEAVER MX 2004

misspelling because you added this spelling to the Check Spelling dictionary. If a prior user has already added blockquote *to the Check Spelling dictionary, it will not be flagged.*

3. Search for and replace text by completing the following steps:

a. Click Edit on the Menu bar and then Find and Replace to open the Find and Replace dialog box.

b. Make sure *Current Document* is selected in the *Find in* text box and *Text* is selected in the *Search* list box.

c. Type Dreamweaver in the *Find* text box.

d. Type Dreamweaver MX 2004 in the *Replace* text box.

e. Click the Find Next button.

f. Move the dialog box if necessary to see *Dreamweaver* highlighted in the document. Click the Replace button to replace *Dreamweaver* with *Dreamweaver MX 2004*. When you have clicked the Replace button, the next occurrence of *Dreamweaver* is highlighted.

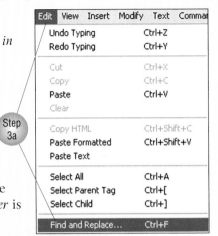

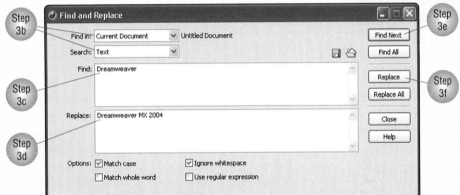

g. Click the Replace button until every instance of *Dreamweaver* has been replaced with *Dreamweaver MX 2004*. Close the Find and Replace dialog box when you are finished.

4. Save **ch2ex15.htm** and then close it.

Using the History Panel

The **History panel** shown in Figure 2.37 can be used to undo, redo, or automate any of the activities performed in open documents when working in Design view. The History panel record for a document remains intact even if the document is saved, but after it is closed, the History panel record is cleared. You can copy actions or a series of actions and paste them into another document, or save them as a command that can be used to automate tasks. The vertical slider can be used to undo or redo a step. Mouse movements are not recorded, but keyboard commands are, so keyboard commands should be used for any mouse movements when recording commands. Clicking Edit on the Menu bar and then Keyboard Shortcuts displays the Keyboard Shortcuts dialog box, which contains a complete list of Dreamweaver MX 2004 keyboard shortcuts. To set the maximize number of actions the History panel will undo, complete the following steps:

1. Click Edit on the Menu bar and then Preferences.
2. Click *General* from the Preferences dialog box *Category* list box.
3. Type the number of undo steps you want the History panel to remember in the *Maximum number of history steps* text box. **Note: The default setting is 50. The higher the number of steps, the more memory is used. This might cause your computer to perform slower.**
4. Click OK to close the Preferences dialog box.

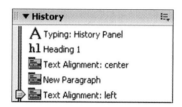

Figure 2.37
History Panel

USING THE HISTORY PANEL

1. Undo and redo actions by completing the following steps:
   a. Click Window on the Menu bar and then History to open the History panel. If necessary, click the History panel Expander arrow to expand it.
   b. Create a new HTML document and use the Save or Save As commands to name and save it as **ch2ex16.htm**.
   c. Click in the Document window, and type The History panel makes it easy to undo and redo steps. A step or series of steps can also be copied and pasted in a document, or saved as a command for later use.
   d. Press Enter twice, and type The vertical slider can be used to undo and redo steps.
   e. Click the vertical slider and move it up the list of actions in the History panel. As you move the vertical slider up the list, the steps are undone.
   f. Move the vertical slider down the list until it is pointing to the last item. All of the steps you performed are redone.

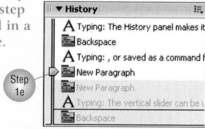

2. Copy and paste commands by completing the following steps:
   a. Hold down the Ctrl key and select all of the steps taken to type the two paragraphs by clicking each step in the History panel. **Hint: If you made corrections during or after typing, you might need to use the scroll bar to select all steps performed.**
   b. Click the History panel Copy button.
   c. Position the insertion point just after the second paragraph and press Enter to create a new line.
   d. Right-click and then click Paste. The copied material appears in the insertion point location.

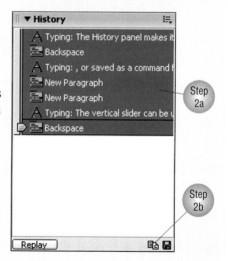

DREAMWEAVER MX 2004

Note: The release version of Dreamweaver MX 2004 contained a bug that prevented Steps 2a–2d from working correctly. If you experience this problem, at Step 2b, click the History panel Replay button instead of clicking the Copy button and then click Replay Steps in the History panel to select it. You can then click the Copy button and proceed with Steps 2c–2d to paste the steps.

3. Create and use a command by completing the following steps:
   a. Place the insertion point just after the second occurrence of the last paragraph and press Enter to begin a new line.
   b. Type Page Design by [Your Name] Copyright 2004.

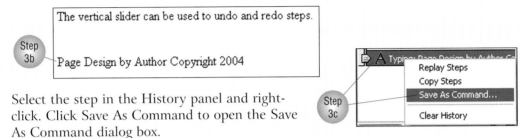

   c. Select the step in the History panel and right-click. Click Save As Command to open the Save As Command dialog box.
   d. Type Copyright in the *Command Name* text box and then click OK to close the dialog box.

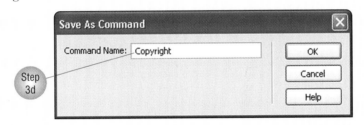

   e. Place the insertion point at the end of the copyright text and press Enter to begin a new line.
   f. Click Commands on the Menu bar and then Copyright. A duplicate of the copyright statement is inserted at the insertion point.

4. Delete a command by completing the following steps:
   a. Click Commands on the Menu bar and then Edit Command List.

   b. Select the *Copyright* command and then click the Delete button. A message box appears warning you that the action cannot be undone. Click the Yes button to proceed.
   c. Click the Close button to close the dialog box.
   d. Close the History panel group when you are finished.

5. Save ch2ex16.htm and then close it.

Inserting Comments

A ***comment*** is a segment of text inserted into HTML code to provide information for anyone viewing and working on the code at a later time. For example, the comment shown in Figure 2.38 serves as a reminder to perform an action at a later date. Comments are not visible when a page is displayed in a browser, but can be viewed by anyone viewing the HTML code that is controlling a Web page.

Comments can be inserted in Code view, Code and Design view, and Design view by placing the insertion point in the desired location and then clicking the Comment button on the Insert bar (Common menu item or tab) as shown in Figure 2.39. In Code view, comment text is entered by typing text between paired comment tags (<!-- -->); in Design view, text is entered using a Comment dialog box. In Design view, comments are marked by a comment marker as shown in Figure 2.40, if the *Comments* check box has been selected in the Preferences dialog box from the *Invisible Elements Category* list box.

Comments can be edited in Code view by removing or adding text between the comment tags. In Design view, comments can be edited using the Comments dialog box, which can be opened by selecting a comment marker. Comments can be removed in Code view by deleting the comment tags and text, and in Design view by selecting and deleting a comment marker.

Figure 2.38
Comment

Figure 2.39
Insert Bar Comment Button

Figure 2.40
Comment Marker

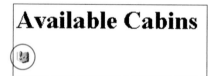

exercise 17

ADDING AND EDITING COMMENTS

1. Make comment markers visible by completing the following steps:
   a. Click Edit on the Menu bar and then Preferences.
   b. Click *Invisible Elements* from the *Category* list box.
   c. Click the *Comments* check box if the check box is empty.

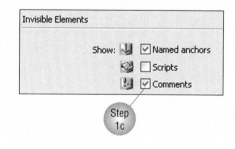

DREAMWEAVER MX 2004

 d. Click OK to close the dialog box.
2. Create a comment by completing the following steps:
 a. Open **ch2ex04-a.htm** and use the Save As command to rename it **ch2ex17.htm**.
 b. Place the insertion point before the first word in the first paragraph *(Lorem)*.
 c. Open the Comment dialog box by clicking the Comment button on the Insert bar (Common menu item or tab).

Step 2c

 d. In the *Comment* text box, type Rewrite this column and insert an image when ready.

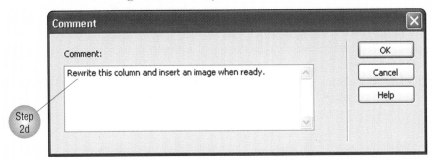

Step 2d

 e. Click OK to close the dialog box. A comment marker appears at the insertion point.

Step 2e

3. Read and edit a comment by completing the following steps:
 a. Open the *Comment* text box in the Property inspector by clicking the comment marker you just inserted. ***Note: Clicking in the document closes the* Comment *text box.***
 b. Type the text **you are** so that the comment reads *Rewrite this column and insert an image when you are ready.*

Step 3b

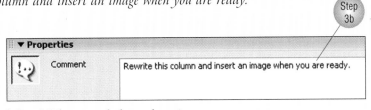

 c. Save **ch2ex17.htm** and then close it.

Using Meta Tags

Meta tags are tags that are placed in the head region of HTML documents just after the title tags (<title> </title>). There are a number of different meta tags, but the description, keywords, and refresh meta tags are probably the most widely used.

 Meta description and keyword tags are used to improve the chances that a Web page will appear near the top of a search engine results page list when someone looking for information uses a search engine to conduct a keyword search. Search engines differ in their treatment of keywords and descriptions, and some ignore them entirely, so it is not a sure-fire method of getting good search engine placement.

A meta description tag should offer a concise description of the contents or subject of a Web page, and the keywords meta tag should contain a list of words, separated by commas, that occur frequently in the site. Figure 2.41 illustrates this concept by showing the description and keywords meta tags for a site offering free graphics.

Meta keywords can be inserted in an HTML document by clicking the Insert bar HTML menu item or tab and then clicking the unlabeled Meta tag button down-pointing arrow. This opens the Meta tag menu as shown in Figure 2.42. The *Meta Tag button* icon changes to reflect the previous item selected from the Meta tag menu. Clicking Keywords opens the Keywords dialog box which can be used to enter keywords describing the document's contents as shown in Figure 2.43. Clicking Description opens the Description dialog box which can be used to enter a short narrative description of the document contents.

The refresh meta tag can be used to instruct a browser to refresh the current page or to redirect viewers to a new page. Refresh is used for pages containing dynamic data or Web cam images that may be updated frequently. Refreshing the page after a specified time interval instructs the page to reload so that the page content can be refreshed. Redirect often is used to direct viewers to a new URL

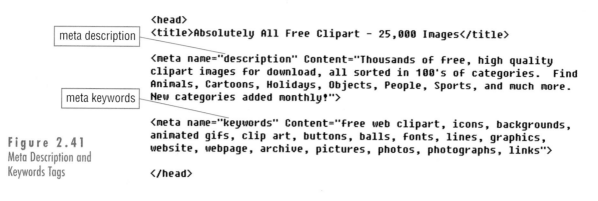

Figure 2.41
Meta Description and
Keywords Tags

Figure 2.42
Insert Bar Meta Tag Menu

Figure 2.43
Keywords Dialog Box

DREAMWEAVER MX 2004

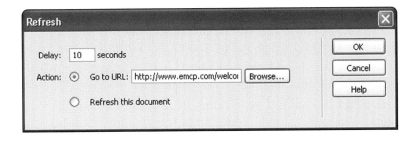

Figure 2.44
Refresh Dialog Box

when a Web site has moved or to create a splash page effect. Splash pages are Web pages that open for a specified time period before a home page opens, and are used to create an interesting introductory effect for a Web site.

Clicking the Insert bar HTML menu item or tab, the Meta tag button down-pointing arrow, and then Refresh opens the Refresh dialog box shown in Figure 2.44. The dialog box lets users specify a URL for the page that viewers will be redirected to, and indicates the number of seconds the page will be displayed before the redirect takes effect. If the goal is to refresh the page, the *Refresh this document* radio button can be selected.

CHAPTER summary

- ➤ The only way to be certain that pages will appear as intended is to use the Preview/Debug in browser button to preview them in different browsers.

- ➤ When a page is previewed, Dreamweaver MX 2004 creates a temporary copy of the file and opens it in the specified browser.

- ➤ The Check Target Browsers feature of Dreamweaver MX 2004 checks documents for any code not supported by specified browsers.

- ➤ Text can be entered into an HTML document by typing text, opening documents directly, copying and pasting text, or importing text from other programs.

- ➤ Text can be formatted using formatting commands available in button form on the Insert bar, by subcommands accessed through the Text command on the Menu bar, or by using the Property inspector.

- ➤ Text documents (.txt extension) and HTML documents can be opened directly in Dreamweaver MX 2004.

- ➤ The Copy, Paste, Copy HTML, Paste HTML, Paste Formatted, and Paste Text commands can be used to copy and paste material into Dreamweaver MX 2004 documents.

- ➤ Microsoft Word and Excel document content can be copied and then pasted into a Dreamweaver MX 2004 document using the Paste Formatted command.

- ➤ Clicking Commands on the Menu bar and then Clean Up HTML or Clean Up Word HTML opens dialog boxes that can be used to remove extraneous code in non-Dreamweaver MX 2004 HTML documents.

- ➤ Tabular data can be imported in Dreamweaver MX 2004 if they are first saved as delimited text files.

- Preformatted text can be used to retain text formatting that HTML might ignore or override, such as for verse or HTML code.
- The *Font* text box drop-down list located in the Property inspector lets you select the font style (also known as font face or typeface) for selected text and any text subsequently entered on the page.
- Text colors can be changed by clicking the text color box in the Property inspector.
- Web-safe colors refers to colors that appear the same in both Netscape and Explorer browsers running on either Windows or Macintosh systems operating in 256-color mode.
- The Color Picker Strikethrough button restores the default text color setting.
- Selected text can be aligned by clicking the Align Left, Align Center, Align Right, or Justify buttons in the Property inspector.
- The Page Properties dialog box Appearance page can be used to specify default background and text colors.
- Dreamweaver MX 2004 features a number of predefined Web-safe background and text color combinations, accessed by clicking Commands on the Menu bar and then Set Color Scheme.
- You can select favorite assets and save them in the Assets panel's *Favorites* list. The panel also automatically saves assets such as images, URLs, and the colors used in a site.
- In HTML, a link consists of starting and ending anchor tags (<a> </a>) and an **href** attribute.
- Absolute paths include the complete URL (Uniform Resource Locator) for a linked document, including the protocol used.
- Document relative paths are used to link documents that are located in the same folder or site.
- Using document relative paths for all documents located in a site allows Dreamweaver MX 2004 to update them automatically if their location changes within the site.
- Links can be created using the Property inspector, the Menu bar, the Insert bar, or the Assets panel.
- The Point to File button allows you to create a link by dragging to a link target file.
- The *Target* list box drop-down list in the Property inspector lets users choose where the target link document will open.
- Anchor links are used to link to locations within a document.
- Before creating an anchor link, a link target (named anchor) must be named.
- A Named Anchor marker will appear at a named anchor location.
- Clicking an e-mail link opens a new blank message window, provided that a mail program has been associated with the browser.
- E-mail links are created using the Email Link dialog box.
- Attributes can be typed into an e-mail link to specify additional recipients, a message subject, and text that will appear in the message body.
- The Link Checker panel located in the Results panel group can be used to report and repair broken links.

- Default link colors can be changed by clicking Modify on the Menu bar, clicking Page Properties, and then using the Links page link color boxes to change their default colors.
- The Property inspector can be used to change a link's path and target window.
- An unordered list places a bullet before each list item, an ordered list numbers each list item, and a definition list contains indented text that can be used to describe each list item.
- Sublists within lists are called nested lists.
- Lists can be created using the List buttons on the Insert bar (Text menu item or tab), the List buttons in the Property inspector, or by clicking Text on the Menu bar and then pointing to List.
- List preferences can be changed using the List Properties dialog box, accessed by clicking Text on the Menu bar, pointing to Lists, and then clicking Properties.
- The Dreamweaver MX 2004 Find and Replace tool allows you to search for text, code, and combinations of text and code in documents or entire sites.
- The Check Spelling dialog box allows you to check spelling in a document while ignoring HTML tags and attributes.
- The History panel can be used to undo, redo, or automate any of the activities performed in open documents when working in Design view.
- A comment is a segment of text inserted into HTML code to provide information for anyone viewing and working on the code at a later time.
- A meta description tag offers a concise description of the contents or subject of a Web page.
- A meta keywords tag contains a list of words, separated by commas, that occur frequently in the site.
- The refresh meta tag can be used to instruct a browser to refresh the current page, or to redirect viewers to a new page

KEY terms

absolute paths File paths that include the complete URL (Uniform Resource Locator) for a linked document, including the protocol used.

accessibility Refers to the issue of people with visual, hearing, physical, or neurological disabilities being able to access Web page content.

anchor links Links to locations within a document.

anchor tags HTML tags (<a>) used to create a hyperlink, along with an **href** attribute identifying the path to the link target.

Assets panel A panel that can be used to store various assets used on a site, such as images, URLs, favorite colors, and so on.

blockquote tags The HTML tags (<blockquote>) used to indent text.

broken links Links containing an invalid path, or a path leading to a document that no longer exists.

Check Spelling dialog box Allows users to check spelling in a document while ignoring HTML tags and attributes.

Check Target Browsers A Dreamweaver MX 2004 tool that checks documents for any code that is not supported by specified browsers.

Color Picker The Web-safe color palette opened by clicking a color box.

Color Wheel button Clicking this button opens the Windows Color Selection palette containing 48 basic colors.

comment A segment of text inserted into HTML code to provide information for anyone viewing or working on the code at a later time.

definition list A list that contains indented text that can be used to describe each list item.

delimited text file A file format that allows tabular data to be imported for use in Dreamweaver MX 2004 documents.

document relative paths File paths used to link documents that are located in the same folder or site.

e-mail link A hyperlink that opens up a preaddressed e-mail message that can be completed and sent by the user.

Eyedropper A tool that can be used to change the color of any selected text by clicking a color from anywhere in a color palette or on the screen.

Find and Replace dialog box Allows users to search for text, code, and combinations of text and code in documents or in entire sites.

font style A font design, such as Arial, Times New Roman, or Courier. Also known as *font face* or *typeface*.

hexadecimal color values Hexadecimal (base 16) values for colors, composed of the pound sign and a combination of six numbers and/or letters composing the hexadecimal value; for example, #FFFFCC produces a light shade of yellow.

History panel A vertical panel that can undo, redo, or automate any of the activities performed in open documents when working in Design view.

href attribute Used with anchor tags to identify the path to a link target.

hyperlink Text or object that, when clicked, takes users to another location on the same page, or to documents located on other servers. Also called *link*.

hypertext documents Documents containing hyperlinks.

link See *hyperlink*.

Link Checker panel A panel located in the Results panel group used to report and repair broken links.

link target The document a hyperlink leads to.

meta tags Special tags placed in the head section of an HTML document. There are a number of different meta tags, but the most popular are the description, keywords, and refresh meta tags. The description and keywords meta tags are used to provide information about Web page content to search engines, while the refresh meta tag is used to refresh the page or redirect the viewer to a new browser.

named anchor The link target for an anchor link.

Named Anchor marker A marker used to indicate a named anchor location.

nested list A list (sublist) within a list.

ordered list A list that places a number next to each list item.

orphan files Any unlinked files in a site.

path The directions that a browser uses to locate files. See *absolute paths* and *document relative paths*.

Point to File button A Property inspector button that can be used to create links by dragging an arrow line to a link target file.

preformatted text Text formatting that retains formatting that HTML code might ignore or override, such as for verse or HTML code.

Preview/Debug in browser button A button on the Document toolbar used to preview the current document in a browser.

primary browser A browser used for previewing that can be opened by pressing the F12 key.

Property inspector A context-sensitive horizontal panel that can be used to format text and create links, work with CSS, and perform other tasks.

Properties panel A horizontal panel that contains the different Property inspectors.

Results panel group A vertical panel group containing the Link Checker and other tools.

secondary browser A browser used for previewing that can be opened by pressing the F12 key while holding down the Ctrl key.

Set Color Scheme Command dialog box Provides access to predefined Web-safe background and text color combinations.

Strikethrough button A Color Picker button that restores default text color settings.

text color box A small, gray, square button found in the Property inspector and many dialog boxes that when clicked opens the Color Picker.

Text Indent button A Property inspector button used to indent text.

Text Outdent button A Property inspector button used to outdent (remove indenting) text.

unordered list A list that places a bullet next to each list item.

URL (Uniform Resource Locator) The address (path) to resources on the World Wide Web (WWW).

Web-safe colors Colors that appear the same in both Netscape and Explorer browsers running on either Windows or Macintosh systems operating in 256-color mode.

World Wide Web (WWW or "The Web") The collection of resources and the community of users using the Hypertext Transfer Protocol (HTTP) on the Internet.

COMMANDS review

Change list preferences	Text, List, Properties
Check spelling	Text, Check Spelling
Check Target Browsers	File, Check Page, Check Target Browsers
Clean up HTML	Commands, Clean Up HTML, or Clean Up Word HTML
Create lists	Text, List, click desired list
Default colors	Modify, Page Properties, *Appearance* category, click desired color box
Find and replace	Edit, Find and Replace
Import tabular data	File, Import, Tabular Data
Insert e-mail link	Insert, Email Link
Insert hyperlink	Insert, Hyperlink
Insert named anchor	Insert, Named Anchor
Keyboard shortcuts list	Edit, Keyboard Shortcuts
Preview a Web page	File, Preview in Browser, click desired browser
Set accessibility preferences	Edit, Preferences, *Accessibility* category
Set color scheme	Commands, Set Color Scheme
Set preview preferences	Edit, Preferences, *Preview in Browser* category

CONCEPTS check

Indicate the correct term or command for each item.

1. A link to a location within a document is called this.
2. This panel is used to store various Web site assets, such as images, URLs, color favorites, and so on.
3. This file path includes the complete URL for a linked document, including the protocol used.
4. Clicking this button lets you open a browser that can be used to preview the current document.
5. This file path is used to link documents located in the same folder or site.
6. This tool is used to select colors from a color palette or anywhere on the screen.
7. Clicking this button restores default font-color settings.
8. This panel can be used to undo and redo steps, as well as save steps as commands that can be stored and used later.
9. This is the term for a list located inside another list.
10. This is the name for a document containing hyperlinks.
11. This panel is used to report and repair broken links.
12. This marker shows the location of a named anchor.
13. This type of list places a number next to each list item.

DREAMWEAVER MX 2004

14. This is the term for the document a link leads to.
15. Clicking this button allows users to drag to a link target.
16. This tool checks documents to let you know if any code is unsupported by specified browsers.
17. This is the term for lists that contain indented text that can be used to describe list items.
18. In the default Dreamweaver MX 2004 setup, the Property inspector uses these rules to format text.
19. This is the term for notes inserted into a document's HTML code.
20. This meta tag can be used to automatically direct the viewer to a new page after a specified period of time elapses.

SKILLS check

Use the Site Definition dialog box to create a separate Dreamweaver site named CH 02 Assessments to keep your assessment work for this chapter. Save the files for the site in a new root folder named ch_02_assessments under the Sites folder you created in Chapter 1, Exercise 3. Download the ch_02_student_files folder from the IRC to the CH 02 Assessments site root folder (ch_02_assessments) and expand it. Delete the compressed folder when you are finished.

Assessment 1 • Apply a Set Color Scheme to a Document

1. Create a new HTML document and use the Save or Save As commands to name it and save it as **ch2sa1.htm**.
2. Use the Set Color Scheme Command dialog box to apply a color scheme to the document. You determine which color scheme to apply.
3. Change the title of the document to *Home Page*.
4. Type a heading using the level-one heading size. Press Enter.
5. Type at least two paragraphs of text.
6. Use the Property inspector to change the paragraph font size to 24 pixels.
7. Use the Property inspector to center the heading and justify the paragraph margins.
8. Create a list with at least four items below the last paragraph. Format the list as an unordered list. Change the list font size to 24 pixels.
9. Save and then close **ch2sa1.htm**.

Assessment 2 • Modify Page Properties

1. Open **ch2sa1.htm** and use the Save As command to rename and save it as **ch2as2.htm**.
2. Use the Page Properties dialog box to change the default page background and text colors. You determine appropriate color choices for the page.
3. Use the Property inspector to change the paragraph text color to a color of your choice.
4. Use the Property inspector to change the paragraph text font style to another style of your choosing.
5. Use the List Properties dialog box to change the list to a numbered list. Format the list in the same font style and size as the paragraphs.

6. Insert the following comment (using comment tags) just after the level-one heading: Look for suitable image to place between heading and text and insert when ready.
7. Save and then close **ch2sa2.htm**.

Assessment 3 • Learn More about Accessibility

1. Log onto the Internet and conduct a search using your favorite search engine for information about Web page accessibility.
2. Find at least six Web sites containing information about the topic that is as current as possible. Record their names and URLs for use in Assessment 4.
3. Search the Dreamweaver Support Center for more information about accessibility. Record the URL for any articles you find related to accessibility for use in Assessment 4.
4. Create a new HTML document and use the Save As command to name and save it as **ch2sa3.htm**.
5. Change the document title to *Accessibility*.
6. Use **ch2sa3.htm** to write a report (at least 250 words) of your findings. Include in the report an unordered list displaying key accessibility concerns.
7. Save and then close **ch2sa3.htm**.

Assessment 4 • Create and Link Documents

1. Open **ch2sa2.htm** and use the Save As command to rename and save it as **ch2sa4-a.htm**.
2. Open **ch2sa3.htm** and use the Save As command to rename and save it as **ch2sa4-b.htm**.
3. Click the *ch2sa4-a.htm* document tab and type Information on Accessibility underneath the list. Format the list in the same font style and size as the paragraphs. Use this text to create a link to **ch2sa4-b.htm**.
4. Click the *ch2sa4-b.htm* document tab and at the top of the page type Home. Use this text to create a link to **ch2sa4-a.htm**.
5. At the bottom of **ch2sa4-b.htm**, write short paragraphs (two to three lines) describing each of the Web sites with information on accessibility that you discovered during your research for Assessment 3. Each paragraph should begin with the name of the Web site, followed by some descriptive text. *Example*: Web Accessibility Initiative (WAI) Home Page ("The home page for the W3C's Web Accessibility Initiative, chockful of information on . . .").
6. Create links to each Web site using the Web site names as the link text.
7. Save and then preview **ch2sa4-a.htm** and **ch2sa4-b.htm** to check the links. Use the Link Checker to check any links that do not work.
8. Save **ch2sa4-a.htm** and **ch2sa4-b.htm** and then close them.

Assessment 5 • Create an E-mail Link

Check with your instructor before completing this assessment. In Step 3, you will need four e-mail addresses. If necessary, use fictitious e-mail addresses.

1. Open **ch2sa4-a.htm** and use the Save As command to rename and save it as **ch2sa5.htm**.
2. Insert an e-mail link at the bottom of the page using your e-mail address.
3. Use the appropriate attributes, punctuation, and/or characters to modify the link to add:
   a. A second e-mail address in addition to your own

DREAMWEAVER MX 2004

b. Two CC and one BCC e-mail addresses

c. *Accessibility* as the subject text of the e-mail message

d. A short message (two or more sentences) describing the accessibility page (**ch2sa4-b.htm**) for the body of the e-mail message

4. Preview the page in a browser. Click the link to check that it works.

5. Save and then close **ch2sa5.htm**.

Assessment 6 • Create and Format a Web Page

1. Create a new HTML document and use the Save or Save As commands to name and save it as **ch2sa6.htm**.

2. Look at the Web page shown in Figure 2.45, and recreate the page in **ch2sa6.htm**. Be careful to duplicate as closely as possible the following:

a. Page background color

b. Heading size, color, and style

c. Text size, color, style, and formatting

d. Paragraph and heading alignment

e. List style

3. Save and then close **ch2sa6.htm**.

Assessment 7 • Use the Check Spelling and Find and Replace Tools

1. Open the student file named **bill_of_rights.htm** and use the Save As command to save it to the ch_02_assessments root folder as **ch2sa7.htm**.

2. Open the Check Spelling dialog box and correct all of the spelling mistakes in the document.

3. Use Find and Replace to find all instances of *amendment* in lowercase *(amendment)* and replace them with *amendment* in uppercase *(Amendment)*.

4. Use Find and Replace to find all instances of *constitution* in lowercase *(constitution)* and replace them with *constitution* in uppercase *(Constitution)*.

5. Save **ch2sa7.htm** and then close it.

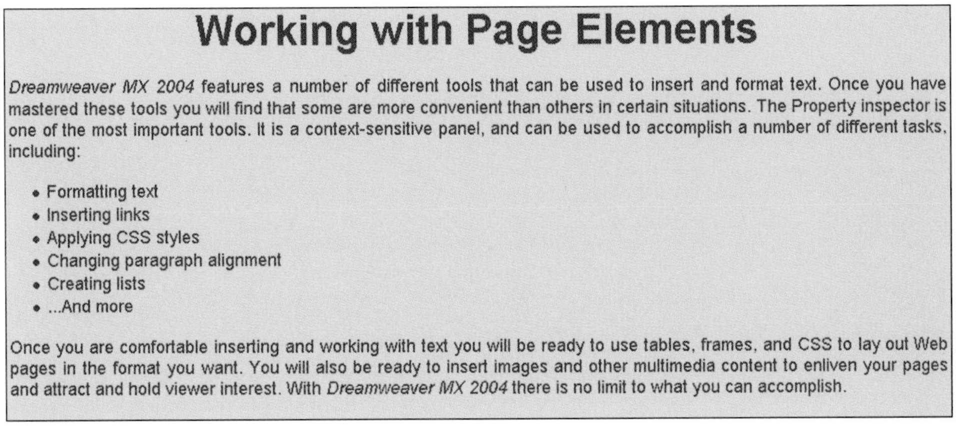

Working with Page Elements

Dreamweaver MX 2004 features a number of different tools that can be used to insert and format text. Once you have mastered these tools you will find that some are more convenient than others in certain situations. The Property inspector is one of the most important tools. It is a context-sensitive panel, and can be used to accomplish a number of different tasks, including:

• Formatting text
• Inserting links
• Applying CSS styles
• Changing paragraph alignment
• Creating lists
• ...And more

Once you are comfortable inserting and working with text you will be ready to use tables, frames, and CSS to lay out Web pages in the format you want. You will also be ready to insert images and other multimedia content to enliven your pages and attract and hold viewer interest. With *Dreamweaver MX 2004* there is no limit to what you can accomplish.

Figure 2.45 • Assessment 6

Assessment 8 • Start Building Your Design Portfolio Site

Use the Site Definition dialog box to create a separate Dreamweaver site named Design Portfolio Project to keep your design portfolio work. Save the files for the site in a new root folder named design_portfolio under the Sites folder you created in Chapter 1, Exercise 3.

1. Use the Files panel integrated file browser to add folders to your site and arrange them to reflect the hierarchy you planned in the design portfolio assessment in Chapter 1 (Assessment 7).
2. Create a basic HTML page and use the Save or Save As commands to name it **index.htm**, and save it to the design portfolio site.
3. Change the title of **index.htm** to *Home Page*.
4. Create a color scheme for your home page that matches the look of the mock-up page you created for the first design portfolio assessment in Chapter 1.
5. Create other files for your Web site by selecting **index.htm** in the Files panel integrated file browser, right-clicking, and then clicking Duplicate from the drop-down menu. Repeat this until you have enough documents for your site.
6. Select each copy of **index.htm**, right-click, and then click Rename to give each copy a new name, such as **page_2.htm**, **hobbies.htm**, **resume.htm**, and so on.
7. Change the title of each document to reflect the content you plan for it. For example, if a page will contain your resume, the title might be *Resume*, or *Resume Page*.
8. Place a link to the home page (**index.htm**) on all of the pages you created.
9. Place links on the home page to the pages you created.
10. Insert comments in each page outlining your plans for the page. For example: <!--*Resume page. Will contain copy of resume and link to resume Word document. Include portrait and links to projects I have worked on.* -->
11. Save and then close all of your Web pages.

WORKING WITH TABLES

PERFORMANCE OBJECTIVES

➤ Understand tables and table elements.

➤ Understand how tables are used for layout control.

➤ Create tables in Standard mode.

➤ Create proportional-width and fixed-width tables.

➤ Select tables and table elements.

➤ Use the Expanded Tables mode to aid table and cell selection.

➤ Use the Tab and arrow keys to navigate inside tables.

➤ Use the Table Property inspector and Table Cell Property inspector to format tables.

➤ Add and delete columns and rows.

➤ Merge and split cells.

➤ Create nested tables.

➤ Format tables using the Format Table command.

➤ Create tables in Layout mode.

➤ Create autostretch tables in Layout mode.

➤ Understand and use spacer images.

➤ Use a grid when working with tables.

➤ Sort table content.

The student files for this chapter are available for download from the Internet Resource Center at www.emcp.com.

Using the skills learned in the first two chapters, you are now able to use Dreamweaver MX 2004 to format page elements so they appear in the color, size, and style that you want. You also have learned to create pages with internal, external, and e-mail links. You might have noticed that your ability to enter content in a document is restricted by the left-to-right, top-to-bottom limitations of HTML code. Tables provide a solution to this problem, allowing you to place content in a document where you want it. After you understand how to use tables for page layout, you are a step closer to creating attractive, professional-looking Web pages.

Understanding Tables

When HTML code was developed, it was assumed that tables would be used to perform their traditional role as a convenient method for organizing and displaying data. However, designers soon discovered that tables could be used to position page elements by inserting them into the matrix formed by table cells, as shown in Figure 3.1. This ability afforded designers a much greater degree of control over *page layout*. Making a table's borders invisible means that viewers are not even aware that a table is being used to control page layout. Cascading Style Sheets (CSS) also can be used to control page layout, and as browser support for CSS improves, it will eventually replace the use of tables for that purpose. In the meantime, tables continue to be the principle method used to control page layout.

Table Components

Tables are grids composed of horizontal *rows* and vertical *columns*, with the space formed by the intersection of each row and column forming a *table cell*, as shown in Figure 3.2. The amount of space between cells is known as *cell spacing*, and the distance between cell content and cell borders is known as *cell padding*. Tables and cell backgrounds can be colored or even can contain a *background image*. *Table borders* can be colored as well, or can be made invisible.

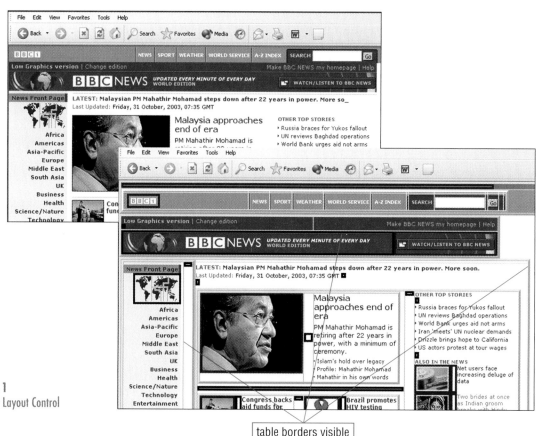

Figure 3.1
Tables Used for Layout Control

table borders visible

DREAMWEAVER MX 2004

Table Dimensions

Tables and the cells they are composed of will shrink to fit their contents unless a width is specified to make them wider than their content. ***Fixed widths*** are indicated in pixels; ***proportional widths*** are indicated as percentages. You also can indicate the height of a cell, but it is better in most circumstances to let browsers determine cell height based on a cell's content. Figure 3.3 shows the effect different table width settings can have on table appearance when viewed in a browser window.

Fixed-width tables and cells are not as fixed as the name implies. If a fixed-width cell's content is wider than its specified width, it will expand to fit the widest portion of its content. For example, a table cell with a width of 200 pixels will expand to 250 pixels if it contains an image that wide. A fixed-width cell also can be squeezed (narrowed in width) if an adjacent cell expands.

Proportional widths are relative sizes. A proportional width for a table indicates the percentage of the browser window the table will occupy. For example, a table width of 80 percent instructs browsers to display the table across 80 percent of their window. A cell with a proportional width occupies the specified percentage of the table's width, whether the table width is specified in pixels or a percentage. Proportional widths allow cells or tables to stretch to occupy their specified percentage of the table or browser window.

Designers must be careful not to create mathematically impossible dimensions by specifying fixed widths for columns whose total exceeds the width specified for the table containing them. For example, a table specified as 350 pixels wide should not contain two columns with a combined width of 400 pixels. Dreamweaver MX 2004 will not correct errors of this type, and tables with impossible dimensions might confuse browsers and produce unexpected results.

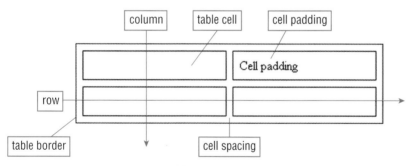

Figure 3.2 • Table Components

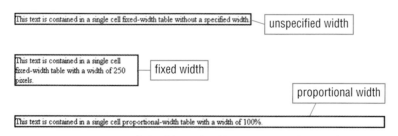

Figure 3.3 • Unspecified-Width, Fixed-Width, and Proportional-Width Tables as Viewed in a Browser

You also can manually resize a selected table by dragging its **table selection handles**, as shown in Figure 3.4. When a table is resized in this way, its individual cells change size proportionately. Clicking and dragging the selection handle located on the right side of a table resizes it horizontally. Clicking and dragging the selection handle located at the bottom of a table resizes it vertically. Tables can be resized in both dimensions simultaneously by clicking and dragging the selection handle in the lower-right corner of a table. Resizing tables by dragging is not an ideal method because it is hard to maintain exact control over the dimensions automatically being created by Dreamweaver MX 2004 as a table is being resized.

When a table has been resized by dragging, its column header display will indicate two sizes. The first size indicates the width specified in the HTML code, and the second size, set in parentheses, indicates the visual width. Clicking the table header display down-pointing arrow opens a menu containing a Make All Widths Consistent command as shown in Figure 3.5. Clicking this command will make the actual width in the HTML code consistent with the visual width. The insertion point must be located inside a table in order to view the table header and table width displays. If they are still not visible after placing the insertion point inside a table, click the Document toolbar View options button, point to Visual Aids, and then make sure that Table Widths is checked.

Table Code

Knowledge of the HTML code used for creating tables is helpful because using the Tag selector is one of the easiest ways to select tables and table components. Basic tables are created in HTML using **table tags** (<table>), with rows controlled by **table row tags** (<tr>), and cells controlled by **table data cell tags** (<td>). Each pair of table row tags must contain at least one pair of table data cell tags. Table, table row, and table data cell tags all can contain attributes that further modify their appearance.

Figure 3.6 shows a basic table and the HTML code used to create it. Note that the empty table cells contain an HTML special character known as a **nonbreaking space** ( ). This character prevents empty cells from collapsing and disappearing from view in some browsers. When content is entered into a cell, Dreamweaver MX 2004 automatically removes the nonbreaking space.

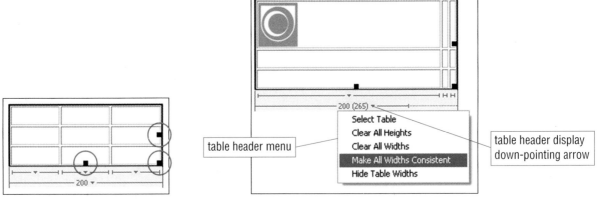

Figure 3.4 • Table Selection Handles

Figure 3.5 • Table Header Display Menu

table header menu

Select Table
Clear All Heights
Clear All Widths
Make All Widths Consistent
Hide Table Widths

table header display down-pointing arrow

Using Tables to Control Page Layout

The look of a page using a table for layout control is dependent on a number of variables that are outside the designer's control, such as the viewer's screen size, screen resolution, and browser window dimensions. With those variables in mind, designers try to create layout tables that will maintain their design integrity to the greatest extent possible when viewed across different browser scenarios.

Designers can control the size of the overall layout by using tables with fixed widths (in pixels), with proportional widths (as a percentage of the screen width), or with a combination of both fixed and proportional widths. Tables containing proportional widths are referred to as *liquid tables* or *flexible tables* because they adjust to fit browser window dimensions.

Fixed-width tables will maintain their appearance when viewed using different screen and browser combinations, provided that a table does not contain empty cells or cells containing content that exceeds their specified width. The drawback to fixed-width tables is that on large screens, there can be a lot of wasted space next to or on either side of the table, depending on table alignment. Conversely, on smaller screens, a portion of the table might disappear off the right side of the browser window.

The advantage to using a table with proportional widths is that the table maintains its relative dimensions no matter what screen and browser combinations the table is viewed in. The drawback to proportional tables is that the designer loses control over lines and spacing as the table and/or column widths stretch or decrease to accommodate different dimensions. Figure 3.7 shows a fixed-width table that is cut off because it stretches beyond the browser's available window width and the same table with a proportional width that has automatically resized to fit the available window width.

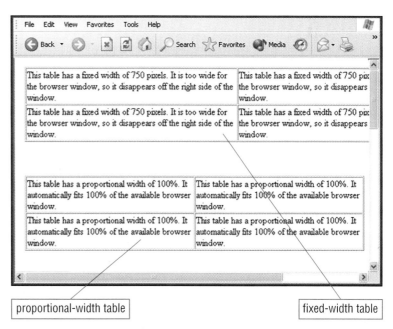

```
<table width="100" border="1"
<tr>
<td width="50">Cats</td>
<td width="50">Dogs</td>
</tr>
<tr>
<td>15</td>
<td>21</td>
</tr>
<tr>
<td> </td>
<td> </td>
</tr>
</table>
```

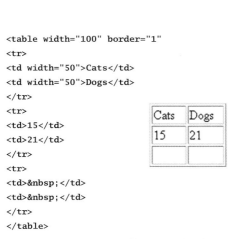

Figure 3.6 • Basic Table HTML Code and Table

Figure 3.7 • Tables with Fixed- and Proportional-Width Columns in a Browser Window

Tables that contain a combination of fixed and proportional widths are a common compromise solution, allowing designers to use fixed widths to maintain control over segments of the table that need to remain stable, while letting other segments of the table flow to fit browser windows. A simple example of this is a two-column table with a fixed-width column containing navigation buttons or links, and a proportional-width column containing text. Figure 3.8 shows such a page under two different browser size configurations. Note how the text location in the column on the right changes as the proportional-width column adjusts to fit the browser window. Because the fixed-width column remains stable, it ensures that the navigation or link layout will appear as intended, with each button or link appearing in the correct location. The proportional column is often used to contain text because a change in column width affects only the length of the lines of text and is therefore not as critical to design considerations.

Designers can use additional table properties to lay out text and images in an attractive manner that will please viewers. Columns can be used to break up lines of text so that a single line does not contain more than the recommended 10 to 12 words. Columns also can be used to separate navigation functions from content, to contain links, or to separate other page content. Cell padding and cell spacing can be used to create *margins* (the space around the outer edges of the document) and a *gutter* (the space between columns of text) as shown in Figure 3.9. Margins prevent text from bumping up against the edge of the browser window; a gutter separates text in adjacent columns. Long tables can slow down page loading, so when possible, it is better to use several tables rather than one long table on a page.

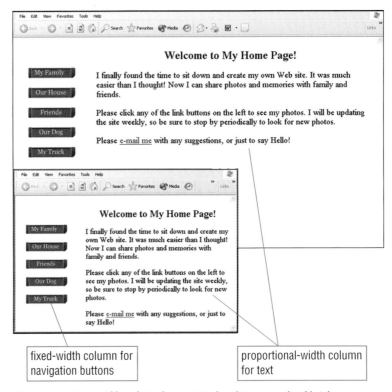

fixed-width column for navigation buttons

proportional-width column for text

Figure 3.8 • Table with Combination Fixed- and Proportional-Width Columns

DREAMWEAVER MX 2004

Creating Tables

You can create tables using the Table dialog box shown in Figure 3.10, opened by clicking Insert on the Menu bar and then Table, or by clicking the Table button on the Insert bar (Common menu item or tab). The dialog box lets users specify the desired number of rows and columns along with table width, cell padding, cell spacing, and border thickness dimensions.

The dialog box also contains ***header*** buttons featuring choices for None, Left (column), Top (row), or Both (column and row). Choosing the None button specifies that the table will not have any column or row headers. The Left button formats the first column as a header column, with text centered and in bold so

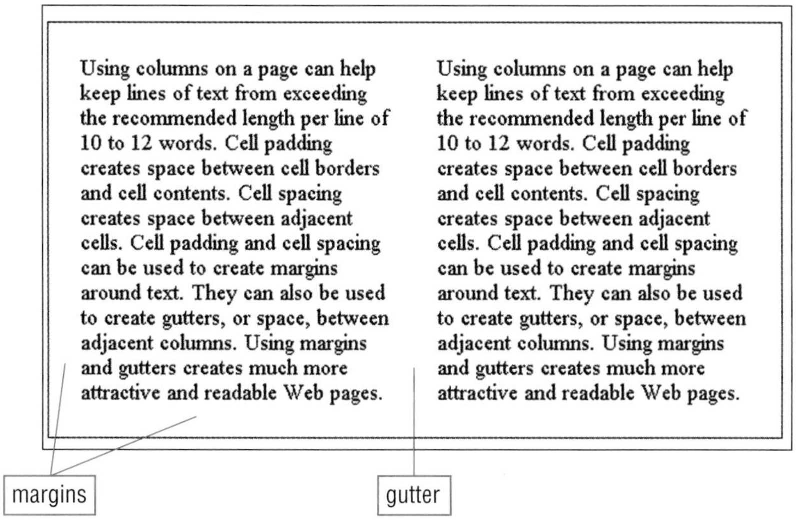

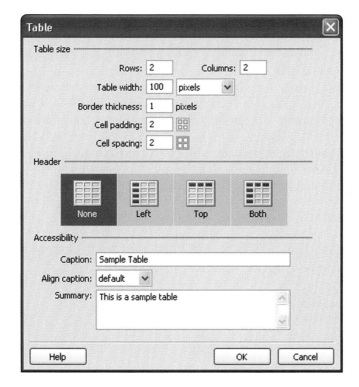

Using columns on a page can help keep lines of text from exceeding the recommended length per line of 10 to 12 words. Cell padding creates space between cell borders and cell contents. Cell spacing creates space between adjacent cells. Cell padding and cell spacing can be used to create margins around text. They can also be used to create gutters, or space, between adjacent columns. Using margins and gutters creates much more attractive and readable Web pages.
Using columns on a page can help keep lines of text from exceeding the recommended length per line of 10 to 12 words. Cell padding creates space between cell borders and cell contents. Cell spacing creates space between adjacent cells. Cell padding and cell spacing can be used to create margins around text. They can also be used to create gutters, or space, between adjacent columns. Using margins and gutters creates much more attractive and readable Web pages.
margins
gutter

Figure 3.9
Using Cell Padding and Cell Spacing to Create Margins and a Gutter

Table
Table size
Rows: 2
Columns: 2
Table width: 100
pixels
Border thickness: 1
pixels
Cell padding: 2
Cell spacing: 2
Header
None
Left
Top
Both
Accessibility
Caption: Sample Table
Align caption: default
Summary: This is a sample table
Help
OK
Cancel

Figure 3.10
Table Dialog Box

that each column cell acts as a header for the adjacent row. The Top button creates header formatting in the top row of the table, so that each row cell acts as a column header. The Both button creates both column and row headers.

Completing the information called for in the *Accessibility* section of the Table dialog box ensures that viewers with disabilities will be able to better understand table content. The Table dialog box accessibility properties are described in the following list.

- **Caption** This text box creates a ***caption*** that functions as a table title. The table title will be displayed outside the table as shown in Figure 3.11.

- **Align caption** Caption alignment choices in the drop-down list are *default* (top), *top, bottom, left,* and *right* title placement.

- **Summary** Text summarizing the table content *(**summary text**)* can be entered in the *Summary* text box. The text will be invisible in browsers, but can be interpreted by screen readers.

After table values have been entered, clicking the OK button places a table at the insertion point in the current document. Dreamweaver MX 2004 remembers user preferences, so the next time the Table dialog box is opened, the settings will reflect the previous choices.

Figure 3.11
Table Caption

Annual Sales	
2003	**2004**
23,500 units	30,300 units

exercise **1**

CREATING A PROPORTIONAL-WIDTH TABLE

Make sure that you are working in the Standard mode table view by clicking View on the Menu bar, pointing to Table Mode, and then verifying that a check mark is next to Standard Mode. *Exercises in this chapter will be completed using Standard mode unless otherwise indicated.*

1. If necessary, start Dreamweaver MX 2004.
2. At a clear document screen, create a new site named CH 03 Exercises to store the exercises you create in this chapter. Name the root folder ch_03_exercises and save it under the Sites folder you created in Chapter 1, Exercise 3. Download the ch_03_student_files folder from the IRC to the CH 03 Exercises site root folder (ch_03_exercises) and expand it. Delete the compressed folder when you are finished. ***Note: Refer to Chapter 1 for instructions on navigating with the Files panel integrated file browser.***
3. Create a proportional-width layout table by completing the following steps:
   a. Create a new HTML document and use the Save or Save As command to name and save it as **ch3ex01.htm**.
   b. Click the Common menu item or tab on the Insert bar.
   c. Click the Insert bar Table button or click it and drag it to the Document window to open the Table dialog box.

d. Type the following values in the Table dialog box:

1) Type 1 in the *Rows* text box.
2) Type 2 in the *Columns* text box.
3) Type 100 in the *Table width* text box. If necessary, click the down-pointing arrow next to the *Table width* list box to select *percent* from the drop-down list.
4) Type 0 in the *Border thickness* text box.
5) Type 8 in the *Cell padding* and *Cell spacing* text boxes.
6) Click the None button in the *Header* section.
7) Leave the *Caption* text box blank because this table is not being used for tabular data.

Steps 3d1–3d9

8) Ignore the *Align caption* list box because there will be no caption for this table.
9) Type A table containing a two-column newsletter in the *Summary* text box.
10) Click the OK button to close the dialog box. **Note: If the table is not visible in the Document window, click the View options button on the Document toolbar, point to Visual Aids, and then make sure there is a check mark next to Table Borders.**

e. Click File on the Menu bar and then New. The New Document dialog box appears.

f. Select *Page Designs* from the *Category* list. **Note: Make sure the General tab is selected.**

g. Select *Commerce: Product Catalog A* from the *Page Designs* list box. **Hint: At the bottom of the Page Designs list box there are left and right arrows and a slider that you can use to scroll and view the document names if they are not completely visible in the list box.**

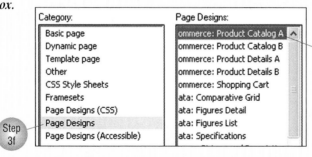

Step 3f

Step 3g

h. Click the Create button to open the *Commerce: Product Catalog A* document in the Document window.

i. Select the paragraph placeholder text. Click Edit on the Menu bar and then Copy to copy the selected text. Close the document when you are finished. Click the No button when the message box asking if you want to save changes to the document appears.

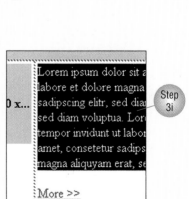

Step 3i

j. With **ch3ex01.htm** as the current document, position the insertion point in the first table cell. Click Edit and then Paste to paste the copied placeholder text in the first cell. Press Enter once and then paste the copied text again to add a second paragraph of placeholder text to the first cell. ***Note: The first cell has expanded to fit its contents and has squeezed the empty second cell.***

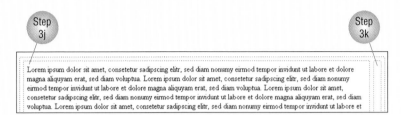

k. Position the insertion point in the second table cell. Repeat the pasting process in Step 3j to paste two copies of the placeholder text in the second table cell. ***Hint: Remember to press Enter once before pasting the copied text for the second time.***

l. Click the Preview/Debug in browser button and then click Preview in iexplore to preview the table you have just created. Note that because its width was specified as 100 percent, the table has expanded to fit the entire width of the browser window. Because no width was specified for the two columns, they have automatically expanded to fit their content. Because the cells contain identical content, each one occupies 50 percent of the total table width. If the width of the cell content differed, the percentage of the total table width occupied by the cells would vary, with one cell shrinking to accommodate the adjacent cell with wider content. Resize the browser window and observe how the table behaves. Close the browser when you are finished.

4. Save **ch3ex01.htm** and then close it.

| CREATING A FIXED-WIDTH TABLE |

1. Create a fixed-width table by completing the following steps:
    a. At a clear document screen, create a new HTML document and use the Save or Save As command to name and save it as **ch3ex02.htm**.
    b. Click the Common menu item or tab on the Insert bar.
    c. Click the Table button or click it and drag it to the Document window to open the Table dialog box.

d. Type the following values in the Table dialog box:

1) Type 6 in the *Rows* text box.
2) Type 7 in the *Columns* text box.
3) Type 350 in the *Table width* text box.
4) Click the down-pointing arrow next to the *Table width* list box and select *pixels* from the drop-down list.
5) Type 1 in the *Border thickness* text box.
6) Type 0 in the *Cell padding* and *Cell spacing* text boxes.
7) Click the Top button in the *Header* section.
8) Type November 2006 in the *Caption* text box. (You are going to create a calendar for that month.)
9) Click the *Align caption* list box down-pointing arrow and select *default* or *top* from the drop-down list.
10) Type A table containing a calendar for November 2006 in the *Summary* text box.
11) Click the OK button to close the dialog box.

e. Position the insertion point in the upper-left table cell and type an uppercase M. Position the insertion point in the next cell and type T. Continue in this fashion until the top row reads *M, T, W, TH, F, SA, SU*, representing the days of the week.

Note that the text you are entering appears in bold and is centered because you selected the Top button in the *Header* section of the Table dialog box.

November 2006						
M	T	W	TH	F	SA	SU

f. Position the insertion point in the first cell below the column headed *W* and type 1 for the first day of the month. Press the Tab key to move to the next cell and type 2. Continue in this fashion until you have entered all of the days of the month to 30.

November 2006						
M	T	W	TH	F	SA	SU
		1	2	3	4	5
6	7	8	9	10	11	12
13	14	15	16	17	18	19
20	21	22	23	24	25	26
27	28	29	30			

g. Click the Preview/Debug in browser button and then click Preview in iexplore to preview the fixed-width table you have just created. Note that unlike the proportional table you created previously, the fixed-width table has not expanded to fit the browser window. Close the browser window when you are finished.

2. Save ch3ex02.htm and then close it.

Selecting Table Elements

Tables and table elements (rows, columns, and cells) must be selected before they can be modified using the Property inspector. You can choose from a variety of different methods for selecting tables and table elements. Some methods might be more convenient than others under certain circumstances, so it is helpful to be familiar with more than one method. Dreamweaver MX 2004 features an ***Expanded Tables mode*** that temporarily adds cell padding and spacing to tables in order to make it easier to view and select table and cell borders. The Expanded Tables mode can be activated by clicking the Insert bar Layout menu item or tab and then clicking the Expanded button. Tables in the current document will then be displayed in Expanded Tables mode as shown in Figure 3.12. Some operations will not appear as expected in Expanded Tables mode, so once you are finished using it to select tables or table cells you should click the exit link as shown in Figure 3.12 to return to Standard mode. You also can return to Standard mode by clicking the Insert bar (Layout menu item or tab) Standard button.

Tables

Clicking inside a table causes the table header display to appear as shown in Figure 3.13. The table header display contains a down-pointing arrow that displays a menu when clicked as shown in Figure 3.13. The Select Table command can then be used to select the table.

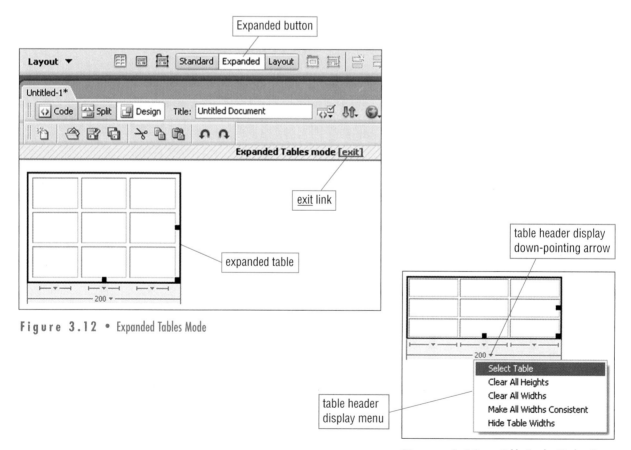

Figure 3.12 • Expanded Tables Mode

Figure 3.13 • Table Header Display Menu

Clicking a table's upper or lower border selects the entire table. When the insertion point is placed over an upper or lower table border, the insertion point will transform into a small table grid icon as shown in Figure 3.14. Selecting a table in this manner is not always as easy as it appears, and it is possible to inadvertently resize or move a table when trying to select it. For that reason, an easier way to select a table is to use the Tag selector to click the table tag. The insertion point must first be positioned inside a table for its table tag (<table>) to appear in the Tag selector. When a table is selected, its outer edge appears outlined in black and its selection handles are visible as shown in Figure 3.15. You also can position the insertion point in a table cell and click Modify, point to Table, and then click Select Table to select a table.

With large tables, it is sometimes difficult to position the insertion point outside the table. Selecting the table and pressing the Left or Right Arrow keys positions the insertion point outside the table, indicated by a blinking black line spanning the height of the table as shown in Figure 3.16.

Cells

Cells can be selected in several ways as well. You can click inside the cell and then click the table data cell tag (<td>) in the Tag selector; click inside a cell, click Edit, and then Select All; or hold down the Ctrl key while clicking inside a cell.

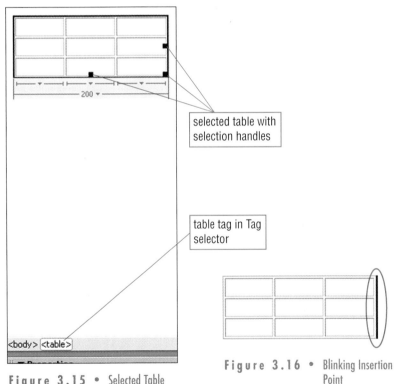

selected table with selection handles

table tag in Tag selector

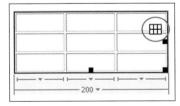

Figure 3.14 • Table Grid Icon

Figure 3.15 • Selected Table

Figure 3.16 • Blinking Insertion Point

Rows and Columns

Placing the insertion point in a column cell and then clicking the column header display down-pointing arrow opens up a menu as shown in Figure 3.17. Clicking the Select Column command will select the column containing the insertion point.

Placing the pointer on the outer border of a row or column causes a selection arrow to appear, as shown in Figure 3.18. After the arrow appears, you can click the mouse button to select the desired row or column.

Another method for selecting rows, columns, or adjacent blocks of cells is to click inside a cell, and without releasing the mouse button, to drag the pointer across the cells to be selected. Releasing the button selects the cells.

A fourth method that can be used to select blocks of cells is to click inside a cell, hold down the Shift key, and then click inside another cell. This selects all of the cells located between the first and last cell selected.

Finally, clicking inside a table and then clicking the desired table row tag (<tr>) in the Tag selector selects the table row it controls.

Nonadjacent Cells

Nonadjacent cells can be selected by holding down the Ctrl key, clicking inside one cell, and then clicking inside the other cells to be selected as shown in Figure 3.19. While performing this operation, clicking inside a cell that is already selected deselects it.

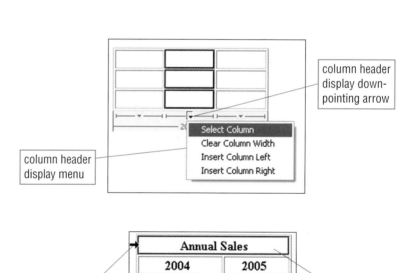

Figure 3.17
Column Header Display Menu

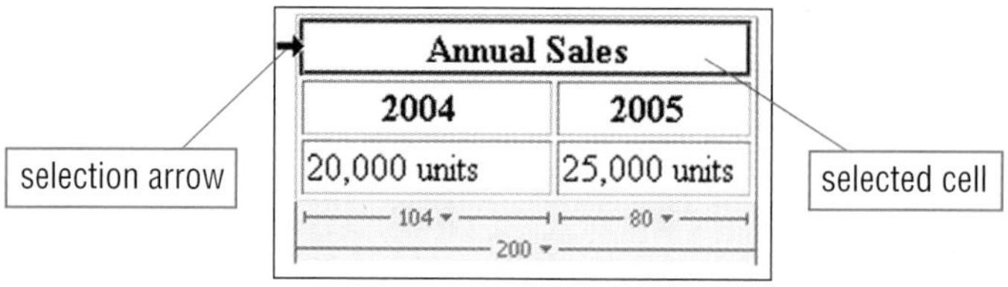

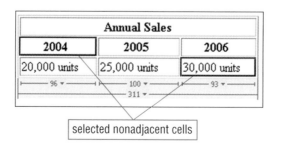

Figure 3.18
Selection Arrow

Figure 3.19
Selected Nonadjacent Cells

1. Select tables and table cells by completing the following steps:
   a. At a clear document screen, open **ch3ex02.htm**. Use the Save As command to rename and save it as **ch3ex03.htm**.
   b. Place the pointer on the left border of the top row of the table until the right-pointing black selection arrow appears, and then click to select the row.
   c. Click the Property inspector *Font* text box down-pointing arrow to open the drop-down list. Click *Arial, Helvetica, sans-serif* to choose that font style for the text in the selected first table row.
   d. Position the insertion point inside the first cell below the Saturday column *(SA)* and drag it across to the next cell and then downward until all of the Saturday and Sunday cells are selected. Click the Bold button in the Property inspector to bold the dates in the selected cells.
   e. Position the insertion point in the cell for Tuesday the 7th, Election Day. Click Edit on the Menu bar and then Select All to highlight the cell. Click the Bold button in the Property inspector to bold *7*. Deselect the cell by clicking outside the table when you are finished.
   f. Hold down the Ctrl key and click inside the cells for the 29th (author Louisa May Alcott's birthday) and the 30th (Thanksgiving Day) to select those nonadjacent cells. Click the Bold button in the Property inspector to bold the dates in those cells.
   g. Click the Preview/Debug in browser button and then click Preview in iexplore to preview the page. Close the browser when you are finished.
2. Save **ch3ex03.htm** and then close it.

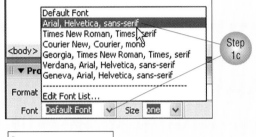

Navigating in Tables

The Tab or arrow keys can be used to navigate within tables. Although both keys move the insertion point through a table, they function in slightly different ways.

Tab Keys

Positioning the insertion point inside a table cell and then pressing the Tab key moves the insertion point to the next cell. Each time the Tab key is pressed, the insertion point moves to the next cell, traveling in a left-to-right, top-to-bottom direction. Holding down the Shift key while pressing the Tab key reverses the tab direction. Pressing the Tab key creates a new row when the last cell in a table is reached. The new row will have the same characteristics as the row immediately above it. Be careful to avoid inadvertently creating new rows when you are navigating with the Tab key.

Arrow Keys

The Up, Down, Left, and Right Arrow keys can be used to navigate inside a table. Unlike the Tab key, the arrow keys first navigate within a cell's contents and then move on to the next cell. For example, if the Down Arrow key is used to navigate in a cell with four lines of text, each press of the key moves the insertion point down one line of text. After the last line has been reached, the insertion point moves to a new cell. The arrow keys cannot be used to create new rows.

exercise 4

NAVIGATING INSIDE TABLES

1. Use the Tab key to navigate between cells and to create new rows by completing the following steps:
   a. At a clear document screen, open **ch3ex01.htm**. Use the Save As command to rename and save it as **ch3ex04.htm**.
   b. Position the insertion point in the upper-left corner of the first table cell.

   Step 1b

   Lorem ipsum dolor s
   sed diam nonumy ei
   dolore magna aliquy

   c. Press the Tab key once to move the insertion point into the next cell. Note that the text in the cell is selected. Press the Tab key again to create a new table row below the first row.

   Step 1c

   ut labore et dolore magna ali
   voluptua.

   d. Hold down the Shift key and press the Tab key until the insertion point moves back into the first table cell.
   e. Click the upper-left corner of the table to deselect the text and position the insertion point.
2. Use the arrow keys to navigate through cell content by completing the following steps:
   a. Select the first word in the first cell *(Lorem)* and click the Bold button in the Property inspector to bold it.
   b. Press the Down Arrow key until the insertion point is moved down three lines. Press the Right Arrow key until the insertion point is located in *Lorem*. ***Note: If the panel groups on the right side of the Document window have been resized, the text might appear on a different line than instructed. Adjust the instructions accordingly.***

   Step 2a

   Lorem ipsum dolo
   sed diam nonumy e
   dolore magna aliqu

   c. Double-click *Lorem* to select it, and then click the Bold button in the Property inspector to bold it.
   d. Continue using the arrow keys to maneuver through the document, and bold every instance of *Lorem*. Note that the Left and Right Arrow keys move the insertion point through the text one character at a time, while the Up and Down Arrow keys move the insertion point up or down one line of text at a time.

   Lorem ipsum dolor sit amet, consetetur sadipscing elitr, sed diam nonumy eirmod tempor invidunt ut labore et dolore magna aliquyam erat, sed diam voluptua. **Lorem** ipsum dolor sit amet, consetetur sadipscing elitr, sed \diam

   Step 2c

3. Save **ch3ex04.htm** and then close it.

DREAMWEAVER MX 2004

Using the Property Inspector to Format Tables and Table Cells

When the Property inspector shown in Figure 3.20 is open, it automatically displays table or cell properties when a table or cell is selected. When a table is selected, the Property inspector opens in Table Property inspector mode; when a cell is selected, it opens in Table Cell Property inspector mode.

When formatting tables, be aware that cell and row background formatting will override table formatting. The order of precedence is cell, row, table. For example, if a cell has been formatted to have a green background, changing the table background color to red will not change the color of the green cell.

Table Property Inspector

The **Table Property inspector** shown in Figure 3.20 is visible when a table is selected. Clicking the down-pointing Expander arrow expands the inspector to make all table or cell properties visible in the Property inspector. When the Table Property inspector is in expanded mode, the Expander arrow turns into an up-pointing Contractor arrow. Clicking the Contractor arrow will contract the Table Property inspector. Table Property inspector properties are described in the following list:

- **Table Id** You can type a name or number to identify a table in this text box. A **table identification** is useful when working with nested tables or with pages containing a number of different tables.

- **Rows** Specifies the number of rows in the table.

- **Cols** Specifies the number of columns in the table.

- **W** Width can be specified as a fixed number of pixels, or as a percentage of the width of the browser window. The default setting is *pixels,* but the down-pointing arrow in the adjacent list box can be used to specify a percentage value.

- **H** Height can be specified as a fixed number of pixels, or as a percentage of the height of the browser window. Not all browsers support specifying a height as a percentage of the total table height. The default setting is *pixels,* but the down-pointing arrow in the adjacent list box can be used to specify a percentage value.

- **CellPad** Specifies the cell padding, the number of pixels of space appearing between a cell's contents and its borders.

- **CellSpace** Specifies the cell spacing, the number of pixels of space appearing between adjacent cell borders.

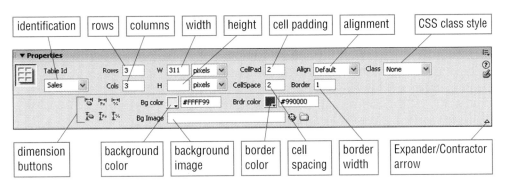

Figure 3.20
Table Property Inspector

- *Align* Specifies the **table alignment**, the table location relative to other elements (text, images, and so on) in the table paragraph. *Left* and *Right* place a table to the left or right of any text or images; *Center* places a table in the center of the page with text appearing above and below the table; and *Default* places the table on the left side of the screen, but without text appearing next to it.

- *Border* Specifies table border width in pixels. If a border value is not entered, most browsers set a table's border thickness at 1 pixel by default. To display a borderless table, the border value should be set at 0. To make a borderless table visible in the Document window, click View options on the Menu bar, point to Visual Aids, and then click to place a check mark next to Table Borders.

- *Class* The *Class* list box displays the CSS class style that is applied to the selected table. This list box will be described more fully in Chapter 6, *Using Cascading Style Sheets (CSS)*.

- *Bg color* Specifies the background color for the entire table. Clicking the color box opens the Color Picker.

- *Bg Image* Specifies a background image file location if a background image is used (covered in Chapter 4, *Working with Images*).

- *Brdr color* Specifies the **border color** for a table. Clicking the color box opens the Color Picker.

- **Dimension Buttons** To the left of the *Bg color* and *Bg Image* text boxes there are six **dimension buttons** that can be used to clear column and row heights, and convert table widths and heights to pixels or percentages.

exercise 5

FORMATTING TABLE PROPERTIES

1. Use the Table Property inspector to format table properties by completing the following steps:
    a. At a clear document screen, open **ch3ex03.htm**. Use the Save As command to rename and save it as **ch3ex05.htm**.
    b. Position the insertion point anywhere inside the table.
    c. Click <table> in the Tag selector to select the table.

Step 1c

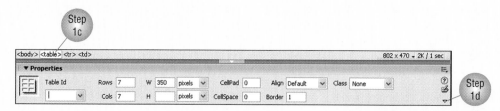

d. If the Table Property inspector is not fully expanded, click the Expander arrow in the lower-right corner of the Table Property inspector to expand it.
e. Type November 2006 Calendar in the *Table Id* text box to identify the table. *Note: The identification you create will appear in the Tag selector next to the body tag (<body>) when you press Enter.*

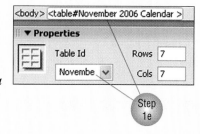

DREAMWEAVER MX 2004

f. Type *5* in the *CellPad* text box to create 5 pixels of space between cell content and cell borders.

g. Click the *Align* list box down-pointing arrow and then click *Center* from the drop-down list to align the table in the center of a browser window.

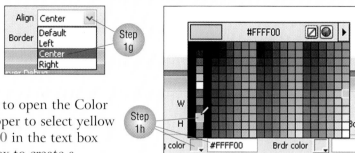

h. Click the *Bg color* color box to open the Color Picker and use the Eyedropper to select yellow #FFFF00, or type *#FFFF00* in the text box next to the *Bg color* color box to create a yellow background for the table.

i. Click the *Brdr color* color box to open the Color Picker and use the Eyedropper to select brown #660033, or type *#660033* in the text box next to the *Brdr color* color box to change the table borders from black to brown.

j. Click the Preview/Debug in browser button and then click Preview in iexplore to preview the table in a browser. Note that the table is now centered in the middle of the browser window, the dates in the cell have moved in further from the cell walls (cell padding), and the table background and border colors you selected have been implemented. Close the browser when you are finished.

2. Save **ch3ex05.htm** and then close it.

Table Cell Property Inspector

The ***Table Cell Property inspector*** is visible when rows, columns, or cells are selected, as shown in Figure 3.21. Some properties will not be visible if the Table Cell Property inspector is not fully expanded. Table Cell Property inspector properties are described in the following list:

*   ***Horz*** Specifies the ***horizontal alignment*** for row, column, or cell content. Options are *Default, Left, Center,* and *Right. Default* usually means a left alignment for normal cells and a center alignment for header cells.

*   ***Vert*** Specifies the ***vertical alignment*** for row, column, or cell content. Options are *Default, Top, Middle, Bottom,* or *Baseline. Baseline* aligns text to the bottom of an image. *Default* usually results in middle alignment.

*   ***W*** Specifies cell width in pixels or as a percent of a table's width or height. To set as a percentage, type a percent sign (%) after the number. Leaving this text box blank instructs a browser to determine an appropriate width based on cell content.

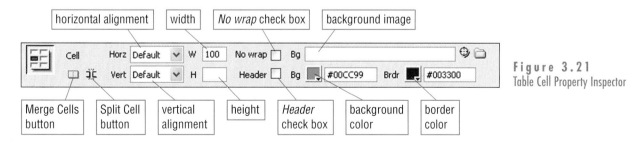

Figure 3.21
Table Cell Property Inspector

- ***H*** Specifies cell height in the same manner as the *W* text box.
- ***No wrap*** Placing a check mark in the *No wrap* check box prevents text from wrapping to a new line when a line exceeds a specified column or table width. If this option is not selected, text will wrap to fit inside a cell, which will expand vertically to accommodate the text.
- ***Header*** Selecting this option centers and bolds cell text, and is used to create table headers.
- ***Bg*** The top *Bg* text box specifies a background image file location for a cell, column, or row (covered in Chapter 4). *Note: The background image* Bg *text box is the one with the Browse for File button next to it.*
- ***Bg*** The bottom *Bg* color box and text box specifies the background color for a cell. Clicking the color box opens the Color Picker.
- ***Brdr*** Specifies cell border color. Clicking the color box opens the Color Picker.
- **Merge Cells Button** The unlabeled ***Merge Cells button*** located on the left side of the Table Cell Property inspector merges selected cells, rows, or columns into one cell. Only adjacent cells can be merged.
- **Split Cell Button** The unlabeled ***Split Cell button*** located on the left side of the Table Cell Property inspector splits a selected cell into two or more cells. Only one cell can be split at a time.

exercise 6 — FORMATTING TABLE ROW, COLUMN, AND CELL PROPERTIES

1. Use the Table Cell Property inspector to format table properties by completing the following steps:
    a. At a clear document screen, open **ch3ex05.htm**. Use the Save As command to rename and save it as **ch3ex06.htm**.
    b. Select the first table row by positioning the insertion point in the first cell of the first row and then dragging it across the row. Alternatively, position the insertion point in the first cell of the first row and click the table row tag (<tr>) in the Tag selector.

Step 1b

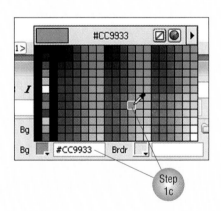

Step 1c

    c. Click the *Bg* color box to open the Color Picker and use the Eyedropper to select light brown #CC9933, or type #CC9933 in the text box next to the *Bg* color box to create a light brown background for the first row.
    d. Position the insertion point in the first cell of the second row, and drag it diagonally downward to the last table cell in the lower-right corner to select the remaining table rows.

DREAMWEAVER MX 2004

e. Click the down-pointing arrow next to the *Horz* list box and click *Center* from the drop-down list to center the text in the selected cells.

f. Select the header row, and type **50** in the *W* text box to format each column at 50 pixels wide.

g. Position the insertion point in the empty cell to the right of the cell containing the last day of the month (30) and drag to the right to select the remaining three empty cells.

h. Click the Table Cell Property inspector Merge Cells button to merge the selected cells into one long cell.

i. Position the insertion point in the cell with *4* (first day of the month below *SA*), and drag it diagonally downward to the cell for the 26th to select the cells with weekend dates.

j. Click the *Bg* color box to open the Color Picker and use the Eyedropper to select white #FFFFFF, or type **#FFFFFF** in the text box next to the *Bg* color box to create a white background for the weekend cells. Deselect the cells by clicking outside the table when you are finished.

k. Hold down the Ctrl key and click the insertion point in the cells for the special days in bold (7th, 29th, and 30th) to select those cells.

l. Click the *Bg* color box to open the Color Picker and use the Eyedropper to select orange #FF6633, or type **#FF6633** in the text box next to the *Bg* color box to create an orange background for the holiday cells.

m. Click the Preview/Debug in browser button and then click Preview in iexplore to preview the changes to the table that you just made. Note that each column is the same width because you entered an identical width for all of the cells in the first row in Step 1f. Close the browser window when you are finished.

2. Save **ch3ex06.htm** and then close it.

Adding and Deleting Rows and Columns

Rows and columns can be added to tables by clicking Modify on the Menu bar, point to Table, and then click Insert Row or Insert Column. Positioning the insertion point in a cell and clicking Insert Row creates a new row directly above the insertion point location. Clicking Insert Column creates a new column directly to the left of the insertion point location.

Columns also can be added by selecting a column and then clicking the table width drop-down arrow to open the column header display menu as shown in Figure 3.22. The menu can then be used to insert a column to the left or right of the selected column.

The Insert Rows or Columns dialog box shown in Figure 3.23 offers more flexibility in inserting and locating new rows and columns. To open the Insert Rows or Columns dialog box, click Modify on the Menu bar, point to Table, and then click Insert Rows or Columns. The Insert Rows or Columns dialog box lets you insert more than one column or row at a time. You also can specify whether you want rows to appear above or below the insertion point, or whether you want columns to appear before or after the insertion point.

You also can access the insert commands by right-clicking when the insertion point is positioned inside a table cell. This opens a context-sensitive menu containing the Table command. Clicking the Table command opens a submenu with insert commands. You also can press the Tab key when the insertion point is positioned in the last cell of a table to create new rows.

The Table Property inspector can be used to insert additional rows or columns in a table by selecting the table and increasing the values in the Table Property inspector *Rows* or *Cols* text boxes.

To delete rows and columns, position the insertion point inside a cell in the row or column to be deleted, click Modify on the Menu bar, point to Table, and then click Delete Row or Delete Column. Another method for deleting rows or columns is to select the entire row or column and then press the Delete or Backspace keys, or click Edit on the Menu bar and then Clear. The Tag selector also can be used to remove rows by selecting a row's table row tag and pressing the Delete or Backspace keys. The Table Property inspector can be used to reduce the number of rows or columns by selecting a table and reducing the values in the *Rows* or *Cols* text boxes. Dreamweaver MX 2004 will not warn you if a row or column to be deleted contains content, so be careful when deleting rows and columns.

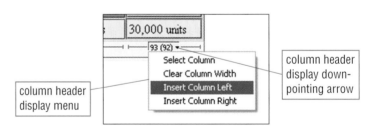

Figure 3.22 • Column Header Display Menu

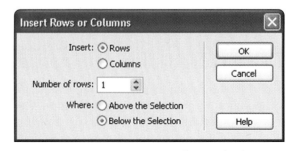

Figure 3.23 • Insert Rows or Columns Dialog Box

1. Add rows and columns to a table by completing the
   following steps:
   a. At a clear document screen, open **ch3ex04.htm**. Use the
      Save As command to rename and save it as
      ch3ex07.htm.
   b. Position the insertion point in the first cell of the first
      table row.
   c. Click Modify on the Menu bar, point to Table,
      and then click Insert Row to insert a row above
      the first row.
   d. If necessary, position the insertion point in the
      first cell of the new row.
   e. Click Modify on the Menu bar, point to Table,
      and then click Insert Column to insert a column
      to the left of the insertion point location.
   f. Position the insertion point in the third column of the first row. Click Modify,
      point to Table, and then click Insert Rows or Columns to open the Insert Rows or
      Columns dialog box.
   g. Select the *Columns* radio button, and leave the default *Number of columns* value as *1*.
      If necessary, click the *After current Column* radio button to indicate where you want
      the column to appear. Click the OK button when you are finished.

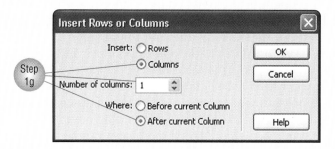

2. Delete table rows and columns by completing the following steps:
   a. Position the insertion point in the last cell of the first row of
      the table.
   b. Click Modify on the Menu bar, point to Table, and then click
      Delete Column to delete the fourth column.
   c. Position the insertion point in the first cell of the last row
      and drag it across all three columns to select the row.

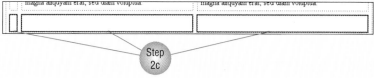

   d. Press the Delete or Backspace keys to delete the last row.

e. Click the Preview/Debug in browser button and then click Preview in iexplore to preview the changes to the table that you just made. Note that the empty first row and first column create additional white space between the text and the top and left margins of the browser screen. Close the browser window when you are finished.

3. Save **ch3ex07.htm** and then close it.

Creating Nested Tables

A *nested table* is a table inserted inside another table as shown in Figure 3.24. The table containing the nested table is known as the *parent table*. Nested tables can be formatted just like any other table, but their width is determined by the width of the table cell they are contained in. Nested tables provide an additional level of control over table appearance and page layout by allowing more precise positioning of table cells, as well as expanding formatting options. For example, with a normal table, all cells share the same cell padding and cell spacing properties, but because nested tables are separate tables with their own formatting, their cell padding and cell spacing properties can differ from the table they are inserted in. Nested tables also can be used to create margins and other areas of white space.

Nested tables can be inserted within other nested tables. As a general rule, tables should not be nested more than three deep. Deeply nested tables slow down page loading and cause some browsers difficulty in interpreting the tables. Because nested table cells can appear tiny in the Document window, they can be difficult or even impossible to select. This is where the Tag selector comes in handy. Positioning the insertion point inside a nested table, maneuvering with arrow keys, and then selecting a cell's tag (<td>) in the Tag selector is usually much easier than using the mouse to locate and select a tiny cell border.

Figure 3.24
Nested Table

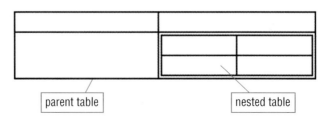

DREAMWEAVER MX 2004

exercise 8

CREATING A NESTED TABLE

1. Create a nested table that can be used to control page layout by completing the following steps:
   a. At a clear document screen, create a new HTML document and use the Save or Save As commands to name and save it as **ch3ex08.htm**.
   b. If necessary, click the Common menu item or tab on the Insert bar.
   c. Click the Table button or click it and drag it to the Document window to open the Table dialog box.
   d. Type the following values in the Table dialog box:
      1) Type 2 in the *Rows* text box.
      2) Type 2 in the *Columns* text box.
      3) Type 100 in the *Table width* text box. If necessary, click the down-pointing arrow next to the *Table width* text box to select *percent* from the drop-down list.
      4) Type 0 in the *Border thickness* text box.
      5) Type 0 in the *Cell padding* and *Cell spacing* text boxes.
      6) Click the None button in the *Header* section.
      7) Type **Parent layout table** in the *Summary* text box.
      8) Click the OK button to close the dialog box.

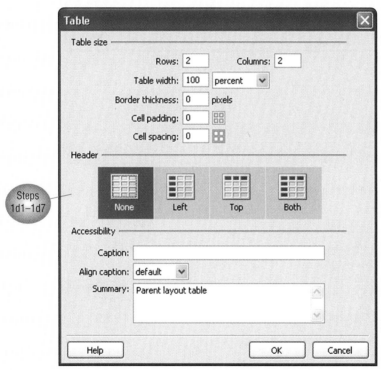

Steps
1d1–1d7

   e. Position the insertion point in the last cell of the second row.
   f. Click the Insert bar (Layout menu item or tab) Table button to open the Table dialog box.

Step
1e

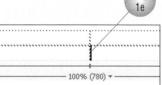

DREAMWEAVER MX 2004

135

Working with Tables

g.   Type 4 in the Table dialog box *Cell padding* and *Cell spacing* text boxes.

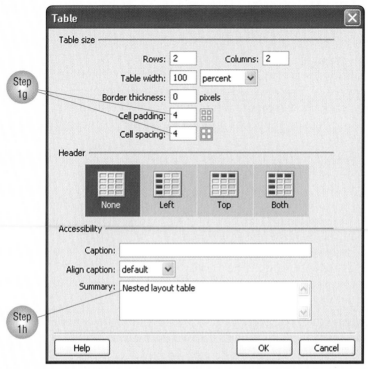

h.   Type **Nested layout table** in the *Summary* text box. Click the OK button to close the dialog box. ***Note: Leave all the other text boxes the same.***

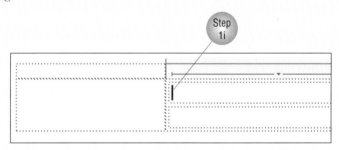

i.   Position the insertion point inside one of the nested table's cells.

j.   Click the nested table's table tag (<table>) in the Tag selector.

k.   Type **Nested Table** in the Table Property inspector *Table Id* text box. Press Enter.

l.   Click the parent table's table tag (<table>) in the Tag selector.

m.   Type **Parent Table** in the Table Property inspector *Table Id* text box. Press Enter.

n.   Position the insertion point in one of the nested table cells. Note that the Tag selector now identifies both the parent and nested tables.

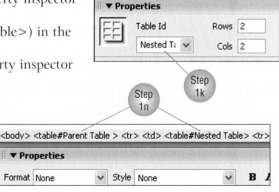

2.   Save **ch3ex08.htm** and then close it. You will use this table in the next chapter to learn about inserting background images.

Using the Format Table Command to Format Tables

The Format Table dialog box shown in Figure 3.25 offers a handy alternative to formatting tables with the Table Property inspector. This dialog box is convenient because it features a number of preset table formatting options that allow you to set all of a selected table's formatting options with a single click. The dialog box also contains color boxes and text boxes that can be used to customize a preset format. With the insertion point as a table, clicking Commands on the Menu bar and then Format Table opens the Format Table dialog box.

Figure 3.25
Format Table Dialog Box

exercise 9

USING THE FORMAT TABLE COMMAND

Step
1d

1. Apply a preset formatting option to a table by completing the following steps:
   a. At a clear document screen, open **ch3ex02.htm**. Use the Save As command to rename and save it as **ch3ex09.htm**.
   b. Position the insertion point in any table cell.
   c. Click Commands on the Menu bar and then Format Table to open the Format Table dialog box. Because this table has a caption, a message will appear stating that the Format Table command cannot be applied to tables with captions. Click the OK button to close the dialog box.
   d. Position the insertion point in the *November 2006* caption. Click <caption> in the Tag selector to select it, and then press the Delete or Backspace keys to remove the tag.

e. Position the insertion point in any cell in the top row of the table.

f. Click Modify on the Menu bar, point to Table, and then click Insert Row to insert a new row above the insertion point location.

g. Click inside the first cell of the new row and then drag to the right to select the first row.

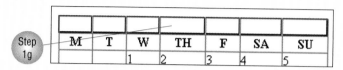

h. Type *50* in the *W* text box to format each column 50 pixels wide. ***Hint: Do not click in the Document window so that the cells remain selected.***

i. Click the Table Cell Property inspector Merge Cells button to merge the first row cells.

j. Click in the first row, and type November 2006.

k. Position the insertion point in any cell in the table.

l. Click Commands on the Menu bar and then Format Table to open the Format Table dialog box.

m. Experiment with five or six table formatting styles by clicking an option (such as *Simple1*) in the list box in the upper-left corner of the dialog box and then clicking the Apply button to see how the formatting option will look with the table in the current document. ***Hint: If the dialog box prevents you from seeing the table's new format, move it to a new location by clicking and dragging its blue Title bar.***

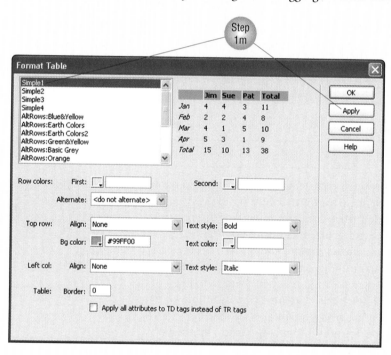

DREAMWEAVER MX 2004

2. Customize a formatting option by completing the following steps:
   a. Click the *Simple4* formatting option from the formatting options list.

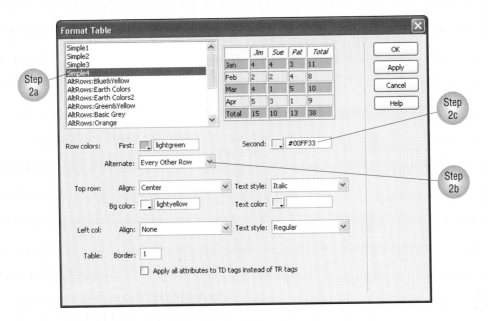

   b. The color boxes and text boxes can be used to customize a formatting option. Click the down-pointing arrow next to the *Alternate* list box and then click *Every Other Row* from the drop-down list to create an alternating row color scheme.
   c. Click the *Second* color box to open the Color Picker and use the Eyedropper to select bright green #00FF33, or type #00FF33 in the text box next to the color box. This will be the second color in the alternate row color scheme.
   d. Click the OK button to close the dialog box and apply the format to the table.
   e. Click the Preview/Debug in browser button and then click Preview in iexplore to preview the page. Close the browser when you are finished.
3. Save **ch3ex09.htm** and then close it.

Creating Tables in Layout Mode

Although tables can be created for page layout purposes in **Standard mode, Layout mode** simplifies this process by letting you draw cells and move them wherever you want. Layout mode also features a convenient **autostretch** function for creating liquid or flexible tables. Existing tables created in Standard mode also can be edited in Layout mode. Dreamweaver MX 2004 automatically creates layout tables using HTML table code, so a table created in Layout mode will look like any other table. One drawback to using Layout mode is that it creates extra code that can make it difficult to troubleshoot when problems occur with a table. For that reason, most experienced Dreamweaver MX 2004 users prefer to create tables in Standard mode.

Layout mode can be enabled when using Design view or Code and Design view by clicking View on the Menu bar, pointing to Table Mode, and then clicking Layout Mode. The light blue *Layout mode bar* shown in Figure 3.26 appears at the top of the Document window to let you know you are no longer working in Standard mode. Another method that can be used to switch to Layout mode is to click the Insert bar Layout button that appears when the Insert bar Layout menu item or tab is selected. Clicking the Layout button shifts the view to Layout mode. Layout mode can be exited by clicking the exit link on the Layout mode bar, clicking the Insert bar Standard button (Layout menu item or tab), or clicking View, pointing to Table Mode, and then clicking Standard Mode.

Drawing Tables and Cells

Tables and cells are created in Layout mode using the Insert bar's *Layout Table button* and *Draw Layout Cell button* (Layout menu item or tab) as shown in Figure 3.26. Clicking the Layout Table button and then moving the insertion point to an empty area of a document changes the insertion point into crosshairs or a plus sign (+) as shown in Figure 3.27. The crosshairs are placed where the table will begin, and clicking and dragging them creates a table. When the table reaches the desired size, releasing the mouse button fixes the table size. When the table is drawn, its width appears in the table header display of the table as shown in Figure 3.28. When cells are created, column widths appear in the column header display.

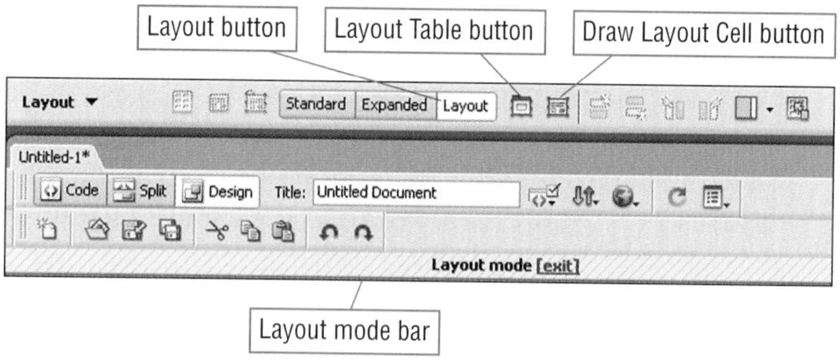

Figure 3.26
Layout Mode

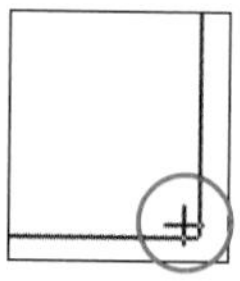

Figure 3.27
Layout Table Crosshairs

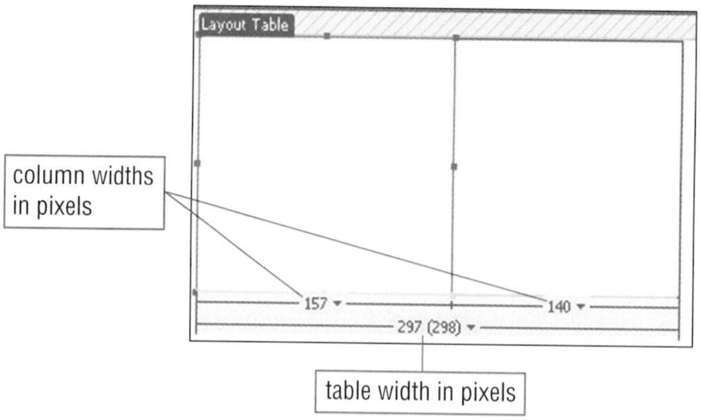

Figure 3.28
Table Dimensions

DREAMWEAVER MX 2004

Layout cells are created by clicking the Draw Layout Cell button and working in the same manner used to create layout tables. If a layout cell is created outside a table, Dreamweaver MX 2004 automatically creates a table to contain it. Layout cells cannot be overlapped. Dreamweaver MX 2004 automatically snaps new cells to existing cells or to the sides of a table when they are drawn within 8 pixels of each other. This option can be temporarily canceled by holding down the Alt key while drawing the cell. Multiple-layout tables and cells can be drawn without having to click a button each time by holding down the Ctrl key when clicking a button. Tables appear outlined in solid green, while cells are outlined with dotted blue lines as shown in Figure 3.29. As cells are created, Dreamweaver MX 2004 automatically creates any additional cells that might be necessary to correctly position cells. These positioning cells appear as gray (empty) cells, and change as new layout cells are entered in a table.

Tables can be nested as long as they are inserted in the gray sections of the parent table that do not already contain layout cells. After the nested table has been inserted in the parent table, the Draw Layout Cell button can be used to create layout cells just as with any other table.

Selecting, Moving, and Resizing Layout Tables and Cells

One of the greatest conveniences of working with tables in Layout mode is the ability to move and resize table cells simply by clicking and dragging. You can move layout cells to new locations within a layout table by clicking on their border and dragging them to the desired location. More precise positioning can be obtained by selecting a cell in Layout mode and pressing an arrow key to move the cell 1 pixel at a time. Holding down the Shift key and pressing an arrow key moves a cell 10 pixels at a time. To select layout cells, place the pointer over the cell's border until it turns red, and then click once. Another method for selecting cells is to hold down the Ctrl key and position the insertion point in the desired cell. The cell border turns red and a single click selects it.

Selection handles appear when tables and cells are selected, as shown in Figure 3.29. You can use these handles to resize by clicking and dragging them in the desired direction. If a layout cell already contains content, it cannot be resized smaller than the content, and tables cannot be resized smaller than their component cells. Selecting a cell and pressing the Delete or Backspace keys will remove it.

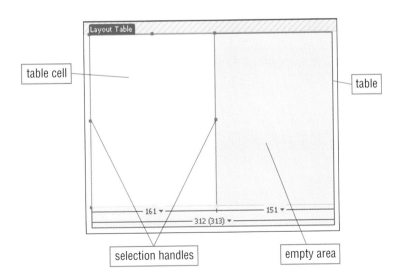

Figure 3.29
Layout Table and Cells

Using Autostretch

Because tables created in Layout mode have fixed widths, they might not appear as intended under certain screen resolution and browser window combinations. Autostretch offers a solution to this problem by enabling the creation of liquid or flexible tables containing one autostretch column that automatically adjusts to fit different browser window sizes, while leaving the remaining columns with fixed widths. If a table is set to autostretch, it will have a width of 100 percent. This percentage cannot be changed within Layout mode, but switching to Standard mode allows you to enter a different value in the Table Property inspector *W* text box.

Figure 3.30
Autostretch Radio Button

An autostretch table can be created in Layout mode by clicking and filling in the *Autostretch* radio button in the Layout Table Property inspector as shown in Figure 3.30. When a layout table is created, it will have a 100 percent width. The first layout cell created in the layout table will also have a specified width of 100 percent. Any remaining columns will have fixed widths. The percentage-width column will stretch to take up 100 percent of any space remaining after any fixed-width cell space is allocated.

Another method for creating autostretch tables is to click on a column header display down-pointing arrow and then to click Make Column Autostretch from the layout column drop-down menu as shown in Figure 3.31.

Adding Spacer Images

Autostretch tables use 1 × 1 pixel transparent GIF files known as ***spacer images*** to prevent fixed-width columns from being squeezed when content is added to an autostretch column. This works because columns containing a cell with a spacer image can shrink only to the spacer image width and no further. When a Layout mode table's fixed-width column is changed to autostretch, Dreamweaver MX 2004 automatically creates an additional table row and inserts spacer images into the new row's fixed-width columns. The width of the spacer images is also changed to match the width of the fixed-width columns containing them. Columns with spacer images are indicated by a double line as shown in Figure 3.32. The new table row containing the spacer images is only 1 pixel in height and therefore is virtually impossible to distinguish in Design view. Because this row is so narrow, it will not affect the appearance of the page when viewed in a browser.

When an autostretch table is created in a site for the first time, a Choose Spacer Image dialog box appears, as shown in Figure 3.33, prompting users to create or locate a spacer image that will be saved in the site and automatically inserted in autostretch tables as needed. This dialog box will not appear if a spacer image has already been saved in the site.

Figure 3.31 • Column Header Display Make Column Autostretch Command

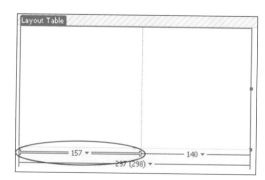

Figure 3.32 • Spacer Image Double Line

DREAMWEAVER MX 2004

To locate or create a spacer image and save it to a site before creating an autostretch table, or to select automatic spacer insertion if that option has been deselected, complete the following steps:

1. Click Edit on the Menu bar and then Preferences to open the Preferences dialog box.

2. Click *Layout Mode* from the *Category* list box to open the Layout Mode page of the Preferences dialog box as shown in Figure 3.34.

3. Click the radio button located between *Autoinsert spacers* and *When making autostretch tables*.

4. If the site you are working in already contains a spacer image, use the Browse button to locate and select it in the *Image file* text box. If the site does not contain a spacer image, click the Create button to create a 1 by 1 transparent GIF (spacer.gif) and save it to the site.

5. Click the OK button to close the Preferences dialog box.

Spacer images can be inserted into tables in Standard mode as well. Positioning the insertion point inside a table cell, clicking Insert on the Menu bar, and then clicking Image opens the Select Image Source dialog box. If a spacer image has

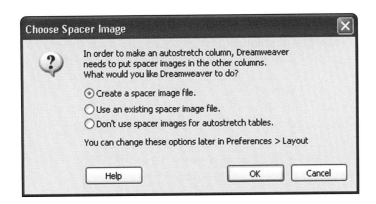

Figure 3.33
Choose Spacer Image Dialog Box

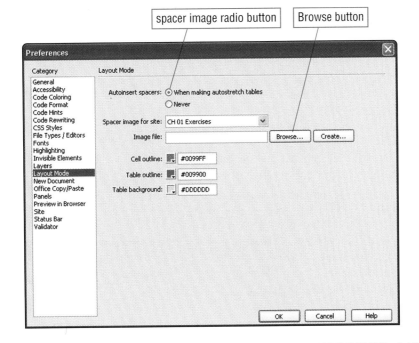

Figure 3.34
Layout Mode Page of the Preferences Dialog Box

already been created and saved in the current site, it appears in the dialog box. After a spacer image is inserted into a cell, its width in pixels can be set by selecting the cell with the spacer image, using the Tag selector to select <img> (the image tag), and then using the Image Property inspector *W* text box to change the width to the desired value.

exercise 10

1. Create a layout table in Layout mode by completing the following steps:
   a. At a clear document screen, create a new HTML document and use the Save or Save As commands to name and save it as **ch3ex10.htm**.
   b. Click the Layout menu item or tab on the Insert bar.
   c. Click the Layout button on the Insert bar. *Note: A message advising users how to insert tables and table cells in Layout mode will appear. Click the OK button to close the message box. If you want to prevent this message from appearing again, click the check box next to* **Don't show me this message** *again.*

Step 1b

Step 1c

   d. Click the Layout Table button on the Insert bar and move the pointer into the Document window where it will change into crosshairs. Position the crosshairs in the upper-left corner of the Document window and then click and drag them across and down the screen so that the table fills the Document window. Do not drag the crosshairs so far that horizontal and vertical scroll bars appear. Release the mouse button to create the table. *Hint: If you drag the crosshairs too far and scroll bars appear, click Edit on the Menu bar and then Undo, and try again.*

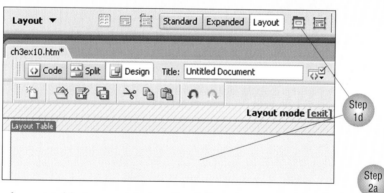

Step 1d

2. Add cells to a layout table by completing the following steps:
   a. Click the Draw Layout Cell button on the Insert bar.
   b. Position the crosshairs in the upper-left corner of the table and drag them across the width of the table and then down until the Window Size indicator on the Status bar indicates that it is 50 pixels high. *Note: If necessary, click View, point to Grid, and then click Snap To Grid to remove the check mark beside Snap To Grid.*

Step 2a

Step 2b

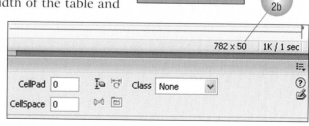

c. Click the Draw Layout Cell button, hold down the Ctrl key, and position the crosshairs so that the horizontal line matches up with the lower border of the row you just created and the vertical line matches up with the left border of the table. The crosshairs will turn orange when they are aligned with a border, although this might be difficult to see. Drag the crosshairs to the right about 1 inch and then down to the bottom of the table. Look at the Window Size indicator to size the width of the column you are creating at 100 pixels. Release the mouse button to fix the column, but keep the Ctrl key pressed. ***Hint: Keeping the Ctrl key pressed allows you to continue creating cells without having to click the Draw Layout Cell button. If you release it, you will have to click the Draw Layout Cell button again.***

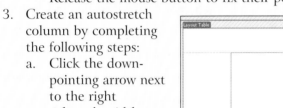

d. Position the crosshairs so that the horizontal line matches up with the lower border of the table row and the vertical line matches up with the right border of the column you just created. Drag the crosshairs to the right border of the table and then down to the bottom of the table. Release the mouse button to fix their position.

3. Create an autostretch column by completing the following steps:

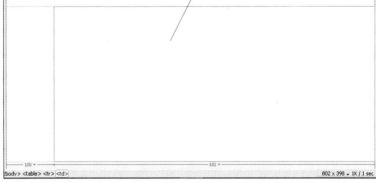

a. Click the down-pointing arrow next to the right column's width indicator to open the column header menu, and then click Make Column Autostretch.

b. If a spacer image has not been created and saved in the current site, a Choose Spacer Image dialog box appears. Click the *Create a spacer image file.* radio button to select it and then click the OK button.

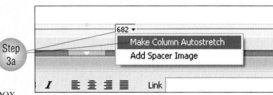

c. The Save Spacer Image File As dialog box appears. Click the Save button to save the spacer image file to the current site and insert it into the left column to prevent the left column from collapsing when the autostretch column expands. ***Note: If the location shown in the dialog box is not the current site, use the Browse for File button to browse and select the current site.***

d. Click the Code button on the Document toolbar. Look in the HTML code and locate the spacer image code in the code for the left column. Note that its width has automatically been made identical to the width of the column it was inserted in—100 pixels.

```
lign="top"><!--DWLayoutEmptyCell-->$nbsp;</td>
l"><img src="spacer.gif" alt="" width="100" height=
```

e. Click the Design button. Note that the bottom of the first column contains a double green line. This indicates that it contains a spacer image. The bottom of the second column contains a single line with a wavy portion in the center of the line. This indicates that it is an autostretch column.

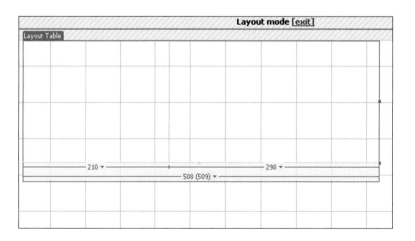

f. Click the Standard button on the Insert bar (Layout menu item or tab).

g. Click the table tag (<table>) in the Tag selector to select the table and then type 1 in the Table Property inspector *Border* text box so that you can view the table in a browser.

h. Click the Preview/Debug in browser button and then click Preview in iexplore to preview the layout table you just created. Note that the table stretches across the entire length of the browser window because creating the autostretch column automatically converts the table width from the fixed width you initially created to a proportional width of 100 percent. At the bottom of the table, you will see a very thin row. The left column of this row contains a transparent spacer image that is 1 pixel high and 100 pixels wide. The spacer image prevents the left column from being squeezed below 100 pixels in width when content is added to the autostretch column. When the table border is reset to *0*, this row will be invisible, and because it is so narrow, it will not interfere with the page design. Close the browser when you are finished.

i. With **ch3ex10.htm** as the current document, select the table, and type 0 in the *Border* text box to remove the border.

4. Save **ch3ex10.htm** and then close it. You will use this table in the next chapter to learn about inserting images in tables.

Using a Grid

A *grid* can be used in Layout and Standard modes to assist in positioning cells and content within tables as shown in Figure 3.35. The grid also has a **Snap to Grid** feature that automatically snaps cells to the nearest grid coordinate when they are created, moved, or resized. The Grid Settings dialog box shown in Figure 3.36 allows you to change grid color, spacing, and line options.

Figure 3.35
Grid

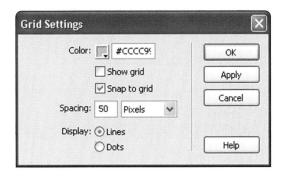

Figure 3.36
Grid Settings Dialog Box

WORKING WITH A GRID

1. Show the grid, activate the Snap to Grid feature, and change grid settings by completing the following steps:
   a. Create a new HTML document.
   b. Click View on the Menu bar, point to Grid, and then click Show Grid to use a grid when working in Standard or Layout table modes. Click View on the Menu bar, point to Grid, and then click Snap To Grid to activate the snap to grid feature.

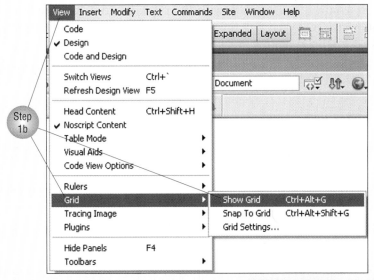

   c. Click View on the Menu bar, point to Grid, and then click Grid Settings to open the Grid Settings dialog box. Type 25 in the *Spacing* text box, and then click *Pixels* from the adjacent drop-down menu if it is not already selected. This changes the size of the grid boxes. Clicking the Apply button lets you see how the settings will appear. Click the OK button to close the dialog box.

2. Work with the grid when creating a table by completing the following steps:
   a. Click the Layout menu item or tab on the Insert bar.

b. Click the Layout button on the Insert bar.
c. Click the Layout Table button and draw a table that fills the Document window but does not cause the horizontal and vertical scroll bars to appear.
d. Click the Draw Layout Cell button and use the crosshairs to slowly move diagonally to the lower right of the Document window. As the right border of the cell nears each vertical grid line, notice how the cell border jumps to the line because of the Snap to Grid feature. As the bottom border of the cell moves downward, it will jump from horizontal grid line to grid line because of the Snap to Grid feature. Release the mouse button to create the cell.

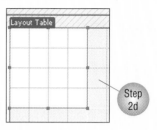

Step 2d

e. Turn off the grid by clicking View, pointing to Grid, and then clicking to remove the check mark next to Show Grid.
f. Click the Layout mode bar <u>exit</u> link to return to Standard mode.
3. Close the file without saving it.

Sorting Table Content

Table content is sorted using the Sort Table dialog box shown in Figure 3.37. Tables can be sorted based on the contents of a single column or two columns. Tables that contain merged cells cannot be sorted. Clicking Commands on the Menu bar and then Sort Table opens the Sort Table dialog box. The Sort Table dialog box properties are described in the following list:

- **Sort by** Use this list box to select the column to be sorted. The drop-down list displays a table's columns. Clicking a column selects it.

- **Order** Columns can be sorted alphabetically or numerically and in ascending or descending order. For example, an alphabetical sort in ascending order would sort from *A* to *Z*, while a descending sort would sort from *Z* to *A*.

- **Then by/Order** A second column can be sorted after the first column. Sorting specifications are set in the same way specifications were set for the first column to be sorted.

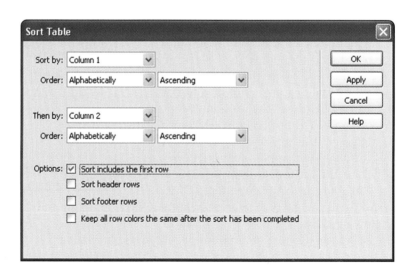

Figure 3.37
Sort Table Dialog Box

DREAMWEAVER MX 2004

- *Sort includes the first row* This option is not selected in the default Dreamweaver MX 2004 setup. It should be selected only if the first row of a table is not a header and contains information that should be sorted.

- *Sort header rows* This sort option includes header rows.

- *Sort footer rows* This sort option includes footer rows.

- *Keep all row colors the same after the sort has been completed* This sort option keeps table row attributes associated with row content. If a row attribute is related to the row content, this option should be selected. For example, if yellow is being used to indicate rows listing products that cost less than $100, selecting this option ensures that those rows remain yellow wherever they are located after sorting. Leaving this option deselected when sorting a table with rows in alternating colors will maintain the alternating color scheme.

SORTING TABLE CONTENT

1. Sort a table's first column alphabetically in ascending order by completing the following steps:
   a. At a clear document screen, open the student file named **sorting.htm** and use the Save As command to rename and save it to the ch_03_exercises root folder as **ch3ex12.htm**.
   b. Position the insertion point in the *American Presidents* table.
   c. Click Commands and then Sort Table to open the Sort Table dialog box. **Hint: You must be in Standard mode to access the Sort Table dialog box.**
   d. Do not change the dialog box settings, which specify an alphabetically ascending sort of column 1.

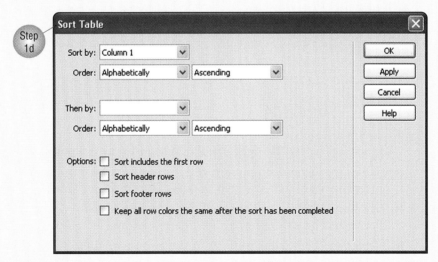

   e. Click the OK button. The list of American presidents will appear in ascending alphabetical order, from *A* to *Z*.
2. Numerically sort a table by completing the following steps:
   a. Position the insertion point in the table containing prices for everyday items.
   b. Click Commands and then Sort Table to open the Sort Table dialog box.

c. Click the down-pointing arrow next to the *Sort by* list box and then click *Column 2* from the drop-down list.

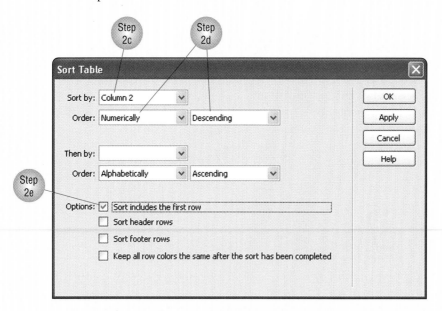

d. Click *Numerically* and *Descending* from the *Order* drop-down list boxes.
e. Click the check box next to *Sort includes first row* in the *Options* section to include the first row in the sort. ***Note: Most tabular tables have a header row that should not be sorted. This table does not use a header row, so enabling this option allows the first row to be included in the sort process.***
f. Click the OK button. The everyday items will now be sorted in numerically descending order, from the most expensive item to the least expensive item.

3. Save **ch3ex12.htm** and then close it.

CHAPTER summary

➤ Tables are grids composed of horizontal rows and vertical columns, with the space created by the intersection of each row and column forming a table cell.

➤ Tables can be used to present tabular data or to control page layout by inserting page elements into the matrix formed by table cells.

➤ The amount of space between cells is known as cell spacing, and the distance between cell content and cell borders is known as cell padding.

➤ Tables and cells will shrink to fit their contents unless a width is specified to make them wider.

➤ Table and table cell widths can be specified using pixels or percentages of the screen.

➤ Proportional widths allow cells or tables to stretch to occupy their specified percentage of the table or browser window.

➤ You can indicate the height of a cell, but it is usually better to let browsers determine cell height based on their content.

- A fixed-width table can expand if the width of its contents is greater than its specified width.

- A fixed-width cell also can be squeezed (narrowed in width) if an adjacent cell expands.

- Selected tables can be resized by dragging their selection handles in the desired direction, although this method is not recommended.

- Clicking the table header menu Make All Widths Consistent command will make the actual width in the HTML code consistent with the visual width if a table has been resized by dragging.

- Dreamweaver MX 2004 inserts an HTML special character known as a nonbreaking space ( ) into empty table cells to prevent the cells from collapsing and disappearing from view in some browsers.

- Tables containing proportional widths are referred to as liquid or flexible tables because they can adjust to fit browser window dimensions.

- Fixed-width tables will maintain their appearance when viewed using different screen and browser combinations, provided that a table does not contain empty cells or cells containing content that exceeds their specified width.

- Tables that contain a combination of fixed and proportional widths let designers maintain control over segments of the table that need to remain stable, while letting other segments of the table flow to fit browser windows.

- Columns can be used to break up lines of text so that a single line does not contain more than the recommended 10 to 12 words, and also to separate navigation functions from content, to contain links, or to separate other page content.

- Cell padding and cell spacing can be used to create margins and a gutter so that text doesn't bump up against the edge of the browser window or adjacent text.

- Completing the information called for in the *Accessibility* section of the Table dialog box ensures that viewers with disabilities will be able to better understand table content.

- Tables and table elements (rows, columns, and cells) must be selected before they can be modified using the Table Cell Property inspector.

- The Insert bar Layout menu item or tab Expanded Tables mode Expanded button can be clicked to make selecting tables and table cells easier.

- Using the Tag selector is the easiest way to select a table or table element.

- When a table is selected, its outer edge appears outlined in black.

- Selecting a table and pressing the Left or Right Arrow keys positions the insertion point outside the table, indicated by a blinking black line spanning the height of the table.

- Placing the pointer on a row or column outer border causes a selection arrow to appear. After the arrow appears, clicking the mouse button will select the desired row or column.

- Nonadjacent cells can be selected by holding down the Ctrl key and clicking inside each cell to be selected.

- The Tab or arrow keys can be used to navigate within tables.

- Holding down the Shift key while pressing the Tab key reverses tab direction.

- Pressing the Tab key creates a new row when the last cell in a table is reached.

- Cell and row background formatting overrides table formatting.

➤ The *Table Id* (table identification) text box is useful when working with nested tables or with pages containing a number of different tables.

➤ Horizontal alignment specifies the horizontal alignment for row, column, or cell content.

➤ Vertical alignment specifies the vertical alignment for row, column, or cell content.

➤ Header rows or columns automatically center and bold text.

➤ The Table Cell Property inspector Merge Cells button can be used to merge selected cells.

➤ The Table Cell Property inspector Split Cell button splits a selected cell into two or more cells. Only one cell can be split at a time.

➤ The Insert Rows or Columns dialog box lets you insert more than one column or row at a time and specify their location.

➤ Insert commands can be accessed by right-clicking when the insertion point is positioned inside a table cell.

➤ A nested table is a table inserted inside another table (known as the parent table).

➤ Nested tables can be formatted just like any other table, but their width is determined by the width of the table cell they are contained in.

➤ Nested tables provide an additional level of control over table appearance and page layout by allowing more precise positioning of table cells, as well as expanding formatting options.

➤ It is generally recommended that tables not be nested more than three deep to avoid slowing down page loading, and because some browsers may have difficulty interpreting deeply nested tables.

➤ The Format Table dialog box offers a handy alternative to formatting tables with the Table Property inspector, and contains color boxes and text boxes for further customization.

➤ Layout mode simplifies designing layout tables by letting you draw cells and move them wherever you want. One drawback to using Layout mode is that it creates extra code that can make it difficult to troubleshoot problems with a table.

➤ Layout mode features a convenient autostretch function for creating liquid or flexible tables.

➤ Existing tables created in Standard mode also can be edited in Layout mode.

➤ A small blue Layout mode bar appears at the top of the Document window to let you know you are working in Layout mode.

➤ Tables and cells are created in Layout mode using the Insert bar's Layout Table and Draw Layout Cell buttons (Layout menu item or tab).

➤ If a layout cell is created outside of a table, Dreamweaver MX 2004 automatically creates a table to contain it.

➤ Layout cells cannot be overlapped.

➤ Dreamweaver MX 2004 automatically snaps new cells to existing cells or to the sides of a table when they are drawn within 8 pixels of each other.

➤ Holding down the Ctrl key when clicking the Draw Layout Cell button allows you to draw cells without having to click the button each time.

- Tables in Layout mode appear outlined in solid green, while cells are outlined with dotted blue lines. Empty areas of a table appear in gray.
- As cells are created in Layout mode, Dreamweaver MX 2004 automatically creates any additional cells that might be necessary to correctly position cells.
- Layout cells can be moved to new locations within a table by clicking their border and dragging them to the desired location.
- Selecting a cell in Layout mode and pressing an arrow key moves a cell 1 pixel at a time and assists in more precise positioning. Holding down the Shift key and pressing an arrow key moves a cell 10 pixels at a time.
- Autostretch enables the creation of liquid or flexible tables containing one autostretch column that automatically adjusts to fit different browser window sizes, while leaving the remaining columns with fixed widths.
- If a table is set to autostretch, it will have a width of 100 percent. This percentage cannot be changed within Layout mode, but switching to Standard mode allows you to enter a different value in the Table Property inspector W text box.
- Autostretch tables use 1 by 1 pixel transparent GIF files known as spacer images to prevent fixed-width columns from being squeezed when content is added to an autostretch column.
- When a Layout mode table fixed-width column is changed to autostretch, Dreamweaver MX 2004 automatically creates an additional table row and inserts spacer images into the new row's fixed-width columns.
- A grid can be used in Layout and Standard modes to assist in positioning cells and content within tables.
- The feature grid also has a Snap to Grid feature that automatically snaps cells to the nearest grid coordinate when they are created, moved, or resized.
- Tables can be sorted based on the contents of a single column or two columns.

KEY terms

autostretch Layout mode function used to create liquid or flexible tables.

background image An image used as a background for a table or table cell.

border color The color of a table border.

caption A title that will be displayed outside a table.

cell padding The distance between cell content and cell borders.

cell spacing The amount of space between cells.

columns Vertical lines of table cells.

dimension buttons Table Property inspector buttons that can be used to clear column and row heights, and convert table widths and heights to pixels or percentages.

Draw Layout Cell button Insert bar button (Layout menu item or tab) used to create table cells in Layout mode.

Expanded Tables mode A viewing mode that makes it easier to select tables and table cells. Expanded Tables mode can be accessed by clicking the Expanded button on the Insert bar (Layout menu item or tab).

fixed widths Widths for tables or table cells indicated as a fixed measurement.

flexible tables See *liquid tables*.

grid A mesh of horizontal and vertical lines that can be used to position table elements and content in Layout and Standard modes.

gutter The space between columns.

header A column or row used to identify column or row content. Header columns and rows automatically center and bold text.

horizontal alignment Specifies the horizontal alignment for row, column, or cell content.

Layout mode Insert bar view that can be used to conveniently create layout tables.

Layout mode bar A light blue bar at the top of the Document window that lets users know they are no longer working in Standard mode.

Layout Table button Insert bar button (Layout menu item or tab) used to create tables in Layout mode.

liquid tables Tables that adjust to fit browser window dimensions. Also called *flexible tables*.

margins The white space around the edges of a document or document contents.

Merge Cells button Table Cell Property inspector button that merges selected cells, rows, or columns into one cell.

nested table A table contained inside another table.

nonbreaking space HTML special character ( ) that prevents empty cells from collapsing and disappearing from view in some browsers.

page layout The placement of page elements on a page.

parent table The table containing a nested table.

proportional widths Widths for tables or table cells indicated as a relative measurement by using a percentage.

rows A horizontal line of table cells.

Snap to Grid A grid feature that automatically snaps table cells or content to the nearest grid coordinate.

spacer images Transparent 1 × 1 pixel GIF files used to prevent fixed-width columns from being squeezed by other columns.

Split Cell button Table Cell Property inspector button that splits a selected cell into two or more cells.

Standard mode Insert bar view used to create tables.

summary text A summary of table content that can be interpreted by screen readers.

table alignment Specifies the table location relative to other elements (text, images, and so on) in the table paragraph.

table borders The lines that define table and cell boundaries. Table borders can be specified to be visible or invisible.

table cell The space formed by the intersection of table rows and columns.

Table Cell Property inspector The Property inspector that is displayed when table cells are selected.

table data cell tags The HTML tags (<td>) used to create table cells.

DREAMWEAVER MX 2004

table identification Used to name tables as an identification aid.

Table Property inspector The Property inspector that is displayed when a table is selected.

table row tags The HTML tags (<tr>) used to create a table row.

tables Grids composed of horizontal rows and vertical columns of cells. Tables are used for displaying data and for layout purposes.

table selection handles Small handles used for dragging and resizing tables.

table tags The HTML tags (<table>) used to create tables.

vertical alignment Specifies the vertical alignment for row, column, or cell content.

COMMANDS review

Add a column	Modify, Table, Insert Column
Add a row	Modify, Table, Insert Row
Create a table	Insert, Table
Delete a column	Modify, Table, Delete Column
Delete a row	Modify, Table, Delete Row
Delete a selected table, row, column, or cell	Edit, Clear
Enable Expanded Tables mode	View, Table Mode, Expanded Tables Mode
Enable Layout mode	View, Table Mode, Layout Mode
Enable snap to grid	View, Grid, Snap To Grid
Enable Standard mode	View, Table Mode, Standard Mode
Make borders visible in Document window	View, Visual Aids, *Table Borders*
Open Format Table dialog box	Commands, Format Table
Open Grid Settings dialog box	View, Grid, Grid Settings
Open Insert Rows or Columns dialog box	Modify, Table, Insert Rows or Columns
Select a cell	Edit, Select All
Select a table	Modify, Table, Select Table
Show a grid	View, Grid, Show Grid
Sort table content	Commands, Sort Table

Indicate the correct term or command for each item.

1. This is the term for the amount of space between cells.
2. These table or cell widths are specified as a percentage.
3. These are the types of tables that expand to fit a browser window.
4. This HTML special character is used to prevent empty table cells from collapsing and disappearing when viewed by some browsers.
5. A table contained inside another table is called this.
6. This term refers to the distance between cell content and cell borders.
7. This key can be used to navigate between cells and create new rows.
8. These Table Property inspector buttons can be used to clear column and row heights, and convert table widths and heights to pixels or percentages.
9. This is the term for a table containing a nested table.
10. This dialog box can be used to format tables using preset formatting options.
11. This view can be used to conveniently create layout tables and allows users to drag cells inside a table.
12. This Layout Table Property inspector radio button is used to create liquid or flexible tables.
13. This is the name of a transparent GIF image used to prevent fixed-width columns from being squeezed by other columns.
14. This term describes the appearance of the pointer when used to create tables and cells in layout mode.
15. These HTML tags are used to create a table.
16. This view feature is used to assist in positioning cells when creating tables.
17. This is the term for the space formed by the intersection of a table row and column.
18. This is dragged to resize a table.
19. These HTML tags are used to create table cells.
20. Holding down this key in Layout mode allows users to use the arrow keys to move selected tables 10 pixels at a time.

SKILLS check

*Use the Site Definition dialog box to create a separate Dreamweaver site named CH 03
Assessments to keep your assessment work for this chapter. Save the files for the site in a
new root folder named ch_03_assessments under the Sites folder you created in Chapter 1,
Exercise 3. Download the ch_03_student_files folder from the IRC to the CH 03 Assessments
site root folder (ch_03_assessments) and expand it. Delete the compressed folder when you
are finished.*

Assessment 1 • Recreate a Class Schedule Table

1. Create a new HTML document and use the Save or Save As commands to name and save it as **ch3sa1.htm**.
2. Recreate the table in Figure 3.38 as closely as possible.
3. Create the table as a fixed-width table, 650 pixels in width.
4. Specify cell spacing and cell padding as 4.
5. Create row and header columns for the days of the week and the class hours.
6. Create a caption for the table as shown and specify default caption alignment.
7. Specify left alignment for the class hours.
8. Specify the font size for the schedule cells as 10.
9. Center align the table.
10. Ensure that the border is visible in the browser window.
11. Save **ch3sa1.htm** and then close it.

Class Schedule

Hour	Mon	Tues	Wed	Thur	Fri
8:00-9:00	History	History	History	History	History
9:00-10:00	Social Studies	Social Studies	Social Studies	Social Studies	Social Studies
10:00-11:00	Computer Sci.	Computer Sci.	Computer Sci.	Computer Sci.	Computer Sci.
11:00-12:00	Chemistry	Chemistry	Chemistry	Chemistry	Chemistry
12:00-1:00	Lunch	Lunch	Lunch	Lunch	Lunch
1:00-2:00	Phy. Ed.	Phy. Ed.	Phy. Ed.	Phy. Ed.	Phy. Ed.
2:00-3:00	Dreamweaver	Dreamweaver	Dreamweaver	Dreamweaver	Dreamweaver
3:00-4:00	Physics	Physics	Physics	Physics	Physics
4:00-5:00	Theater	Theater	Theater	Theater	Theater
5:00-6:00	·	·	·	·	·

Figure 3.38 • Assessment 1

Assessment 2 • Create Nested Tables

1. Create a new HTML document and use the Save or Save As commands to name and save it as **ch3sa2.htm**.
2. Recreate the table in Figure 3.39 as closely as possible, and insert the text exactly as shown.
3. Start by creating a seven-row, two-column table in Standard mode. Specify the width for the table as 100 percent. Merge cells as necessary.
4. Specify a 4-pixel-wide border for the parent table.
5. Specify a red border for the first row.
6. Horizontally and vertically align the text as noted in the table.
7. Nest three tables inside the table as indicated, and center align the text in the nested tables. Specify a 1-pixel-wide border for the nested tables.
8. Specify cell spacing of 4 pixels and cell padding of 0 pixels for Nested Table 1.
9. Specify cell spacing of 0 pixels and cell padding of 0 pixels for Nested Table 2.
10. Specify cell spacing of 0 pixels cell padding of 4 pixels for Nested Table 3, and set the width of its border at 0 pixels.
11. Specify a light yellow (#FFFF66) background for Nested Table 2.
12. Specify a light orange (#FFCC33) for the table background.
13. Save **ch3sa2.htm** and then close it.

Assessment 3 • Format a Table

1. Open **ch3sa1.htm** and use the Save As command to rename and save it as **ch3sa3.htm**.
2. Change the row header font style to *Arial, Helvetica, sans-serif*.
3. Specify a light brown (#CC9966) for the row header background color.
4. Specify a yellow (#FFFF99) for the table background color.
5. Change cell spacing and cell padding to *2*.
6. Horizontally center align the schedule cells (the cells with the activity description).
7. Use the Tag selector to remove the table caption.
8. Insert a new row above the header row.
9. Merge the cells of the new row.

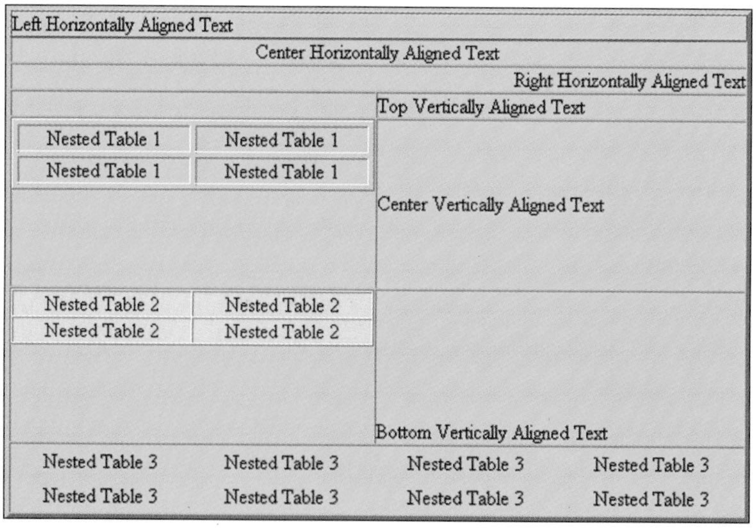

Figure 3.39
Assessment 2

Left Horizontally Aligned Text			
Center Horizontally Aligned Text			
Right Horizontally Aligned Text			
Top Vertically Aligned Text			
Nested Table 1	Nested Table 1		
Nested Table 1	Nested Table 1	Center Vertically Aligned Text	
Nested Table 2	Nested Table 2		
Nested Table 2	Nested Table 2		
		Bottom Vertically Aligned Text	
Nested Table 3	Nested Table 3	Nested Table 3	Nested Table 3
Nested Table 3	Nested Table 3	Nested Table 3	Nested Table 3

10. Type **Class Schedule** in the first row.
11. Format Class Schedule in the level-one heading size (<h1>).
12. Save **ch3sa3.htm** and then close it.

Assessment 4 • Create a Table in Layout Mode

1. Create a new HTML document and use the Save or Save As commands to name and save it as **ch3sa4.htm**.
2. Use Figure 3.40 as a guide to creating a table in Layout mode. You may insert your own text or text provided by your instructor instead of using the placeholder text shown in Figure 3.40.
3. Specify the second column as an autostretch column. *Note: Dreamweaver MX 2004 automatically creates the very narrow row at the bottom of the table to accommodate the spacer image it creates when autostretch is used.*
4. Create links to **ch3sa1.htm**, **ch3sa2.htm**, and **ch3sa3.htm** in the left column. You may create links to documents of your own choosing if you want, including external pages.
5. Specify level-one heading size for the header text.
6. Specify a font size of 2 for the footer text.
7. Justify the right column text.
8. Save **ch3sa4.htm** and then close it.

Assessment 5 • Work with a Page Design Table

1. Create a new HTML document using the Text: Article D page design. Use the Save or Save As commands to name the file **ch3sa5.htm** and save it.
2. Replace the placeholder text with your own text or text that your instructor provides.
3. Change the text and background color for the parent table and three nested tables in this document. Choose an attractive combination of colors. Seek feedback from your classmates about your color choices.
4. Change the font style used in the document. Seek classmate feedback to help you decide which font style, colors, and sizes are easiest to read.
5. Add one more row to the bottom of the document.
6. Merge the cells in the new row and insert text into the row. Change the color of the text in the new row.
7. Save **ch3sa5.htm** and then close it.

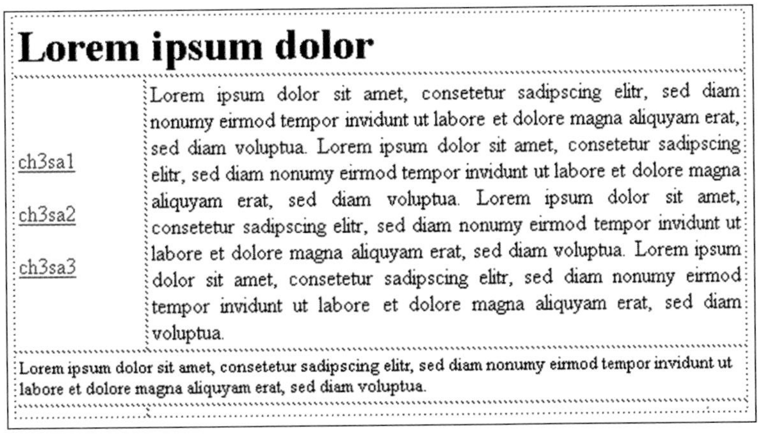

Lorem ipsum dolor

ch3sa1

ch3sa2

ch3sa3

Lorem ipsum dolor sit amet, consetetur sadipscing elitr, sed diam nonumy eirmod tempor invidunt ut labore et dolore magna aliquyam erat, sed diam voluptua. Lorem ipsum dolor sit amet, consetetur sadipscing elitr, sed diam nonumy eirmod tempor invidunt ut labore et dolore magna aliquyam erat, sed diam voluptua. Lorem ipsum dolor sit amet, consetetur sadipscing elitr, sed diam nonumy eirmod tempor invidunt ut labore et dolore magna aliquyam erat, sed diam voluptua. Lorem ipsum dolor sit amet, consetetur sadipscing elitr, sed diam nonumy eirmod tempor invidunt ut labore et dolore magna aliquyam erat, sed diam voluptua.

Lorem ipsum dolor sit amet, consetetur sadipscing elitr, sed diam nonumy eirmod tempor invidunt ut labore et dolore magna aliquyam erat, sed diam voluptua.

Figure 3.40
Assessment 4

Assessment 6 • Format a Data Table

1. At a clear document screen, open the student file named **table.htm** and use the Save As command to rename and save it to the ch_03_assessments root folder as **ch3sa6.htm**.
2. Delete the empty fourth column.
3. Merge the top row cells.
4. Center align *Sales,* and specify its size as a level-one heading.
5. Bold the left column and second row text.
6. Center align the second row text.
7. Right align the cells with sales figures.
8. Insert a row below the last row. Merge the cells of the new row.
9. Type Note: March 2004 results due to fire.
10. Specify the text size for the last row as 10.
11. Save **ch3sa6.htm** and then close it.

Assessment 7 • Add Tables to Your Design Portfolio

Save the files for this assessment in the design_portfolio root folder under the Sites folder you created in Chapter 1, Exercise 3.

1. Create and format a table that can be used to implement the design "look" you planned for your design portfolio in Chapter 1, Assessment 7. Assess how much control you need to exert over your page layout, and where you need to exert control, and choose the type of table needed accordingly.
2. Create and format a table that you can used to present tabular data on one or more of your pages. Format the table to fit in with your design look.
3. Look through the pages you have created so far, read the planning comments you inserted in those pages, and begin using the tables you have created for page layout and tabular data presentation for your other design portfolio site pages as required.

WORKING WITH IMAGES

PERFORMANCE OBJECTIVES

➤ Understand the different types of images suitable for Web page use.
➤ Insert images in Web page documents.
➤ Create accessible images.
➤ Create a <u>D</u> link (description link).
➤ Use image placeholders in the page-design process.
➤ Use the Image Property inspector and Tag Editor - Img dialog box to modify image properties.
➤ Create image links.
➤ Create image maps.
➤ Perform simple image editing tasks within the Dreamweaver MX 2004 environment.
➤ Insert page background images.
➤ Insert table and table cell background images.
➤ Create rollovers.
➤ Build a Web photo album.
➤ Work with tracing images.
➤ Use the Assets panel to store and manage images.

The student files for this chapter are available for download from the Internet Resource Center at www.emcp.com.

After you have learned how to insert, format, and lay out text, you are ready to use images to enhance the appearance of the Web pages you create. The proper use of images in Web pages increases the chances of attracting and maintaining viewer interest. Images can make a Web page more attractive, provide information, or facilitate an interactive experience when used as buttons, links, or image maps. Many images fulfill all of these roles at the same time. Images also can supplement text, or even eliminate the need for text altogether.

Understanding Images

Web page images are not saved as part of a Web page document. Instead, they are located in separate files, with an HTML *image tag* (<img>) and *source attribute (src)* in a document directing the browser to an image file location so that the file can be retrieved and displayed as part of a Web page as shown in Figure 4.1. Because a Web page with images is made up of multiple files, the time required for the browser to retrieve all of the necessary elements to display the complete page is a function of the size of all of the various files involved. It is important that image file sizes are kept relatively small to ensure that a Web page does not take too long to load. Many experts recommend that a single Web page be no larger than 100 kilobytes (KB) in size, with smaller sizes being preferable. Thus the file size of an HTML page plus all of its images added together should be less than 100 KB whenever possible. The excessive use of images on a page should also be avoided to keep down the cumulative file size. The exception to this rule is if the same image is repeated on a page. That does not increase loading time because the image file needs to be loaded only once by a browser.

Many different digital image formats exist, some of which are unsuitable for use on Web pages. The ideal image format for Web pages uses a compression technique that produces small image files and is supported by all browsers. The three image formats that meet these requirements are GIF (Graphics Interchange Format), JPEG (Joint Photographic Experts Group), and PNG (Portable Network Graphics).

GIF images are the most commonly used on the Web. The GIF format has several variations. One allows interlacing and transparency. *Interlacing* allows images to be displayed gradually, somewhat like a picture slowly coming into focus as shown in Figure 4.2. *Transparency* allows the background color of a Web page to show through an image as shown in Figure 4.3. A more recent GIF variation produces *animated* (moving) *graphics*. The GIF format supports only 256 colors, so it might not be suitable for all images. As a general rule, GIF is the best format for displaying drawings or illustrations.

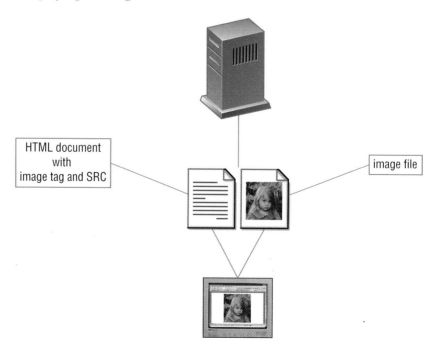

Figure 4.1
How Images Are Displayed

Figure 4.2
Interlaced GIF Image Loading

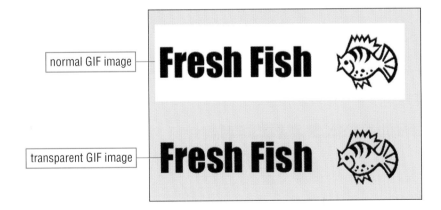

normal GIF image

transparent GIF image

Figure 4.3
Normal and Transparent GIF
Images

JPEG images support more than 16 million colors and are the best format for photographs. When used to display large images, a JPEG file will be smaller than a comparable GIF file because of the compression technology used.

PNG images offer interlacing and transparency, and produce smaller file sizes than the GIF or JPEG formats. Currently PNG images are supported only by browser versions 4.0 and above. The PNG format is the native image format for Fireworks MX 2004, but until browser support improves, it is probably better to use GIF and JPEG image files in most circumstances.

Inserting Images

The Select Image Source dialog box shown in Figure 4.4 is used to locate image files. After you complete the information in the dialog box and click OK, Dreamweaver MX 2004 inserts an image tag and source attribute at the insertion point as shown in Figure 4.5 (visible only in Code view or Code and Design view) so that an image will appear in the document when it is displayed in a browser. You can open the Select Image Source dialog box by clicking Insert on the Menu bar and then Image, or by clicking the Insert bar Images button (Common menu item or tab) down-pointing arrow as shown in Figure 4.6. This opens a menu of image-related commands. Clicking the Image command opens the Select Image Source dialog box. The Images button always displays the icon of the last image command selected. For example, once you select Image from the menu the Image command

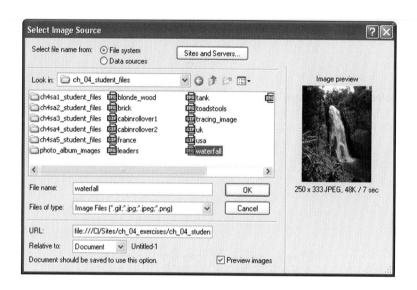

Figure 4.4
Select Image Source
Dialog Box

Figure 4.5
Image Tag and
Source Attribute

```
<body>
<img src="ch_04_student_files/photo_album_images/citroen.jpg" width="434" height="325"></body>
</html>
```

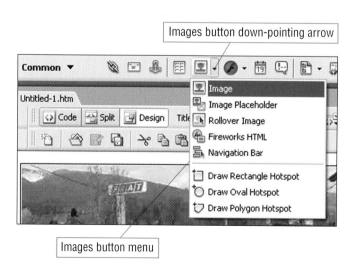

Figure 4.6
Insert Bar Images Button
and Menu

icon will be displayed on the Images button. Hovering the mouse pointer over the Images button will display a tooltip identifying the function of the button as shown in Figure 4.7. Images also can be inserted by dragging the Images button from the Insert bar to the current document.

The Select Image Source dialog box can be used to specify the following properties:

- **Select file name from File system or Data sources** Click the *File system* radio button unless you are using dynamic images from a database recordset.

- **Look in** Browse to find the image file location.

- **File name** The image file name appears in this text box.

- **Files of type** Shows the file type.

- **URL** Shows the path to the image file.

- **Relative to** This drop-down list can be used to save the file relative to the document or the site root. *Document* (document-relative path) should be chosen when working with documents located in the same site. *Root* (root-relative path) is suitable for large Web sites that might be hosted on more than one server.

After an image has been selected, the dialog box displays a **thumbnail** (a much smaller copy of the image) as shown in Figure 4.8 if the *Preview images* check box has been selected. The image's dimensions in pixels are displayed as well. Clicking OK inserts the image on the page at the insertion point. If the document has not been saved yet, a message will appear advising that the document should be saved so that a document-relative path for the image can be created. Dreamweaver MX 2004 uses a temporary path until the file is saved. Clicking OK closes the message box. If the image file is located outside the document's root folder, another message box will appear advising that a copy of the image file should be saved to the root folder. Clicking the Yes button opens a Copy File As dialog box that can be used to browse and locate the desired root folder. Clicking the Save button completes

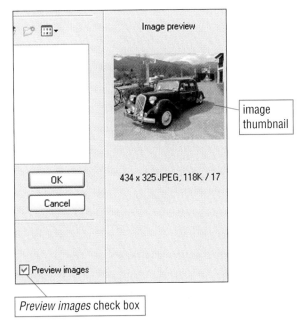

Figure 4.7 • Images Button Tooltip   **Figure 4.8** • Image Thumbnail Preview

the process, and the image appears in the document. If the *Images* check box has been selected in the Preferences dialog box Accessibility page, the Image Tag Accessibility Attributes dialog box will open at this point and can be completed as described in the following section. Clicking Cancel inserts the image without creating any accessibility attributes.

INSERTING AN IMAGE

1. If necessary, start Dreamweaver MX 2004.
2. At a clear document screen, create a new site named CH 04 Exercises to store the exercises you create in this chapter. Name the root folder ch_04_exercises and save it under the Sites folder you created in Chapter 1, Exercise 3. Download the ch_04_student_files folder from the IRC to the CH 04 Exercises site root folder (ch_04_exercises) and expand it. Delete the compressed folder when you are finished. ***Note: Refer to Chapter 1 for instructions on navigating with the Files panel integrated file browser.***
3. Insert an image into an HTML document by completing the following steps:
   a. Create a new HTML document and use the Save or Save As commands to name and save it as **ch4ex01.htm**.
   b. Click Edit on the Menu bar and then Preferences to open the Preferences dialog box. Click *Accessibility* in the *Category* list box and make sure that there is a check mark in the *Images* check box in order to enable accessibility preferences for images. ***Note: Instructions on selecting this preference are contained in the "Ensuring Accessibility" section of Chapter 2.***
   c. Click Insert on the Menu bar and then Image to open the Select Image Source dialog box.
   d. Use the Select Image Source dialog box to browse and locate the student file named **toadstools.jpg** in the ch_04_student_files folder. Click the OK button to insert the image into the document. ***Note: If you insert an image into an unsaved document, Dreamweaver MX 2004 will advise you to save it first so that a document-relative path can be created. If an image being inserted is located outside the root folder for the document it is being inserted in, Dreamweaver MX 2004 will advise you to save it in the root folder for the document.***

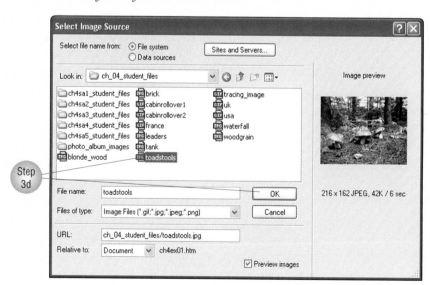

e. The Image Tag Accessibility Attributes dialog box appears after you click the OK button in the Select Image Source dialog box. Type the following text in the dialog box:
1) Type Toadstools in the Forest in the *Alternate text* text box.

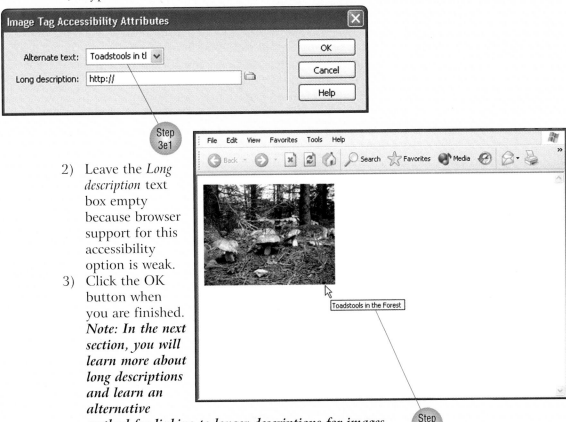

2) Leave the *Long description* text box empty because browser support for this accessibility option is weak.
3) Click the OK button when you are finished. **Note: In the next section, you will learn more about long descriptions and learn an alternative method for linking to longer descriptions for images.**

f. Click the Preview/Debug in browser button and then click Preview in iexplore to see how the image looks on the page. Hover the pointer over the image to see the alternate description you created. Close the browser when you are finished.

4. Save **ch4ex01.htm** but do not close it.

Ensuring Image Accessibility

If *Images* has been selected in the *Accessibility Category* list box, an Image Tag Accessibility Attributes dialog box containing *Alternate text* and *Long description* text boxes will appear during the image-insertion process.

An ***alternate text description*** for the image will be interpreted by screen readers and will also appear in the latest browser versions as a descriptive tooltip when the pointer is moved over the image. Alternate text should be limited to less than 50 characters. The goal of alternate text should be to describe the meaning of an image, so alternate text descriptions should do more than just provide a label. For example, typing *flowers* as an alternate description for an image is insufficient. The meaning or use of the image should be provided instead, such as "This is a sample floral arrangement available at our store."

Alternate text also can be entered when using the Image Property inspector or Tag Editor - Img dialog box to modify image properties. If an image does not add meaning to a page, it is not necessary to create an alternate description; however, to let those with screen readers know that the image is irrelevant to understanding the page content, type an asterisk (*) in the *Alternate text* text box.

A ***long description*** is used to indicate a path to a file containing a long description of the image as shown in Figure 4.9. This is useful when the information conveyed by an image is important to the meaning of a page and the 50 characters maximum recommended for alternate text is insufficient. When the image is clicked in a browser, the long description file opens.

The long description feature is currently poorly supported by browsers, but there is an alternative way of creating a longer description for images or other page elements known as a ***D̲ link (description link)***. A D̲ link is a hyperlink linking to a long description file and is positioned next to the image as shown in Figure 4.10. Clicking the D̲ link opens the file with the longer description, which can be an HTML file containing a text-only description, or a file containing the image with longer descriptive text such as the example shown in Figure 4.9.

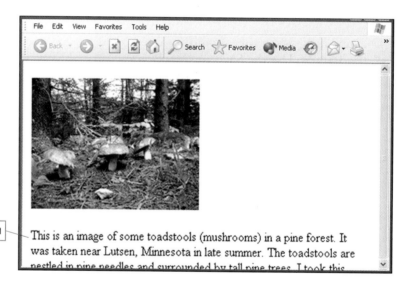

Figure 4.9
Long Description Example

long description

Figure 4.10
D̲ Link (Description Link)

1. Create a <u>D</u> link by completing the following steps:

   a. With **ch4ex01.htm** as the current document, use the Save As command to rename and save it as **ch4ex02.htm**.

   b. Use the Save As command to rename and save **ch4ex02.htm** as **ch4ex02-a.htm**.

   c. Position the insertion point to the right of the image in **ch4ex02-a.htm**, and press Enter to move the insertion point below the image.

Step 1c

   d. Type This is an image of some toadstools (mushrooms) in a pine forest. It was taken near Lutsen, Minnesota in late summer. The toadstools are nestled in pine needles and surrounded by tall pine trees. I took this photo while on a long walk in the woods. I didn't see much wildlife, but there was a variety of interesting plant life, including these toadstools. Use the Save command to save the document when you are finished typing the text, and then close it.

Step 1e

   e. Open **ch4ex02.htm**. Position the insertion point to the right of the image. Type D.

   f. Select the *D* you just typed. With the Files panel open and displaying the contents of the CH 04 Exercises site, click the Property inspector Point to File button and point to *ch4ex02-a.htm* to create a link (the <u>D</u> link).

Step 1f

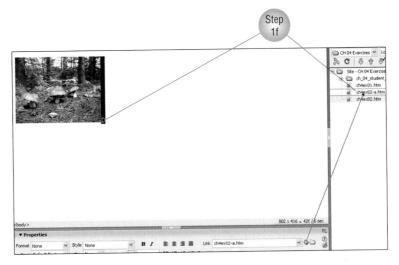

g. Click the Preview/Debug in browser button and then click Preview in iexplore to preview **ch4ex02.htm** in a browser. Click the <u>D</u> link. Document **ch4ex02-a.htm** opens in the browser window, with the long description located below the image. Close the browser when you are finished.

2. Save **ch4ex02.htm** and then close it.

Step 1g

Inserting Image Placeholders

Ideas about which images to use and where they should be placed occur frequently during the page-design process. To see how image size and placement will affect overall page design, it is necessary to place images on a page. Although this is the ideal solution, an image often needs to be created or obtained before this can be done, and the time spent doing that can adversely affect the flow of the design process. To streamline the design process, temporary **image placeholders** can be placed in a document wherever images are planned, as shown in Figure 4.11. The placeholder's dimensions (width by height) in pixels are displayed inside the placeholder. Image placeholders can be inserted by clicking Insert on the Menu bar and then Image Placeholder, or by clicking the Image Placeholder button on the Insert bar (Common menu item or tab) to open the Image Placeholder dialog box shown in Figure 4.12. Dragging the Image Placeholder button to the Document window also opens the Image Placeholder dialog box. The dialog box is used to give placeholders a name, specify their dimensions and color, and provide alternate text descriptions. Image placeholders can be replaced by an actual image after a replacement image is available, and the placeholder's alternate text description will be automatically transferred to the replacement image.

After an image placeholder has been inserted, its dimensions can be adjusted by selecting it and then dragging the horizontal, vertical, or diagonal resize handles in the desired direction. Entering new values in the Image Property inspector or Tag Editor - Img dialog box *Width* and *Height* text boxes is another way to change placeholder dimensions. Setting placeholder dimensions allows you to visualize how an image with those dimensions will fit in with the overall page layout. However, when a placeholder is replaced by an image, the new image is inserted in its actual dimensions, not in the placeholder dimensions. To maintain page layout integrity,

DREAMWEAVER MX 2004

it is important that placeholder dimensions either match the dimensions of the image that will replace it, that an image editor is used to modify replacement image dimensions to match placeholder dimensions, or that the replacement image is resized to match the placeholder dimensions and then resampled.

Both the Image Property inspector and the Tag Editor - Img dialog box can be used to change image placeholder properties, which are the same as image properties. Dreamweaver MX 2004 has a quirk that prevents the *Align* list box drop-down list from working when the Image Property inspector is used in conjunction with image placeholders, so the Tag Editor - Img dialog box must be used to change those settings. The Tag Editor - Img dialog box also can be used to change most image placeholder properties, with the exception of links and target windows, which must be changed using the Image Property inspector. Right-clicking an image placeholder and clicking Edit Tag <img> opens the Tag Editor - Img dialog box.

You can replace an image placeholder with an image by double-clicking the placeholder to open the Select Image Source dialog box that can be used to browse and locate the image that will replace the placeholder. Click the OK button to place the image on the page in the placeholder location. If you want to create an image to replace the image placeholder, click the Create button in the Image Property inspector as shown in Figure 4.13 to open Fireworks if that program is installed on your computer or local network. Two other methods can be used to replace image placeholders with images: selecting an image placeholder and then using the Image Property inspector *Src* text box Point to File button to locate an image in the Files panel, or clicking the Image Property inspector *Src* text box Browse for File button to locate an image using the Select Image Source dialog box.

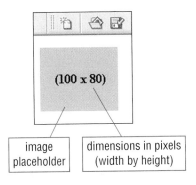

Figure 4.11
Image Placeholder

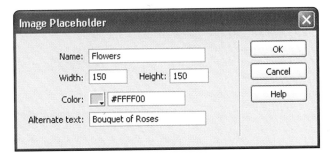

Figure 4.12
Image Placeholder Dialog Box

Figure 4.13
Image Property Inspector
Create Button

exercise **3**

1. Insert an image placeholder by completing the following steps:
   a. At a clear document screen, open **ch3ex10.htm** and use the Save As command to rename and save it to the ch_04_exercises root folder as **ch4ex03.htm**.
   b. Position the insertion point in the second column of the second row of the table.
   c. Click Insert on the Menu bar, point to Image Objects, and then click Image Placeholder to open the Image Placeholder dialog box. Type the following values in the dialog box:

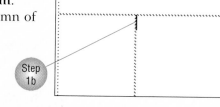

Step 1b

   1) Type **Waterfall** in the *Name* text box.
   2) Type **250** in the *Width* text box.
   3) Type **333** in the *Height* text box.
   4) Leave the *Color* text box blank.
   5) Type **A Waterfall** in the *Alternate text* text box.

Steps 1c1–1c5

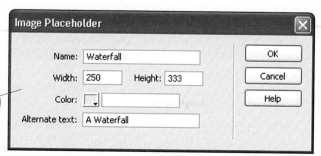

   d. Click the OK button when you are finished. The image placeholder appears in the document. *Note: The **Color** text box can be used to select a color for the image placeholder. When working with a large amount of images, you might find it helpful to color-code image placeholders by image type, subject, source, and so on.*

2. Replace an image placeholder with an image by completing the following steps:
   a. Double-click the image placeholder to open the Select Image Source dialog box.
   b. Locate and select the student file named **waterfall.jpg** in the ch_04_student_files folder. Click the OK button to replace the image placeholder with the **waterfall.jpg** image.
   c. Click the Preview/Debug in browser button and then click Preview in iexplore to see how the image looks on the page. Close the browser when you are finished.

3. Save **ch4ex03.htm** and then close it.

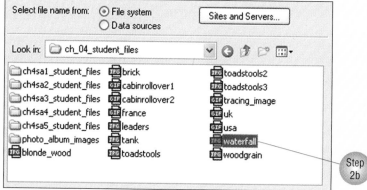

Step 2b

Defining Image Properties

When images are selected, the fully expanded Image Property inspector displays image properties as shown in Figure 4.14. Values can be entered in the text boxes or selected from drop-down lists. Image properties also can be modified by

DREAMWEAVER MX 2004

selecting an image, clicking Modify on the Menu bar, and then Edit Tag. This opens the Tag Editor - Img dialog box as shown in Figure 4.15. To see the Tag Editor - Img dialog box image properties, the *General* category must be selected. The Image Property inspector contains abbreviated descriptions for image property text boxes, while the Tag Editor - Img dialog box contains full descriptions. Each of these editing tools shares most image properties, but a few image properties are unique to one or the other as noted in the following sections.

Width and Height

The width and height of an image in pixels are automatically displayed in the *Width (W)* and *Height (H)* text boxes. A browser will still display an image without this information, but it might take longer because the browser must download the image first in order to estimate the size of the image file, increasing the time it takes to load the text on a page. Changing the width and height specifications in an image tag, or resizing an image by dragging its resize handles, does not affect the file's size in bytes and can lead to image distortion as shown in Figure 4.16 if the ratio between width and height is not maintained. Even if the correct ratio is

image name

Figure 4.14
Image Property Inspector

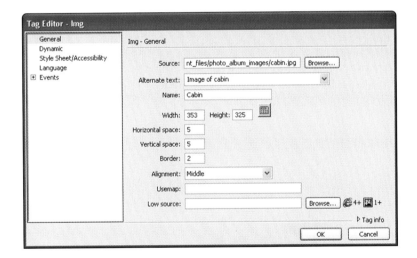

Figure 4.15
Tag Editor - Img Dialog Box

distorted image

Figure 4.16
Image Distortion

maintained, some browsers will ignore width and height settings and instead display the image using its actual dimensions. The resized image can then be inserted into a document. Clicking the Reset Size button will restore an image to its original dimensions if its dimensions have been changed. The Reset Size button appears only when an image's dimensions have been changed.

A resized image's actual size can be changed to reflect its visual size using the Image Property inspector Resample button (discussed in the upcoming "Resample Button" section). Another method that can be used to resize images is to resize them in an image editor that can be accessed through the Edit button (discussed in the upcoming "Edit/Create Button" section).

Image Path

The *Source (Src)* text box contains the path to the selected image. In both the Image Property inspector and the Tag Editor - Img dialog box, you can type a new path in the *Source* text box, or you can use the Point to File and Browse for File buttons (Image Property inspector) or Browse button (Tag Editor - Img dialog box) to locate a new path. Although you can type the path, this is not recommended because it is easy to make a mistake.

Alternate Text

Alternate text can be typed in the *Alternate text (Alt)* text box so that viewers using screen readers can make sense of an image. Alternate text should be less than 50 characters, and consist of a concise description of the image, such as Image of Tree, Image of the White House, and so on, as shown in Figure 4.17. Longer descriptions can be contained in <u>D</u> links as described earlier in the "Ensuring Image Accessibility" section of this chapter. If alternate text has already been created for a selected image, it appears in the text box and can be modified if desired.

CSS Class Style

The *Class* list box, available only in the Image Property inspector, displays the CSS class style if a style is applied to the selected image. This list box will be described more fully in Chapter 6, *Using Cascading Style Sheets (CSS)*.

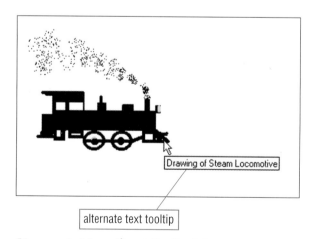

Drawing of Steam Locomotive

alternate text tooltip

Figure 4.17 • Alternate Text Description

DREAMWEAVER MX 2004

Image Link

An image can function as a link if the image is selected and a path to a link target is entered in the Image Property inspector's *Link* text box. The link target path can be typed, or it can be located using the Point to File or Browse for File buttons.

Horizontal and Vertical Space

The *Horizontal space (H space)* and *Vertical space (V space)* text boxes can be used to add space between an image and any adjacent text or page elements. Entering a number in either box adds that number of pixels of space to the left and right of an image *(horizontal space),* or above and below an image *(vertical space),* as shown in Figure 4.18.

Target Browser Window

If an image is being used as a link, the browser window that the link target opens in can be specified by clicking the desired choice from the *Target* text box drop-down list in the Image Property inspector. The *_self* option is the default, and will load the target link file in the same window as the linking document. The *_blank* option displays the target link file in a new browser window. The *_parent* and *_top* options will be described in Chapter 5, *Working with Frames*.

Image Border

Entering a value in the *Border* text box creates a black border around an image measured in pixels. Higher border values produce thicker borders.

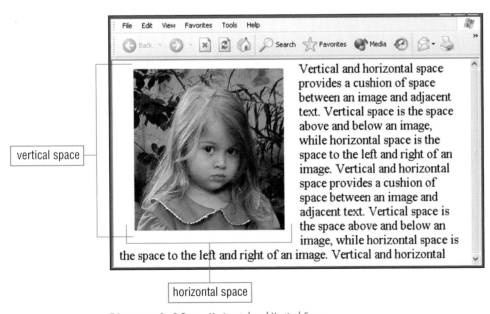

Figure 4.18 • Horizontal and Vertical Space

Image Alignment

The options in the *Alignment* or *Align* list box drop-down lists can be used to align an image in relation to the other elements located in the same paragraph or line as the image. Figure 4.19 shows image and text placement when different image alignment values are chosen. As you can see from the examples, the difference between some of these values is very slight. The alignment values are described in the following list:

- *Default* Browsers usually interpret **default image alignment** as a baseline alignment, aligning text or elements to the bottom of an image.
- *Baseline* **Baseline image alignment** aligns the baseline of text or elements to the bottom of a selected image.
- *Top* **Top image alignment** aligns the top of an image with the top of the tallest portion of an image or text.
- *Middle* **Middle image alignment** aligns the middle of the image with the baseline of an image or text.
- *Bottom* Like baseline image alignment, **bottom image alignment** aligns the baseline of text or elements to the bottom of a selected object.
- *TextTop* **Text top image alignment** aligns the top of an image with the top of the tallest character in a line of text.
- *Absolute Middle* **Absolute middle image alignment** aligns the middle of an image with the middle of the text.
- *Absolute Bottom* **Absolute bottom image alignment** aligns the bottom of an image with the bottom of a line of text, including portions of the text that descend below the text baseline, such as *y* or *g*.
- *Left* **Left image alignment** aligns an image to the left margin, with text wrapped around the image to the right. If a paragraph does not reach the bottom of the image, text from a following paragraph (if any) is pulled up next to the image. To prevent this from happening, press Enter to add additional paragraph tags (<p>).

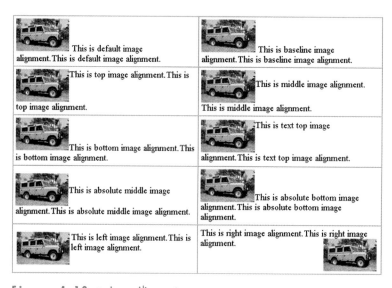

F i g u r e 4 . 1 9 • Image Alignments

- ***Right*** ***Right image alignment*** aligns an image to the right margin with text wrapped around the image to the left. Press Enter to add paragraph tags to prevent a following paragraph from being pulled up next to the image if the first paragraph ends short of the image bottom.

Low Source Image

The *Low source (Low Src)* text box can be used to indicate a path to a lower resolution copy of the main image that will load first, letting viewers preview the image while waiting for the main image to load. Low source paths can be typed or located and selected using the Point to File and Browse for File buttons in the Image Property inspector, or the Browse button in the Tag Editor - Img dialog box. A ***low source image*** is usually a black-and-white version of the main image as shown in Figure 4.20. The small browser icons (shown in Figure 4.21) to the right of the *Low source* text box in the Tag Editor - Img dialog box show the browser versions that support this tag: Internet Explorer v. 4 and up, Netscape v. 1 and up.

Figure 4.20 • Low Source Image

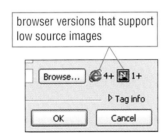

Figure 4.21 • Tag Editor - Img Dialog Box Low Source Tag Browser Support

Image Maps and Hotspot Buttons

The *Map* text box in the Image Property inspector is used to enter a name for an image map. **Image maps** are images containing **hotspots** that link to other documents when clicked. The hotspot buttons shown in Figure 4.22 are used to create image hotspots. When you move the insertion point to an image after clicking a hotspot button, the insertion point transforms into **crosshairs** (+). Clicking and dragging the crosshairs to create the desired shape and then releasing the mouse button completes the hotspot. The Polygon Hotspot Tool creates irregular shapes. Clicking the Polygon Hotspot Tool periodically around the irregular shape and then clicking the starting point will create an irregular hotspot as shown in Figure 4.22. After a hotspot has been created, the Pointer Hotspot Tool can be used to move it. The Hotspot Property inspector displays a *Link* text box for typing in a link target, and Point to File and Browse for File buttons for browsing and locating a link target for the hotspot. The *Target* text box is used to specify the browser window that the hotspot link target document will open in, and the *Alt* text box is used to type

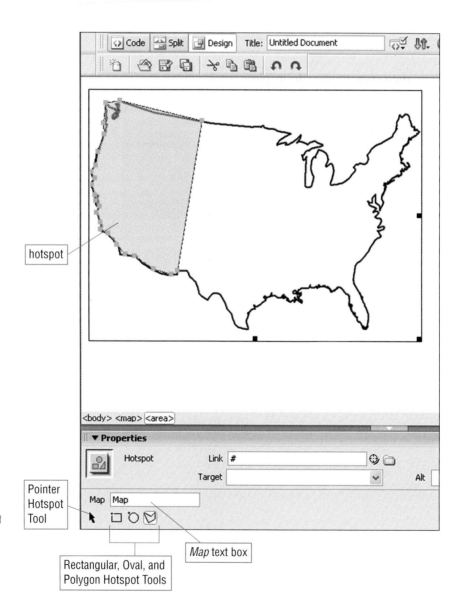

Figure 4.22
Creating an Image Hotspot

or locate alternate text describing the hotspot. In the Tag Editor - Img dialog box, the map name is displayed in the *Usemap* text box.

Image Name

The *Name* text box is used to type a name for identifying an image in the HTML code for a page. In the Image Property inspector, this box is unlabeled, and appears in the upper-left corner of the inspector to the right of the image thumbnail as shown previously in Figure 4.14.

exercise 4

CHANGING IMAGE PROPERTIES

1. Change image dimensions by completing the following steps:
   a. At a clear document screen, open **ch4ex01.htm** and use the Save As command to rename and save it as **ch4ex04.htm**.
   b. Click the image to select it.
   c. Change the image width by typing 400 in the Image Property inspector *W* text box.

   Step 1c

   d. Click the Preview/Debug in browser button and then click Preview in iexplore to view the page. The image appears distorted because you have changed the ratio between the image's width and height. Using an image editor is the easiest and most reliable method of changing image dimensions before an image is inserted in a document. Close the browser when you are finished.

   e. Click the image in **ch4ex04.htm** and then click the Image Property inspector Reset Size button to restore the image to its actual dimensions. *Note: The 400-pixel dimension is bold, indicating that this dimension does not match the actual width of the image.*

   Step 1d

   Step 1e

   f. Click the Preview/Debug in browser button and then click Preview in iexplore to view the image again. It is now displayed in its original dimensions. Close the browser when you are finished.

2. Change an image's horizontal and vertical space by completing the following steps:
   a. Position the insertion point to the right of the image and type **Vertical space adds a cushion of space above and below an image. Horizontal space adds a cushion of space to the left and to the right of an image.**

Vertical space

cushion of space to the left and to the right of an im

Step 2a

b. Click the image to select it.

c. Type **20** in the Image Property inspector *V Space* text box to add vertical space above and below the image.

d. Type **20** in the Image Property inspector *H Space* text box to add horizontal space to the left and to the right of the image.

e. Click the Preview/Debug in browser button and then click Preview in iexplore to view the image. Note that now a cushion of space is surrounding the image. Close the browser when you are finished.

3. Change image alignment by completing the following steps:

a. Click the image to select it.

b. Click the *Align* list box down-pointing arrow in the Image Property inspector to open the *Align* drop-down list and then click *Middle*. Note how the text behaves. Click other choices to familiarize yourself with the different alignment options.

c. When you are finished experimenting with the different alignment options, click the *Left* alignment option. Note that the vertical spacing at the top of the image makes the text appear above the image rather than in line with it.

d. Select the image and type **0** in the Image Property inspector *V Space* text box to change the vertical spacing from 20 pixels to 0 pixels. The text will now appear almost in line with the image.

4. Add a border to an image by completing the following steps:

a. Click the image to select it.

b. Type **5** in the Image Property inspector *Border* text box.

c. Click the Preview/Debug in browser button and then click Preview in iexplore to view the image. A thick black border now surrounds the image. Close the browser when you are finished.

5. Save **ch4ex04.htm** but do not close it.

1. Create an image link by completing the following steps:
   a. With **ch4ex04.htm** in the current window, use the Save As command to rename and save it as **ch4ex05.htm**.
   b. Click the image to select it.
   c. With the Files panel open, click the Image Property inspector *Link* text box Point to File button and point to *ch4ex02-a.htm* to create a link to this file with the long description. Note that the image border changes to a dark blue.

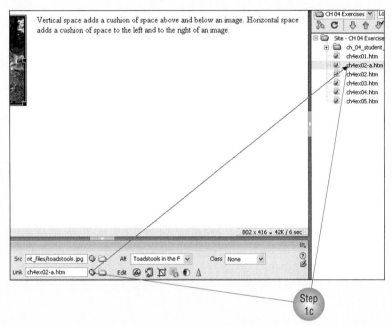

   d. Type **0** in the Image Property inspector *Border* text box to remove the border around the image.

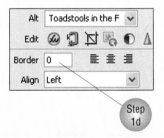

   e. Click the Preview/Debug in browser button and then click Preview in iexplore to view the image.
   f. Click the image. Document **ch4ex02-a.htm** opens in the browser window. Close the browser window when you are finished.
2. Save **ch4ex05.htm** and then close it.

1. Create an image map by completing the following steps:

   a. At a clear document screen, open the student file named **image_map.htm** in the ch_04_student_files folder and use the Save As command to rename and save it to the ch_04_exercises root folder as **ch4ex06.htm**.

   b. With **ch4ex06.htm** as the current document, click one of the stamps to select the image. *Note: All three stamps are located in the same image, so you can click any stamp to select the image.*

   c. Click the Image Property inspector Polygon Hotspot Tool button and move the insertion point up to the first stamp image until it turns into crosshairs. *Note: A message advising you to create an alternate text description may appear. Since a description is already contained in the* Alt *text box, click the OK button to close the message whenever it appears.*

   d. Place the crosshairs on the upper-left corner of the first stamp and click once. Move the crosshairs to the lower-left corner of the stamp and click again. Continue moving the crosshairs to each corner of the first stamp and click in each corner. As you do this, you will see the blue hotspot outline forming. *Hint: If you make a mistake, start over again by clicking Edit on the Menu bar and then Undo, or click the Undo button on the Standard toolbar if the toolbar is displayed.*

   e. With the Files panel open, click the Hotspot Property inspector *Link* text box Point to File button and drag the arrow line over to the student file named **de_gaulle.htm** in the ch_04_student_files folder to create a hotspot link for the first stamp.

   f. Click the Rectangular Hotspot Tool button and move the crosshairs up to the last stamp on the right. Place the crosshairs in the upper-left corner of the stamp and drag it diagonally down to the lower-right corner to create the hotspot outline.

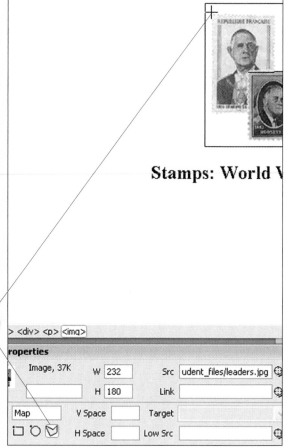

Step 1c

Step 1d

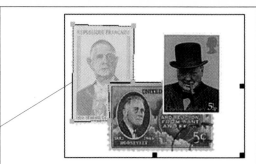

Step 1f

DREAMWEAVER MX 2004

g. Click the Hotspot Property inspector *Link* text box Browse for File button to browse and locate the student file named **churchill.htm** in the ch_04_student_files folder. Click the OK button to complete the hotspot link. *Hint: You can use either the Point to File method or the Browse for File button method to create links. For external links, you must type a URL.*

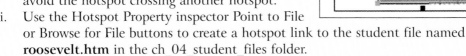

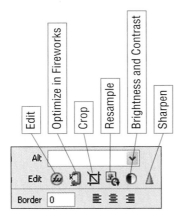

Step 1h

h. Click the Image Property inspector Polygon Hotspot Tool button and move the pointer to the middle stamp. Place the crosshairs at the intersection of the middle stamp and Churchill's shoulder, and work in a clockwise direction to avoid the hotspot crossing another hotspot.

i. Use the Hotspot Property inspector Point to File or Browse for File buttons to create a hotspot link to the student file named **roosevelt.htm** in the ch_04_student_files folder.

j. Click the Preview/Debug in browser button and then click Preview in iexplore to view the document. Move the pointer to one of the stamps. A Link Select hand appears. Click once to open the file linked to the hotspot. Click the browser Back button to return to the hotspot document and check that the other two stamp hotspots work. Close the browser when you are finished.

2. Save **ch4ex06.htm** and then close it.

Image Property Inspector Image Editing Buttons

The Image Property inspector includes a number of buttons identified in Figure 4.23. These buttons can be used to perform image editing functions. Users can use the Edit button to work with one or more external image editor, or use other image editing buttons to perform simple image editing within the Dreamweaver MX 2004 environment.

Edit Button

Selecting an image and clicking the Edit button opens an image editor that can be used to modify the selected image. If an image placeholder is selected, the Edit

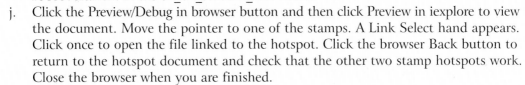

Figure 4.23
Image Property Inspector
Image Editing Buttons

button appears as the Create button. Clicking the Create button opens an image editor that can be used to create an image that will replace the placeholder. Users can specify different image editors as the default image editors for different image formats. For example, provided the applications were installed on your computer or local network, you could specify Photoshop as the default image editor for GIF images, and Fireworks for JPEG images.

exercise **7**

SELECTING IMAGE EDITOR PREFERENCES

Check with your instructor to find out which program or programs should be set as the image editor or editors for GIF, JPG, and PNG files.

1. Select default image editors for different image formats by completing the following steps:
   a. Click Edit on the Menu bar and then Preferences to open the Preferences dialog box.
   b. Select *File Types / Editors* from the *Category* list box on the left side of the dialog box.
   c. Click an image file type (*.png, .gif,* or *.jpg .jpe .jpeg*) in the *Extensions* list box that will be matched to an image editor that will be used to edit that type of file.

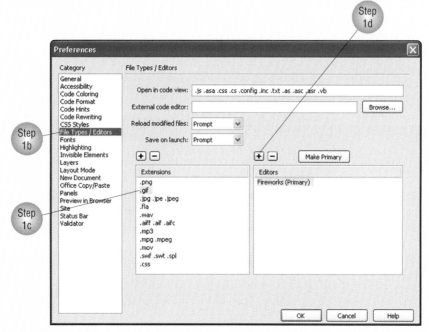

   d. Click the Add (+) button above the *Editors* list box to open the Select External Editor dialog box.

DREAMWEAVER MX 2004

e. Use the Select External Editor dialog box to browse and locate the image editor you want. Click Open to choose the image editor as the image editor for the image file type you chose in Step 1c. The Delete (–) buttons above the *Extensions* and *Editors* list boxes can be used to remove an extension or editor. ***Note: You can add more than one image editor to the Editors list box. If that is the case, you can make one editor***

the primary editor by clicking it and then clicking the Make Primary button. A primary editor opens whenever the image file type it is linked to is edited. If more than one type of editor is listed for a file type, the other editors can be accessed by right-clicking an image, pointing to Edit With, and then clicking the Browse button to locate and open an image editor.

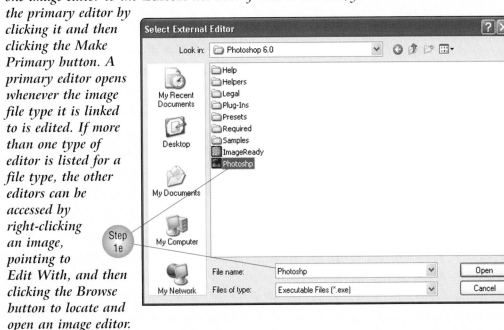

Step 1e

2. Click the OK button to close the dialog box.

Optimize in Fireworks Button

Images can be optimized in Fireworks if Fireworks is installed on your computer or local network. Clicking the Optimize in Fireworks button opens the Fireworks Optimize dialog box. The dialog box can be used to perform a number of different image editing functions aimed at optimizing images so that they contain the right mix of color, compression, and quality. Available functions include changing the file format, cropping the image, changing colors, and so on. If a file format is changed, a dialog box will ask you if you want to update any references to the image. Simply clicking the Update button will automatically optimize an image without the need to specify any variables. An optimized image will appear the same as it did previously, but its file size usually will be smaller.

exercise **8**

OPTIMIZING IMAGES WITH FIREWORKS

1. Use the Optimize in Fireworks button to optimize an image by completing the following steps:
   a. Create a new HTML document and use the Save or Save As commands to name and save it as **ch4ex08.htm**.

b. Right-click the student file named **toadstools.jpg** in the Files panel, point to Edit, and then click Duplicate to make a duplicate of **toadstools.jpg** named **Copy of toadstools.jpg**.

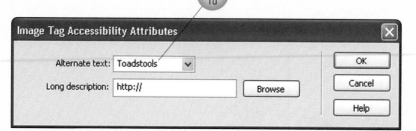

c. Right-click *Copy of toadstools.jpg,* point to Edit, and then click Rename to rename it **toadstools2.jpg**.

d. Click *toadstools.jpg* and drag it to the Document window to insert it in **ch4ex08.htm**. Type Toadstools in the Image Tag Accessibility Attributes dialog box *Alternate text* text box and then click the OK button to close the dialog box.

e. Press Enter to move the insertion point below the image.

f. Click *toadstools2.jpg* and drag it to the Document window to insert it in **ch4ex08.htm** below **toadstools.jpg**. Type Toadstools in the Image Tag Accessibility Attributes dialog box *Alternate text* text box and then click the OK button to close the dialog box.

g. Click **toadstools.jpg** in the Document window and note that the Image Property inspector indicates that the file size of the image is 42 kilobytes. Click **toadstools2.jpg** and note that its file size is the same.

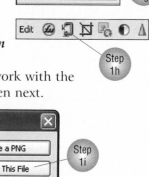

h. Click **toadstools2.jpg** in the Document window to select it, and then click the Optimize in Fireworks button in the Image Property inspector to begin the image optimization process. ***Note: If Fireworks is not installed, a message will appear informing you that Fireworks needs to be installed in order for the Optimize in Fireworks button to work.***

i. Click the Find Source dialog box Use This File button to work with the selected image. The Fireworks Optimize dialog box will open next.

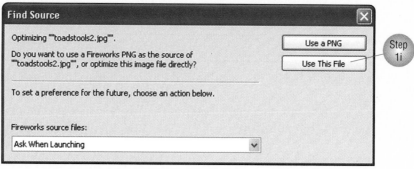

j.   Click the Fireworks Optimize dialog box Update button to optimize **toadstools2.jpg**. The dialog box will close.

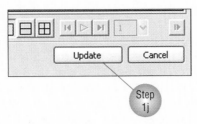

k.   If necessary, click **toadstools2.jpg** to select it. Note that its file size is now 29 kilobytes.

l.   Click the Preview/Debug in browser button and then click Preview in iexplore to view the document. Although the two images appear identical, the file size of the **toadstools2.jpg** image is 13 kilobytes smaller than the file size of **toadstools.jpg** (29 kilobytes vs. 42 kilobytes). ***Note: Images with smaller file sizes will load more quickly in browsers and save space on a server, so it pays to optimize images.*** Close the browser when you are finished.

2.   Save **ch4ex08.htm** and then close it.

Crop Button

The Crop button allows you to crop images by selecting them, clicking the Crop button, and then using the crop handles to move the crop bounding image so that it covers the portion of the image that you wish to remain after cropping as shown in Figure 4.24. Double-clicking, clicking the Crop button again, or pressing Enter crops the picture by removing the portion of an image that lies outside the crop bounding image. Cropping will permanently change an image, so you may wish to save a copy of the original image. Cropping of an image can be undone by clicking Edit on the Menu bar and then Undo crop. Once Dreamweaver MX 2004 is closed, any cropping of an image will be permanent.

crop bounding image   crop handles

Figure 4.24
Crop Bounding Image

Resample Button

Resizing an image changes the visual size of the image in the Document window, but does not change its actual file size. Clicking the Resample button makes the actual size of a selected resized image match its visual size. For example, a 100 by 100 pixel image could be resized by dragging its selection handles so that its width and height dimensions appear as *200* in the Document window *W* and *H* text boxes. However, the actual size of the image would remain the same, and browsers might not display the image as intended. Clicking the Resample button overcomes this difficulty by resampling the image so that its actual size matches the size displayed in the Document window. Resampling can be undone by clicking Edit on the Menu bar and then Undo. The Resample button is faded and inoperative unless a resized image is selected.

Brightness and Contrast Button

Clicking the Brightness and Contrast button opens the Brightness/Contrast dialog box as shown in Figure 4.25. Clicking and dragging the *Brightness* and *Contract* scale indicators changes brightness and contrast values. Alternatively, new values can be typed directly into the text boxes next to each indicator.

Sharpen Button

Sharpening increases the number of pixels around an image's edge to give it more definition and make it appear sharper. Clicking the Sharpen button opens the Sharpen dialog box shown in Figure 4.26. The *Sharpen* scale indicator can be clicked and dragged to change the sharpness value, or a value can be typed directly into the text box next to the indicator.

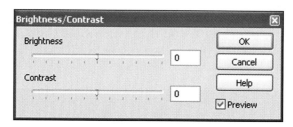

Figure 4.25 • Brightness/Contrast Dialog Box

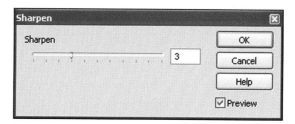

Figure 4.26 • Sharpen Dialog Box

1. Crop an image within the Dreamweaver environment by completing the following steps:
   a. Create a new HTML document and use the Save or Save As commands to name and save it as **ch4ex09.htm**.
   b. Make a duplicate of **toadstools.jpg**, rename it **toadstools3.jpg**, and insert it into **ch4ex09.htm**. *Hint: See Exercise 8, Steps 1b–1d for instructions on doing this.*
   c. Select the image and then click the Image Property inspector Crop button. A message will appear informing you that the changes you are about to make will permanently affect the selected image. Click the OK button to close the message. *Note: Click the OK button to close this message whenever you see it.*

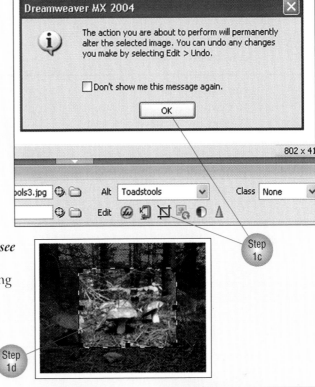

   d. Click and drag the crop bounding image crop handles toward the center of the image to crop the image so that only the three toadstools in the center of the image are visible. Click the Crop button again to implement the crop. The image contained within the boundaries of the crop bounding image will appear in the document.

2. Resample a resized image by completing the following steps:
   a. Select the image and drag the diagonal selection handle outward to expand the image about half an inch. Note that the image appears slightly blurry. Although you have enlarged the image in the Document window, its file size remains the same, and it will be difficult to predict how it will display when viewed in a browser.

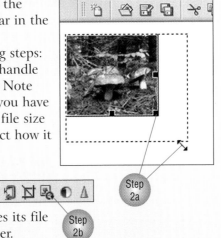

   b. With the image selected, click the Resample button. The image should now appear somewhat more focused. In addition, the image size as displayed now matches its file size so the image will display properly in a browser.

3. Change image brightness and contrast values by completing the following steps:
   a. Select the image.
   b. Click the Image Property inspector Brightness and Contrast button to open the Brightness/Contrast dialog box.

c. Experiment by clicking and dragging the *Brightness* and *Contrast* sliders to change those values. As you move the sliders, the changes will be visible in the Document window. When you are finished, specify the image brightness at 40 and the contrast at 43. Click the OK button to close the dialog box.

4. Sharpen an image by completing the following steps:

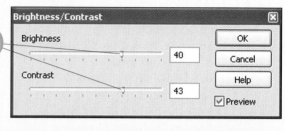

Step 3c

a. Select the image.

b. Click the Image Property inspector Sharpen button to open the Sharpen dialog box.

Step 4b

c. Click and drag the *Sharpen* slider to change the image sharpness. As you move the slider, you can see the changes to the image sharpness take effect. When you are finished, specify the image sharpness as 5. Click the OK button to close the dialog box.

Step 4c

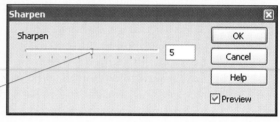

5. Save **ch4ex09.htm** and then close it.

Creating a Page Background Image

The Page Properties dialog box Appearance page shown in Figure 4.27 can be used to insert a ***background image,*** an image that fills an entire page. If the image is not large enough to fill the entire page by itself, it will ***tile*** (repeat) on the page until it does, as shown in Figure 4.28. With the large monitors in use today, an image should be at least 1,000 pixels wide and 600 pixels high to avoid tiling. Large background images can slow page loading, so ensure that the image file size is as small as possible. Because background images can drown out page content, be careful to choose an image that allows the page content to be easily read and that does not clash with it. Background images can be modified using any image editor.

Clicking Modify on the Menu bar and then Page Properties opens the Page Properties dialog box, which opens to the Appearance page by default. The dialog box also can be opened by clicking the Properties button in the Image Property inspector, or by right-clicking in a document and then clicking Page Properties. The

Figure 4.27
Page Properties Dialog Box

Background image Browse button

DREAMWEAVER MX 2004

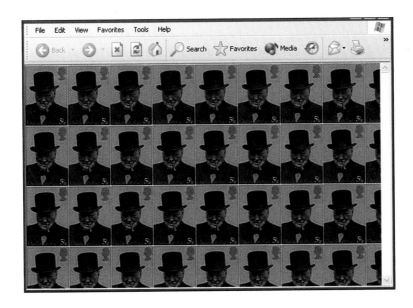

Figure 4.28
Tiled Background Image

Background image text box appears on the Page Properties dialog box Appearance page. The Browse button next to the *Background image* text box can then be used to browse and select a background image. Cascading Style Sheets can be used for a greater degree of control over background image properties and will be covered in Chapter 6, *Using Cascading Style Sheets (CSS)*.

exercise 10

ADDING A BACKGROUND IMAGE TO A WEB PAGE

1. Add a tiled background image to a Web page by completing the following steps:
   a. At a clear document screen, open **ch4ex06.htm** and use the Save As command to rename and save it as **ch4ex10.htm**.
   b. Click Modify on the Menu bar and then Page Properties to open the Page Properties dialog box. If necessary, click *Appearance* in the *Category* list box to select it.
   c. Click the Browse button next to the *Background image* text box to open the Select Image Source dialog box.
   d. Use the Select Image Source dialog box to locate the student file named **woodgrain.jpg** in the ch_04_student_files folder, and select it as the page background image. Click the OK button to close the Select Image Source dialog box.

   Step 1c

   Step 1d

   e. Click the OK button to close the Page Properties dialog box.
   f. Click the Preview/Debug in browser button and then click Preview in iexplore to view the page in a browser. If you take a close look at the page, you will see that because of the small size of the image, it has tiled, or repeated itself, across the page. Close the browser when you are finished.
   g. Save **ch4ex10.htm** and then close it.

2. Add a nontiling background image to a Web page by completing the following steps:
   a. At a clear document screen, open **ch4ex06.htm** and use the Save As command to rename and save it as **ch4ex010-a.htm**.
   b. Complete Steps 1b–1e to locate the student file named **tank.jpg** in the ch_04_student_files folder and select it as the page background image.
   c. Click the Preview/Debug in browser button and then click Preview in iexplore to view the page in a browser. Note that the image does not tile because it is large enough to occupy the entire window, but the image's white space blends into the image in an unattractive way. Close the browser when you are finished.

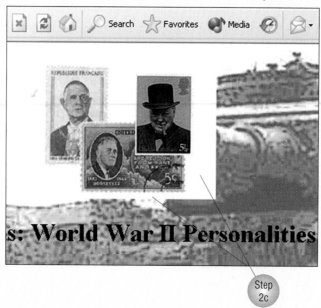

Step 2c

   d. In the Document window, click the image in **ch4ex010-a.htm** to select it. *Hint: Click the white space around stamps, not the stamps. If you click one of the stamps, the Hotspot Property inspector appears instead of the Image Property inspector.*
   e. Type 5 in the Image Property inspector *Border* text box.

Step 2e

   f. Click the Preview/Debug in browser button and then click Preview in iexplore to view the page in a browser. The border helps delineate the image and make the page more attractive. Close the browser when you are finished.

Step 2f

3. Save **ch4ex010-a.htm** and then close it.

Creating Table and Table Cell Background Images

Background images can be added to tables and table cells by selecting them and using the Image Property inspector Point to File or Browse for File buttons to browse to and locate the desired background image.

1. Insert background images into tables, nested tables, and table cells by completing the following steps:

   a. At a clear document screen, open **ch3ex08.htm** and use the Save As command to rename and save it to the ch_04_exercises root folder as **ch4ex11.htm**.

   Step 1b

   b. Click inside the first column of the first table row.

   c. Click <table#Parent Table> in the Tag selector to select the parent table.

   Step 1c

   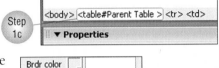

   d. Use the Table Property inspector *Bg Image* text box Point to File or Browse for File buttons to browse and locate the student file named **brick.jpg** in the ch_04_student_files folder, and select it as the table background image. Note that the background image covers the entire table, including the nested table portion of the table.

   e. Position the insertion point in the second column of the second table row. ***Hint: With the background in place, it may be difficult to distinguish the rows and columns. To make viewing easier, click the Insert bar Layout menu item or tab and then click the Expanded button. When you are finished selecting items, click the Standard button to return to Standard mode.***

   Step 1d   Step 1e

   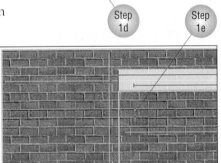

   f. Click <table#Nested Table> in the Tag selector to select the nested table.

   Step 1f

   g. Use the Table Property inspector *Bg Image* text box Point to File or Browse for File buttons to browse and locate the student file named **woodgrain.jpg** in the ch_04_student_files folder and select it as the table background image. Note that the nested table background image overrides the parent table background image.

   Step 1h

   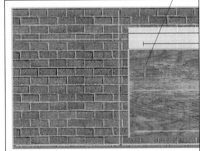

   h. If necessary, position the insertion point in the second column of the second table row again.

   i. Use the Table Cell Property inspector *Bg* text box Point to File or Browse for File buttons to browse and select the student file named **blonde_wood.jpg** in the ch_04_student_files folder and select it as the table cell background image. The selected table cell now has its own background image that overrides the parent and nested table background images.

   Step 1i

   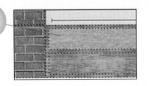

2. Save **ch4ex11.htm** and then close it.

Applying Behaviors to Images

Behaviors allow you to create **interactive Web pages** that let viewers change various aspects of a Web page or perform tasks. Dreamweaver MX 2004 uses JavaScript code to create behaviors. A behavior **event**, such as placing the pointer over an image, is used in conjunction with an **action** that will take place when the event occurs. In the case of a rollover image, an image that changes when the pointer rolls over it, the event is the hovering of the pointer over the image, and the action is the image changing once this event takes place.

Three behaviors are associated with images: preload images, swap image, and swap image restore. **Preload images** ensures that an image will be loaded in the browser and ready when an event requiring an action takes place. If an image is not preloaded, there might be a delay in the action triggered by an event because the browser must search for and load the image. **Swap image** is used to swap or replace one image with another. **Swap image restore** instructs a browser to display the original source image when a swap image event is over. If swap image restore is not selected, the second image in a swapped image set will remain on display rather than revert to the pre-event image. These three behaviors can be used to create rollovers, navigation bars, and other image effects.

The easiest way to add behaviors to images is by using the Insert bar (Common menu item or tab) Rollover Image or Navigation Bar commands located on the Images button drop-down menu as shown in Figure 4.29, or by clicking Insert on the Menu bar, pointing to Image Objects, and then clicking Rollover Image or Navigation Bar. Behaviors can be modified using the Behaviors panel located under the Tag panel group. Creating navigation bars is covered in Chapter 5, *Working with Frames*.

Rollover images are images that change when the mouse pointer is moved across the image when viewed in a browser. The change in appearance is accomplished by using two images: a **primary image** that appears when the page is first displayed, and a **secondary image** that appears when the pointer is moved across the primary image. In the Insert Rollover Image dialog box, Dreamweaver MX 2004 refers to primary images as original images and secondary images as rollover images. A common use for rollovers is to create buttons that appear to be illuminated or dimmed when clicked. When used for that purpose, a link is made to another document that will open when the rollover image is clicked. Rollover images should be the same size. If images with different sizes are used in a rollover image pair, Dreamweaver MX 2004 automatically resizes the secondary image to match the primary image. Rollover images will not function when viewed in the Document window, so they need to be previewed in a browser to see that they work as intended.

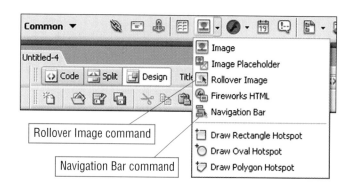

Figure 4.29
Rollover Image and
Navigation Bar Buttons

DREAMWEAVER MX 2004

Clicking the Insert bar (Common menu item or tab) Images button down-pointing arrow and then clicking Rollover Image from the drop-down menu or dragging the Rollover Image button or command to a document opens the Insert Rollover Image dialog box shown in Figure 4.30. Clicking Insert on the Menu bar, pointing to Image Objects, and then clicking Rollover Image is another way to open the dialog box.

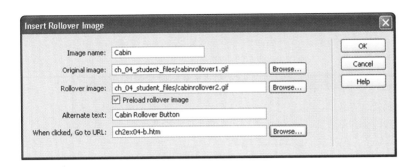

exercise 12

CREATING A ROLLOVER IMAGE

1. Create a rollover image by completing the following steps:
   a. At a clear document screen, open **ch4ex03.htm** and use the Save As command to rename and save it as **ch4ex12.htm**.
   b. Position the insertion point in the first column of the second row of the table.
   c. Click the Common menu item or tab on the Insert bar.
   d. Click the Images button down-pointing arrow and then click Rollover Image from the drop-down menu to open the Insert Rollover Image dialog box.

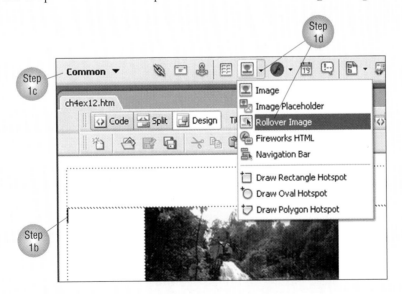

e. Type **Cabin Rollover Image** in the *Image name* text box.

f. Use the *Original image* and *Rollover image* text box Browse buttons to browse and select the student files named **cabinrollover1.gif** and **cabinrollover2.gif** in the ch_04_student_files folder. **Cabinrollover1.gif** goes in the *Original image* text box and **cabinrollover2.gif** goes in the *Rollover image* text box.

g. If a check mark is not in the *Preload rollover image* check box, click it to select that option.

h. Type **Rollover image of cabin** in the *Alternate text* text box.

i. Click the *When clicked, Go to URL* text box Browse button to browse and locate **ch4ex02.htm**.

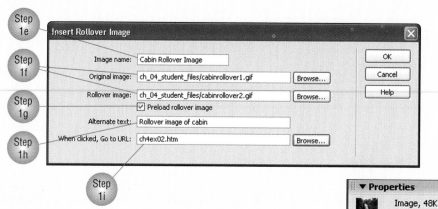

j. Click the OK button to make a link from the rollover image to **ch4ex02.htm**. Click the OK button to close the Insert Rollover Image dialog box.

k. In the Document window, click the waterfall image in the second column to select it, and type **20** in the Image Property inspector *H Space* text box to create some space between the rollover image and the adjacent image.

l. Click the Preview/Debug in browser button and then click Preview in iexplore to view the document. Move the pointer over the rollover image to see the image change. Click the image to link to **ch4ex02.htm**. Close the browser when you are finished.

2. Save **ch4ex12.htm** and then close it.

Creating a Web Photo Album

A **Web photo album** consists of a Web page with thumbnail image links to all of the photos in the album. Clicking a thumbnail opens a new page containing a larger copy of the image, and, if desired, the page can include navigation links as shown in Figure 4.31. During the Web photo album creation process, Dreamweaver MX 2004 automatically opens Fireworks MX 2004 to create the thumbnails and larger images, provided that Fireworks MX 2004 is installed on your computer. A **source images folder** containing all of the images that will be placed in the Web photo album must be chosen before the Web photo album creation process can begin. All folder images in formats recognized by the Create Web Photo Album command (GIF, JPG, JPEG, PNG, PSD, TIF, or TIFF) are included in the album. Clicking Commands on the Menu bar and then Create Web Photo Album opens the Create Web Photo Album dialog box shown in Figure 4.32. The dialog box allows you to set the following Web photo album properties:

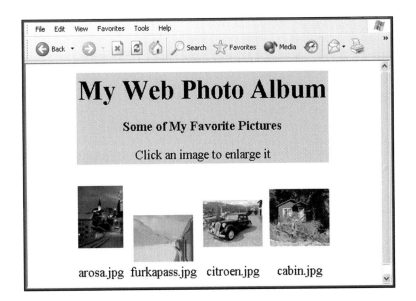

Figure 4.31
Web Photo Album Page

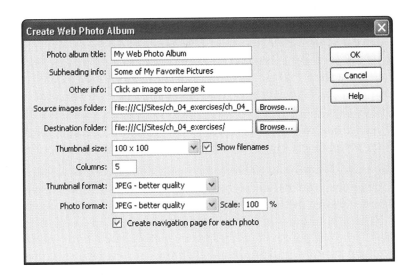

Figure 4.32
Create Web Photo Album
Dialog Box

- *Photo album title/Subheading info/Other info* Three lines of text can appear on the Web photo album page. The title is displayed in H1 text, the subheading in H4 text, and other information in a browser's default text size. Web photo albums must contain a title, but subheading and other information text are optional.

- *Source images folder* The *Source images folder* text box contains the path to the folder containing the images that will be used to create the Web photo album. The Browse button can be used to locate and select the folder. The folder does not have to be located in a site.

- *Destination folder* This text box is used to locate and select the **destination folder,** the folder in a site where the Web photo album pages and associated documents will be stored. The Browse button can be used to locate and select the folder. *Note: If the destination folder already contains a photo album, Dreamweaver MX 2004 might overwrite any of the thumbnail and image files that share the same name and extension as images in the new Web photo album. This problem can be avoided by either saving the new Web photo album to a different folder or by* *ensuring that the images in the new album do not share names with images in the existing album. Dreamweaver MX 2004 displays a warning before writing over an image file, so you can choose not to write over a file.*

- **Thumbnail size** Use the drop-down list to choose the size of the thumbnail images that will appear on the Web photo album page. There are five dimensions to choose from, ranging in size from 36 × 36 pixels to 200 × 200 pixels. Image file names appear under the thumbnails unless the check mark is removed from the *Show filenames* check box.

- **Columns** Thumbnail images are displayed in columns across the Web photo album Web page. You can type the number of columns desired, but should avoid creating pages that are so wide that viewers must scroll horizontally across the page to see all of the thumbnails. Choosing smaller thumbnails means that more columns can fit on a page without the need for scrolling.

- **Thumbnail format/Photo format** Choose from four different image file formats for the thumbnail and image files in the drop-down list: *GIF webSnap 128, GIF webSnap 256, JPEG - better quality,* and *JPEG - smaller file.* As a general rule, GIF images are best suited for drawings or illustrations, while JPEG images are best for photographs.

- **Scale** A scale of 100 percent means that Web photo album images will be the same size as the original images they were created from. You might want to reduce the scale depending on the size of the original images. Increasing the scale more than 100 percent will result in reduced image quality. *Note: If you want all images to appear in the same size, the images must be resized to the same size using an image editor before an album is created.*

- **Create navigation page for each photo** If this option is checked, Dreamweaver MX 2004 places <u>Back</u>, <u>Home</u>, and <u>Next</u> navigation links on each album page.

Clicking the OK button begins the Web photo album creation process after all of the dialog box properties have been set. Fireworks MX 2004 opens and a Batch Progress message box appears to let you know which images are being processed. When the process is finished, a Dreamweaver MX 2004 message box tells you that the Web photo album has been created. The album will not work in the Document window, so you should click the Preview/Debug in browser button and then click Preview in iexplore to preview the pages in a browser.

exercise **13**

CREATING A WEB PHOTO ALBUM

1. Create a Web photo album by completing the following steps:
   a. At a clear document screen, create a new HTML document.
   b. Click Commands on the Menu bar and then Create Web Photo Album to open the Create Web Photo Album dialog box.

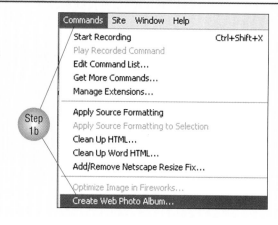

DREAMWEAVER MX 2004

c. Type **My Web Photo Album** in the dialog box *Photo album title* text box.

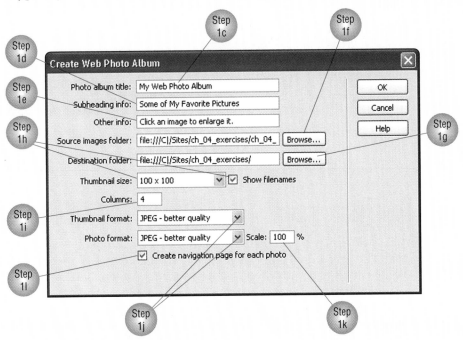

d. Type **Some of My Favorite Pictures** in the *Subheading info* text box.
e. Type **Click an image to enlarge it.** in the *Other info* text box.
f. Click the *Source images folder* text box Browse button to open the Choose a folder dialog box. Browse and locate the photo_album_images folder located inside the ch_04_student_files folder. This folder contains the photos to be placed in the photo album. After you have located the folder, double-click the folder to place it in the *Select* text box and then click the Select button. ***Note: When you have located the folder, its contents will not be visible in the Choose a folder dialog box. When creating photo albums, you should use the Files panel or another file browser to verify that a folder contains the images you want to include in the photo album.***
g. Click the *Destination folder* text box Browse button to open the Choose a folder dialog box. Browse and locate the ch_04_exercises root folder. After you have located the folder, double-click the folder to place it in the *Select* text box and then click the Select button.
h. Click the *Thumbnail size* list box down-pointing arrow and, if necessary, select *100 × 100* from the drop-down list. Make sure that the *Show filenames* check box contains a check mark.
i. Type **4** in the *Columns* text box to display the four images across a page.
j. If necessary, click the down-pointing arrows next to the *Thumbnail format* and *Photo format* list boxes to open their drop-down lists and select *JPEG - better quality*.
k. If necessary, type **100** in the *Scale* text box.
l. Make sure there is a check mark in the *Create navigation page for each photo* check box.
m. Click the OK button. Fireworks MX 2004 opens and creates the images and thumbnails for the Web photo album, and Dreamweaver MX 2004 creates and saves a Web photo album page named **index.htm**. When the process is finished, a message box reading *Album created* appears. Click the OK button to close the message box. ***Note: Dreamweaver MX 2004 also automatically creates subfolders named images, pages, and thumbnails to contain all of the material contained in the Web photo album.***

n. Right-click the Fireworks button on the Taskbar, and then click Close to close Fireworks.

o. Click the Preview/Debug in browser button and then click Preview in iexplore to view the photo album. Click the links and images to see that they work. Close the browser when you are finished.

2. Close **index.htm**.

Step 1n

Using Tracing Images

Web page designers often create prototype page layouts by sketching them with pen and paper or in a graphics program. ***Tracing images*** is a method that facilitates the transition from prototype layout to actual page by letting designers copy a prototype layout as if they were using tracing paper. Any GIF, JPEG, or PNG image can be used as a tracing image. Hand sketches can be scanned and saved for use as tracing images as long as they are saved in a recognized image format. After an image is inserted as a tracing image, it appears in the Document window at a user-specified level of transparency so that tables or layers can be placed over it to emulate a tracing image layout as shown in Figure 4.33. The tracing image process cannot create an exact reproduction of the page, but is useful as a fairly close guide to positioning. If a document already has a background image, it will block a tracing image, so the tracing image process should be completed before inserting a background image.

You can insert tracing images by clicking Modify on the Menu bar and then Page Properties to open the Page Properties dialog box. The dialog box contains a *Tracing image* text box as shown in Figure 4.34. Use the Browse button to the right of the text box to locate and select the tracing image. After the tracing image has been selected, you can adjust its degree of transparency using the *Transparency* slider. Click the OK button in the Page Properties dialog box to insert the tracing

Figure 4.33
A Web Page Used as a Tracing Image

DREAMWEAVER MX 2004

image in the current document. After clicking the OK button, a dialog box prompts you to save a copy of the image to the current document's root folder if that has not been done yet.

Tracing images also can be inserted by clicking View on the Menu bar, pointing to Tracing Image, and then clicking Load. This opens the Select Image Source dialog box that can be used to locate and select the tracing image. If the image is located outside the current document's root folder, a dialog box appears prompting you to save a copy of the image to the root folder. After that, the Page Properties dialog box automatically opens, allowing you to set the desired transparency level for the tracing image you have chosen.

The left corner of a tracing image is positioned starting at the upper-left corner of the document. Tracing image position can be adjusted by clicking View, pointing to Tracing Image, and then clicking Adjust Position. This opens the Adjust Tracing Image Position dialog box shown in Figure 4.35. The dialog box can be used to enter *x* and *y* coordinates to move the tracing image. The original *x* and *y* coordinates of an inserted tracing image are *0,0*. Tracing image positioning can be reset to *0,0* at any time by clicking View, pointing to Tracing Image, and then clicking Reset Position. The tracing image position also can be adjusted while the Adjust Tracing Image Position dialog box is open by using the arrow keys to move it 1 pixel at a time. Holding down the Shift key while pressing an arrow key moves the tracing image 5 pixels at a time. Tracing images also can be made to line up with a selected page element (such as a table, layer, or image) by clicking View, pointing to Tracing Image, and then clicking Align with Selection.

Tracing images are not visible in browsers, but can be removed after a design is complete by removing the path to the image in the Page Properties dialog box *Tracing image* text box.

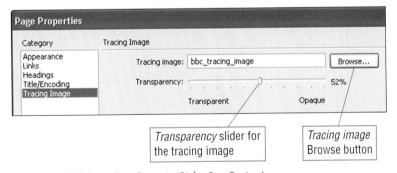

Figure 4.34 • Page Properties Dialog Box–Tracing Image

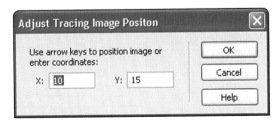

Figure 4.35 • Adjust Tracing Image Position Dialog Box

1. Use a tracing image to create a layout table by completing the following steps:
   a. At a clear document screen, create a new HTML document and use the Save or Save As commands to name and save it as **ch4ex14.htm**.
   b. Click Modify on the Menu bar and then Page Properties to open the Page Properties dialog box. If necessary, click *Tracing Image* in the dialog box *Category* list box.

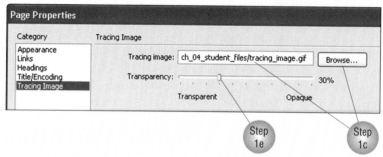

   c. Click the *Tracing image* Browse button to open the Select Image Source dialog box.
   d. Browse and locate the student file named **tracing_image.gif** in the ch_04_student_files folder. Click the Select Image Source dialog box OK button after you have located the image.
   e. Click the *Transparency* slider and drag it to 30 percent.
   f. Click the Page Properties dialog box OK button. The tracing image appears in the Document window.
   g. Click the Layout menu item or tab on the Insert bar, and then click the Layout button. ***Note: Click OK if the Getting Started in Layout View message box appears.***
   h. Click the Layout Table button and position the crosshairs in the upper-left corner of the tracing image. Drag the crosshairs diagonally down the page until you reach the bottom of the tracing image. Release the mouse button to complete the table.

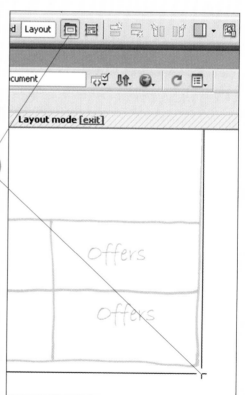

   i. Click the Draw Layout Cell button to draw table cells over the table cells pictured in the tracing image. ***Hint: Holding down the Ctrl key when clicking the Draw Layout Cell button allows you to draw cells without having to click the button each time. Note: If you draw a table cell incorrectly, click Edit on the Menu bar and then Undo. Resizing layout cells was discussed in Chapter 3.***
   j. When the layout table is complete, click the Standard View button on the Insert bar.
   k. Click inside the table and then click <table> in the Tag selector to select the table.

l. Type 1 in the Table Property inspector *Border* text box so that you can see the table when you preview it in a browser. ***Note: When tables are used for page layout they usually have invisible borders.***

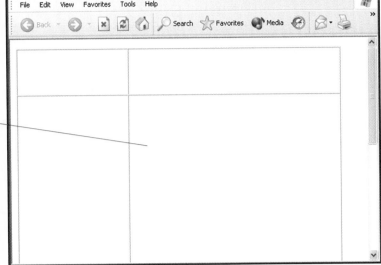

m. Click the Preview/Debug in browser button and then click Preview in iexplore to view the page. Note that the tracing image is not visible when the page is viewed in a browser. Close the browser when you are finished.

2. Save **ch4ex14.htm** and then close it.

Using the Assets Panel to Manage Images

Dreamweaver MX 2004 automatically stores all of the images used in the current site in the Assets panel. The list of images can be viewed by clicking the Images button located on the left side of the Assets panel and then clicking the *Site* radio button as shown in Figure 4.36. Clicking an image displays it as a thumbnail at the top of the panel.

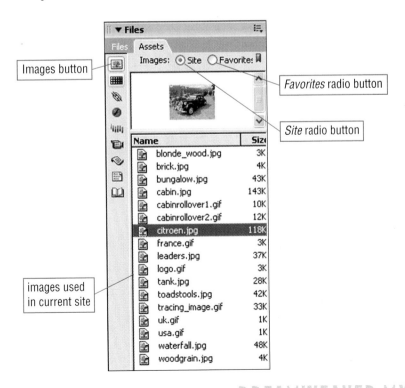

Figure 4.36
Assets Panel

Images listed in the Assets panel can be inserted into a current document by clicking the image listing and dragging it to the document, or by placing the insertion point in the desired image location, clicking the image listing, and then clicking the Insert button at the bottom of the panel.

Favorites List

Large sites can contain so many assets that you might have trouble locating an asset you want to use. To avoid this problem, you can save frequently used assets, including images, to the ***Assets panel Favorites list***. The Favorites list works just like the Site list, but it is more manageable because you can control the content of the list. You can view images stored in the Favorites list by clicking the Images button on the left side of the Assets panel and then clicking the *Favorites* radio button as shown in Figure 4.36.

Images in the Document window can be added to the Favorites list by selecting the image, right-clicking, and then clicking Add to Image Favorites as shown in Figure 4.37 or by selecting an image and then clicking the Assets panel Add to Favorites button (Site list view) located in the lower-right corner of the panel as shown in Figure 4.38. Images already listed in the Site list can be copied to the Favorites list by selecting an image listing and clicking the Assets panel Add to Favorites button (Site list view) or by selecting an image listing, right-clicking, and then clicking Add to Favorites. Assets can be removed from the Favorites list by selecting the asset and clicking the Assets panel Remove from Favorites button (Favorites list view) located in the lower-right corner of the panel as shown in Figure 4.39.

Favorites List Folders

You can have even more control over your images by using ***Favorites list folders*** to categorize them. For example, folders could be created under the Favorites list

Figure 4.37 • Add to Image Favorites Context Menu Command

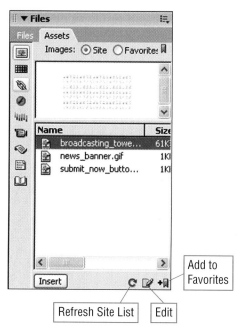

Figure 4.38 • Assets Panel Site List View

DREAMWEAVER MX 2004

to store images by topic, such as cats, flags, or people as shown in Figure 4.39. You can create folders by clicking the New Favorites Folder button located in the lower-left corner of the Assets panel when in Favorites list view. After the folder appears in the Favorites list, you can type a name for the folder. To remove folders and their contents, select them and click the Remove from Favorites button.

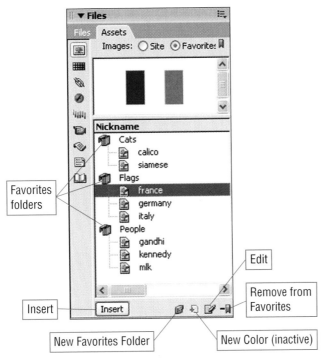

Favorites folders

Insert

New Favorites Folder

Edit

Remove from Favorites

New Color (inactive)

Figure 4.39
Assets Panel Favorites List View

 exercise 15

USING THE ASSETS PANEL TO MANAGE IMAGES

1. Use the Assets panel to insert images by completing the following steps:
   a. At a clear document screen, create a new HTML document and use the Save or Save As commands to name and save it as **ch4ex15.htm**.
   b. With the Files panel open, click the Assets panel tab and then the Images button on the left side of the Assets panel.
   c. Click the *Site* radio button to see a list of all of the images in use at the current site.
   d. Click *citroen.jpg* and look for its thumbnail image at the top of the Assets panel.
   e. Click and drag *citroen.jpg* over to the Document window to insert it in **ch4ex15.htm**.
   f. An Image Tag Accessibility Attributes dialog box appears after dragging the image if the *Images* check box option has been selected in the Preferences dialog box Accessibility page. Type **Citroen automobile** in the *Alternate text* text box and then click the OK button.

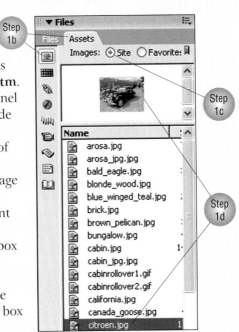

Step 1b

Step 1c

Step 1d

g. Position the insertion point to the right of the image and press Enter to place the insertion point below the image.

h. Click *cabin.jpg* and then click the Insert button at the bottom of the Assets panel to insert the cabin image below the car image in **ch4ex15.htm**. Type **Cabin** in the Image Tag Accessibility Attributes dialog box *Alternate text* text box and then click the OK button.

2. Add and remove Assets panel favorite images by completing the following steps:

a. Right-click the car image and then click Add to Image Favorites from the context-sensitive menu that appears. The Assets panel switches to the Favorites list view and shows that the car image has been saved to the Favorites list as *citroen*.

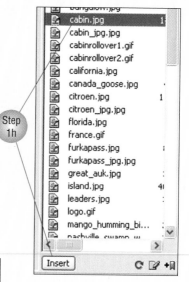

Step 1h

Step 2a

b. Click the Assets panel *Site* radio button to view the images used in the current site again.

c. Click *cabin.jpg*.

d. Click the Add to Favorites button in the lower-right corner of the Assets panel in Site list view. A message box might appear advising that the image has been added to the Favorites list and that it can be viewed by clicking the *Favorites* radio button. Click the OK button to close the message box if necessary. ***Note: The message box has a check box that can be checked if you do not want to see the message box again. If someone has already placed a check mark in this box, you will not see this message.***

e. Click the *Favorites* radio button to verify that *cabin* was added to the Favorites list.

3. Create an Assets panel Favorites folder by completing the following steps:

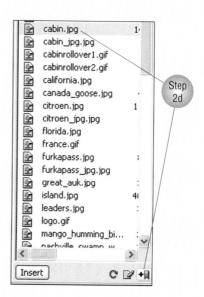

Step 2d

DREAMWEAVER MX 2004

a. Click the New Favorites Folder button located at the bottom-left side of the Assets panel (Favorites list view).

b. Type **Country Images** over the untitled text next to the new folder image.

c. Click *cabin* and drag it to the Country Images folder. The Assets panel Favorites list view now shows *cabin* stored under the Country Images folder.

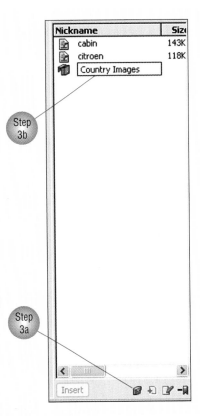

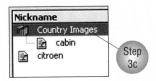

d. Delete the Country Images folder by selecting it and then clicking the Remove from Favorites button in the lower-right corner of the Assets panel (Favorites list view) or by pressing the Delete or Backspace keys. *Note: The images within the folder are also deleted.*

4. Save **ch4ex15.htm** and then close it.

CHAPTER summary

➤ Web page images are located separately from HTML documents, with an HTML image tag (<img>) and source attribute (**src**) directing the browser to an image file location so that the file can be retrieved and displayed in the document containing the image tag and source attribute.

➤ The time required for a browser to display a Web page is a function of the size of all of the various files involved.

➤ The file size of an HTML page plus all of its images added together should be less than 100 KB whenever possible.

➤ If the same image is repeated on a page, it does not increase loading time because the image file needs to be loaded only once by a browser.

➤ The three image formats supported by all browsers are GIF (Graphics Interchange Format), JPEG (Joint Photographic Experts Group), and PNG (Portable Network Graphics).

➤ GIF variations feature interlacing (gradual appearance when loading), transparency (background colors can show through the image), and animation.

➤ GIF is the best format for displaying drawings or illustrations, and JPEG is the best format for displaying photographs.

➤ Because of the compression technology used, a JPEG file will be smaller than a comparable GIF file when used to display large images.

➤ PNG images offer interlacing and transparency, and produce smaller file sizes than GIF or JPEG formats, but are not as well supported.

➤ After an image has been selected, the Select Images Source dialog box displays a thumbnail (a much smaller copy of the image) if the *Preview images* check box has been selected.

➤ Image alternate text descriptions will be interpreted by screen readers, and they will also appear in the latest browser versions as a descriptive tooltip when the pointer is moved over the image.

➤ Alternate text should be limited to less than 50 characters.

➤ A <u>D</u> link (description link) is a hyperlink positioned next to an image and linking to a long description file.

➤ To streamline the design process, temporary image placeholders can be placed in a document wherever images are planned.

➤ Placeholder alternate text is automatically transferred to the image replacing it.

➤ After an image placeholder has been inserted, its dimensions can be adjusted by selecting it and then dragging the horizontal, vertical, or diagonal resize handles in the desired direction.

➤ Entering new values in the Image Property inspector *W* and *H* text boxes or Tag Editor - Img dialog box *Width* and *Height* text boxes is another way to change placeholder dimensions.

➤ When a placeholder is replaced by an image, the new image is inserted in its actual dimensions, not in the placeholder dimensions.

➤ Both the Image Property inspector and the Tag Editor - Img dialog box can be used to change image and image placeholder properties.

➤ An image placeholder can be replaced with an image by double-clicking the placeholder.

➤ A browser will still display an image without width and height information, but it might take longer because the browser must first download the image in order to estimate the size of the image file.

➤ Changing the height and width specifications of an image tag or resizing an image by dragging its resize handles does not affect the file's size in bytes, and might create image distortion.

➤ Images should be resized by using an image editor or by using the Image Property inspector Resample button to resample the resized image.

➤ An image can function as a link if a path to a link target is entered in the Image Property inspector *Link* text box.

➤ Selecting an image and clicking the Image Property inspector Edit button opens an image editor that can be used to modify the selected image.

➤ Clicking the Image Property inspector Reset Size button restores an image's original dimensions if they have been modified by resizing or by typing new dimensions.

➤ Vertical space adds a cushion of space above and below an image, while horizontal space adds a cushion of space to the left and to the right of an image.

➤ If an image is being used as a link, you can specify the browser window that the link target opens in by clicking the desired choice from the Image Property inspector *Target* drop-down list.

➤ Image alignment affects the position of an image in relation to surrounding text or page elements.

➤ Low source images are usually black-and-white versions of an image that load before the main image.

DREAMWEAVER MX 2004

➤ Image maps are images containing hotspots that link to other documents when clicked.

➤ An image editor can be opened to work with images by clicking the Image Property inspector Edit button.

➤ Simple image editing such as cropping, adjusting brightness and contrast, and increasing or decreasing image sharpness can be performed within the Dreamweaver MX 2004 environment by using Image Property inspector Crop, Brightness and Contract, and Sharpen buttons.

➤ The Page Properties dialog box can be used to insert an image that will fill the background of a page.

➤ If a background image is not large enough to fill the entire page, it will tile (repeat) on the page.

➤ With the large monitors in use today, an image should be at least 1,000 pixels wide and 600 pixels high to avoid tiling.

➤ Large background images can slow page loading, so designers should ensure that the image file size is as small as possible.

➤ Background images can be added to tables and table cells by selecting them and using the Image Property inspector Point to File or Browse for File buttons to browse to and locate the desired background image.

➤ Behaviors allow the creation of interactive Web pages that let viewers change various aspects of a page or perform tasks.

➤ Behavior events, such as placing the pointer over an image, are used in conjunction with an action that will take place when the event occurs.

➤ Three behaviors are associated with images: preload images, swap image, and swap image restore. Preload images ensures that an image will be loaded in the browser and ready when an event requiring an action takes place. Swap image is used to swap or replace one image with another. Swap image restore instructs a browser to display the original source image when a swap image event is over.

➤ The easiest way to add behaviors to images is by using the Rollover Image or Navigation Bar commands on the Insert bar (Common menu item or tab) Images button drop-down menu.

➤ Behaviors can be modified using the Behaviors panel located under the Tag panel group.

➤ Rollover images are images that change when the mouse pointer is moved across the image when viewed in a browser.

➤ Rollovers consist of two images: a primary image that appears when the page is first displayed and a secondary image that appears when the pointer is moved across the primary image.

➤ If images with different sizes are used in a rollover image pair, Dreamweaver MX 2004 automatically resizes the secondary image to match the primary image.

➤ Web photo albums consist of a Web page with thumbnails image links for all of the photos in the album.

➤ During the Web photo album creation process, Dreamweaver MX 2004 automatically opens Fireworks MX 2004 to create the thumbnail and larger-size album images, provided that Fireworks MX 2004 is installed on your computer.

➤ Tracing images is a method that facilitates the transition from prototype layout to actual page by letting designers copy a prototype layout as if they were using tracing paper.

➤ Any GIF, JPEG, or PNG image can be used as a tracing image.

➤ After an image is inserted as a tracing image, it appears in the Document window at a user-specified level of transparency so that tables or layers can be placed over it to emulate a tracing image layout.

➤ Holding down the Shift key while pressing an arrow key moves the tracing image 5 pixels at a time.

➤ Tracing images are not visible in browsers, but can be removed after a design is complete by removing the path to the image in the Page Properties *Tracing image* text box.

➤ Dreamweaver MX 2004 automatically stores all of the images used in the current site in the Assets panel.

➤ Images listed in the Assets panel can be inserted into a current document by clicking the image listing and dragging it to the document or by placing the insertion point in the desired image location, clicking the image listing, and then clicking the Insert button at the bottom of the panel.

➤ A degree of image management can be obtained by using Favorites list folders to further categorize images.

KEY terms

absolute bottom image alignment Aligns the bottom of an image with the bottom of a line of text, including portions of the text that descend below the text baseline, such as *y* or *g*.

absolute middle image alignment Aligns the middle of an image with the middle of the text.

action See *behaviors*.

alternate text description Accessibility feature that provides a description of an image that is interpreted by screen readers, and also appears in the latest browser versions as a descriptive tooltip when the pointer is moved over the image.

animated graphics Images that appear to move, created by using multiple images that change incrementally.

Assets panel Favorites list Frequently used assets such as images or URLs can be saved in the Assets panel Favorites list and reused.

background image An image that fills the background of a page.

baseline image alignment Aligns the baseline of text or elements to the bottom of a selected image.

behaviors JavaScript code that enables the creation of interactive Web pages. Behaviors consist of events that trigger actions, such as a mouse hovering over an image (event) that causes a new image to appear (action).

bottom image alignment Like baseline, aligns the baseline of text or elements to the bottom of a selected object.

crosshairs (plus sign) Pointer shape (+) when designing tables in Layout mode, creating hotspots, working with layers, and other activities.

D link (description link) A hyperlink linking to a long description file and positioned next to the image. A D link is an alternative to using a long description, which is poorly supported by browsers.

default image alignment Browsers usually interpret default as a baseline alignment, aligning text or elements to the bottom of an image.

destination folder The folder where Web photo album pages and associated documents are stored.

event See *behaviors*.

Favorites list folders Folders that can be used to organize assets in the Assets panel Favorites list.

GIF images Most commonly used image format on the Web, with several varieties that support interlacing, transparency, or animation.

horizontal space A cushion of space to the left and to the right of an image.

hotspots Areas of an image map that link to other documents when clicked. Also called *image maps*.

image maps Images containing hotspots that link to other documents when clicked. See *hotspots*.

image placeholders Dreamweaver MX 2004 feature that allows users to visualize how images will work on a page by inserting a temporary placeholder in a planned image location. The placeholder can later be replaced by an image.

image tag The HTML tag (<img>) used in conjunction with a source attribute (**src**) to direct a browser to an image file location so that the file can be retrieved and displayed as part of a Web page.

interactive Web pages Web pages that allow users to interact with pages by performing tasks or changing page content.

interlacing Feature of some GIF images that allow them to be displayed gradually, somewhat like a picture slowly coming into focus.

JPEG images Image file format that is best for photographs.

left image alignment Aligns an image to the left margin, with text wrapped around the image to the right.

long description Image accessibility feature providing a link to a file containing a longer description of an image.

low source image A smaller file size version of an image that loads first, often in black and white. The purpose is to let people with slower Internet connections see an image without having to wait for the image to fully download.

middle image alignment Aligns the middle of an image with the baseline of an image or text.

PNG images Image format that offers interlacing and transparency, and produces smaller file sizes than the GIF or JPEG formats.

preload images Behavior that ensures that an image will be loaded in the browser and ready when an event requiring an action takes place. See *behaviors*.

primary image Image that first appears when a rollover image is displayed. Referred to in Dreamweaver MX 2004 as the original image.

right image alignment Aligns an image to the right margin, with text wrapped around the image to the left.

rollover images Images that change when the mouse pointer is moved across the image when viewed in a browser.

secondary image The image that appears when the pointer is moved across the primary image. Referred to in Dreamweaver MX 2004 as the rollover image.

source attribute (src) An image tag (<img>) attribute that contains the path to an image.

source images folder The folder containing the images that will be used to create a Web photo album.

swap image A behavior that swaps (exchanges) one image for another when an event triggers this action.

swap image restore A behavior that instructs a browser to display the original source image when a swap image event is over. See *behaviors*.

text top image alignment Aligns the top of an image with the top of the tallest character in a line of text.

thumbnail A much smaller duplicate of an image used to allow viewers to see what the full-size image looks like. Thumbnails are usually linked to the full-size image.

tile The effect of a background image repeating (tiling) across a page if it is not large enough to fill the page.

top image alignment Aligns the top of an image with the top of the tallest portion of an image or text.

tracing images Images used as patterns to recreate page layouts.

transparency Feature of some GIF images that allows the background color of a Web page to show through one color of the image.

vertical space A cushion of space above and below an image.

Web photo album A collection of Web pages consisting of a page with thumbnail image links to full-page images.

COMMANDS review

Add background image	Modify, Page Properties, *Appearance* category
Adjust image brightness and contrast	Modify, Image, Brightness/Contrast
Adjust tracing image position	View, Tracing Image, Adjust Position
Align tracing image	View, Tracing Image, Align with Selection
Create navigation bar	Insert, Image Objects, Navigation Bar
Create rollover image	Insert, Image Objects, Rollover Image
Create Web photo album	Commands, Create Web Photo Album
Crop an image	Modify, Image, Crop
Insert image	Insert, Image
Insert image placeholder	Insert, Image Placeholder
Make tracing images visible	View, Tracing Image, Show
Optimize an image in Fireworks	Modify, Image, Optimize Image in Fireworks
Resample an image	Modify, Image, Resample
Reset tracing image position	View, Tracing Image, Reset Position
Sharpen an image	Modify, Image, Sharpen
Use an external image editor	Edit, Edit with External Editor
Work with a tracing image	View, Tracing Image, Load

CONCEPTS check

Indicate the correct term or command for each item.

1. This type of image format is best suited for drawings or illustrations.
2. This type of link can be used as an alternative to using a long description for an image.
3. Using these allows users to see how images will work with their page layout plans.
4. This hotspot tool can be used to create irregularly shaped hotspots.
5. What is the term for the cushion of space that can be specified to appear on the left and right side of an image?
6. This is the portion of an image map that contains a link to another document.
7. This is the term for the effect produced when a background image is too small to fill a page.
8. What type of image format is best suited for photographs?
9. What is the term for an image that changes appearance when the pointer is hovered over it?
10. When working with behaviors, this triggers an action.
11. This type of image can be used to help with the Web page design process.
12. This panel stores all of the images used in a site.
13. This is a feature of one type of GIF format that allows images to load on a page as if they were slowly coming into focus.
14. This image format supports interlacing and transparency, but is not well supported by browsers.
15. Images are inserted into HTML documents using this HTML tag and attribute.
16. When working with behaviors, an event triggers this.
17. This accessibility feature provides a short description for an image that can be read by screen readers or seen as a tooltip in the latest browser versions.
18. Web pages should be under this size.
19. This is the term for an image containing hotspots linked to other documents.
20. What is the term for the cushion of space that can be specified to appear at the top and bottom of an image?

SKILLS check

Use the Site Definition dialog box to create a separate Dreamweaver site named CH 04 Assessments to keep your assessment work for this chapter. Save the files for the site in a new root folder named ch_04_assessments under the Sites folder you created in Chapter 1, Exercise 3. Download the ch_04_student_files folder from the IRC to the CH 04 Assessments site root folder (ch_04_assessments) and expand it. Delete the compressed folder when you are finished.

Assessment 1 • Insert and Format Images

1. Open the student file named **resort_page.htm** located in the ch4sa1_student_files subfolder. Use the Save As command to rename and save it to the ch_04_assessments root folder as **ch4sa1.htm**.
2. Locate the student file named **logo.gif** in the ch4sa1_student_files subfolder, and insert it into the top row of the table in **ch4sa1.htm**. Create an alternate text description for the image consisting of the following word: *Logo*.

3. Place the insertion point in the first column of the second table row and insert the student file named **seaview.jpg** (located in ch4sa1_student_files). Create an alternate text description for the image consisting of the following words: *View from bungalow*. ***Note: Alternate text also can be created by selecting an image and typing it in the Property inspector* Alt *text box.***

4. Place the insertion point in the second column of the second table row and insert the student file named **bungalow.jpg** (located in ch4sa1_student_files). Create an alternate text description consisting of the following words: *View of bungalow*.

5. Use the Image Property inspector Align Center button to center align all three images.

6. Add a border of 4 pixels to the **seaview.jpg** and **bungalow.jpg** images.

7. Link **seaview.jpg** to the student file named **island.htm** located in the ch4sa1_student_files folder.

8. Link **bungalow.jpg** to the student file named **room.htm** located in the ch4sa1_student_files folder.

9. Click the Preview/Debug in browser button and then click Preview in iexplore to preview **ch4sa1.htm** and check that the image links work. Close the browser when you are finished.

10. Save **ch4sa1.htm** and then close it.

Assessment 2 • Insert Table and Table Cell Background Images

1. Open **ch4sa1.htm** and use the Save As command to rename and save it as **ch4sa2.htm**.

2. Create a table background image using the student file named **water.gif** located in the ch4sa2_student_files subfolder. ***Note: A message box will appear advising you that the document should be saved first in order to create a document-relative path. Whenever you see this message, click the OK button to close it. A document-relative path will be created when you save the document at the end of the exercise.***

3. Position the insertion point in the bottom row of the table in **ch4sa2.htm** and select it by clicking <tr> in the Tag selector. Create a cell background image for that row using the student file named **palm.gif** located in the ch4sa2_student_files subfolder.

4. Click the Preview/Debug in browser button and then click Preview in iexplore to preview **ch4sa2.htm**. Close the browser when you are finished.

5. Save **ch4sa2.htm** and then close it.

Assessment 3 • Create an Image Map

1. Create a new HTML document and use the Save or Save As commands to name and save it as **ch4sa3.htm**.

2. Locate the student file named **usa.gif** in the ch4sa3_student_files subfolder, and insert it in **ch4sa3.htm**. Create an alternate text description for the image consisting of the following words: *Map of USA*.

3. Center align the image in the document.

4. Locate and open the four state student files (for example, **california.htm**, **new_york.htm**, and so on) in the ch4sa3_student_files subfolder, and use the Save As command to add *-3* to their names (for example, **california-3.htm**). Save them to the ch_04_assessments root folder. ***Hint: Click the Yes button to update links when prompted.***

DREAMWEAVER MX 2004

5. With **ch4sa3.htm** as the current document, use the appropriate hotspot tool to make an image map of the state of California. Link the hotspot to the student file named **california-3.htm**. Chose _blank_ from the *Target* text box drop-down list. Create an alternate text description consisting of the following word: *California*.

6. Repeat Step 5 to create image maps for Florida, New York, and Ohio. Link the image maps to the student files for each state (for example, **new_york-3.htm**, and so on). Chose _blank_ from the *Target* text box drop-down list for each image map. Create an alternate text description for each state consisting of the name of the state.

7. Switch to each of the state files (for example, **california-3.htm**) and specify absolute middle image alignment for the flag images in each file. Save and then close each file when you are finished.

8. Click the Preview/Debug in browser button and then click Preview in iexplore to preview **ch4sa3.htm** and check that the hotspots work. Close the browser when you are finished.

9. Save **ch4sa3.htm** and then close it.

Assessment 4 • Create a Web Photo Album

1. Create a new HTML document.
2. Create a Web photo album with the following specifications:
   a. *Photo album title:* Audubon Birds
   b. *Subheading info:* Created by [your name]
   c. *Other info:* [today's date]
   d. *Source images folder: ch4sa4_student_files*
   e. *Destination folder: ch_04_assessments*
   f. *Thumbnail size: 72 × 72*
   g. *Columns: 5*
   h. *Scale: 100%*
3. Specify a white background for the table at the top of the document containing the photo album information, change the font color to a dark green, and center align the text.
4. Open each of the bird HTML pages (for example, **wild_turkey_jpg.htm**, and so on) located in the pages subfolder that Dreamweaver MX has created, and center the table containing the bird image. Save and then close each document when you are finished.
5. Click the Preview/Debug in browser button and then click Preview in iexplore to preview the Web photo album and verify that the links work. Close the browser when you are finished.
6. Save **index.htm** and then close it.

Assessment 5 • Create Rollover Images

1. Create a new HTML document and use the Save or Save As commands to name and save it as **ch4sa5.htm**.
2. Create a series of three rollover images at the top of the page using the button images located in the ch4sa5_student_files subfolder. Use the image appended with *-1* for the original image, and the image appended *-2* for the rollover image. Create appropriate names and alternative text for each button, for example, *page_1* for the image name and *Page 1* for the alternate text description. Create the following links for each rollover image button:

    a. Page 1: **ch4sa2.htm**
    b. Page 2: **ch4sa3.htm**
    c. Page 3: **index.htm**
3. Center the buttons horizontally in the document.
4. Include a heading for the page below the rollover image buttons, followed by a paragraph explaining the various skills you have learned in this chapter. Format the document to make it attractive and easy to read.
5. Save **ch4sa5.htm** and then close it.

Assessment 6 • Design Portfolio

Save all documents created in this assessment in the site you created in Chapter 2 for your design portfolio project.

1. Use the comments relating to image placement that you inserted in your design portfolio pages in Chapter 2 as a guide to image placeholder insertion for your design portfolio pages. Create alternate text descriptions for all of your images. Resize the placeholders to fit in with your page layout plans.
2. Gather the images you want to use on the site and use an image editor to adjust their size to fit the size indicated by the appropriate placeholder.
3. Replace the placeholders with the images you have resized.
4. Change image alignment so that the image position in relationship to text matches your page design requirements.
5. Add at least one image map to your design portfolio site.
6. Use a background image for at least one page or table on a page.
7. Add a <u>D</u> link next to at least two images or tables and create longer description files that will be the target links for the <u>D</u> links.
8. As you build your design portfolio Web site, ask other students to evaluate your design ideas. Let them test drive your pages and report their findings to you. It is always a good idea to have others evaluate your work before launching it on the Internet.

DREAMWEAVER MX 2004

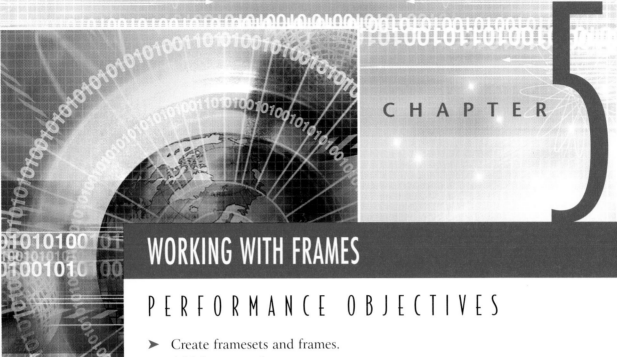

WORKING WITH FRAMES

PERFORMANCE OBJECTIVES

➤ Create framesets and frames.
➤ Add frames to framesets.
➤ Open documents in a frame.
➤ Save, delete, and select framesets and frames.
➤ Use the Frames panel.
➤ Use the Frameset Property inspector to modify frameset properties.
➤ Use the Frame Property inspector to modify frame properties.
➤ Use links to change frame content.
➤ Create and modify navigation bars.
➤ Create accessible frames with frame titles and noframes content.

The student files for this chapter are available for download from the Internet Resource Center at www.emcp.com.

Frames-based pages enhance Web page functionality by allowing more than one HTML document to appear on the same page at the same time. Using frames opens up all kinds of possibilities for page design. Unfortunately, frames have acquired a poor reputation with some users for a number of reasons, including poor browser support when frames first began being used, the need for more complicated coding, difficulties in bookmarking or printing frames, and the fact that most search engines cannot search frame content.

Many of the objections based on these reasons are not as valid as they once were. More than 99 percent of the browsers in use today can handle frames, and programs such as Dreamweaver MX 2004 make creating and working with frames easy. The latest browser versions allow individual frames to be bookmarked and printed by right-clicking a frame. The use of meta tags and noframes content in framesets can offset problems related to search engines.

This chapter shows you how to create frames so you can decide whether to use them when designing Web pages.

Understanding Frames

In appearance, frames are like tables, a matrix or grid formed by intersecting horizontal and vertical lines forming rows and columns as shown in Figure 5.1. Frames even share some characteristics with tables, such as the capability to nest frames within frames, or to use invisible borders so that casual users are not even aware that a Web page uses frames. The resemblance to tables ends there, however, as frames can accomplish tasks that tables cannot, such as creating page regions that remain static (unchanging), while other page region content varies.

Frames are page regions that contain an HTML document; a single page can contain two or more frames. Thus, with frames, a single Web page can display content from two or more HTML documents at a time. All of the frames on a page are specified in a *frameset*, an HTML document that controls frame layout and properties but does not appear in a browser. Instead of containing body tags (<body>) like normal HTML documents, a frameset document uses *frameset tags* (<frameset>) to create a frameset. Each frameset must contain a minimum of two frames, indicated by using a single *frame tag* (<frame>). Like image tags (<img>), frame tags use a source attribute (**src**) to locate an HTML file and open it in the frame. The documents needed to instruct a browser to display two frames on the screen consist of a frameset document and the two HTML documents that will appear in the frames specified in the frameset document, as shown in Figure 5.2. When frames are created in Dreamweaver MX 2004, a frameset document is created as well as the HTML documents that will appear in the frames specified in the frameset document.

One of the most important features of frames is that the documents appearing in frames can contain links, and a link on a document in one frame can be specified to open a new document in the same frame, in another frame, or in a new browser window.

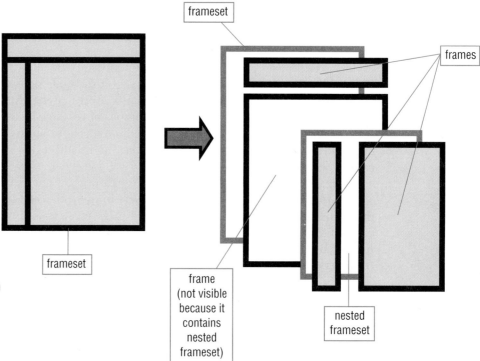

Figure 5.1
Frameset Exploded Diagram

DREAMWEAVER MX 2004

A popular use for frames is to create a Web page containing a top row that functions as a *heading* or *banner area*, a left column that contains a navigation bar or navigation links, and a central or main frame area that contains changing content as shown in Figure 5.3. The navigation frame contains links to different

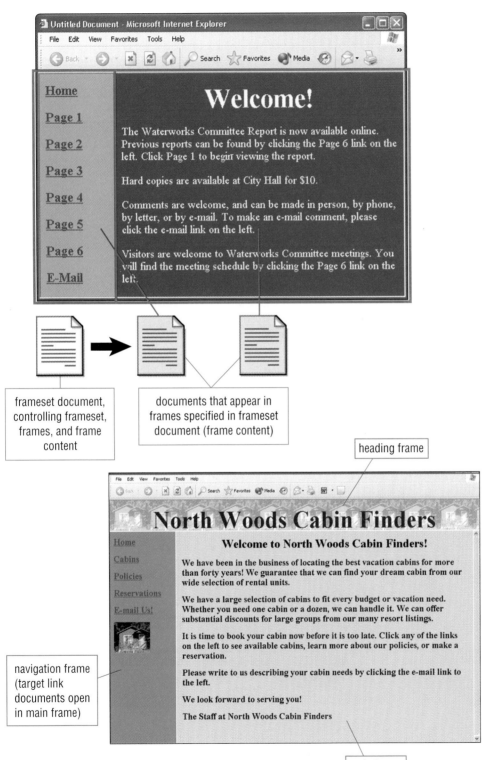

Figure 5.2
How Frames Work

frameset document, controlling frameset, frames, and frame content

documents that appear in frames specified in frameset document (frame content)

heading frame

navigation frame (target link documents open in main frame)

main frame

Figure 5.3
A Popular Web Page Frame Design

HTML pages that will appear in the main frame of the Web page when a link is clicked. The advantage of using frames in this way is that the heading and navigation frames can remain constant because browsers do not need to reload those pages when the main frame content changes. One benefit for viewers is that they will not experience the flicker or jump in navigation bars or links that may occur when viewing navigation bars or links on conventional pages that need to reload.

Frames also can be used to create stable or stationary areas at the bottom of the screen so that content in this bottom frame will be visible whatever the length of the page content and no matter how a browser is resized, as shown in Figure 5.4

You are limited only by your own creativity in designing frame layouts; there is no limit to the number of frames that a frameset can contain. However, excessive frames can make navigation difficult for viewers, squeeze the space available in the browser window, and make it difficult to troubleshoot problems. To avoid those problems, framesets should contain no more than three frames. In recognition of this advice, the predefined framesets available in Dreamweaver MX 2004 do not exceed this number.

Creating Framesets and Frames

You can design framesets and frames from scratch or you can use **predefined framesets**. Using predefined framesets can save a lot of time, but you might enjoy the flexibility of creating your own frameset designs. Either way, Dreamweaver MX 2004 makes creating framesets and frames easy.

Before working with frames, make sure that **frame borders** are visible when working in the Document window as shown in Figure 5.5. These borders are not the same as the frame borders that can be specified as being visible or invisible in browsers. To make frame borders visible in the Document window, complete the following steps:

1. Click the View options button at the end of the Document toolbar as shown in Figure 5.6.
2. Point to Visual Aids on the drop-down menu.
3. Make sure a check mark appears to the left of Frame Borders. If not, click Frame Borders to enable it.

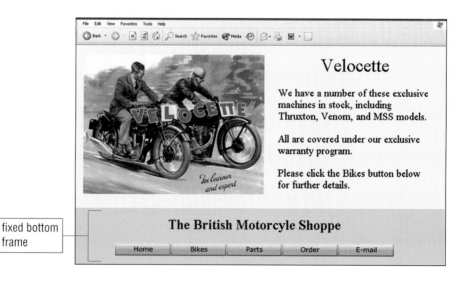

Figure 5.4
A Web Page Using Frames to Create Fixed Bottom Page Content

fixed bottom frame

New Framesets

A new frameset is designed with a document open (current) in the Document window. This document will be included in one of the frames when the frameset is created.

Click Modify on the Menu bar and then point to Frameset to open the Frameset submenu shown in Figure 5.7. Click one of the submenu commands to create a frameset and frames, with the current document included in one of the

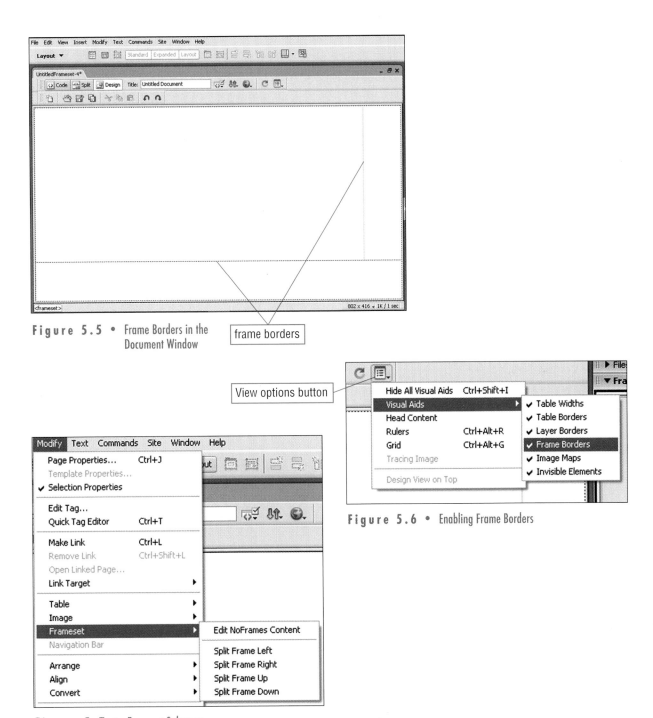

Figure 5.5 • Frame Borders in the Document Window

frame borders

View options button

Figure 5.6 • Enabling Frame Borders

Figure 5.7 • Frameset Submenu

frames. Table 5.1 shows the frame location of the open document when the different commands are used.

Adding Frames to a Frameset Building a frameset using the Frameset command results in a frameset with two frames; however, the same commands that were used to build the frameset can be used to add frames by splitting existing frames. Any frameset in which the number of frames varies between rows or columns will automatically contain nested framesets. Clicking Modify on the Menu bar, pointing to Frameset, and then clicking a command from the submenu shown in Figure 5.7 is one way to split frames.

Frames also can be added to a frameset by dragging a frameset border and moving it toward the center of the Document window as shown in Figure 5.8. Dragging a horizontal border splits a frame horizontally, whereas dragging a vertical

Table 5.1 • Open Document Frame Locations

Frameset Submenu Command	Open Document Location	Example
Split Frame Left	Open document contained in left frame	
Split Frame Right	Open document contained in right frame	
Split Frame Up	Open document contained in top frame	
Split Frame Down	Open document contained in bottom frame	

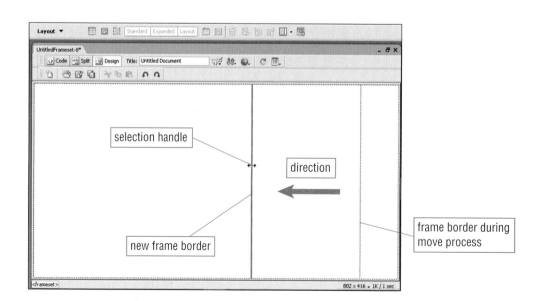

Figure 5.8
Dragging to Split a Frame

DREAMWEAVER MX 2004

border splits a frame vertically. If a frame border is located inside the frameset, holding down the Alt key while dragging it splits the frame. A frame also can be split into four frames by positioning the insertion point on a frame corner until it turns into the *move icon,* and then dragging the move icon toward the center of the frame as shown in Figure 5.9. Because this method results in a frameset containing more than three frames, it is not recommended.

Finally, clicking Insert on the Menu bar, pointing to HTML, pointing to Frames, and then clicking Left, Right, Top, or Bottom creates a single frame in the desired direction, calculated from the insertion point.

Opening Documents in a Frame   After a frame has been created, a document inside a frame can be replaced by positioning the insertion point in the desired frame, clicking File on the Menu bar, and then Open in Frame. This opens the Select HTML File dialog box shown in Figure 5.10, which can then be used to locate and select an HTML file that will open in the frame containing the insertion

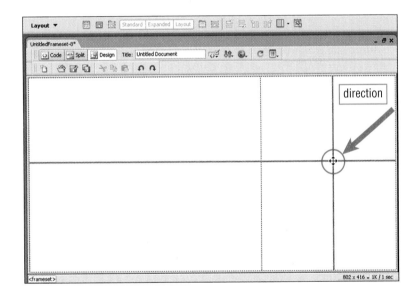

Figure 5.9
Frame Move Icon

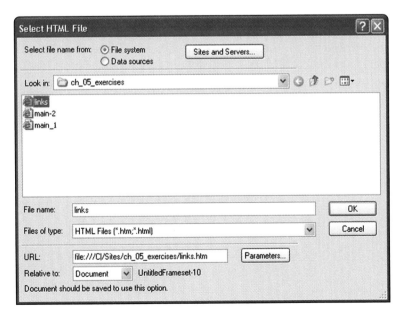

Figure 5.10
Select HTML File Dialog Box

point. The Frame Property inspector *Src* (Source) text box also can be used to change a frame document as described in the "Using the Frame Property Inspector to Change Frame Properties" section later in this chapter.

Changing Frame Document Background Color Although frame properties are set using the Frame Property inspector, the background color of a frame is determined by the document contained in the frame. Click in a frame, click Modify on the Menu bar, and then Page Properties to open the Page Properties dialog box. Clicking *Appearance* in the dialog box *Category* list box displays the *Background* color box. The *Background* color box can then be clicked to open the Color Picker and select a new page background color.

Saving Framesets and Frames Unlike regular HTML pages, framesets and frame documents must be saved before they can be previewed in a browser. Because a frameset consists of more than one document, the saving process is slightly more involved than when saving a regular HTML document. When framesets and frames are created, Dreamweaver MX 2004 gives them temporary names such as UntitledFrameset-1.htm, UntitledFrame-2.htm, and so on. A document that was open while the frameset was created is now enclosed in a frame and maintains its name. You should create your own names for frames and framesets because the temporary names are similar enough to cause confusion.

The Document toolbar *Title* text box can be used to enter a title for each document. Document titles should not be confused with frame titles, an accessibility feature described later in this chapter.

Framesets and frames can be selected and saved individually by clicking File on the Menu bar and then clicking the Save Frameset or Save Frameset As commands for framesets, or the Save Frame or Save Frame As commands for frames. If a frameset or a frame is being saved for the first time, either of the two save options can be used.

After a frameset or frame has been saved, choosing Save Frameset As or Save Frame As creates a copy of the frameset or frame that can be renamed. Methods for selecting framesets and frames are covered in the "Selecting Framesets and Frames" section of this chapter.

Using the Save All command saves all open framesets and frames. If a frameset is being saved for the first time, a heavy border appears around the frameset in the Document window, and a Save As dialog box opens that can be used to name the frameset as shown in Figure 5.11. After the frameset has been saved, the Save As dialog box reappears for any frames that have not yet been saved. A heavy border appears around each frame as it is being saved. Under most circumstances, you should use the Save All command periodically to ensure that all framesets and frame documents are saved.

Deleting Framesets and Frames Frames can be deleted by dragging them out of the Document window or by dragging them to a frame border. A message box appears asking whether you want to save a document if the frame contains unsaved content. Closing a frameset without saving deletes the frameset. To delete a saved frameset, delete the file in the Files panel.

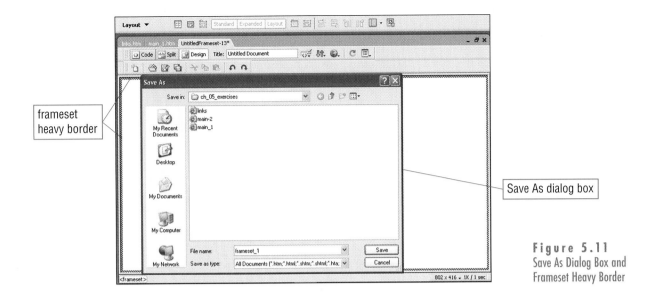

framed label: **frameset heavy border**

label: **Save As dialog box**

Figure 5.11
Save As Dialog Box and
Frameset Heavy Border

exercise 1

CREATING A NEW FRAMESET

1. If necessary, start Dreamweaver MX 2004.
2. At a clear document screen, create a new site named CH 05 Exercises to store the exercises you create in this chapter. Name the root folder ch_05_exercises and save it under the Sites folder you created in Chapter 1, Exercise 3. Download the ch_05_student_files folder from the IRC to the CH 05 Exercises site root folder (ch_05_exercises) and expand it. Delete the compressed folder when you are finished. ***Note: Refer to Chapter 1 for instructions on navigating with the Files panel integrated file browser.***
3. Create a frame-based Web page by completing the following steps:
   a. Open the student file named **main_page.htm**.
   b. Click File on the Menu bar and then Save As to rename the document **main_page-1.htm** and save it to the ch_05_exercises root folder. The ch_05_student_files folder appears by default in the Save As dialog box *Save in* text box, so click the Up One Level button to place the ch_05_exercises root folder in the *Save in* text box.
   c. Click Modify on the Menu bar, point to Frameset, and then click Split Frame Down to place **main_page-1.htm** inside a frame on the page.

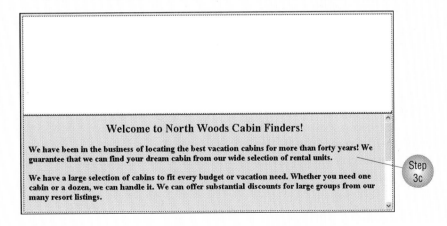

Step 3b

Step 3c

d. Position the insertion point in **main_page-1.htm** and click Modify on the Menu bar, point to Frameset, and then click Split Frame Right to place **main_page-1.htm** inside the right side of a two-column row. The frameset you have created has a single row at the top, and then a two-column row below that.

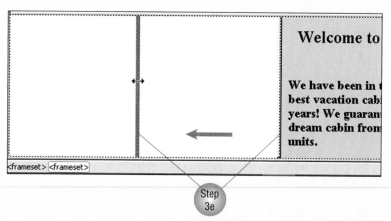

Step 3e

e. Click the left border of the frame containing **main_page-1.htm**, drag it halfway toward the left frameset border, and then release it.

f. Position the insertion point in the top frame of the frameset.

g. Click File and then Open in Frame to open the Select HTML File dialog box. Double-click the student file named **heading_page.htm**, or click the file and then click the OK button to open it in the top frame. A message appears advising you that a document needs to be saved before a document-relative path can be created, and that Dreamweaver MX 2004 will use a temporary path until the document is saved. Click the OK button to close the message box. *Note: Be sure to click the Open in Frame command and not the Open command.*

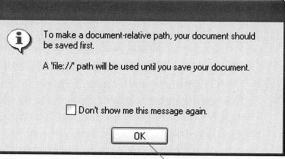

Step 3g

Step 3h

h. Use the Save Frame As command on the File menu to rename the frame **heading_page-1.htm** and save it to the ch_05_exercises root folder.

i. Position the insertion point in the frame column to the left of the frame column containing **main_page-1.htm**.

j. Click File and then Open in Frame to open the Select HTML File dialog box. Double-click the student file named **navigation_page.htm**, or click the file and then click the OK button. The same message that appeared in Step 3g will appear on your screen. Click the OK button to close the message box and place **navigation_page.htm** in the left column.

k. Use the Save Frame As command to rename the frame **navigation_page-1.htm** and save it to the ch_05_exercises root folder.

l. Click File and then Save All to open the Save As dialog box. Click the *Save in* text box down-pointing arrow to locate the ch_05_exercises root folder and place it in the *Save in* text box. The frameset document default name appears in the dialog box *File name* text box. Type ch5ex01.htm in the text box and click the Save button to save the document. ***Note: Because the HTML documents that appear in the frameset's frames have already been named and saved, the Save All command saves them automatically without requiring any further user input.***

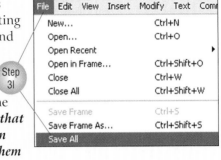

m. Click the Preview/Debug in browser button and then click Preview in iexplore to view the page in a Web browser. Note that the top frame height is taller than necessary and shows the tiling of the cabin image. Frame borders are visible, and can be resized by clicking and dragging. You will learn how to adjust these and other frameset and frame properties in upcoming exercises. Close the browser when you are finished.

4. Click File and then Close to close **ch5ex01.htm**.

Predefined Framesets

You can create predefined framesets in three different ways: by using the Insert bar Frames button menu (Layout menu item or tab), by using the HTML and then Frames commands on the Insert menu, or by using the *Framesets* options in the New Document dialog box.

The Insert bar can be used to create predefined framesets by clicking the Insert bar Layout menu item or tab with a document open in the Document window, clicking the Frames button down-pointing arrow, and then clicking a predefined frameset command from the menu that appears as shown in Figure 5.12. The Frames button also can be dragged to the Document window to create a frameset. The Frames button displays the icon of the last predefined frame command to be selected. Hovering the pointer over the button activates a tooltip that displays the current function of the Frames button.

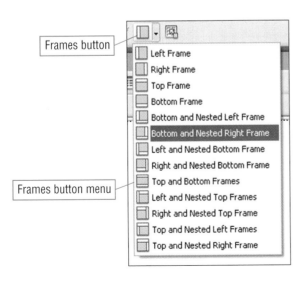

Figure 5.12
Insert Bar Frames
Button Menu

A predefined frameset can be created with a document open in the Document window by clicking Insert on the Menu bar, pointing to HTML, pointing to Frames, and then clicking one of the frameset options from the submenu shown in Figure 5.13.

The New Document dialog box can be used to create framesets without a document open in the Document window by clicking File on the Menu bar and then New. Clicking *Framesets* in the *Category* list box displays more than a dozen predefined framesets, and an outline of each frameset appears in the *Preview* section of the dialog box as shown in Figure 5.14.

After a predefined frameset has been created, frame borders can be dragged to new locations. Frames also can be split in the same manner used when creating a new frameset. The process of saving a predefined frameset and frames is the same as the one used when saving a new frameset.

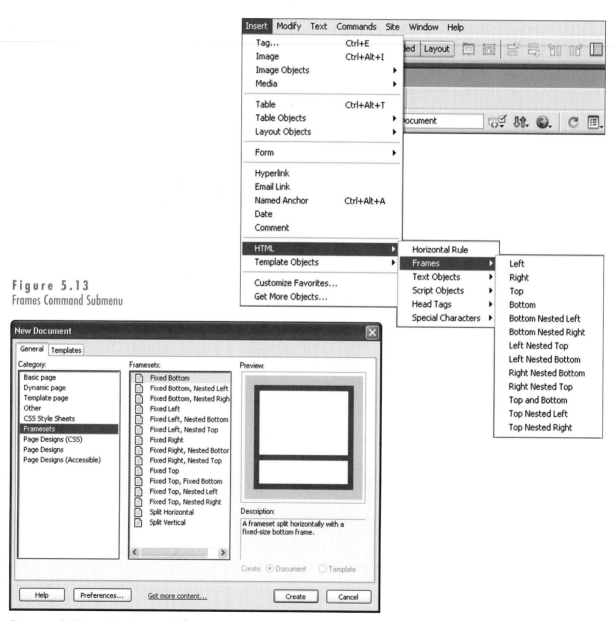

Figure 5.13
Frames Command Submenu

Figure 5.14 • New Document Dialog Box Frameset Options

DREAMWEAVER MX 2004

Dreamweaver MX 2004 automatically provides frame names for each frame in a predefined frameset. These names appear in the Property inspector *Target* text box drop-down list and are used when specifying the frame that a target link document will open in. Frame names can be changed by typing a new name in the Frame Property inspector *Frame name* text box, as described in the "Using the Frame Property Inspector to Change Frame Properties" section of this chapter.

exercise **2**

1. Use a predefined frameset to create a frame-based Web page by completing the following steps:

    a. At a clear document screen, click File on the Menu bar and then New to open the New Document dialog box. Click *Framesets* in the *Category* list box, and then *Fixed Top, Fixed Bottom* in the *Framesets* list box. An image and preview of the frameset appears on the right side of the dialog box. Click the Create button to create the frameset.

    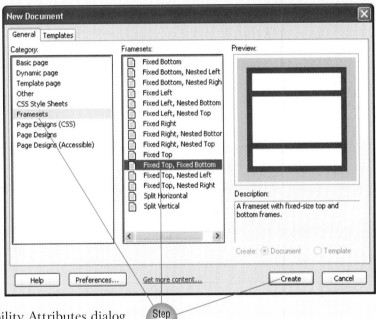

    Step 1a

    b. A Frame Tag Accessibility Attributes dialog box appears after you click the Create button if the *Frames* option has been enabled in the Preferences dialog box Accessibility page. ***Note: Instructions on selecting this preference are contained in the "Ensuring Accessibility" section of Chapter 2.*** Click the down-pointing arrow next to the *Frame* list box to open a drop-down list of predefined frame names. Below the *Frame* list box is a *Title* text box that can be used to enter a title for each frame. Click each frame name from the list and then type the following titles for the frames in the *Title* text box. Do not click the OK button until you are finished:

        1) Type **Navigation Frame** for *bottomFrame*.
        2) Type **Heading Frame** for *topFrame*.
        3) Type **Main Frame** for *mainFrame*.

    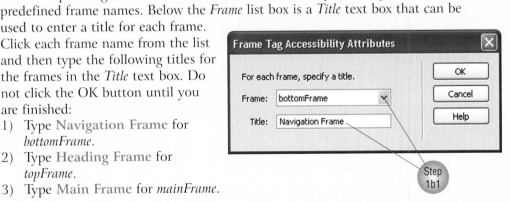

    Step 1b1

c. Position the insertion point in the top frame of the frameset. Click File and then Open in Frame to open the Select HTML File dialog box. Double-click the student file named **heading_page.htm**, or click the file and then click the OK button to open it in the top frame. Click the OK button to close the message box that appears.

d. Use the Save Frame As command to rename the frame **heading_page-2.htm** and save it to the ch_05_exercises root folder.

e. Position the insertion point in the middle frame of the frameset. Click File and then Open in Frame. Double-click the student file named **alternative_main_page.htm**, or click the file and then click the OK button to open it in the middle frame. Click the OK button to close the message box that appears.

f. Use the Save Frame As command to rename the frame **alternative_main_page-2.htm** and save it to the ch_05_exercises root folder.

g. Position the insertion point in the bottom frame of the frameset. Click File and then Open in Frame. Double-click the file named **bottom_navigation_page.htm**, or click the file and then click the OK button to open it in the bottom frame. Click the OK button to close the message box that appears. *Note: The bottom frame is empty because you will be inserting a navigation bar in this document in Exercise 7.*

h. Use the Save Frame As command to rename the frame **bottom_navigation_page-2.htm** and save it to the ch_05_exercises root folder.

i. Click File and then Save All to open the Save As dialog box. The Frameset document appears in the dialog box *File name* text box. Type ch5ex02.htm in the text box and click the Save button to save the document to the ch_05_exercises root folder.

j. Click the Preview/Debug in browser button and then click Preview in iexplore to view the page in a Web browser. Note that the top and bottom frames are fixed and that no scroll bars appear next to those frames. The middle frame contains the **main_page.htm** document, and because there is not enough space in the middle frame to display the document in its entirety, a scroll bar appears on the right side of the frame. The frame borders in this predefined frameset are also invisible. Close the browser when you are finished.

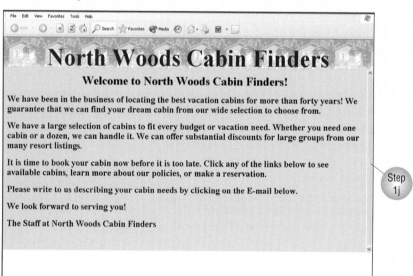

Step 1j

2. Click File and then Close to close **ch5ex02.htm**.

DREAMWEAVER MX 2004

Selecting Framesets and Frames

Frameset and frame properties can be changed using the Frameset or Frame Property inspectors, but before that can be done, a frameset or frame must be selected. Note that positioning the insertion point inside a frame selects the document in a frame, not the frame itself.

Framesets

Framesets can be selected in a number of different ways. Using the **Frames panel** is probably the easiest method. If the panel is closed, it can be opened by clicking Window on the Menu bar and then clicking Frames from the submenu. When an HTML document containing a frameset is the current document in the Document window, the Frames panel shows the structure of the frameset and the frames and nested framesets it contains in outline form. The name of each frame appears in the center of each frame as shown in Figure 5.15.

A frameset can be selected by clicking its outside border in the Frames panel. When the frameset is selected, the frameset border in the Frames panel is surrounded by a thick black line, a dotted line appears around the frameset and the frameset's frames in the Document window, the frameset tag appears outlined in white in the Tag selector, and the Frameset Property inspector opens as shown in Figure 5.16. The Frames panel also can be used to select a frameset by clicking in one of the frames in the Frames panel and then selecting <frameset> in the Tag selector. If the frameset contains a nested frameset, more than one <frameset> might appear in the Tag selector, but this depends on whether a parent or a nested frameset frame was selected.

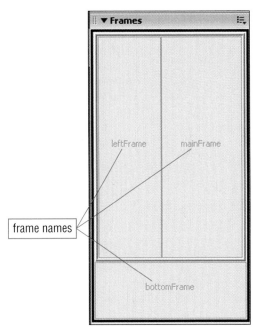

Figure 5.15 • Frames Panel

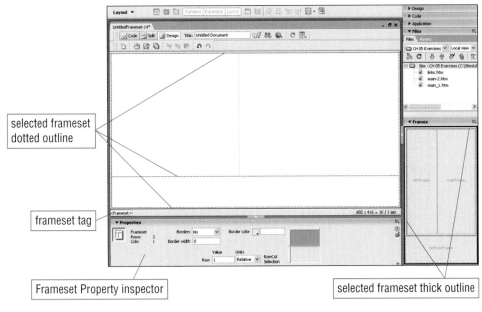

Figure 5.16
Selected Frameset in the Frames Panel

Holding down the Alt key and clicking in a frame in the Document window causes one or more frameset tags (<frameset>) to appear in the Tag selector, again depending on whether or not the frameset contains a nested frameset, and depending on the frame that was clicked. After a frameset tag appears in the Tag selector, clicking it selects the frameset controlled by that tag and opens the Frameset Property inspector. It is also possible to select a frameset by clicking a frameset border in the Document window, but this can sometimes be difficult, particularly if the Document window is not fully expanded or if the frameset contains a number of nested frames.

Frames

Selecting frames with the Frames panel works in a similar manner to the method used for selecting framesets. Clicking inside a frame in the Frames panel places a thin black line around the frame, places a dotted line around the frame in the Document window, and opens the Frame Property inspector as shown in Figure 5.17. You do not have to click <frame> in the Tag selector because it is selected automatically. Frames also can be selected by holding down the Alt key and clicking inside a frame in the Document window. If the Alt key is not held down, this action selects only the HTML document that will appear in the frame.

It is important to understand the difference between selecting a frame and selecting an HTML document that will appear in a frame. When a frame is selected, the Frame Property inspector opens. Switching to Code view shows the frame portion of the frameset code highlighted in black in the frameset document. This is the code that will change when changes are typed in the Frame Property inspector. When an HTML document that will appear in a frame is selected, the Property inspector will be in its normal HTML document mode. Switching to Code view shows the code for a normal HTML document.

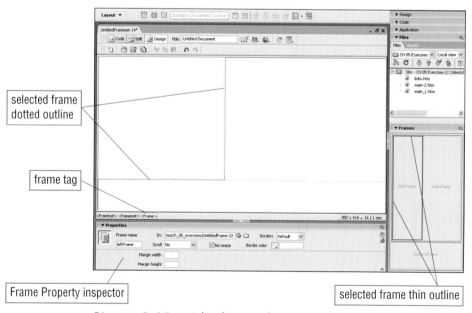

Figure 5.17 • Selected Frame in the Frames Panel

DREAMWEAVER MX 2004

1. Select framesets and frames by completing the following steps:
   a. At a clear document screen, open **ch5ex01.htm**.
   b. If the Frames panel is not open, click Window and then Frames to open it.
   c. Position the pointer in the upper-left edge of the frameset border in the Frames panel and click. A <frameset> appears in the Tag selector, the Property inspector displays frameset properties, and the frameset in the Frames panel is indicated by a thick black line. In the Document window, the frameset is outlined with a thin dotted line. The frameset tag in the Tag selector appears outlined in white to indicate that the frameset has been selected.

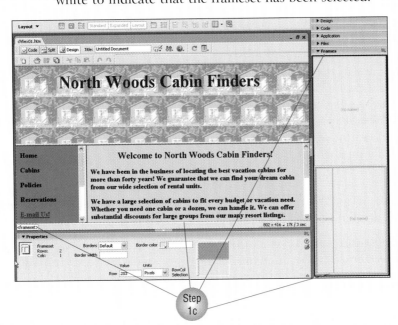

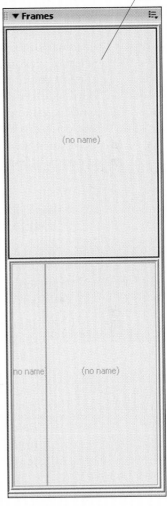

   d. Position the pointer inside the top frame depicted in the Frames panel and click. The frame's tag appears next to <frameset> in the Tag selector, and the Property inspector now displays frame properties. The frame tag in the Tag selector appears outlined in white to indicate that the frame has been selected. The bold outline around the frameset in the Frames panel disappears, and the frame is outlined by a thin black line. In the Document window, the frame is outlined with a thin dotted line.
   e. Position the pointer inside one of the two frames that form the second row of the frameset in the Frames panel and click. Looking at the Tag selector, you will now see two frameset tags displayed in addition to the highlighted (outlined in white) <frame> of the selected frame. This indicates that the selected frame is contained inside a frameset that is nested (contained) in a parent frameset. Nesting framesets is the only way to create rows or columns with

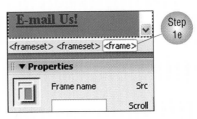

varying numbers of frames, so the two frames forming the two columns of the second row of the frameset are contained inside a nested frame.

   f.   Position the insertion point on the border just above either of the two lower framesets depicted in the Frames panel and click. The second <frameset> in the Tag selector is outlined in white to indicate that it is the frameset that has been selected, and a thick black line appears around the nested frameset. The nested frameset is surrounded by a thin dotted line in the Document window.

   g.   Move the insertion point over to the Document window and position it inside the top frame. Note that the Property inspector now displays normal HTML document properties, and that the Tag selector shows HTML document tags. This is because you have selected the document that will be displayed in a frame, but not the frame itself.

   h.   Hold down the Alt key, position the pointer inside the top frame, and then click to select the frame. The Property inspector now displays the frame's properties, and the Tag selector shows its <frame> outline in white, indicating the frame has been selected. The parent frameset for the frame is located to the left of the <frame> in the Tag selector, but it is not outlined in white, indicating that it is not selected.

   i.   Click <frameset> in the Tag selector. The Property inspector displays frameset properties, and <frameset> is outlined in white, indicating that the frameset is selected.

2.   Close **ch5ex01.htm** without saving it.

Using the Frameset Property Inspector to Change Frameset Properties

When a frameset has been selected, the Property inspector appears as the *Frameset Property inspector* as shown in Figure 5.18. It is a good idea to set frameset properties first because some of these settings can affect frame properties. Frameset Property inspector properties are described in the following list.

- **Borders** You can specify whether or not frames will appear with three-dimensional borders when viewed in a browser. The *Borders* list box choices are *Yes, No,* and *Default. Default* leaves the decision of whether or not to display borders up to the browser. Frame borders also can be set using the Frame Property inspector, which will override any choice made in the Frameset Property inspector.

- **Border width** A width in pixels can be specified for the frameset border using the *Border width* text box.

- **Border color** Clicking the color box opens the Color Picker. You can use the Color Picker Eyedropper to select a border color from the palette, or you can type a hexadecimal color value in the *Border color* text box.

- **Row** or **Column** The *Value* text box and *Units* list box are located at the bottom of the Frameset Property inspector as shown in Figure 5.18. *Column* or *Row* appears to the left of the *Value* and *Units* boxes, depending on whether

Figure 5.18
Frameset Property Inspector

a column or row is selected in the *RowCol Selection* area to the right of the *Value* and *Units* boxes as shown in Figure 5.19. Clicking a row tab selects that row of frames, and clicking a column tab selects that column so that dimensional values and units can be entered into the *Value* and *Units* boxes.

The height and width of frames is set in the Frameset Property inspector instead of the Frame Property inspector because all of the frames in a row must be the same height and all of the frames in a column must be the same width. Entering a value in the *Value* text box tells the browser how much row height or column width to allocate for a selected row or column. The *Units* list box lets you choose between *Pixels, Percent,* and *Relative.*

Pixels specifies a fixed size for a frame, and should be used for frames that need to maintain fixed dimensions, such as a column used to contain a navigation bar, or a row used as a heading or banner area. Pixel specifications take precedence over percentage and relative values, meaning that a browser first allocates space for fixed rows and columns before considering the spatial needs of rows and columns with percentage or relative values.

Percent specifies the percentage of the total frameset width or height that a selected column or row will occupy. Percentages are calculated from any space remaining after a browser allocates space for columns and rows with pixel values.

Relative specifies a value that is relative to the width or height of other frames in a frameset. For example, if the first column in a two-column frameset has a relative value of 1, and the second column has a relative value of 2, the second column will occupy two thirds of the available browser width and the first column one third. **Relative values** allocate any space remaining after space has been allocated for frames with pixel or percentage values.

Just like tables, a popular frameset format is to combine fixed frames with flexible frames. For example, a frameset with a row at the top, a column on the left, and a frame serving as the main frame will often have the top row and left column set in pixels so their dimensions remain the same, while the main frame is set as a percentage or relative value so that it can adjust to fit browser screens.

Most Dreamweaver MX 2004 predefined framesets use a combination of fixed and relative values for the frames that form frameset rows and columns. For example, the predefined Top and Nested Right Frame parent frameset pictured in Figure 5.20 has a top frame set to 80 pixels, while the bottom frame is set to

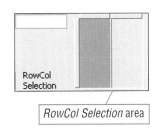

RowCol Selection area

Figure 5.19
Frameset Property Inspector
RowCol Selection Area

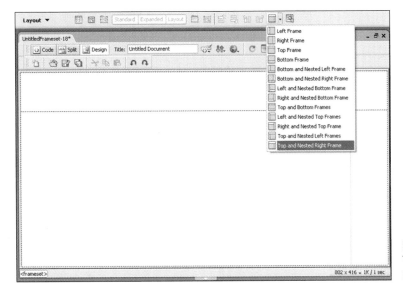

Figure 5.20
Top and Nested Right Frame
Frameset

a relative value of 1. The nested frameset contains a left column with a relative value of 1 and a right column set at 80 pixels.

Allocating space can be confusing, so for most users, the best solution is to let Dreamweaver MX 2004 do the work by using predefined framesets.

exercise

4

MODIFYING FRAMESET PROPERTIES

1. Modify frameset properties by completing the following steps:

   a. At a clear document screen, open **ch5ex01.htm**. Click the parent frameset border in the Frames panel to select it, and use the Save Frameset As command to rename and save it as **ch5ex04.htm**.

   b. Click inside the top frame of the frameset in the Document window and then use the Save Frame As command to rename the frame **heading_page-4.htm**. Do this for the remaining two frames, renaming them by changing the -1 after the frame name to -4.

   c. Click the parent frameset border in the Frames panel to select it again, and then click the down-pointing arrow next to the Frameset Property inspector *Borders* list box to open the drop-down list. Click *No* so that no borders appear around the frameset.

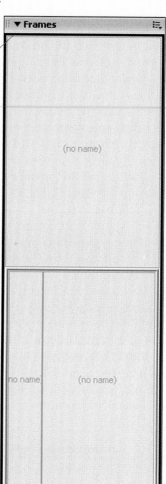

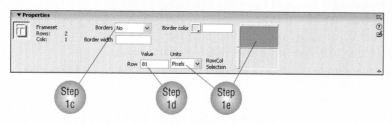

   d. Click the first row in the *RowCol Selection* area and then type 81 in the *Value* text box. This is the height of the background image in the **heading_page-4.htm** document that appears in the top frame.

   e. Click the down-pointing arrow to the right of the *Units* list box to open the drop-down list and click *Pixels* if necessary. Notice in the *RowCol Selection* area, the top row is darker than the bottom row, and the *Value* text box label reads *Row*. This indicates that you are setting a fixed height for that row.

   f. Click the bottom row in the *RowCol Selection* area.

   g. Type 1 in the *Value* text box.

   h. Click the down-pointing arrow to the right of the *Units* list box to open the drop-down list and click *Relative*.

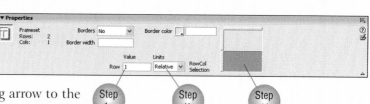

DREAMWEAVER MX 2004

i. Click inside one of the two column frames in the Frames panel and then click the <frameset> nearest the <frame> outlined in white in the Tag selector to select the nested frameset. The *RowCol Selection* area shows the two columns of the nested frameset.

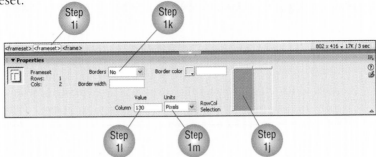

j. Select the first column in the *RowCol Selection* area by clicking it.
k. Click the down-pointing arrow next to the *Borders* list box to open the drop-down list and click *No*.
l. Type 130 in the *Value* text box. Notice that the *Value* text box label reads *Column*.
m. Click the down-pointing arrow to the right of the *Units* list box to open the drop-down list and click *Pixels* if necessary.
n. Select the second column in the *RowCol Selection* area by clicking it.
o. Type 1 in the *Value* text box.
p. Click the down-pointing arrow to the right of the *Units* list box to open the drop-down list and click *Relative*.
q. Select the parent frameset in the Frames panel, click File on the Menu bar, and then click Save Frameset to save the frameset changes you have made.
r. Click the Preview/Debug in browser button and then click Preview in iexplore to view the page in a Web browser. Note that the background image tiling can no longer be seen in the heading row because its height setting is the same as the background image height. The navigation column is also narrower because its width was set to allow for the widest element and fixed in pixels. Finally, the frame borders no longer appear because that option has been disabled. Close the browser when you are finished.

2. Save **ch5ex04.htm** but do not close it.

Using the Frame Property Inspector to Change Frame Properties

When a frame has been selected, the Property inspector appears as the **Frame Property inspector** as shown in Figure 5.21. Frame Property inspector properties are described in the following list:

Figure 5.21 • Frame Property Inspector

- **Frame name** When a link is created to open a document in a frame, the target frame is identified by its *frame name,* which appears in the Property inspector *Target* text box drop-down list as shown in Figure 5.22. Frame names are case-sensitive and must begin with a letter, not a number. If a frame name contains more than one word, the words should be connected using underscores (_).

- **Src (Source)** The *Src* text box contains the path to a file that will appear in the selected frame. A file path can be placed in the text box by using the Point to File or Browse for File buttons to browse and locate the desired file. Another method for changing the file displayed in a frame is to position the insertion point in a frame, click File, and then Open in Frame. This opens the Select HTML File dialog box, which can be used to browse and locate a document that will replace the document open in the frame.

- **Borders** The *Borders* list box specifies whether or not the current frame will display a border when viewed in a browser. Available options are *Yes, No,* and *Default.* Frame borders override frameset border options, with the exception of when a frame is set to default. In that case, most browsers display borders unless the parent frameset's border is specified as *No.* A border is invisible only if all frames sharing the border have a *No* border property, or if a parent frameset border property is specified as *No* and the border properties for frames sharing the border are set to *Default.*

- **Scroll** The *Scroll* list box specifies whether or not **scroll bars** appear in a frame. Scroll bars let users move the contents of a frame horizontally or vertically. Figure 5.23 shows an example of a vertical scroll bar. The four choices for this property are *Yes, No, Auto,* and *Default.* Specifying *Yes* displays scroll bars in a frame even if a document in a frame can be read without scrolling. Specifying *No* turns off scroll bars, even if a document in a frame is too large to be read without scrolling. If there is any possibility of that happening, *No* should not be specified. *Default* does not set a value and lets browsers use their own default value for scrolling. Choosing *Auto* means that browsers display scroll bars only when they are necessary; in other words, when the content of a document in a frame cannot be read without scrolling. Most browsers default to *Auto,* so choosing *Auto* or *Default* usually produces the same results—scroll bars appear if there is not enough room to display the entire frame content.

Figure 5.22 • Property Inspector *Target* Drop-Down List

Figure 5.23 • Vertical Scroll Bar

DREAMWEAVER MX 2004

- *No resize* A check mark in the **No resize *check box*** prevents viewers from resizing a frame in a browser. This does not affect the ability of Dreamweaver MX 2004 users to resize frames when working in Document view.

- *Border color* The *Border color* color box and text box specifies frame border color and applies the color to all borders that touch the selected frame. Frame border color overrides a frameset border color.

- *Margin width* and *Margin height* Entering a pixel value in the *Margin width* and *Margin height* text boxes creates margin space inside the frame, just like cell padding for tables.

1. Modify frame properties by completing the following steps:
   a. With **ch5ex04.htm** in the current Document window, select the frameset, click File on the Menu bar, and then click Save Frameset As to rename and save it as **ch5ex05.htm**.
   b. Click inside the top frame of the frameset in the Document window and then use the Save Frame As command to rename the frame **heading_page-5.htm**. Do this for the remaining two frames, renaming them by changing the -4 after the frame name to -5.
   c. Hold down the Alt key and click in the top frame to select it. Type heading_frame in the *Frame name* text box, located on the upper-left side of the Frame Property inspector. Note that you are creating a frame name that will appear in the *Target* text box drop-down list when linking documents. This is not the same as the name in the *Src* text box, *heading_page-5.htm,* which is the name of the document that appears in the frame.

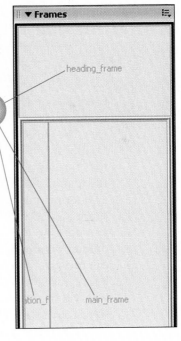

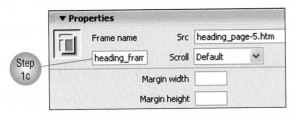

   d. Hold down the Alt key and click in the left column. Type navigation_frame in the *Frame name* text box.
   e. Hold down the Alt key and click in the right column. Type main_frame in the *Frame name* text box. Look in the Frames panel and you will see that each frame now appears with its new frame name.

f. Hold down the Alt key and click in the left column (navigation_frame) to select it, and open the Frame Property inspector. Click the down-pointing arrow next to the *Scroll* list box and click *No* from the drop-down list that appears. This turns off the scroll bar function for this frame. Click to place a check mark in the *No resize* check box to prevent users from resizing the navigation frame in their browsers. Click the down-pointing arrow next to the *Borders* list box and click *No* from the drop-down list that appears.

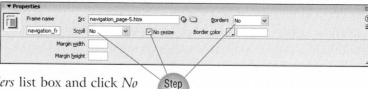

Step 1f

g. Hold down the Alt key and click in the top row (heading_frame) to select it. Choose the same options for the top row as you did for the left column in Step 1f.

h. Hold down the Alt key and click in the right column (main_frame) to select it. Type 15 in the *Margin width* and *Margin height* text boxes to enable that amount of space in pixels around documents that will be opened in this frame. Click the down-pointing arrow next to the *Borders* list box and click *No* from the drop-down list that appears. Click to place a check mark in the *No resize* check box to prevent users from resizing the main frame in their browsers. Do not change the *Scroll* list box choice *(Default)* because the main frame will need to display a scroll bar to view its contents.

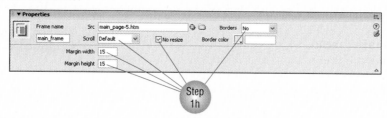

Step 1h

i. Click File and then Save All to save the frame changes you have made.

j. Click the Preview/Debug in browser button and then click Preview in iexplore to view the page in a Web browser. Note that the content of the main frame has a wider margin of space around it. If you position the pointer on any of the invisible borders between the frames, you will be unable to resize them because you selected the *No resize* option in the Frame Property inspector. Close the browser when you are finished.

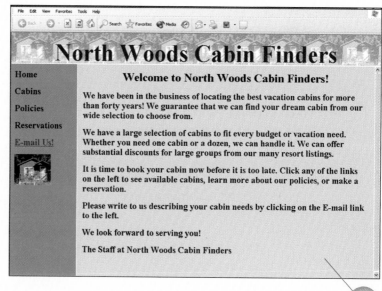

Step 1j

2. Save **ch5ex05.htm** but do not close it.

Using Links to Change Frame Content

The ability to use links to change frame content is one of the outstanding features of frames. This means that a link in one frame can be used to change the content of another frame. The most common application of this ability is a navigation bar in one frame that can be used to open documents in other frames. When a frameset's borders are invisible, most viewers will not know they are viewing a frames-based page.

Links are created using the Property inspector in the same way that links are created for normal HTML documents. However, with frames, the *Target* text box drop-down list includes frame names in addition to normal target options such as *_blank* and *_parent,* as shown previously in Figure 5.22. There are a number of choices in the *Target* text box:

- *_blank* opens the target link document in a new browser window.

- *_parent* opens the target link document in the parent frameset of the frame containing the link.

- *_self* opens the target link document in the link frame (the same as leaving the *Target* text box blank).

- *_top* opens the target link document in the current browser window (produces the same effect as *_parent*).

- Clicking a frame name from the *Target* drop-down list opens a target link in that frame.

- Not selecting a target means that *_self* will be the default, so the target link will open in the same frame as the link.

When linking to external Web pages, you should specify *_top* or *_blank* so that viewers do not think the pages are part of your site. It is always a good idea to advise viewers when a link will take them away from a site. Commercial sites often have a disclaimer (as shown in Figure 5.24) advising viewers that a link is to a document outside the site, and that the company is not responsible for the content of the target link.

Figure 5.24 • External Web Site Disclaimer

1. Create links to change frame content by completing the following steps:
   a. Make sure that the Files panel is open and displaying the contents of the ch_05_exercises root folder.
   b. With **ch5ex05.htm** open in the Document window, select the parent frameset, click File on the Menu bar, and then click Save Frameset As to rename and save it as **ch5ex06.htm**.
   c. Click inside the top frame of the frameset in the Document window and then use the Save Frame As command to rename the frame **heading_page-6.htm**. Do this for the remaining two frames, renaming them by changing the -5 after the frame name to -6.
   d. Select the *Home* text in the navigation frame. Use the Property inspector Point to File button to drag the arrow to *main_page-6.htm* in the Files panel. When the file is highlighted, release the mouse button to create a link.

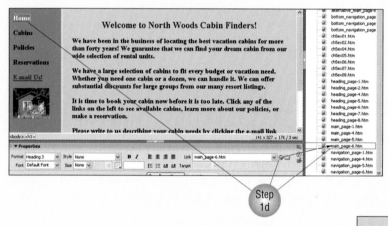

   e. Click the down-pointing arrow next to the *Target* text box to open the drop-down list and click *main_frame*. The link you have created will open the **main_page-6.htm** document in the frame named main_frame when the Home link is clicked in a browser window. *Note: You should see all of the frame names that you created in the* **Target** *text box. If a name is missing, select the frame and type a name for the frame in the* **Frame** name *text box in the upper-left corner of the Frame Property inspector*.
   f. Follow the sequence described in Steps 1d–1e to create links from *Cabins* to *cabin_page.htm,* from *Policies* to *policies_page.htm,* and from *Reservations* to *reservations_page.htm*. For each of these links, choose *main_frame* from the *Target* text box drop-down list. The e-mail link has already been created, so you do not need to do that. *Hint: The files to be linked to are located in the ch_05_student_files folder*.
   g. Click File on the Menu bar and then Save All to save the changes you have made.
   h. Click the Preview/Debug in browser button and then click Preview in iexplore to view the page in a Web browser. Click each of the links. The new pages should appear in the main frame. Clicking the e-mail link opens an e-mail message form with a preaddressed subject header if the browser you are using is configured to work with an e-mail program. Close the browser when you are finished.
2. Close **ch5ex06.htm**.

Creating Navigation Bars

Navigation bars are a slightly more complex version of image rollovers, and are often used in conjunction with frames. They can be created and inserted horizontally or vertically. Figure 5.25 shows an example of a horizontal navigation bar. Navigation bars are composed of a series of images, with each *navigation bar element* being composed of up to four different images as shown in Figure 5.26. Each image is used to create an *element display state,* such as bright or dimmed, that lets users know the current status of the element. Navigation bars are used with frames because users can experience all four states when a navigation bar is placed in a static frame. If a navigation bar is placed on a conventional HTML page, some states will not be seen because when a navigation bar element is clicked, a new document will replace the page containing the navigation bar.

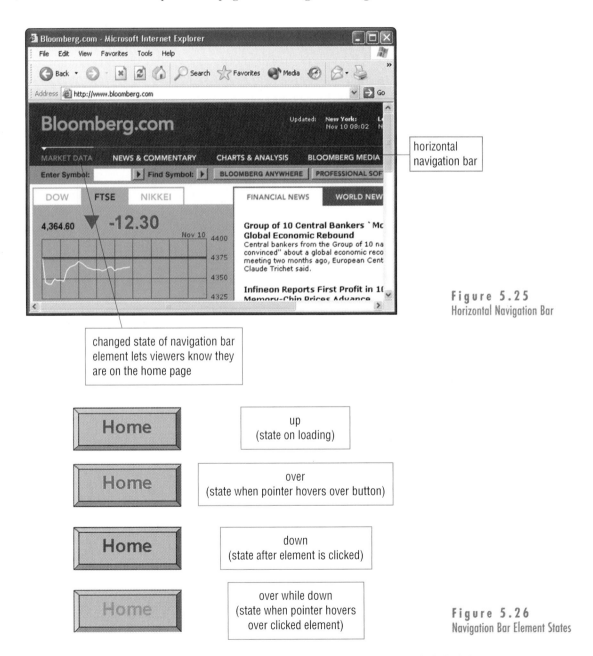

horizontal
navigation bar

Figure 5.25
Horizontal Navigation Bar

changed state of navigation bar
element lets viewers know they
are on the home page

up
(state on loading)

over
(state when pointer hovers over button)

down
(state after element is clicked)

over while down
(state when pointer hovers
over clicked element)

Figure 5.26
Navigation Bar Element States

The four element display states are described in the following list:

- **Up image** The image that appears when the page loads.
- **Over image** The image that appears when the pointer is moved over the up image.
- **Down image** The image that appears after an element has been clicked.
- **Over while down image** The image that appears when the pointer is moved across an element that has already been clicked.

When used for buttons, each image can be the same, but in a different shade or color. For example, an over image might be slightly brighter than an up image to let viewers know that the button is interactive. After the over image is clicked, a down image might be darker to show that the navigation bar element has been selected. Finally, an over while down image might be faded to show that it has already been clicked. It is not necessary to use all four display states, and some designers find using three sufficient.

Clicking the Images button down-pointing arrow on the Insert bar (Common menu item or tab) and then clicking the Navigation Bar command or dragging the navigation bar button to the Document window opens the Insert Navigation Bar dialog box shown in Figure 5.27. Clicking Insert on the Menu bar, pointing to Image Objects, and then clicking Navigation Bar is another way to open this dialog box.

Selecting a navigation bar, clicking Modify on the Menu bar, and then Navigation Bar opens the Modify Navigation Bar dialog box that can be used to change navigation bar properties. The Modify Navigation Bar dialog box does not contain the *Insert* list box that was used to specify horizontal or vertical navigation bar placement when the navigation bar was created, so it is not possible to change that property by using this dialog box. The only way to change from horizontal to vertical placement or vice versa is to delete the navigation bar and recreate it, making sure to indicate the desired horizontal or vertical placement in the Insert Navigation Bar dialog box *Insert* list box.

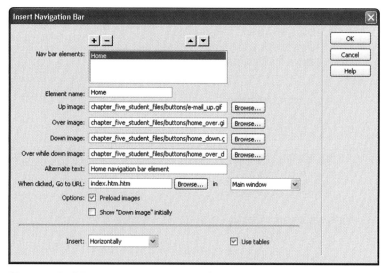

Figure 5.27 • Insert Navigation Bar Dialog Box

1. Add an element to a navigation bar by completing the following steps:
   a. At a clear document screen, open **ch5ex02.htm**, select the frameset, and use the Save Frameset As command to rename and save it as **ch5ex07.htm**.
   b. Click inside the top frame of the frameset in the Document window and then use the Save Frame As command to rename the frame **heading_page-7.htm**. Do this for the remaining two frames, renaming them by changing the -2 after the frame name to -7.
   c. Position the insertion point in the upper-left corner of the bottom frame (bottom_navigation_page-7.htm).

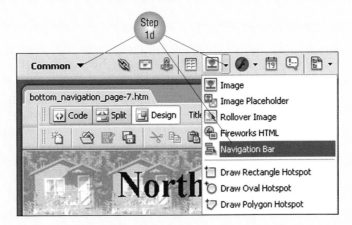

   d. Click the Insert bar Common menu item or tab, the Images button down-pointing arrow, and then Navigation Bar on the submenu to open the Insert Navigation Bar dialog box.

   e. Type **Home** in the dialog box *Element name* text box.
   f. Use the *Up image* text box Browse button to browse and locate the **home_up.gif** file in the ch_05_student_files subfolder named buttons. Click the OK button after you have selected the image. *Hint: All of the buttons are in the buttons folder.*

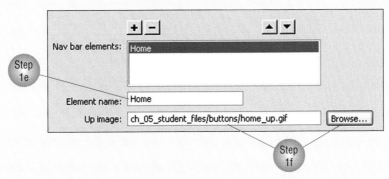

   g. Use the *Over image* text box Browse button to browse and select the **home_over.gif** file and then click the OK button.
   h. Use the *Down image* text box Browse button to browse and select the **home_down.gif** file and then click the OK button.

i. Use the *Over while down image* text box Browse button to browse and select the **home_over_down.gif** file and then click the OK button.

j. Type **Home navigation bar element** in the *Alternate text* text box.

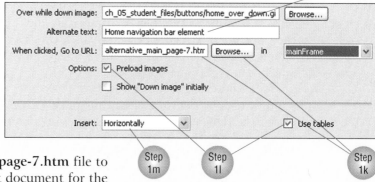

k. Click the *When clicked, Go to URL* text box Browse button to browse and locate the **alternative_main_page-7.htm** file to create a link to that document for the Home element. Click the down-pointing arrow next to the *in* list box located to the right of the Browse button and select *mainFrame* from the drop-down list. ***Hint: Be careful not to select* mainWindow *or the document will open in the main browser window instead of the main frame of the frameset.***

l. Make sure that the *Preload images* and *Use tables* check boxes contain check marks. Leave the *Show "Down image" initially* check box empty.

m. Click the *Insert* list box down-pointing arrow and select *Horizontally* to insert the navigation bar elements in a row. ***Note: Selecting* Vertically *inserts the elements in column form.*** Do not click the OK button when you are finished with the Home element. ***Hint: If you click the OK button, click Modify on the Menu bar and then Navigation Bar to open the Modify Navigation Bar dialog box, which is similar to the Insert Navigation Bar dialog box. Alternatively, select the navigation bar element you just created and then click the Insert bar Navigation Bar button. A message will appear advising that only one navigation bar can appear on a page, and asking if you want to modify the existing navigation bar. Click the OK button to open the Modify Navigation Bar dialog box. The Modify Navigation Bar dialog box does not allow you to change horizontal and vertical placement, so be careful to select the desired placement style when you are creating the navigation bar or you will have to recreate it if you want to change it.***

2. Add additional elements to the navigation bar by completing the following steps:

a. Click the Plus (+) button at the top of the dialog box.

b. Follow Steps 1e–1k to create the Cabins navigation bar element. Type **Cabins** in the *Element name* text box, and then select the appropriate cabin image, for example, **cabins_up.gif** for the *Up image,* and so on. Don't forget to type **Cabins navigation bar element** in the *Alternate text* text box, link the Cabins element to the student file named **cabin_page.htm**, and then select *mainFrame*. When you are finished with the Cabins element, click the Plus (+) button again and repeat Steps 1e–1k for the Policies and Reservations elements. Type the appropriate text in the *Alternate text* text box, and link the elements to the appropriate document, for example, policies to the student file named **policies_page.htm**, and so on. Proceed in this manner to create an e-mail element, but instead of browsing for a link, type mailto:nwcf@emcp.net?subject=I Have a Question! in the *When clicked, Go to URL* text box. Select *Main window* so that the e-mail message will open in its own window. ***Note: Omit the hyphen when typing*** **E-mail** *in the* **Element Name** ***text box.***

c. Click the OK button when you are finished entering all of the elements.

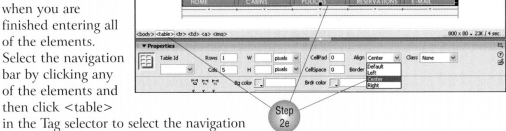

d. Select the navigation bar by clicking any of the elements and then click <table> in the Tag selector to select the navigation bar table. The Property inspector transforms into the Table Property inspector because the navigation bar elements are contained in the selected table.

e. Click the down-pointing arrow next to the *Align* list box and then click *Center* from the drop-down list to center the navigation bar on the page.

f. Click File and then Save All to save the changes you have made.

g. Click the Preview/Debug in browser button and then click Preview in iexplore to view the page in a Web browser. Click the navigation bar elements to verify that they change states and that the links work. Check that the e-mail link opens a new blank message window with a predefined subject line. ***Hint: If no message window opens, check your browser options to determine whether a mail program has been associated with the browser.*** Close the browser when you are finished.

3. Close **ch5ex07.htm**.

Creating Accessible Frames with Frame Titles and Noframes Content

Screen readers vary in the ways that they deal with frames. Some read frames in a linear fashion, one frame after another; others read all of the frames on a page as if they were all from the same document; and still others present users with a list of frames that they can then select for reading. To make frames as accessible as possible, you should provide descriptive frame titles that will help listeners identify the location and meaning of the content being read. For example, a frame with a title *navigation bar* is helpful, whereas a title such as *topframe* is not because it provides no indication of the content of the frame.

Frame titles should not be confused with frame names, which are used to identify the frame a target link will open in when making links, and are not the same as document titles. With the *Frames* check box option selected on the Accessibility Preferences page, a ***Frame Tag Accessibility Attributes dialog box*** will appear when creating predefined framesets as shown in Figure 5.28. The dialog box can be used to enter a frame title for each frame.

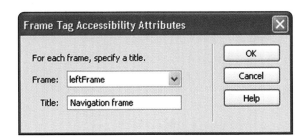

Figure 5.28
Frame Tag Accessibility Attributes Dialog Box

When creating a new frameset from scratch, the dialog box does not appear. Frame titles can be created by switching to Code view and typing title="Frame Title" just before the closing frame angle bracket (>); for example, **<frame src="heading_page.htm" title="Heading Frame">**.

The use of *noframes content* in a frameset is another method of ensuring access to the information in a frames-based Web page. Each frameset page contains a noframes area that can be used to place information describing the content of the frames on the page. This can consist of long text descriptions or links to frames or other HTML documents. Noframes content does not appear in browsers, but it will be read by screen readers. Noframes content also can be seen by those using text-based browsers. Figure 5.29 shows the empty noframes portion of a frameset in Code view. Text entered in noframes view is contained between the two noframes tags.

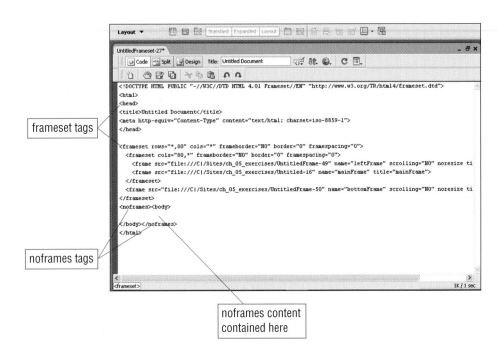

Figure 5.29
Frameset Noframes Area in Code View

frameset tags

noframes tags

noframes content contained here

exercise **8**   CREATING FRAME TITLES AND NOFRAMES CONTENT

1. Create noframes content by completing the following steps:
   a. At a clear document screen, open **ch5ex07.htm**. Click the parent frameset border in the Frames panel to select it, and use the Save Frameset As command to rename and save it as **ch5ex08.htm**.
   b. Click inside the top frame of the frameset in the Document window and then use the Save Frame As command to rename the frame **heading_page-8.htm**. Do this for the remaining two frames, renaming them by changing the -7 after the frame name to -8.
   c. Select the text in **alternative_main_page-8.htm** and copy it by clicking Edit on the Menu bar and then click Copy, or by right-clicking and clicking Copy from the context-sensitive menu.

d. Click Modify on the Menu bar, point to Frameset, and then click Edit NoFrames Content. The Document window is cleared, and a thin gray bar reading *NoFrames Content* appears at the top of the window.

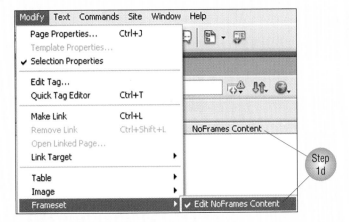

Step 1d

e. Position the insertion point in the *NoFrames Content* window. Click Edit on the Menu bar and then click Paste Text to paste the material copied from **alternative_main_page-8.htm**.

f. Press the Enter key to create a new line after the last line of text (*The Staff at North Woods Cabin Finders*), and then type Click these links to find more information: Cabins, Policies, and Reservations. Click Here to e-mail us.

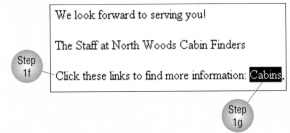

Step 1f

Step 1g

g. Select *Cabins* (do not select the comma), and with the Files panel open, use the Property inspector Point to File button to link to the student file named **cabin_page.htm**. Click the link and then select *_blank* from the Property inspector *Target* text box drop-down list so that the document will open in a new window.

h. Repeat Step 1g to create links for *Policies* and *Reservations*, linking to the appropriate document, for example, *Policies* to the student file named **policies_page.htm**, and so on. Select the *_blank* target window for these links as well.

i. Select *Here* in the *Click Here to e-mail us.* text and type mailto:nwcf@emcp.net?subject=I Have a Question! in the Property inspector *Link* text box to create an e-mail link.

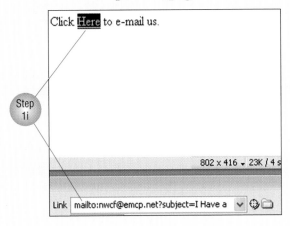

Step 1i

j. Click Modify on the Menu bar, point to Frameset, and then click Edit NoFrames Content to exit the noframes view.

k. Click File and then Save All to save the changes you have made.

1. Use the Frames panel to select the parent frameset in **ch5ex08.htm**. Click the Code button. The frameset and its contents will be highlighted. Just below the closing frameset tag (</frameset>), you will see the opening noframes tag (<noframes>) followed by the content you just entered. The noframes content is not visible in your browser, and is accessible only to those using screen readers and browsers that cannot handle frames. Click the Design button when you are finished.

2. Close **ch5ex08.htm**.

```
</head>

<frameset rows="80,*,80" frameborder="NO" border="0" framespac
    <frame src="heading_page-8.htm" name="topFrame" scrolling="N
    <frame src="alternative_main_page-8.htm" name="mainFrame" ti
    <frame src="bottom_navigation_page-8.htm" name="bottomFrame"
</frameset>
<noframes><body>
Welcome to North Woods Cabin Finders!
<p>We have been in the business of locating the best vacation
<p>We have a large selection of cabins to fit every budget or
<p>It is time to book your cabin now before it is too late. Cl
<p>Please write to us describing your cabin needs by clicking
<p>We look forward to serving you!</p>
<p>The Staff at North Woods Cabin Finders</p>
<p>Click these links to find more information: <a href="ch_05_
</body></noframes>
```

Step 1I

CHAPTER summary

➤ More than 99 percent of the browsers in use today can handle frames.

➤ The latest browser versions allow individual frames to be bookmarked and printed by right-clicking a frame.

➤ With frames, a single Web page can display content from two or more HTML documents at a time.

➤ All of the frames on a page are specified in a frameset, an HTML document that controls frame layout and properties but does not appear in a browser window.

➤ Each frameset must contain a minimum of two frames, indicated by using a single frame tag (<frame>).

➤ Like image tags (<img>), frame tags use a source attribute (**src**) to locate an HTML file and open it in the frame.

➤ A link in a document in one frame can be specified to open a new document in the same frame, in another frame, or in a new browser window.

➤ Heading and navigation frames can remain constant because browsers do not need to reload those pages when the main frame content changes.

➤ Frames can be used to create stable or stationary areas at the bottom of the screen so that content of this bottom frame will be visible whatever the length of the page content and no matter how a browser is resized.

➤ Excessive frames can make navigation difficult for viewers, squeeze the space available in the browser window, and make it difficult to troubleshoot problems.

➤ Framesets should contain no more than three frames.

- Framesets and frames can be designed from scratch or can be created using predefined framesets.

- Before working with frames, you should use the View options button to make sure that frame borders are visible when working in the Document window.

- When framesets are created using the Insert bar Frames button (Layout menu item or tab) or the Frames command on the Insert menu, a new document must be open in the Document window. The document open in the Document window will be contained in one of the frameset's frames.

- Framesets can be created using the New Document dialog box without a new document open in the Document window.

- Building a frameset using the Frameset command results in a frameset with two frames.

- The Frameset commands can be used to add frames to a frameset by splitting existing frames.

- Any frameset in which the number of frames varies between rows or columns will automatically contain nested framesets.

- Frames also can be added to a frameset by dragging a frameset border and moving it toward the center of the Document window.

- Dragging a horizontal border splits a frame horizontally, while dragging a vertical border splits a frame vertically.

- If a frame border is located inside a frameset, holding down the Alt key while dragging it splits the frame.

- A frame also can be split into four frames by positioning the insertion point on a frame corner until it turns into the move icon, and then dragging the move icon. Because this method results in a frameset containing more than three frames, it is not recommended.

- The Frame Property inspector *Src* text box can be used to browse and locate a frame document source.

- The background color of a frame is determined by the document contained in the frame.

- Framesets and frame documents must be saved before they can be previewed in a browser.

- Dreamweaver MX 2004 gives framesets and frames temporary file names, such as UntitledFrameset-1.htm, UntitledFrame-2.htm, and so on, but you should create your own file names because the temporary names are similar enough to cause confusion.

- The Document toolbar *Title* text box can be used to enter a title for each document. Document titles should not be confused with frame titles.

- After a frameset or frame has been saved, choosing Save Frameset As or Save Frame As creates a copy of the frameset or frame that can be renamed.

- Using the Save All command saves all open framesets and frames. It is a good habit to use the Save All command periodically to ensure that all framesets and frame documents are saved.

- Frames can be deleted by dragging them out of the Document window, or by dragging them to a frame border.

- Closing a frameset without saving it deletes it.

- To delete a saved frameset, delete the file in the Files panel.

➤ You can create predefined framesets by using the Insert bar Frames button (Layout menu item or tab), by using the Frames command on the Insert menu, or by using the framesets options available through the New Document dialog box.

➤ The Insert bar Frames button (Layout menu item or tab) can be dragged to the Document window to create a frameset. The frameset created depends on the last Frames button command selected from the Frames button submenu.

➤ After a predefined frameset has been created, frame borders can be dragged to new locations.

➤ Dreamweaver MX 2004 automatically provides frame names for each frame in a predefined frameset.

➤ Frame names appear in the Frame Property inspector *Target* text box drop-down list, and are used when specifying the frame that a target link document will open in.

➤ Selected frameset and frame properties can be changed using the Frameset or Frame Property inspectors.

➤ Positioning the insertion point inside a frame selects the document in a frame, not the frame itself.

➤ The Frames panel can be displayed by clicking Window on the Menu bar and then Frames.

➤ The Frames panel shows the structure of the frameset and the frames and nested framesets it contains in outline form.

➤ A frameset can be selected by clicking a frameset outside border in the Frames panel.

➤ The Frames panel can be used to select a frameset by clicking in one of the frames in the Frames panel and then selecting <frameset> in the Tag selector.

➤ If a frameset contains a nested frameset tag, it might appear in the Tag selector depending on whether a parent or a nested frameset frame was selected.

➤ Holding down the Alt key and clicking in a frame in the Document window causes one or more frameset tags to appear in the Tag selector.

➤ After a frameset tag appears in the Tag selector, clicking it selects the frameset that tag controls and opens the Frameset Property inspector.

➤ Framesets can be selected by clicking a frameset border in the Document window, but this can sometimes be difficult to do.

➤ Clicking inside a frame in the Frames panel places a thin black line around a frame, places a dotted line around the frame in the Document window, and opens the Frame Property inspector.

➤ Frames also can be selected by holding down the Alt key and clicking inside a frame in the Document window. If the Alt key is not held down, this action selects only the HTML document that will appear in the frame.

➤ When a frameset has been selected, the Property inspector appears as the Frameset Property inspector.

➤ When a frame has been selected, the Property inspector appears as the Frame Property inspector.

➤ You should set frameset properties first because some of the settings can affect frame properties.

- Relative frame values are relative to the width or height of other frames in a frameset.

- Most Dreamweaver MX 2004 predefined framesets use a combination of fixed and relative values for the frames that form frameset rows and columns.

- Links can be used to change the content of another frame.

- When a link is made to a frame, the target frame is identified by its frame name, which appears in the Property inspector *Target* text box drop-down list.

- Frame names are case-sensitive and must begin with a letter, not a number. If a frame name contains more than one word, the words should be connected using underscores (_).

- Links are created using the Property inspector in the same way that links are created for normal HTML documents.

- Navigation bars are a slightly more complex version of image rollovers, and navigation bars are often used in conjunction with frames.

- Navigation bars are composed of a series of images, with each navigation bar element being composed of up to four different images.

- The four different navigation bar element display states are up, over, down, and over while down.

- Clicking the Images button on the Insert bar (Common menu item or tab) and then Navigation Bar from the submenu opens the Insert Navigation Bar dialog box.

- To make frames as accessible as possible, you should provide descriptive frame titles that will help listeners identify the location and meaning of the content being read.

- Frame titles should not be confused with frame names, which are used to identify the frame a target link will open in when making links, and are not the same as the document titles used to identify HTML documents.

- With the *Frames* check box option selected on the Accessibility Preferences page, a Frame Tag Accessibility Attributes dialog box will appear when creating predefined framesets.

- Frame titles can be created by switching to Code view and typing a title in a frame tag.

- The use of noframes content in a frameset is another method of ensuring access to the information in a frame-based Web page.

- Noframes content does not appear in browsers, but will be read by screen readers, and also can be seen by those using text-based browsers.

banner area See *heading*.

element display state The appearance of a button or element in a navigation bar, correlated to the current status of the element link, for example, clicked or unclicked.

frame borders Three-dimensional frame borders that can be specified to appear when frames are displayed in a browser window.

frame name Target link frames are identified by frame names, which appear in the Property inspector *Target* text box drop-down list.

Frame Property inspector The Property inspector that is displayed when a frame is selected.

frames Page regions containing an HTML document as specified in a frameset document.

frameset An HTML document that controls frame layout and properties.

Frameset Property inspector Property inspector mode used to modify frameset properties.

frameset tags The tags (<frameset>) used to create framesets.

Frames panel A panel used for selecting framesets and frames.

frame tag The tag (<frame>) used to create frames in a frameset document.

Frame Tag Accessibility Attributes dialog box Dialog box that can be used to create frame titles.

frame titles Titles used to identify frames for accessibility.

heading Area at the top of a Web page used to contain a heading or introductory text and/or image for a Web site. Also called *banner area*.

move icon An icon that appears when clicking the corner of a frame and dragging to resize it.

navigation bar element A button on a navigation bar.

navigation bars A slightly more complex version of image rollovers, often used in conjunction with frames for navigation link purposes.

noframes content An area in a frameset that can be used to place content or links to content for viewers using browsers that cannot view frames.

***No resize* check box** A check mark in this Frame Property inspector check box prevents viewers from resizing a frame in a browser.

predefined framesets Ready-made framesets available by using the Insert bar frame buttons, or by clicking Insert and then Frames.

relative values Frame dimension values that are relative to the width or height of other frames in a frameset.

scroll bars Horizontal or vertical bars next to frames that are used to scroll (move up and down, or left to right) and view frame content.

COMMANDS review

Create a frameset	Modify, Frameset
Create a predefined frameset	Insert, HTML, Frames, or File, New
Create noframes content	Modify, Frameset, Edit NoFrames Content
Modify a navigation bar	Modify, Navigation Bar
Open a document in a frame	File, Open in Frame
Open the Frames panel	Window, Frames
Save a frame	File, Save Frame or Save Frame As
Save a frameset	File, Save Frameset or Save Frameset As
Save frameset and frames	File, Save All
Split a frameset	Modify, Frameset

CONCEPTS check

Indicate the correct term or command for each item.

1. This command can be used to save a frameset and frame documents at the same time.
2. An HTML document that controls frame layout and properties is called this.
3. This is the term for page regions in HTML documents that can contain other HTML documents.
4. This panel can be used to select framesets and frames.
5. Depending on whether or not a frameset has been previously saved, one or both of these commands can be used to save a frameset.
6. This indicates a selected frameset or frame in the Document window when using the Save All command to save a frameset and frames for the first time.
7. This is the term for a frameset located inside another frameset.
8. Frameset tags replace these tags in a frameset document.
9. Frame names appear in this Property inspector text box.
10. The Frames panel is displayed by clicking this Menu bar command and then clicking Frames from the drop-down menu that appears.
11. Frames can be deleted from a frameset by doing this.
12. Framesets can be created without a document open in the Document window when using this dialog box.
13. This Insert bar button can be used to create predefined framesets.
14. Frame names can be created or changed using this Frame Property inspector text box.
15. If the *Frames* check box has been enabled on the Preferences page, this dialog box will appear after a predefined frameset is inserted on a page.
16. Frame titles serve this function.
17. Frames can be selected by holding down this key and clicking inside a frame in the Document window.
18. Dimensions for a frame are relative to this.
19. When allocating space, browsers first calculate frames with values specified using this value unit.
20. Frame names longer than one word can be connected using this character.

SKILLS check

Use the Site Definition dialog box to create a separate Dreamweaver site named CH 05 Assessments to keep your assessment work for this chapter. Save the files for the site in a new root folder named ch_05_assessments under the Sites folder you created in Chapter 1, Exercise 3. Download the ch_05_student_files folder from the IRC to the CH 05 Assessments site root folder (ch_05_assessments) and expand it. Delete the compressed folder when you are finished.

Assessment 1 • Create a Frameset and Frames

1. The company you work for has asked you to create a frameset page containing three frames. One frame will function as a horizontal heading or banner area at the top of the page. The main page content will be contained in a vertical frame on the right, while the frame on the left will contain a vertical navigation bar that can be used to change the content of the main frame. Create the frameset and save it as **ch5sa1_frameset.htm**. Save the three frame documents as **ch5sa1_frame_1.htm** (the banner frame), **ch5sa1_frame_2.htm** (the main content frame), and **ch5sa1_frame_3.htm** (the navigation frame). Use the Frame Property inspector to create a frame name for each frame to help you identify its function.
2. Specify a background color for each of the three frames, and be sure to choose three colors that create an attractive combination.
3. Specify a default font size, style, and color for each page. The font color you choose for each page can vary depending on the page background color.
4. If necessary, make the frame borders invisible.
5. Save the documents but do not close them.

Assessment 2 • Add Content to the Frames

1. Use the Save Frameset As and Save Frame As commands to rename the frameset and frames from Assessment 1 by changing the *ch5sa1* portion of each name to *ch5sa2* (for example, frameset **ch5sa1_frameset.htm** will become **ch5sa2_frameset.htm**, and so on).
2. Think of a name for your company, create an attractive banner or header frame containing the company name, and insert it in the banner frame (**ch5sa2_frame_1.htm**). Customers will see this page at the top of every document in the site, so it should include a background image or color to make it as attractive as possible.
3. Enter content in the main content frame document (**ch5sa2_frame_2.htm**) that will serve as the introductory page for the frameset. The content should introduce the company and its products, and explain how the navigation buttons can be used to change the content in the main frame.
4. Create three new HTML documents and save them as **ch5sa2_frame_2-a.htm, ch5sa2_frame_2-b.htm**, and **ch5sa2_frame_2-c.htm**. Each of these pages will contain content about the company's products or services. Use your imagination, and then enter content in these pages. For example, if you decided that the company you worked for was an automobile dealer, each of these pages could contain information on a different model of car. Each page should contain at least one image. The purpose of these pages is to attract customer interest, so design them to be as attractive as possible.

DREAMWEAVER MX 2004

5. Preview the framesets and frames in a browser to make sure that they appear as you intended. Troubleshoot and repair if necessary.
6. Save the documents but do not close them.

Assessment 3 • Create and Insert a Vertical Navigation Bar

1. Use the Save Frameset As and Save Frame As commands to rename the frameset and frames from Assessment 2 by changing the *ch5sa2* portion of each name to *ch5sa3* (for example, frameset **ch5sa2_frameset.htm** will become **ch5sa3_frameset.htm**, and so on). *Hint: Do not forget to open and rename ch5sa2_frame_2-a.htm, ch5sa2_frame_2-b.htm, and ch5sa2_frame_2-c.htm as ch5sa3_frame_2-a.htm, ch5sa3_frame_2-b.htm, and ch5sa3_frame_2-c.htm.*

2. Create a vertical navigation bar in the left vertical frame (**ch5sa3_frame_3.htm**) using the buttons located in the ch_05_student_files folder subfolder named assessment buttons. Link the Home button to the opening document in the main frame (**ch5sa3_frame_2.htm**) using the four element display states. Link the three remaining buttons (**page1_up_sa3.gif**, and so on) so that they open the **ch5sa3_frame_2-a.htm**, **ch5sa3_frame_2-b.htm**, and **ch5sa3_frame_2-c.htm** documents in the main frame. *Note: Include alternate text for each button. Hint: The documents should open in the main frame of the frameset.*

3. Save all of the documents and then preview the frameset in a browser. Check that the links work and troubleshoot if necessary. *Note: Resize the navigation bar frame if necessary to display the buttons fully. In order to be able to resize borders, make sure that they are visible in the Document window by clicking the View options button, pointing to Visual Aids, and then making sure there is a check mark next to Frame Borders.*

4. Save the documents but do not close them.

Assessment 4 • Add Noframes Content to a Frameset and Frame Titles to Frames

1. Use the Save Frameset As and Save Frame As commands to rename the frameset and frames 1 and 3 from Assessment 3 by changing the *ch5sa3* portion of each name to *ch5sa4* (for example, frameset **ch5sa3_frameset.htm** will become **ch5sa4_frameset.htm**, and so on). *Note: Do not rename ch5sa3_frame_2, ch5sa3_frame_2-a.htm, ch5sa3_frame_2-b.htm, and ch5sa3_frame_2-c.htm because that would break the previously created navigation bar links to those pages. If you do rename these documents you will have to recreate the navigation bar links by using the Modify Navigation Bar dialog box.*

2. Create noframes content in the form of links to each of the four documents that appear in the main frame. Each link should be preceded by a description of the link. For example, the link to the noframes content for the introductory page in the main frame (**ch5sa3_frame_2.htm**) might read: *Click this Link to view the main introductory page containing information about products.* **Hint: Remember to click the link and then select -blank from the Property inspector Target text box drop-down list so that the document will open in a new window.**

3. Save and close all of the documents.

Assessment 5 • Add Frames to Your Design Portfolio

1. Add at least one frameset to your design portfolio, making sure to format it so that the frames that it contains are in line with the style you created for your site pages. One of the frameset frames should contain navigation buttons or links to change the content of at least one of the frames in the frameset.

USING CASCADING STYLE SHEETS (CSS)

PERFORMANCE OBJECTIVES

- ➤ Understand Cascading Style Sheets (CSS).
- ➤ Create inline, internal, and external style sheets.
- ➤ Attach external style sheets to documents.
- ➤ Create grouped (multiple) selectors.
- ➤ Create contextual selectors.
- ➤ Create Class (Custom) styles.
- ➤ Create Pseudo selectors.
- ➤ Use predefined style sheets.
- ➤ Export styles.
- ➤ Edit and remove styles and style sheets.

The student files for this chapter are available for download from the Internet Resource Center at www.emcp.com.

Cascading Style Sheets (CSS) work by applying formatting rules (styles) to page elements. CSS styles can be applied to a document in any of three different ways: as an external style sheet that can be attached to one or more documents, inserted in the head section of a document, or contained inside a tag.

The great advantage of CSS is that changes made to a style sheet change the formatting in every document that is attached to the sheet or to the formatting in the document containing the sheet if the style sheet is contained in the head section of a document. With font tags, any changes would have to be made manually wherever formatting was required. The need to make formatting changes on each page can be a very time-consuming task on a large site, so the convenience of using CSS for large sites is easy to see.

Although CSS is the future, acceptance by the Web community has been slower than anticipated because of problems with browser support and the necessity of learning a new skill for those who are comfortable using older methods of dealing with formatting. Positioning page elements with CSS can be tricky, and a common compromise solution in use today is to combine tables for page layout with CSS for formatting. Although the full range of what CSS can accomplish is beyond the scope of this book, you will learn enough to make designing Web pages much easier.

Setting the Dreamweaver MX 2004 CSS Formatting Default

Unlike Dreamweaver MX, the default Dreamweaver MX 2004 setup uses CSS styles inserted in the head section of a document to implement formatting changes applied using the Property inspector or Menu bar commands. Figure 6.1 shows the Code and Design view of a document in which the text color, background color, and font size have been formatted using the Property inspector. In the Code view portion you can see the CSS styles that have been placed in the head section and body of the document to effect the formatting changes.

Before continuing further, you should verify that the use of CSS for formatting is the default setting for the copy of Dreamweaver MX 2004 you are using. Verify that automatic CSS formatting is enabled by completing the following steps:

1. Click Edit on the Menu bar and then Preferences.
2. If necessary, click *General* in the *Category* list box.
3. Look to see if a check mark is placed in the check box next to *Use CSS instead of HTML tags*. If the check box is empty, click it to place a check mark in it and enable CSS formatting.
4. Click the Preferences dialog box OK button to close it.

While Dreamweaver MX 2004 allows you to use CSS automatically when working with the Property inspector or Menu bar commands, you will find that creating and editing your own CSS style sheets and CSS styles provides even greater flexibility and increased control over the appearance of the Web page documents you create.

Understanding CSS

In HTML, **structural tags**, such as paragraph tags (<p>), are used to indicate the structure of Web page content so that browsers can interpret and display the content. For example, a pair of paragraph tags enables the browser to identify the material between the paired tags as a paragraph. Structural tags cannot tell browsers exactly how the content should be displayed, and browsers often vary in the ways they display page content. To exert more control over the way browsers display content, **presentational tags**, such as the font tag (<font>), were developed.

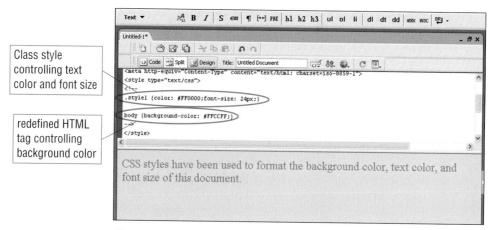

Class style controlling text color and font size

redefined HTML tag controlling background color

Figure 6.1 • HTML Document Showing CSS Styles

Thus, if a designer wants a paragraph to appear in a red font, the HTML code would look like this:

```
<p><font color="#FF0000">This text is red.</font></p>
```

In this example, the font tag includes a **color** attribute and a value for that attribute (#FF0000, the hexadecimal code for red). A single font tag could contain a number of other attributes and values, such as **face** to indicate the font style, and **size** to indicate the font size. This short piece of code becomes even longer if a coder decides that the text should appear in a size 4, Arial font face:

```
<p><font color="#FF0000" size="4" face="Arial,
Helvetica, sans-serif">This text is red.</font></p>
```

This example, multiplied many times throughout a Web page, illustrates how presentational markup creates crowded and confusing code, code that can slow down page loading.

Another drawback to using the presentational tag approach to instruct browsers how to display page content is that adding presentational markup is a time-consuming task, even more so when changes need to be made. Imagine a site consisting of 100 different Web pages with each page containing some examples of green, level-one heading text. If a decision is made that the headings should be red instead, each page would have to be opened and the changes made to each occurrence of paired level-one heading tags. That exercise could take hours, if not days, and it would be easy to miss some of the heading tags that needed modification.

By separating HTML structure from presentation, CSS offers a much more efficient method of instructing browsers how to display Web pages. Instead of requiring presentational tags and attributes scattered throughout an HMTL document, CSS contains instructions known as *CSS styles* or *CSS rules*. These styles can be used *inline* (inside a tag), as an *internal style sheet* (*embedded* in the head section of an HTML document), or as an *external style sheet* that can be attached to any number of HTML documents.

The real beauty of CSS is found in external style sheets and the way they can be linked to HTML documents to control how browsers display their content. Whereas changing a green, level-one heading to a red heading in a large Web site of traditionally formatted pages might take hours, with an external style sheet linked to all of the pages in the Web site, you would need to change only the style in the style sheet dealing with level-one headings. This is one of the reasons that the W3C recommends using external styles sheets whenever possible. In addition to this obvious convenience, CSS also allows you easily to do things that are difficult or impossible to do with ordinary HTML, such as removing the underlining from hyperlinks.

CSS Styles

Internal and external style sheets usually consist of a number of different CSS styles, with each style instructing a browser how to display different elements of page content. Because styles also can be placed inside tags (inline styles), or embedded in the head section of an HTML document (internal style sheets), the use of the word *sheet* can be confusing. For that reason it is helpful to keep in mind that a style sheet is a collection of one or more styles, which might not be located in a separate "sheet" or document, as is the case with an external style sheet.

CSS styles are composed of a selector and a declaration and are the basic building blocks of style sheets. A *selector* frequently, but not always, redefines or modifies an existing HTML tag and can be created for any HTML tag or element. Selectors are followed by *declarations* that declare and define the properties of the tag that the selector is redefining. Declarations are composed of a *property* (`color`, `size`, and so on) and a *value* (`blue`, `+4`, and so on) for the property being set. Declarations are contained inside what the W3C refers to as curly braces ({ }). For example, a selector that calls for the text in a paragraph to be brown would look like this: `p { color: #330000;}`. In this example, the paragraph tag is the selector, `color` is the property, and `#330000` (hexadecimal code for brown) is the value. This selector has redefined the paragraph tag by specifying the color of any text appearing between paired paragraph tags. The semicolon after the last declaration in this example is optional, but it is used by Dreamweaver MX 2004.

Selectors can contain more than one declaration. If you want a paragraph to appear with a yellow background, you can add a declaration to the previous example by using a semicolon to separate it from the first declaration:

```
p { color: #330000; background-color: #FFFF99;}
```

Selectors can also redefine more than one tag at the same time by separating the tags with commas. When a selector redefines more than one tag at a time it is known as a *grouped* or *multiple selector*. The following example of a grouped selector redefines both level-one and level-two heading tags so that both appear in red:

```
h1, h2 { color: #FF0000; }
```

Selectors can also be created that can be applied to any tag. Such a selector is called a *Class style* or *Custom style*. Instead of a tag as the selector, the Class style is given a name beginning with a period, such as `.style1`. For example, the Class style `.style1 { color: #FF0000; font-family: Arial, Helvetica, sans-serif; }` could be applied to any text-related tag to make the controlled element appear in a red Arial font style.

Selectors that work only when certain conditions are met are known as *contextual selectors*. A contextual selector's formatting will be applied only when the conditions stated in the contextual selector style are met, such as `h1 strong {color: #00FF00;}`. This contextual style would format level-one heading text in green (`#00FF00`) only if the level-one heading text was also formatted using strong tags. If a document containing this contextual selector (or attached to an external style sheet containing the contextual selector) contained examples of level-one headings, only those level-one headings that were also formatted using the strong tag would appear in green.

Finally, there are selectors known as *Pseudo classes*. Pseudo classes are selectors that are active when an event takes place, such as hovering the pointer over a link, and they are used primarily to change hyperlink properties. For example, the Pseudo class selector `a:link {text-decoration: none;}` will remove the underlining from links on a page.

Cascading and Hierarchy

Style sheets are referred to as *cascading* because of the hierarchical order in which they are interpreted by browsers. Styles closer to the structural code (HTML tags) in a document generally take precedence over styles located farther away. Therefore, inline styles (located inside HTML tags) take precedence over internal styles (located in HTML document head sections), and internal styles in turn take precedence over styles contained in external style sheets. Thus, when rule conflicts occur, the rule closer to the actual code wins. Despite this approach, you should always avoid creating redundant or conflicting rules.

Although font tags use a different approach to formatting text, they will override CSS styles because they work at the tag level. In fact, any tag-level formatting will override a style. If a CSS style does not work, some tag formatting might need to be removed before the style can take effect.

The concept of *inheritance* is related to cascading. Inheritance means that a closer style can inherit rules from styles located higher up the style chain as long as those styles do not conflict with the closer style's own rules. For example, if an external style sheet specifies left alignment, an internal style sheet would follow (inherit) that rule as long as it did not contain a conflicting rule, such as a rule specifying right alignment.

More than one external style sheet can be attached to a document or series of documents. Although it is a good idea to use a single external style sheet, some designers create separate external style sheets, each dealing with a separate presentational aspect. For example, two separate style sheets could be attached to the documents in a Web site, with one sheet dealing with text formatting and the other dealing with table formatting. When more than one external style sheet is attached to documents, the order in which they were attached becomes important. In case of a rule conflict, rules in the most recently attached external style sheet take precedence.

Creating a New External Style Sheet

If you are comfortable coding directly in HTML, you can create new external style sheets by clicking File on the Menu bar and then New to open the New Document dialog box as shown in Figure 6.2. Clicking *Basic page* in the *Category* list box and then *CSS* in the *Basic page* list box opens a new CSS document in the Document window in Code view. You should save and name the CSS document before applying styles to it by using the Save or Save As commands. Because external style sheets

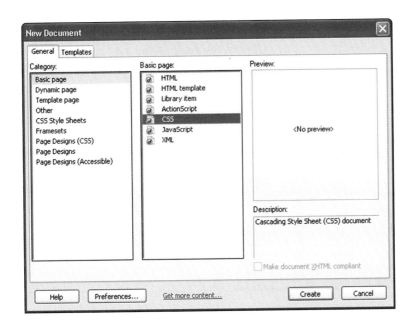

Figure 6.2
New Document Dialog Box
Basic CSS Page

are not HTML documents, they have their own file extension (.css). Whenever possible, choose names that describe what the style sheet does. For example, if a style sheet deals primarily with tables, you might name it table_properties.css. If you use a number of different external style sheets in a site, you should store them in a separate folder.

Fortunately for noncoders, Dreamweaver MX 2004 makes it easy to use panels and dialog boxes to create external style sheets and CSS styles. To create an external style sheet, open the CSS Styles panel located inside the Design panel group and click the CSS Styles tab. If the Design panel group is not open, you can display it by clicking Window on the Menu bar and then CSS Styles.

Click the New CSS Style button located at the bottom of the CSS Styles panel to begin creating the style sheet by opening the New CSS Style dialog box shown in Figure 6.3. Another method for opening the dialog box is to click Text on the Menu bar, point to CSS Styles, and then click New. An HTML document must be open in the current window for the New button to be enabled.

If a CSS document has already been created and is the current document, click the *This document only* radio button at the bottom of the dialog box to add styles to the CSS document. If an HTML document is open in the Document window and the *Define in (New Style Sheet File)* radio button is clicked, Dreamweaver MX 2004 creates a new external style sheet and automatically attaches it to the HTML document. You are prompted to provide a name for the style sheet to save it to the appropriate location.

The Property inspector also can be used to create an external style sheet with an HTML document open in the Document window by clicking the *Style* list box down-pointing arrow and then *Manage Styles* from the list that appears as shown in Figure 6.4. This opens the Edit Style Sheet dialog box as shown in Figure 6.5. Clicking the dialog box New button opens the New CSS Style dialog box, which functions just as it does when opened using the CSS Styles panel.

Redefining HTML Tags

Working in an upward motion in the New CSS Style dialog box, you are given three style choices: *Advanced (IDs, contextual selectors, etc)*, *Tag (redefines the look of a specific tag)*, or *Class (can apply to any tag)*. *Advanced (IDs, contextual selectors, etc)* and *Class (can apply to any tag)* are described in later sections of this chapter. Selecting *Tag (redefines the look of a specific tag)* allows you to create selectors for tags of your choosing. Click the down-pointing arrow to the right of the *Tag* text box to open a drop-down list of HTML tags as shown in Figure 6.6. Click a tag and then click the OK button to open the CSS Style Definition dialog box, which can be used to redefine the chosen tag.

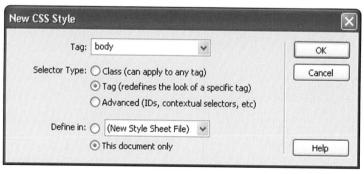

Figure 6.3 • New CSS Style Dialog Box

Figure 6.4 • Property Inspector *Style* List Box List

DREAMWEAVER MX 2004

The name of the CSS Style Definition dialog box reflects the tag that was selected when using the New CSS Style dialog box. For example, if *body* was selected from the *Tag* text box drop-down list, the dialog box would appear as the CSS Style definition for body dialog box as shown in Figure 6.7.

When the Page Properties dialog box is used to format page properties, Dreamweaver MX 2004 redefines tags to include the specified formatting properties. Figure 6.8 shows a redefined body tag in the head section of an HTML document that was formatted to display a yellow page background using the Property inspector.

Figure 6.5 • Edit Style Sheet Dialog Box

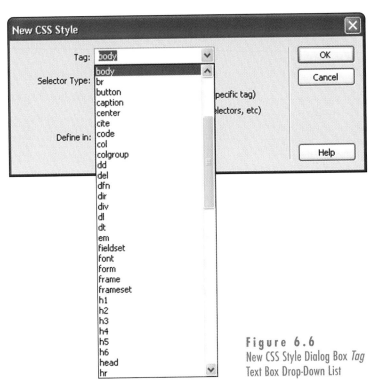

Figure 6.6
New CSS Style Dialog Box *Tag*
Text Box Drop-Down List

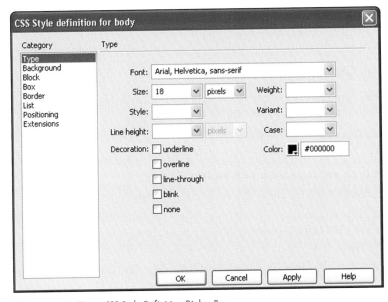

Figure 6.7 • CSS Style Definition Dialog Box

Figure 6.8 • Redefined Body Tag in an
HTML Document

Using the CSS Style Definition Dialog Box

The CSS Style Definition dialog box has eight different categories, and selecting a category changes the properties that can be defined in the dialog box. Although the eight categories are briefly described in the following list, it is beyond the scope of this chapter to fully describe each category. However, clicking the dialog box Help button opens a Using Dreamweaver page that describes the various properties and values of each dialog box category as shown in Figure 6.9.

- **Type** Specifies font and text properties.
- **Background** Specifies a color or image as an element background.
- **Block** Specifies text formatting such as word and letter spacing, alignment, and indentation.
- **Box** Specifies element placement.
- **Border** Specifies element border properties, such as line, color, and thickness.
- **List** Specifies number and bullet formats and positions.
- **Positioning** Specifies layer positioning.
- **Extensions** Controls page breaks, insertion point appearance, and extension style attributes. Browser support for these features is mixed.

You might be overwhelmed by the choices available, but in many cases, creating a style can involve specifying only one or two different properties from a category and the other properties can be left empty. A style can be defined using properties from only one of the category windows if desired. Not all of the CSS properties that can be defined will take effect in the Document window, so the only way to be sure that a style has been implemented is to preview a page in a browser.

You should click the dialog box OK button only when you are finished defining a style. Another tag can be defined as a selector and added to a style sheet by clicking the New CSS Style button in the CSS Styles panel again and repeating the steps used to define the first selector. After the process is complete, save the document before closing it.

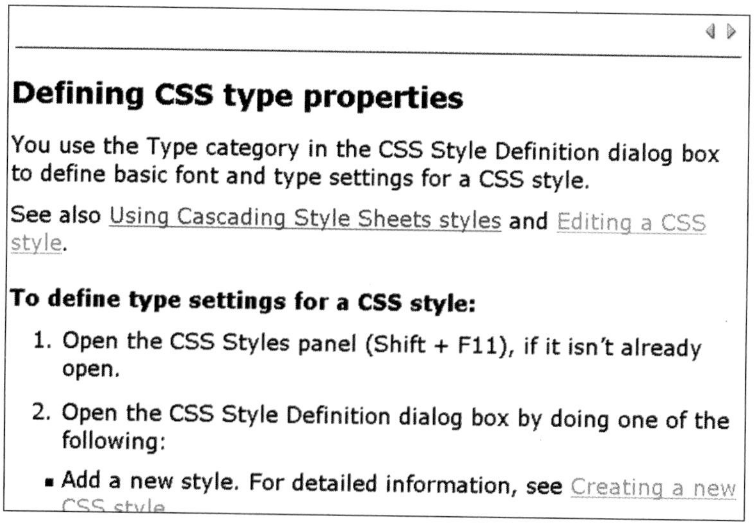

Defining CSS type properties

You use the Type category in the CSS Style Definition dialog box to define basic font and type settings for a CSS style.

See also Using Cascading Style Sheets styles and Editing a CSS style.

To define type settings for a CSS style:

1. Open the CSS Styles panel (Shift + F11), if it isn't already open.

2. Open the CSS Style Definition dialog box by doing one of the following:

   ■ Add a new style. For detailed information, see Creating a new CSS style

Figure 6.9 • CSS Style Definition Dialog Box CSS Type Category Help Page

Attaching an External Style Sheet to a Document

After an external style sheet has been created, it can be attached to a document by clicking the Attach Style Sheet button located at the bottom-right corner of the CSS Styles panel as shown in Figure 6.10. This opens the Attach External Style Sheet dialog box shown in Figure 6.11. The dialog box Browse button can be used to browse and locate the desired style sheet. Only files with .css extensions can be attached as style sheets. The dialog box contains two radio buttons, *Link* and *Import*. *Link* is the default choice that should be selected in almost all cases.

Figure 6.10
CSS Styles Panel Attach Style Sheet Button

The Attach External Style Sheet dialog box also can be opened by clicking Text on the Menu bar, pointing to CSS Styles, and then clicking Manage Styles. This opens the Edit Style Sheet dialog box. Clicking the dialog box Attach button opens the Attach External Style Sheet dialog box.

The Property inspector also can be used to attach an external style sheet to a document by clicking the down-pointing arrow next to *Styles* list box and then clicking *Manage Styles*. This opens the Attach External Style Sheet dialog box. The dialog box Browse button then can be used to browse and locate a CSS style sheet that will be attached to the current document.

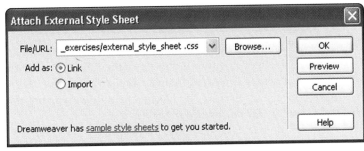

Figure 6.11 • Attach External Style Sheet Dialog Box

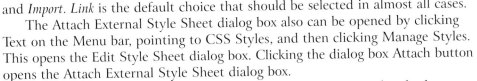

CREATING AND ATTACHING AN EXTERNAL STYLE SHEET

1. If necessary, start Dreamweaver MX 2004.
2. At a clear document screen, create a new site named CH 06 Exercises to store the exercises you create in this chapter. Name the root folder ch_06_exercises and save it under the Sites folder you created in Chapter 1, Exercise 3. Download the ch_06_student_files folder from the IRC to the CH 06 Exercises site root folder (ch_06_exercises) and expand it. Delete the compressed folder when you are finished. *Note: Refer to Chapter 1 for instructions on navigating with the Files panel integrated file browser.*
3. Redefine an HTML tag to create a style in an external style sheet that automatically will be attached to the current document by completing the following steps:
   a. At a clear document screen, open the student file named **css_styles_sampler.htm** and use the Save As command to rename and save it to the ch_06_exercises root folder as **ch6ex01.htm**.

b. If necessary, click the CSS Styles tab in the Design panel group to make sure that it is the active panel. *Hint: If the Design panel group is not open, click Window on the Menu bar and then CSS Styles. The Design panel group will open with the CSS Styles panel as the active panel.*

c. Click the New CSS Style button located in the lower-right corner of the CSS Styles panel to open the New CSS Style dialog box.

d. If necessary, at the bottom of the dialog box, click the *Define in (New Style Sheet File)* radio button.

e. Click the *Tag (redefines the look of a specific tag)* radio button.

f. Click the down-pointing arrow next to the *Tag* text box to open the *Tag* drop-down list. Click *body* to redefine this tag, and then click the OK button when you are finished. The Save Style Sheet File As dialog box opens so that the external style sheet document can be named and saved. *Note: All of the content of an HTML document is located between the starting and ending body tags. Because ch6ex01.htm was open in the Document window during the creation process, the style sheet is automatically attached to it.*

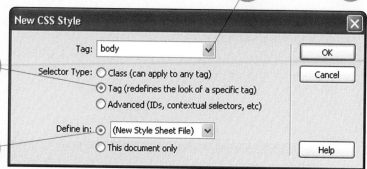

g. Type external_style_sheet in the *File name* text box, locate the ch_06_exercises folder, and then click the Save button to save the document. The CSS Style Definition dialog box opens so that styles can be created and placed in the style sheet.

h. Click *Type* in the *Category* list box, if it is not already selected.

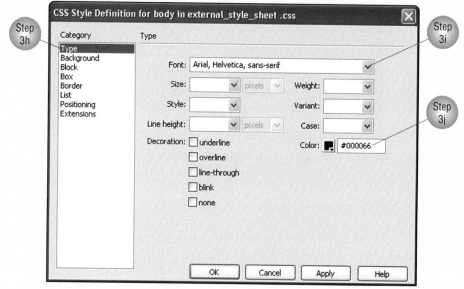

i. Click the down-pointing arrow to the right of the *Font* text box and then click *Arial, Helvetica, sans-serif* from the drop-down list that appears.

DREAMWEAVER MX 2004

j.   Type #000066 (a dark blue) in the text box next to the *Color* color box.

k.   Click *Background* in the *Category* list box.

l.   Type #00FFFF (a light blue) in the text box next to the *Background color* color box.

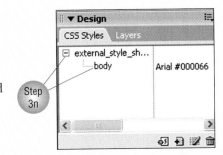

m.   Click the OK button to close the dialog box.

n.   Look in the CSS Styles panel and note that it displays the external style sheet that is attached to it *(external_style_sheet)* and the body style it contains. ***Note: If necessary, click the Plus (+) button beside* external_style_sheet *to expand and display the body style.***

o.   Click the Preview/Debug in browser button and then click Preview in iexplore to see how the style you have created will be displayed. The document should have a light blue background and dark blue Arial text. Close the browser when you are finished.

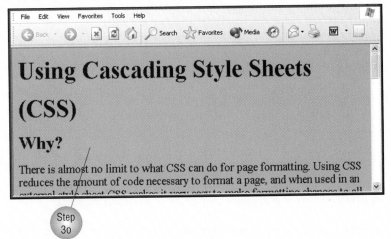

4.   Add more styles to an existing external style sheet by completing the following steps:

a.   With **ch6ex01.htm** open in the Document window, click the New CSS Style button to open the New CSS Style dialog box. The *Define in* list box contains the name of the attached style sheet, and the radio button is selected. The *Tag (redefines the look of a specific tag)* radio button is also selected. ***Note: If these radio buttons are not selected, be sure to select them.***

b.   Click the down-pointing arrow next to the New CSS Style dialog box *Tag* text box to open the *Tag* drop-down list. Click *h1* to redefine the level-one heading HTML tag—the largest heading size. Click the OK button to open the CSS Style Definition dialog box.

c.   Click *Block* in the *Category* list box.

d.   Click the down-pointing arrow next to the *Text align* text box and click *center* from the drop-down list that appears.

e.   Click the OK button in the CSS Style Definition dialog box to close the dialog box.

f.   Click the New CSS Style button again to open the New CSS Style dialog box.

g.   Click the down-pointing arrow next to the New CSS Style dialog box *Tag* text box to open the *Tag* drop-down list. Click *li* to redefine the list item HTML tag. Click the OK button to open the CSS Style Definition dialog box.

h.   Click *List* in the *Category* list box.

i. Use the Browse button located to the right of the *Bullet image* text box to open the Select Image Source dialog box. Browse and locate the student file named **blue_bullet.gif** in the ch_06_student_files folder. Click the OK button after you have selected the file.

j. Click the OK button in the CSS Style Definition dialog box to close the dialog box.

Step 4i

Category	List
Type	
Background	Type: [▾]
Block	
Box	Bullet image: ch_06_student_files/blue_bull▾ [Browse...]
Border	
List	Position: [▾]
Positioning	
Extensions	

k. Click the New CSS Style button to reopen the New CSS Style dialog box. Choose *table* from the *Tag* drop-down list to redefine the table HTML tag. Click the OK button to open the CSS Style Definition dialog box.

l. Click *Background* in the *Category* list box. **Note: Because you are redefining the table tag, you are setting the background properties for that tag. This will not affect the background properties of the body tag that you redefined previously.**

m. Type **#66CCFF** (a medium shade of blue) in the *Background color* text box.

Step 4m

Background color: [ ] #66CCFF

n. Click *Border* in the *Category* list box.

o. Click the down-pointing arrow next to the *Top* text box in the *Style* section and then click *solid* from the drop-down list.

p. Click the down-pointing arrow in the *Width* section *Top* text box and then click *medium* from the drop-down list.

q. Type **#0000FF** (a dark blue) in the text box located in the *Color* section.

Border		
Style	Width	Color
☑ Same for all	☑ Same for all	☑ Same for all
Top: solid ▾	medium ▾ pixels ▾	#0000FF

Step 4o **Step 4p** **Step 4q**

r. Click the OK button in the CSS Style Definition dialog box to close the dialog box.

s. Click the New CSS Style button to reopen the New CSS Style dialog box. Choose *img* from the *Tag* drop-down list to redefine the image HTML tag. Click the OK button to open the CSS Style Definition dialog box.

t. Click *Border* in the *Category* list box. **Note: Because you are redefining the image tag, you are setting the border properties for that tag. This will not affect the border properties of the table tag that you redefined previously.**

u. Click the down-pointing arrow next to the *Top* text box in the *Style* section and click *outset* from the drop-down list.

v. Type **50** in the *Width* section *Top* text box. If *pixels* does not automatically appear in the unit list box, click the down-pointing arrow and then click *pixels* from the drop-down list.

w. Type **#0066FF** (a light blue) in the *Top* text box next to the color box in the *Color* section. Click

Step 4u **Step 4v** **Step 4w**

Category	Border		
Type			
Background	Style	Width	Color
Block	☑ Same for all	☑ Same for all	☐ Same for all
Box			
Border	Top: outset ▾	50 ▾ pixels ▾	#0066FF
List	Right: outset ▾	50 ▾ pixels ▾	#0066FF
Positioning	Bottom: outset ▾	50 ▾ pixels ▾	#0066FF
Extensions	Left: outset ▾	50 ▾ pixels ▾	#0066FF

DREAMWEAVER MX 2004

the *Same for all* check box located in the *Color* section to remove its check mark. The *Right, Bottom,* and *Left* text boxes will now contain *#0066FF*. Click the OK button in the CSS Style Definition dialog box to close the dialog box. **Note: The image border in the document will look different when displayed in a browser window.**

    x. Click the Preview/Debug in browser button and then click Preview in iexplore to preview **ch6ex01.htm**. The table should now have a dark blue border with a medium blue background, the image should be surrounded by a three-dimensional blue border, and the list should feature the image bullets you specified. Close the browser when you are finished.

5. Save **ch6ex01.htm** but do not close it.
6. Save **external_style_sheet.css** and close it.

Grouping Selectors

Often you might want different selectors to share the same properties and values. Rather than create different selectors with the same properties and values, selectors can be grouped to create a single selector. This is done by separating the tags that compose the selector with commas, as shown in the following example, which would direct browsers to display the three heading tags in blue, underlined, Times New Roman font:

```
h1,h2,h3 {font-family: "Times New Roman", Times,
    serif;color: #0000CC;text-decoration: underline;}
```

You can create grouped or multiple selectors by clicking the New CSS Style button to open the New CSS Style dialog box. Click the *Advanced (IDs, contextual selectors, etc)* radio button as shown in Figure 6.12. After this is done, type the desired tags, separated by commas, in the *Selector* text box. This step can be confusing because the text box does not clear between uses, and if the dialog box was previously used to create another type of selector, it might already contain a tag or Class style name. Additionally, rather than listing tags, the *Selector* text box drop-down list displays only four Pseudo class link states. (Pseudo classes can be used to modify hyperlinks and will be described later in this chapter.) After clicking the *Advanced (IDs, contextual selectors, etc)* radio button, you should ignore any text in the text box and enter the desired tags, being careful to separate each tag with a comma. If the grouped selectors are to be contained in an external style sheet, click the *Define in* radio button. If the grouped selectors are to be contained in the head section of the current document, click the *This document only* radio button. Click the OK button to open the CSS Style Definition dialog box where you can specify the desired properties and values for the tags.

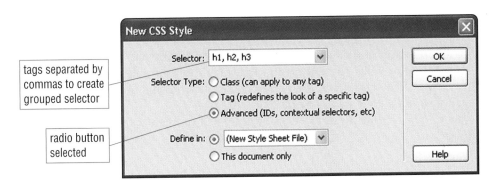

Figure 6.12
Creating a Grouped Selector

exercise 2

1. Add a grouped (multiple) selector to the previously created external style sheet by completing the following steps:

   a. With **ch6ex01.htm** open in the Document window, use the Save As command to rename and save it as **ch6ex02.htm**. Close the document when you are finished.

   b. Use the Files panel integrated file browser to locate the **external_style_sheet.css** file in the ch_06_exercises root folder. Right-click this file, point to Edit, and then click Duplicate from the context menu that appears to create a duplicate of the style sheet.

   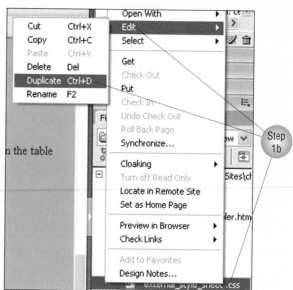

   Step 1b

   c. Click the duplicate style sheet to select it *(Copy of external_style_sheet.css),* right-click, point to Edit, and then click Rename from the context menu. Rename the file **external_style_sheet-2.css**. *Hint: Make sure you are renaming the duplicate copy and not the original.*

   Step 1c

   d. Open **ch6ex02.htm**, select *external_style_sheet.css* in the CSS Styles panel window, and then click the Trash Can button to detach it from the document. ***Note: This removes the style sheet from this document only. The style sheet will not be deleted and can still be found in the ch_06_exercises root folder. All of the formatting that was applied using external_style_sheet.css will disappear from the document.***

   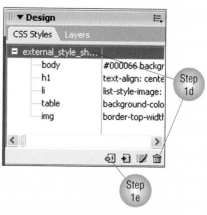

   Step 1d

   Step 1e

   e. Click the Attach Style Sheet button in the CSS Styles panel to open the Attach External Style Sheet dialog box. Click the Browse button to open the Select Style Sheet File dialog box. Use the dialog box to locate **external_style_sheet-2.css** in the ch_06_exercises root folder. Click the file to place it in the *File name* text box, and then click the OK button.

   f. The Attach External Style Sheet dialog box reappears, showing *external_style_sheet-2.css* in the *File/URL* text box. Click the OK button to attach the style sheet to **ch6ex02.htm**. *Note: The reason you are renaming and reattaching the style sheet is so that changes you make to it will not affect ch6ex01.htm.*

   g. Click the New CSS Style button in the CSS Styles panel to open the New CSS Style dialog box.

h. Click the *Define in* radio button next to the list box containing the name of the external style sheet if it is not already selected. This adds the multiple selector you are about to create to the external style sheet.

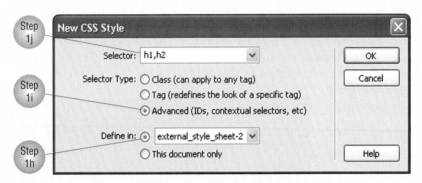

i. Click the *Advanced (IDs, contextual selectors, etc)* radio button.
j. Position the insertion point inside the *Selector* text box and select any text that might be there. Type h1,h2. Be sure to separate the tags with a comma. Click the OK button to close the dialog box. The CSS Style Definition dialog box opens.
k. Click *Type* in the *Category* list box, if necessary.

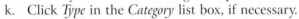

l. Click the *underline* check box in the *Decoration* section to place a check mark in the check box. Click the OK button to close the dialog box.

m. Click the Preview/ Debug in browser button and then click Preview in iexplore to preview the page. The level-one heading that appears at the top of the page and the two smaller level-two headings below it are underlined. Close the browser when you are finished.

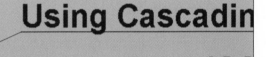

n. In the Document window, scroll down to the bottom of the page and position the insertion point just after the last sentence in the document. Press the Enter key to move the insertion point down one line.
o. Type Heading Test. Press the Enter key to move the insertion point down one more line, and type Heading Test again. Repeat these instructions one more time until *Heading Test* appears on three separate lines at the bottom of the document.

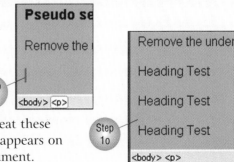

p. Select the first *Heading Test* text. Click the Insert bar Text menu item or tab, and then click the h1 button. Note that it will be centered because the level-one heading tag was redefined with a center align value in Exercise 1.

q. Select the second *Heading Test* text, and then click the h2 button.

r. Select the third *Heading Test* text, and then click the h3 button.

s. Click the Preview/Debug in browser button and then click Preview in iexplore to view the page in a Web browser. Scroll to the bottom of the page. The level-one and level-two *Heading Test* text is underlined. This demonstrates that the style you just created is adding underlining to any level-one and level-two heading tags in the document. The level-three heading is not underlined because it has not been redefined. Close the browser when you are finished.

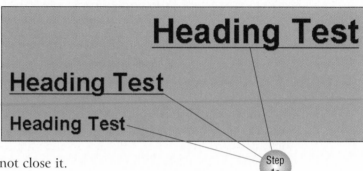

2. Save **ch6ex02.htm** but do not close it.

3. Save **external_style_sheet-2.css** and close it.

Creating Contextual Selectors

Contextual selectors instruct browsers to apply a style only when certain conditions are met. For example, although a style sheet might contain a style specifying that all level-one headings appear in purple text, a contextual selector could be placed in a style sheet to specify that all level-one heading tags containing strong tags appear in red text. When a browser interprets a page attached to the style sheet, it displays all level-one headings in purple, but when it encounters a level-one heading containing strong tags, the browser follows the contextual selector instructions and displays the heading in red. Contextual selectors can be created by following the same steps that were used to create a grouped selector—except that each tag should be separated by a space rather than a comma when entering tags in the *Selector* text box.

exercise 3

ADDING CONTEXTUAL SELECTORS TO A STYLE SHEET

1. Add a contextual selector to the previously created external style sheet by completing the following steps:

a. With **ch6ex02.htm** open in the Document window, use the Save As command to rename and save it as **ch6ex03.htm**. Close the document when you are finished.

b. Follow Steps 1b–1f from Exercise 2 to:
   1) Make a duplicate copy of **external_style_sheet-2.css**.
   2) Rename the duplicate copy **external_style_sheet-3.css**.
   3) Detach **external_style_sheet-2.css** from **ch6ex03.htm**.
   4) Attach **external_style_sheet-3.css** to **ch6ex03.htm**.

c. With **ch6ex03.htm** open in the Document window, click the New CSS Style button in the CSS Styles panel to open the New CSS Style dialog box.

d. Click the *Define in* radio button next to the list box containing the name of the external style sheet if it is not already selected. This adds the contextual selector you are about to create to the external style sheet.

e. Click the *Advanced (IDs, contextual selectors, etc)* radio button.

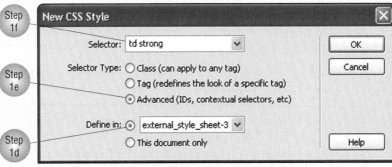

f. Position the insertion point inside the *Selector* text box and select any text that might be there. Type **td strong**. Make sure there is a space between these two items but do not use a comma. Click the OK button to close the dialog box. The CSS Style Definition dialog box opens. ***Note: You are creating a contextual selector that will apply a rule whenever strong tags—(bold effect)—are found inside paired table data tags. If you place a comma between these two tag names, you will create a multiple selector that will define properties for the table data tags and strong tags.***

g. Click *Type* in the *Category* list box, if necessary.

h. Type **#FF0000** (red) in the *Color* text box. Click the OK button to close the dialog box.

i. Click the Preview/Debug in browser button and then click Preview in iexplore to view the page. The bold text located inside the table appears in red because it was created using strong tags. The strong tags are located inside table data tags, and the contextual selector you just created changes text to red whenever these two tags are found together. Close the browser when you are finished.

2. Save **ch6ex03.htm** but do not close it.

3. Save **external_style_sheet-3.css** and then close it.

Creating Class Styles

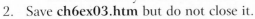

When a selector is used to redefine an HMTL tag and create a style, the style is applied to every instance of the tag in the document the style is contained in or attached to. For example, if a style redefining the paragraph tag calls for all paragraphs to appear in red text, all of the text enclosed by paragraph tags in a document controlled by the style will appear in red.

Sometimes, however, you might want to have some paragraphs appear in another text color. Class styles provide a solution for this type of situation by allowing you to create a style with its own name rather than a tag name. The

Class style contains properties and values that can be applied to any tag. Thus, a Class style calling for green text could be created and applied to a paragraph in a document with an internal or attached external style calling for paragraphs to have red text. Because the Class style is inserted inline, it is closer to the tag level than an internal or external style and therefore overrides their formatting instructions. When you use the Property inspector or Menu bar commands to format text, Dreamweaver MX 2004 implements the formatting using Class styles, but you can also create and use your own Class styles.

Class style names begin with a period, so a Class style to change paragraph text color to green might be named .paragraphgreen to help identify its function. Dreamweaver MX 2004 automatically adds a period before a Class style name if you forget to type one. Class style names cannot begin with a number or character, and should contain no spaces, punctuation, or special characters. When Dreamweaver MX 2004 creates a Class style in response to Property inspector or Menu bar formatting commands, they are named *.style* and followed by a number indicating their order of creation, such as *.style1*, *.style2*, and so on.

After a Class style has been created in a style sheet, it appears in the CSS Styles panel as shown in Figure 6.13. A Class style can be applied to selected text by clicking the Class style name in the CSS Styles panel, right-clicking, and then clicking Apply. This action inserts the Class style into the document as an inline style, meaning that it will be contained inside an HTML tag. Another way to apply a Class style to selected text is to right-click the desired text, point to CSS Styles from the context menu that appears, and then click a Class style name displayed in the submenu that appears as shown in Figure 6.14.

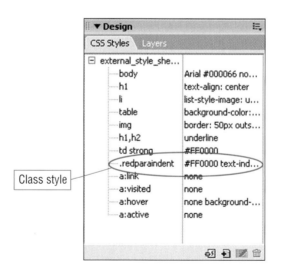

Figure 6.13
Class Style in the CSS Styles Panel

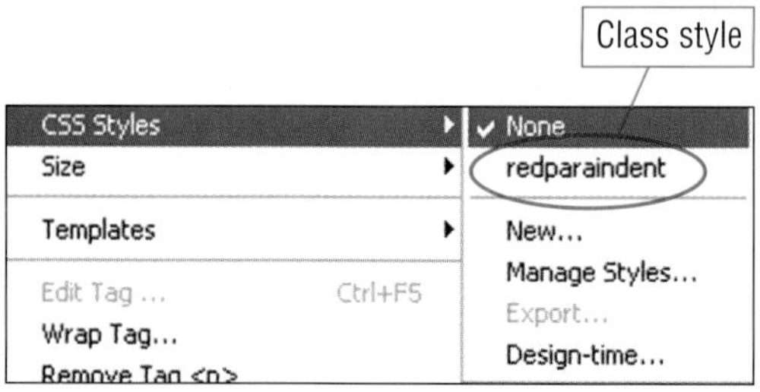

Figure 6.14
Class Style Name on Context Menu

DREAMWEAVER MX 2004

1. Add a Class style to the previously created external style sheet by completing the following steps:

   a. With **ch6ex03.htm** open in the Document window, click the Save As command to rename and save it as **ch6ex04.htm**. Close the document when you are finished.

   b. Follow Steps 1b–1f from Exercise 2 to:
      1) Make a duplicate copy of **external_style_sheet-3.css**.
      2) Rename the duplicate copy **external_style_sheet-4.css**.
      3) Detach **external_style_sheet-3.css** from **ch6ex04.htm**.
      4) Attach **external_style_sheet-4.css** to **ch6ex04.htm**.

   c. Click the New CSS Style button in the CSS Styles panel to open the New CSS Style dialog box.

   d. Click the *Define in* radio button next to the list box containing the name of the external style sheet if it is not already selected. This adds the Class style you are about to create to the external style sheet.

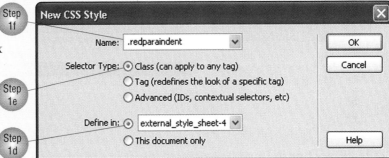

   e. Click the *Class (can apply to any tag)* radio button.

   f. Type **.redparaindent** in the *Name* text box. ***Note: Dreamweaver MX 2004 automatically adds a period before the name if you do not type one.*** Click the OK button to close the dialog box. The CSS Style Definition dialog box opens.

   g. Click *Type* in the *Category* list box, if necessary.

   h. Type **#FF0000** (red) in the *Color* text box.

   i. Click *Block* in the *Category* list box.

   j. Type **50** in the *Text indent* text box. Click the down-pointing arrow next to the list box to open the unit drop-down list and click *pixels*. Click the OK button to close the dialog box.

   k. Select the text in the document reading: *Change the text color of this sentence and indent it.* **Hint: The sentence is located just below the table.**

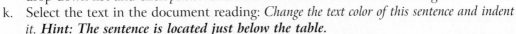

   l. Right-click the selected text, point to CSS Styles, and then click redparaindent from the context menu that appears. ***Note: While the period in front of the Class style does not appear when displayed in the context menu and in the document (Code view), it does appear when viewed in the CSS Styles panel.***

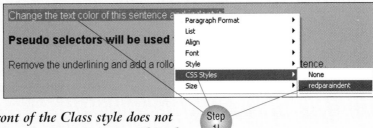

m. Click the Preview/Debug in browser button and then click Preview in iexplore to view the page. The selected sentence appears in indented red text. Close the browser when you are finished.

A Custom style will be used to:

Change the text color of this sentence and indent it.

Pseudo selectors will be used to:

n. In the Document window, select the indented red text and then click the Code button. Note that the *redparaindent* Class style has been applied inside the paragraph tags for the selected text, making this an inline style. Click the Design button when you are finished.

```
<h3 class="special">A Custom style will be used to:</h3>

<p class="redparaindent">Change the text color of this sentence and indent it.</p>
<h3 class="special">Pseudo selectors will be used to:</h3>
```

Step 1n

2. Save **ch6ex04.htm** but do not close it.
3. Save **external_style_sheet-4.css** and then close it.

Modifying Hyperlinks with Pseudo Classes

When the concept of hyperlinking documents was new, it was necessary to call attention to hyperlinks by having them appear in a different color, usually blue, and then underlining them. As hyperlinks are now a familiar concept, many people think that underlining hyperlinks detracts from the appearance of a page. Prior to CSS, nothing could be done to change this, but underlining can be removed from links by using a type of CSS style known as a Pseudo class. Pseudo classes are styles that are active when an event takes place, such as hovering the pointer over a link, and are primarily used to change hyperlink properties.

Pseudo classes for links are created using the New CSS Style dialog box by selecting the *Advanced (IDs, contextual selectors, etc)* radio button. Clicking the down-pointing arrow next to the *Selector* text box opens a drop-down list displaying four link states: *a:link, a:visited, a:hover,* and *a:active* as shown in Figure 6.15. Clicking a state and then the dialog box OK button opens the CSS Style Definition dialog box. The *Decoration* category can be used to define the appearance of the selected link state. If the *a:link* state is selected, the *Decoration* category can be used to remove underlining from links by clicking the *None* check box to enable it. The links' states should be defined in the order in which they appear in the drop-down list or the effects will interfere with each other.

Another method that can be used to modify hyperlinks is to click Modify on the Menu bar and then click Page Properties, or click the Property inspector Page Properties button to open the Page Properties dialog box. Clicking *Links* in the *Category* list box displays the Page Properties dialog box Links page, which can be

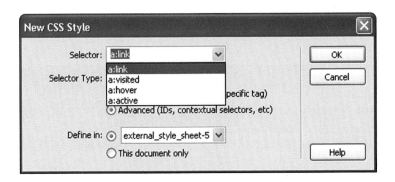

Figure 6.15
Selector Text Box Drop-
Down List

used to define hyperlink properties. Removing link underlining can be accomplished
by clicking the Underline Style dialog box down-pointing arrow and then clicking
Never underline from the menu that appears.

exercise **5**

MODIFYING HYPERLINKS WITH PSEUDO CLASSES

1. Add Pseudo class styles to the previously created external style sheet by completing the
   following steps:
   a. With **ch6ex04.htm** open in the Document window, click the Save As command to
      rename and save it as **ch6ex05.htm**. Close the document when you are finished.
   b. Follow Steps 1b–1f from Exercise 2 to:
      1) Make a duplicate copy of **external_style_sheet-4.css**.
      2) Rename the duplicate copy **external_style_sheet-5.css**.
      3) Detach **external_style_sheet-4.css** from **ch6ex05.htm**.
      4) Attach **external_style_sheet-5.css** to **ch6ex05.htm**.
   c. Select the word *link* in the last sentence in the document and type
      http://www.cnn.com in the Property inspector *Link* text box to create a link to an
      external Web site. ***Note: If you want to use another external URL, ask your
      instructor first.***

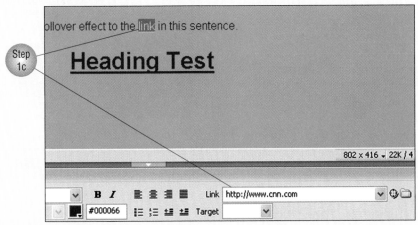

   d. Click the New CSS Style button in the CSS Styles panel to open the New CSS
      Style dialog box.

e. Click the *Define in* radio button next to the list box containing the name of the external style sheet if it is not already selected. This adds the Pseudo class styles you are about to create to the external style sheet.

Step 1g

Step 1f

Step 1e

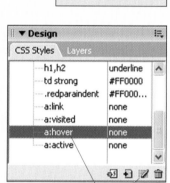

f. Click the *Advanced (IDs, contextual selectors, etc)* radio button.

g. Click the down-pointing arrow next to the *Selector* text box to open the drop-down list and click *a:link*. Click the OK button to close the dialog box. The CSS Style Definition dialog box opens.

h. Click *Type* in the *Category* list box, if necessary.

Step 1i

i. Click the check box next to the *none* option in the *Decoration* area of the dialog box to place a check mark in the check box. Click OK to close the dialog box.

j. Repeat Steps 1d–1i to select the *none* option for *a:visited* from the *Selector* text box drop-down list.

k. Repeat Steps 1d–1i to select the *none* option for *a:hover* from the *Selector* text box drop-down list.

l. Repeat Steps 1d–1i to select the *none* option for *a:active* from the *Selector* text box drop-down list.

m. Click *a:hover* in the CSS Styles panel and then click the Edit Style Sheet button to open the CSS Styles Definition dialog box. **Hint: If the external style sheet listing in the CSS Styles panel is not expanded, click the Plus (+) button next to it to expand it. Use the scroll bar to scroll down and find the a:hover style.**

n. Click *Background* in the *Category* list box, and then type #FFFF00 (yellow) in the *Background color* text box. Click the OK button to close the dialog box.

Step 1m

Step 1o

o. Click the Preview/Debug in browser button and then click Preview in iexplore to preview the page. The link should appear without any underlining. Placing the pointer over the link causes it to appear with a yellow background. Close the browser when you are finished. **Note: If you are not using the latest browser version, the link might still be underlined. You must be connected to the Internet for the external link to work.**

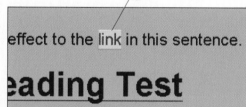

2. Save and close **ch6ex05.htm** and **external_style_sheet-5.css**.

Using Predefined Style Sheets

Although it is not difficult to create your own style sheets, Dreamweaver MX 2004 offers the convenience of **predefined CSS style sheets** that can be used as is or modified to suit your preferences. You can create predefined CSS style sheets by clicking File on the Menu bar and then New to open the New Document dialog box as shown in Figure 6.16. Clicking *CSS Style Sheets* in the *Category* list box displays a number of different predefined style sheets in the *CSS Style Sheets* list box. The right side of the dialog box displays a preview of the selected style sheet with a brief description below. Clicking the Create button opens the style in the Document window in Code view, where it can be modified or saved right away using the Save or Save As commands to name and save the document. After it has been named and saved, the style sheet can be attached to HTML documents.

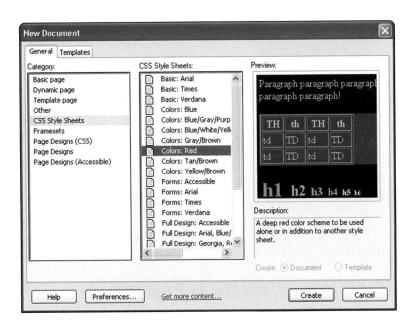

Figure 6.16
New Document Dialog Box
CSS Style Sheets

exercise **6**

CREATING PREDEFINED STYLE SHEETS

1. Create a predefined style sheet and attach it to a document by completing the following steps:
   a. Click File on the Menu bar and then New to open the New Document dialog box.
   b. Click *CSS Style Sheets* in the *Category* list box, and then *Colors: Blue/Gray/Purple* in the *CSS Style Sheets* list box. Click the Create button to open the document in the Document window. The Document window automatically shifts to Code view when a CSS document is created.

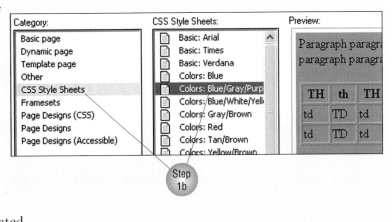

c. Scroll to the top of the document and note the different selectors the style sheet contains as you scroll back down.

d. Click File and then use the Save or Save As commands to name and save the document as **pre_defined_style_sheet.css** to the ch_06_exercises root folder. Close the document when you are finished.

e. Open the student file named **css_styles_sampler.htm** in the ch_06_student_files folder and use the Save As command to save it to the ch_06_exercises root folder as **ch6ex06.htm**.

f. Click the Attach Style Sheet button located in the lower-right corner of the CSS Styles panel to open the Attach External Style Sheet dialog box.

g. Click the dialog box Browse button to open the Select Style Sheet File dialog box. Browse and select *pre_defined_style_sheet.css*. Click the OK button after you locate the file name.

h. The file name now appears in the *File/URL* text box in the Attach External Style Sheet dialog box. Make sure that the *Link* radio button is selected. Click the OK button to attach the style sheet to the current document, **ch6ex06.htm**.

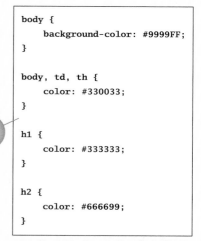

Step
1c

```
body {
    background-color: #9999FF;
}

body, td, th {
    color: #330033;
}

h1 {
    color: #333333;
}

h2 {
    color: #666699;
}
```

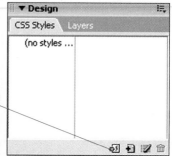

Step
1f

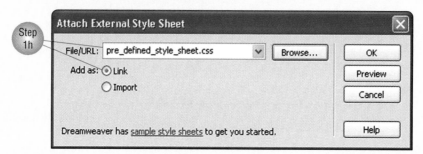

Step
1h

i. Click the Preview/Debug in browser button and then click Preview in iexplore to view the page. The styles specified in the style sheet have automatically been applied to the relevant tags in **ch6ex06.htm**. Close the browser when you are finished.

2. Save **ch6ex06.htm** and then close it.

Step
1i

DREAMWEAVER MX 2004

Creating an Internal or Embedded Style Sheet

As their names imply, internal or embedded style sheets are located inside HTML documents. They are contained in the head section located at the top of an HTML document as shown in Figure 6.17 and can be used to control the formatting of the entire document. Because internal styles are contained inside a document, they have no effect on other documents located in the same site as the document with the internal style sheet. However, if you later decide to apply an internal style sheet to other pages, the internal style sheet can be exported to create an external style sheet. The external style sheet then can be attached to other HTML documents.

With an HTML document open in the Document window, clicking the New CSS Style button in the CSS Styles panel begins the internal style sheet creation process. The New CSS Style dialog box opens and the *This document only* radio button should be clicked to place the styles that will be created in the head section of the document. The process is then the same as the process used to create an external style sheet, with the difference being that the styles appear in the head section of the document rather than on an external style sheet.

With an HTML document open in the Document window, the Property inspector also can be used to create an internal style sheet by clicking the down-pointing arrow next to the *Style* list box and then clicking *Manage Styles* from the drop-down list that appears. This opens the Edit Style Sheet dialog box. Clicking the dialog box New button opens the New CSS Style dialog box. To create an internal style, select the *This document only* radio button. If you select the *Define in (New Style Sheet File)* radio button, an external file sheet is created and attached to the current document.

```
<html>
<head>
<title>Untitled Document</title>
<meta http-equiv="Content-Type" content="text/html; charset=iso-8559-1">
<style type="text/css">
<!--
h1 {color: #FF0000;}
p {font-family: Arial, Helvetica, sans-serif;font-size: 18px;}
body {background-color: #FFFFCC;}
-->
</style>
</head>
```

Figure 6.17
Internal Style Sheet in Head Section of HTML Document

internal style sheet

exercise 7

CREATING AN INTERNAL STYLE SHEET

1. Create an internal style sheet by completing the following steps:
    a. Open the student file named **css_styles_sampler.htm** in the ch_06_student_files folder and use the Save As command to rename and save it to the ch_06_exercises root folder as **ch6ex07.htm**.
    b. Click the New CSS Style button in the CSS Styles panel.

c. Click the *This document only* radio button.

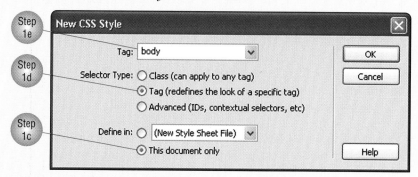

d. Click the *Tag (redefines the look of a specific tag)* radio button.
e. Click the down-pointing arrow next to the *Tag* text box to open the *Tag* drop-down list. Click *body* to redefine this tag, then click the OK button to open the CSS Style Definition dialog box.
f. Click *Type* in the *Category* list box, if necessary.
g. Click the down-pointing arrow to the right of the *Font* text box and then click *Georgia, Times New Roman, Times, serif* from the drop-down list that appears.

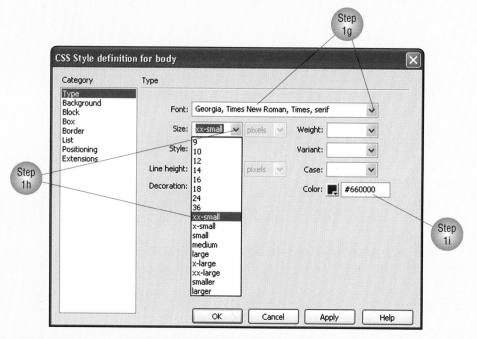

h. Click the down-pointing arrow to the right of the *Size* text box and then click *xx-small* from the drop-down list that appears.
i. Type **#660000** (a dark brown) in the *Color* text box.
j. Click *Background* in the *Category* list box.
k. Type **#FFFFCC** (a light yellow) in the *Background color* text box. Click the OK button to close the CSS Style Definition dialog box.

l. Click the Preview/Debug in browser button and then click Preview in iexplore to preview the page. The text appears somewhat smaller and in brown, and the page background is a light yellow. Close the browser when you are finished.

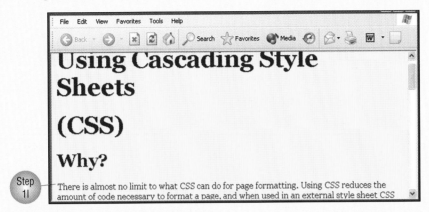

m. Click the Code button. Scroll to the top of the document and locate the first head tag (<head>). A line or two below that, you will see the selector (style rule) that makes up the internal style sheet you just created. Click the Design button when you are finished.

```
<head>
<title>Untitled Document</title>
<meta http-equiv="Content-Type" content="text/html; charset=iso-8859-1">

<style type="text/css">
<!--
body {
    font-family: Georgia, "Times New Roman", Times, serif;
    font-size: xx-small;
    color: #660000;
    background-color: #FFFFCC;
}
-->
</style>
</head>
```

Step 1m

2. Save **ch6ex07.htm** but do not close it.

Exporting Styles

You can use several methods to export an internal style so that it can be converted into an external style sheet that can be attached to other HTML documents. With the document containing the internal style sheet open in the Document window, the HTML document and the style sheets it contains appear in the CSS Styles panel. Click the style sheet name, right-click to open a context menu, and then click the Export Style Sheet command to open the Export Styles As CSS File dialog box shown in Figure 6.18. In this dialog box, you can name the new file and locate a folder where the file should be saved. Another way to open the Export Styles As CSS File dialog box is to click File on the Menu bar, point to Export, and then click CSS Styles.

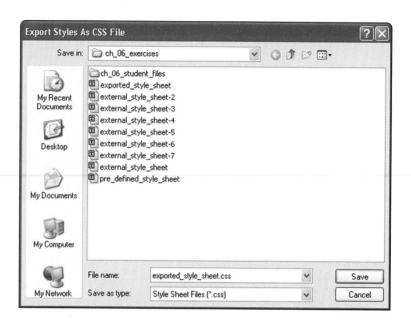

Figure 6.18
Export Styles As CSS File
Dialog Box

1. Export an internal style sheet, name and save it, and attach it to another document by completing the following steps:
   a. With **ch6ex07.htm** open in the Document window, right-click the style listed in the CSS Styles panel *(<style>)*, and the click Export from the context menu that appears.

b. Type exported_style_sheet.css in the *File name* text box and browse and locate the ch_06_exercises root folder, if necessary. Click the Save button to save the style. ***Note: If you do not type a .css extension, Dreamweaver MX 2004 does it for you.***

c. Close **ch6ex07.htm**.

d. Open **ch3ex01.htm** and use the Save As command to rename it **ch6ex08.htm** and save it to the ch_06_exercises root folder. ***Hint: Be careful not to open ch6ex01.htm by mistake. Look for ch3ex01.htm in your ch_03_exercises root folder.***

e. Click the Attach Style Sheet button in the CSS Styles panel to open the Attach External Style Sheet dialog box.

f. Click the Browse button to open the Select Style Sheet File dialog box. Locate the ch_06_exercises root folder, if necessary. All of the external style sheets that are saved in the ch_06_exercises root folder appear in the dialog box window.

1) Click *exported_style_sheet.css* and then click OK to attach the style sheet to **ch6ex08.htm**, or double-click the style sheet file name to attach it. The Attach External Style Sheet dialog box appears with the style sheet file name in the *File/URL* text box.

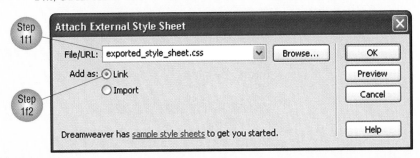

2) Make sure the *Link* radio button is selected, and then click OK to close the dialog box.

g. Click the Preview/Debug in browser button and then click Preview in iexplore to preview the page. The formatting rules that were once contained inside the head section of **ch6ex07.htm** have been exported to create an external style sheet, and now that the external style sheet is attached to **ch6ex08.htm**, the document contains the same background and text color as **ch6ex07.htm**.

2. Save **ch6ex08.htm** and then close it.

Editing CSS Styles

CSS styles can be edited manually in Code view, but it is far easier for most users to edit them using the Relevant CSS or CSS Properties panels. These two panels are referred to in Dreamweaver MX 2004 as tabs, but they are panels located in the Tag panel group. The two panels are almost identical, but the ***Relevant CSS panel*** is displayed when a CSS element is selected in a document whereas the CSS Properties panel is displayed when a CSS style is selected in the CSS Styles panel. To display either of these panels, you first need to click Window on the Menu bar and then Tag Inspector to open the Tag panel group. The Relevant CSS panel will be displayed by default, but clicking a CSS rule in the CSS Styles panel will display the ***CSS Properties panel***.

As shown in Figure 6.19, the top half of the Relevant CSS panel displays the tag selected in the Document window and any style rule applied to it. The lower half of the panel displays all of the properties that can be associated with the selected tag. Properties that have been defined are shown in blue. If a property is inapplicable to the selected page element, it will appear with a red strikethrough line. Holding the mouse pointer over the inapplicable property will display a tooltip explaining why the property is inapplicable as shown in Figure 6.20. In the default Dreamweaver MX 2004 setup, properties are listed alphabetically with defined properties appearing at the top of the list in blue. Clicking the Show category view button displays the properties sorted under eight different categories: font, background, block, border, box, list, positioning, and extensions. Defined properties under each category appear at the top of the list in blue.

Depending on the property, clicking in the blank space next to a property in the lower half of either panel causes a text box, text box and down-pointing arrow, or color box to appear as shown in Figure 6.21. Clicking a down-pointing arrow displays a menu of possible values for the selected property. Clicking a value sets that value for the property. If a property contains a color box as shown in

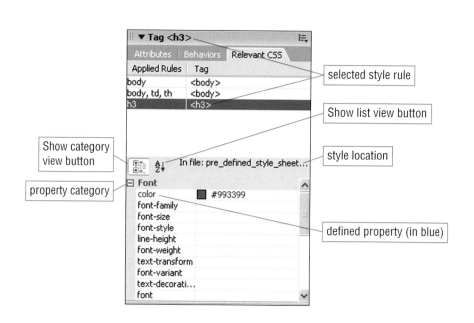

Figure 6.19
Relevant CSS Panel

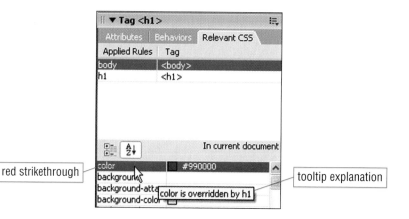

Figure 6.20
Inapplicable Property
Explanatory Tooltip

DREAMWEAVER MX 2004

Figure 6.21, clicking it opens the Color Picker, which can be used to select a new color for the property. A blank text box can be typed in directly. Changes made in the Relevant CSS panel or CSS Properties panel will be displayed immediately in the Document window.

Other than the difference in the method used to display the two panels, the principal differences between the Relevant CSS panel and the CSS Properties panel are that the CSS Properties panel opens in Category view instead of List view by default, and the CSS Properties panel does not contains an upper panel view. In most other respects, the panel functions like the Relevant CSS panel.

Another method that can be used to edit a style is to select the style in the CSS Styles panel and then click the Edit Style button located in the lower right-hand corner of the CSS Styles panel as shown in Figure 6.22. This opens the CSS Style Definition dialog box. The dialog box then can be used to set property values for the selected style using the same methods that were used to create a new style.

With a document open in the Document window, a CSS style can be edited by clicking Text on the Menu bar, pointing to CSS Styles, and then clicking Manage Styles. This opens the Edit Style Sheet dialog box shown in Figure 6.23. Clicking a style sheet name in the list box and then clicking the Edit button displays all of the style rules contained in the style sheet. When an internal or inline style is selected and the Edit button is clicked, the CSS Style Definition dialog box will appear and can be used to edit the style. If a style is contained in an external style sheet, the external style sheet name must be clicked first so that all the style rules that it contains appear in the dialog box. Style rules then can be selected and the Edit button clicked to open the CSS Style Definition dialog box.

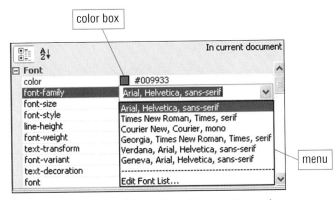

Figure 6.21 • Relevant CSS Panel Property Menu and Color Box

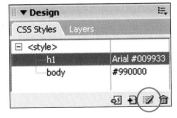

Figure 6.22 • CSS Styles Panel Edit Style Button

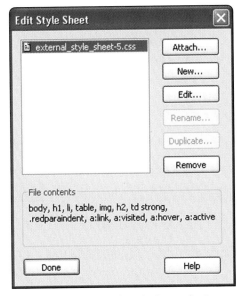

Figure 6.23 • Edit Style Sheet Dialog Box

To change the tags redefined by a selector, you must work in Code view. After you locate the selector in Code view, you can replace selectors with other selectors by typing a new tag over the old one. Tags also can be added to a selector to create a grouped (multiple) selector, or to add to an existing grouped selector.

exercise 9

1. Edit a style sheet by completing the following steps:
   a. Open **ch6ex05.htm** and use the Save As command to rename and save it as **ch6ex09.htm**. Close the document when you are finished.
   b. Follow Steps 1b–1f from Exercise 2 to:
      1) Make a duplicate copy of **external_style_sheet-5.css**.
      2) Rename the duplicate copy **external_style_sheet-6.css**.
      3) Detach **external_style_sheet-5.css** from **ch6ex09.htm**.
      4) Attach **external_style_sheet-6.css** to **ch6ex09.htm**.
   c. Click Window on the Menu bar and then Tag Inspector to open the Tag panel group.
   d. If necessary, click the Relevant CSS panel tab to display it.
   e. Click *body* in the Relevant CSS panel.
   f. If necessary, click the *Font* category to expand it and then click in the blank text box next to the color box. Type **#FF0000** (red) over the existing color code *(#000066)*. **Hint: Select the existing color code and then type the new color code.**
   g. Click *body* again in the Relevant CSS panel.
   h. Click the *Background* category to expand it.
   i. Click in the blank text box next to the color box and type **#FFCCFF** (light red). Click the OK button.
   j. Click the Preview/Debug in Browser button and then click Preview in iexplore to view the page. The document now appears with the text and background color formatting you specified using the Relevant CSS panel. Close the browser when you are finished.

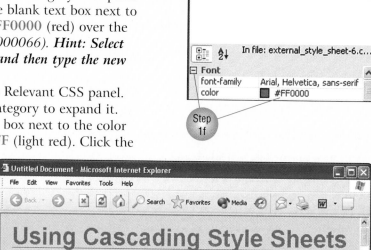

Step 1e

Step 1f

Step 1j

2. Edit the tags redefined by a selector in Code view by completing the following steps:
   a. Without closing **ch6ex09.htm**, open **external_style_sheet-6.css**.

DREAMWEAVER MX 2004

b. Scroll down the page and locate the grouped selector you created earlier for the level-one and level-two heading tags and type ,h3 after the level-two heading tag.

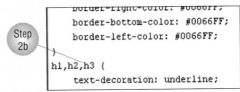

Step 2b

c. Save and then close the document.
d. Click the Preview/Debug in browser button, click Preview in iexplore, and then scroll down to the bottom of the page. The level-three heading (the last line on the page) is now underlined because it is included in the grouped selector that redefined the level-one headings and level-two headings. Close the browser when you are finished.

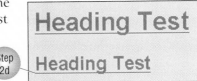

Step 2d

3. Save **ch06ex09.htm** and then close it.

Removing Styles and Style Sheets

Style sheets can be removed from a document by clicking the style sheet listing in the CSS Styles panel and then clicking the Trash Can button as shown in Figure 6.24. If the style sheet being deleted is an inline or internal style, it is removed from the document and permanently deleted. Removing an external style sheet detaches it from the document, but the style sheet is not deleted and can still be seen in the Files panel.

Individual styles from an internal or external style sheet can be deleted by clicking the style name and then clicking the CSS Styles panel Trash Can button. Deleting a style cannot be undone after the Trash Can button is selected.

The CSS Property inspector can be used to edit styles by clicking the *Style* list box down-pointing arrow and then *Manage Styles* from the menu that appears. This opens the Edit Style Sheet dialog box. Styles contained in or attached to the open document will appear in the dialog box. Selecting the style and then clicking the Remove button will remove the style.

Every instance of a Class style application can be removed from a document by clicking the Class style listing in the CSS Styles panel and then clicking the Trash Can button. This deletes the style from the CSS Styles panel and removes any formatting that was applied using the style.

The CSS Property inspector also can be used to remove individual instances of a Class style application by clicking the text where a Class style was applied, clicking the *Style* list box down-pointing arrow, and then clicking *None* from the drop-down list that appears as shown in Figure 6.25.

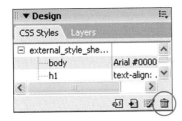

Figure 6.24 • CSS Styles Panel Trash Can Button

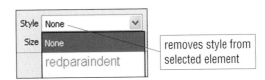

Figure 6.25 • CSS Property Inspector *Style* List Box Menu

1. Remove styles and style sheets by completing the following steps:
    a. Open **ch6ex05.htm** and use the Save As command to rename and save it as **ch6ex10.htm**. Close the document when you are finished.
    b. Follow Steps 1b–1f from Exercise 2 to:
        1) Make a duplicate copy of **external_style_sheet-5.css**.
        2) Rename the duplicate copy **external_style_sheet-7.css**.
        3) Detach **external_style_sheet-5.css** from **ch6ex10.htm**.
        4) Attach **external_style_sheet-7.css** to **ch6ex10.htm**.

Step 1c

    c. Click the Plus (+) button next to the external style sheet listing in the CSS Styles panel to expand it if necessary. The styles contained in the **external_style_sheet-7.css** style sheet document are displayed. Scroll down the list of styles contained in the style sheet and click *a:hover* to select it.
    d. Click the Trash Can button in the CSS Styles panel to delete the style from the style sheet.

Step 1d

    e. Click the Preview/Debug in browser button and then click Preview in iexplore to preview the page. Scroll down to near the bottom of the page where the link is located. The *a:hover* Pseudo class style was used to add a yellow background to the link when the mouse hovers over it. Because you just deleted *a:hover* Pseudo class style, the link on the page is not highlighted in yellow when you move the mouse over it. Close the browser when you are finished.

Step 1e

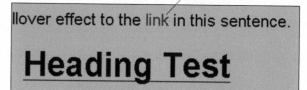

2. Use the CSS Styles Property inspector to remove styles by completing the following steps:
    a. Click the down-pointing arrow next to the Property inspector *Style* list box and then click *Manage Styles* to open the Edit Style Sheet dialog box.
    b. Click the style sheet name *(external_style_sheet-7.css)* in the Edit Style Sheet dialog box and then click the Edit button to open a dialog box displaying all of the styles contained in the style sheet.
    c. Click *h1,h2* to select that style and then click the Remove button. Click the Done button when you are finished. Click the Edit Style Sheet dialog box Done button. ***Hint: You can remove other styles before clicking the Done***

Step 2c

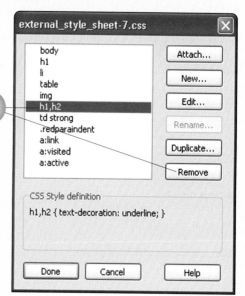

button. If you decide you do not want to remove a style after all, click the Cancel button instead of the Done button and no styles will be removed from the style sheet.

d. Click the Preview/Debug in browser button and then click Preview in iexplore to view the page. Note that the level-one and level-two headings are no longer underlined because the grouped selector you just removed was the style that redefined those tags to display with underlining. Close the browser when you are finished.

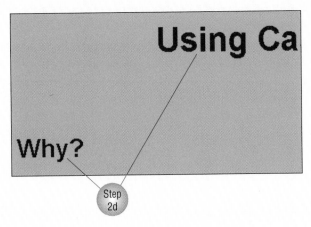

Step
2d

3. Remove a Class style by completing the following steps:
   a. Select the sentence in the document that appears in red indented text, or position the insertion point anywhere in the sentence text. The Property inspector *Style* list box shows that the selected sentence is formatted using the .redparaindent class style.
   b. Click the Property inspector *Style* list box down-pointing arrow and then click *None* from the drop-down list that appears to remove the Class style formatting from the selected sentence.

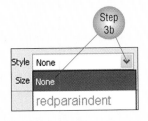

Step
3b

   c. Click the Preview/Debug in browser button and then click Preview in iexplore to preview the page. The Class style that applied the indented red text formatting to the sentence that was selected in the Document window has been removed, so the sentence now appears flush left and in the same color text as the rest of the document. Close the browser when you are finished.

A Custom style will be used to:

Change the text color of this sentence and indent it.

Step
3c

Pseudo selectors will be used to:

4. Save and close **ch6ex10.htm** and **external_style_sheet-7.css**.

CHAPTER summary

➤ The most popular method of using CSS involves placing styles in a separate style sheet that can be attached to any number of HTML documents.

➤ Positioning page elements with CSS can be tricky, and a common compromise solution in use today is to combine tables for page layout with CSS for formatting.

➤ By separating HTML structure from presentation, CSS offers a much more efficient method of instructing browsers how to display Web pages.

➤ Instead of requiring presentational tags and attributes scattered throughout an HMTL document, CSS contains instructions, known as CSS styles or CSS rules, that are referred to and applied by browsers.

➤ CSS styles can be used inline (inside a tag), as an internal style sheet (embedded in the head section of a Web page), or as an external style sheet that can be attached to any number of HTML documents.

➤ Designers can do things easily with CSS that are difficult or impossible to do with ordinary HTML, such as removing the underlining from hyperlinks.

➤ CSS styles are the basic building blocks of CSS that determine how a tag being defined by a style will be interpreted and displayed by browsers.

➤ A CSS selector redefines or modifies an existing HTML tag and can be created for any HTML tag or element, such as a paragraph tag (<p>).

➤ Declarations declare and define the properties of the tag that a selector is redefining. They are composed of a property (**color**, **size**, and so on) and a value (**blue**, **+4**, and so on) for the property being set.

➤ A style sheet is a collection of one or more styles that might not be located in a separate "sheet" or document as is the case with an external style sheet.

➤ Style sheets are referred to as cascading because of the hierarchical order in which they are interpreted by browsers.

➤ Styles closer to the structural code (HTML tags) in a document take precedence over style sheets located farther away.

➤ If a CSS style does not work, it might be because previous tag formatting needs to be removed before the style can take effect.

➤ Inheritance means that a closer style can inherit rules from styles located higher up the style chain, as long as the higher style rules do not conflict with the closer style's own rules.

➤ More than one external style sheet can be attached to a document or series of documents.

➤ When more than one external style sheet is attached to documents, the order in which they were attached becomes important. In case of a rule conflict, rules in the last external style sheet attached take precedence.

➤ Because external style sheets are not HTML documents, they have their own file extension (.css).

➤ If a number of different external style sheets are used in a site, you should store them in a separate folder.

- Not all of the CSS properties that can be defined will take effect in the Document window, so the only way to be sure that a style has been implemented is to preview a page in a browser.

- After an external style sheet has been created, it can be attached to a document by clicking the Attach Style Sheet button located at the bottom of the CSS Styles panel.

- Rather than create different selectors with the same properties and values, selectors can be grouped to create a single selector by separating the tags that the selector redefines with commas.

- Contextual selectors can be used to instruct browsers to apply a style only when certain conditions are met, such as specifying that all level-one heading tags containing strong tags appear in red text.

- Class styles, also known as Custom styles, allow you to create a selector with its own name rather than a tag name. The Class style contains properties and values that can be applied to any tag.

- Pseudo class styles can be used to change aspects of link appearance, such as size and color.

- Dreamweaver MX 2004 offers you the convenience of predefined CSS style sheets that can be used as is or modified to suit your preferences. After the style sheet has been named and saved, it can be attached to any HTML document.

- Internal or embedded style sheets are located inside the head section located at the top of an HTML document.

- Because internal styles are contained inside a document, they have no effect on other documents located in the same site as the document with the internal style sheet.

- Internal style sheets can be exported to create an external style sheet that then can be attached to other documents.

- Because a style sheet is composed of a collection of styles, each style must be edited individually.

- When the Tag panel group is open, the Relevant CSS panel is displayed when a CSS element is selected in a document. The Relevant CSS panel can be used to edit CSS style properties.

- When the Tag panel group is open, the CSS Properties panel is displayed when a CSS style is selected in the CSS Styles panel. The CSS Properties panel can be used to edit CSS style properties.

- To change the tags redefined by a selector, it is necessary to work in Code view.

- Removing an external style sheet detaches it from the document, but the style sheet is not deleted and still appears in the Files panel.

- Individual styles can be deleted by clicking the style name and then clicking the CSS Styles panel Trash Can button.

- Every instance of a Class style application can be removed from a document by clicking the Class style listing in the CSS Styles panel and then clicking the Trash Can button.

- Individual instances of a Class style application can be removed by clicking anywhere in the text where a Class style was applied, and then clicking *None* in the CSS Property inspector *Style* list box list.

cascading Refers to the hierarchical order in which style sheets are interpreted by browsers, as in *Cascading Style Sheets (CSS)*.

Cascading Style Sheets (CSS) The term for a collection of one or more CSS styles or rules. A cascading style sheet can be a separate document (an *external style sheet*), or located inside the head section of an HTML document (*internal or embedded style sheet*).

Class style A type of style that is not tag specific.

contextual selectors A type of CSS selector used to instruct browsers to apply a style only when certain tag combinations are encountered, such as when level-one heading tags (<h1>) contain strong tags (<strong>).

CSS Properties panel A panel that can be used to edit CSS style properties. To use the panel the Tag panel group must be open and a CSS style must be selected in the CSS Styles panel.

CSS rules See *CSS styles*.

CSS styles Formatting rules used to redefine HTML tag properties and values. Also known as *CSS rules*.

Custom style See *Class style*.

declarations Declarations declare and define the properties of a tag that a selector is redefining, and are composed of *properties* and *values*.

embedded style sheet See *internal style sheet*.

external style sheet A style sheet located in a separate document.

grouped selector A CSS selector that redefines more than one tag at a time. Also called *multiple selector*.

inheritance Refers to the way a style can inherit rules from styles located higher up the style chain as long as they do not conflict with its own rules.

inline style CSS style located inside an HTML tag.

internal style sheet A CSS style sheet located (embedded) in the head section of an HTML document.

multiple selector See *grouped selector*.

predefined CSS style sheets Ready-made style sheets that can be used as is or modified to suit preferences.

presentational tags HTML tags, such as the font tag (<font>), that control the appearance of elements when they are displayed by browsers.

property A tag characteristic, such as `color`, `size`, `width`, and so on.

Pseudo classes A type of style that is active when an event takes place, such as hovering the pointer over a link. Primarily used to change hyperlink properties.

Relevant CSS panel A panel that can be used to edit CSS style properties. To use the panel the Tag panel group must be open and a page element selected in a document. The Relevant CSS panel will display any styles controlling the selected element.

selector Selectors redefine or modify HTML tags to create a CSS style or rule.

structural tags HTML tags, such as paragraph tags (<p>) or table tags (<table>), used to indicate the structure of Web page content so that browsers can interpret and display page elements.

value A tag property option, such as **green** or **red** for a **color** property, or **+4** for a **size** property.

COMMANDS review

Attach a style sheet	Text, CSS Styles, Manage Styles, Attach
Create a new style sheet	Text, CSS Styles, Manage Styles, New
Edit a style sheet	Text, CSS Styles, select style, Edit
Export a style sheet	File, Export, CSS Styles
Open the CSS Styles panel	Window, CSS Styles
Open the Relevant CSS panel	Window, Tag Inspector, select page element
Open the CSS Properties panel	Window, Tag Inspector, select CSS style in CSS Styles panel

CONCEPTS check

Indicate the correct term or command for each item.

1. This panel group must be open in order to use the Relevant CSS panel or CSS Properties panel.
2. This type of HTML tag indicates the structure of Web page content.
3. This type of HTML tag controls the way a browser displays Web page content.
4. This type of style sheet is located in the head section of an HTML document.
5. This is the term for a style that is located inside an HTML tag.
6. This is the term for a style sheet that can be attached to HTML documents.
7. A declaration contains these two components.
8. This is the term for the hierarchical way that browsers interpret style sheets.
9. The CSS Styles panels are located inside this panel group.
10. This type of selector instructs browsers to apply formatting rules only when specified tag combinations are encountered.
11. This type of style can be applied to any tag.
12. To use the CSS Properties panel a CSS style must be selected in this panel.
13. The Relevant CSS panel and the CSS Properties panels can display properties in either of these two views.
14. This type of selector redefines more than one tag at a time.
15. This concept describes the way that styles accept formatting rules from other styles located higher up the style chain, as long as they do not contain conflicting rules.
16. When a selector contains more than one declaration, they are separated using this punctuation mark.
17. External style sheets appear with this file extension.
18. The tags redefined by a selector can be edited in this view.
19. This is used to separate tags redefined by a contextual selector.
20. When Class styles are displayed in the CSS Styles panel, they begin with this punctuation mark.

SKILLS check

Use the Site Definition dialog box to create a separate Dreamweaver site named CH 06 Assessments to keep your assessment work for this chapter. Save the files for the site in a new root folder named ch_06_assessments under the Sites folder you created in Chapter 1, Exercise 3. Download the ch_06_student_files folder from the IRC to the CH 06 Assessments site root folder (ch_06_assessments) and expand it. Delete the compressed folder when you are finished.

Assessment 1 • Create an Internal CSS Style Sheet

1. Open the student file named **css_styles_sampler.htm** and use the Save As command to rename and save it as **ch6sa1.htm** in the ch_06_assessments root folder.
2. Create an internal (embedded) CSS style sheet with the following properties:

    - **Background Color**   #CC66FF (light purple)
    - **Font**   Times New Roman, Times, serif
    - **Font Color**   #330000 (dark purple)
    - **Image Border**   Style—ridge; Width—25 pixels; Color—#990000 (dark red) for all
    - **Table Text Color**   #990033 (dark purple)
    - **Table Background Color** #FF66CC (pinkish red)
    - **Table Border Color**   #CC0033 (dark pink)

3. Create a grouped (multiple) selector that specifies center alignment for all level-one, level-two, and level-three heading tags.
4. Create a Custom (Class) style with a Background color property of #66FFFF (light blue) and a solid blue border (#000099). Type an appropriate name for the Class style. Apply this Class style to all of the level-three headings in the document.
5. Save **ch6sa1.htm** and then close it.

Assessment 2 • Export an Internal Style Sheet and Attach It to Another Document

1. Open **ch6sa1.htm**.
2. Export the internal styles contained in **ch6sa1.htm** to create an external style sheet named **ch6sa2_style_sheet.css**. Close **ch6sa1.htm** when you are finished.
3. Open the student file named **css_styles_sampler_2.htm** and use the Save As command to rename and save it as **ch6sa2.htm** in the ch_06_assessments root folder.
4. Attach **ch6sa2_style_sheet.css** to **ch6sa2.htm**.
5. Apply the Class style contained in the style sheet to each of the amendment headings (*Amendment I, Amendment II,* and so on).
6. Save **ch6sa2.htm** and then close it.

Assessment 3 • Create a Predefined Style Sheet, Edit It, and Apply It to an Existing HTML Document

1. Use the New Document dialog box to create a Blue/Gray/Purple predefined CSS style sheet. Use the Save As command to name the style **style_control.css** and save it to the ch_06_assessments root folder.

2. Add redefined HTML tags to the style sheet with the following values:
   - **img tag:** solid medium border in black (#000000)
   - **table tag:** inset thin border in dark purple (#663333)
   - **li tag:** link to **blue_bullet.gif** image in ch_06_student_files folder

3. Edit the redefined h1 tag style so that it is center aligned.
4. Save and close **style_control.css**.
5. Create a new HTML document and name and save it to the ch_06_assessments root folder as **ch6sa3.htm**.
6. Add two paragraphs of text to the document.
7. Create level-one headings for each paragraph.
8. Add a table with a border value of 1 to the document.
9. Add an image to the document.
10. Create a list in the document.
11. Attach **style_control.css** to **ch6sa3.htm**.
12. Save **ch6sa3.htm** and then close it.

Assessment 4 • Create and Attach Predefined Style Sheets

1. Create a predefined *Basic:Times* CSS style sheet, and use the Save As command to rename it **ch6sa4-a.css** and save it to the ch_06_assessments root folder. Close the document when you are finished.
2. Create a predefined *Colors:Gray/Brown* style sheet, and use the Save As command to rename it **ch6sa4-b.css** and save it to the ch_06_assessments root folder. Close the document when you are finished.
3. Create a predefined *Link Effects* style sheet, and use the Save As command to rename it **ch6sa4-c.css** and save it to the ch_06_assessments root folder. Close the document when you are finished.
4. Open **ch6ex05.htm**, and use the Save As command to rename it **ch6sa4.htm** and save it to the ch_06_assessments root folder.
5. Detach the style sheet attached to **ch6sa4.htm**.
6. Attach the **ch6sa4-a.css**, **ch6sa4-b.css**, and **ch6sa4-c.css** style sheets to **ch6sa4.htm**.
7. Save **ch6sa4.htm** and then close it.

Assessment 5 • Remove CSS Styles from a Document

1. Open **ch6ex05.htm** and use the Save As command to rename it **ch6sa5.htm** and save it to the ch_06_assessments root folder.
2. Make a copy of **external_style_sheet-5.css** and paste it into the ch_06_assessments root folder. Rename the copy **external_style_sheet-ch6.css**. Detach **external_style_sheet-5.css** from **ch6sa5.htm**. Attach **external_style_sheet-ch6.css** to **ch6sa5.htm**. *Note: If you skip this step, any changes made to external_style_sheet-ch6.css will affect the appearance of ch6ex05.htm since it is attached to the sheet.*
3. Remove the *redparaindent* Class style.
4. Remove the *td strong* contextual selector style.
5. Remove the redefined *img* style.
6. Remove the redefined *h1* style.
7. Save **ch6sa5.htm** and **external_style_sheet-ch6.css** and then close both documents.

Assessment 6 • Apply CSS to Your Design Portfolio

1. Create a CSS style sheet to apply page design basics (background and text color, font style and size, image borders, table text, background color, border color, and so on) to the pages, or a group of pages, of your design portfolio project.
2. Add a Class style that changes the text color and indent and apply it to at least one line of text on any page of your design portfolio project.
3. Add Pseudo class styles that remove underlining for links and cause at least one link to appear with a colored background when the insertion point is hovered over it.
4. Create a predefined style sheet and attach it to at least one page of your design portfolio project.
5. Edit the predefined style sheet by changing at least one color (type, background, and so on).

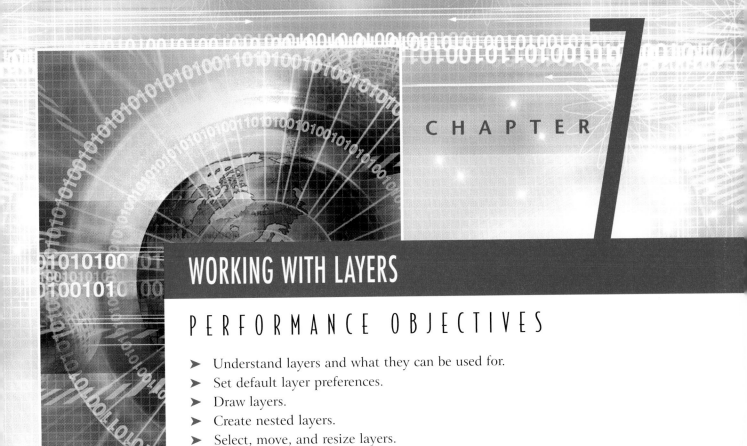

WORKING WITH LAYERS

PERFORMANCE OBJECTIVES

➤ Understand layers and what they can be used for.
➤ Set default layer preferences.
➤ Draw layers.
➤ Create nested layers.
➤ Select, move, and resize layers.
➤ Align multiple layers.
➤ Insert content into layers.
➤ Use the Property inspector to specify layer properties.
➤ Add behaviors to layers.

The student files for this chapter are available for download from the Internet Resource Center at www.emcp.com.

Layers can be thought of as transparent containers used to contain almost any type of page content, much like the text boxes that can be created in Microsoft Word. Unlike other HTML elements, the placement of a layer on a page is not determined by its location in the HTML code of a document. Instead, layers are positioned using left and top coordinates relative to the upper-left corner of a page. Using coordinates for positioning creates some interesting possibilities, including overlapping layers. The default Dreamweaver MX 2004 setup creates layers using division tags with absolute or relative positioning.

Although the vast majority of browsers in use today support layers, some variation remains in how the different browsers and browser versions interpret layers. Dreamweaver MX 2004 does its best to ensure cross-browser compatibility whenever possible, but sometimes layers will function differently when viewed in different browsers. For that reason, it is especially important that you preview pages with layers in a number of different browsers before publishing your Web site.

Browser support for page layouts created using layers is still mixed, so many experts advise the use of tables, frames, or CSS Positioning (CSS-P) for page-layout control. Layers also can be converted to tables, but the results are not always satisfactory. It is better to create tables directly rather than convert layers to tables.

In this chapter, you will learn how to use layers to create a number of interesting effects, including overlapped images, layers that can be dragged by viewers, and pop-up message windows.

Understanding Layers

A layer is indicated in an HTML document using paired ***division tags*** (<div> </div>) located in the body area of the page, as shown in Figure 7.1. Inside these tags are left and top ***layer coordinates*** that specify the location of the layer in relationship to the upper-left corner of an HTML document or the upper-left corner of another layer in the case of nested layers. Because layers are positioned using coordinates, their location on a Web page is unrelated to the location of the code used to create the layer in the HTML document. The coordinates fix layer positions so that they will maintain their position on a page in a browser window even if the window is resized. For example, a layer with a top coordinate of 50 pixels and a left coordinate of 50 pixels will appear in the browser window at the same location and in the same size no matter how the browser window is resized, as shown in Figure 7.2.

Specifying the same coordinate values for different layers places them one on top of the other in a page. Layers can be hidden or visible, and behaviors can be used to make hidden layers visible or visible layers hidden, allowing for interesting effects such as page content that appears or disappears when navigation buttons are clicked.

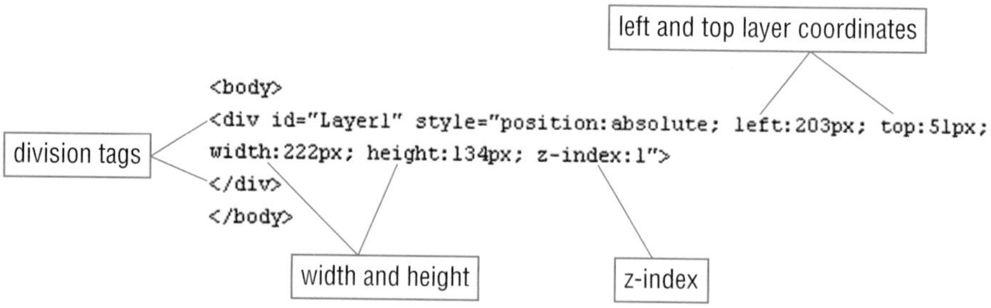

Figure 7.1
Layer Code in Code View

```
<body>
<div id="Layer1" style="position:absolute; left:203px; top:51px;
width:222px; height:134px; z-index:1">
</div>
</body>
```

left and top layer coordinates

division tags

width and height

z-index

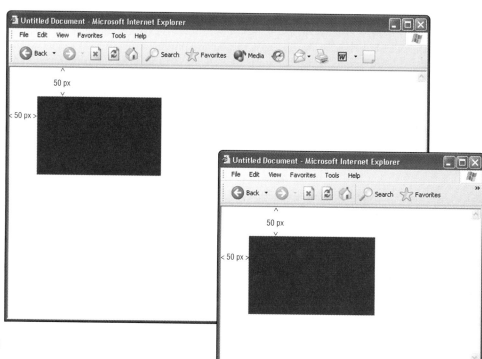

Figure 7.2
Fixed (Absolute) Positioning
of Layers

The layer's width and z-index are specified inside division tags. The ***z-index*** indicates the order in which a layer will appear when it is stacked over other layers. A layer with a higher z-index value will appear above a layer with a lower value, as shown in Figure 7.3. Z-index values do not have to be consecutive, but the relative values determine the stacking order. For example, the ***stacking order*** of three layers with z-index values of 1, 2, and 3 would be the same if they had z-index values of 3, 7, and 9.

Setting Default Layer Preferences

You can specify layer preferences using the Preferences dialog box as shown in Figure 7.4. The dialog box is opened by clicking Edit on the Menu bar and then Preferences. Clicking *Layers* in the *Category* list box displays the Layers page listing the following layer properties that you can set:

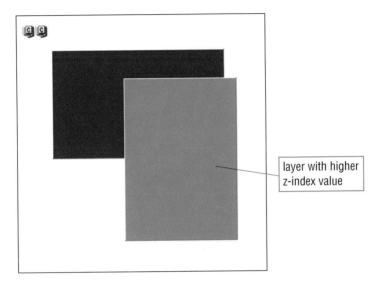

layer with higher z-index value

Figure 7.3
Stacked Layers

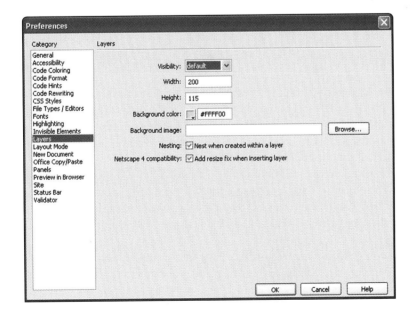

Figure 7.4
Preferences Dialog Box
Layers Page

- *Visibility* This preference specifies the initial visibility of a layer. The four choices are *default, inherit, visible,* and *hidden.* When *default* is specified, most browsers will use *inherit.* When *inherit* is specified, the visibility specified for a layer's parent layer is applied. The *visible* option makes a layer visible, whatever the visibility specification of a parent layer. The *hidden* option hides a layer, whatever the visibility specification of a parent layer.

- *Width* and *Height* These preferences specify the default height and width for layers created by inserting rather than drawing a layer.

- *Background color* This preference specifies a default background color for layers. Clicking the down-pointing arrow opens a color palette, or you can type a hexadecimal color code in the text box.

- *Background image* The *Background image* Browse button can be used to browse and locate an image that will appear as the default background for layers.

- *Nesting* Placing a check mark in the check box enables Dreamweaver MX 2004 to nest layers when the insertion point is placed inside a layer, and a new layer is drawn. If this check box does not contain a check mark, placing the insertion point inside a layer and then drawing a layer creates an overlapping layer but does not nest the layer inside the original layer. If this button is not selected, layers can be nested by dragging the Draw Layer button inside an existing layer or by clicking Insert on the Menu bar, pointing to Layout Objects, and then clicking Layer.

- *Netscape 4 compatibility* Placing a check mark in the check box enables Dreamweaver MX 2004 to insert special JavaScript code in the head area of a document to fix a resizing problem inherent in Netscape 4 browsers.

The exercises in this chapter assume that the following layer preferences have been specified:

> *Visibility: default*
> *Width: 200* (the default dimension)
> *Height: 115* (the default dimension)
> *Background color:* empty (no background color specified)
> *Background image:* empty (no background image specified)
> *Nesting:* enabled by placing a check mark in the check box
> *Netscape 4 compatibility:* enabled by placing a check mark in the check box

Creating Layers

You can use several methods to create layers. You can draw layers anywhere in a document by clicking the Draw Layer button on the Insert bar (Layout menu item or tab) as shown in Figure 7.5. When you move the pointer into the Document window, it transforms into crosshairs. The crosshairs can be used to draw a layer by clicking and holding down the mouse button and dragging the crosshairs diagonally in any direction across the Document window. When you reach the desired layer size, release the mouse button to insert the layer. Holding down the Ctrl key before or after clicking the Draw Layer button allows you to create multiple layers without having to click the Draw Layer button each time. Releasing the Ctrl key stops the multiple-layer drawing capability.

Layers also can be inserted into a page at the insertion point location by clicking Insert on the Menu bar, pointing to Layout Objects, and then clicking Layer, or by dragging the Insert bar Draw Layer button into the Document window. A layer appears at the insertion point location with the default dimensions specified in the Preferences dialog box Layers page.

After a layer has been created, it appears in the Document window as a faintly outlined box or rectangle as shown in Figure 7.5. If you cannot see layers, you need to make them visible by completing the following steps:

1. Click the View options button on the Document toolbar.
2. Point to Visual Aids from the drop-down menu.
3. Click to place a check mark next to Layer borders to make layers visible. Removing the check mark next to Layer borders will hide layers.

Because newly created layers do not contain any content, they are not visible when viewed in a browser window unless a layer background color has been specified. When content is inserted in a layer, the content is visible when the layer is viewed in a browser. If the content does not occupy the entire area of a layer, the remaining area is transparent, unless a layer background color has been specified.

When layers are created, yellow *layer-code markers* appear (as shown in Figure 7.5) if the *Invisible Elements* option has been selected using the View options button and the *Anchor points for layers* check box is selected in the Preferences dialog box Invisible Elements page as shown in Figure 7.6. A layer can be deleted by deleting its corresponding layer-code marker, and right-clicking a layer-code marker opens a context menu with commands related to layers. Layer-code markers can make page elements shift position, although this occurs only in the Document window and does not affect layer positioning when a document is viewed in a browser. The exercises in this chapter assume that layer-code markers have been enabled.

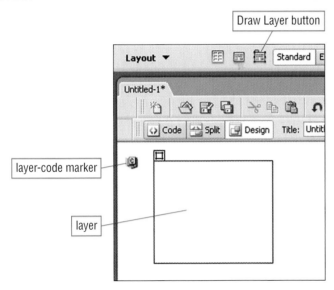

Figure 7.5
Draw Layer Button, Layer, and Layer-Code Marker

Figure 7.6
Preferences Dialog Box Invisible Elements Page

Layers can be deleted by selecting them and then pressing the Delete or Backspace keys or by selecting a layer's layer-code marker and pressing the Delete or Backspace keys to delete both the layer-code marker and its corresponding layer. When deleting many layers, hold down the Delete or Backspace keys to speed up the process by deleting layers simply by clicking them.

exercise

CREATING LAYERS

1. If necessary, start Dreamweaver MX 2004.
2. At a clear document screen, create a new site named CH 07 Exercises to store the exercises you create in this chapter. Name the root folder ch_07_exercises and save it under the Sites folder you created in Chapter 1, Exercise 3. Download the ch_07_student_files folder from the IRC to the CH 07 Exercises site root folder (ch_07_exercises) and expand it. Delete the compressed folder when you are finished. ***Note: Refer to Chapter 1 for instructions on navigating with the Files panel integrated file browser.***
3. Draw and insert layers by completing the following steps:
   a. Create a new HTML document and use the Save or Save As commands to name and save it as **ch7ex01.htm**.
   b. Click the Layout menu item or tab on the Insert bar and then click the Draw Layer button.
   c. Bring the pointer down to the Document window where it turns into crosshairs. Near the top-left corner of the screen, click and then drag the crosshairs diagonally downward to begin drawing a layer. Draw a layer that is approximately 1 inch wide and 1 inch high. When you are finished, release the mouse button. ***Note: The size and position of the layers that you draw in this exercise are not critical because you will be using the Layer Property inspector later to specify those properties.***
   d. Repeat Step 3c seven more times to place a total of eight small layers on the screen. The location of the layers is not important at this point as you will be repositioning them in a subsequent exercise. ***Hint: Speed up this process by holding down the Ctrl key and clicking the Draw Layer button to draw these layers. This method allows you to draw layers without having to click the Draw Layer button each time.***
4. Save **ch7ex01.htm** and then close it.

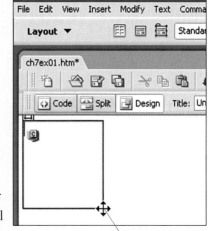

Creating Nested Layers

The concept of nested layers is similar to nested tables and frames. A ***nested layer*** is contained inside another layer. The layer nested inside another layer is referred to as a ***child layer,*** and the layer it is contained in is referred to as the ***parent layer***. A nested layer moves with its parent layer when the parent layer is moved and inherits its visibility properties from the parent layer as well. A child layer can be selected and moved independently of its parent layer so that it

DREAMWEAVER MX 2004

appears completely separated from the parent layer. However, the code for the child layer is still nested inside the code for the parent layer, and the child layer still inherits the parent layer's visibility property. If the Minus (–) button next to a parent layer name is displayed, nested layers are indicated in the Layers panel by a line connecting the layers as shown in Figure 7.7. If you see a Plus (+) button, click it to see the names of any nested layers attached to the layer.

If the *Nesting* option has been enabled in the Preferences dialog box Layers page as shown in Figure 7.8, you can nest a layer by positioning the insertion point inside a layer and clicking the Draw Layer button.

If the *Nesting* option has not been enabled, you can nest a layer by positioning the insertion point inside a layer and then dragging the Draw Layer button to a point inside the layer, or by clicking Insert on the Menu bar, pointing to Layout Objects, and then clicking Layer. When the *Nesting* option is not enabled, clicking the Draw Layer button will draw a layer inside a layer, but the layer created covers or overlaps the original layer and is not nested. Look at the Layers panel to see the nesting status of a selected layer.

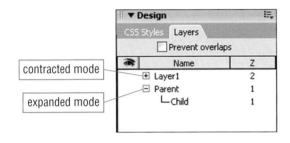

Figure 7.7
Nested Layers in the Layers Panel

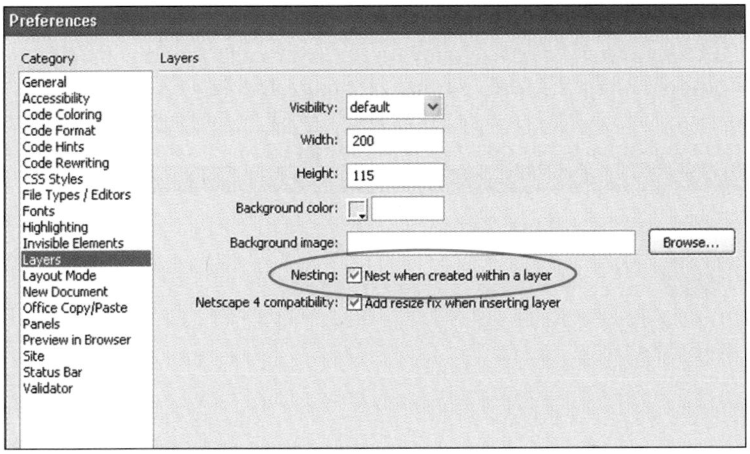

Figure 7.8
Preferences Dialog Box Layers Page

exercise 2

CREATING A NESTED LAYER

1. Create a nested layer by completing the following steps:
   a. Create a new HTML document and use the Save or Save As commands to name and save it as **ch7ex02.htm**.
   b. Click the Draw Layer button on the Insert bar (Layout menu item or tab) and draw a layer that is approximately 2 inches by 2 inches in diameter. ***Hint: Do not worry about the size or location of the layer you create as you will be modifying those properties in a later exercise.***

c. Click Window on the Menu bar and then Layers to open the Layers panel.

d. Double-click the new layer name *(Layer1)* in the Layers panel and rename it *puzzle*.

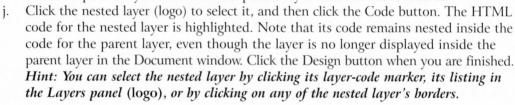

Step 1d

Step 1e

e. Position the insertion point inside the layer you just created.

f. Click the Draw Layer button on the Insert bar (Layout menu item or tab) and drag the button into the large layer. A nested layer appears inside the large layer. Look at the Layers panel and observe that the new layer's nested status is indicated by a line attaching it to the parent layer *(puzzle)*.

g. Double-click the new layer name *(Layer1)* in the Layers panel and rename it *logo*.

h. Click the parent layer (puzzle) to select it, click one of its borders, and drag the parent layer 1 inch to the right. Note that the nested layer stays with it.

Step 1f

i. Click the nested layer, and drag it back to the left until it is no longer inside its parent layer. Note that the parent layer does not move with it.

j. Click the nested layer (logo) to select it, and then click the Code button. The HTML code for the nested layer is highlighted. Note that its code remains nested inside the code for the parent layer, even though the layer is no longer displayed inside the parent layer in the Document window. Click the Design button when you are finished. ***Hint: You can select the nested layer by clicking its layer-code marker, its listing in the Layers panel (logo), or by clicking on any of the nested layer's borders.***

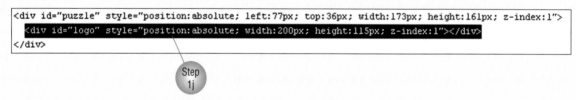

Step 1j

2. Save **ch7ex02.htm** and close it.

Selecting Layers

As previously noted, if layer-code markers are visible, they can be clicked to select their corresponding layer. Layers also can be selected by moving the insertion point across a layer's border until the move pointer appears as shown in Figure 7.9. Clicking the move pointer selects the layer. When a layer is selected, small black boxes appear on each of its borders and corners as shown in Figure 7.9. You also can select layers by holding down the Shift key while clicking inside a layer.

The ***Layers panel*** shown in Figure 7.10 also can be used to select layers. If the Layers panel is not open, click Window on the Menu bar and then Layers to open it. The Layers panel appears inside the Design panel group. Each layer on a page is indicated in the Layers panel under a default name, such as *Layer1, Layer2,*

and so on. Clicking a layer listing in the Layers panel selects the corresponding layer in the Document window, which is indicated in the same fashion as layers selected using the selection methods described earlier.

The Layers panel also indicates default *layer visibility* status. An open eye indicates that a layer is visible, while a closed eye indicates that it is hidden. Changing visibility status is discussed in the "Show-Hide Layers" section of this chapter.

The z-index for each layer is also displayed. Layers with higher values appear above layers with lower values when layers are stacked or overlap. You can change the z-index value for a layer by clicking it and typing a new value or by using the Layer Property inspector to type in new z-index values. It is also possible to change a layer's z-index by dragging it up or down in the Layers panel. Dragging a layer upward increases the z-index number, while dragging it downward reduces it.

You can change default layer names by double-clicking them and typing a new name. Be sure to rename layers descriptively so that their functions are easy to identify. For example, a layer used as background might be named *background,* while layers used as navigation buttons could be named *button1, button2,* and so on. **Layer names** cannot contain spaces and should be composed only of letters and/or numbers. The Layer Property inspector also can be used to change layer names.

The Layers panel also contains a **Prevent overlaps** *check box*. When this check box contains a check mark, layers cannot be overlapped.

Moving Layers

Layers can be moved by placing the insertion point over a layer border until the move pointer appears and then clicking and dragging the layer to the desired location. Layers also can be moved 1 pixel at a time by selecting them and then pressing the Up, Down, Left, or Right Arrow keys to move the layer in the desired direction. If the Shift key is held down while the arrow keys are pressed, layers can be moved 5 pixels at a time. Layers also can be moved by changing their left and top coordinates in the Layer Property inspector. Layers cannot be moved so that they overlap if the *Prevent overlaps* check box is checked in the Layers panel.

When a layer is selected using the Layers panel, it can be moved by clicking the layer box located near the upper-left corner of the layer as shown in Figure 7.11 to make the move pointer appear. The layer then can be dragged to a new position. If the layer box is not clicked, the layer is resized when a border is dragged.

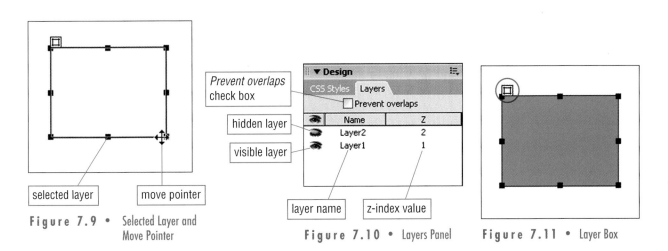

Figure 7.9 • Selected Layer and Move Pointer

Figure 7.10 • Layers Panel

Figure 7.11 • Layer Box

Resizing Layers

You can resize layers by selecting them and then dragging one of the resize handles that appears as shown in Figure 7.12. If you hold down the Ctrl key, the Down Arrow key and Right Arrow key also can be used to resize a selected layer 1 pixel at a time. The Up Arrow key and Left Arrow key have no effect, however, because this method only resizes a layer by expanding the bottom or right borders.

Layers also can be resized by changing their width and height dimensions in the Layer Property inspector. Multiple layers can be resized to the same dimensions by selecting them and then entering new width and height dimensions in the Layer Property inspector. More than one layer can be selected at a time by holding down the Shift key while clicking layer borders. As each layer is selected, the small black boxes appearing on its borders and corners turn white, with the last layer selected displaying the standard black boxes, as shown in Figure 7.13.

Another method you can use to modify the width and height of more than one layer at a time is to select the layers, click Modify on the Menu bar, point to Align, and then click either Make Same Width or Make Same Height. The width or height dimension for all of the selected layers will be changed to match the corresponding dimensions of the last layer selected, which is indicated by black boxes on its borders and corners.

Aligning Layers

Dreamweaver MX 2004 provides an easy way to align layer borders at the same time. After you select a group of layers, click Modify on the Menu bar, point to Align, and then click Left, Right, Top, or Bottom to align the chosen border of all of the selected layers to the corresponding border of the last layer selected. Depending on the layer position and the border that was aligned, layers might appear stacked as shown in Figure 7.14, but the appropriate arrow keys can be used to separate them after selecting each layer. Holding down the Shift key while clicking an arrow speeds up the moving process by moving layers 5 pixels at a time.

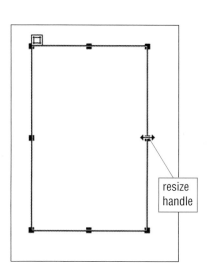

resize handle

Figure 7.12 • Using Resize Handles to Resize a Layer

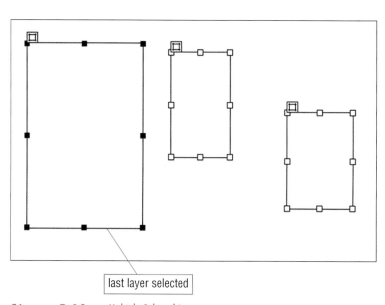

last layer selected

Figure 7.13 • Multiple Selected Layers

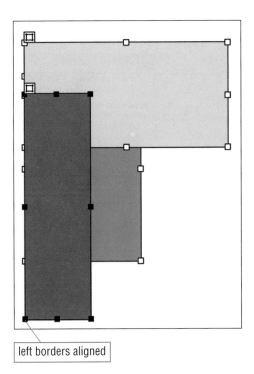

Figure 7.14
Aligned Layers

left borders aligned

exercise 3

SELECTING, MOVING, RESIZING, ALIGNING, AND RENAMING LAYERS

1. Select, move, resize, align, and rename layers by completing the following steps:
   a. Open **ch7ex01.htm** and use the Save As command to rename and save it as **ch7ex03.htm**.
   b. Move the insertion point across the layer border of the layer nearest to the left side of the page and click when the move pointer appears in order to select the layer. Drag the layer so that its top and left borders are almost, but not quite, touching the left and top edges of the screen. Click in the Document window to deselect the layer.
   c. Hold down the Shift key and select each of the eight layers. It is important that the layer on the left be the last one selected. *Note: Seven of the layers have small white boxes on their borders and corners and the leftmost one has small black boxes. The black boxes indicate the layer that was selected last.*

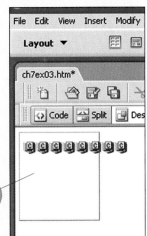

Step 1b

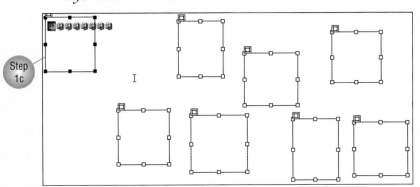

Step 1c

d. Click Modify on the Menu bar, point to Align, and then click Top to align the top border of the layers.

e. Double-click *Layer1* in the Layers panel to select it and then type **piece1** to rename the layer.

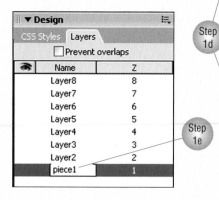

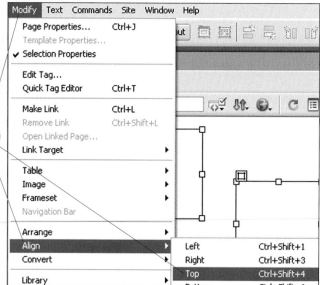

f. Repeat Step 1e to rename each layer *piece2, piece3,* and so on until all of the layers have been renamed.

g. Move the insertion point across the border of any one of the layers and click when the move pointer appears to select the layer.

h. Position the insertion point over the little black box in the lower-right corner of the selected layer until a resize arrow appears. Click the resize arrow and use it to drag the lower-right corner of the layer diagonally until the layer is about twice its original size.

i. Select another layer and click the border to drag the layer down the screen approximately 1 inch. ***Note: The layer must be selected for the move pointer to appear. Do not click on a black box or you will resize the layer.***

2. Save **ch7ex03.htm** but do not close it.

Inserting Content into Layers

Layers can contain almost any kind of content, including text, images, tables, and multimedia. Frames are one of the few types of content that layers cannot contain. Text can be inserted into layers by positioning the insertion point inside a layer and then typing. Copied text can be pasted into layers by positioning the insertion point inside a layer, right-clicking, and then clicking Paste from the context menu that appears. You also can paste copied text into layers by positioning the insertion point inside a layer, clicking Edit on the Menu bar, and then Paste. Images, multimedia, and tables can be inserted by clicking Insert on the Menu bar, and then clicking Image or Table or pointing to Media as desired.

When selecting a layer with content, it is easy to inadvertently select the content instead of the layer. To avoid this possibility, you can use the Layers panel to select layers, or you can click a layer's layer-code marker.

1. Insert content into layers by completing the following steps:
   a. With **ch7ex03.htm** as the current document, use the Save As command to rename and save it as **ch7ex04.htm**.
   b. Click inside the piece1 layer to place the insertion point inside the layer.
   c. Click Insert on the Menu bar and then click Image. Use the Select Image Source dialog box to browse and locate the student file named **puzzle_piece_1.gif** in the ch_07_student_files folder and then click the OK button.

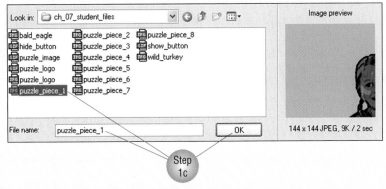

   d. An Image Tag Accessibility Attributes dialog box appears if the *Images* option has been selected in the Preferences dialog box Accessibility page. ***Note: Instructions on selecting this preference are contained in the "Ensuring Accessibility" section of Chapter 2.*** Type Puzzle Piece 1 in the *Alternate text* text box and then click OK to close the dialog box.

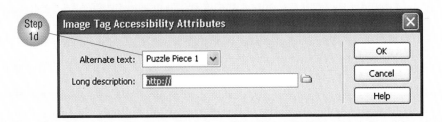

   e. Follow Steps 1b–1d to insert the matching images in the remaining layers, for example, **puzzle_piece_2.gif** for the piece2 layer and so on. Type the appropriate alternate text name for each of these layers, for example, Puzzle Piece 2 for the piece2 layer and so on. ***Hint: Because some of the layers are overlapped, the easiest way to select them is to click a layer name in the Layers panel. You can then place the insertion point in the selected layer in order to insert an image.***
2. Save **ch7ex04.htm** but do not close it.

Using the Layer Property Inspector to Specify Layer Properties

When layers are selected, the Layer Property inspector appears as shown in Figure 7.15. The different layer properties that can be specified using the Layer Property inspector are described in the following list:

- **Layer ID** This text box identifies a layer's name. New layers appear with default names, such as *Layer1, Layer2,* and so on. A new name can be created for a layer, or a previously named layer can be renamed by typing a new name in the *Layer ID* text box.

- **L and T** Left *(L)* and top *(T)* are the coordinates used for positioning a layer on a page, or in the case of nested layers, within another layer. The values are indicated in pixels *(px)*. Left is the leftmost position of a layer and top is the topmost. For example, a left value of 0 specifies that a layer's left border will be 0 pixels away from the left edge of a browser screen or parent layer border, and a top value of 0 pixels specifies that a layer's top border will be 0 pixels from the top edge of a browser screen or the top border of a parent layer. Figure 7.16 shows a layer with left and top values of 50 pixels, and a nested layer with child layer left and top values of 0 pixels.

- **W and H** The width *(W)* and height *(H)* text boxes specify the dimensions of a layer in pixels. Percentage values can be entered by replacing *px* (pixel) with % (a percent sign). Not all browsers interpret percentage values for layers in the same way, so be careful to preview results using different browsers and browser versions when specifying a percentage value.

- **Z-Index** This text box specifies the stacking order of the layer shown in the *Layer ID* text box. A higher number indicates that a layer will appear on top of a layer with a lower number when the layers are stacked or overlap. The numbers do not have to be consecutive. A layer's z-index number can be changed by typing a new number over the old number. A layer's z-index number also can be changed using the Layers panel.

- **Bg image** The *Bg image* text box specifies a background image for a layer. The Browse for File button can be clicked to browse and locate a background image.

- **Vis** The *Vis* text box specifies the initial visibility of a layer. The four choices are *default, inherit, visible,* and *hidden.* When *default* is specified, most browsers will use *inherit.* The *inherit* option follows the visibility specified for a layer's parent layer. The *visible* option makes a layer visible, whatever the visibility specification of a parent layer. *Hidden* hides a layer, whatever the visibility specification of a parent layer.

- **Bg color** The *Bg color* color box and text box specifies a background color for a layer. Leaving this text box blank (the default option) specifies a transparent layer.

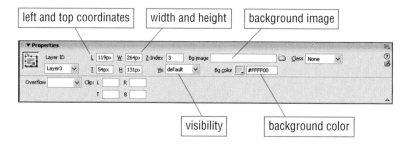

Figure 7.15
Layer Property Inspector

DREAMWEAVER MX 2004

- *Overflow* The **overflow property** determines what happens when layer content exceeds its specified dimensions. The *visible* option stretches a layer to display extra content, while *hidden* hides extra content. Specifying *scroll* adds scroll bars to a layer, even if they are unnecessary. Specifying *auto* instructs browsers to add scroll bars only when a layer's content exceeds its specified dimensions.

- *Clip* The **clip property** determines the visible portion of a layer. Specifying left *(L)*, right *(R)*, top *(T)*, and bottom *(B)* coordinates for a clip creates a rectangle or box inside a layer that contains the layer content that will be visible in a browser window. For example, a layer 100 pixels wide by 80 pixels high with left and top values of 0 pixels and right and bottom values of 100 and 40 pixels would display only the top half of the contents of the layer as shown in Figure 7.17. Clipping can be used to mask or crop portions of an image, but it is more frequently used for scripting purposes.

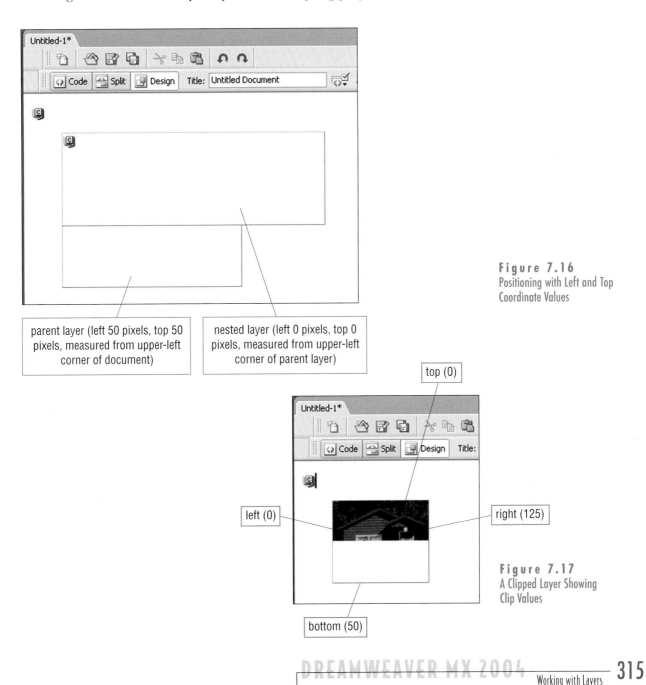

parent layer (left 50 pixels, top 50 pixels, measured from upper-left corner of document)

nested layer (left 0 pixels, top 0 pixels, measured from upper-left corner of parent layer)

Figure 7.16
Positioning with Left and Top Coordinate Values

top (0)

left (0)

right (125)

bottom (50)

Figure 7.17
A Clipped Layer Showing Clip Values

1. Use the Layer Property inspector to resize layers to match the dimensions of their contents by completing the following steps:
   a. With **ch7ex04.htm** as the current document, use the Save As command to rename and save it as **ch7ex05.htm**.

   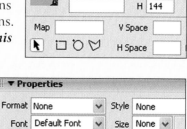

   Step 1b

   b. Click inside one of the layers to select an image. The Property inspector transforms into the Image Property inspector and displays the width and height dimensions for the image. Write down or remember the dimensions. *Note: Each image is the same size, so you need to do this only once.*

   c. Hold down the Shift key and then click all of the layers in the Layers panel to select those layers.

   d. Locate the *W* (width) and *H* (height) text boxes in the Layer Property inspector and enter the image dimensions that you recorded in Step 1b. This sizes all of the layers at once so that they are an exact fit for their content. *Hint: Be careful not to enter these values in the* L *(left) and* T *(top) text boxes. Note: You do not need to type* px *(pixel) in the coordinate text boxes because Dreamweaver MX 2004 assumes pixels unless another unit of measure is entered.*

   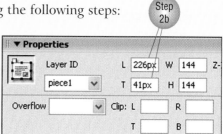

   Step 1d

2. Specify coordinates to position layers by completing the following steps:

   Step 2b

   a. Select the piece1 layer.
   b. Locate the Layer Property inspector *L* and *T* text boxes and type 226 in the *L* text box and 41 in the *T* text box.

   c. Repeat Step 2b to enter the following coordinates for the remaining layers:

piece2	L 221 T 213
piece3	L 347 T 97
piece4	L 543 T 25
piece5	L 520 T 258
piece6	L 414 T 215
piece7	L 667 T 120
piece8	L 709 T 259

   d. Click the Preview/Debug in browser button and then click Preview in iexplore to view the document in a browser window. Note that some of the layers overlap. Whether or not a layer appears above or below another layer depends on its z-index number. A higher z-index number layer will appear above a layer with a lower number. Close the browser window when you are finished. *Note: Layers are supported by IE and Netscape 4.0 versions and up, but even the latest browser versions can differ in the way they interpret layers.*

   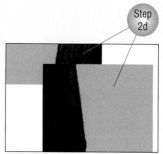

   Step 2d

3. Save **ch7ex05.htm** but do not close it.

Adding Behaviors to Layers

Behaviors use *JavaScript* code to create events and actions that can be associated with layers to make them interactive, but Dreamweaver MX 2004 graphical interface tools enable you to attach behaviors to layers without knowing JavaScript.

When a viewer performs an event, an associated action is performed. Clicking a layer or hovering the pointer over a layer are two examples of viewer-performed events that could be used to trigger an action, such as opening an HTML document in a new browser window, making a hidden layer visible, or opening a pop-up message. More than one action can be assigned to an event. For example, a behavior could be created that opens an HTML document in a new browser window when a layer is clicked, and another behavior could be created for the same event (clicking the layer) that displays a pop-up message. Clicking the layer would then simultaneously open a new document in the browser window and display a pop-up message.

To add behaviors to layers, you use the *Behaviors panel*. Click Window on the Menu bar, and then Behaviors to open the panel, which is located inside the Design panel group. After you select a layer, a behavior can be attached to it by clicking the Behavior panel Plus (+) button. This opens a drop-down menu displaying the behaviors that can be attached to the layer as shown in Figure 7.18. Click a behavior to open a contextual dialog box that can be used to define behavior properties. For example, if the Go To URL behavior is selected, a Go To URL dialog box opens. The dialog box contains a Browse button that can be used to browse and locate a URL that will open when the behavior is activated. After you close the dialog box, the behavior appears in the Behaviors panel, as shown in Figure 7.19.

Figure 7.18
Behaviors Drop-Down Menu

Figure 7.19 • Behavior Events and Actions in the Behaviors Panel

Near the very bottom of the list is a Show Events For command. Clicking this command allows you to change the events listed in the drop-down menu to events supported by specific browser versions, such as Netscape 3.0 or Internet Explorer 6.0. The selection of available events varies depending on the browser version selected. You can click an event to select it.

Behaviors are divided into two parts, an event and an action. An event triggers an action. Clicking an event in the Behaviors panel selects it and displays a down-pointing arrow. Clicking the down-pointing arrow opens a drop-down list with a long series of event types to choose from as shown in Figure 7.20. If the previously described Go To URL action was attached to a layer, the event used to trigger the action might be onClick, which would trigger the action when the layer is clicked, or onMouseOver, which would trigger the action when the mouse pointer is rolled over the layer.

Draggable Layers

A **Drag behavior** can be attached to layers so that viewers can use the mouse to drag them in the browser window. This behavior can be used to create puzzles, games, and other interactive activities. Clicking the Drag Layer command from the Behaviors panel drop-down Behaviors menu opens the Drag Layer dialog box as shown in Figure 7.21. Properties can be entered to specify the area in which a layer can be dragged, the area where the layer should be dropped, and how close a layer needs to be to a drop area for it to drop into place.

Figure 7.20
Events Drop-Down Menu

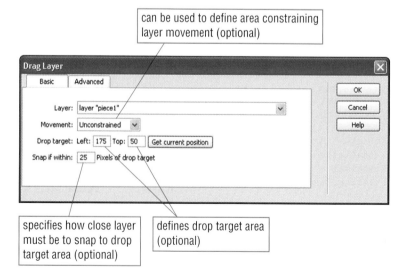

Figure 7.21
Drag Layer Dialog Box

1. Use the Drag behavior to make a jig-saw puzzle that can be assembled by viewers by completing the following steps:

   a. With **ch7ex05.htm** as the current document, use the Save As command to rename and save it as **ch7ex06.htm**.

   b. Click Window on the Menu bar and then Behaviors to open the Tag panel group.

   c. Click the Behaviors panel Plus (+) button and then point to Show Events For from the drop-down menu.

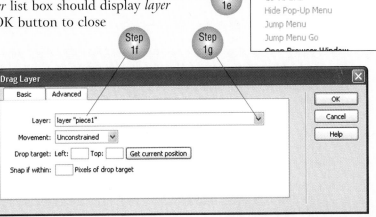

   d. Click IE 6.0 from the context menu that appears to specify behaviors supported by Internet Explorer versions 6.0 onward. *Note: The behaviors that will be available for use are determined by the browser type you are selecting. Consult with your instructor if you are not using a recent version of Internet Explorer.*

   e. With none of the images or layers selected, click the Plus (+) button in the Behaviors panel and click Drag Layer to open the Drag Layer dialog box. *Hint: Clicking the body tag in the Tag selector is an easy way to ensure that no layers are selected.*

   f. The dialog box *Layer* list box should display *layer "piece1"*. Click the OK button to close the dialog box.

   g. Repeat Steps 1e–1f to enable the drag behavior for each layer. Click the dialog box *Layer* list box down-pointing arrow to select each new layer from the list that appears.

   h. Look at the Behaviors panel to verify that onLoad is the event specified for the drag action. If not, click the event and then click the down-pointing arrow that appears. Select *onLoad* from the list that appears. Do this for each layer.

   i. Click the Preview/Debug in browser button and then click Preview in iexplore to view the document in a browser window. Click the puzzle pieces and drag them to reassemble the puzzle. Close the browser when you are finished.

2. Save **ch7ex06.htm** but do not close it.

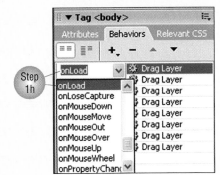

Pop-up Message Windows

Pop-up messages are small dialog boxes as shown in Figure 7.22 that pop up when an event triggers this action. Pop-up messages can be used only to contain a message, and the only choice a viewer has is to click the OK button to close the pop-up message. Clicking the Popup Message command on the Behaviors panel Behaviors drop-down list opens a Popup Message dialog box as shown in Figure 7.23. The text for the pop-up message can be typed in the *Message* text box. More than one pop-up message can be attached to the same event. In that case, messages appear consecutively, with each message appearing after the previous pop-up message is closed.

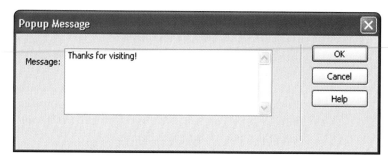

Figure 7.22 • Pop-up Message   **Figure 7.23** • Popup Message Dialog Box

CREATING A POP-UP MESSAGE

1. Create a pop-up message by completing the following steps:
   a. With **ch7ex06.htm** as the current document, use the Save As command to rename and save it as **ch7ex07.htm**.
   b. With none of the layers selected, click the Plus (+) button in the Behaviors panel and then click Popup Message to open the Popup Message dialog box.
   c. Type To assemble the puzzle, click a piece and drag it in any direction. in the Popup Message dialog box *Message* text box. Click the OK button to close the dialog box.

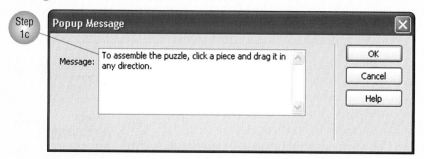

   d. If the event in the Behaviors panel for the Popup Message is not onLoad, click the event and then click the down-pointing arrow to select *onLoad* from the list that appears.

e. Click the Preview/Debug in browser button and then click Preview in iexplore to view the document in a browser window. The pop-up message will appear when the page loads in the browser window. Click the OK button to close it. Click and drag the pieces to reassemble the puzzle. Close the browser when you are finished.

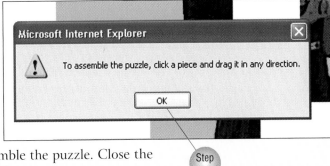

Step 1e

2. Save **ch7ex7.htm** but do not close it.

Show-Hide Layers

The *Show-Hide Layers behavior* can be used to cause a hidden layer to show or a visible layer to hide. Clicking the Show-Hide Layers command on the Behaviors panel Behaviors drop-down list opens the Show-Hide Layers dialog box. The appropriate layer can be selected in the *Named layers* text box, and then either the Show or Hide buttons can be clicked to specify that action when an event occurs.

exercise 8

SHOWING AND HIDING LAYERS

1. Show and hide layers by completing the following steps:
   a. With **ch7ex07.htm** as the current document, use the Save As command to rename and save it as **ch7ex08.htm**.
   b. Drag any puzzle pieces occupying the upper-left corner of the Document window to another spot in the document so that the upper-left corner of the document is empty.

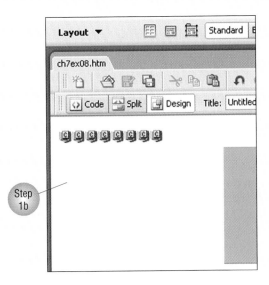

Step 1b

c. Hold down the Ctrl key, click the Draw Layer button, and then draw two small layers in the upper-left corner of the document, one above the other. The size and position of the layers are not critical because they will be specified in the Layer Property inspector.

d. Click inside the top layer, click Insert on the Menu bar, and then click Image to open the Select Image Source dialog box. Use the dialog box to browse and locate the student file named **show_button.gif** in the ch_07_student_files folder. Click the OK button to close the dialog box.

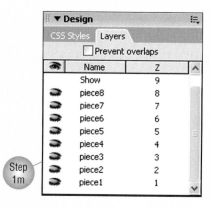

e. Type Show Button in the Image Tag Accessibility Attributes dialog box *Alternate text* text box and then click OK to close the dialog box.

f. Repeat Step 1d for the second layer, and insert the student file named **hide_button.gif**.

g. Type Hide Button in the Image Tag Accessibility Attributes dialog box *Alternate text* text box and then click OK to close the dialog box.

h. Select the layer containing the show_button image and then double-click the layer name in the Layers panel and rename it *Show*.

i. Select the layer containing the hide_button image and then double-click the layer name in the Layers panel and rename it *Hide*.

j. Click the show_button image and write down or remember its dimensions. (The show and hide images are the same size.)

k. Select the Show layer and type the width and height dimensions in the Layer Property inspector corresponding to those of the image it contains. Do the same for the Hide layer.

l. Type the following left and top values for the Show and Hide layers:

    Show *L:* 20   *T:* 15
    Hide   *L:* 20   *T:* 80

m. Click next to each puzzle piece layer listing (*piece1* through *piece8*) in the empty column below the eye image in the Layers panel. Each click changes the default visibility status of a layer: a closed eye for hidden, an open eye for visible, and blank for default. Click until you see a closed eye next to each puzzle piece. As the closed eye appears, the corresponding layer disappears from the screen. The layer still exists, and clicking its layer-code marker makes it visible in the Document window. However, when the document is viewed in a browser, any layers with a default visibility of *hidden* will not be visible.

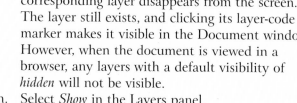

n. Select *Show* in the Layers panel.

o. Click the Plus (+) button in the Behaviors panel and then click Show-Hide Layers. Select *layer "piece1"* in the *Named layers* text box. Click the Show button so that an event will trigger the show behavior for that layer. Repeat this process for piece2 through piece8 (the puzzle piece layers). Click the OK button when you are finished. **Hint: If you make a mistake, you can change it by clicking another button. To remove any status information, click the Default button until there is no status next to the layer name. Note: If Show-Hide Layers is dimmed, click Show Events For, select your browser version, and then click the Plus (+) button again to select Show-Hide Layers. The Show-Hide Layers behavior is supported by most browser versions.**

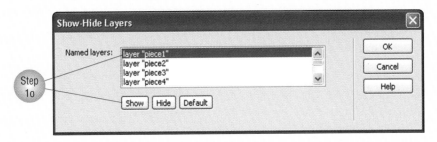

p. Select *Hide* in the Layers panel.
q. Click the Plus (+) button in the Behaviors panel and then click Show-Hide Layers. Select *layer "piece1"* in the *Named layers* text box. Click the Hide button so that an event will trigger a hide action for that layer. Repeat this process for piece2 through piece8. Click the OK button when you are finished.
r. Click the Preview/Debug in browser button and then click Preview in iexplore to view the document in a browser window. The browser window displays only the Show and Hide buttons. Clicking the Show button makes the puzzle pieces visible. Clicking the Hide button hides them again. Close the browser when you are finished.

2. Save **ch7ex08.htm** and then close it.

Go To URL

The *Go To URL behavior* can be attached to a layer so that a layer event (clicking, hovering over, and so on) opens an HTML document in the same browser window. When the Go To URL behavior is clicked, the Go To URL dialog box shown in Figure 7.24 appears. You can click the Browse button to browse and locate another HTML file. The *Open in* text box is inoperative, so the only choice is for the document to open in the same browser window.

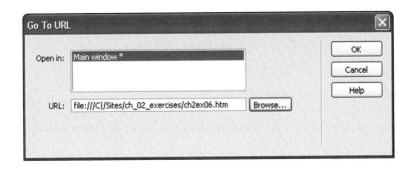

Figure 7.24
Go To URL Dialog Box

1. Use the Behaviors panel to attach a URL behavior to a layer by completing the following steps:

   a. Open **ch7ex02.htm** and use the Save As command to rename and save it as **ch7ex09.htm**.

   b. Click inside the parent layer (puzzle) to position the insertion point and insert the **puzzle_image.gif** image from the ch_07_student_files folder.

   c. Type Jig-Saw Puzzle Image in the Image Tag Accessibility Attributes *Alternate text* text box.

   d. Click inside the nested layer (logo) to position the insertion point and then insert the **puzzle_logo.gif** image from the ch_07_student_files folder.

   e. Type Puzzle Logo in the Image Tag Accessibility Attributes *Alternate text* text box.

   f. Click the puzzle_logo image to select it and display the Image Property inspector.

   g. Click the Image Property inspector Optimize in Fireworks button.

   h. Click the Find Source dialog box Use This File button.

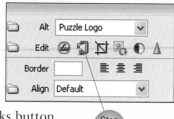

Step 1g

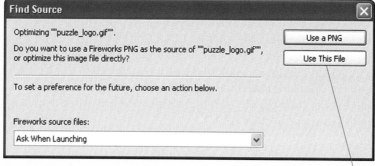

Step 1h

   i. Click the *Transparency* list box down-pointing arrow and if necessary select *Alpha Transparency* to change the image from a normal GIF file to a transparent GIF file. Click the Update button to complete the process. Because the image is now a transparent GIF and because the layer it is contained in has no background color, the image in the parent layer (puzzle) now shows through the nested layer image.

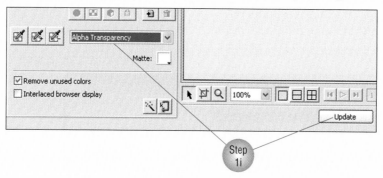

Step 1i

   j. Select the images and write down the width and height values displayed in the Image Property inspector for each image.

k. Select each layer and enter the width and height values for the image it contains in the Layer Property inspector *W* and *H* text boxes.

l. Select the nested layer (logo) and move it so that its lower half overlaps the top of the parent layer (puzzle).

Step 1l

m. Click the parent layer (puzzle) in the Layers panel to select it.

n. Click the Behaviors panel Plus (+) button to display the behaviors list.

o. Click Go To URL from the drop-down menu.

p. Click the Select File dialog box *URL* text box Browse button to locate **ch7ex08.htm**. Click the OK button to close the dialog box.

q. Click the Go To URL dialog box OK button to close it.

Step 1q

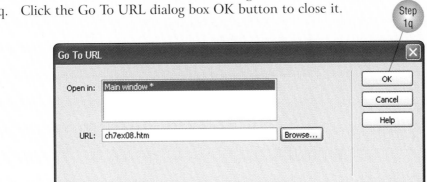

r. Click the Preview/Debug in browser button and then Preview in iexplore to preview the page in a browser.

s. Click inside the puzzle to activate the link to **ch7ex08.htm**. Close the browser when you are finished.

2. Save **ch7ex09.htm** and then close it.

Converting Layers to Tables

Although it is possible to convert layers into tables, or tables into layers, it is not recommended because the conversion process produces unwieldy code that is difficult to edit. If tables are to be used for page layout, it is much better to design them in Standard mode. Learning CSS Positioning (CSS-P) for layer positioning is an even better and more forward-looking strategy.

Layers can be converted to tables, or vice versa, by clicking Modify on the Menu bar, pointing to Convert, and then clicking either Layers to Table or Tables to Layers. Either the Convert Layers to Table dialog box or the Convert Tables to Layers dialog box will open as shown in Figures 7.25 and 7.26, depending on the command that was chosen. The desired options can be chosen using the dialog boxes. Nested layers cannot be converted to tables.

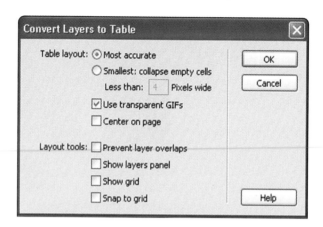

Figure 7.25
Convert Layers to Table Dialog Box

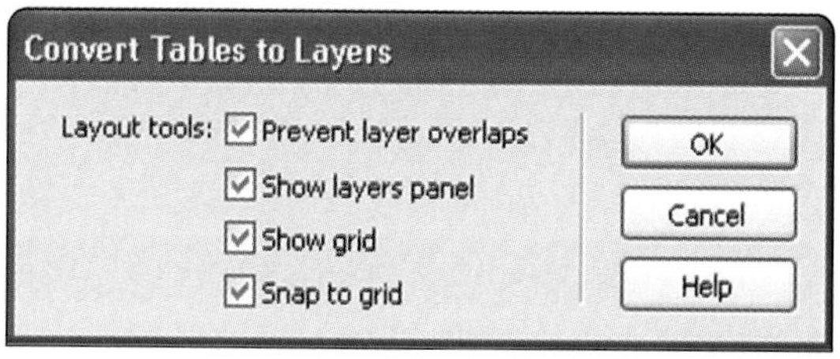

Figure 7.26
Convert Tables to Layers Dialog Box

CHAPTER summary

➤ Layers can be thought of as transparent containers that can be used to contain almost any type of page content, much like the text boxes that can be created in Word.

➤ Layers are positioned using left and top coordinates that specify the location of a layer in relationship to the upper-left corner of an HTML document, or the upper-left corner of another layer in the case of nested layers.

➤ Browser support for page layouts created using layers is still mixed, so many experts advise the continued use of tables or frames for page-layout control.

➤ Dreamweaver MX 2004 creates layers in HTML documents using paired division tags (<div> </div>) located in the body area of the document.

➤ Layer position on a Web page remains the same even when a browser is resized.

➤ Specifying the same coordinate values for different layers stacks them one on top of the other in a page.

➤ Layers can be hidden or visible, and behaviors can be used to make hidden layers visible or visible layers hidden, allowing for interesting effects such as page content that appears or disappears when navigation buttons are clicked.

DREAMWEAVER MX 2004

- A layer's z-index value indicates the order in which a layer will appear when it is stacked over other layers. A layer with a higher z-index value will appear on top of a layer with a lower value.

- The Preferences dialog box can be used to specify layer preferences.

- After a layer has been created, it appears in the Document window as a faintly outlined box or rectangle.

- Because newly created layers do not contain any content, they are not visible when viewed in a browser window unless a layer background color has been specified.

- If a layer's content does not occupy the entire area of a layer, the remaining area is transparent, unless a layer background color has been specified.

- When layers are created, yellow layer-code markers will appear if the *Invisible Elements* option has been selected using the View options button and the *Anchor points for layers* check box is selected in the Preferences dialog box Invisible Elements page.

- Layer-code markers can make page elements shift position, although this occurs only in the Document window and does not affect layer positioning when a document is viewed in a browser.

- The Layers panel indicates layer default visibility status. An open eye indicates that a layer is visible, while a closed eye indicates that it is hidden.

- You should always rename layers descriptively so that their function is easy to identify. Layer names cannot contain spaces, and they should be composed only of letters and/or numbers.

- The Layers panel contains a *Prevent overlaps* check box. When this check box contains a check mark, layers cannot be overlapped.

- The concept of nested layers is similar to nested tables and frames. A nested layer is contained inside another layer.

- The layer nested inside another layer is referred to as a child layer, and the layer it is contained in is referred to as the parent layer.

- A nested layer moves with its parent layer when the parent layer is moved, and it inherits its visibility properties from the parent layer as well.

- A child layer can be selected and moved independently of its parent layer so that it appears completely separate from the parent layer. However, the code for the child layer is still nested inside the code for the parent layer, and the child layer still inherits the parent layer's visibility property.

- The overflow property in the Layer Property inspector specifies layer behavior in the event that layer content exceeds its specified dimensions.

- The clip property in the Layer Property inspector specifies the visible portion of a layer.

- Behaviors use JavaScript code to create events and actions that can be associated with layers to make them interactive.

- When a viewer performs an event, an associated action is performed.

- More than one action can be assigned to an event.

- The Go To URL behavior can be attached to a layer so that a layer event (clicking, hovering over, and so on) opens an HTML document in the same browser window.

➤ A Drag behavior can be attached to layers so that viewers can use the mouse to drag the layers in the browser window.

➤ Pop-up messages are small dialog boxes that pop up when an event triggers that action.

➤ The Show-Hide Layers behavior can be used to cause a hidden layer to show, or a visible layer to hide.

➤ Although it is possible to convert layers into tables, or tables into layers, it is not recommended because the conversion process produces unwieldy code that is difficult to edit. If tables are to be used for page layout, it is much better to design them in Standard mode.

KEY terms

behaviors Events and actions that can be associated with HTML elements to make them interactive.

Behaviors panel A panel that allows you to attach behaviors to HTML elements.

child layer Term used to describe a nested layer.

clip property Layer property that specifies the visible portion of a layer.

division tags The HTML tags (<div> </div>) that provide structure and content for block-level content in a document. Dreamweaver MX 2004 uses division tags to create layers.

Drag behavior A behavior that can be attached to layers so that viewers can use the mouse to drag the layers in the browser window.

Go To URL behavior A behavior that can be attached to a layer so that a layer event (clicking, hovering over, and so on) opens an HTML document in the same browser window.

JavaScript A scripting language that allows interactive behavior.

layer-code markers Small yellow markers that indicate the presence of a layer on a page. They can be used to select or delete a layer. Right-clicking a layer-code marker opens a context menu.

layer coordinates Coordinates that specify the position of a layer in relationship to the upper-left corner of an HTML document, or the upper-left corner of another layer in the case of nested layers.

layer names Layer names cannot contain spaces and should be composed only of letters and/or numbers. You should rename layers descriptively so that their functions are easy to identify.

Layers panel A panel that can be used to select, rename, and change z-index and visibility status for layers. It also contains a *Prevent overlaps* check box that can be used to prevent layers from overlapping.

layer visibility Layer property that specifies the default visibility status of a layer. The four possibilities are *default, inherit, visible,* and *hidden*.

nested layer A layer contained inside another layer. Not the same as a layer that overlaps another layer. The code for a nested layer (child layer) is contained inside the code for its parent layer.

overflow property Layer property that specifies layer behavior in the event that layer content exceeds its specified dimensions.

parent layer Term used to describe a layer that contains a nested layer (child layer).

pop-up messages Behavior that causes small dialog boxes to pop up when an event triggers this action.

Prevent overlaps **check box** A Layers panel check box that prevents layers from overlapping when enabled.

Show-Hide Layers behavior A behavior that can be used to cause a hidden layer to show or a visible layer to hide.

stacking order The order in which layers are stacked, determined by their z-index values.

z-index Determines the order in which a layer will appear when it is stacked over other layers. A layer with a higher z-index value appears on top of a layer with a lower value.

COMMANDS review

Align layer borders	Modify, Align, and then Left, Right, Top, or Bottom
Convert layers to tables	Modify, Convert, Layers to Table
Convert tables to layers	Modify, Convert, Tables to Layers
Insert a layer	Insert, Layout Objects, Layer
Insert content into layers	Insert, and then choose object
Resize multiple layers	Modify, Align, Make Same Width or Make Same Height
Specify layer preferences	Edit, Preferences, Layers Page

CONCEPTS check

Indicate the correct term or command for each item.

1. These are the four different possibilities for the default layer visibility property.
2. The Layers panel is located inside this panel group.
3. This is the default tag that Dreamweaver MX 2004 uses to create layers in HTML code.
4. This behavior can be used to show layers with a default visibility property of hidden.
5. Behaviors consist of these two components.
6. A behavior event triggers this.
7. Layers can be inserted in a document by clicking Insert on the Menu bar, pointing to Layout Objects, and then clicking Layer, or by doing this.
8. Specifying this default visibility status for a nested layer (child layer) makes its visibility property the same as its parent layer's property.
9. When more than one layer is selected, the last layer selected is distinguished from the other selected layers in this way.
10. This layer should be dragged to move a nested layer set together without changing their position relative to each other.
11. This value determines the stacking order of layers.

12. This Layer Property inspector property determines the visible portion of a layer.
13. This Layer Property inspector property determines what happens when layer content exceeds a layer's dimensions.
14. This scripting language is used to create behaviors in Dreamweaver MX 2004.
15. These two coordinates determine layer page positioning.
16. Layer coordinates determine layer position in relationship to this.
17. If two layers are stacked, one has a z-index value of 2, and the other has a z-index value of 1, the layer with this z-index value will appear on top of the other when the page they are in is displayed in a browser.
18. Holding down this key after clicking the Draw Layer button lets you draw layers without having to click the Draw Layer button each time.
19. The number of spaces a layer name can contain.
20. More than one layer can be selected at a time by holding down this key.

SKILLS check

Use the Site Definition dialog box to create a separate Dreamweaver site named CH 07 Assessments to keep your assessment work for this chapter. Save the files for the site in a new root folder named ch_07_assessments under the Sites folder you created in Chapter 1, Exercise 3. Download the ch_07_student_files folder from the IRC to the CH 07 Assessments site root folder (ch_07_assessments) and expand it. Delete the compressed folder when you are finished.

Assessment 1 • Create Layers and Insert Images into Layers

1. Create a new HTML document and use the Save or Save As commands to name and save the document as **ch7sa1.htm**.
2. Insert or draw a layer anywhere on the page.
3. Create a nested layer within the layer drawn in Step 2.
4. Use a free graphics site to locate and save two images, or locate two of your own images and save them to the CH 07 Assessments site.
5. Insert one image into the parent layer, and the other into the nested layer. Create appropriate alternate text descriptions for each image.
6. Rename the layers.
7. Resize the layers so that their dimensions match the size of the images they contain.
8. Drag the parent layer to a position in the Document window that you like.
9. Drag the nested layer to position it in a location you like.
10. Click the Preview/Debug in browser button and then click Preview in iexplore to view the results. If you do not like the positioning, close the browser and readjust the position of the layers. Click the Preview/Debug in browser button and then click Preview in iexplore again to view the results. Close the browser when you are finished.
11. Save **ch7sa1.htm** and then close it.

Assessment 2 • Create a Jig-saw Puzzle

1. Create a new HTML document and use the Save or Save As commands to name and save the document as **ch7sa2.htm**.
2. Insert or draw nine layers in the document.
3. Use a free graphics site to find and save an image that you can make into a jig-saw puzzle consisting of nine pieces, or use an image you already have. Use a graphics editor to create the nine puzzle-piece images. Alternatively, insert a letter into each layer to make the puzzle create a nine-letter word when the puzzle pieces are rearranged.
4. Insert the images into the layers and resize each layer to fit the size of the image it contains. If you are using letters instead of images, enlarge the letters and center-align them. Change the background color of each layer.
   Note: An image puzzle should be arranged so that the completed puzzle consists of a three-row, three-column square when finished. A word puzzle should consist of nine pieces in a row. Each letter puzzle piece should be the same size, but image puzzle pieces can contain irregular shapes.
5. Add a Drag behavior to each layer. Make the drag behavior start when the document loads in a browser (onLoad).
6. Scramble the pieces in the document by dragging to random locations in the Document window.
7. Click the Preview/Debug in browser button and then click Preview in iexplore to test the puzzle to ensure that all pieces are draggable. Close the browser when you are finished.
8. Save **ch7sa2.htm** and then close it.

Assessment 3 • Add the Show-Hide Behavior to Layers

1. Create a new HTML document and use the Save or Save As commands to name and save the document as **ch7sa3.htm**.
2. Insert or draw three small layers at the top or along the left side of the document. These layers serve as buttons to show or hide other layers that you will create later.
3. Make the three layers the same size. At the same time, set their left and top coordinates so that the three layers are all evenly spaced at the top of the document or along the left side of the document.
4. Use a free graphics site to find and save at least three images of oil paintings by famous artists and save them to the CH 07 Assessments site.
5. Create different background colors for each layer button.
6. Insert text into each layer button with the name of an artist or artwork that the button will be used to open and close.
7. Resize the text and center align it.
8. Insert or draw a layer in the center of the document.
9. Insert one of the artwork images into the layer. Resize the layer to match the image dimensions.
10. Create additional layers on top of the layer you just drew, and insert the remaining artwork images into each layer. Resize each layer to match the size of the image it contains.
11. Align the top and left borders of the artwork layers.
12. Set the default visibility property of the artwork layers as hidden.

13. Select the first layer button and use the Show-Hide Layers behavior to make its corresponding layer show on a mouseover event. For example, the van Gogh button would show the layer containing a van Gogh painting. Attach another Show-Hide behavior to make its corresponding layer hide on a mouseout event. Repeat this step for each button and its corresponding artwork layer.

14. Click the Preview/Debug in browser button and then click Preview in iexplore to check the document. Hovering the mouse pointer over a button should cause its corresponding artwork layer to show, while moving the mouse pointer off a button should cause the artwork layer to disappear. Close the browser when you are finished.

15. Save **ch7sa3.htm** and then close it.

Assessment 4 • Create a Preload Layer

1. Open any HTML document that you have created previously and save it to the CH 07 Assessments site as **ch7sa4.htm**.

2. Create a layer that completely covers the page contents of **ch7sa4.htm**. Use the Layer Property inspector to change the background color of the layer so that the contents of **ch7sa4.htm** are not visible. Name the layer *Preload*.

3. Click the Preview/Debug in browser button and then Preview in iexplore to verify that the layer obscures the contents of **ch7sa4.htm**. If it does not, close the browser and return to Dreamweaver MX 2004 to adjust the layer and check again using the browser. Close the browser window when you are finished.

4. Type a message in the layer, such as Please wait while the page loads. or Loading. Use the Property inspector to increase the font size of the message and to center it. ***Note: Change the text color if necessary so that the text is legible with the background color you have selected.***

5. If **ch7sa4.htm** contains any layers in addition to the Preload layer use the Layers panel to click and drag the Preload layer to the top of the list of layers so that it has the highest z-index number.

6. Use the Show-Hide behavior to hide the Preload layer. ***Hint: Make sure that the layer is not selected when you do this. Clicking the body tag is an easy way to do that.***

7. Make sure that the event for the hide behavior is *onLoad*. If it is not, click the down-pointing arrow next to the event to select *onLoad* from the list that appears.

8. Save **ch7sa4.htm** and then close it. ***Note: If you preview ch7sa4.htm in a browser the page will load so quickly that you probably will not see the preload layer message. However, when the page is located on a server those with slow connection speeds will see the preload message before the page loads.***

Assessment 5 • Add Layers to Your Design Portfolio

Save all documents created in this assessment in the site you created in Chapter 2 for your design portfolio project.

1. Use layers to contain and position images on some of the existing pages in your design portfolio, or create new pages to contain these layers and add them to the portfolio.

2. Use the Show-Hide Layers behavior to show and hide a layer on at least one page of your design portfolio. The event or events that trigger this behavior are up to you.

DREAMWEAVER MX 2004

USING TEMPLATES AND LIBRARY ITEMS

PERFORMANCE OBJECTIVES

- ➤ Understand how template and library items work.
- ➤ Create templates from new and existing documents.
- ➤ Insert editable regions, repeating regions, and repeating table regions into templates.
- ➤ Create new documents from templates.
- ➤ Attach existing documents to templates.
- ➤ Create editable tag attributes.
- ➤ Create nested templates.
- ➤ Update templates and documents created from templates.
- ➤ Set template preferences.
- ➤ Create library items.
- ➤ Insert library items into documents.
- ➤ Edit library items.

The student files for this chapter are available for download from the Internet Resource Center at www.emcp.com.

For viewers to know that the different Web pages they visit belong to the same Web site, there should be a continuity of design between the pages. If no two Web pages in a Web site share any design traits, viewers will be as confused and disoriented as they would be if they were to read a newspaper in which no two pages shared any design similarities. A good Web site provides visual cues that let viewers know that a page belongs to the Web site. This can take the form of similarities in background colors, images, logos, page layouts, font styles and colors, or navigation schemes. For designers, this involves employing repeated content, and when working on a large Web site, this could involve a lot of duplicated effort. This is where Dreamweaver MX 2004 templates and library items come in handy. Templates and library items make it easy to create repeated or duplicate content. That alone would be enough to justify their use, but there is an additional benefit to using templates and library items. When a change is made to a template, the change will be implemented in any document attached to the template, and when a library item is updated, the update will be implemented in any document where the library item was inserted. Like Cascading Style Sheets (CSS), this drastically simplifies the task of making site-wide changes to documents.

Understanding Templates

Most Dreamweaver MX 2004 users are familiar with the concept of a template—a document used as a pattern to create other documents. The predefined page-design documents in Dreamweaver MX 2004 function as templates. You select a page design you like, create it, save it under a different name, and then change the document's placeholder content. Dreamweaver MX 2004 templates function in a similar way, but with several key differences.

Dreamweaver MX 2004 templates contain *locked regions* that prevent users from making changes to any content in the locked region. In fact, when a template is created, the entire document is locked, with the exception of the document title. After the template is created, users must designate regions of the document that will be editable. HTML documents created from a template are attached automatically to the template and contain locked and *editable regions* as shown in Figure 8.1. Editable regions are indicated by a colored tab containing the name of the editable region; an outlined rectangle indicates the region of the document that can be edited. Positioning the insertion point inside this rectangle allows users to enter content in the normal fashion. If the editable region contains placeholder text, it can be left in place, deleted, or typed over. The pointer turns into a *prohibited sign* as shown in Figure 8.1 when it moves over a locked region.

Creating locked and editable regions allows designers great control over the appearance of documents created from the template and helps them preserve the integrity of the pages they design by protecting them from unauthorized alteration. For example, a newsletter template could be created that allows subsequent users to create documents based on the template. Editable regions in those documents would allow the users to change the date and issue number at the top of the document and the content of the document, but not the basic page layout or the banner content at the top of the document. Basing the newsletter on a template results in a newsletter layout that remains consistent from issue to issue, and the designer would not have to worry about unauthorized modifications to the newsletter layout.

When a document is created from a template in Dreamweaver MX 2004, it is automatically attached to the template, somewhat like the way a style sheet is attached to an HTML document. Documents created from a template are called

Figure 8.1
Editable and Locked Regions in a Document Created from a Template

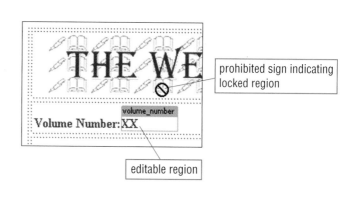

prohibited sign indicating locked region

editable region

instances, and instances can be saved as templates (to create nested templates) or as HTML documents. Changes to any of the locked regions of the template or the addition of new editable regions will be propagated (passed on) to any document created using the template, whether it is another template or an HTML document. Using the newsletter example, if the designer wanted to make a change only to the locked banner area at the top of the document, the template document would have to be modified. The change would then be implemented in any document attached to that template.

Editable regions in nested templates or HTML documents created from a template are independent of the parent template, so any changes to an editable region in a template have no effect on the editable region in any documents created from that template. For example, imagine an editable region in a template containing the words *Enter content here.* A document attached to this template contains an editable region with those words contained in the rectangular editable region box. If the template is modified by bolding the text in the editable region, that change does not appear in the document attached to it. In fact, even if the editable region is removed from the template, it would still appear in the attached document. However, if a new editable region is inserted in the template, or if any locked content is modified, those changes are propagated to any attached documents when the template is saved.

Creating Templates

Dreamweaver MX 2004 templates can be created from a new blank HTML document or by using an existing document. Editable regions in templates do not have to contain any text, but it is often a good idea to create placeholder or instructional text that lets users know the purpose of an editable region, such as *Enter report body text here.* or *Enter disclaimer text here.* as shown in Figure 8.2.

When templates are created, Dreamweaver MX 2004 creates a new **Templates folder** that will be stored in the root folder of the current site, unless another site is chosen. The Templates folder should not be moved and templates should not be moved out of the Templates folder. Doing either of those things can have a negative effect on the paths between templates and the documents created from them.

Templates have a special **.dwt file extension** to distinguish them from ordinary HTML documents as shown in Figure 8.3. Template names should be lowercase and should not contain special characters or spaces. Hyphens or underscores can be used to separate words in template names.

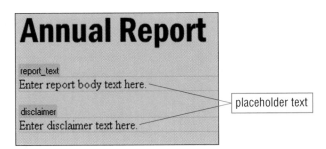

Figure 8.2 • Template Placeholder and Instructional Content

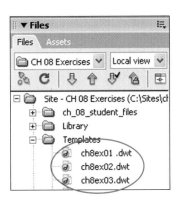

Figure 8.3 • Template Files in the Templates Folder

Templates can be created from scratch by opening a basic HTML document and then using the Save as Template command to save the document as a Dreamweaver MX 2004 template. You do not need to indicate the folder for the template to be saved in because all templates are stored in a site's automatically created Templates folder. During the saving process, a message box appears advising that the document does not contain editable regions. You can save a document without editable regions, and in fact, it is a good idea to do this right away before adding any editable regions. Because there is no purpose in creating and using a template without editable regions, the reminder is there to prompt users who might inadvertently think they had just created a template with an editable region. It is easy to mistake the Save As command for the Save as Template command. Mistakenly selecting the Save As command results in an ordinary HTML document with an .htm extension.

The Assets panel also can be used to create a template based on a blank document by clicking the Assets panel Templates button and then the New Template button located at the bottom of the panel as shown in Figure 8.4. If the Assets panel is not open, you can click Window on the Menu bar and then Assets. Right-clicking inside the panel will also bring up a context menu with the New Template command if the panel is in the Templates category. After you click the New Template button, a new template listing appears in the panel with its default name selected, and you can type a new name for the template. After renaming the template, double-click it to open the template in the Document window as a template document with a .dwt extension.

The Insert bar (Common menu item or tab) contains commands for all Template functions. These commands can be accessed by clicking the Templates button down-pointing arrow as shown in Figure 8.5. Clicking the Make Template command opens the Save As Template dialog box that also can be opened by clicking File and then Save as Template. The Templates button will display the most recent template command chosen from the command menu. Hovering the mouse pointer over the Templates button lets you know its current status, such as *Templates: Editable Region*.

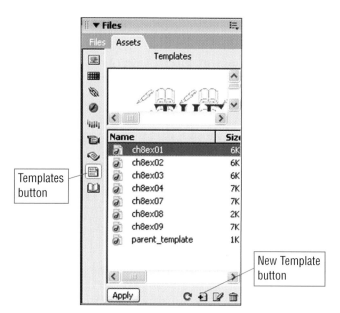

Figure 8.4 • Assets Panel Templates and New Template Buttons

Figure 8.5 • Insert Bar Templates Button Menu (Common Menu Item or Tab)

DREAMWEAVER MX 2004

Creating a template from an existing document is the same as creating a template from a new document, except that you can select existing content and make it editable while leaving other content locked, as described in the next section of this chapter. The existing HTML document is transformed into a template by using the Save as Template command instead of the Save or Save As commands.

exercise **1**

1. If necessary, start Dreamweaver MX 2004.
2. At a clear document screen, create a new site named CH 08 Exercises to store the exercises you create in this chapter. Name the root folder ch_08_exercises and save it under the Sites folder you created in Chapter 1, Exercise 3. Download the ch_08_student_files folder from the IRC to the CH 08 Exercises site root folder (ch_08_exercises) and expand it. Delete the compressed folder when you are finished. ***Note: Refer to Chapter 1 for instructions on navigating with the Files panel integrated file browser.***
3. Create a template from an existing HTML document by completing the following steps:
   a. Open the **newsletter.htm** student file in the ch_08_student_files folder.
   b. Click File on the Menu bar and then Save as Template to open the Save As Template dialog box.
   c. Click the down-pointing arrow next to the *Site* list box and locate *CH 08 Exercises* if necessary.

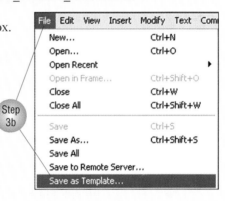

Step 3c

Step 3b

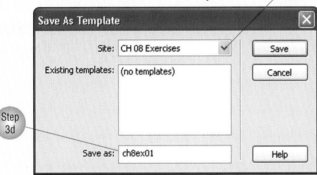

Step 3d

   d. Type **ch8ex01** in the *Save as* text box and then click the Save button.
   e. Open the Files panel. Note that Dreamweaver MX 2004 has created a Templates folder. Click the Plus (+) button next to the Templates folder to see its contents. The template you have just created is displayed with a .dwt extension, indicating that it is a template document. ***Hint: Click the Files panel Refresh button if you do not see the Templates folder.***
   f. Click the Assets panel tab to open the Assets panel and then click the Templates button. The template you just created is displayed in the panel. Any template created in the current site is stored in the Templates folder and displayed in the Assets panel.

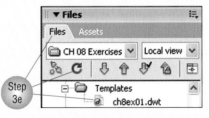

Step 3e

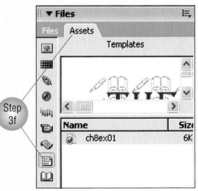

Step 3f

g. Click File on the Menu bar and then Close to close **ch8ex01.dwt**. A message box appears advising you that the document does not contain any editable regions. Click the dialog box Cancel button to stop the file closing process. A new message appears advising that editable regions can be created by clicking Insert on the Menu bar and then pointing to Template Objects. Click the OK button to close the message box.

4. Leave **ch8ex01.dwt** open in the Document window.

Creating Editable Regions

For a template to be useful, you should designate at least one editable region in the document. Four types of regions can be created in a template: editable regions, repeating regions, repeating tables, and optional regions. *Optional regions* appear or do not appear in a template based on conditional statements; they can be locked or editable. Creating the conditional statements required for optional regions requires writing expressions, which are based on a subset of JavaScript. Because that knowledge is beyond the scope of this book, creating optional regions will not be discussed.

Editable Regions

As its name implies, an editable region can be edited in documents created from a template. If an editable region is inserted in a normal HTML document, a message appears informing you that the document will be saved automatically as a template document as shown in Figure 8.6.

The placement of the editable region in selected page content is important. When saving the template, you might see the message box shown in Figure 8.7 informing you that you have placed the editable region inside block element tags, such as paired paragraph tags. If this is the case, you cannot create a new paragraph when working with the editable region in a document created from the template. If you want users to be able to create new block elements, the editable region must be placed outside the block tags, as advised by the message box. For example, if an entire paragraph is selected and designated as an editable region,

Figure 8.6
Template Saving Message

DREAMWEAVER MX 2004

338 Chapter 8

you could create a new document based on the template and then create new paragraphs when working in the editable region. However, if only a portion of the paragraph was selected and designated as an editable region, users working with a new document based on that template could not create a new paragraph in the editable region, and they would see a message box advising them of that fact if they attempt to do that.

Switching to Code view when creating editable regions will reveal whether an editable region is contained inside or outside paired block tags as shown in Figure 8.8. The Tag selector can be used to ensure that an editable region encompasses an entire block level tag if that is desired. Clicking a block tag in the Tag selector highlights the content it controls in the Document window, and an editable region then can be created.

Editable regions can be created within a template by first positioning the insertion point in the desired location or by selecting page content (text, an image, a layer, and so on) and clicking Insert on the Menu bar, pointing to Template Objects, and then clicking Editable Region.

The Insert bar also can be used to insert editable regions by clicking the Templates button and then clicking the Editable Region command as shown previously in Figure 8.5. Right-clicking, pointing to Templates, and then clicking New Editable Region is another way to create editable regions.

After any of these methods have been performed, the New Editable Region dialog box appears as shown in Figure 8.9, prompting you to create a name for the editable region. This name will appear in a small blue tab over an editable region rectangle outlined in blue. If you do not choose a name, a default name

Figure 8.7
Inside Block Tag Message Box

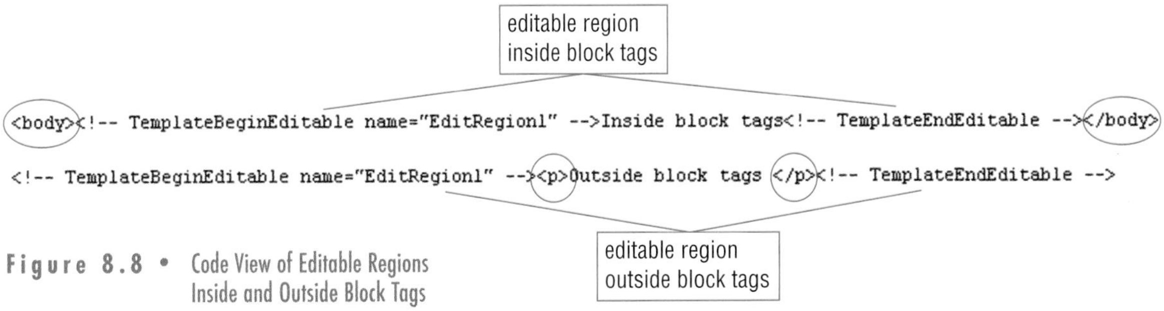

Figure 8.8 • Code View of Editable Regions
Inside and Outside Block Tags

Figure 8.9
New Editable Region
Dialog Box

will appear, such as *EditRegion1*. Editable region names should be lowercase and contain no spaces or special characters. Hyphens or underscores can be used to separate words in the name if desired. If page content was selected when creating the editable region, it will appear inside the editable region box as shown in Figure 8.10. If no page content was selected, the name of the editable region will appear inside the editable region box. *Note: If no outline color is visible, check to see that the Invisible Elements option has been enabled by clicking the Document toolbar View options button and then pointing to Visual Aids to see if a check mark appears next to Invisible Elements. If an outline color is still not visible, look in the "Setting Template Preferences" section near the end of this chapter to learn how to determine whether the Show check boxes for editable, nested, and locked template regions have been disabled.*

Editable region names can be changed by selecting the editable region and typing a new name in the Template Property inspector *Name* text box as shown in Figure 8.11.

Editable regions can be removed from templates by selecting the region and clicking Modify on the Menu bar, pointing to Templates, and then clicking Remove Template Markup. Although the corresponding editable region will remain in any document attached to the template, new documents created from the template will not contain the editable region that was removed.

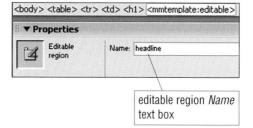

Figure 8.10
Editable Regions

Figure 8.11
Template Property Inspector

exercise 2

CREATING EDITABLE REGIONS

1. Create editable regions in a template by completing the following steps:
   a. With **ch8ex01.dwt** as the current document, use the Save as Template command to rename and save it as **ch8ex02.dwt**. *Note: The message box advising that there are no editable regions in the template will appear. Click the OK button to close the message box.*
   b. Position the insertion point just after *Volume Number:*.

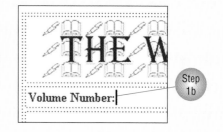

c. Click the Insert bar (Common menu item or tab) Templates button down-pointing arrow and then click the Editable Region command to create an editable region. The New Editable Region dialog box appears.

d. Type **volume_number** in the New Editable Region dialog box *Name* text box. Click the OK button to close the dialog box.

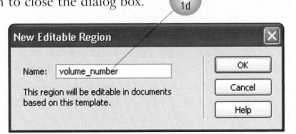

Step 1d

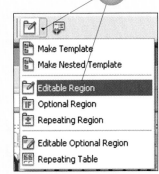

Step 1c

e. Select *Month, Date, Year* in the same table row and then repeat Steps 1c and 1d to create an editable region. Name this editable region *date*.

f. Select *Headline* in the next row and then repeat Steps 1c and 1d to create an editable region. Name the region *headline*.

g. Position the insertion point anywhere inside the text of the first column.

h. Click <p> in the Tag selector and then repeat Steps 1c and 1d to create an editable region in the first column. Name the region *column_1*. ***Note: Selecting the division tag would have included the image in the editable region. By selecting the paragraph tag only, the text content of the first column will be an editable region. Leaving the image outside the editable region means it will be locked when instances (HTML documents) are created from this template. Later, you will make some of the image attributes editable even though the image itself is locked.***

i. Position the insertion point inside the text of the second column.

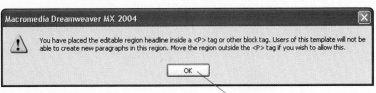

Step 1h

j. Click <p> in the Tag selector to select the content of the second column and then repeat Steps 1c and 1d to create an editable region in the second column. Name the region *column_2.*

k. Select *2004* at the bottom of the document and then repeat Steps 1c and 1d to create an editable region. Name the region *copyright_date*.

l. Click File on the Menu bar and then Save. A message appears advising that the headline editable region is contained inside paragraph or block tags and that users will not be able to create new paragraphs when working with instances created from this template.

In this circumstance, that is fine because this is a headline area, and you probably do not want a two-line headline. Click the OK button to close the dialog box. ***Note: This message will appear whenever documents with editable regions inside block tags are saved or resaved. It is just a reminder, so click the OK button whenever it appears.***

Step 1l

2. Leave **ch8ex02.dwt** open in the Document window.

Repeating Regions

When you are using a document attached to a template, ***repeating regions*** allow you to repeat a region simply by clicking the Plus (+) button shown in Figure 8.12. The repeated region can be removed by clicking the Minus (–) button. The Up Arrow and Down Arrow buttons can be used to change the order of the repeated regions. A repeating region is not editable unless it has been specifically designated as a repeating region. It is possible to remove the editable region from a repeating region by clicking the Minus (–) button too many times, but it can be restored by clicking the Undo button on the Standard toolbar.

You can create repeating regions in several ways. You can select content or position the insertion point at the desired location, click Insert on the Menu bar, point to Template Objects, and then click Editable Region. Clicking the Insert bar Templates button Editable Region command also creates a repeating region. If a document already has been saved as a template, you can right-click the selected text to bring up a context menu with a Templates command. Point to this command and then New Repeating Region on the submenu to create a repeating region.

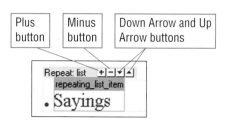

Figure 8.12
Repeating Regions Buttons

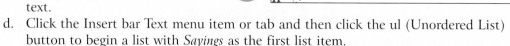

exercise **3**　　　　　　　　　　　　　　　　　　　　　　**CREATING REPEATING REGIONS**

1. Create a repeating region in a template by completing the following steps:
   a. With **ch8ex02.dwt** as the current document, use the Save as Template command to rename and save it as **ch8ex03.dwt**.
   b. Position the insertion point just to the right of *This Week's Favorite Sayings:* and press Enter to move the insertion point down.
   c. Type **Sayings** and then select the text.
   d. Click the Insert bar Text menu item or tab and then click the ul (Unordered List) button to begin a list with *Sayings* as the first list item.

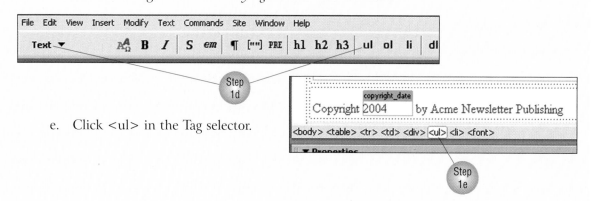

   e. Click <ul> in the Tag selector.

DREAMWEAVER MX 2004

f. Click the Insert bar (Common menu item or tab) Templates button down-pointing arrow and then click the Repeating Region command to open the New Repeating Region dialog box.

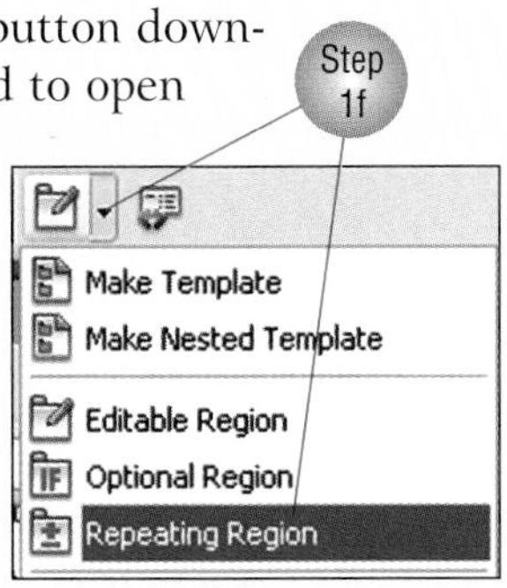

g. Type list in the New Repeating Region dialog box *Name* text box and then click the OK button to close the dialog box.

h. Click *Sayings* to deselect it. Position the insertion point inside *Sayings* and then click <font> in the Tag selector to select only the text in the repeating region. ***Hint: The trick here is to select only the* Sayings *text and nothing else. To be sure, click the Code button and determine whether only* Sayings *is selected. Return to Design view after you have checked.***

i. Click the Insert bar Templates button down-pointing arrow and then the Editable Region command to open the New Editable Region dialog box.

j. Type repeating_list_item in the New Editable Region dialog box *Name* text box and then click the OK button to close the dialog box.

k. Click File on the Menu bar and then Save. Click OK to close the message box.

2. Leave **ch8ex03.dwt** open in the Document window.

Repeating Tables

Repeating tables allow you to define the rows of a table that will repeat when the repeating table Plus (+) button is clicked. When the repeating table insertion commands are clicked, an Insert Repeating Table dialog box appears as shown in Figure 8.13. You can enter the appropriate values and choices, including designating which table rows will repeat and which will not. The repeating rows are created automatically as editable regions. Editable regions can be added to table cells in nonrepeating rows or removed from cells in repeating rows.

You can create repeating tables by clicking Insert on the Menu bar, pointing to Template Objects, and then clicking Repeating Table. You also can click the Insert bar Templates button Repeating Table command to create a repeating table. There is no context menu command for creating a repeating table.

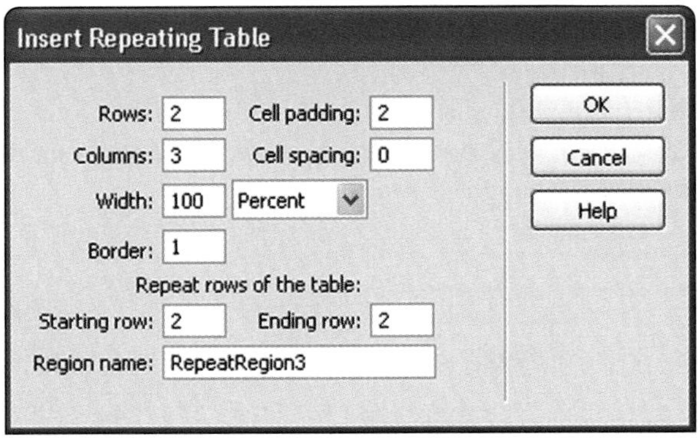

Figure 8.13 • Insert Repeating Table Dialog Box

1. Create a repeating table region in a template by completing the following steps:

   a. With **ch8ex03.dwt** as the current document, use the Save as Template command to rename and save it as **ch8ex04.dwt**.

   b. Position the insertion point below the repeating region you created in Exercise 3. *Hint: Ensure that the insertion point is no longer positioned in the repeating region by checking that the Tag inspector displays the paragraph tag. If the paragraph tag is not visible, the insertion point is located inside the repeating region.*

   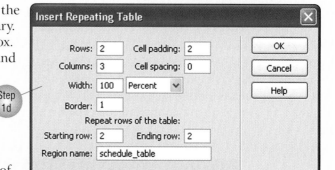

   Step 1b

   c. Click the Insert bar Templates button down-pointing arrow and then click the Repeating Table command to open the Insert Repeating Table dialog box.

   Step 1c

   d. Type the following values in the dialog box:
      1) Type 2 in the *Rows* text box.
      2) Type 3 in the *Columns* text box.
      3) Type 2 in the *Cell padding* text box.
      4) Leave the *Cell spacing* text box empty or type 0 in the text box.
      5) Type 100 in the *Width* text box and select *Percent* from the drop-down menu if necessary.
      6) Type 1 in the *Border* text box.
      7) Type 2 in the *Starting row* and *Ending row* text boxes.
      8) Type schedule_table in the *Region name* text box.

      Step 1d

      9) Click the OK button when you are finished.

   e. Type Time in the first column of the first table row, Program in the second column of the first table row, and Channel in the third column of the first table row. *Hint: The first column will be obscured partly by the repeat region tab, but clicking just above it will allow you to select the column.*

   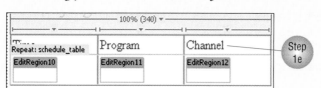

   Step 1e

   Step 1f

   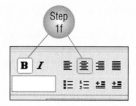

   f. Select the first row of the table, and use the Property inspector to center and bold the text you just entered.

g. Position the insertion point inside the first table column of the first row and type 35% in the Table Cell Property inspector *W* text box. ***Hint: Do not place the insertion point inside the editable regions.***

h. Position the insertion point inside the second column of the first row and type 50% in the Table Cell Property inspector *W* text box.

i. Position the insertion point inside the third column of the first row and type 15% in the Table Cell Property inspector *W* text box.

j. Click the first editable region tab in the table to select it. Type time in the Property inspector *Name* text box.

k. Repeat Step 1j to rename the next two remaining editable regions in the table *program* and *channel*.

2. Save **ch8ex04.dwt** and then close it.

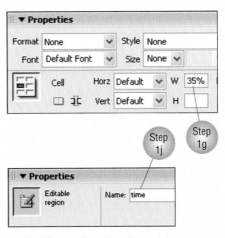

Attaching a New Document to a Template

A document must be attached to a template to take advantage of the power that templates have to offer. Using the Assets panel located inside the Files panel group is one way to create new documents based on templates. Templates do not have their own panel, but you can access the Templates category of the Assets panel by clicking the Templates button located on the left side of the Assets panel as shown in Figure 8.14. The Templates category shows all of the templates available in the current site. Right-click a template name in the Assets panel list box and then click New from Template to create an instance based on the template. Instances then can be saved as ordinary HTML documents, or as another template if a nested template is desired. (Creating nested templates is discussed later in this chapter.) Be careful not to confuse the New Template command with the New from Template command on the context menu.

Another way you can create an instance based on an existing template is to click File on the Menu bar and then New to open the New from Template dialog

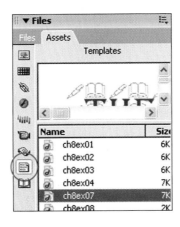

Figure 8.14
Assets Panel Templates Button

box as shown in Figure 8.15. Clicking the Templates tab shows Dreamweaver sites on the left side of the dialog box. Clicking a site name shows any templates available in that site in a list box, and a preview of the template also appears. If a description has been created for the template, it appears below the preview. Double-clicking a template name opens it in the Document window. Single-clicking a template name and then clicking the Create button also opens a template in the Document window. After the template is open, it then can be modified and saved using the Save as Template command to make it a nested template.

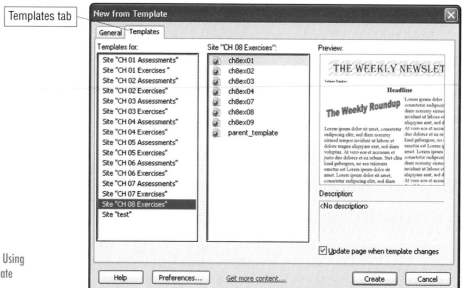

Figure 8.15
Creating a Template Using the New from Template Dialog Box

exercise **5**

USING A TEMPLATE TO CREATE AN INSTANCE

1. Create an instance from a template by completing the following steps:
   a. At a clear document screen, open the Assets panel and click the Templates button if necessary.
   b. Right-click *ch8ex04* and then click New from Template.
   c. Click File on the Menu bar and then Save As to rename and save the instance you have just created as **ch8ex05.htm** in the CH 08 Exercises root folder (ch_08_exercises). *Hint: Be sure that you do not inadvertently save the file under the Templates folder.*

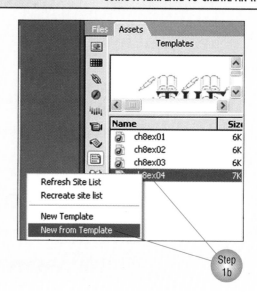

d. Move the pointer around the screen. Note how it turns into a prohibited sign when it hovers over locked portions of the document, but it turns into an insertion point when over an editable region.

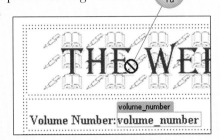
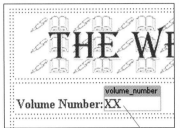

Step 1d

Step 1e

e. Select the text in the *volume_number* editable region and type XX.

f. Press Enter. A message appears advising that the change you just tried to make (entering a paragraph tag) is prohibited because the code is locked and the change will be discarded. This is because this editable region was created inside block tags, in this case the table data cell tags (<td> </td>), for the table cell the editable tag is located in. ***Note: If you had wanted users to be able to create new paragraphs in this editable region, selecting the cell's table data cell tag in the Tag selector and then creating an editable region would have placed the editable tag outside the block tags and allowed new paragraphs to be created.*** Click OK to close the message box.

g. Select *XX* and click the Code button on the Document toolbar. Note that the comment tags that indicate the editable region are inside the paired table data cell tags. Click the Design button when you are finished.

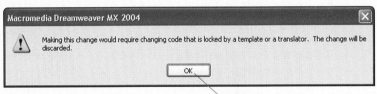

Step 1f

```
<tr>
  <td><font color="#660066"><strong>Volume Number:<!-- InstanceBeginEditable name="volume_number " -->XX
<!-- InstanceEndEditable --></strong></font></td>
  <td>
```

Step 1g

h. Select the text in the *date* editable region and type the current month, date, and year. This editable tag is located between block tags and a new paragraph cannot be created.

i. Select the text in the *headline* editable region and type a headline of your choice for the newsletter. Like the previous two editable tags, this editable tag is located between block tags and a new paragraph cannot be created.

j. Select the text in the *column1* editable region and type a line or two of text. Press Enter. A new paragraph is created because this editable region was created outside block tags, in this case paragraph tags. Click the Code button and note that the comment tags for this editable region are located outside paragraph tags. Click the Design button when you are finished.

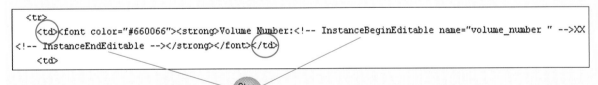

Step 1j

```
<!-- InstanceBeginEditable name="column_1" -->
<p><font color="#660066" size="5">New paragraph.</font></p>
<p><font color="#660066" size="5">New paragraph. </font></p>
<!-- InstanceEndEditable --></div></td>
```

k. Type at least three paragraphs of newsletter text in the first column of the document and do the same for the second column editable region. ***Hint: Select the text in the* column2 *editable region before you type your paragraphs.***

l. Select the text in the *list* repeating editable region and type A stitch in time saves nine. Click the Plus (+) button when you are finished to repeat the editable region. ***Hint: Do not press Enter. If you do, a message appears advising that the change you just tried to make cannot be made because it is locked out. This is because this repeating editable region was created inside block tags.***

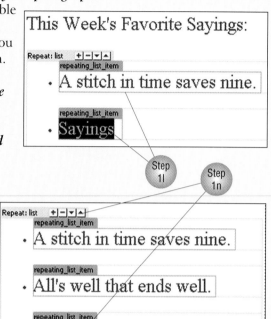

m. Type All's well that ends well. in the repeated editable region. Click the Plus (+) button again, and type two or three more sayings of your choice.

n. Place the insertion point in the last saying you entered and then click the Up Arrow button to move the saying so that it is the first in the list.

o. Place the insertion point in *A stitch in time saves nine.* and then use the Down Arrow button to move it so that it is the last item in the list.

p. Place the insertion point inside the repeating table *time* editable region and type 8:00-9:00.

q. Place the insertion point inside the repeating table *program* editable region and type Morning News.

r. Place the insertion point inside the repeating table *channel* editable region and type 11.

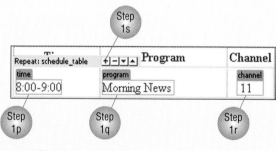

s. Click the repeating table Plus (+) button to create a new row. Type a time, program name, and channel of your choice. Click the Plus (+) button again, and create three more program listings.

t. Select the text in the *copyright date* editable region and type the current year.

u. Click the Preview/Debug in browser button and then click Preview in iexplore to preview the document. Close the browser when you are finished.

2. Save **ch8ex05.htm** and then close it.

Attaching a Template to an Existing Document

An existing document can be attached to a template by making the document the current document in the Document window, clicking Modify on the Menu bar, pointing to Templates, and then clicking Apply Templates to Page. This opens the Select Template dialog box as shown in Figure 8.16. You then can select the site that a desired template is located in by clicking the *Site* list box down-pointing arrow. A list of all of the templates in the chosen site appears. Click a site name and then click the select button to attach the template to the current document.

An Inconsistent Region Names dialog box as shown in Figure 8.17 might appear. The purpose of this dialog box is to resolve (reconcile) the regions in the current document with the regions in the template it was attached to. This can happen either when a document without any editable regions is attached to a template or when a document that was created from another template contains regions whose names differ from the regions in the new template being attached to the document. To view regions in the template document that the region highlighted in the Inconsistent Region Names dialog box list box can be moved to, click the *Move content to new region* list box down-pointing arrow. You also can click the Use for all button to move all of the unresolved regions in the list box to a region selected from the drop-down list. Clicking *Nowhere* from the drop-down list discards a region displayed in the list box.

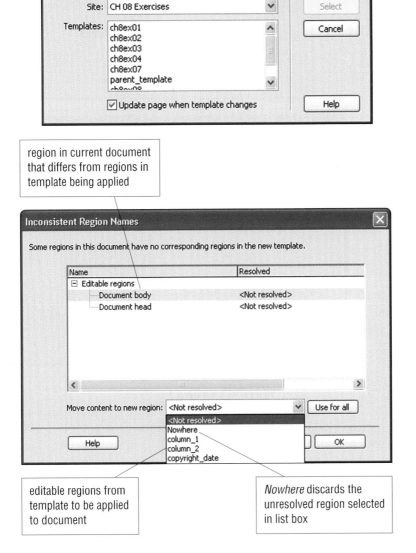

Figure 8.16
Select Template Dialog Box

region in current document that differs from regions in template being applied

Figure 8.17
Inconsistent Region Names
Dialog Box

editable regions from template to be applied to document

Nowhere discards the unresolved region selected in list box

1. Attach a template to an existing document by completing the following steps:
   a. At a clear document screen, open the student file named **previous_version.htm** in the ch_08_student_files folder. Use the Save As command to rename and save it as **ch8ex06.htm** in the ch_08_exercises root folder. Note that this document is similar to the newsletter template you created but with several differences. This document contains only one column, and the content of the column is contained in an editable region named *body*. The volume content is contained in an editable region named *volume,* whereas it is named *volume_number* in the template that will be applied to this document.
   b. Click Modify on the Menu bar, point to Templates, and then click Apply Template to Page to open the Select Template dialog box.
   c. Click *ch8ex04* and then click the Select button. The Inconsistent Region Names dialog box appears because of the previously described mismatch between some regions in the existing document and the template being applied to it.

   Step 1c

   Select Template

   Site: CH 08 Exercises

   Templates: ch8ex01
   ch8ex02
   ch8ex03
   ch8ex04

   Select
   Cancel

   ☑ Update page when template changes

   Help

   d. Click *body* from the list box to select it. This region name appears in the list because the document contains an editable region named *body* that does not occur in the template being applied to this document. Note that the *Resolved* column shows that *body* is not resolved, meaning that Dreamweaver MX 2004 needs your assistance in deciding where to place this material.

   Step 1d

   Inconsistent Region Names

   Some regions in this document have no corresponding regions in the new template.

Name	Resolved
⊟ Editable regions	
body	<Not resolved>
volume	<Not resolved>

   Move content to new region: <Not resolved>   Use for all

   <Not resolved>
   Nowhere
   column_1
   column_2
   copyright_date
   date
   doctitle
   head
   headline
   volume_number

   Help   OK

   Step 1f   **Step 1e**

   e. Click the down-pointing arrow next to the *Move content to new region* list box. All of the regions in the template being applied to the existing document are displayed. *Hint: Choosing* **Nowhere** *discards content from content selected in the list box.*
   f. Click *column_1* from the drop-down list to move the content in the *body* editable region to the *column_1* editable region that will be applied to the existing document by the template.

g. Click *volume* from the list box to select it.

h. Click the down-pointing arrow next to the *Move content to new region* list box, scroll down the list until you see *volume_number,* and then click it. This moves the content of the *volume* editable region in the existing document to the *volume_number*

Step 1h

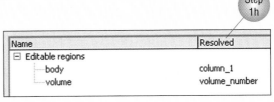

editable region that will be applied by the template. Look at the list box and note that it now shows where the mismatched regions will be placed when the template is applied to the existing document. Click the OK button to close the dialog box.

i. Look at the document in the Document window. The template regions have been applied to the document. Content from regions in the existing document that did not match regions in the template have been moved to the template regions you specified. The content from the *body* region has been placed in the *column_1* editable region, and the content of the *volume* editable region has been applied to the *volume_number* editable region. In the previous document, the headline *Twentieth Anniversary Issue* was not contained in a separate editable region, so it will appear in the *column_1* editable region along with the other content that was moved there from the *body* editable region.

2. Format the document by completing the following steps:

a. Move the *Twentieth Anniversary Issue* headline to the new *headline* editable region, by selecting it, right-clicking, and then clicking Cut. Select the text in the *headline* editable region, right-click, and then select Paste.

b. Position the insertion point where the *Twentieth Anniversary Issue* headline was formerly located and press the Delete key to move the paragraph text up into the area where the headline was. The text in the first paragraph enlarges because it is in the area controlled by the level-one heading tag that previously controlled the heading.

c. Remove the level-one heading formatting from the first column text, by selecting the first paragraph text and then clicking the Code button. Delete the paired level-one heading tags (**`<h1 align="center">`** **`</h1>`**) to remove the formatting. Click the Design button when you are finished.

```
<h1 align="center"><font color="#660066" size="5">It has been twenty years s
issue of the Weekly Newsletter first appeared. How time flies. The first
issues were typed using an old IBM typewriter, and then reproduced using
a mimeograph machine. It was a very time-consuming method of producing
a newsletter, but that is what everyone had to put up with.</font></h1>
```

Step 2c

d. Cut the *column_1* editable region content beginning with *This issue is a special one . . .* and ending with *. . . our readers want.,* and move it to the *column_2* editable region by pasting it over the placeholder text.

3. Save **ch8ex06.htm** and then close it.

Creating Editable Tag Attributes

When creating templates, it is possible to allow users to change selected attributes of text or page content that are otherwise locked when working on a document based on the template. For example, an image could be locked, but specified image attributes such as **border**, **width**, **height**, or **align** could be made into *editable tag attributes*. Although the image could not be removed or changed in a document based on the template, those attributes could be changed to add a border to the image or change the width, height, or alignment of the image.

To modify an attribute, you must select the desired page content. Click Modify on the Menu bar, point to Templates, and then click Make Attribute Editable to open the Editable Tag Attributes dialog box as shown in Figure 8.18. The list of attributes associated with the tag controlling the selected content appears in the *Attribute* list box, and they can be viewed by clicking the down-pointing arrow. To make an attribute editable, click the *Make attribute editable* check box to place a check mark in the box; the *Label, Type,* and *Default* boxes will all become active. The *Label* text box should be used to create a new distinctive name for the attribute. The *Type* list box lets you specify the type of value that can be entered for the attribute, such as text, a URL, or a number. The *Default* text box displays the current default value for the current attribute, which can be changed if desired. Click the OK button to complete the process.

If an attribute is not listed in the *Attribute* list box, clicking the Add button allows you to add an attribute to the list. The attribute must be one that is allowed with the tag whose attributes are being made editable. You can use the Reference panel to see the attributes that can be used with a particular tag. Open the Reference panel by clicking Window on the Menu bar and then Reference. Clicking the Reference panel *Tag* list box down-pointing arrow displays a list of HTML tags. After you choose a tag, click the down-pointing arrow in the unlabeled text box next to the *Tag* list box to display a list of all attributes associated with the tag that was selected in the *Tag* list box as shown in Figure 8.19.

Locked content with one or more editable attributes can be edited by clicking Modify on the Menu bar and then pointing to Template Properties. This opens the Template Properties dialog box as shown in Figure 8.20. The dialog box displays any attributes in the document that can be modified. Clicking an attribute activates a text box at the bottom of the dialog box, and new values for the attribute can

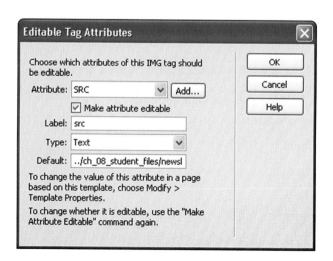

Figure 8.18
Editable Tag Attributes
Dialog Box

DREAMWEAVER MX 2004

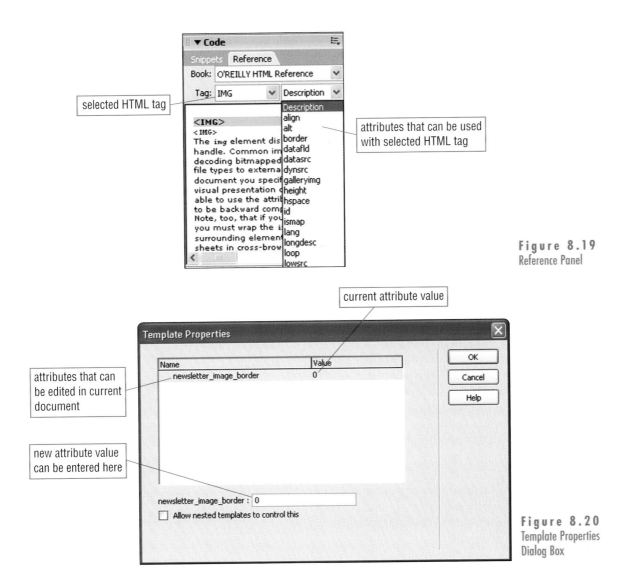

selected HTML tag

attributes that can be used
with selected HTML tag

Figure 8.19
Reference Panel

current attribute value

attributes that can
be edited in current
document

new attribute value
can be entered here

Figure 8.20
Template Properties
Dialog Box

be typed in the text box. The text box name changes to match the name of the
attribute being modified. Clicking the OK button completes the process and
closes the dialog box.

exercise 7

CREATING EDITABLE TAG ATTRIBUTES

1. Create editable tag attributes by completing the following steps:
   a. At a clear document screen, open **ch8ex04.dwt** and
      use the Save as Template command to rename and
      save it as **ch8ex07.dwt**.
   b. Select the newsletter banner image at the top of the
      document by clicking it.
   c. Click Modify, point to Templates, and then click
      Make Attribute Editable to open the Editable Tag
      Attributes dialog box.

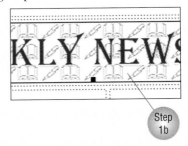

Step
1b

d. Click the down-pointing arrow next to the *Attribute* list box to see the current attributes associated with the selected image. Note that the attributes listed are *SRC* (used to indicate the path to the image), *WIDTH*, and *HEIGHT*. These are the attributes currrently associated with this image. Close the Editable Tag Attributes dialog box by clicking the Cancel button.

e. Click Window on the Menu bar and then Reference to open the Reference panel.

f. Click the down-pointing arrow next to the Reference panel *Tag* list box to see a drop-down list of HTML tags. Locate and click *IMG* from the list.

g. Click the down-pointing arrow next to the list box located to the right of the *Tag* list box to see a drop-down list of all attributes that can be associated with the image tag. Locate and click *border* from the drop-down list. Read the description about the border attribute that appears in the Reference panel.

h. Reopen the Editable Tag Attributes dialog box by repeating Steps 1b and 1c. ***Hint: Make sure that the newsletter banner image is still selected.***

i. Click the Add button in the Editable Tag Attributes dialog box to open a small dialog box with a text box that can be used to add a new editable attribute to the drop-down list for the selected newsletter banner image.

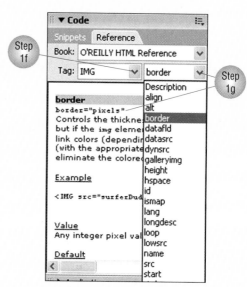

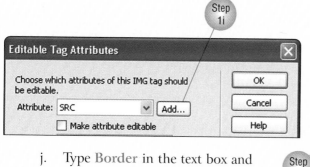

j. Type Border in the text box and then click the OK button.

DREAMWEAVER MX 2004

k. In the Editable Tag Attributes dialog box, click the *Make attribute editable* check box to enable it if necessary.

l. Type newsletter_image_border in the *Label* text box. **Hint: It is important to**

provide a distinctive name
for editable attributes.
When changing an editable
attribute in an instance,
the Template Properties
dialog box lists all editable
attributes in a document. If
any names are the same, it
will be impossible to tell
which page element an
attribute will be applied to.

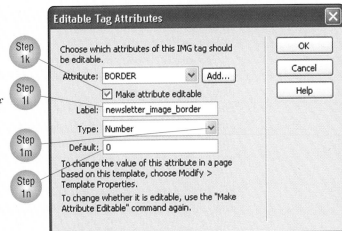

m. Click the *Type* list box down-pointing arrow and select *Number* from the drop-down list.

n. Type 0 in the *Default* text box.

o. Click the OK button to close the dialog box.

p. Save **ch8ex07.dwt** and then close it.

q. Open the Assets panel, click the Templates button, and right-click *ch8ex07*. Click New from Template to create an instance from **ch8ex07.dwt**.

r. Click Modify on the Menu bar and then Template Properties to open the Template Properties dialog box.

s. Click *newsletter_image_border* in the Template Properties dialog box to select it. A

border text box
appears. Type 4 in
the text box to
specify a border 4
pixels wide for the
newsletter
banner and
then click the
OK button to
close the dialog box.
Note that the
newsletter banner
image is now
surrounded by the
border that you
specified.

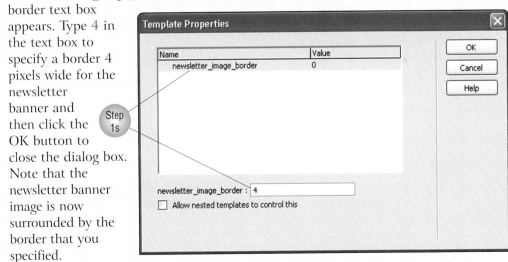

t. Click File on the Menu bar and then Save or Save As to rename and save the instance as **ch8ex07.htm**.

2. Close **ch8ex07.htm**.

Creating Nested Templates

Templates can be nested inside other templates to offer more control over editable content and to streamline the page-design process. Imagine a Web site that offers stamps for sale. The owner of the site wants to create a uniform look for the site. A template could be created so that all of the pages of the site shared the same banner area and introductory content. The banner and introductory content areas could be left locked so that no changes could be made to these areas in any instances created using this template, while an editable region or editable regions could be inserted that would allow users to insert additional page content as shown in Figure 8.21.

Next, the owner might want the site to have some pages that contain some information on stamps by country. There will be one page for each country, so using a template would speed up the page-creation process. This is where **nested templates** come into play. An instance can be created from the **parent template**, and country content can be added to the editable region of the instance. A new editable region can be inserted at the end of the instance's inherited editable region. The instance then can be saved as a template. Dreamweaver MX 2004 automatically makes this template a nested template of the parent template. New HTML documents based on this nested template will inherit the locked banner and introduction areas from the parent template. The country information also will be locked because when the editable region was inserted into the editable region inherited from the parent template, any content already in that region was locked as well. The result would be a document with all areas locked except for the editable region at the bottom as shown in Figure 8.22. Nested templates could be created for other countries by following this same process.

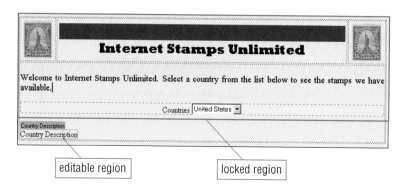

Figure 8.21
Parent Template

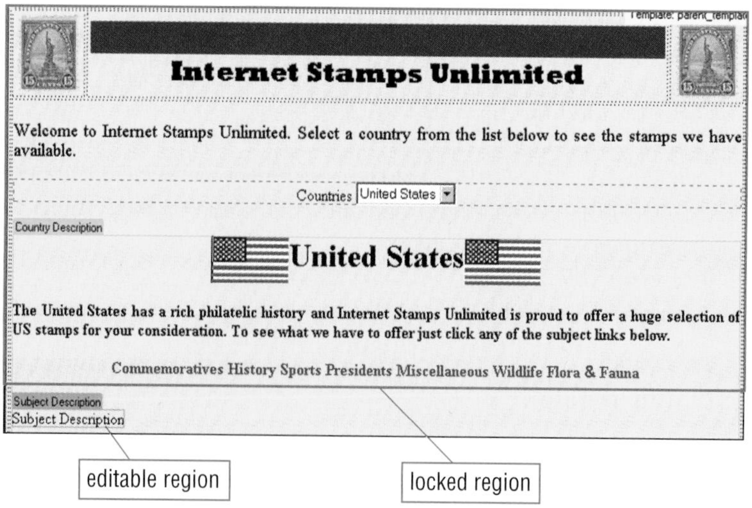

Figure 8.22
First Nested Template

DREAMWEAVER MX 2004

Now imagine that the owner wants each country page to contain a series of links by category so that viewers can click them to see the stamps available under each link. The categories can vary by country, so a template for that would be helpful as well. To create such a template, an instance can be created based on the nested template that was created previously. The links can be entered in the document's editable region, and a new editable region can be inserted after that. Using the Save as Template command will save this instance as a nested template of the first nested template. All of the content inherited from the parent template and the first nested template will be locked in this second nested template, and the only editable region will be the one inserted when this template was created. The end result is a template that can be used to create documents that will display the inherited banner, introductory content, country information, links in locked regions, and the new editable region as shown in Figure 8.23. This new editable region could be used to insert images of stamps, creating Web pages like the one shown in Figure 8.24.

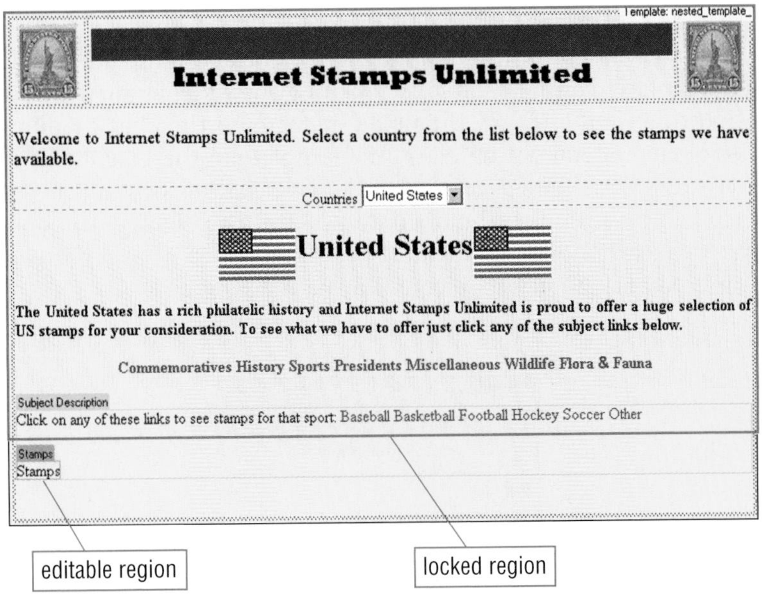

editable region   locked region

Figure 8.23
Second Nested Template

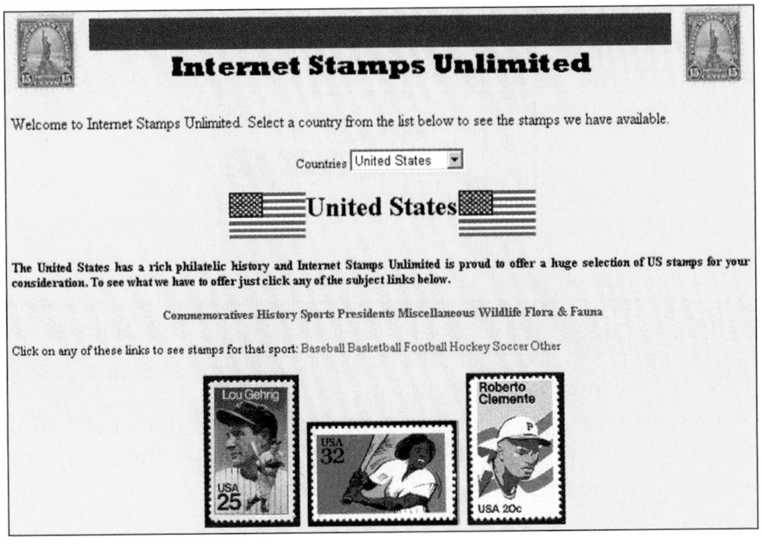

Figure 8.24
Web Page Created Using
Nested Templates

You could also accomplish this by creating normal HTML documents and using them as templates, but documents created from Dreamweaver MX 2004 templates have the advantage of being linked to the template that was used to create them. If the template the document was created from is a nested template, that template also will be linked to its parent template, and so on. This means that if the designer of the stamp Web site pages makes a change to the parent template containing the banner and introductory content, those changes will be propagated to any templates that were based on it and also to any HTML documents that were created based on those templates. Any change made to the first nested template will be propagated to any documents created from that template and to the second nested template and any documents created from that template. For example, after all of the pages for the stamp site are created, the designer could open the parent template and insert links for all of the countries in the country list. Nested templates based on the parent template are updated automatically with the new link information, as are any documents created based on those nested templates. The first nested template then could be opened and the category links created. The second nested template based on this nested template is updated automatically with the new link information, as are any documents created based on the first and second nested templates.

Nested templates can be created by opening the Assets panel, clicking the Templates button, right-clicking a template name, and then clicking New from Template to open a document based on the template in the Document window as shown in Figure 8.25. Changes can be made to locked regions and new editable regions then can be added to the document. After the changes are complete, clicking the Save as Template command saves the document as a nested template of the parent template that was selected in the Assets panel.

Figure 8.25
Using the Assets Panel to Create a Nested Template

CREATING NESTED TEMPLATES

1. Create a nested template by completing the following steps:
   a. At a clear document screen, open the **parent_template.dwt** student file and use the Save As command to save it to the Templates folder without changing its name. Close the document when you are finished.

DREAMWEAVER MX 2004

b. Open the Assets panel and click the Templates button, if necessary. Right-click *parent_template,* and then click New from Template to create an instance from that template in the Document window.

c. Position the insertion point to the right of *Title* in the instance, and press the Enter key to move the insertion point down the document.

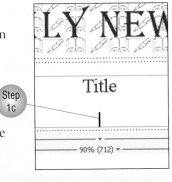

Step 1c

d. Click the Insert bar (Common menu item or tab) Templates button down-pointing arrow and then click the Editable Region command to insert an editable region. A message appears advising that Dreamweaver MX 2004 automatically will convert the instance into a template document. Click OK to close the message box. *Note: If the* **Don't show me this message again** *check box was previously checked, this dialog box will not appear.*

e. Type classifieds in the New Editable Region dialog box *Name* text box when it appears. Click OK to close the dialog box and create the editable region.

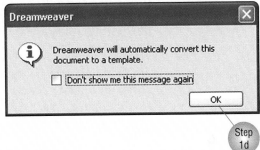

Step 1d

Step 1e

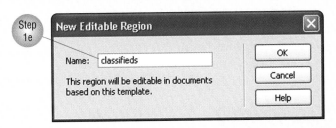

Step 1f

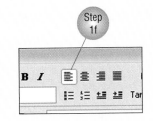

f. Click the Property inspector Left Align button to left align the editable region.

g. Click File on the Menu bar and then Save to open the Save As Template dialog box. Name the document **ch8ex08** and click the Save button. *Note: The Save As Template dialog box opens because Dreamweaver MX 2004 automatically saves any instances into which editable regions have been inserted as a template, as the earlier message box advised. If no editable regions were inserted in this instance, clicking the Save button would cause the Save As dialog box to open and the document would be saved with a normal HTML extension.*

h. Look at the document and note that the title region is now highlighted in orange. This indicates that it is no longer editable and is now locked. The orange outline is visible only in the Document window and will not show up in instances created from this nested template. Blue outlining indicates that a region is editable. Look at the upper-right corner of the document and note that it indicates that parent_template is the parent template for this nested template. Close **ch8ex08.dwt** when you are finished.

Step 1h

i. Open the Assets panel and click the Templates button, if necessary. Right-click *ch8ex08* and then click New from

Template to create an instance from this nested template. Note that the title region is now locked. Moving the pointer over it changes the pointer into the prohibited sign. The new editable region you just inserted is fully editable. The parent template can be used to create instances in which the title can be changed to create new sections of the newsletter, such as the classified section you just created. Nested templates then can be created from the instances to enter content under the newly created sections.

2. Close the instance without saving it.

Updating Template-Based Documents and Detaching Templates from Documents

When a template is updated, you can decide whether you want templates attached to the template to be updated as well. When changes are made and a template is saved, an Update Template Files dialog box appears asking if you want to update any templates attached to the template as shown in Figure 8.26. The dialog box lists templates or documents that will be affected by changes to the template. Clicking the Update button updates those documents to reflect any changes. An Update Pages dialog box then appears, displaying the results of the updating process as shown in Figure 8.27. If updating is not desired, click the Don't Update button in the Update Template Files dialog box.

The newsletter referred to earlier in this chapter provides an example of an occasion when you might not want a change to a template to be propagated to

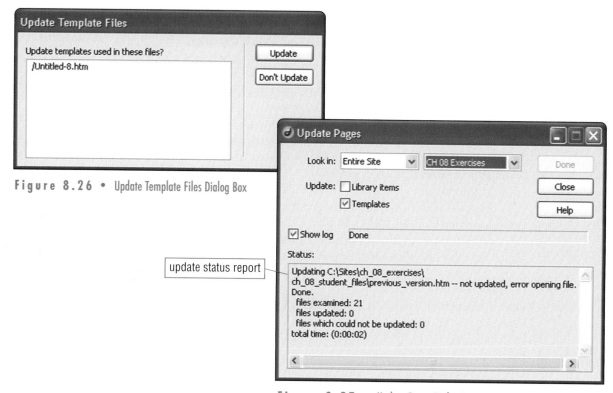

Figure 8.26 • Update Template Files Dialog Box

Figure 8.27 • Update Pages Dialog Box

documents that were created from that template. If changes were made to the banner area of the newsletter template, propagating the change to documents created from the template in the past would mean that previous issues of the newsletter would appear with the new banner changes, which would not be historically accurate. Instead, you could choose not to propagate the change to those documents. New issues created from the modified template would reflect the changes made to the banner, while the previous issues of the newsletter would appear the same as they did when they were originally issued.

Template changes can be propagated to documents attached to the template on an individual basis. After the changes have been made and the template saved without propagating the changes, click Modify on the Menu bar, point to Templates, and then click Update Current Page to update only the current document.

If the template changes are to be applied to some templates and not others, you can open the modified template in the Document window and then click Modify on the Menu bar, point to Templates, and then click Update Pages to open the Update Pages dialog box. Click the *Look in* list box down-pointing arrow and then click *Files That Use* from the drop-down list that appears. Click the down-pointing arrow of the list box located to the right of the *Look in* list box to open a drop-down list of the template files in the site. Click a template listing and then click the Start button to update the selected templates and any HTML documents based on that template.

You also can open a document and then use Menu bar commands to open the template it is attached to. With the document as the current document in the Document window, click Modify on the Menu bar, point to Templates, and then click Open Attached Template to open any template that is attached to the document. The template can then be modified and saved using the methods described previously.

You can detach documents from templates by making them the current document in the Document window and clicking Modify on the Menu bar, pointing to Templates, and then clicking Detach from Template. A detached document retains its template content but is no longer updatable.

exercise 9

1. Update a template and the documents attached to it by completing the following steps:
   a. At a clear document screen, open **ch8ex04.dwt** and use the Save as Template command to rename and save it as **ch8ex09.dwt**.
   b. Open the Assets panel and click the Templates button, if necessary. Right-click *ch8ex09*, and then click New from Template to create an instance.
   c. Click File on the Menu bar and then Save As to rename and save the instance as **ch8ex09.htm**. Close it when you are finished.
   d. With **ch8ex09.dwt** as the current document, click the newsletter image at the top of the document to select it and then delete it by pressing the Delete key.

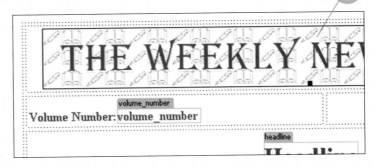

Step 1d

e. With the insertion point positioned in the table row that the deleted image was in, click Insert on the Menu bar and then Image to open the Select Image Source dialog box. Locate the student file named **newsletter_banner_2.gif** and then click the OK button. Type new banner in the *Alternate text* text box and then click the OK button.

f. Click File on the Menu bar and then Save. The Update Template Files dialog box appears asking if you want to update the file (**ch8ex09.htm**) attached to the template. Click the Update button to update **ch8ex09.htm**.

g. Look at the Update Pages dialog box that appears after the Update Template Files dialog box closes. Note that it lists the status of any attempt to update files attached to a template. Click the Close button to close the dialog box.

h. Open **ch8ex09.htm**. Note that it has been updated automatically; the newsletter banner is now the same as the one you just inserted in the template attached to this document. Close the document when you are finished.

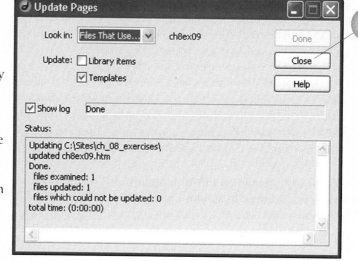

2. Close **ch8ex09.dwt**.

Creating Links in Templates

When a template is created from an existing document containing document-relative links, Dreamweaver MX 2004 must update the links because the template document will be saved in the Templates folder that is created automatically by Dreamweaver MX 2004. This does not cause any problems, but it does mean that links in template files should be created using the Point to File or Browse for File buttons rather than by typing them in the *Link* text box because it is easy to type the wrong path. The only exception would be for external URLs, which must be typed in the *Link* text box.

Setting Template Preferences

The colors used to highlight the outlines for editable and locked regions can be changed using the Preferences dialog box. Clicking Edit, pointing to Preferences, and then clicking *Highlighting* from the *Category* list box displays color boxes next to the *Editable regions, Nested editable,* and *Locked regions* text boxes at the top of the dialog box as shown in Figure 8.28. Clicking the appropriate color box opens the Color Picker, and the Eyedropper can be used to select the desired color. The *Show* check boxes next to both the *Editable regions* text box and the *Locked regions* text box are enabled in the default Dreamweaver MX 2004 setup. If you do not want outline colors to be visible in Document window, the check mark in these check boxes should be removed.

Understanding Library Items

Library items are sections of code that can be created, saved, and then inserted in documents whenever needed. In this way, they perform like the assets that can be saved in the Assets panel and reused. Unlike assets, however, library items share the updating feature of templates. When a library item is updated, the changes are propagated to every copy of the library item that was inserted in any document in a site. This capability makes library items ideal for frequently used page content that might need updating at some point.

A good example of the kind of content that would make an ideal library item is a company address or slogan that is used frequently throughout the documents in a Web site. The ability to insert an address or slogan at the click of a button would save a lot of time and effort, but an even greater benefit is that any changes to the address or slogan could be implemented throughout the site simply by making the change to the address or slogan library item. Because library items are stored sections of code, they are not limited to text, so they can be images, tables, URLs, or just about any type of content that might be found in an HTML document.

When a library item is created in a site for the first time, Dreamweaver MX 2004 creates a **Library folder** to store all of the library items in that site and assigns library items an **.lbi file extension** as shown in Figure 8.29. Library items in one site will not be accessible to other sites, but a Library folder from one site can be copied to another site and used in that site. Links in library items might not work if the library item is moved to another site; any images in library items must be copied to the new site for those library items to work.

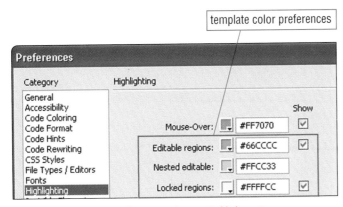

template color preferences

Figure 8.28 • Preferences Dialog Box Highlighting Page

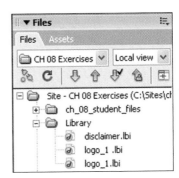

Figure 8.29 • Assets Panel Library Folder and Library Items

Creating Library Items

The first step in creating a library item is to select the page content that is to be saved as a library item. After the desired content has been selected, you can save it as a library item by clicking Modify on the Menu bar, pointing to Library, and then clicking Add Object to Library. The Assets panel opens automatically and displays the new library item listing in the Library category list. The default library item name is highlighted, and a new name can be typed as shown in Figure 8.30.

New library items also can be created by dragging selected content into the Library category of the Assets panel. This causes a library item name to appear, and it can be renamed as described previously.

A third way of creating a library item is to select the content that will become the library item and then click the New Library Item button at the bottom of the Assets panel when it displays the Library category. This creates a new library item name in the panel, and you can rename it using the same procedure that was used in the previous methods.

The Assets panel is located inside the Files panel group. If the Files panel group is closed, click Window on the Menu bar and then Assets to open it. The Files panel opens and displays the Assets panel. Clicking the Library button on the bottom-left side of the Assets panel displays the Assets panel Library category.

Adding Library Items to Documents

Library items can be added to documents by positioning the insertion point in the desired location and then dragging the library item into the Document window. A common mistake is to try to drag or insert a library item from its file listing in the Files panel, so make sure that the Assets panel is open and that it is displaying the Library category, accessed by clicking the Library button located on the lower-left side of the panel.

You also can click the library item in the Assets panel and then click the Assets panel Insert button as shown in Figure 8.30 to insert a library item at the insertion point. Double-clicking a library item in the Assets panel will not insert it in a document. Instead, the library item's .lbi file opens in the Document window, where it can be edited as described later in this section.

Most library items appear shaded in light yellow when they are inserted into a document as shown in Figure 8.31. The highlighting color can be changed by clicking Edit on the Menu bar, clicking Preferences, and then clicking

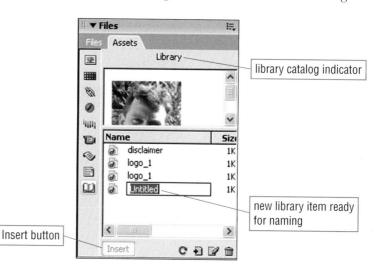

Figure 8.30
Assets Panel Library Category

DREAMWEAVER MX 2004

Highlighting from the Preferences dialog box *Category* list box. The fourth text box, *Library items,* allows you to use the Color Picker and Eyedropper to change the library item highlighting color as shown in Figure 8.32. If no highlighting is desired, remove the check mark from the *Show* check box next to the *Library items* text box.

Editing Library Items

Library items can be edited by double-clicking the library item in the Assets panel or by clicking it and then clicking the Edit button at the bottom of the panel. Either of these methods opens the library item document in the Document window. You also can open a library item file by selecting the library item in a document and then clicking the Open button in the Library Item Property inspector as shown in Figure 8.33.

Changes can be made to the library item once the library item file is the current document. Click File on the Menu bar and then Save. If the library item has not been inserted in a document, it will be saved. If the library item has been inserted in documents, the Update Library Items dialog box will open as shown in Figure 8.34. You can choose to update all instances of the library item in documents in the current site by clicking the Update button, or choose not to update by clicking the Don't Update button. The current document in the Document window can be updated by clicking Modify on the Menu bar, pointing to Library, and then clicking Update Current Page.

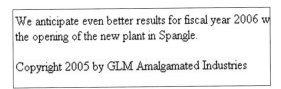

Figure 8.31 • Highlighted Library Item in Document

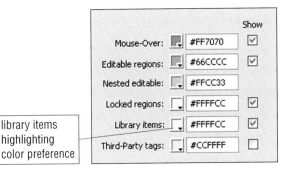

library items highlighting color preference

Figure 8.32 • Preferences Dialog Box Highlighting Page Color Settings

Figure 8.33 • Library Item Property Inspector

copy of library item to be updated in this document

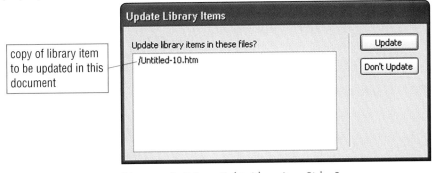

Figure 8.34 • Update Library Items Dialog Box

To update all documents in a site or all of the documents that use a library item, click Modify on the Menu bar, point to Library, and then click Update Pages. This opens the Update Pages dialog box as shown in Figure 8.35. The *Library items* check box should contain a check mark. If not, click to enable it. Using the *Look in* list box down-pointing arrow, choose between *Entire Site* and *Files That Use*. If you choose *Entire Site,* use the down-pointing arrow in the list box to the right of the *Look in* list box to locate the site that will be updated. If you choose *Files That Use,* use this same list box to locate the library item that will be updated. To begin the updating process, click the Start button and a report appears in the *Status* section of the dialog box as shown in Figure 8.36.

Library items can be renamed by clicking the name. After a brief pause, the library item name is highlighted and a new name can be typed.

To delete a library item, click it and then press the Delete key or click the Trash Can button in the Assets panel. Deleting a library item does not remove any copies of the item that have been inserted in documents, but it does mean that the copies can no longer be updated.

You can restore a deleted library item by selecting a copy of the library item that has been inserted in a document and then clicking the Recreate button in the Library Item Property inspector as shown previously in Figure 8.33. The Library Item Property inspector also can be used to detach a library item that has been

library item will be updated in all files in this site

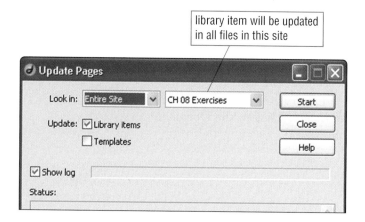

Figure 8.35
Update Pages Dialog Box

status report on updated documents containing selected library item update

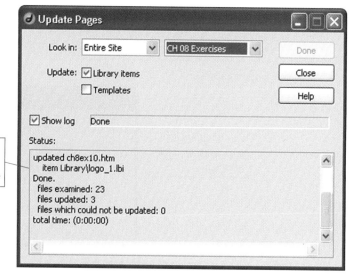

Figure 8.36
Update Pages Dialog Box
Status Report

DREAMWEAVER MX 2004

inserted in a document from the original library item in the Assets panel by clicking the Detach from original button. Doing this means that the item can no longer be updated. Clicking the Library Item Open button in the Library Item Property inspector opens the library item file so that it can be edited.

exercise 10

1. Create a library item by completing the following steps:
   a. At a clear document screen, open the student file named **library_item_source.htm** in the ch_08_student_files folder.
   b. If necessary, open the Assets panel by clicking Window on the Menu bar and then Assets.
   c. Click the Assets panel Library button in the lower-left corner of the panel to display the Library category, if necessary.
   d. Click the GML logo at the top of the document in the Document window and drag it to the Assets panel. *Hint: It doesn't matter if you drag it to the upper or lower pane of the Assets panel Library category.*

   Step 1c

   e. With the library item name (Untitled) still highlighted in the Assets panel Library category, type logo_1 to rename it. *Hint: A library item can always be renamed by right-clicking its listing in the Assets panel Library category and clicking Rename from the context menu that appears.*
   f. Select the *Disclaimer of Liability* heading and paragraph text in the Document window, click Modify on the Menu bar, point to Library, and then click Add Object to Library. Repeat Step 1e to rename the library item *disclaimer*. Click in the Document window to deselect the heading and paragraph text. *Hint: In the future, you can use this method or the method described in Step 1d to create library items.*
   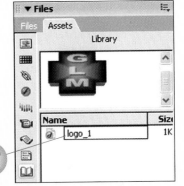

   Step 1e

   g. Click File on the Menu bar and then Close to close **library_item_source.htm**. A message appears asking if you want to save the changes you made to **library_item_source.htm**. If you look at the document, you will see that the image and the disclaimer text are highlighted in yellow, meaning they are now library items. Because this document is being used as a source for library items and does not need to change to reflect any updates to those items, click the No button so that the changes to the document will not be saved.
   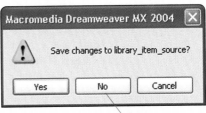

   Step 1g

2. Insert a library item into a document by completing the following steps:
   a. At a clear document screen, open the **glm_home_page.htm** student file and use the Save As command to rename and save it as **ch8ex10.htm** in the ch_08_exercises root folder.
   b. Click *logo_1* in the Assets panel Library category and drag the library item over to the empty table cell to the left of the *Welcome to GLM Page* text in **ch8ex10.htm**. The logo is inserted as a library item in that location. It is highlighted in light yellow to indicate that it is a library item.

   Step 2b

c. Repeat Step 2b to drag *logo_1* from the Assets panel Library category to the empty table cell to the right of the *Welcome to GLM Page* text.

d. Move the Document window vertical scroll bar down until you can see the empty table row at the bottom of **ch8ex10.htm**. Position the insertion point in the table row.

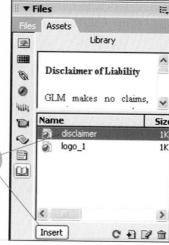

Step 2e

e. Click *disclaimer* in the Assets panel Library category and then click the Assets panel Library category Insert button to insert the library item. Like the logos, the disclaimer text is highlighted in yellow to indicate that it is a library item. ***Note: You can use this method or the method described in Step 2b to insert library items in the future.***

f. Save **ch8ex10.htm**, click the Preview/Debug in browser button and then click Preview in iexplore to preview the document. Note that the yellow library item highlighting is no longer visible. Close the browser when you are finished.

g. Close **ch8ex10.htm**.

3. Edit a library item by completing the following steps:

Step 3a

a. Double-click *logo_1* in the Assets panel Library category to open the library item's file in the Document window. Note that it has an .lbi extension, identifying it as a library item.

b. Click the logo to select it and then press the Delete key to delete it from the document.

c. Click Insert on the Menu bar and then Image to open the Select Image Source dialog box. Locate the student file named **logo_2.gif** and then click the OK button. Type logo 2 in the *Alternate text* text box and then click the OK button to insert it in the document.

d. Click File on the Menu bar and then Save to save the changes to the document. An Update Library Items message appears, asking if you want to update the documents in its list box. Click the Update button to update **ch8ex10.htm**.

Step 3d

Update Library Items

Update library items in these files?

/ch8ex10.htm

Update

Don't Update

e. Click the Close button to close the Update Pages dialog box that appears. The dialog box shows the status of any updating that was completed.

f. Click File on the Menu bar and then Close to close the library item document.

g. Double-click *disclaimer* in the Assets panel Library category to open the library item in the Document window.

h. Delete the second sentence in the disclaimer, *The company expressly disclaims liability for errors and omissions in the contents of this Web site*.

i. Click File on the Menu bar and then Save to save the changes to the document. An Update Library Items message appears asking if you want to update the documents in its list box. Click the Update button to update **ch8ex10.htm**.

j. Click the Close button to close the Update Pages dialog box.

DREAMWEAVER MX 2004

k. Click File and then Close to close the document.

l. Open **ch8ex10.htm**. Note that both copies of the logo in the document have been updated to reflect the change you made to the logo_1 library item and that the disclaimer has been updated to reflect the changes you made to that library item as well.

m. Close **ch8ex10.htm**.

4. Delete and restore a library item by completing the following steps:

a. Click *logo_1* in the Assets panel Library category to select the library item.

b. Click the Assets panel Trash Can button to delete library item.

Step 4b

c. A message appears asking if you are sure you want to delete the library item. Click the Yes button. *Note: This will not affect any copies of the library item that were inserted in any documents, but it will mean that the library item cannot be used again to insert more copies unless it is recreated.*

Step 4c

d. At a clear document screen, open **ch8ex10.htm**. Note that the logo_1 copies are still in place. Click one of the logo_1 copies to select it. *Hint: When the image is selected, it will appear to have a dotted background, not resizing handles.*

e. Click the Recreate button in the Library Item Property inspector to recreate the deleted logo_1 library item.

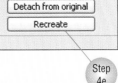

Step 4e

f. Look in the Assets panel Library category to verify that the logo_1 library item has been recreated.

5. Close **ch8ex10.htm**.

CHAPTER summary

➤ When a template is created, the entire document is locked. With the exception of the document title, you must designate regions of the document that will be editable in documents created from the template.

➤ Creating locked and editable regions allows designers great control over the appearance of documents created from a template and helps them preserve the integrity of the pages they design by protecting them from unauthorized alteration.

➤ Documents created from a template are called instances, and instances can be saved as templates (to create nested templates) or as HTML documents.

➤ HTML documents and templates created from instances are attached automatically to the template, and changes to the locked region or the addition of new editable regions in the parent template are propagated (passed on) to these documents.

➤ Editable regions are indicated by a colored tab containing the name of the editable region and an outlined rectangle that indicates the region of the document that can be edited.

- The pointer turns into a prohibited sign when it moves over a locked region in a document created from a template.

- Changes to any of the locked regions of a template or the addition of new editable regions are propagated to any document created using the template, whether it is another template or an HTML document.

- Editable regions in nested templates or HTML documents created from a template are independent of the parent template, so any changes to an editable region in a template have no effect on the editable region in any documents created from that template.

- Editable regions in templates do not have to contain any text, but it is often a good idea to create placeholder or instructional text that lets users know the purpose of an editable region.

- When templates are created, Dreamweaver MX 2004 creates a new Templates folder that is stored in the root folder of the current site, unless another site is chosen.

- The Templates folder should not be moved and templates should not be moved out of the Templates folder.

- Templates have a special .dwt extension to distinguish them from ordinary HTML documents.

- Template names should be lowercase and should not contain special characters or spaces. Hyphens or underscores can be used to separate names in template names.

- Creating a template from an existing document is the same as creating a template from a new document, except that users can select existing content and make it editable, while leaving other content locked.

- Four types of regions can be created in a template: editable regions, repeating regions, repeating tables, and optional regions.

- Editable regions create a region that can be edited in documents created from a template.

- Repeating regions allow those using a document attached to a template to repeat a region, which can be locked or editable.

- Repeating tables allows you to define the portions of a table that will repeat.

- Optional regions appear or do not appear in a template based on conditional statements; they can be locked or editable.

- Editable regions need to be placed outside block tags if the template designer wants users to be able to create new block elements in documents created from the template.

- Switching to Code view when creating editable regions reveals whether an editable region is contained inside or outside a block tag.

- Selecting a block tag in the Tag selector ensures that an editable region encompasses an entire block level tag if that is desired.

- Editable region names should be lowercase and contain no spaces or special characters. Hyphens or underscores can be used to separate words in the name if desired.

- If page content was selected when creating the editable region, it will appear inside the editable region box.

- If no page content was selected, the name of the editable region will appear inside the editable region box.

- Although an editable region removed from a template will remain in any document attached to the template, new documents created from the template will not contain the editable region that was removed.

- Templates do not have their own panel, but the Templates category of the Assets panel can be accessed by clicking the Templates button located on the left side of the Assets panel.

- Existing documents can be attached to templates, but regions in the existing document must be resolved (reconciled) with the regions in the template it is being attached to.

- When creating templates, you can allow users to change selected attributes of text or page content that are otherwise locked by creating editable tag attributes.

- The Reference panel can be used to find the attributes that can be used with a particular tag.

- Templates can be nested inside other templates to offer more control over editable content and to streamline the page-design process.

- When a template is created from a template, it is linked to its parent template, and changes to the locked regions or the addition of new editable regions in the parent template are propagated to the nested template.

- When a template is updated, you can decide whether you want templates that are attached to the template to be updated as well.

- Template changes can be propagated to documents attached to the template on an individual basis.

- Documents can be detached from templates if desired. A detached document retains its template content, but it is no longer updateable.

- Links in template files should be created using the Point to File or Browse for File buttons rather than by typing them in the *Link* text box because it is easy to type the wrong path. The only exception would be for external URLs, which must be typed in the *Link* text box.

- The colors used to highlight the outlines for editable and locked regions can be changed using the Preferences dialog box.

- Library items are sections of code that can be created, saved, and then inserted in documents whenever needed.

- When a library item is updated, the changes are propagated to every copy of the library item that was inserted in any document in a site.

- Because library items are stored sections of code, they are not limited to text; they can be images, tables, URLs or just about any type of content that might be found in an HTML document.

- When a library item is created in a site for the first time, Dreamweaver MX 2004 creates a Library folder to store all of the library items in that site and assigns library items an .lbi file extension.

- Clicking the Library button located on the bottom-left side of the Assets panel displays the Assets panel Library category.

- Most library items appear shaded in light yellow when they are inserted into a document. The Preferences dialog box Highlighting page can be used to change the Library item highlighting color.

KEY terms

Dreamweaver MX 2004 templates Special templates in Dreamweaver MX 2004 that can be used to create new documents or templates (nested templates). Documents created from a template automatically are attached to it, and changes to a template's locked regions or the addition of new editable regions are propagated (passed on) to documents created from the template.

.dwt file extension The file extension for Dreamweaver MX 2004 templates.

editable regions Areas of a template that can be edited in a document created from a template. See *locked regions*.

editable tag attributes Attributes of locked regions in templates that can be made editable in documents created from a template.

instances Documents created from templates that can be saved as nested templates or HTML documents.

.lbi file extension The file extension for library items.

Library folder A folder automatically created by Dreamweaver MX 2004 to store all of the library items created in a site.

library items Sections of code that can be created, saved, and then inserted in documents whenever needed.

locked regions Areas of a template that prevent users from making changes to any content in the locked region in a document created from the template. See *editable regions*.

nested templates Templates created from another template. Nested templates inherit the parent table's locked and editable regions.

optional regions Template regions that appear or do not appear in a document created from a template based on conditional statements. They can be locked or editable.

parent template The template a nested template was created from. Changes to a parent table's locked regions, or the addition of new editable regions, are propagated (passed on) to nested templates.

prohibited sign The insertion point turns into a prohibited sign (a circle with a diagonal slash) when moved over a locked area in a document created from a template to indicate that the content cannot be edited.

repeating regions Areas of a document created from a template that can be repeated if desired. The repeating region can be locked or editable.

repeating tables Areas in a document created from a template that allow users to repeat specified table rows and control which table cells are editable.

Templates folder A folder automatically created by Dreamweaver MX 2004 to store the templates created in a site.

COMMANDS review

Attach a template to an existing document	Modify, Templates, Apply Template to Page
Create a library item	Modify, Library, Add Object to Library
Create a new template instance	File, New, Templates tab
Create an editable tag attribute	Modify, Templates, Make Attribute Editable
Detach a template from a document	Modify, Templates, Detach from Template
Insert a repeating region	Insert, Template Objects, Repeating Region
Insert a repeating table	Insert, Template Objects, Repeating Table
Insert an editable region	Insert, Template Objects, Editable Region
Modify an editable attribute in a template instance	Modify, Template Properties
Open a template attached to a document	Modify, Templates, Open Attached Template
Open the Assets panel Library items	Window, Assets, Library button
Open the Assets panel Templates category	Window, Assets, Templates button
Remove an editable region	Modify, Templates, Remove Template Markup
Save a template as an HTML document	File, Save As
Save an HTML document as a template	File, Save as Template
Set template preferences	Edit, Preferences, *Highlighting* category
Update a template	Modify, Templates, Update Pages
Update all documents using a library item	Modify, Library, Update Pages
Update the current document	Modify, Templates, Update Current Page
Update the current document library item	Modify, Library, Update Current Page

CONCEPTS check

Indicate the correct term or command for each item.

1. This is the term for a document created from a template.
2. The term for a region in a template that cannot be edited is referred to as this.
3. This is the term used for a region in a template that can be duplicated by clicking a button.

4. A table in a template with rows that can be repeated is called this.
5. This is a template created from another template.
6. A nested template is created from this template.
7. This is the file extension for template documents.
8. This is the file extension for library items.
9. This is what the Up Arrow and Down Arrow buttons in a repeating region or repeating table can be used for.
10. When a template is attached to an existing document, this is what must be done with any inconsistent regions in the existing document.
11. Locked region content attributes that can be changed in documents created from a template are referred to as this.
12. This panel can be used to find information about HTML tags and their attributes.
13. Changes to this type of region in a template will not be propagated to documents created from the template.
14. Template instances can be saved as either of these two document types.
15. Template and library item color preferences can be changed by clicking Edit on the Menu bar, clicking Preferences, and then clicking this category from the Preferences dialog box *Category* list box.
16. This is the key difference between assets and library items.
17. When a template is created for the first time, Dreamweaver MX 2004 automatically creates this folder.
18. When a library item is created for the first time, Dreamweaver MX 2004 automatically creates this folder.
19. Clicking a copy of a deleted library item in a document and then clicking this button in the Library Item Property inspector can recreate the deleted library item in the Assets panel Library category.
20. This will happen if a library item listing in the Library category of the Assets panel is double-clicked.

SKILLS check

Use the Site Definition dialog box to create a separate Dreamweaver site named CH 08 Assessments to keep your assessment work for this chapter. Save the files for the site in a new root folder named ch_08_assessments under the Sites folder you created in Chapter 1, Exercise 3. Download the ch_08_student_files folder from the IRC to the CH 08 Assessments site root folder (ch_08_assessments) and expand it. Delete the compressed folder when you are finished.

Assessment 1 • Use an Existing Document to Create a Company Newsletter Template

1. Open the student file named **company_newsletter.htm** in the ch_08_student_files folder Ch8sa1_student_files subfolder and use the Save as Template command to rename and save it as **ch8sa1.dwt** to your CH 08 Assessments site.
2. Format the page layout to develop an attractive page design by changing the table background colors; font style, size, color, and so on. Not all table cells have to be the same color, and the text can vary in style, size, and color as well.

3. Create the following editable regions for selected table content. Provide each editable region with a name that indicates its function, for example, *director_image, body_text,* and so on.
   a. Select the *A monthly newsletter for GLM employees* text just below the banner image placeholder at the top of the page and make it an editable region inside the block tags controlling it.
   b. Select the *Summer 2005* text and make it an editable region inside the block tags controlling it.
   c. Select the *Message from the director* text and make it an editable region outside the block tags controlling it.
   d. Select the *Article 1* text and make it an editable region outside the block tags controlling it. Repeat this step for every instance of the *Article* text on the page, *Article 2, Article 3,* and so on.
   e. Select the *Welcome to the first issue of our newsletter!* text and make it an editable region inside the block tags controlling it.
   f. Select the *Quotation* text and make it an editable region inside the block tags controlling it.
   g. Select the *Header Text* text and make it an editable region inside the block tags controlling it.
   h. Select the *Body text* text and make it an editable region outside the block tags controlling it.
   i. Select the *John Doe, Editor* text and make it an editable region inside the block tags controlling it.
   j. Select the *Information about newsletter here* text and make it an editable region outside the block tags controlling it.
4. Make all image placeholders editable regions.
5. Save **ch8sa1.dwt** and then close it.
6. Create an instance from **ch8sa1.dwt** and use the Save As command to save it as **ch8sa1.htm**.
7. Create a prototype newspaper page by entering content into the editable regions. Use the student file named **banner_image.gif** to replace the banner image placeholder. Use the student files named staff_photo (for example, **staff_photo1_100x100.gif**) to replace the staff photo placeholder images (for example, 90 by 90, 100 by 100, and so on).
8. Enter appropriate text in the editable text regions of the newsletter.
9. Save **ch8sa1.htm** and then close it when you are finished.

Assessment 2 • Use a New Document to Create a Catalog Page Template with an Editable Repeating Table

1. Create a new HTML document and use the Save as Template command to save it as **ch8sa2.dwt**.
2. You are working for a company that publishes an online catalog and the company has requested that you create a catalog page template that can be used to feature several products on each page, with an image of each product and product details. Create the template by doing the following:
   a. Format the page background color and text to make an attractive page design.
   b. Insert introductory text at the top of the page that will be contained in a locked region when instances are created from this template. This text could consist of the company name and a slogan, a company logo

and name, and so on—anything that a company would be likely to put at the top of its catalog pages.

c. Insert a Home button or link and make it an editable region so that documents created from this page can be linked to a home page.

d. Insert a two-row, five-column repeating table, and make the second row a repeating row.

e. Type Image in the first cell of the first table row, Product in the second cell of the first table row, Description in the third cell, Product ID in the fourth cell, and Price in the fifth cell to create column headings.

f. Center and bold the text you just entered in the first row.

g. Insert an image placeholder 100 by 100 pixels in size in the first cell of the second table row (the repeating row).

h. Select the second table row (the repeating row), click the *Vert* list box down-pointing arrow, and then click *Top*.

i. Save **ch8sa2.dwt** and then close it.

3. Create an instance from **ch8sa2.dwt** and use the Save As command to save it as **ch8sa2.htm**.

4. Replace the image placeholder with one of the product student files located in the Ch8sa2_student_files subfolder of the ch_08_exercises folder, and then enter suitable product details for each product under the appropriate column headings.

5. Click the Plus (+) button to create at least four more product listings. Replace the image placeholders and type in suitable product details for each product.

6. Save **ch8sa2.htm** and then close it.

Assessment 3 • Create a Parent Template and Nested Templates

1. The hotel chain that you work for has asked you to create a template that can be used by all of its affiliate hotels. The company wants a template that contains the company logo or image, company name, and a short slogan or paragraph of introductory text that is suitable as a basic page design for every page in the Web site. This template would contain an editable region that could be used by the affiliate hotels to create their own pages describing their hotels.

The affiliate hotels then would be furnished with this template. They would enter content describing their hotels in the editable region of the template, including an image, and then create a new editable region. This template would be saved as a nested template of the parent template created by the hotel chain. The affiliate hotels then could use this nested template to create pages that would further describe the amenities their hotels have to offer, such as room features, restaurants, recreational facilities, and so on.

Do the following to fulfill this task:

a. Create an attractive HTML page design for the hotel chain. The page should include a logo or image of your choosing and some introductory text for the hotel chain. Include at least five buttons or links, and make them editable regions so that documents created from this template could be linked to other pages. Include an editable region that will be used by the affiliate hotels to enter their own content. Use the Save as Template command to save this document as **ch8sa3.dwt** and then close it.

b. Create an instance from **ch8sa3.dwt** and use the Save as Template command to save it as **ch8sa3_nested.dwt**.

c. Enter content for an affiliate hotel, including an image, in the nested template's editable region, and then insert a new editable region below the content you just entered. Save **ch8sa3_nested.dwt** and then close it when you are finished.

d. Create an instance from **ch8as3_nested.dwt** and use the Save As command to rename and save it as **ch8as3.htm**.

e. Enter content describing one of the hotel's amenities in the page's editable region.

2. Save **ch8sa3.htm** and then close it.

Assessment 4 • Create Editable Attributes in an Existing Template

1. The catalog company that you work for has several different catalogs, and it wants each catalog to have a distinctive "look." The company likes the repeating table catalog page you designed, but wants the people who work on the page to have some flexibility in deciding the appearance of the table. Fulfill this task by doing the following:

a. Open **ch8sa2.dwt** and use the Save As or Save as Template commands to rename and save it as **ch8sa4.dwt**.

b. Make the following table attributes editable and use default values of your choosing:
   - `border`
   - `cellspacing`
   - `cellpadding`

c. Add the following attributes to the table tag to make them editable:
   - `bgcolor`
   - `bordercolor`

2. Save **ch8sa4.dwt** and then close it.

3. Create an instance from **ch8sa4.dwt** and use the Save As command to rename and save it as **ch8sa4.htm**.

4. Change the values of the table attributes that you made editable to change the appearance of the table.

5. Save **ch8sa4.htm** and then close it.

Assessment 5 • Save, Insert, and Modify Library Items

1. Select at least five images from any HTML documents you have created and use them to create library items.

2. Select at least five text samples and save them as library items.

3. Create a new HTML document and use the Save or Save As command to name and save it as **ch8sa5.htm**.

4. Format the page to make an attractive page design.

5. Save **ch8sa5.htm** and then use the Save As command to create two new copies of ch8sa5.htm and name them **ch8sa5-a.htm** and **ch8sa5-b.htm**.

6. Enter text content of your choosing (a story, description text) in the pages, and use each of the image and text library items you save in Steps 1 and 2 at least once. ***Note: Don't worry if the text library items do not make sense in the context you are using them, because you will be modifying them soon.***

7. Save the documents and click the Preview/Debug in browser button and then click Preview in iexplore to view and print a copy of each page. ***Note: Use the browser's Print command to print a copy of a page.***

8. Open each library item and modify it. For the images, this means swapping the image with another image; for the text, this means editing it to change the text. Save each library item and click the Update button each time to update any documents containing the library item.

9. Click the Preview/Debug in browser button and then click Preview in iexplore to view and print a copy of each page to show the changes to the library items on the pages.

10. Save and close the documents.

Assessment 6 • Add Templates and Library Items to Your Design Portfolio

Save all documents created in this assessment in the design_portfolio root folder of your Design Portfolio site.

1. Create a templates page for your design portfolio that uses an editable repeating table to contain information on references URLs. For example, the table could contain one column for the URL, one column for the site name, and a third column for a description of the site. Format this document to fit it with the design theme for your pages.

2. Create an instance from the template and save it as an HTML page in your design portfolio site.

3. Enter URL content to fill at least one page.

4. Examine the documents in your Web site and look for any repeated use of images or page content. Create library items using those items and then replace the repeated items with library copies so that they can be updated easily whenever necessary. The library items also can be used when creating new pages.

ADDING MEDIA ELEMENTS

PERFORMANCE OBJECTIVES

➤ Understand multimedia and how it can be used.
➤ Play movies and animations within the Dreamweaver MX 2004 environment.
➤ Insert Flash content.
➤ Create and insert Flash buttons.
➤ Create and insert Flash text.
➤ Insert Shockwave content.
➤ Insert Java applets.
➤ Create and modify multimedia parameters and values.
➤ Insert ActiveX controls.
➤ Insert plugins.
➤ Add sound to a Web page.

The student files for this chapter are available for download from the Internet Resource Center at www.emcp.com.

In its strictest sense, multimedia means the use of more than one type of media. A Web page with text and images could be an example of multimedia. In the Web context, multimedia generally refers to the use of media beyond text and images, such as video, audio, animated graphics, and even hypertext. Used wisely, multimedia in Web pages can provide viewers with an enhanced viewing experience. Web page viewing can even become an interactive experience, with Flash, Shockwave, or Java applets letting viewers use their input to control their viewing experience. This can take the form of games, calculators, animations, or any number of other different interactive activities.

In the early days of the Web, the use of multimedia in Web pages was constrained by technical considerations, but as capabilities improve, multimedia is appearing on more and more Web pages. There is still wide variation in the ability of viewers to enjoy Web pages integrating multimedia, so care needs to be taken to ensure that potential viewers will be able to take advantage of the multimedia in your Web pages. You should also be wary of overwhelming viewers with too much multimedia. When designing Web pages, carefully consider why multimedia is being used and whether it will enhance the viewer experience or needlessly complicate it.

In this chapter, you will learn how to embed various types of media in your Web pages to make the pages more attractive and useful to potential viewers. Although it is always possible to create links to media, embedding media using embed tags and object tags provides a greater degree of control over how the media is displayed.

Understanding Media Elements

Web browsers are *HTML interpreters,* meaning that their job is to interpret and display the HTML code contained in Web page documents. This means that on their own, browsers are limited to displaying text and images. For any type of media beyond this, browsers must look for assistance to display the material. This assistance can take the form of programs that work within the browser to display different media, such as JavaScript or Java applets, the use of stand-alone programs known as helper applications, or the use of ActiveX controls and Netscape-style plugins.

JavaScript

JavaScript is a scripting programming language that resides within an HTML document. The use of JavaScript enables a browser to change page content dynamically in response to viewer input. Mouseover events/actions and form validation are two examples of the types of interactive functions that JavaScript can enable. More recently, JavaScript has been combined with HTML and CSS-P (Cascading Style Sheets-Positioning) to create *dynamic HTML (DHTML)*. You have already used DHTML in Dreamweaver MX 2004 when working with behaviors such as rollover images or navigation bars in Chapter 4.

JavaScript is located between script tags (<script>) and is placed in the head region (and sometimes body section) of a document as shown in Figure 9.1. JavaScript is supported by most browsers, but DHTML is supported only by the latest browser versions (version 4 and up).

```
<!DOCTYPE HTML PUBLIC "-//W3C//DTD HTML 4.01 Transitional//EN"
"http://www.w3.org/TR/html4/loose.dtd">
<html>
<head>
<title>Untitled Document</title>
<meta http-equiv="Content-Type" content="text/html; charset=iso-8859-1">
<script language="JavaScript" type="text/JavaScript">
<!--
function MM_swapImgRestore() { //v3.0
  var i,x,a=document.MM_sr; for(i=0;a&&i<a.length&&(x=a[i])&&x.oSrc;i++) x.src=x.oSrc;
}

function MM_preloadImages() { //v3.0
  var d=document; if(d.images){ if(!d.MM_p) d.MM_p=new Array();
    var i,j=d.MM_p.length,a=MM_preloadImages.arguments; for(i=0; i<a.length; i++)
    if (a[i].indexOf("#")!=0){ d.MM_p[j]=new Image; d.MM_p[j++].src=a[i];}}
```

Figure 9.1
Rollover JavaScript

swapImgRestore
(rollover effect)

Java Applets

Another method that can be used to enable browsers to display other media is to use the Java programming language to create Java applets. *Java applets* are small applications (programs) as shown in Figure 9.2 that can run inside a browser window. They can be used to provide an interactive experience, including audio and video. Although programming Java applets is fairly complicated, installing and using them is not. Java applets are available through a number of sites on the Internet for free or for a small license fee.

Helper Applications

Helper applications are stand-alone programs that browsers can call on to display different media content. Whenever a browser encounters a file, it looks at its file extension to determine its *MIME (Multipurpose Internet Mail Extension)* type. Table 9.1 shows some of the more commonly encountered MIME types and their extensions. Browsers use the MIME type to determine how a file will be displayed. If a file contains an extension that the browser can handle, such as .htm or .gif, then the browser has no problem displaying the file content. However, if a file is a MIME type that the browser cannot display on its own, it must look for a helper application that can be used to display the file content. For example, if the browser is asked to display a Microsoft Word document with a .doc extension, it will look for a copy of the Word program on the computer it is resident on and will open

```
<body>
<applet code="tinyHScroll.class" height=40 width=150>
<param  name="DELAY" value="25">
<param  name="YPOS" value="24">
<param  name="FONTNAME" value="Courier">
<param  name="FONTSIZE" value="24">
<param  name="MESSAGE" value="A product of One Wolf WebArt.">
<param  name="FGRED" value="255">
<param  name="FGGREEN" value="255">
<param  name="FGBLUE" value="255">
<param  name="BGRED" value="0">
<param  name="BGGREEN" value="0">
<param  name="BGBLUE" value="0">
</applet>
</body>
```

Figure 9.2
Java Applet Code

Table 9.1 • Some Common Media MIME Types and File Name Extensions

File Extension	MIME Type
.avi	Microsoft Audio Video
.dcr	Shockwave
.mid, .midi	Musical Instrument Digital Interface
.mov	Quicktime
.mp2, .mp3	Audio MPEG (Moving Pictures Experts Group)
.ra, .ram, .rm	RealAudio
.swf	Flash
.wav	Waveform Sound
.mpe, .mpg, .mpeg	Video MPEG (Moving Pictures Experts Group)

that program to display the file. Adobe PDF files provide another common example of the need for browsers to use helper applications. Whenever a browser encounters a file with a .pdf extension, it looks for a copy of Adobe Acrobat Reader and opens the program to display the file as shown in Figure 9.3.

Plugins and ActiveX Controls

Plugins are small programs that extend the capability of browsers in dealing with different types of media. They differ from helper applications in that they are not stand-alone programs like Microsoft Word or Adobe Acrobat. Instead, the sole purpose of a plugin is to enable a browser to deal with specific types of Web page content that the plugin is designed to handle.

Plugins reside in a browser's *Plugins folder*, located inside the browser's application folder as shown in Figure 9.4, where they can be called on when needed. For example, when a browser encounters a file with an extension such as .swf (used by Flash content), it looks for and opens the Flash player plugin located in its plugins file. It is difficult to predict exactly how a browser might deal with a given media type because even the same browser versions can be configured to handle plugins differently. Browsers come with some plugins already installed, and new plugins can be downloaded to a browser's Plugins folder when needed.

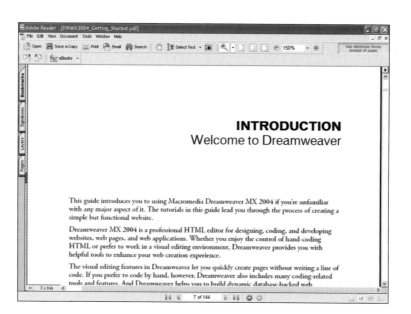

Figure 9.3
Adobe Acrobat File
Displayed in Acrobat Reader

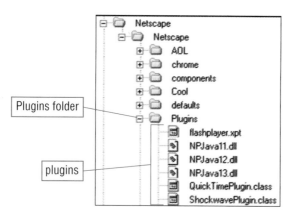

Figure 9.4
Browser Plugins Folder

DREAMWEAVER MX 2004

The two most common browser plugin types are *Netscape-style plugins* and *ActiveX controls*. Netscape originally developed the browser plugin concept for its Navigator browser, and Microsoft later developed ActiveX controls for use in its Internet Explorer browser. Two key differences between these two types of plugins are the type of tag they use to insert media into Web pages and the scripting language used for communication between a browser and a plugin or ActiveX control. Netscape-style plugins use the *embed tag* (<embed>) to insert media and JavaScript for communication, while ActiveX controls use the *object tag* (<object>) and VBScript for communication.

Before the advent of ActiveX controls, Internet Explorer supported Netscape-style plugins, but not long after ActiveX controls came into being, Internet Explorer dropped this support. What this means is that when Internet Explorer encounters an embed tag, it looks for an ActiveX control to handle the content indicated by the tag. If the browser cannot find an ActiveX control to handle the content, the content is not displayed.

The use of plugins can cause problems if viewers do not have a required plugin installed in the browser they are using. If a browser cannot find the correct plugin, the viewer will be looking at a blank screen, a static placeholder image, or a message advising the viewer that the needed plugin cannot be found as shown in Figure 9.5. One way to avoid that possibility is to specify a URL where a copy of the needed plugin can be found. If the browser cannot find a called-for plugin, it will automatically go to the URL, offering viewers the option of downloading and installing the needed plugin. After the plugin is installed in the browser's Plugins folder, this process will not need to be repeated.

Some types of media have both ActiveX controls and plugins that can be used to display media in browsers. When that is the case, Dreamweaver MX 2004 inserts the media, such as Shockwave or Flash movies, using both Netscape plugin tags (embed tags) and ActiveX tags (object tags) as shown in Figure 9.6. When this is done, Internet Explorer uses the ActiveX control specified, while Netscape browsers ignore the ActiveX control and look for the plugin needed to display the object inserted in the page using embed tags.

To ensure that the content you are adding to your pages will be accessible to your viewers, you should preview the pages in as many browser versions as you can. It is also a good idea to offer alternatives for viewers who might not be able to take advantage of content requiring plugins, such as a link to similar material in a different format or an explanation of what the plugin content contains.

Figure 9.5 • Missing Plugin Message

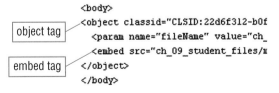

Figure 9.6 • Media Inserted Using Object and Embed Tags

Playing Media within Dreamweaver MX 2004

When movies and animations are inserted within Dreamweaver MX 2004 documents, the Property inspector displays a Play button as shown in Figure 9.7. The button can be clicked to play the media so that it can be previewed within the Dreamweaver MX 2004 environment. The Play button transforms into a Stop button after the media begins playing; clicking the Stop button stops the preview.

Dreamweaver MX 2004 uses Netscape-style plugins for previewing, so when the Play button is selected, it first looks for the appropriate Netscape-style plugin in its Plugins folder. If the appropriate plugin cannot be found, Dreamweaver MX 2004 then searches the Plugins folders of all of the browsers installed on the computer. If a movie or animation relies exclusively on an ActiveX control, it will not be previewable within Dreamweaver MX 2004. If Internet Explorer is the only browser installed on your computer, you will not be able to preview movies and animations in Dreamweaver MX 2004 because Internet Explorer uses ActiveX controls. There are two solutions to this problem:

- Install a copy of the latest Netscape browser on your computer so that Dreamweaver MX 2004 can search for and use the Netscape-style plugins that come with that program.
- Download a needed plugin and copy its class file to the Dreamweaver MX 2004 Plugins folder.

Using the Insert Bar Media Button

Dreamweaver MX 2004 makes it easy for you to insert and work with multimedia by offering an Insert bar (Common menu item or tab) Media button for inserting some of the most popular media types. Clicking the Media button down-pointing arrow displays a drop-down menu with different media-related commands, such as Flash, Flash Text, and so on. The Media button always displays the icon of the last media command selected from the drop-down menu. Although you also can insert media by clicking Insert on the Menu bar and then clicking Media, you will probably find the Insert bar more convenient for inserting media into Web pages. Figure 9.8 shows the Insert bar Media button drop-down menu. Each command and its function will be described in the subsequent sections of this chapter.

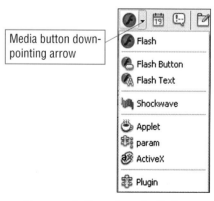

Figure 9.8 • Insert Bar Media Button Drop-Down

Figure 9.7 • Property Inspector Play Button

DREAMWEAVER MX 2004

Flash Media

The Flash command can be used to insert Flash movies and animations into Web pages. **Flash MX 2004** is the latest version of the Flash program, and it is part of the Macromedia suite of programs that includes Dreamweaver MX 2004. Flash MX 2004 can be used to create videos, interactive animations, and other types of rich Internet applications. You can install Flash content even if you do not have Flash MX 2004 installed on your computer. Flash content is also available free or for a fee, so even if you do not know how to create it, you can still install it on your Web pages.

Clicking the Insert bar Flash command opens the Select File dialog box. The dialog box can be used to locate a desired Flash file, which has an .swf file extension. After you select the Flash file, click the OK button to close the dialog box and insert the file. An Object Tag Accessibility Attributes dialog box appears as shown in Figure 9.9 if the *Media* check box has been enabled using the Preferences dialog box Accessibility page. The dialog box can be used to provide a title, access key, and tab index for the Flash movie, although these accessibility features might not work with Flash content in some browsers. The title, access key, and tab index accessibility features were described in the "Using the Menu Bar to Insert Links" section of Chapter 2.

After the Flash movie has been inserted in a document, it appears as a placeholder as shown in Figure 9.10. Selecting the placeholder displays the Flash Property inspector as shown in Figure 9.11. Click the *Align* list box down-pointing arrow to see a list of different alignment properties for the movie. These properties are the same as the alignment properties for images described in the "Image Alignment" section of Chapter 4.

The Flash Property inspector also can be used to change the width and height of the Flash movie and to specify horizontal and vertical space around the movie. When a Flash movie is inserted, Dreamweaver MX 2004 automatically determines the dimensions of the movie and enters them in the *W* (width) and *H* (height) text boxes. Changing these dimensions affects the quality of the movie's appearance.

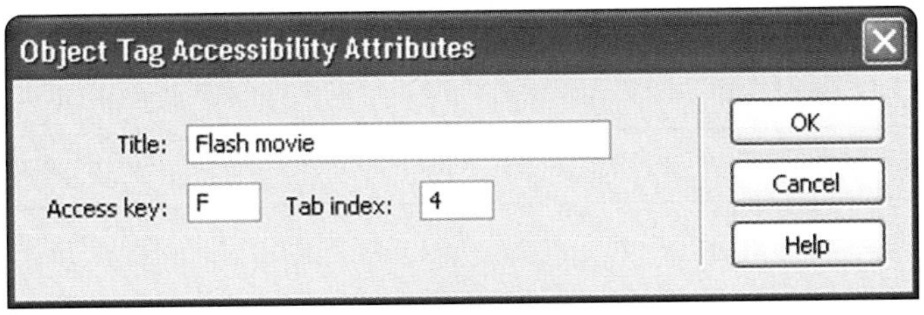

Figure 9.9
Object Tag Accessibility Attributes Dialog Box

Figure 9.10
Flash Placeholder

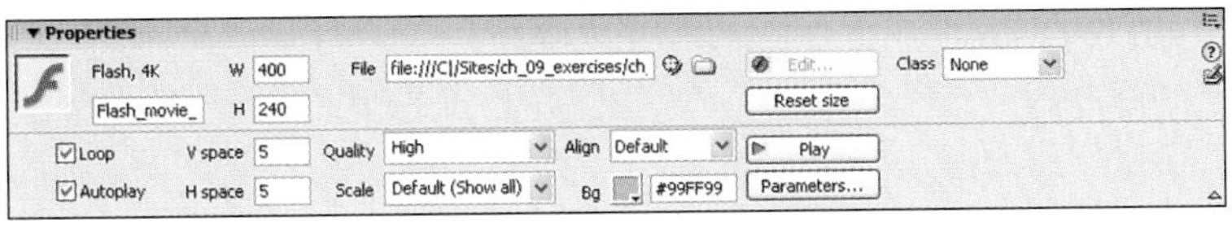

Figure 9.11
Flash Property Inspector

If Flash MX 2004 is also installed on your computer, the *Src* text box automatically displays a link to the Flash source document if it is available, which will have an .fla file extension. Flash files cannot be edited in their .swf format, but clicking the Flash Property inspector Edit button opens the Flash file source document in Flash MX 2004 so you can edit it. If the Flash source document is not available, the *Src* text box will not appear and the Edit button will be visible but inactive.

The Flash Property inspector *Quality* text box lets you choose a quality setting for the Flash movie. The choices available by clicking the *Quality* text box down-pointing arrow are *Low, Auto Low, Auto High,* and *High.* The default setting is *High. High* emphasizes appearance over speed, while *Low* emphasizes speed over appearance. *Auto Low* emphasizes speed at first but will improve appearance if that is possible, whereas *Auto High* starts out emphasizing both speed and appearance, with speed being sacrificed if that becomes necessary.

The Flash Property inspector *Scale* list box lets you choose how the Flash movie will be displayed within the specified width and height **parameters**. The three choices are *Default (Show all), No border,* and *Exact fit. Default (Show all)* displays the entire movie. *No border* fits the movie into the dimensions specified without borders showing and maintains the original aspect ratio—the relationship between the specified width and height properties. *Exact fit* scales the movie to the dimensions that have been set, regardless of the aspect ratio, and it can lead to distortion of the movie.

The *Loop* check box should be enabled if you want the Flash movie to play continuously by repeating whenever it reaches the end. The *Autoplay* check box should be enabled if you want the Flash movie to start playing automatically as soon as the page loads. These controls take effect only if the Flash movie does not have its own internal scripting for these controls.

The Flash Property inspector Parameters button can be used to specify parameters and **values** for the Flash movie by using the Parameters dialog box. The parameters that can be specified are determined by the designer of the Flash movie, although some parameters, such as background transparency, can be specified in any case.

exercise

1

INSERTING FLASH MEDIA

The exercises in this chapter assume that the Media *check box has been enabled using the Preferences dialog box Accessibility page. Instructions on selecting this preference are contained in the "Ensuring Accessibility" section of Chapter 2.*

1. If necessary, start Dreamweaver MX 2004.
2. At a clear document screen, create a new site named CH 09 Exercises to store the exercises you create in this chapter. Name the root folder ch_09_exercises and save it under the Sites folder you created in Chapter 1, Exercise 3. Download the ch_09_student_files folder from the IRC to the CH 09 Exercises site root folder (ch_09_exercises) and expand it. Delete the compressed folder when you are finished. ***Note: Refer to Chapter 1 for instructions on navigating with the Files panel integrated file browser.***
3. Insert a Flash animation by completing the following steps:
   a. Create an HTML document and use the Save or Save As command to name and save it as **ch9ex01.htm**.

DREAMWEAVER MX 2004

b. If necessary, click the Insert bar Common menu item or tab, and then click the Media button down-pointing arrow to display the media menu. Click the Flash command to open the Select File dialog box. Use the dialog box to locate the **flash.swf** student file located in the ch_09_student_files subfolder named flash. Click the file to place it in the dialog box *File name* text box. Click the OK button to close the dialog box.

c. Type **Flash animation** in the Object Tag Accessibility Attributes dialog box *Title* text box. Type **A** in the *Access key* text box and then **1** in the *Tab index* text box. Click the OK button to close the dialog box when you are finished.

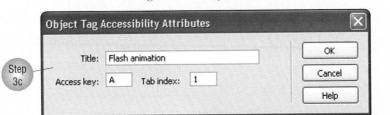

d. Click the Preview/Debug in browser button and then click Preview in iexplore to preview the page. You should see a black-and-white animation with text and light gray blocks that appear and disappear over and over. Close the browser when you are finished.

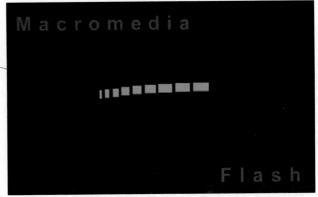

e. Click the Flash animation placeholder in **ch9ex01.htm** to select it and display the Flash Property inspector.

f. Click the Flash Property inspector Parameters button to open the Parameters dialog box. ***Hint: If the Parameters button is not visible, click the Expander arrow located in the lower-right corner of the Property inspector to expand it.***

g. Click below the *Parameter* column head and type **bgcolor**.

h. Click below the *Value* column head and type **FF0000** to specify a red background color. Click the OK button to close the dialog box when you are finished.

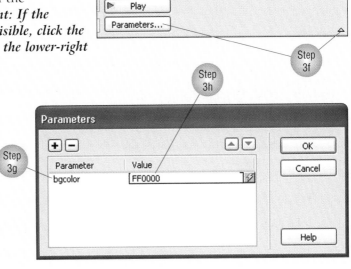

i.   Click the Preview/Debug in browser button and then click Preview in iexplore to preview the page. The Flash animation should have a red background. Close the browser when you are finished.

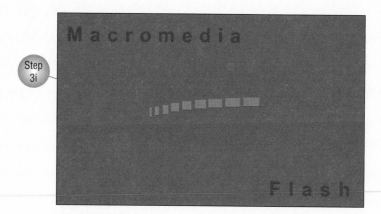

j.   Click the Flash animation placeholder in **ch9ex01.htm** to select it and display the Flash Property inspector.

k.   Click the Flash Property inspector Parameters button to open the Parameters dialog box. Type **wmode** in the *Parameter* column and **transparent** in the *Value* column. Click the OK button to close the dialog box when you are finished.

l.   Click the Preview/Debug in browser button and then click Preview in iexplore to preview the page. The Flash animation background is transparent (invisible), and you should see only the gray text and blocks. Close the browser when you are finished.

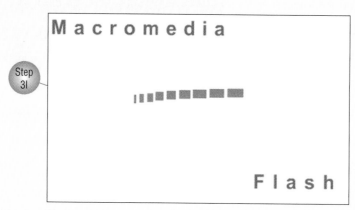

m.   Click the Flash animation placeholder in **ch9ex01.htm** to select it and display the Flash Property inspector.

n.   Click the Flash Property inspector Parameters button to open the Parameters dialog box. Click the Plus (+) button and type **loop** in the *Parameter* column and **False** in the *Value* column. Click the OK button to close the dialog box when you are finished.

o.   Click the Preview/Debug in browser button and then click Preview in iexplore to preview the page. The Flash animation should play once and then stop. Close the browser when you are finished.

4.   Save **ch9ex01.htm** and then close it.

Flash Buttons

The Insert bar Flash Button command allows you to create and insert interactive Flash buttons within the Dreamweaver MX 2004 environment. **Flash buttons** function somewhat like rollover images in that they have two states such as the example shown in Figure 9.12. They differ from rollover images in that they can display animation when clicked. They also can be linked to another URL so that they can function as hyperlinks.

If the current document has not yet been saved when the Flash Button command is clicked, a message appears advising you to save the document first. If the current document already has been saved, the Insert Flash Button dialog box opens as shown in Figure 9.13. The *Style* list box arrows can be used to scroll and locate a desired button style. Clicking a button style listing displays a sample of the button in the *Sample* preview box at the top of the dialog box. The *Button text* text box is used to enter the text that will appear in the button, such as *Home, Page One,* and so on. The dialog box also contains *Font* and *Size* text boxes that can be used to specify the font style and size of the button text entered in the *Button text* text box. The *Link* text box can be used to type a URL, or the adjacent Browse button can be clicked to open the Select File dialog box to browse and locate a file that will be linked to the button. You can click the down-pointing arrow to the right of the *Target* list box to display a list of target windows for the linked file to open in. These target windows are the same as the target windows described previously in the "Using Links to Change Frame Content" section of Chapter 5.

When you click the *Bg color* color box, you can use the Eyedropper to select a background color for the button. You can also type in a desired color in the *Bg color* text box. Some Flash buttons have a white border that is not visible in the *Sample* preview box, but the border will be visible when the button is inserted in a

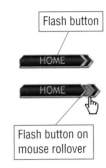

Flash button

Flash button on mouse rollover

Figure 9.12
Flash Buttons

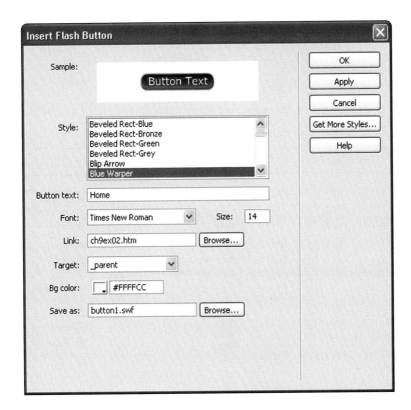

Figure 9.13
Insert Flash Button Dialog Box

Web page with a nonwhite background color as shown in Figure 9.14. To ensure that a button border will not be visible, you can click the *Bg color* color box to open the color palette and use the Eyedropper to select the background color of the page that the Flash button is being inserted in.

Click the Apply button to see how the button will look on the page. If you are satisfied, you can then click the OK button to insert the Flash button. If the *Media* check box has been enabled using the Preferences dialog box Accessibility page, a Flash Accessibility Attributes dialog box appears as shown in Figure 9.15. The dialog box can be used to provide a title, access key, and tab index for the Flash button. Depending on the browser you are using, you might find that these accessibility attributes do not work with Flash.

Use the *Save as* text box in the Insert Flash Button dialog box to provide a new name for the button if you do not want to use the default name. Flash buttons with document-relative links must be saved to the same directory as the current document.

To edit a Flash button, select the button and then click the Edit button in the Flash Button Property inspector shown in Figure 9.16. This opens the Insert Flash Button dialog box so you can make the necessary changes.

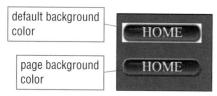

Figure 9.14 • Flash Buttons with Page Background Border Color and Default Border Color (White)

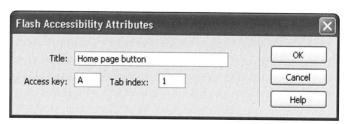

Figure 9.15 • Flash Accessibility Attributes Dialog Box

Figure 9.16 • Flash Button Property Inspector

exercise

CREATING AND INSERTING FLASH BUTTONS

1. Create Flash buttons by completing the following steps:
    a. At a clear document screen, open the **flash_button_document.htm** student file and use the Save As command to rename and save it to the ch_09_exercises root folder as **ch9ex02.htm**.
    b. Position the insertion point in the upper-left corner of the document.
    c. Click the Insert bar (Common menu item or tab) Media button down-pointing arrow and then the Flash Button command to open the Insert Flash Button dialog box.

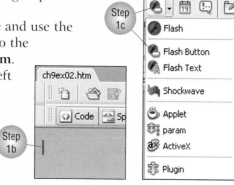

DREAMWEAVER MX 2004

d. Click the *Style* list box down-pointing arrow and scroll down the list of button types until you reach *Slider*. Click *Slider* to select it.

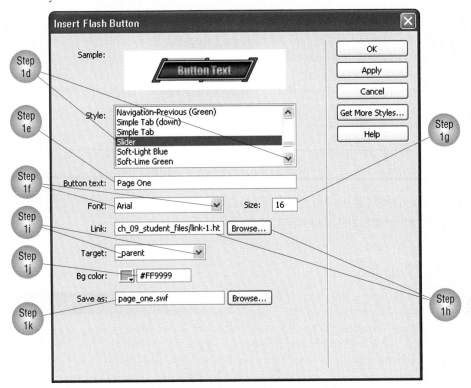

e. Type **Page One** in the *Button text* text box.
f. Click the *Font* list box down-pointing arrow to open the drop-down list of available font styles. Select *Arial* from the list.
g. Type **16** in the *Size* text box if necessary.
h. Click the Browse button next to the *Link* text box to open the Select file dialog box. Use the Select file dialog box to browse and locate the **link-1.htm** file in the ch_09_student_files folder. Click the file to place it in the *File name* text box and then click the OK button to close the dialog box.
i. Click the *Target* list box down-pointing arrow and select *_parent* from the drop-down list.
j. Click the *Bg color* color box and use the Eyedropper to select the document background color (#FF9999) as the background color for the Flash button you are creating or type **#FF9999** in the text box.
k. Change the default button name in the *Save as* text box to read *page_one.swf*. Click the OK button when you are finished.
l. Type **Page one button** in the Flash Accessibility Attributes dialog box *Title* text box, **A** in the *Access key* text box, and **1** in the *Tab index* text box. Click the OK button when you are finished. ***Note: The accessibility features might not work as intended in your browser.***

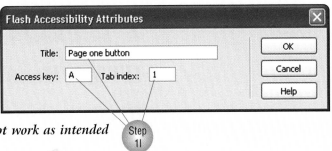

m. Position the insertion point to the right of the Page One button and then repeat Steps 1c–1l to create Flash buttons named Page Two and Page Three. Link these buttons to the appropriate student files (**link-2.htm** and **link-3.htm**). Use the Flash Accessibility Attributes dialog box to name each button after its function (for example, *Page two button* for the button linking to **link-2.htm**), and assign an access key letter of *B* for the Page Two button and *C* for the Page Three button. Assign a tab index number of *2* for the Page Two button, and *3* for the Page Three button.

n. With none of the buttons selected, click the Property inspector Align Center button to center align the buttons on the page.

o. Click the Preview/Debug in browser button and then click Preview in iexplore to preview the Web page. Click one of the buttons. The button will animate, and if your browser is sound-enabled, you will hear a sound effect when the button is clicked. Clicking a button sends you to the link target document. Close the browser when you are finished.

2. Save **ch9ex02.htm** and then close it.

Flash Text

The Insert bar Flash Text command lets you insert a text-only Flash movie. Although the **Flash text** is created using a movie format, it does not move, but it can display a rollover effect by choosing a rollover color. For example, if the Flash text color is black and the rollover color is yellow, the Flash text turns from black to yellow when the mouse pointer is rolled over it. Another advantage of Flash text is that it can be used to insert text into Web pages in font sizes that could not be displayed using the font sizes normally available to a browser as shown in Figure 9.17.

As is the case when the Flash Button command is clicked, if the current document has not yet been saved, clicking the Flash Text button causes a message box to appear advising you to save the document first. If the document has already been saved, the Insert Flash Text dialog box as shown in Figure 9.18 appears. Use the *Font* list box and the *Size* text box at the top of the dialog box to choose a style and size for the text that will appear in the Flash text movie that you are creating. Clicking the *Font* list box down-pointing arrow displays a list of the fonts available. You can use the *Color* text box to enter a hexadecimal color code for the Flash text and the *Rollover color* text box to enter a hexadecimal color for the Flash text when the mouse rolls over it in the browser window. Type the text for the Flash text movie in the *Text* text box. If the *Show font* check box is enabled, the text you enter in the *Text* text box appears in the font style you selected using the *Font* list box. If the *Show font* check box is not enabled, text entered in the *Text* text box always

FLASH TEXT

HTML Heading 1 Text

HTML Heading 2 Text

HTML Heading 3 Text

Figure 9.17
Flash Text and HTML Text

DREAMWEAVER MX 2004

appears in the same font style no matter what font is selected in the *Font* list box. The *Link, Target, Bg color,* and *Save as* boxes all function in the same way as they do in the Insert Flash Button dialog box.

Flash text cannot be edited like normal HTML text because it is actually a Flash movie inserted using object tags. Flash text can be edited by double-clicking the text, which causes the Insert Flash Text dialog box to open. You then can change the text in the *Text* text box or any of the formatting that was specified when the Flash text was created.

Text or objects inserted next to Flash text will be affected as they would when inserted next to an image. Text or objects appear with baseline alignment by default as shown in Figure 9.19. To change the Flash text alignment, the Flash text must be selected to make the Flash Text Property inspector shown in Figure 9.20 appear.

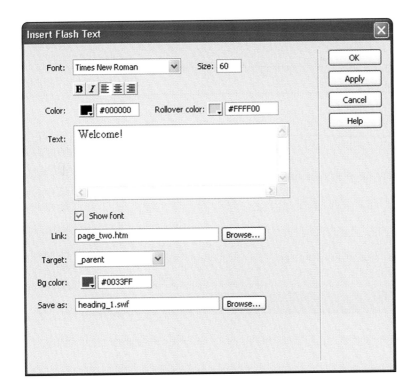

Figure 9.18
Insert Flash Text Dialog Box

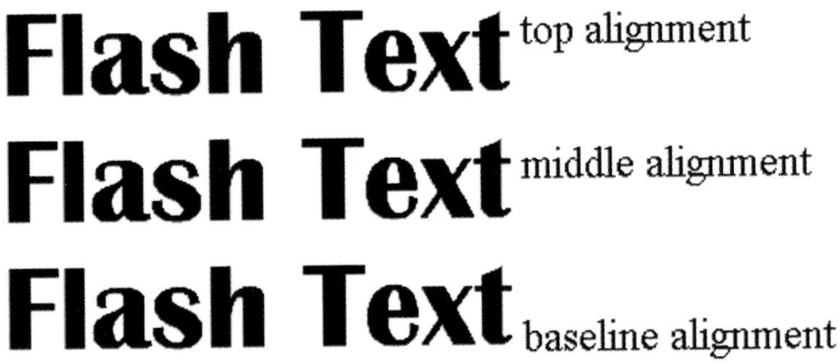

Figure 9.19
Flash Text and HTML Text Default Alignment

Figure 9.20
Flash Text Property Inspector

Because Flash text is a Flash movie, the Flash Text Property inspector is almost identical to the Flash Button Property inspector, lacking only the *Loop* and *Autoplay* check boxes. The *Align* list box contains a list of different alignment values. These values are the same as the alignment values for images described in Chapter 4. The Flash Text Property inspector also can be used to select a URL link for the Flash text, change the width and height of the Flash text, and specify horizontal and vertical space for the Flash text.

The Flash Text Property inspector *Quality* text box lets you choose a quality setting for the Flash text. The choices available are the same as those available in the Flash Button Property inspector.

The Flash Text Property inspector *Scale* text box lets you choose how the text will be displayed within the parameters determined by the width and height specified for the Flash text. The choices and their functions are the same as those available in the Flash Button Property inspector.

CREATING AND INSERTING FLASH TEXT

1. Create and insert Flash text by completing the following steps:
   a. Open the **flash_text_document.htm** student file in the ch_09_student_files folder and use the Save As command to rename and save it to the ch_09_exercises folder as **ch9ex03.htm**.
   b. Position the insertion point in the upper-left corner of the document.
   c. If necessary, click the Insert bar Common menu item or tab, click the Media button down-pointing arrow, and then click the Flash Text command to open the Insert Flash Text dialog box.
   d. Click the *Font* list box down-pointing arrow to see the drop-down list of available font styles. Select *Times New Roman* from the list.

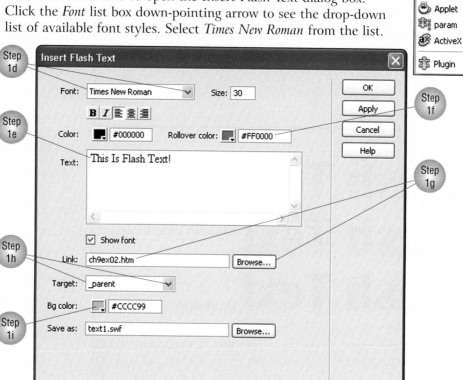

e. Type This Is Flash Text! in the *Text* text box.

f. Click the *Rollover color* color box and use the Eyedropper to select red (#FF0000) or type #FF0000 in the *Rollover color* text box.

g. Click the Browse button next to the *Link* text box to open the Select file dialog box. Locate and click the **ch9ex02.htm** file to place it in the *File name* text box, and then click the OK button to close the Select file dialog box.

h. Click the *Target* list box down-pointing arrow and select *_parent* from the drop-down list.

i. Click the *Bg color* color box and use the Eyedropper to select the document background color (#CCCC99) as the background color for the Flash text you are creating.

j. Click the OK button to close the Insert Flash Text dialog box.

k. Type This Is Flash Text! in the Flash Accessibility Attributes dialog box *Title* text box, A in the *Access key* text box, and 1 in the *Tab index* text box. Click the OK button when you are finished.

l. Click the Preview/Debug in browser button and then click Preview in iexplore to view the Flash text. Click the Flash text to see the rollover effect and link to the **ch9ex02.htm** page. Close the browser when you are finished.

m. With **ch9ex03.htm** as the current document, click the Flash text to select it.

n. Click the Flash Text Property inspector Edit button to open the Insert Flash Text dialog box.

o. Type 60 in the dialog box *Size* text box.

p. Type #993300 in the dialog box *Color* text box. Click the OK button to close the dialog box when you are finished. The Flash Accessibility Attributes dialog box appears again. Because you are not changing these attributes, click the OK button to close it.

q. Click the Preview/Debug in browser button and then click Preview in iexplore to view the Flash text and observe the changes you made to the font size and color.

2. Save **ch9ex03.htm** and then close it.

Shockwave

Shockwave is a Macromedia movie file format. Shockwave plugins exist in both Netscape-style plugins and ActiveX control forms, so Dreamweaver MX 2004 inserts Shockwave movies using both embed tags and object tags. Because Shockwave plugins are widely distributed, the chances that viewers will have one on their computer are very high.

Clicking the Insert bar Shockwave command opens the Select File dialog box. The dialog box can be used to locate the Shockwave file, which has a .dcr file extension. After the desired Shockwave file has been selected, you can click the OK button. If the *Media* check box has been enabled on the Preferences dialog box Accessibility page, an Object Tag Accessibility Attributes dialog box will appear, and the dialog box can be used to provide a title, access key, and tab index for the Shockwave movie.

Selecting the placeholder displays the Shockwave Property inspector shown in Figure 9.21. Unlike Flash movies, Dreamweaver MX 2004 cannot determine the correct dimensions of the Shockwave movie automatically. If the correct dimensions

Figure 9.21
Shockwave Property Inspector

are known, they can be entered in the Shockwave Property inspector *W* and *H* text boxes. If the dimensions are not known, you can experiment until you find the correct dimensions by entering estimated dimensions in the *W* and *H* text boxes and then previewing the movie to determine whether it appears in its entirety or with portions cut off. Start by changing one dimension. For example, if you entered a width of 200 pixels, but the movie is still cut off on one side, return to the Shockwave Property inspector, increase the width dimension, and preview it again. If the entire movie is visible, reduce the width dimension until a portion of the movie is not visible, and then increase the dimension just enough to make it visible again. Repeating this process allows you to determine the correct width for the movie. The same process then can be used to determine the correct height of the movie.

The Shockwave Property inspector Browse for File button next to the *File* text box can be used to browse for and locate a file that can be linked to the Shockwave movie. When a Shockwave movie is linked in this manner, it functions like a hyperlink; when it is clicked, viewers are forwarded to the link target document. The *V space, H space, Align,* and *Bg* boxes function in the same manner as in the other media Property inspectors.

Clicking the Shockwave Property inspector Parameters button opens the Parameters dialog box shown in Figure 9.22. Clicking the Parameters dialog box Plus (+) button opens the Select Parameter Value dialog box shown in Figure 9.23. Clicking the *Name* text box down-pointing arrow displays a list of all of the parameters associated with the Shockwave movie. Selecting a parameter places it in the *Name* text box. The *Value* text box down-pointing arrow then can be clicked to display the possible values for the parameter as shown in Figure 9.24. In Figure 9.24, the *AutoStart* value is *true,* which means that this parameter determines that the Shockwave movie will play automatically when the page containing the movie is loaded in a browser. Changing the value to *false* prevents the movie from playing automatically. After a parameter and value have been specified, clicking the OK buttons closes the Select Parameter Value and Parameters dialog boxes.

Figure 9.22
Parameters Dialog Box

Figure 9.23
Select Parameter Value
Dialog Box *Name* List

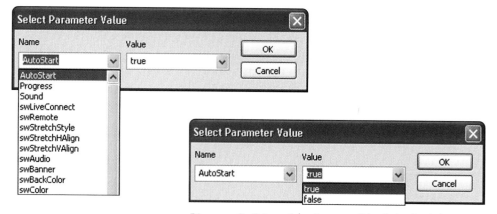

Figure 9.24 • Select Parameter Value Dialog Box *Value* List

DREAMWEAVER MX 2004

1. Insert a Shockwave animation by completing the following steps:

   a. Create an HTML document and use the Save or Save As command to name and save it as **ch9ex04.htm**.

   b. If necessary, click the Insert bar Common menu item or tab, click the Media button, and then click the Shockwave command to open the Select File dialog box. Use the dialog box to locate the **shockwave.dcr** student file located in the ch_09_student_files subfolder named shockwave. Click the file to place it in the dialog box *File name* text box. Click the OK button to close the dialog box.

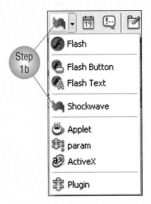

   c. Type Shockwave animation in the Object Tag Accessibility Attributes dialog box *Title* text box. Type A in the *Access key* text box and then 1 in the *Tab index* text box. Click the OK button to close the dialog box when you are finished.

   d. Type 475 in the Shockwave Property inspector *W* text box and 320 in the *H* text box. **Hint: If you deselected the Shockwave placeholder, you need to select it so that the Shockwave Property inspector is displayed.**

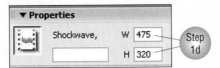

   e. Click the Preview/Debug in browser button and then click Preview in iexplore to preview the page. You should see a black-and-white animation with large gray Shockwave text moving diagonally across the screen and smaller Macromedia text moving from left to right. Close the browser when you are finished.

   f. Click the Shockwave animation in **ch9ex04.htm** to select it and display the Shockwave Property inspector.

   g. Click the Shockwave Property inspector Parameters button to open the Parameters dialog box.

h. Click the Parameters dialog box Plus (+) button to open the Select Parameter Value dialog box. Click the *Name* text box down-pointing arrow to select *swText* from the list of parameters that appears. ***Note: Even though you will see a long list of parameters, you can change only parameter values that the Shockwave file designer called for when the file was created. This file has been designed so that you can change the swText and sw1 parameter values.***

i. Type your name in the *Value* text box. Click the OK button to close the Select Parameter Value dialog box when you are finished. Click the OK button to close the Parameters dialog box.

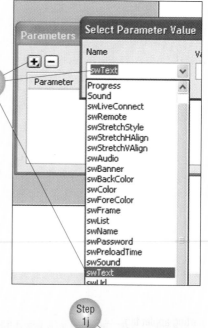

j. Click the Preview/Debug in browser button and then click Preview in iexplore to preview the page. When the animation opens, look for the *Shockwave* text in the upper-right corner of the animation. This will transform into your name shortly after the file starts playing. Close the browser when you are finished.

k. Click the Shockwave animation in **ch9ex04.htm** to select it and display the Shockwave Property inspector.

l. Click the Shockwave Property inspector Parameters button to open the Parameters dialog box.

m. Click the Parameters dialog box Plus (+) button to open the Select Parameter Value dialog box.

n. Click the *Name* text box down-pointing arrow to select *sw1* from the list. Type **False** in the *Value* text box. Click the OK button to close the Select Value Parameter dialog box when you are finished. Click the OK button to close the Parameters dialog box.

o. Click the Preview/Debug in browser button and then click Preview in iexplore to preview the page. The large Shockwave text that moved diagonally has disappeared. Close the browser when you are finished.

2. Save **ch9ex04.htm** and then close it.

Applets

Applets are self-contained mini-programs written using the Java programming language. Applets can be composed of a number of different files, but all applets contain at least one class file, identified by its .class extension. Applet code, known as a statement or instruction, is placed within the body tags of an HTML document and contains information calling for the applet class file or files and defining the applet parameters as shown in Figure 9.25. Java-enabled browsers then can read the applet statement in an HTML document and execute (run) the applet. The applet programmer determines whether or not an applet contains parameters. Some applets do not contain any parameters, while others contain quite a few, as shown in Figure 9.25.

Programming Java applets is a complex task, but many applets are available on the Internet for free or for a small fee. These applets usually are available by downloading a zipped (compressed) file containing all of the files necessary for the applet to run. The zipped file is unzipped (uncompressed) and installed in a folder in your site. Applets typically come with directions describing how the applet is to be installed as shown in Figure 9.26. Follow the directions carefully because the slightest variance from the instructions can cause an applet to fail.

starting applet tag   class file

```
<body>
<applet archive="bookflip.jar" code="bookflip.class" width="140" height="305">
<param name="credits" value="Applet by Fabio Ciucci (www.anfyjava.com)">
<param name="regcode" value="NO">          ; Registration code (if you have it)
<param name="regnewframe" value="YES">      ; Reglink opened in new frame?
<param name="regframename" value="_blank">  ; Name of new frame for reglink
<param name="res" value="1">                ; resolution (1-8)
<param name="image1" value="book1.jpg">     ; Image 1 to load
<param name="image2" value="book2.jpg">     ; Image 2 to load
<param name="image3" value="book3.jpg">     ; Image 3 to load
<param name="link1" value="http://www.anfyjava.com">  ; Link 1
<param name="link2" value="NO">                       ; Link 2
```

parameter   value

Figure 9.25
Applet Code with Parameters

```
           BookFlip - Copyright (C) by Fabio Ciucci 1998/99

This applet can execute a "book flip" transition between any identically
sized GIF or JPG images.

It is based on original code by Dolf Van Der Schaar, which is used under
license.

*****************************************************************************

NECESSARY FILES.

Apart from bookflip images, and an optional overlay image, the following
3 ".class" files must be uploaded:

bookflip.class
Lware.class
anfy.class

Plus, bookflip.jar for speedy loading on recent browsers.

*****************************************************************************

EXAMPLE.

Insert the <applet> tag in your html document as follows to add this applet
to your page (Comments after the ";" symbol are code explanations and
```

Figure 9.26
Applet Directions

The Insert bar Applet command can be used to insert an applet class file. Any parameters for the applet then can be inserted using the Applet Property inspector Parameters button. Because an applet can have more than a dozen different parameters, this is a very slow way to insert an applet. In most circumstances, it is much easier to follow the directions that come with the applet and copy and paste the supplied applet code into the body section of an HTML document. After the instructions are inserted, a placeholder the size of the applet appears in the Document window as shown in Figure 9.27. The applet files should be located in the same folder as the HTML document with the applet statement.

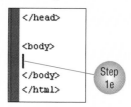

Figure 9.27
Applet Placeholder

If an applet has parameters, they can be modified by selecting the applet to display the Applet Property inspector. Clicking the Parameters button opens the Parameters dialog box, and the parameters and values associated with the applet can be changed using the method described in the "Shockwave" section of this chapter.

---

exercise **5**

INSERTING AND WORKING WITH JAVA APPLETS

1. Insert a Java applet by completing the following steps:
    a. At a clear document screen, create a new HTML document and use the Save or Save As commands to name and save it as **ch9ex05.htm**.
    b. Click File on the Menu bar and then click Open. Use the Open dialog box to locate and select the ch_09_student_files folder, double-click the java_applet folder, and then double-click *tinyhscroll_applet_code.txt* to open the file in the Document window.

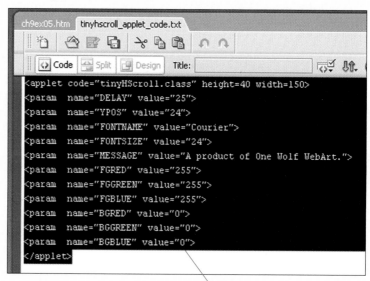

    c. Select and copy the applet code and then close the **tinyhscroll_applet_code.txt** file.
    d. With **ch9ex05.htm** as the current document, click the Code button.
    e. Position the insertion point between the body tags (<body> </body>) and paste the applet code you copied by right-clicking and then clicking Paste.
    f. Click File on the Menu bar and then Save to save **ch9ex05.htm**.

g. Click the Design button. A Java applet placeholder appears at the top of the screen.

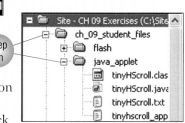

h. Open the Files panel integrated file browser and locate the java_applet folder inside the ch_09_student_files folder. If the folder is not already expanded, click the Plus (+) button next to the java_applet folder to display its contents.

i. Click *tinyHScroll.class*. Hold down the Ctrl key and click *tinyHScroll.java*. Release the Ctrl key after the files are selected. **Hint: Holding down the Ctrl key allows you to select both files at the same time.**

j. Right-click the selected applet files, point to Edit, and then click Copy from the context menu that appears.

k. Select the ch_09_exercises root folder in the Files panel integrated browser, right-click, point to Edit, and then click Paste from the context menu to paste the applet files to the root folder.
Note: You are copying these files because the document containing the applet code (ch9ex05.htm) and the applet files must reside in the same folder. The applet would also work if ch9ex05.htm was saved to the java_applet folder because all of the files would be in the same folder.

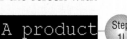

l. Click the Preview/Debug in browser button and then click Preview in iexplore to preview the Web page. A black box should appear at the top of the screen with white text scrolling from right to left across the box.
Close the browser when you are finished.

2. Save **ch9ex05.htm** but do not close it.

exercise 6

ADDING PARAMETERS TO A JAVA APPLET

1. Specify parameters for a Java applet by completing the following steps:
   a. With **ch9ex05.htm** as the current document, use the Save As command to rename and save it as **ch9ex06.htm**.
   b. Click File on the Menu bar and then click Open. Use the Open dialog box to locate and select the ch_09_student_files folder, double-click the java_applet folder, and then double-click *tinyHScroll* to open the file in the Document window.

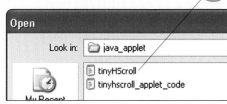

   c. Print a copy of the **tinyHScroll** file by clicking File on the Menu bar, clicking Print Code, and then clicking OK. This file contains instructions about changing the Java applet parameters and adding new ones. Read the instructions and familiarize yourself with the contents. Close the document when you are finished.

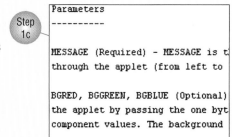

d. With **ch9ex06.htm** as the current document, click the Java applet placeholder to select it and display the Applet Property inspector.

e. Click the Applet Property inspector Parameters button to open the Parameters dialog box.

f. Locate *YPOS* in the *Parameter* column of the Parameters dialog box. Click the value next to the YPOS parameter to select it and type 30 to center the text stream vertically inside the black box.

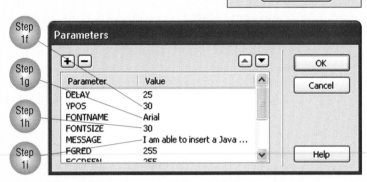

g. Locate *FONTNAME* in the *Parameter* column in the dialog box. Click the value next to the FONTNAME parameter to select it and type Arial to change the font style.

h. Locate *MESSAGE* in the *Parameter* column. Click the value next to the MESSAGE parameter to select it and type I am able to insert a Java applet and modify its parameters. to overwrite the existing text.

i. Locate *FONTSIZE* in the *Parameter* column. Click the value next to the FONTSIZE parameter to select it and type 30 to overwrite the existing number and change the font size. Click the OK button to close the Parameters dialog box.

j. Type 350 in the Applet Property inspector *W* text box to widen the applet black box.

k. Deselect the applet placeholder and then click the Property inspector Align Center button to align the applet to the center of the page.

l. Click the Preview/Debug in browser button and then click Preview in iexplore to preview the Web page. The applet should appear wider and centered on the screen. The message value you typed should appear in the new font style and size you specified. Close the browser when you are finished.

2. Save **ch9ex06.htm** but do not close it.

Parameters

The Insert bar Parameter (Param) command can be used to insert parameters and values one at a time into the code for media content located between embed tags or object tags. The command should be used in Code view or Code and Design view because you need to position the insertion point in the correct location within the code. When you click the Parameter (Param) command, the Tag Editor - Param dialog box shown in Figure 9.28 appears. With *General* selected in the list box, the dialog box displays *Name* and *Value* text boxes. A parameter such as *autoStart* can be typed in the *Name* text box and a corresponding value such as *False* can be typed in the *Value* text box. True and false are the equivalent of on and off, with

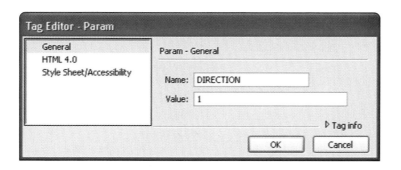

Figure 9.28
Tag Editor - Param Dialog Box

true being on and false being off. An autoStart parameter value of False means that the plugin will not play the specified content automatically when the page it is contained in is loaded.

If you are comfortable entering code directly, you will probably find it much more convenient to type parameters and values directly in Code view or Code and Design view. Because multiple parameters and values can be entered using the Parameters dialog box (accessed through the Property inspector Parameters button), most Dreamweaver MX 2004 users probably will prefer using that method.

exercise 7

USING THE INSERT BAR PARAMETER (PARAM) COMMAND TO INSERT PARAMETERS AND VALUES

1. Use the Insert bar Parameter (Param) command to add a parameter and value to a media object by completing the following steps:

   a. With **ch9ex06.htm** as the current document, use the Save As command to rename and save it as **ch9ex07.htm**.

   b. Select the applet placeholder.

   c. Click the Code button. The applet code is highlighted.

   d. Position the insertion point just after the bracket closing the last parameter and press the Enter key to move the insertion point down one line.

   e. Click the Insert bar (Common menu item or tab) Media button down-pointing arrow and then click the Param (Parameter) command to open the Tag Editor - Param dialog box.

f. Type **DIRECTION** in the *Name* text box and type 1 in the *Value* text box. Click the OK button to close the dialog box. *Note: If you look at the instructions in the tinyHscroll.txt file that you printed, you will see that the applet can take an optional parameter named* **DIRECTION** *that controls the direction that the text scrolls across the black box. This parameter and its value were not included in the applet code that you pasted in ch9ex05.htm, so you are adding them now by using the Tag Editor - Param dialog box. The* **DIRECTION** *parameter and value could also be added using the Parameters dialog box or by entering the code in directly when in Code view.*

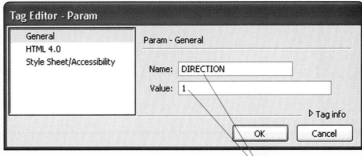

Step 1f

g. Click the Preview/Debug in browser button and then click Preview in iexplore to preview the Web page. The applet text now will scroll from left to right because you specified a value of 1 for the DIRECTION parameter, which the instructions that came with the applet indicated will cause the text to scroll in this direction. Close the browser when you are finished.

h. Click the Design button to return the Document window to Design view.

2. Save **ch9ex07.htm** and then close it.

Plugins

The Insert bar Media button drop-down menu contains commands for inserting ActiveX controls and Netscape-style plugins as shown in Figure 9.29. When ActiveX controls are inserted, there is an option to insert embed tags in addition to the object tags used by the ActiveX control, which increases the chances that viewers will have a browser plugin that can handle the content being inserted.

Clicking the Insert bar ActiveX command causes the Object Tag Accessibility Attributes dialog box to open, which can be used to provide a title, access key, and tab index for the ActiveX control that is being inserted. After the dialog box is closed, an ActiveX placeholder with dimensions of 32 by 32 pixels appears at the insertion point in the document.

The ActiveX Property inspector shown in Figure 9.30 is displayed when you select the placeholder. The *ClassID* text box is used to select or type the name of the ActiveX control that will handle the media object being inserted. Clicking the *ClassID* text box down-pointing arrow displays a list of class IDs. The default Dreamweaver MX 2004 setup *ClassID* text box list contains class IDs for RealPlayer, Shockwave, and Flash. Other class IDs must be typed or pasted in the text box. After a class ID has been entered in the text box, it is added to the drop-down list and ready for future use.

Figure 9.30
ActiveX Property Inspector

A width and height for the ActiveX control can be entered in the *W* and *H* text boxes. If the correct width and height are not known, you must experiment to find the correct dimensions just as you did when using the Insert bar Shockwave button to insert a Shockwave movie. The *Align, V space,* and *H space* boxes perform the same functions as they do in the other media Property inspectors. The Parameters button is used to add parameters and values to the ActiveX control. The parameters and values that can be added depend on the type of ActiveX control being inserted. Common parameters and values for the Windows Media Player that can be entered using the Parameters dialog box are shown in Table 9.2.

The Parameters dialog box should be used to create a fileName parameter and value so that the ActiveX control knows which file to play as shown in Figure 9.31. Other parameters can be entered as desired. For example, entering an autoStart parameter value of False means that the controls for the ActiveX control have to be used to start the media.

The *Base* text box in the ActiveX Property inspector can be used to type or paste in a URL for downloading the specified ActiveX control in the event the control is not already installed in the user's browser. This makes it easy for viewers to download and install the needed ActiveX control if it is missing from their browser.

Table 9.2 • Windows Media Player Parameters and Values

Parameter	Value	Description
autoRewind	*True* or *False*	Specifies whether the media will rewind when finished.
autoStart	*True* or *False*	Specifies whether the media will start when the page is loaded.
balance	*–100–100*	Specifies speaker balance. A value of 0 plays sound equally from a pair of speakers.
clickToPlay	*True* or *False*	Specifies whether the ActiveX will play when clicked.
fileName	Name of file and extension, for example, *movie.mpg*	The file that will be played by the ActiveX control.
loop	*True* or *False*	Specifies whether the movie will loop (repeat).
mute	*True* or *False*	Specifies whether sound will be audible.
playCount	*Number*	The number of times the media will loop (repeat).
showControls	*True* or *False*	Specifies whether controls associated with the ActiveX control will be visible.
transparentAtStart	*True* or *False*	Specifies whether the ActiveX control will be visible.
uimode	*Full, Mini,* or *None*	Specifies the controller appearance.
url	*URL*	Used for streaming media.
volume	*0–100*	Specifies sound volume.

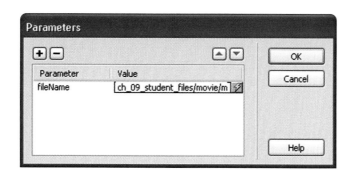

Figure 9.31
Entering a FileName Parameter and Value in the Parameters Dialog Box

The *Data* text box is for the URL of the source file for the media object, but is not required by many ActiveX controls. The *ID* text box is used for scripting purposes and is optional.

The ActiveX Property inspector offers the option of including embed tags to make the object accessible to Netscape users. Placing a check mark in the *Embed* check box automatically enters embed tags within the object tags created for the ActiveX control, and the file path to the content specified by the ActiveX control automatically appears in the *Src* text box. Any parameters and values that were specified for the ActiveX control are repeated between the embed tags. If you look at the code for the ActiveX control as shown in Figure 9.32, you will see the embed tags within the object tag code, along with the source path to the file.

Be sure the *Embed* check box option is enabled. Otherwise Netscape users will be unable to view the media that was inserted because Netscape does not work with plugins inserted using object tags. It is a good idea to enable the *Embed* check box to ensure that as many viewers as possible can access your page content.

The *Alt img* text box Browse for File button can be used to browse and select an image that will be displayed in the event the viewer's browser does not support the ActiveX control. If the *Embed* check box is enabled, this feature will not work.

```
<object classid="CLSID:22d6f312-b0f6-11d0-94ab-0080c74c7e95" codebase="http:/
    <param name="fileName" value="ch_09_student_files/movie/movie.mpg">
    <param name="mute" value="true">
    <param name="autoStart" value="false">
    <param name="autoRewind" value="True">
    <embed src="ch_09_student_files/movie/movie.mpg" width="320" height="290"
    autostart="false" filename="ch_09_student_files/movie/movie.mpg"
    mute="true" autorewind="True"></embed>
```

Figure 9.32
Plugin Code Inside
ActiveX Control Code

embed tag src
file path

Plugin code inside
ActiveX code

exercise **8**

INSERTING AN ACTIVEX CONTROL

1. Use an ActiveX control to embed an MPEG movie by completing the following steps:
   a. At a clear document screen, create a new HTML document and use the Save or Save As commands to name and save it as **ch9ex08.htm**.
   b. Click the Insert bar (Common menu item or tab) Media button down-pointing arrow and then click the ActiveX command.
   c. Type Movie in the Object Tag Accessibility Attributes dialog box *Title* text box, **A** in the *Access key* text box, and 1 in the *Tab index* text box. Click OK to close the dialog box.

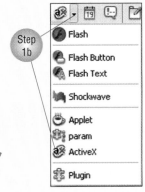

Step 1b

DREAMWEAVER MX 2004

d. In the ActiveX Property inspector, click the *ClassID* text box down-pointing arrow to view the default ActiveX control class IDs. Because class IDs are available for only RealAudio, Shockwave, and Flash in the default Dreamweaver MX 2004 installation, you need to enter the class ID for the Windows Media Player that will be used to play the movie you will be embedding in the document with the ActiveX control. Type CLSID:22d6f312-b0f6-11d0-94ab-0080c74c7e95. *Hint: Type the class ID exactly as it is printed here, being careful to enter lowercase and uppercase characters as required.*

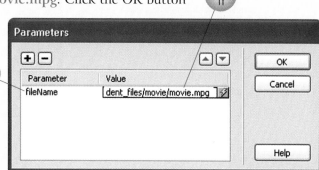

e. Click the ActiveX Property inspector Parameters button to open the Parameters dialog box. Click the Plus (+) button and type fileName in the space just below *Parameter*.

f. Click in the space just below *Value* and type ch_09_student_files/movie/movie.mpg. Click the OK button to close the dialog box *Hint: Whenever you type the file path that will be played by the ActiveX control, you must be sure to enter the correct file path or the ActiveX control will not be able to locate the file.*

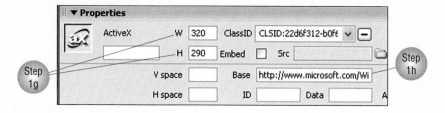

g. Type 320 in the ActiveX Property inspector *W* text box, and 290 in the *H* text box.

h. Type http://www.microsoft.com/Windows/Downloads/Contents/MediaPlayer/ in the *Base* text box.

i. Click the *Embed* check box to place a check mark in it.

j. The correct path to the **movie.mpg** file should appear in the *Src* text box. If it does not, click the *Src* text box Browse for File button to open the Select Netscape Plug-In File dialog box. Use the dialog box to browse and locate the **movie.mpg** file in the movie subfolder of the ch_09_student_files folder. Click the file to place it in the *File name* text box and then click the OK button to close the dialog box.

k. Click the Preview/Debug in browser button and then click Preview in iexplore to preview the Web page. If you are using a recent version of Internet Explorer, the Windows Media Player should appear and the movie should start and play by itself. Close the browser when you are finished.

2. Save **ch9ex08.htm** but do not close it.

1. Add parameters to an ActiveX control by completing the following steps:

   a. With **ch9ex08.htm** open in the Document window, use the Save As command to rename and save it as **ch9ex09.htm**.

   b. Click the ActiveX placeholder to select it.

   c. Click the ActiveX Property inspector Parameters button to open the Parameters dialog box.

   d. Click the Parameters dialog box Plus (+) button. Type mute in the *Parameter* column and then type True in the *Value* column.

   e. Click the Plus (+) button again and type autoStart in the *Parameter* column and type False in the *Value* column.

   f. Click the Plus (+) button again and type autoRewind in the *Parameter* column and type True in the *Value* column. Click OK to close the dialog box.

   g. Click the Preview/Debug in browser button and then click Preview in iexplore to preview the Web page. The Windows Media Player appears, but it does not play automatically. To play the movie, click the right-pointing arrow in the lower-left corner of the player. The movie plays, but the sound is muted because you added this parameter and specified a value of True. The player shows the speaker icon covered by a green prohibited sign to show that the movie sound has been muted, or turned off. Clicking the prohibited sign restores the sound. When the movie finishes, it rewinds to the beginning, reflecting the autoRewind parameter and corresponding True value you specified. Close the browser when you are finished.

2. Save **ch9ex09.htm** and then close it.

Adding Audio (Sound) to Web Pages

A number of different audio file formats are available for Internet use, including .aif, .mid, .midi, .mp2, .mp3, and .wav files. The ability of a user's browser to handle audio varies greatly and depends on a number of different variables, including the plugins installed in the browser, whether or not the computer is equipped with a sound card and the type of sound card installed, whether or not sound settings are enabled, whether it has speakers, and so on. The huge number of variables means that it is highly likely that some viewers will not be able to enjoy audio on your Web pages.

A drawback to embedding audio in Web pages is that many people find background audio intrusive, so it should be used only in the appropriate circumstances, perhaps related to a Web page theme. For example, a page on the old West might feature a country music theme. In many cases, it might be preferable to add a link to an audio file so that your viewers can determine whether or not they want to hear the audio.

Although there are many different ways to embed sound files on Web pages, using a plugin is one of the simpler and more effective ways. For instance, the plugin can be made invisible so that it will not be seen in the viewer's browser. When a plugin is selected, the Plugins Property inspector is displayed as shown in Figure 9.33.

Figure 9.33
Plugins Property Inspector

USING A PLUGIN TO ADD AUDIO TO A WEB PAGE

1. Add background music to a Web page by completing the following steps:
   a. At a clear document screen, create a new HTML document and use the Save or Save As commands to name and save it as **ch9ex10.htm**.
   b. Click the Insert bar (Common menu item or tab) Media button down-pointing arrow and then click the Plugin command.
   c. Use the Select File dialog box to browse and locate the student file named **sweet_dreams.wav** in the wav subfolder of the ch_09_student files folder. Click the file to place it in the *File name* text box and then click the OK button to close the dialog box.
   d. If necessary, click the plugin placeholder to select it and click the Parameters button in the Plugins Property inspector.
   e. Click the Plus (+) button, and then type autoStart in the *Parameter* column and type True in the *Value* column.
   f. Repeat Step 1e to type the following parameters and values:
      1) Type Loop and True.
      2) Type Hidden and True. Click the OK button to close the dialog box when you are finished.

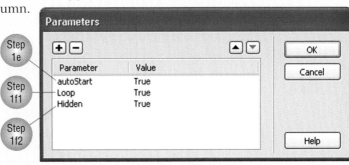

g. Type 2 in the Plugin Property inspector *W* and *H* text boxes. ***Note: Some older browser versions ignore the hidden parameter and value, so changing the width and height values to 2 ensures that if the browser ignores the hidden parameter, the plugin will still be invisible or barely visible.***

h. Click the Preview/Debug in browser button and then click Preview in iexplore to preview the page. The music in the .wav file should play in the background. ***Note: As noted earlier in the "Adding Audio (Sound) to Web Pages" section, a number of different factors can prevent an audio file from playing. If you do not hear any music, check to see that the computer has a sound card and speakers installed and that the browser has the correct plugin to deal with .wav files.*** Close the browser when you are finished.

2. Save **ch9ex10.htm** and then close it.

CHAPTER summary

➤ In the Web context, multimedia generally refers to the use of media beyond text and images, such as video, audio, animated graphics, and even hypertext.

➤ The use of multimedia in Web pages can provide viewers with an enhanced viewing experience, but there is also a danger of overwhelming viewers with too much multimedia.

➤ When designing Web pages, carefully consider why multimedia is being used and whether it will enhance the viewer experience or needlessly complicate it.

➤ Web browsers are HTML interpreters, and they must look for assistance in displaying content other than text or images through the use of programs that work within the browser to display different media, the use of stand-alone programs known as helper applications, or the use of ActiveX controls and Netscape-style plugins.

➤ JavaScript enables a browser to change page content dynamically in response to viewer input. Mouseover events/actions and form validation are two examples of the types of interactive functions that JavaScript can enable.

➤ JavaScript has been combined with HTML and CSS-P to create DHTML, which is used to create behaviors in Dreamweaver MX 2004.

➤ Java applets are small applications (programs) that can run inside a browser window. Java applets can be used to provide interactive experiences that include audio and video.

➤ Helper applications are stand-alone programs that browsers can call on to display different media content.

➤ Whenever a browser encounters a file, it looks at its file extension to determine its MIME (Multipurpose Internet Mail Extension) type.

➤ If a file is a MIME type that the browser cannot display on its own, it must look for a helper application that can be used to display the file content.

➤ Plugins are small programs that extend the capability of browsers in dealing with different types of media; they differ from helper applications in that they are not stand-alone programs.

➤ Plugins reside in a browser's Plugins folder located inside the browser's application folder, where they can be called on when needed.

➤ Because even the same browser versions can be configured to handle plugins differently, it is difficult to predict exactly how a browser might deal with a given media type.

➤ Browsers come with plugins already installed, and new plugins can be downloaded to a browser's Plugins folder when needed.

➤ The two most common browser plugin types are Netscape-style plugins and ActiveX controls.

➤ Netscape-style plugins use the embed tag (<embed>) to insert media and JavaScript for communication, while ActiveX uses the object tag (<object>) and VBScript for communication.

➤ When Internet Explorer encounters an embed tag, it looks for an ActiveX control to handle the content indicated by the tag. If an ActiveX control to handle the content cannot be found, the content will not be displayed.

➤ If a browser cannot find the correct plugin, the viewer will be looking at a blank screen, a static placeholder image, or a message advising that the needed plugin cannot be found.

➤ One way to avoid the problem of missing plugins is to specify a URL where a copy of the needed plugin can be found and downloaded.

➤ Dreamweaver MX 2004 inserts some media, such as Shockwave or Flash movies, using both Netscape plugin tags (embed tags) and ActiveX tags (object tags). When this is done, Internet Explorer uses the ActiveX control specified by the object tag, while Netscape browsers ignore the ActiveX control and look for the plugin needed to display the object inserted in the page using embed tags.

➤ To ensure that the content you are adding to your pages will be accessible to your viewers, preview the pages in as many browser versions as you can.

➤ It is a good idea to offer alternatives for viewers who might not be able to take advantage of content requiring plugins, such as a link to similar material in a different format or an explanation of what the plugin content contains.

➤ When movies and animations are inserted within Dreamweaver MX 2004 documents, the Property inspector displays a Play button, which can be clicked to play the media so that it can be previewed within the Dreamweaver MX 2004 environment.

➤ Dreamweaver MX 2004 uses Netscape-style plugins for previewing. When the Play button is selected, Dreamweaver MX 2004 first looks for the appropriate Netscape-style plugin in its Plugins folder. If the appropriate plugin cannot be found, Dreamweaver MX 2004 then searches the Plugins folders of all of the browsers installed on the computer. If a movie or animation relies exclusively on an ActiveX control, it will not be previewable within Dreamweaver MX 2004.

➤ If Internet Explorer is the only browser installed on your computer, you will not be able to preview movies and animations in Dreamweaver MX 2004 because Internet Explorer uses ActiveX controls. There are two solutions to this problem: installing a copy of the latest Netscape browser on your computer so that Dreamweaver MX 2004 can search for and use the Netscape-style plugins that come with that program, or downloading needed plugins and copying their class file to the Dreamweaver MX 2004 Plugins folder.

- Dreamweaver MX 2004 makes it easy for you to insert and work with multimedia by offering an Insert bar Media button (Common menu item or tab) featuring commands for inserting some of the most popular media types.

- The Insert bar can be used to insert Flash movies, Flash buttons, Flash text, Shockwave content, Java applets, ActiveX controls, plugins, and parameters and values.

- When media is inserted in a document, it is represented by a placeholder.

- Selecting media in the Document window changes the Property inspector display to reflect the different content properties.

- When a Flash movie is inserted, Dreamweaver MX 2004 automatically determines the dimensions of the movie and enters them in the width and height text boxes.

- Flash files cannot be edited in their .swf format, but clicking the Flash Property inspector Edit button opens Flash and allows you to edit the Flash file source document with the .fla extension if it is available on the computer.

- The Property inspector Parameters button can be used to specify parameters and values for selected media content.

- Flash buttons function somewhat like rollover images in that they have two states, but they differ from rollover images in that they can display animation when clicked.

- Flash buttons also can be linked to another URL so that they can function as a hyperlink.

- Flash text can be used to insert text into Web pages in font styles and sizes that could not be displayed using the fonts normally available to a browser.

- Flash text cannot be edited like normal HTML text because it is actually a Flash movie inserted using object tags.

- Flash text can be edited by double-clicking the text, which causes the Insert Flash Text dialog box to open.

- Text or objects inserted next to Flash text will be affected as they would when inserted next to an image, with text or objects appearing with baseline alignment by default.

- Because Flash text is a Flash movie, the Flash Text Property inspector is almost identical to the Flash Button Property inspector, lacking only the *Loop* and *Autoplay* check boxes.

- Shockwave plugins exist in both Netscape-style plugin and ActiveX control form, so Dreamweaver MX 2004 inserts Shockwave movies using both embed tags and object tags.

- Dreamweaver MX 2004 cannot determine the correct dimensions of the Shockwave movie automatically, so the correct dimensions must be entered in the Shockwave Property inspector *W* and *H* text boxes. If the dimensions are not known, you can experiment until you find the correct dimensions by entering estimated dimensions in the *W* and *H* text boxes.

- Java applets can be composed of a number of different files, but all applets contain at least one class file, identified by its .class extension.

- Applet code, known as a statement or instruction, is placed within the body tags of an HTML document. It contains information calling for the applet class files, and defines the applet parameters.

➤ Many applets are available on the Internet free or for a small fee, and are usually available by downloading a zipped (compressed) file containing all of the files necessary for the applet.

➤ Applets usually come with directions describing how the applet is to be installed. Follow the directions carefully, because the slightest variance from the instructions can cause an applet to fail.

➤ In most cases, it is much easier to follow the directions that come with the applet and copy and paste the supplied applet code into the body section of an HTML document than to use the Applet button.

➤ Applet files should be located in the same folder as the HTML document with the applet statement.

➤ The Insert bar Parameter (Param) button can be used to insert parameters and values one at a time into the code for media content located between embed tags or object tags.

➤ If you are comfortable entering code directly, you will probably find it much more convenient to type parameters and values directly in Code view, or enter them by using the Property inspector's Parameters button.

➤ The ActiveX Property inspector *ClassID* text box is used to select or type the name of the ActiveX control that will handle the media object being inserted.

➤ The ActiveX Property inspector Parameters button should be used to open the Parameters dialog box to create a fileName parameter and value so that the ActiveX control knows which file to play.

➤ The ActiveX Property inspector *Base* text box can be used to type or paste a URL for downloading the specified ActiveX control in the event the control is not already installed in the user's browser.

➤ The ActiveX Property inspector offers the option of including embed tags to make the object accessible to Netscape users.

➤ A number of different audio file formats are available for Internet use, including .aif, .mid, .midi, .mp2, .mp3, and .wav files.

➤ The ability of a user's browser to handle audio varies greatly, and depends on a number of different variables, including the plugins installed in the browser, whether or not the computer is equipped with a sound card, the type of sound card installed, whether or not sound settings are enabled, and so on.

➤ A drawback to embedding audio in Web pages is that many people find this intrusive, so it should be used only in the appropriate circumstances, perhaps related to a Web page theme.

➤ In many cases, it might be preferable to add a link to an audio file so that your viewers can determine whether or not they want to hear the audio.

➤ There are many different ways to embed sound files on Web pages, but using a plugin is one of the simpler and more effective ways. The plugin can be made invisible so that it will not be seen in the viewer's browser.

ActiveX controls A plugin type developed by Microsoft and embedded in documents using object tags.

applets Small applications (programs) that can run inside a browser window to provide an interactive experience, including audio and video.

dynamic HTML (DHTML) A combination of JavaScript, HTML, and CSS-P used to create behaviors in Dreamweaver MX 2004.

embed tag The HTML tag (<embed>) used to embed Netscape-style plugins.

Flash buttons Interactive buttons that function somewhat like rollover images, but with the ability to display animation when clicked. They also can be linked to other documents.

Flash MX 2004 The latest version of the Flash program, and part of the Macromedia suite of programs that includes Dreamweaver MX 2004. Flash MX 2004 can be used to create videos, interactive animations, and other types of rich Internet applications.

Flash text Special text created in a Flash movie format. Flash text can be used to insert text into Web pages in font sizes that could not be displayed using the fonts normally available in a browser.

helper applications Stand-alone programs that browsers can call on to display different media types.

HTML interpreters The function of Web browsers, meaning that their job is to interpret and display the HTML code contained in Web page documents.

Java applets Applets are small applications (programs) that can run inside a browser window. They can be used to provide an interactive experience, including audio and video.

JavaScript A scripting programming language that resides within an HTML document. The use of JavaScript enables a browser to dynamically change page content in response to viewer input.

MIME (Multipurpose Internet Mail Extension) Each file has an extension that indicates its MIME type and determines how it will be displayed by a browser.

Netscape-style plugins A plugin type developed by Netscape and embedded in documents using embed tags.

object tag The HTML tag (<object>) used to embed ActiveX controls.

parameters Characteristics such as color, width, file name, and so on.

plugins Small programs that extend the capability of browsers in dealing with different types of media. They differ from helper applications in that they are not stand-alone programs like Microsoft Word or Adobe Acrobat.

Plugins folder The browser folder where plugins are stored.

Shockwave A Macromedia movie and animation file format.

values These define parameters, such as **blue** for a color parameter, **hello.gif** for a file name parameter, and so on.

| Insert media | Insert, Media, select media type |

Indicate the correct term or command for each item.

1. Browsers can display this type of document content without the assistance of other programs.
2. This is another name for an HTML interpreter.
3. This is a scripted programming language that resides within an HTML document and is used to change page content dynamically in response to user input.
4. Dynamic HTML (DHTML) is created using these three components.
5. This is the name for small programs that run inside the browser window to create interactive video and audio experiences.
6. This is the term used to describe stand-alone programs that browsers can call on to display different media types.
7. Browsers determine this by looking at a file's extension.
8. These are small programs that extend the capability of browsers in dealing with different types of media.
9. This is the HTML tag used to insert ActiveX controls.
10. This is the HTML tag used to insert plugins.
11. This is the plugin developed by Microsoft and used by its Internet Explorer browser.
12. This is the name of the folder used by browsers to store plugins.
13. This is the file extension used by Flash content.
14. Shockwave content uses this file extension.
15. Dreamweaver MX 2004 uses these tags to insert Flash and Shockwave content automatically in documents.
16. Dreamweaver MX 2004 uses this kind of plugin for previewing movies and animations within the Dreamweaver MX 2004 environment.
17. This Flash Property inspector check box should be checked if you want a Flash movie or animation to repeat.
18. Clicking this Property inspector button allows Dreamweaver MX 2004 users to change or add parameters to media content.
19. Click this button on the Insert bar to view media commands.
20. This scripting language is used by plugins to communicate with the browser.

SKILLS check

Use the Site Definition dialog box to create a separate Dreamweaver site named CH 09 Assessments to keep your assessment work for this chapter. Save the files for the site in a new root folder named ch_09_assessments under the Sites folder you created in Chapter 1, Exercise 3. Download the ch_09_student_files folder from the IRC to the CH 09 Assessments site root folder (ch_09_assessments) and expand it. Delete the compressed folder when you are finished.

Assessment 1 • Create Flash Buttons

1. Create a new HTML document and use the Save or Save As commands to name and save it as **ch9sa1.htm**.
2. Change the page background color to *#FFFFCC*.
3. Create a set of three different Flash buttons, arranged vertically on the left side of the document, with specifications as noted in the following steps. ***Hint: To arrange the buttons vertically, close the Insert Flash Button dialog box after creating a button, press the Enter key to move down the insertion point, and then reopen the Insert Flash Button dialog box to create the next button.***
   a. Specify the *Blip Arrow* button style.
   b. Create button text of your choosing by typing a name for the button in the *Button text* text box. The button name should be related to the document it will be linked to in the upcoming Step 3e. For example, if you link to the file named **link-1.htm**, you could name the button *link-1.htm*.
   c. Specify the *Arial* font style.
   d. Specify a font size of *16*.
   e. Create links from the buttons to the student files named **link-1.htm**, **link-2.htm**, and **link-3.htm**. ***Hint: Make sure you create links to the files in the ch_09_student_files folder located in the ch_09_assessments folder.***
   f. Specify *_parent* as the target window.
   g. Match the button background color to the page background color.
   h. Use the Insert Flash Button dialog box *Save as* text box to provide a name for each button that helps identify its function. For example, if you link it to the file named **link-1.htm**, you could name it *link-1.swf*.
   i. Use the Flash Accessibility Attributes dialog box that appears after each button is created to provide a name, access key letter, and tab index number for each button. For example, the first button could be named *Button link to link-1.htm*, with an access key letter of *A* and a tab index of *1*.
   j. Preview to ensure that the buttons link properly. ***Hint: If the Flash button links do not work when you preview them, use the Parameters dialog box to remove the base parameter for each button.***
4. Save **ch9sa1.htm** and then close it.

Assessment 2 • Create Flash Text

1. Open **ch9sa1.htm** and use the Save As command to rename and save it as **ch9sa2.htm**.
2. Position the insertion point to the left of the first Flash button and press Enter twice to move the buttons down the document.
3. Position the insertion point in the upper-left corner of the document above the first Flash button.

DREAMWEAVER MX 2004

4. Create a Flash text headline of your choosing using the following specifications:
   a. Specify the *Arial* font style.
   b. Specify a font size of *60*.
   c. Specify a text color of *#660000*.
   d. Specify a rollover color of *#CC9900*.
   e. Link the Flash text headline to an external URL of your choosing. **Hint: *You must type an absolute path (the complete URL) for the external link.***
   f. Specify *_parent* as the target window.
   g. Match the button background color to the page background color.
   h. Use the Insert Flash Button dialog box *Save as* text box to provide a name for the headline that helps identify its function, such as *headline.swf*.
   i. Use the Flash Accessibility Attributes dialog box that appears after the Flash text is created to provide a name, access key letter, and tab index number for the headline. For example, the Flash text could be named *Headline.* Choose an access key letter and a tab index number that have not already been used for the Flash buttons you created in Assessment 1.
   j. Center the Flash text headline on the page.
   k. Preview to ensure that the Flash text effects and link work properly.
5. Save **ch9sa2.htm** and then close it.

Assessment 3 • Modify Applet Parameters and Values

1. Create a new HTML document and use the Save or Save As commands to name and save it as **ch9sa3.htm**.
2. Change the background color of the page to black *(#000000)*.
3. Follow Exercise 5, Steps 1b–1k to insert a Java applet. For Step 1k, paste the two applet files in the ch_09_assessments folder.
4. Change the applet parameter values as specified here:
   a. Change the FONTNAME parameter value to *Arial*.
   b. Change the FONTSIZE parameter value to *30*.
   c. Type Scrolling text with animated gif butterfly image. as the MESSAGE parameter value. Click the Parameters dialog box OK button when you are finished.
5. Copy the student file named **butterfly.gif** from the ch_09_student_files folder and place the copy in the ch_09_assessments root folder. *Note: The file must be in the same folder as the document and all of the files related to the applet.*
6. Create a parameter named BACKGROUND with a value of **butterfly.gif**.
7. Change the applet width and height to *225* pixels.
8. Center the applet on the page.
9. Preview the applet in a browser to ensure that it works.
10. Save **ch9sa3.htm** and then close it.

Assessment 4 • Download a Java Applet and Insert It in a Document

1. Create a new HTML document and use the Save or Save As commands to name and save it as **ch9sa4.htm**.
2. Log on to the Web and go to a site offering free Java applets, such as www.javaboutique.internet.com, www.javapowered.com, or www.javafile.com.
3. Find an applet that you like and follow the instructions on the page to download it to your ch_09_assessments root folder. Most applet files are compressed and will have a .zip extension. You need a special program to unzip the files before they can be used. The Web pages offering free applets usually have a link to a free program that can be used to unzip the files, such

as PKUNZIP. If the computer you are working on cannot unzip the file, download and install a program that can do that. ***Hint: Some sites require you to copy the applet code from a Web page so that you can paste it in your document, while others include the applet code in one of the documents included in the downloaded files. Read the instructions carefully so that you know where to find the applet code.***

4. Follow the directions for the applet to insert it into **ch9sa4.htm**. Test the applet by viewing it in a browser to determine whether it works. Remember that all of the applet files and the document with the applet code should be in the same folder.
5. Save **ch9sa4.htm** and then close it.

Assessment 5 • Insert Flash Content in a Document

1. Create a new HTML document and use the Save or Save As commands to name and save it as **ch9sa5.htm**.
2. Log on to the Web and go to a site offering free Flash content, such as www.weaselcircus.com/freecontent.shtml or www.webdevstore.com/freebies/free_games.htm.
3. Find Flash content that you like and follow the instructions on the page to download it to your ch_09_assessments root folder. Most of the Flash files are compressed and will have a .zip extension. You will need to unzip them using the same kind of program you used to unzip the Java applet material in Assessment 4.
4. Follow the directions for the Flash content to insert it into **ch9sa5.htm**. Preview the Flash content in a browser to determine whether it works.
5. Save **ch9sa5.htm** and then close it.

Assessment 6 • Insert a Movie Using an ActiveX Control and Plugin

1. Create a new HTML document and use the Save or Save As commands to name and save it as **ch9sa6.htm**.
2. Create an Active X plugin and specify the following parameters and values:
   a. Parameter: *fileName*   Value: *ch_09_student_files/movie/electra.mpeg*
   b. Parameter: *autoStart*   Value: *False*
3. Select the Windows Media Player class ID *(CLSID:22d6f312-b0f6-11d0-94ab-0080c74c7e95).*
4. Click the *Embed* check box option to insert plugin code within the ActiveX code.
5. Type 320 in the ActiveX Property inspector *W* text box, and 290 in the *H* text box.
6. Click the Preview/Debug in browser button and then iexplore to see that a media player appears and that the movie plays when the Play button is clicked. ***Note: The movie does not have a soundtrack.***
7. Save **ch9sa6.htm** and then close it.

Assessment 7 • Add Multimedia Items to Your Design Portfolio

Save all documents created in this assessment in the design_portfolio root folder of your Design Portfolio site.

1. Use the skills you have learned in this chapter to add some examples of multimedia content to your design portfolio Web site. Include at least one Java applet, one Flash movie, and some Flash text.

DREAMWEAVER MX 2004

CREATING FORMS

PERFORMANCE OBJECTIVES

➤ Understand forms and form objects.

➤ Create forms and insert a table inside a form.

➤ Create single-line, multiple-line, and password text fields.

➤ Create hidden fields.

➤ Create check boxes.

➤ Create radio buttons and radio button groups.

➤ Create menus.

➤ Create lists.

➤ Create jump menus.

➤ Use the image field form object to create graphical form buttons.

➤ Insert a file field for file uploading.

➤ Create form Submit and Reset buttons.

➤ Attach Validate Form behaviors to forms and form objects.

The student files for this chapter are available for download from the Internet Resource Center at www.emcp.com.

Forms help create a truly interactive Internet experience by allowing visitors to communicate with Web site owners. You have already used forms on Web pages if you have ever filled out an online survey, made a comment in a Web page guest book, or ordered products from a Web site.

Most forms contain a combination of different form controls, or form objects as they are called in Dreamweaver MX 2004, such as text boxes, check boxes, radio buttons, menus, and lists. Text boxes can be created to let those submitting forms provide open-ended answers, while radio buttons, check boxes, menus, and lists can be used to provide more structured answers.

In this chapter, you will learn how to use Dreamweaver MX 2004 Menu bar commands and Insert bar buttons to create forms. You also will learn how to attach behaviors to your forms and/or form objects so that the information they contain can be validated before being submitted. These behaviors are known as client-side scripts because they are created using a scripting language contained in the HTML document and executed by the user's browser instead of a server.

Processing the data in completed forms requires the use of scripts such as CGI (Common Gateway Interface). These scripts are located on a server and are known as server-side scripts. The server-side script you use, and how it should be used, must be determined in consultation with the administrator of the server that will be used to host your Web site.

Understanding Forms

Forms are created in HTML documents using paired *form tags* (<form>) as shown in Figure 10.1. The form tags define the form and contain the form objects that form users will use to input data. Table 10.1 shows the seven possible attributes that form tags can use to provide instructions on how the form data is to be processed.

After a form has been created, *input tags* (<input>) are used to insert form objects within the area defined by the form tags. Input tags contain type attributes that indicate the type of form object being inserted, such as `type="file"` or `type="checkbox"`. The different form objects that can be created are shown in Figure 10.2.

A *Submit button* must be added to the form so that users can submit the form for processing when they are finished. You also should include a *Reset button* that can be used to reset the form if the user wants to start over again.

Figure 10.1
Form Code

```
<form name="form1" method="post" action="">
    <label for="textfield">Name</label>
    <input type="text" name="textfield" accesskey="A" tabindex="1" id="textfield">
</form>
```

Table 10.1 • Form Tag Attributes

Attribute	Function
`accept`	Specifies allowable file types for uploading when using the file input control.
`accept-charset`	Tells the server which character sets it must accept from a client form.
`action`	Specifies the URL that will direct the form to a CGI program or to an HTML page containing server-side scripts.
`enctype`	Specifies a MIME type for the data being submitted with the form.
`method`	Specifies whether a form will be submitted using GET or POST methods. The GET method has been deprecated, and the POST method is recommended. The POST method is also more secure than the GET method.
`name`	Specifies a name for the form element. This name is used when writing scripts that refer to the form or its controls.
`target`	Specifies the window that an HTML document with form results will be loaded in. The default setting returns the document to the window containing the form.

DREAMWEAVER MX 2004

When a form is submitted, the user's browser gathers the form answers and uses the URL specified in the form tag **action** *attribute* to send them to the server for processing by a server-side script. After the answers are processed, most scripts specify that an acknowledgment page be returned and opened in the browser window specified by the form tag **target** *attribute*.

Planning Forms

Before you create a form, you should consider several factors. Careful planning before you begin creating a form will save a lot of time later on and will help ensure that your form gathers the information you are looking for.

Questions should be phrased as clearly as possible to avoid ambiguity or confusion, and the choices for answering a question should be appropriate to the question being asked. For example, yes/no questions should use a radio button group so that users can select only *Yes* or *No,* not both *Yes* and *No.* If you are asking users to select an answer from a group of possible answers, make sure that the answers reflect all of the possible choices. For example, the form object list or menu for a question asking users to select the state they live in should let users choose from all 50 states.

Labels for form objects should be clear. For example, if you want users to provide their first and last name in the same text box, the text box should be labeled *Full Name* or *First and Last Names.* If the text box is labeled *Name,* some users might provide their first name, some their last name, and others their full name.

Forms should be designed so that users will not be confused about which questions relate to which form objects. One method for creating neat forms is to use tables, as shown in Figure 10.3. Placing a table inside a form allows you to control the design and create an attractive and easy-to-follow form.

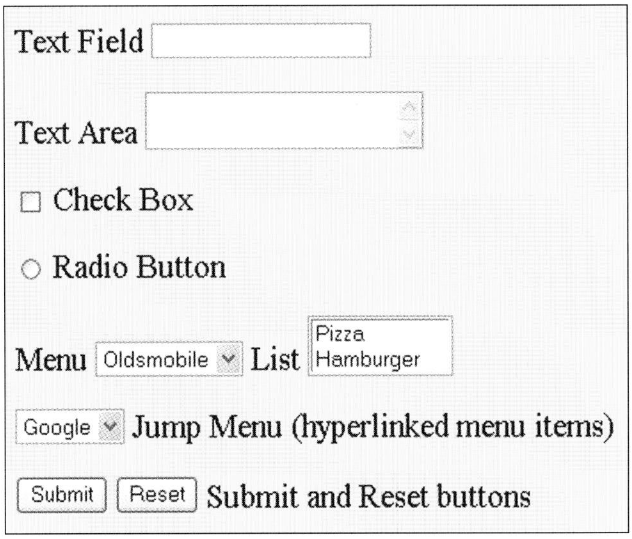

Figure 10.2 • Form Objects

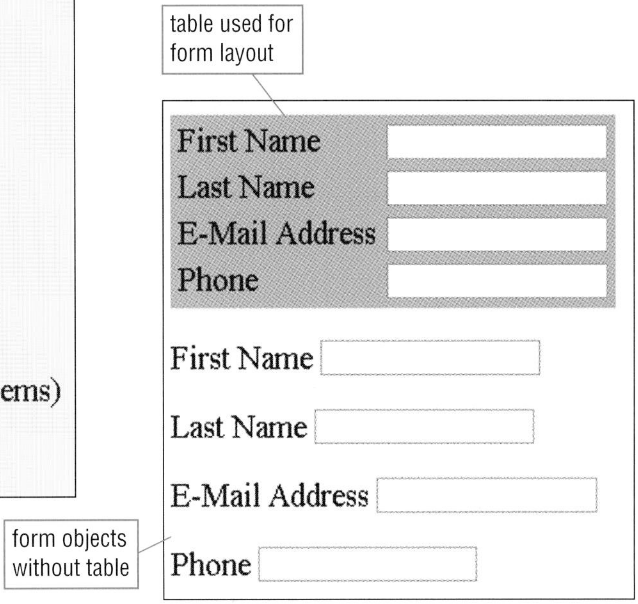

Figure 10.3 • Form Layout with and without a Table

Clearly state the purpose of the questions and consider including a privacy statement as shown in Figure 10.4 to let users know that you will not abuse the information they are providing.

Instructions on how to complete the form should be clear and easy to understand. Never assume that the people completing your forms already know how to complete them.

Finally, before a form is uploaded to a Web site, it should be tested by having other people fill it out. Testing a form is a good way to make sure that other users will understand your form and that the form will elicit the information you are seeking.

Creating Forms

You can use Menu bar commands and Insert bar buttons to create forms and insert form objects. Clicking Insert on the Menu bar and then pointing to Form opens a submenu that displays form and form object commands as shown in Figure 10.5.

The Insert bar buttons shown in Figure 10.6 also can be used to insert forms and form objects when the Insert bar Forms menu item or tab has been selected. You can either click Insert bar buttons to insert a form or form object at the insertion point, or click and drag a button to the desired location in a document.

After the insertion point has been positioned in the desired location, a form can be inserted by clicking Insert on the Menu bar, pointing to Form, and then clicking Form from the submenu; by clicking the Insert bar Forms menu item or tab and then clicking the Form button; or by clicking and dragging the Insert bar Form button to the desired location.

Dotted red lines represent the form borders as shown in Figure 10.7. If the borders are not visible, click View options on the Document toolbar, point to Visual Aids, and then make sure that there is a check mark beside Invisible Elements in the menu that appears.

After a form has been inserted, the form can be selected by clicking its border. The Property inspector then displays form properties as shown in Figure 10.8. A default name appears in the Form Property inspector *Form name* text box. This name is used for identification purposes with scripting languages. If you create a

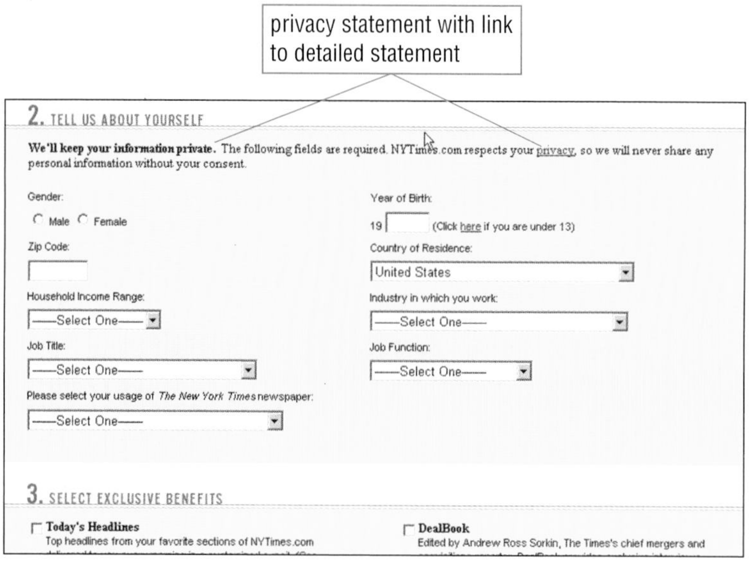

Figure 10.4
Form with Privacy Statement

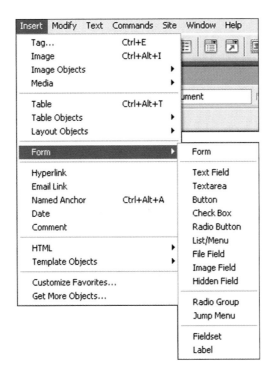

Figure 10.5
Form Menu Bar Commands

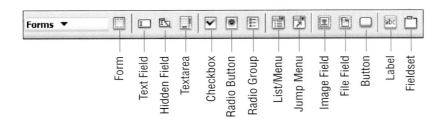

Figure 10.6
Insert Bar Form and Form Objects Buttons (Forms Menu Item or Tab)

Figure 10.7
Form Border

Figure 10.8
Form Property Inspector

new name by typing over the old one, do not use spaces or special characters. Try to create names that will help you identify the form or form object. Some scripting languages have reserved words that cannot be used when naming forms or form objects. If you know which scripting language will be used in conjunction with your form, you can check to make sure that you do not use any of the script's reserved words.

The Form Property inspector *Action* text box is used to specify the path to the dynamic page or script that will be used to process the form. You can leave this text box blank until you know the details about which scripts your Web host supports.

The *Method* text box is used to specify the method for transmitting form data, *GET, POST,* or *Default*. The method you choose (**GET method** or **POST method**) might be determined by the server that will be hosting your form pages, so you will need to research that information when you are choosing a Web host. The GET method should not be used for long forms or for confidential data such as credit card numbers or passwords. The GET method has been deprecated by the W3W, but it is still widely used. The default method setting *(Default)* allows a browser to use its default setting for transmitting form data, which is usually the GET method.

The *Enctype* text box is used to specify a MIME type for data submitted for processing. The default setting is *application/x-www-form-urlencode* and is usually used with the POST method. When you use a file upload form object, you should select *multipart/form-data*.

The *Target* text box selects the window that will be used to display data returned by the server processing the form. The target names have the same function as they do in the other Property inspectors, such as *_blank* to open a document in a new browser window.

A table can be inserted inside a form by positioning the insertion point inside the form and then clicking the Insert bar (Common menu item or tab) Table button. Using a table affords better control over form layout and design.

If a form object is inserted outside a form, a message appears asking if you want to add a form tag as shown in Figure 10.9. For best results, form objects should always be contained inside form tags, so clicking the Yes button in the message box is recommended.

Figure 10.9
Add Form Tag Message Box

CREATING A FORM AND INSERTING A TABLE INSIDE A FORM

1. If necessary, start Dreamweaver MX 2004.
2. At a clear document screen, create a new site named CH 10 Exercises to store the exercises you create in this chapter. Name the root folder ch_10_exercises and save it under the Sites folder you created in Chapter 1, Exercise 3. Download the ch_10_student_files folder from the IRC to the CH 10 Exercises site root folder (ch_10_exercises) and expand it. Delete the compressed folder when you are finished. *Note: Refer to Chapter 1 for instructions on navigating with the Files panel integrated file browser.*
3. Create a form and insert a table inside the form by completing the following steps:
   a. Open the student file named **form_doc.htm**. Click File on the Menu bar and then click Save As to rename the document **ch10ex01.htm** and save it to the ch_10_exercises root folder.

b. Position the insertion point after the last line of the paragraph and press Enter to move the insertion point below the paragraph.

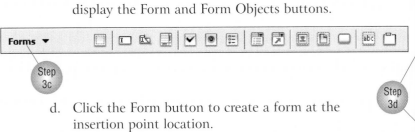

Step 3b

c. Click the Insert bar Forms menu item or tab to display the Form and Form Objects buttons.

Step 3c

d. Click the Form button to create a form at the insertion point location.

e. Click the Insert bar Common menu item or tab and then click the Table button to open the Table dialog box.

Step 3d

Please fill out this survey to the b
text box and typing. Radio butto
radio button, or by clicking direct
bottom of the page. When you a
not be released to third parties.

Step 3e

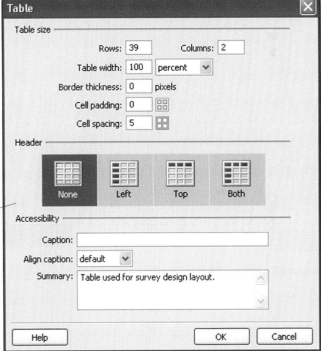

f. Enter the following values in the Table dialog box:
1) *Rows:* 39
2) *Columns:* 2
3) *Table width:* 100 *percent*
4) *Border thickness:* 0
5) *Cell padding:* 0
6) *Cell spacing:* 5
7) Click the None button in the *Header* section.
8) Type **Table used for survey design layout.** in the *Summary* text box. Click the OK button to close the dialog box. ***Hint: Leave the* Caption *text box blank since this table does not need a caption. The* Align caption *list box should display* default.**

Steps 3f1–3f8

g. Click the insertion point anywhere outside the table. Note that the table is outlined by dotted red lines, showing that it is contained inside the form.

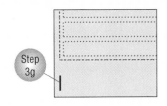

Step 3g

4. Save **ch10ex01.htm** but do not close it.

Creating Text Fields

Text fields allow form users to enter ***alphanumeric*** (letters and/or numbers) data in a text box as shown in Figure 10.10. A text field can be inserted in a form by clicking Insert on the Menu bar, pointing to Form, and then clicking Text Field, or by clicking the Insert bar (Forms menu item or tab) Text Field button.

When a form object is inserted, the Input Tag Accessibility Attributes dialog box appears, as shown in Figure 10.11, if the *Form objects* option has been enabled using the Preferences dialog box Accessibility page. The dialog box can be used to specify a label for the text box and to indicate how the label is attached to the text field. You can type a label name in the *Label* text box and click one of the *Position* radio buttons to position the label either before or after the form object. Three *Style* radio buttons are related to the label. *Wrap with label tag* wraps the form object between paired ***label tags*** (<label>). *Attach label tag using 'for' attribute* uses the label tag **for** attribute to associate the label with the form object. In some browsers, this allows users to click anywhere in the label to enable radio buttons and check boxes, and it is the recommended method to use to increase accessibility. The radio button also will be surrounded by a focus rectangle when selected as shown in Figure 10.12. Selecting the *No label tag* radio button in the Input Tag Accessibility Attributes dialog box inserts the form object without label tags. The dialog box also can be used to indicate an access key and a tab index for the form object.

Selecting a text field displays the Text Field Property inspector as shown in Figure 10.13. You use the *TextField* text box to provide a unique name for the text field just as you do when inserting a form. The *Char width* text box default setting limits a text field's visible length to 20 characters. This means that even though a user can type in more than 20 characters, only 20 will be visible in the text field. This has no effect on the information sent for processing. If you want more characters to be visible in the text field, you can type a number greater than 20 in the *Char width* text box.

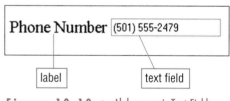

Figure 10.10 • Alphanumeric Text Field

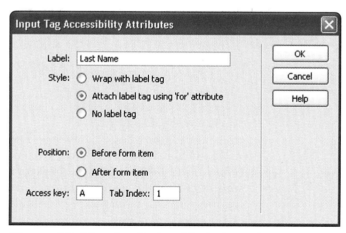

Figure 10.11 • Input Tag Accessibility Attributes Dialog Box

Figure 10.12
Focus Rectangle

Figure 10.13 • Text Field Property Inspector

DREAMWEAVER MX 2004

The *Max Chars* text box can be used to specify a maximum number of characters that a user can enter in the text field. Leaving this text box blank lets users enter an unlimited amount of characters in the text field. If a limit is specified, users are prohibited from entering any characters in excess of the limit.

Selecting the *Single line* radio button creates a **single-line text field**. Selecting the *Multi line* radio button displays the text field as a **multiple-line text field** as shown in Figure 10.14. You also can create a multiple-line text field by clicking the Insert bar (Forms menu item or tab) Textarea button, or by clicking Insert, pointing to Form, and then clicking Textarea.

When a multiple-line text field is created, the *Wrap* text box is enabled. The *Default* setting for the *Wrap* text box prevents text from wrapping to a new line when the width of the text field is exceeded. Instead, text scrolls to the left when it exceeds the margins of the text field. *Off* functions the same as the *Default* setting. *Virtual* causes text to wrap to a new line when the width of the text field is exceeded. However, when the data is sent for processing, it is submitted as a single line. Choosing *Physical* allows text to wrap and also wraps data sent for processing.

Clicking the *Password* radio button causes text entered in the text field to appear as bullets or as asterisks as shown in Figure 10.15. This is not the same as encrypting information, and therefore it should not be used to protect valuable information such as credit card numbers or passwords. The purpose of this feature is to prevent people from viewing entered text by looking over the form user's shoulder or from viewing the text if the form is printed. When the *Password* radio button is selected, the text field automatically appears as a single line.

The *Init val* text box can be used to enter default text that will appear in the text field. Default text is often placeholder text used to provide instructions or a sample of the type of text that should be entered in the text field. For example, a text box labeled *Address* might contain default text such as *Enter your street address here*.

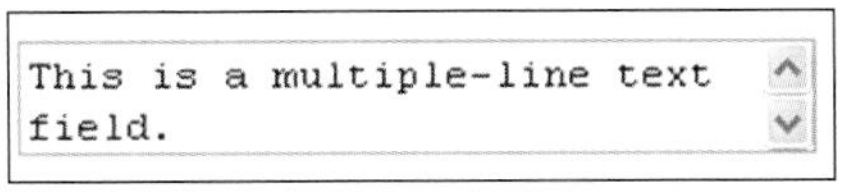

This is a multiple-line text
field.

Figure 10.14 • Multiple-Line Text Field

Date of Birth (MM/DD/YY) ••••••••

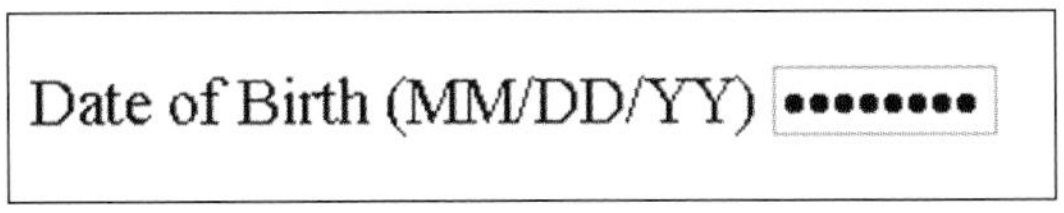

Figure 10.15 • Text Field Entry with Password Feature Enabled

---

CREATING SINGLE-LINE TEXT FIELDS

1. Create single-line text fields by completing the following steps:
   a. With **ch10ex01.htm** as the current document, use the Save As command to rename and save it as **ch10ex02.htm**.
   b. Position the insertion point in the first row of the first table column.
   c. If necessary, click the Insert bar Forms menu item or tab and then click the Text Field button.

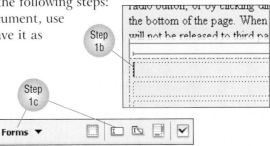

Step 1b

Step 1c

Forms ▼

d. The Input Tag Accessibility Attributes dialog box appears if the *Form objects* option has been selected in the Preferences dialog box Accessibility page. ***Note: Instructions on selecting this preference are contained in the "Ensuring Accessibility" section of Chapter 2.*** Complete the dialog box by doing the following:

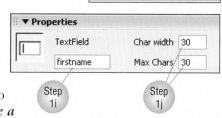

Steps 1d1–1d5

1) Type **First Name** in the *Label* text box.
2) Click the *Attach label tag using 'for' attribute* radio button to enable it.
3) Click the *Before form item* radio button to enable it if necessary.
4) Type **A** in the *Access key* text box and **1** in the *Tab Index* text box. ***Note: This dialog box will appear for all of the form objects you insert. For each subsequent form object, type the next access key letter and tab index number. For example, the access key for the next form object inserted in the form will be B, and the tab index will be 2. This is the last time the exercise instructions will instruct you to do this.***
5) Click the OK button to close the dialog box.

e. Click to the right of the text field to deselect the label and the text field.

f. Click the text field to select it, and without releasing the mouse button, drag it over to the right column.

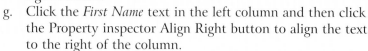

Step 1f Step 1g

g. Click the *First Name* text in the left column and then click the Property inspector Align Right button to align the text to the right of the column.

h. Click within the *First Name* text field to select it.

i. Type **firstname** in the Text Field Property inspector *TextField* text box.

j. Type **30** in the Text Field Property inspector *Char width* and *Max Chars* text boxes.

Step 1i Step 1j

k. Position the insertion point in the third row of the first column and repeat Steps 1c–1j to create a text field named *Last Name*. Use the Text Field Property inspector *TextField* text box to name the text field *lastname*. ***Note: Always create a text field name immediately after creating the text field. If you create a text field without creating a text field name in the Text Field Property inspector TextField text box and then create another text field, a quirk prevents the text field name from functioning correctly in a subsequently created text field, even though the correct text field name appears in the TextField text box. If you encounter this problem, the solution is to go into Code view and change the text field's ID so that it matches the name you created for it. For example, if the code for the text field reads*** `<label for="label">Last Name</label><input type="text" name="lastname" id="label">`, ***change the ID to match the name, e.g.*** `id="lastname"`.

DREAMWEAVER MX 2004

l. Position the insertion point in the fifth row of the first column and repeat Steps 1c–1j to create a text field named *E-Mail Address*. Use the Text Field Property inspector *TextField* text box to name the text field *emailaddress*.

m. Click the Preview/Debug in browser button and then click Preview in iexplore to preview the page. Type in the text boxes to determine whether they work. Close the browser when you are finished.

2. Save **ch10ex02.htm** but do not close it.

CREATING MULTIPLE-LINE TEXT FIELDS

1. Create multiple-line text fields by completing the following steps:

a. With **ch10ex02.htm** as the current document, use the Save As command to rename and save it as **ch10ex03.htm**.

b. Position the insertion point in the left table column two rows below the *E-Mail Address* text and type Please describe what you like about the Internet.

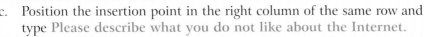

c. Position the insertion point in the right column of the same row and type Please describe what you do not like about the Internet.

d. Position the insertion point in the text you just typed and then click <tr> in the Tag selector to select the table row.

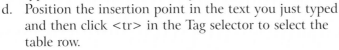

e. Click the Property inspector Align Center button to center the text in the row.

f. Position the insertion point in the left table column two rows below the *Please describe what you like about the Internet.* text.

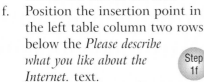

g. Click the Insert bar (Forms menu item or tab) Textarea button to open the Input Tag Accessibility Attributes dialog box.

h. Leave the *Label* text box blank and then click the *No label tag* radio button. Click the OK button to close the dialog box.

i. Click the multiple-line text field to select it. Type 40 in the Text Field Property inspector *Char width* text box. Name the multiple-line text field *likes*.

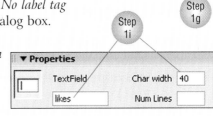

j. Position the insertion point in the right column of the same row. Repeat Steps 1g–1i to create another multiple-line text field. Name the text field *dislikes*.

k. Position the insertion point anywhere in the row containing the multiple-line text fields and click <tr> in the Tag selector to select the table row.

l. Click the Property inspector Align Center button to center the multiple-line text fields.

m. Click the Preview/Debug in browser button and then click Preview in iexplore to preview the page. Type text in the multiple-line text boxes to determine whether they work. Close the browser when you are finished.

2. Save **ch10ex03.htm** but do not close it.

1. Create a password text field by completing the following steps:
   a. With **ch10ex03.htm** as the current document, use the Save As command to rename and save it as **ch10ex04.htm**.
   b. Position the insertion point in the left column, two rows below the multiple-line text box.

   Step 1b

   c. Type **Please enter your birth date using this format: MM/DD/YY (for example, 09/21/85 for September 21, 1985)**.
   d. Position the insertion point anywhere in the text you just entered and click <tr> in the Tag selector to select the row.
   e. Click the Table Row Property inspector Merge button to merge the two columns in the row.
   f. Position the insertion point in the left column, two rows below the text.

   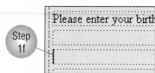

   Step 1f

   g. If necessary, click the Insert bar Forms menu item or tab and then click the Text Field button.

   Step 1e

   h. Leave the Input Tag Accessibility Attributes dialog box *Label* text box blank and then click the *No label tag* radio button. Click the OK button to close the dialog box.
   i. Type **birthdate** in the Text Field Property inspector *TextField* text box.

   Step 1i   Step 1j   Step 1k

   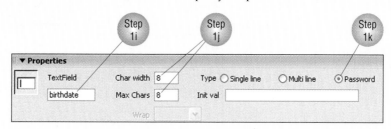

   j. Type **8** in the *Char width* and *Max Chars* text boxes.
   k. If necessary, select the text field and then click the *Password* radio button in the Text Field Property inspector to enable it.
   l. Position the insertion point anywhere in the same row as the password text field and click <tr> in the Tag selector to select the row.
   m. Click the Table Row Property inspector Merge button to merge the two columns in the row.
   n. Click the Table Row Property inspector Align Center button to center the password text field.
   o. Click the Preview/Debug in browser button and then click Preview in iexplore to preview the page. Type a date in the password text box. As you type, you should see asterisks or bullets appear instead of alphanumeric text. Close the browser when you are finished.

   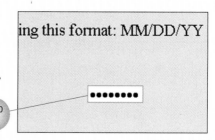

   Step 1o

2. Save **ch10ex04.htm** but do not close it.

Creating Hidden Fields

Hidden fields are used to transmit data that is provided by the Web page, instead of data provided by the user. A common use for hidden fields is to pass on instructions to a server, such as the e-mail address that processed form data should be sent to. Hidden fields are not displayed in a browser, but they are visible in the Dreamweaver MX 2004 Document window as a marker as shown in Figure 10.16. If the marker is not visible, you must click View options on the Document toolbar, point to Visual Aids, and then make sure that there is a check mark beside Invisible Elements in the menu that appears. If a hidden field is still invisible, click Edit on the Menu bar and then click Preferences to open the Preferences dialog box. Click *Invisible Elements* from the dialog box *Category* list box and then make sure that the *Hidden form fields* check box is enabled.

Hidden fields can be inserted by positioning the insertion point in a form and clicking Insert on the Menu bar, pointing to Form, and then clicking Hidden Field, or by clicking the Insert bar (Forms menu item or tab) Hidden Field button. This inserts a *hidden field marker* as shown in Figure 10.16. Selecting the marker displays the Hidden Field Property inspector shown in Figure 10.17. You can type a name and a value for the hidden field and a value in the Hidden Field Property inspector. For example, a hidden field could be used to specify an e-mail address where the form results will be sent after processing, such as `input type="hidden" name="recipient" value="name@emcp.net"`.

Figure 10.16
Hidden Field Marker

Figure 10.17 • Hidden Field Property Inspector

exercise 5

CREATING A HIDDEN FIELD

1. Create a hidden field by completing the following steps:
   a. With **ch10ex04.htm** as the current document, use the Save As command to rename and save it as **ch10ex05.htm**.
   b. Position the insertion point in the row just before the last row of the left table column.
   c. If necessary, click the Insert bar Forms menu item or tab and then click the Hidden Field button.
   d. Type *recipient* in the Hidden Field Property inspector *HiddenField* text box. ***Hint: The Hidden Field Property inspector should be displayed. If not, click the hidden field marker in the document to select it.***
   e. Type your e-mail address in the Hidden Field Property inspector *Value* text box.

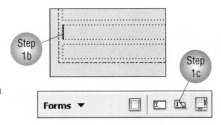

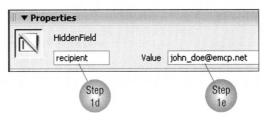

f. Click the Code button to look at the code. Note that the hidden field input tag type is **"hidden"**, which means it will not be visible when the document is viewed in a browser. Click the Design button when you are finished.

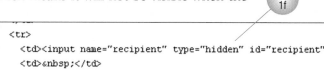

Step 1f

```
<tr>
    <td><input name="recipient" type="hidden" id="recipient"
    <td> </td>
```

g. Click the Preview/Debug in browser button and then click Preview in iexplore to preview the page and verify that the hidden field is not displayed on the page. Close the browser when you are finished.

2. Save **ch10ex05.htm** but do not close it.

Creating Check Boxes

You can create ***check boxes*** by clicking Insert on the Menu bar, pointing to Form, and then clicking Check Box, or by clicking the Insert bar (Forms menu item or tab) Checkbox button. Selecting the check box displays the Check Box Property inspector shown in Figure 10.18.

You should enter a unique name in the *CheckBox name* text box for scripting identification purposes. The *Checked value* text box is used to enter a value for the check box. For example, for a *Yes* check box a value of *1* could be entered, and for a *No* check box a value of *0* could be entered. Check boxes used to rate satisfaction such as *Poor, Good,* and *Excellent* could have corresponding checked values of *1, 2,* and *3.*

Enabling the *Checked* radio button places a check mark in the form check box when the form is viewed in a browser as shown in Figure 10.19. This can be used to create a default answer that users can change if the default answer does not reflect their answer.

Figure 10.19
Default Check Box Selection

Figure 10.18 • Check Box Property Inspector

exercise 6

CREATING CHECK BOXES

1. Create check boxes by completing the following steps:
   a. With **ch10ex05.htm** as the current document, use the Save As command to rename and save it as **ch10ex06.htm**.
   b. Position the insertion point in the left table column two rows below the password text field.

DREAMWEAVER MX 2004

c. Type Which of the following electronic appliances do you own? (Check all that apply.)

Which of the following electronic appliances do you own? (Check all that apply.)

Step 1c

d. Position the insertion point in the left column, two rows below the text you just entered.

Step 1e

e. Click the Insert bar (Forms menu item or tab) Checkbox button.

Forms ▼

f. Type CD Player in the Input Tag Accessibility Attributes dialog box *Label* text box. Click the *Attach label tag using 'for' attribute* radio button and then click the *After form item* radio button. Click the OK button to close the dialog box.

g. Repeat Steps 1e–1f to create check boxes for *DVD Player, VCR, Computer,* and *None of the Above* in each of the rows immediately below the one you just created.

Step 1f

Input Tag Accessibility Attributes

Label: CD Player

Style: ○ Wrap with label tag
       ● Attach label tag using 'for' attribute
       ○ No label tag

Position: ○ Before form item
          ● After form item

Access key: [ ]   Tab Index: [ ]

OK
Cancel
Help

h. Select the *CD Player* check box to display the Check Box Property inspector. Type cd in the *CheckBox name* text box and CD in the *Checked value* text box. Click the *Unchecked* radio button to enable it

Step 1h

▼ Properties

CheckBox name   Checked value CD   Initial state ○ Checked
cd   ● Unchecked

if necessary, which will display the checkbox without a check mark in it.

i. Repeat Step 1h for the other check box items. Name them *dvd, vcr, computer,* and *none*. Specify checked values of *DVD, VCR, Computer,* and *None*.

j. Click the Code button. For each check box item look for **label for=** and change the word between the quotation marks to match the check box item name. For example, the CD check box item ID is **"cd"**, so you must change **label for="checkbox"** to **label for="cd"**. Click the Design button when you are finished. *Note: If the label for value does not match the check box item ID, users will not be able to click the check box text to add a check mark when viewing the form in a browser.*

Step 1j

```
<tr>
    <td><input type="checkbox" name="cd" value="CD" id="cd" acce
    <label for="cd">CD Player </label></td>
    <td> </td>
```

k. Click the Preview/Debug in browser button and then click Preview in iexplore to preview the page and verify that the check boxes work. Because you wrapped label tags around the check box form object using the **for** attribute, you should be able to click a check box label to select it depending on your browser type and version. Close the browser when you are finished.

2. Save **ch10ex06.htm** but do not close it.

Creating Radio Buttons

Radio buttons can be inserted by clicking Insert on the Menu bar, pointing to Form, and then clicking Radio Button, or by clicking the Insert bar (Forms menu item or tab) Radio Button button. When radio buttons are inserted, they are named *radiobutton*. When radio buttons have the same name, only one of the radio buttons can be selected at a time. For example, if *Yes* and *No* radio buttons have the same name, clicking the *Yes* button selects it, but clicking the *No* button deselects the *Yes* button and selects the *No* button. If one of the two radio button names is changed, the buttons function like check boxes and both radio buttons can be selected at the same time.

Radio button groups are useful for questions with only one correct answer in a list of possible answers. For example, a question asking a user to indicate his age group might have choices for the following age groups: *1–20, 21–40, 41–60,* and *61+*. If a radio button group is used, only one of these age groups can be chosen; however, if check boxes were used, more than one age group could be selected, and the data received would have to be discarded if two age groups were selected since that is physically impossible.

Clicking Insert on the Menu bar, pointing to Form, and then clicking Radio Group, or clicking the Insert bar (Forms menu item or tab) Radio Group button opens the Radio Group dialog box shown in Figure 10.20. The Radio Group dialog box also allows you to choose whether you want radio buttons to be inserted using line breaks or a table. If table is selected, a single column table is created, with the radio buttons on the left and the labels on the right.

When an individual or grouped radio button is selected, the Radio Button Property inspector is displayed as shown in Figure 10.21. This Property inspector is almost identical to the Check Box Property inspector, and it offers you the option of naming the radio button, specifying a value for the button, and specifying an initial state.

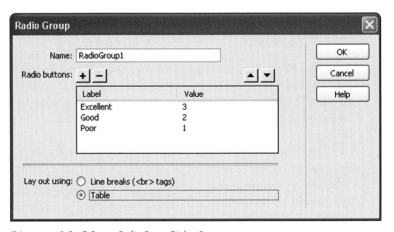

Figure 10.20 • Radio Group Dialog Box

Figure 10.21 • Radio Button Property Inspector

DREAMWEAVER MX 2004

1. Create a radio button group by completing the following steps:
   a. With **ch10ex06.htm** as the current document, use the Save As command to rename and save it as **ch10ex07.htm**.
   b. Position the insertion point two rows below the last check box item *(None of the Above)* and type How many hours a week do you use the Internet? (Check one.)

   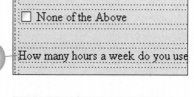

   c. Position the insertion point two rows below the text you just entered.
   d. Click the Insert bar (Forms menu item or tab) Radio Group button.

   e. Do not change *RadioGroup1* in the Radio Group dialog box *Name* text box. Click *Radio* in the *Radio buttons* text box *Label* column to select it, and then type More than 75. Click *radio* in the *Value* column to select it, and then type 75+.

   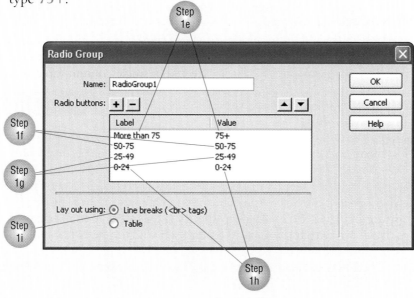

   f. Select *Radio* in the next row of the *Label* column and type 50-75. Select *radio* in the *Value* column and type 50-75.
   g. Click the dialog box Plus (+) button to add another radio button label and value pair. Give this radio button a label and value of 25-49.
   h. Click the Plus (+) button one more time to create another radio button label and value set and give it a label and value of 0-24.
   i. Click the *Line breaks (
 tags)* radio button to enable it if it is not already enabled. Click the OK button to close the dialog box.

j. Click the Code button. The Radio Group dialog box did not provide an option for creating an access key letter and tab index number for the radio group, but you can create them in Code view by locating the radio group input tag and then typing accesskey="L" tabindex="12" inside the tag. Click the Design button when you are finished creating access key letters and tab index numbers for all four radio buttons. *Hint: If you have not been creating access key numbers and tab index letters for the form objects as instructed in Exercise 2, Step 1d4, you can use this method to create them in Code view.*

```
        <input type="radio" name="RadioGroup1" value="75+" accesskey="L" tabindex="12" >
More than 75</label>
        <br>
```

Step
1j

k. Click the Preview/Debug in browser button and then click Preview in iexplore to preview the page. Click one of the radio button labels or the radio button to select it. Next, click another radio button. The radio button you previously selected should deselect, and the one you just clicked should be selected. Close the browser when you are finished.

2. Save **ch10ex07.htm** but do not close it.

Creating Menus and Lists

Form lists and menus can be inserted by clicking Insert on the Menu bar, pointing to Form, and then clicking List/Menu, or by clicking the Insert bar (Forms menu item or tab) List/Menu button. Lists differ from menus in that a *menu* displays a drop-down list when its down-pointing arrow is clicked as shown in Figure 10.22, while a *list* allows users to use navigation arrows to scroll through list items as shown in Figure 10.23. You can specify the number of items that will be visible in a list. A list with a scroll bar is often used when there is not enough room on a page for a drop-down list to appear. Lists also can be configured to allow users to select more than one item from a list at a time by pressing the Ctrl key (Windows) or Cmd key (Mac) when making a selection from the list.

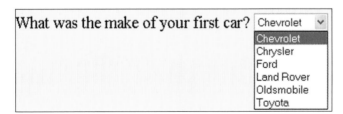

Figure 10.22 • Form Menu

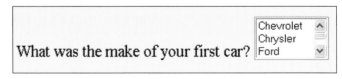

Figure 10.23 • Form List

DREAMWEAVER MX 2004

Selecting a list/menu form object displays the List/Menu Property inspector shown in Figure 10.24. The *List/Menu* text box can be used to provide a name for the list or menu for scripting identification purposes. The *Menu* radio button is selected by default.

Menu items and their values can be added to the menu by clicking the List/Menu Property inspector List Values button. This button opens the List Values dialog box as shown in Figure 10.25. Enter a menu item by clicking below the *Item Label* column head of the list box, and attach a value to the item by clicking below the *Value* column head of the list box and typing the value. Additional menu items and values can be added by clicking the Plus (+) button, and an item and value can be removed by clicking the Minus (–) button. Click the OK button to close the dialog box.

The List/Menu Property inspector *Initially selected* list box displays the menu items created for the list. Selecting one of these items causes it to be the default item displayed when the menu is viewed in a browser window.

If you need a list, select the *List* radio button. This causes the List/Form Property inspector to display a *Height* text box and an *Allow multiple* check box. The *Height* text box is used to specify the number of items that will be displayed in the list without the need to scroll. For example, if *3* is specified, the list will display three items, as shown in Figure 10.26. Placing a check mark in the *Allow multiple* check box allows users to select more than one item in a list by pressing the Ctrl key when making a selection.

You can click the List Values button to open the List Values dialog box so that list items and values can be created in the same manner used when working with a menu. The *Initially selected* list box functions as it does when used with menus.

Figure 10.24
List/Menu Property Inspector

Figure 10.25
List Values Dialog Box

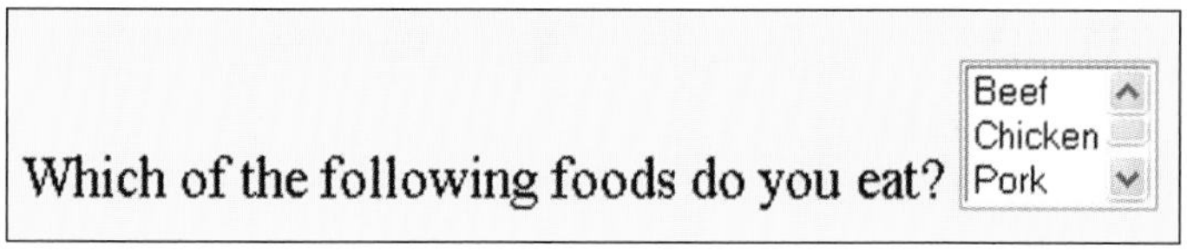

Which of the following foods do you eat? Beef / Chicken / Pork

Figure 10.26
List with a *Height* Text Box
Setting of 3

1. Create a menu by completing the following steps:
   a. With **ch10ex07.htm** as the current document, use the Save As command to rename and save it as **ch10ex08.htm**.
   b. Position the insertion point two rows below the last item in the radio group. Type Please indicate your favorite time to use the Internet. (Click the down-pointing arrow and select your favorite time.)

   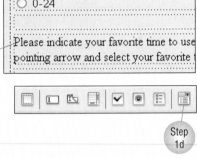

   Step 1b

   c. Position the insertion point in the left column, two rows below the text you just entered.
   d. Click the Insert bar (Forms menu item or tab) List/Menu button.

   Step 1d

   e. Click the Input Tag Accessibility Attributes dialog box *No label tag* radio button. Click the OK button to close the dialog box when you are finished. ***Hint: Do not forget to type an access key letter and tab index number.***

   Step 1e

   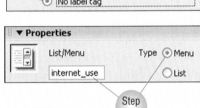

   f. Click the menu you inserted in the document to select it and display the List/Menu Property inspector.
   g. Type internet_use in the List/Menu Property inspector *List/Menu* text box. Click the *Menu* radio button to enable it if necessary.

   Step 1g

   h. Click the List/Menu Property inspector List Values button to open the List Values dialog box. Click just below the *Item Label* column head and type I like to use the Internet in the morning. Click just below the *Value* column head and type morning.

   Step 1h

   Step 1i

   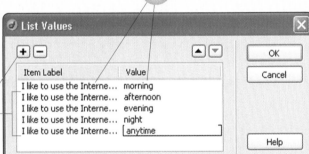

   i. Click the List Values dialog box Plus (+) button to type additional *Item Label/Value* pairs as follows:
      1) *Item Label*: I like to use the Internet in the afternoon.   *Value:* afternoon
      2) *Item Label:* I like to use the Internet in the evening.   *Value:* evening
      3) *Item Label:* I like to use the Internet at night.   *Value:* night
      4) *Item Label:* I like to use the Internet anytime.   *Value:* anytime

      Click the OK button to close the dialog box when you are finished.
   j. Click the Preview/Debug in browser button and then click Preview in iexplore to preview the page. Check the menu to see that it works. Close the browser when you are finished.
2. Save **ch10ex08.htm** but do not close it.

1. Create a list by completing the following steps:
   a. With **ch10ex08.htm** as the current document, use the Save As command to rename and save it as **ch10ex09.htm**.
   b. Position the insertion point in the left column, two rows below the menu text box. Type Select the computer brands you own or have owned in the past. (Hold down the Ctrl key (Windows) or Cmd key (Mac) when making a selection to select more than one brand.)

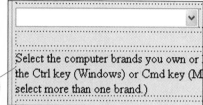

Step 1b

   c. Position the insertion point in the left column, two rows below the text you just entered.
   d. Click the Insert bar (Forms menu item or tab) List/Menu button.
   e. Click the Input Tag Accessibility Attributes dialog box *No label tag* radio button. Click OK to close the dialog box. ***Hint: Do not forget to type an access key letter and tab index number.***
   f. Click the list you inserted in the document to select it and display the List/Menu Property inspector.
   g. Type computer_brands in the List/Menu Property inspector *List/Menu* text box. Click the *List* radio button to enable it if necessary. Click the *Allow multiple* check box to enable it. Type 6 in the *Height* text box.

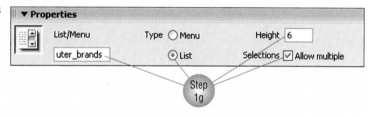

Step 1g

   h. Click the List/Menu Property inspector List Values button to open the List Values dialog box. Type the following *Item Label* and *Value* pairs:
      1) *Item Label:* Dell   *Value:* Dell
      2) *Item Label:* Compaq   *Value:* Compaq
      3) *Item Label:* Mac   *Value:* Mac
      4) *Item Label:* IBM   *Value:* IBM
      5) *Item Label:* Toshiba   *Value:* Toshiba
      6) *Item Label:* Other   *Value:* Other

Step 1i

   i. Use the List Values dialog box up- and down-pointing arrows to place the computer names in alphabetical order. Leave *Other* at the end of the list. Click the OK button to close the dialog box when you are finished.

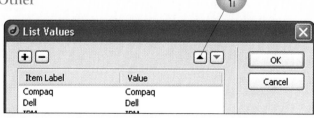

   j. Click the Preview/Debug in browser button and then click Preview in iexplore to preview the page. Check the list to see that it works. By holding down the Ctrl key, you should be able to select more than one computer brand from the list. Close the browser when you are finished.
2. Save **ch10ex09.htm** and then close it.

Creating Jump Menus

A *jump menu* has menu items that function as hyperlinks that can be used to link to other documents or to anchor links. Because the JavaScript that makes this possible is located inside the HTML document, jump menus work without server-side scripts.

Jump menus can be inserted by clicking Insert on the Menu bar, pointing to Form, and then clicking Jump Menu, or by clicking the Insert bar (Forms menu item or tab) Jump Menu button. This opens the Insert Jump Menu dialog box shown in Figure 10.27. You can type jump menu items in the *Text* text box and change their position in the list by clicking the up- and down-pointing arrows located to the upper-right of the *Menu items* text box.

You can click the Browse button next to the *When selected, go to URL* text box to open the Select File dialog box. You can use the Select File dialog box to browse and locate a file that will be linked to the list item. Selecting the file name places it in the *File name* text box. If the jump menu item is to be linked to a named anchor or to a file with an absolute path, these items can be typed directly in the *When selected, go to URL* text box. A pound sign (#) must precede a named anchor name.

The *Open URLs in* list box lets you specify a window or frame that a linked file will appear in. If the jump menu is located in a normal HTML document, the choice will be *Main window,* but if the jump menu is located in a document with frames, you can choose from the different frame names that appear.

The *Menu name* text box enables you to type a name for the jump menu. When the jump menu is selected, a jump menu name can be created or changed by typing a name in the *List/Menu* text box in the List/Menu Property inspector.

When selected, the *Insert go button after menu* check box places a **Go button** to the right of the jump menu as shown in Figure 10.28. Including a Go button is useful because the link selected in the jump menu by default will not jump when clicked. Inserting a Go button lets users click it to jump to any link in the jump menu list, even the one selected by default.

The *Select first item after URL change* check box should be selected if you want the jump menu to revert to displaying its default item after a selection has been made.

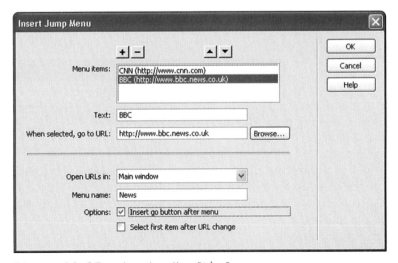

Figure 10.27 • Insert Jump Menu Dialog Box

Figure 10.28
Jump Menu Go Button

DREAMWEAVER MX 2004

Jump menu items can be edited by selecting the jump menu and using the Jump Menu Property inspector to edit the list values. To edit the jump menu behavior, you will need to select the jump menu and then go to the Behaviors panel to double-click *Jump Menu Go* in the unlabeled actions column as shown in Figure 10.29. This opens the Jump Menu dialog box shown in Figure 10.30. This dialog box differs from the Insert Jump Menu dialog box in that it does not contain a provision for inserting a Go button and lacks the *Menu name* text box. A jump menu can be named or renamed by selecting the jump menu and typing in the Property inspector *List/Menu* text box.

A Go button can be added to a jump menu that already has been created by inserting a button after the jump menu and then using the Behaviors panel to attach a Jump Menu Go behavior to it. You will learn how to create buttons in the "Creating Buttons" section later in this chapter.

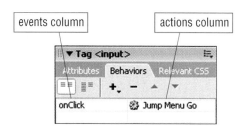

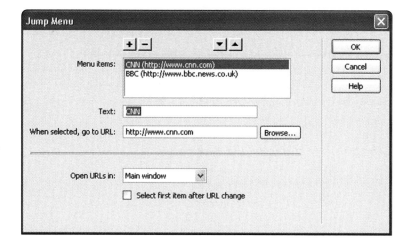

Figure 10.29
Behaviors Panel Jump Menu Behavior

Figure 10.30
Jump Menu Dialog Box

CREATING A JUMP MENU

1. Create a jump menu by completing the following steps:
   a. Open the student file named **news_source.htm**. Use the Save As command to rename the document as **ch10ex10.htm** and save it to the ch_10_exercises root folder. The ch_10_student_files folder appears by default in the *Save As* dialog box *Save in* text box, so click the dialog box Up One Level button to place the ch_10_exercises root folder in the *Save in* text box.

b. Position the insertion point in the center of the page between the *NEWS* headline and the image.

c. Click the Insert bar (Forms menu item or tab) Jump Menu button to open the Insert Jump Menu dialog box.

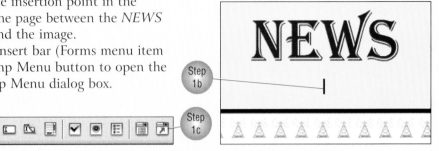

Step 1b

Step 1c

d. Enter the following information in the Insert Jump Menu dialog box:

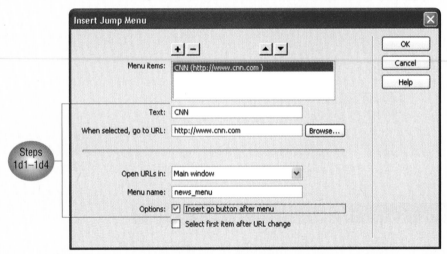

Steps 1d1–1d4

1) Type CNN in the dialog box *Text* text box.
2) Type http://www.cnn.com in the *When selected, go to URL* text box.
3) Type news_menu in the *Menu name* text box.
4) Click the *Insert go button after menu* check box to select it.

e. Repeat Steps 1d1 and 1d2 to create the following additional jump menu items and lists. ***Hint: Click the Plus (+) button to add each pair.***
   1) *Text:* CBS   *URL:* http://www.cbs.com
   2) *Text:* FOX   *URL:* http://www.foxnews.com
   3) *Text:* LATIMES   *URL:* http://www.latimes.com
   4) *Text:* NPR   *URL:* http://www.npr.org

f. Use the List Values dialog box up- and down-pointing arrows to alphabetize the jump menu items. Click the OK button to close the dialog box when you are finished.

g. Click the Preview/Debug in browser button and then click Preview in iexplore to preview the page. Go online and check to see that the jump menu links work. Use your browser's Back button to return to your page after each news page opens. Close the browser when you are finished.

2. Save **ch10ex10.htm** and then close it.

Creating Image Fields

An ***image field*** is used to create a graphical Submit button. You create an image field by positioning the insertion point inside a form, clicking Insert on the Menu bar, pointing to Form, and then clicking Image Field, or by clicking the Insert bar

DREAMWEAVER MX 2004

(Forms menu item or tab) Image Field button. This opens the Select Image Source dialog box so you can browse and locate an image that will act as an image field. After you locate the image, click it to place it in the *File name* text box. Click the OK button to close the dialog box. After you have selected the image, type submit button in the Image Field Property inspector *ImageField* text box as shown in Figure 10.31. You also can create an alternate description for the image by typing one in the *Alt* text box.

Figure 10.31
Image Field Property
Inspector

exercise 11

CREATING A GRAPHICAL SUBMIT BUTTON

1. Create a graphical Submit button by completing the following steps:
   a. Open **ch10ex09.htm** and use the Save As command to rename and save it as **ch10ex11.htm**.
   b. Position the insertion point in the last row of the left table column. ***Hint: Position it just below the hidden field marker.***
   c. Click the Insert bar (Forms menu item or tab) Image Field button.
   d. Use the Select Image Source dialog box that appears to browse and locate the student file named **submit_now_button.gif**. Click the file when you have located it to place it in the *File name* text box and then click the OK button to close the dialog box.
   e. Click the Input Tag Accessibility Attributes *No label tag* radio button. Do not enter an access key letter or tab index number because you will be replacing this button in another exercise. Click the OK button to close the dialog box.
   f. If necessary, click the button to select it and then type submit_button in the Image Field Property inspector *ImageField* text box. ***Note: Only submit is supported for this behavior. You cannot create a graphical Reset button by typing*** reset ***in the*** ImageField ***text box.***
   g. Type Form submit button in the Image Field Property inspector *Alt* text box to provide an alternate description for the button.

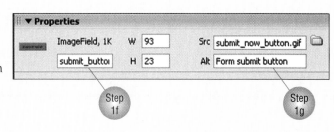

   h. Click the Preview/Debug in browser button and then click Preview in iexplore to preview the page. Clicking the Submit button just reopens the page because the page is not on a server and no form tag `action` attribute links the page to a server-side script. After the page is on a server that supports scripts and the form contains the appropriate form tag `action` attribute, the Submit button will send the form data to the specified dynamic page or script for processing. Close the browser when you are finished.
2. Save **ch10ex11.htm** but do not close it.

Creating File Fields for File Uploads

The **file field** allows you to upload a file when a form is submitted. File fields can be inserted by positioning the insertion point inside a form, clicking Insert on the Menu bar, pointing to Form, and then clicking File Field, or by clicking the Insert bar (Forms menu item or tab) File Field button. Inserting a file field places a text box and Browse button in the document as shown in Figure 10.32. Clicking the Browse button opens a Choose file dialog box used to browse and locate the file to be uploaded as shown in Figure 10.33. Before inserting a file field, you must check with your server administrator to determine whether anonymous file uploads are permitted, and to find out about any special instructions necessary for making the file field work with the server. The Form Property inspector *Method* text box should be set to *POST* if a file field is inserted in a form. The File Field Property inspector *Max Chars* text box should be left empty to ensure that a long file name will not be cut off if it is too long. If you browse for a file, the file name will be accepted even if it is longer than the number of characters specified in the *Max Chars* text box.

Figure 10.32
File Field Text Box and Browse Button

Figure 10.33
Choose File Dialog Box

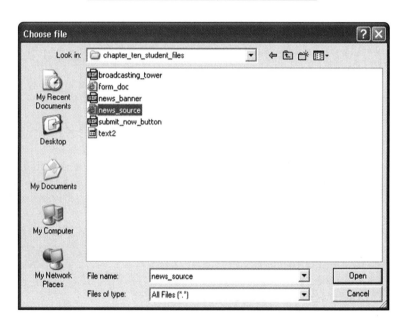

 CREATING A FILE FIELD

1. Create a file field by completing the following steps:
   a. With **ch10ex11.htm** as the current document, use the Save As command to rename and save it as **ch10ex12.htm**.
   b. Position the insertion point two rows below the *List* text box and type Use the Browse button to locate a file and select it for uploading.

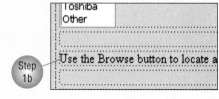

c. Position the insertion point in the left table column two rows below the text you just entered. *Hint: This is the row just above the hidden field marker, which is not visible when the document is viewed in a browser window.*

d. Click the Insert bar (Forms menu item or tab) File Field button.

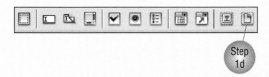

Step 1d

e. Click the *No label tag* radio button in the Input Tag Accessibility Attributes dialog box. Click the OK button to close the dialog box. *Hint: Do not forget to type an access key letter and tab index number.*

f. If necessary, select the file field, and then type file_field in the File Field Property inspector *FileField name* text box.

g. Click the Preview/Debug in browser button and then click Preview in iexplore to preview the page. Click the Browse button to open the Choose file dialog box. Select a file to place it in the *File name* text box and then click the Open button to place the path to the file in the file field text box on the page. Close the browser when you are finished.

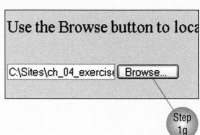

Step 1g

2. Save **ch10ex12.htm** but do not close it.

Creating Buttons

Dreamweaver MX 2004 makes inserting Submit and Reset buttons for forms very convenient. You can insert buttons by positioning the insertion point inside a form, clicking Insert on the Menu bar, pointing to Form, and then clicking Button, or by clicking the Insert bar (Forms menu item or tab) Button button. After a button has been selected, the Button Property inspector appears as shown in Figure 10.34. A Submit button is created by default. When the form containing the button is viewed in a browser and the Submit button is clicked, the form data is submitted to the dynamic page or script specified in the form tag **action** attribute.

The Submit button can be changed to a Reset button by selecting it and then clicking the Button Property inspector *Reset form* radio button. When the form is viewed in a browser window, clicking the Reset button removes any data entered and restores the form to the way it appeared when it was first opened. The Button Property inspector also contains a *None* radio button that can be used to create a button without any action. The Button Property inspector *Label* text box can be used to change the text that appears on a button. For example, the default Submit button could be changed to read *Send Now* by typing Send Now in the *Label* text box.

Figure 10.34 • Button Property Inspector

CREATING SUBMIT AND RESET BUTTONS

1. Create Submit and Reset buttons by completing the following steps:
   a. With **ch10ex12.htm** as the current document, use the Save As command to rename and save it as **ch10ex13.htm**.
   b. Select the Submit Now button and then press the Delete key to delete it.
   c. With the insertion point located where the Submit Now button was, click the Insert bar (Forms menu item or tab) Button button.

   d. Click the Input Tag Accessibility Attributes *No label tag* radio button. Click the OK button to close the dialog box. ***Hint: Do not forget to type an access key letter and tab index number.***
   e. Position the insertion point in the right column of the same row and click the Insert bar (Forms menu item or tab) Button button again.
   f. Repeat Step 1d.
   g. If necessary, select the Submit button you just inserted to display the Button Property inspector. Click the *Reset form* radio button to enable it. The Submit button changes to a Reset button.

   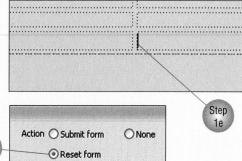

   h. Click the Preview/Debug in browser button and then click Preview in iexplore to preview the page. Fill out a few of the text boxes and select some of the check boxes. Click the Reset button. The changes you made will be cleared. Close the browser when you are finished.
2. Save **ch10ex13.htm** but do not close it.

Applying Labels to Form Objects

Selecting a form object and then clicking Insert on the Menu bar, pointing to Form, and then clicking Label, or clicking the Insert bar (Forms menu item or tab) Label button wraps label tags around the form object. If you have enabled the *Form objects* accessibility option in the Preferences dialog box Accessibility page, you already have the option of wrapping labels around form objects by using the Input Tag Accessibility Attributes dialog box. The Label command or button does not add a **for** attribute or a label name, so those must be added in Code view or Code and Design view if desired. For most users, creating form objects with the *Form objects* accessibility option enabled is an easier method of adding labels and **for** attributes to form objects, as described in the "Creating Text Fields" section earlier in this chapter.

Understanding the Fieldset Button

The last button in the Insert bar Forms category is the Fieldset button. Fieldset tags (<fieldset>) are container tags that can be used to identify form objects dealing with related information. For example, imagine a form with two sections:

one containing form objects related to personal information such as name, address, and so on, and the other containing form objects related to opinions. Fieldset tags could be used to identify and logically separate the form objects into *Personal Information* and *Opinion* sections. Because the content of fieldset tags can be read by screen readers, their primary function is to improve accessibility for users with visual disabilities.

When the Fieldset button is clicked, the Document window changes to Code and Design view, and a Fieldset dialog box appears. The Fieldset dialog box contains a single *Label* text box that can be used to type text that can identify a group of form objects. The fieldset tags are inserted with legend tags that bracket the text that will identify the group of form objects:

```
<fieldset><legend>Personal Information</legend></fieldset>
```

The *Personal Information* text will appear in the Design view portion of the split Code and Design view screen.

Attaching the Validate Form Behavior to Forms

You can attach a Validate Form behavior to a form object and/or a Submit button using the Behaviors panel. The **Validate Form behavior** works only with text field form objects, and every text field in a form must have a unique name for it to work properly. When attached to a text field, the Validate Form behavior checks whether a user has entered data of the type specified when the Validate Form behavior was created. For example, Validate Form behaviors can be specified that determine whether any data has been entered in a text field, numeric data has been entered, numeric data within a specified range has been entered, or an e-mail address has been entered.

If the appropriate data was not entered, a message box appears in the browser window as shown in Figure 10.35 when the user leaves the text field. The message box references the text field name, which is another reason to create descriptive names for form objects, such as address_1 for the first of two address text fields, or email_address for a text field that will contain an e-mail address.

The Validate Form behavior also can be attached to a Submit button. The behavior operates when the Submit button is clicked and determines whether text fields contain data as specified in the Validate Form behavior attached to the Submit button. If any of the text fields do not contain the required data, the user will not be able to submit the form and must go back and fix the improper or missing data before resubmitting.

You can attach Validate Form behaviors to text fields and the Submit button at the same time. This is a good idea because even though a warning message appears when a Validate Form behavior attached to a text field detects incorrect or missing data, it is possible for users to move on to the next text field. That means that an incomplete or inappropriately filled out form could still be submitted. However, if a Validate Form behavior has also been attached to the Submit button,

Figure 10.35
Validate Form Behavior
Message Box

it can check for correct data as well. This acts as a fail-safe measure, providing a reminder to users when they make a mistake in filling in a text field, and preventing them from submitting an incorrectly filled out form.

The Validate Form behavior can be attached to a text field by selecting the field, clicking the Behaviors panel Plus (+) button as shown in Figure 10.36, and then clicking Validate Behavior from the drop-down list that appears. This opens the Validate Form dialog box shown in Figure 10.37.

The named fields in the form containing the selected text field appear in the dialog box *Named fields* list box. The named field for the selected text field should be selected from the list, and will not necessarily be the one highlighted in the list box. Clicking the *Required* check box indicates that a value is required for the text field. One of four *Accept* radio buttons can be enabled to validate whether any data is acceptable *(Anything)*, a number must be entered *(Number)*, an e-mail address must be entered *(Email address)*, or a number in a range must be entered *(Number from)*. If *Number from* is enabled, the starting number for the number range must be entered in the text box to the left of *to*, and the ending number entered in the text box to the right of *to*. The Validate Form behavior works exactly the same when it is attached to a Submit button.

Figure 10.36 • Behaviors Panel Plus (+) Button

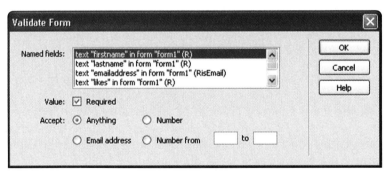

Figure 10.37 • Validate Form Dialog Box

exercise 14

ATTACHING THE VALIDATE FORM BEHAVIOR

1. Attach the Validate Form behavior to text fields and the Submit button by completing the following steps:
   a. With **ch10ex13.htm** as the current document, use the Save As command to rename and save it as **ch10ex14.htm**.
   b. Click the *First Name* text field in the Document window to select it, click the Behaviors panel Plus (+) button, and then click Validate Form to open the Validate Form dialog box. *Hint: If the Behaviors panel is not visible, click Window on the Menu bar and then Behaviors to open the panel.*

c.   Make sure that *text "firstname" in form "form1"* is selected in the *Named fields* list box. Click the *Required* check box to enable it, and in the *Accept* section click the *Anything* radio button to enable it. Click the OK button to close the dialog box.

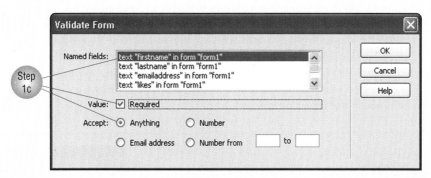

d.   Look for the *Validate Form* event and action in the Behaviors panel. If the event is not *onBlur,* click the Events down-pointing arrow and select it from the list.

e.   Repeat Steps 1b–1d for the remaining text fields, being sure to select the named field from the dialog box *Named fields* list box that matches the selected text field. In the *Accept* section of the dialog box, choose the following radio buttons:
   *   "lastname": *Anything* radio button
   *   "emailaddress": *Email address* radio button
   *   "likes": *Anything* radio button
   *   "dislikes": *Anything* radio button
   *   "birthdate": *Number* radio button

   Hint: It is easy to forget to click the Required check box, which must be clicked each time, so be sure to remember to do that. Also be sure to check the Behaviors panel to see that the event specified is onBlur for every text field.

f.   Select the Submit button, click the Behaviors panel Plus (+) button, and then click Validate Form to open the Validate Form dialog box.

g.   Repeat Steps 1c and 1e, but this time, do not close the dialog box after you are finished specifying a validation behavior for a named field. Instead, select the next named field from the *Named fields* list box, click the *Required* check box, and then click the appropriate radio button. Continue until a Validate Form behavior has been specified for every named field.

h.   Look for the *Validate Form* event and action in the Behaviors panel. If the event is not *onClick,* click the *Events* down-pointing arrow to select it from the list.

i.   Click the Preview/Debug in browser button and then click Preview in iexplore to preview the page.

j.   Position the insertion point in the *First Name* text box and then press the Tab key. You should see a message stating that a first name is required. Click the OK button to close the message box.

k.   Type your first name in the text box and then use the Tab key to move to the *Last Name* text box.

l.   Press the Tab key. You should see a message informing you that you must enter a last name. Type your last name.

m.   Press the Tab key to move through the remaining form objects. Each of the text fields should cause a message box to appear if you do not enter the appropriate text. Leave the remaining fields empty. *Hint: If you do not see a message for any of the text fields, it is probably because you did not enable the* Required *check box in the* Validate Form *dialog box or because the event was not set to* onBlur *in the* Behaviors *panel. To change the event, click the down-pointing arrow next to the event. To open the* Validate Form *dialog box again, click* Validate Form *in the actions column of the Behaviors panel.*

n.   Click the Submit button. A message box should appear informing you that data is missing for all of the text fields except the first and last name text fields that you completed. Click the OK button. *Hint: If the Submit button Validate Form behavior does not work correctly, check to see that the* Required *check box was enabled for every item in the* Validate Form *dialog box, and that the event in the Behaviors panel is specified as* onClick.

o.   Close the browser when you are finished.

2.   Save **ch10ex14.htm** and then close it.

CHAPTER summary

➤   Forms help create a truly interactive Internet experience by allowing visitors to communicate with Web site owners.

➤   Most forms contain a combination of different form controls, or form objects as they are referred to in Dreamweaver MX 2004, such as text boxes, check boxes, radio buttons, menus, and lists.

➤   Text fields can be created that let those submitting forms provide open-ended answers while radio buttons, check boxes, menus, and lists can be used to provide more structured answers.

➤   Processing form data in completed forms requires the use of scripts such as CGI (Common Gateway Interface). These scripts are located on a server and are known as server-side scripts.

➤   The server-side script you use, and how it should be used, must be determined in consultation with the administrator of the server that will be used to host your Web site.

➤   Forms are created in HTML documents using paired form tags (<form>). The form tags define the form and contain the form objects that users will use to input data.

➤   After a form has been created, input tags (<input>) are used to insert form objects within the area defined by the form tags.

➤   Input tags contain **type** attributes that indicate the type of form object being inserted, such as **type="file"** or **type="checkbox"**.

➤   A Submit button must be added to the form so that users can submit the form for processing when they are finished. You also should include a Reset button that can be used to reset the form if the user wants to start over again.

➤ When a form is submitted, the user's browser gathers the form answers and uses the URL specified in the form tag **action** attribute to send them to the server for processing by a server-side script.

➤ After the answers are processed, most scripts specify that an acknowledgment page be returned and opened in the browser window specified by the form tag **target** attribute.

➤ Careful planning before you begin creating a form will save a lot of time later on and help ensure that your form gathers the information you are looking for.

➤ Questions should be phrased as clearly as possible to avoid ambiguity or confusion, and the choices for answering a question should be appropriate to the question being asked.

➤ If you are asking users to select an answer from a group of possible answers, make sure that the answers reflect all of the possible choices.

➤ Forms should be designed so that users will not be confused about which questions relate to which form objects.

➤ Placing a table inside a form allows you to control the design and create an attractive and easy-to-follow form.

➤ Clearly state the purpose for which the questions are being asked, and consider adding a privacy statement to let users know that you will not abuse the information they are providing.

➤ Instructions on how to complete the form should be clear and easy to understand. Never assume that the people completing your form already know how to complete it.

➤ Before a form is uploaded to a Web site, it should be tested by having other people fill it out.

➤ Form borders are represented by dotted red lines when viewed in the Document window. If form borders are not visible, click View options on the Document toolbar, point to Visual Aids, and then make sure that there is a check mark beside Invisible Elements in the menu that appears.

➤ After a form has been inserted, the form can be selected by clicking its border.

➤ Forms and form objects should be provided with names for use with scripting languages.

➤ Do not use spaces or special characters for form or form object names, and try to create names that will help you identify the form or form object.

➤ Some scripting languages have reserved words that cannot be used when naming forms or form objects.

➤ The Form Property inspector *Action* text box is used to specify the path to the dynamic page or script that will be used to process a form.

➤ The Form Property inspector *Method* text box is used to specify the method for transmitting form data. The options are *GET, POST,* and *Default*.

➤ The GET method should not be used for long forms or for confidential data such as credit card numbers or passwords.

➤ The Form Property inspector *Enctype* text box is used to specify a MIME type for data submitted for processing. The default setting is *application/x-www-form-urlencode* and is usually used with the POST method.

➤ The Form Property inspector *Target* text box is used to select the window that will be used to display data returned by the server processing the form.

The target names have the same function as they do in the other Property inspectors, such as *_blank* to open a document in a new browser window.

➤ A table can be inserted inside a form by positioning the insertion point inside the form and then clicking the Insert bar (Common menu item or tab) Table button.

➤ If a form object is inserted outside a form, a message appears asking you if you want to add a form tag. For best results, form objects should always be contained inside form tags.

➤ Text fields allow form users to enter alphanumeric (letters and/or numbers) data.

➤ When a form object is inserted, an Input Tag Accessibility Attributes dialog box will appear if the *Form objects* option has been enabled using the Preferences dialog box Accessibility page.

➤ Hidden fields are used to transmit data that is provided by the Web page, instead of data entered by the user. A common use for hidden fields is to pass on instructions to a server, such as the e-mail address that processed form data should be sent to. Hidden fields are not displayed in a browser but are visible in the Dreamweaver MX 2004 Document window as a hidden field marker.

➤ More than one check box can be checked at a time, so they are suitable for questions that may have more than one answer.

➤ When radio buttons have the same name, only one of the radio buttons can be selected at a time. This makes them useful for questions with only one correct answer.

➤ Radio buttons are often inserted as radio button groups.

➤ Menus display a drop-down list when their down-pointing arrow is clicked, and only one item can be selected from a menu list at a time.

➤ Lists are scrollable, and they can be formatted so that more than one list item can be selected at a time.

➤ A jump menu is a menu in which the items function as hyperlinks that can be used to link to other documents or to anchor links. Because the JavaScript that makes this possible is located inside the HTML document, jump menus work without server-side scripts.

➤ A Go button can be added to a jump menu that already has been created by inserting a button after the jump menu and then using the Behaviors panel to attach a Jump Menu Go behavior to it.

➤ The file field allows users to upload a file when a form is submitted. When a file field is inserted in a document, a text box and Browse button appear.

➤ Before inserting a file field, you must check with your server administrator to determine whether anonymous file uploads are permitted, and to find out about any special instructions necessary for making the file field work with the server.

➤ The Form Property inspector *Method* text box should be set to *POST* if a file field is inserted in a form, and the File Field Property inspector *Max Chars* text box should be left empty to ensure that a long file name will not be cut off if it is too long when using a file field.

➤ Submit and Reset buttons can be inserted in forms so that users can submit forms or reset them if they want to restart the form.

➤ Labels can be wrapped around form objects to attach them to the form object. When this is done with check boxes and radio buttons and a **for** attribute is specified, the check boxes and radio buttons can be selected by clicking their label or the check box or radio button.

➤ The Insert bar Fieldset button is an accessibility feature that can be used to identify related form objects.

➤ The Behaviors panel can be used to attach a Validate Form behavior to a form object and/or a Submit button.

➤ The Validate Form behavior works only with text field form objects, and it is important that every text field in a form have a unique name for it to work properly.

➤ When attached to a text field, the Validate Form behavior determines whether a user has entered data of the type specified when the Validate Form behavior was created.

➤ The Validate Form behavior also can be attached to a Submit button.

➤ It is possible to attach Validate Form behaviors to both text fields and to the Submit button at the same time, so that each form object will be validated as the user moves the insertion point away from it, and again when the form is submitted.

KEY terms

action attribute Form tag attribute used to specify a path to the dynamic page or script that will be used to process the form data.

alphanumeric Text consisting of letters and/or numbers.

check boxes A form object consisting of a small box that can be checked with a check mark to enable it.

file field Form object that creates a text box and Browse button that allow users to upload a file when a form is submitted.

form tags The HTML tags (<form>) used to create forms.

GET method A method for transmitting form data. The GET method should not be used for long forms, or for confidential data such as credit card numbers or passwords. The GET method has been deprecated, and the POST method should be used if possible. The GET method is selected using the Form Property inspector.

Go button A button that can be added to a jump menu to select the default item in the jump menu.

hidden field marker An icon to indicate a hidden field.

hidden fields Form objects used to transmit data that is provided by the Web page rather than the user.

image field A form object that can be used create a graphical Submit button.

input tags The HTML tags (<input>) used to insert form objects (elements) in forms.

jump menu A form menu in which the items function as hyperlinks that can be used to link to other documents or to anchor links.

label tags The HTML tags (<label>) that can be wrapped around a form object input tag. When a **for** attribute is specified, check boxes and radio buttons can be selected by clicking their label.

list A form object that users can scroll to view the list items. Lists can be formatted to allow more than one list item to be selected at a time.

menu A form object that displays a drop-down list of items. Only one item can be selected from the list.

multiple-line text field A form object text field more than one line high.

POST method A method used to transmit form data. The POST method is suitable for use with confidential data. The POST method is selected using the Form Property inspector.

radio buttons Small round form objects that can be enabled by clicking. When radio buttons have the same name, only one button can be enabled at a time, so they are suitable for questions with only one correct answer. Radio buttons are often inserted as radio button groups.

Reset button Button used to reset a form.

single-line text field A form object text field one line high.

Submit button Button used to submit form data for processing.

target attribute Form tag attribute that specifies the browser window that processed form results will be returned to.

Validate Form behavior A behavior that can be attached to form objects or to a form to validate form data before it is submitted for processing.

COMMANDS review

Insert form	Insert, Form, Form
Insert form objects	Insert, Form, select from submenu

CONCEPTS check

Indicate the correct term or command for each item.

1. This is the term for a script processed by a server.
2. This is the tag used to create forms.
3. This is the tag used to create form objects.
4. This is a button used to send form data for processing.
5. These two methods can be used to transmit form data for processing.
6. This method of transmitting form data for processing has been deprecated by the W3W.
7. This type of form object is used to pass data to a server that is not entered by the form user.
8. This button is used to clear data from a form.
9. This is the name of the Behaviors panel event that should be specified when the Validate Form behavior is attached to a form object.
10. These buttons are often grouped so that only one button in the group can be selected at a time.
11. This is the term for a script processed by a browser.
12. This type of menu contains menu items that are linked to other documents or named anchors.

13. This form object can be used to insert an image that can be formatted as a Submit button.
14. This form object can be used to insert a text box and Browse button that can be used to upload files.
15. This behavior can be attached to form objects or to a Submit button to validate form data before it is sent for processing.
16. This input tag attribute is used to indicate the type of form object specified.
17. Clicking this selects a form.
18. This attribute is used to specify the path to a server where form data will be processed.
19. This should be done before a form is uploaded to a server.
20. Form buttons are located under this Insert bar menu item or tab.

SKILLS check

Use the Site Definition dialog box to create a separate Dreamweaver site named CH 10 Assessments to keep your assessment work for this chapter. Save the files for the site in a new root folder named ch_10_assessments under the Sites folder you created in Chapter 1, Exercise 3.

In Assessments 1–7 you will create a survey form that will be added to your Design Portfolio Web site. In Assessment 8, you will create a jump menu that will also be added to the site. In Assessment 9, you will add the survey form and jump menu to your Design Portfolio Web site.

Assessment 1 • Plan a Survey, Create a Form, and Insert a Table

1. Think about the information you would like to know about the people viewing your Design Portfolio Web site. Write down or record the kinds of information you would like to elicit and develop a list of at least 20 different questions. Some examples:
    • What is your age?
    • How did you discover my Design Portfolio Web site?
    • What do you think of my Web site design theme?
    • What do you think of the font styles I used?
    • Do you have any suggestions for improvement?
2. Write down the type of form object or objects you would use for each question. Some examples:
    • Birth date: text field
    • Age group: radio button group
    • Opinion of Design Portfolio Web site: radio button group or menu
    • Things viewers like about the site: check boxes or list
    • Suggestions or comments: multiple-line text field
3. Create an HTML document and use the Save or Save As command to save it as **ch10sa1.htm**.
4. Format the document to match your Design Portfolio Web site design theme.
5. Type a short introduction to the survey that includes instructions and information about why you are asking the questions and what you will do with the answers.
6. Insert a form into the document.
7. Insert a table into the form. Start with a basic two-column, multirow table. You can modify the table later.
8. Save **ch10sa1.htm** but do not close it.

Assessment 2 • Add Text Fields and Check Boxes

1. With **ch10sa1.htm** as the current document, use the Save As command to rename and save it as **ch10sa2.htm**.
2. Create text fields for a last name, a first name, and an e-mail address. Use the Text Field Property inspector *TextField* text box to name them *lastname*, *firstname*, and *email*. **Note: Always create a text field name immediately after creating the text field. If you create a text field without creating a text field name in the Text Field Property inspector TextField *text box and then create another text field, a quirk prevents the text field name from functioning correctly in a subsequently created text field, even though the correct text field name appears in the TextField *text box. If you encounter this problem, the solution is to go into Code view and change the text field's ID so that it matches the name you created for it. For example, if the code for the text field reads* `<label for="label">Last Name</label><input type="text" name="lastname" id="label">`, *change the ID to match the name, e.g.* `id="lastname"`.
3. Add at least three different check box groups to your survey form, with each group consisting of at least five check box items. Check boxes are useful for answering questions for which more than one answer is possible. Place a label before or after each check box, and attach a label tag to each check box form object using the **for** attribute.
4. Save **ch10sa2.htm** but do not close it.

Assessment 3 • Add Radio Buttons

1. With **ch10sa2.htm** as the current document, use the Save As command to rename and save it as **ch10sa3.htm**.
2. Add at least four radio button groups to the survey form. Remember that radio button groups are used for questions that can have only one answer, such as age group, so select appropriate questions. Insert the radio button groups using line break tags.
3. Save **ch10sa3.htm** but do not close it.

Assessment 4 • Add Menus

1. With **ch10sa3.htm** as the current document, use the Save As command to rename and save it as **ch10sa4.htm**.
2. Add at least two menus to the survey form. Each menu should contain at least four different menu items. Only one menu item can be chosen from the menu, so choose questions that are appropriate for this type of form object.
3. Save **ch10sa4.htm** but do not close it.

Assessment 5 • Add Lists

1. With **ch10sa4.htm** as the current document, use the Save As command to rename and save it as **ch10sa5.htm**.
2. Add at least two lists to the survey form. Format the lists so that multiple list items can be selected. Each list should be at least two lines high and contain a minimum of five items. Lists that allow multiple-item selections are suitable for questions that can have more than one possible answer, so choose questions that are appropriate for this kind of form object.
3. Save **ch10sa5.htm** but do not close it.

DREAMWEAVER MX 2004

Assessment 6 • Add Multiple Line and Password Text Fields

1. With **ch10sa5.htm** as the current document, use the Save As command to rename and save it as **ch10sa6.htm**.
2. Add at least one multiple-line text field and one password text field to your survey form. The password text field should be for an answer to a question that viewers might not want others to see, such as answers concerning their age, income group, and so on.
3. Save **ch10sa6.htm** but do not close it.

Assessment 7 • Attach Validate Form Behaviors to the Text Field Form Objects and the Submit Button

1. With **ch10sa6.htm** as the current document, use the Save As command to rename and save it as **ch10sa7.htm**.
2. Attach a Validate Form behavior to the *First Name, Last Name,* and *E-Mail* text fields. Make sure that you specify the appropriate validation action. For example, for the *E-Mail* text field you would select the *E-Mail address* validation option. Make sure the event is *onBlur* for each text field.
3. Create Submit and Reset buttons, and attach Validate Form behaviors to the Submit button for each of the three text fields as well.
4. Have at least three of your classmates try out your survey form. Use their feedback to improve the survey form and correct any mistakes.
5. Save **ch10sa7.htm** and then close it.

Assessment 8 • Create a Jump Menu

1. Create a new HTML document and use the Save or Save As command to save it as **ch10sa8.htm**.
2. Format the page to match your Design Portfolio Web site design theme.
3. Create a jump menu that links to at least five different search engines. Add a Go button to the jump menu. *Note: Ask your instructor if you can link to other sites if you want.*
4. Go online to verify that the jump menu links work.
5. Save **ch10sa8.htm** and then close it

Assessment 9 • Add the Survey Form and Jump Menu to Your Design Portfolio Web Site

1. Add the survey form that you created in Assessments 1 through 7 to your Design Portfolio Web site. Create links to the page as appropriate.
2. Add the jump menu page that you created in Assessment 8 to your Design Portfolio Web site. Create links to the page as appropriate.

Appendix

DEFINING A REMOTE SITE AND USING FTP TO UPLOAD WEB PAGES

After you finalize your Web site, you are ready to publish it on a server so that other people can view it. Dreamweaver MX 2004 simplifies this task by letting you define a remote site so that uploading your Web site can be done at the click of a button. Defining a remote site takes only a few minutes, provided that you have the correct information at hand. After a remote site has been defined, you will not need to do it again unless there has been a change to any of the information you entered. The best source for information about publishing your pages is usually provided by your Web host administrator. Many Web hosts have an information page containing answers to commonly asked questions and a contact e-mail address that can be used to seek answers to additional questions.

Defining a Remote Site

In Chapter 1, Exercise 3, you learned how to use the Dreamweaver MX 2004 Site Definition Wizard to define (create) a local site for storing and working on documents. A local site allows you to take advantage of convenient Dreamweaver MX 2004 features such as automatic link updating, file management, and file sharing. After you finalize the documents in your local site, you are ready to use the Site Definition Wizard to define a *remote site* that will reside on a server so that others can view it. You can define a remote site by completing the following steps:

1. Click Site on the Menu bar and then click Manage Sites to open the Manage Sites dialog box shown in Figure A.1.

Figure A.1
Manage Sites Dialog Box

2. Select the site to be edited in the Manage Sites dialog box and then click the Edit button to open the Site Definition dialog box (the Site Definition Wizard) shown in Figure A.2. *Note: The Site Definition dialog box Title bar incorporates the name of the site being defined (Site Definition for [site name]).*

3. Click the Advanced tab and then click *Remote Info* from the *Category* list box to open the dialog box Remote Info page as shown in Figure A.2.

5. Click the *Access* list box down-pointing arrow in the Site Definition dialog box to select the method to use to upload your site files. The following choices are available from the drop-down list shown in Figure A.3:

- **None** When you defined your local site in Chapter 2, you selected *None,* and that should be the current default. With *None* selected, you can still upload files using an independent **File Transfer Protocol (FTP)** program, but you will not be able to take advantage of the built-in Dreamweaver MX 2004 FTP program.
- **FTP** Selecting FTP lets you use the built-in Dreamweaver MX 2004 FTP to upload files to a remote server.
- **Local/Network** This option should be selected if you are publishing your site on an intranet where the server is located on your local network.

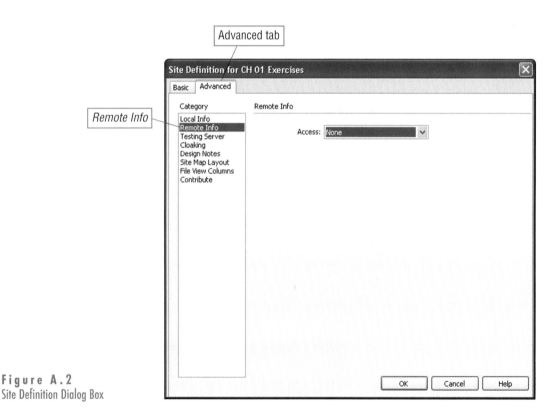

Figure A.2
Site Definition Dialog Box

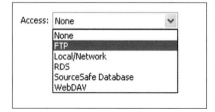

Figure A.3
Site Definition *Access* List Box Drop-Down List Choices

- **RDS (Remote Development Services)** This option is used with ColdFusion.
- **SourceSafe Database** This option is used for Web servers using a SourceSafe database.
- **WebDAV (Web-based Distributed Authoring and Versioning)** This option is used for Web servers using the WebDAV protocol.

The access choice you make determines the subsequent information you will need to specify in the Site Definition dialog box. Most people use the FTP method to upload their Web site documents, so this method is described here. Before defining your remote site, find out and write down the required server address, host directory, login name, and password information from your Web host so you can refer to it when needed. Figure A.4 shows a portion of a registration notification from a free site-hosting service providing FTP login information. Passwords usually are sent separately by e-mail for security reasons. The *FTP host,* the address of the server that hosts a Web site, and login information are not always identified using these terms, so if you are unsure what to use when you define your remote site, write to the Web host administrator for clarification.

6. With *FTP* selected in the *Access* list box, the Site Definition dialog box Remote Info page appears as shown in Figure A.5. You will need to specify some or all of the following information:

- **FTP host** Type the address of the server that will host your Web site in this text box, such as *ftp.angelfire.com*.
- **Host directory** Type the path to the folder that will contain your site's root directory in this text box. If you do not know the folder, you should leave it blank. If you experience a problem connecting, ask your Web host administrator for the correct host directory and type that here.

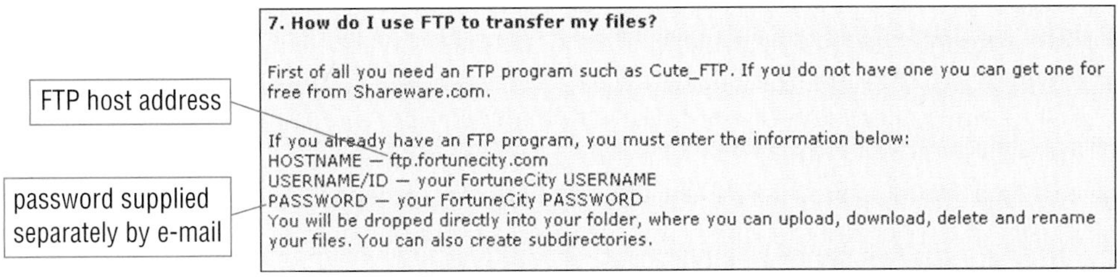

FTP host address

password supplied separately by e-mail

7. How do I use FTP to transfer my files?

First of all you need an FTP program such as Cute_FTP. If you do not have one you can get one for free from Shareware.com.

If you already have an FTP program, you must enter the information below:
HOSTNAME — ftp.fortunecity.com
USERNAME/ID — your FortuneCity USERNAME
PASSWORD — your FortuneCity PASSWORD
You will be dropped directly into your folder, where you can upload, download, delete and rename your files. You can also create subdirectories.

Figure A.4
Web Host Registration Notification Page

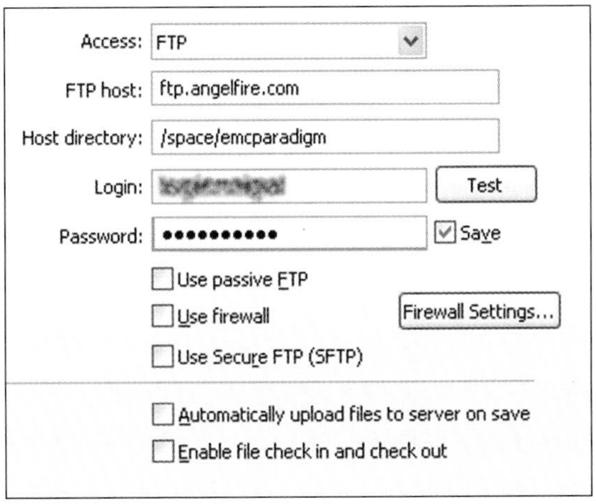

Access: FTP
FTP host: ftp.angelfire.com
Host directory: /space/emcparadigm
Login:
Password: •••••••••   ☑ Save   Test
☐ Use passive FTP
☐ Use firewall   Firewall Settings...
☐ Use Secure FTP (SFTP)

☐ Automatically upload files to server on save
☐ Enable file check in and check out

Figure A.5
Site Definition Dialog Box Remote Info Page

- *Login* Type the login name used to connect to the FTP server in this text box. This login name is sometimes referred to by Web hosts as your user name.
- *Password* Type the password needed to connect to the FTP server in this text box. Placing a check mark in the *Save* check box indicates that you will not need to enter your password again, but it also means that others can gain unauthorized access to your site if they use your computer. The *Save* check box is automatically enabled when you enter your password, so if you do not want this feature enabled, you will have to click the check box to remove the check mark.
- *Use passive FTP* If you are working on a network, you should ask your network administrator if this is required.
- *Use firewall* If you are working on a network, you should ask your network administrator if this is required.
- *Use Secure FTP (SFTP)* Selecting this option enables the use of encryption and public keys to protect your login information. This option will work only if your testing server uses a SFTP server.
- *Automatically upload files to server on save* Selecting this option means that files will be uploaded to the server automatically when they are saved.
- *Enable file check in and check out* This option is used for collaborative efforts in which more than one person might be working with the documents on a site. Checking documents in and out helps ensure that only one person can make changes to document at a time.

When you are finished, click the OK button to close the Site Definition dialog box. The Manage Sites dialog box is still open, so you will need to click the Done button to close it.

Putting (Uploading) Files

After a remote site has been defined, you are ready to connect to your host server to *put* (upload) or *get* (download) files. The desired site should be selected in the list box on the left side of the Files panel, and *Remote view* should be selected in the list box on the right side of the Files panel as shown in Figure A.6. If you have not yet defined a remote site for the local site you selected, a hyperlink message advises that you must define a remote site as shown in Figure A.7. Clicking the blue hyperlink portion of the message opens the Remote Info page of the Site Definition dialog box, which can be completed as previously described.

Working with the Files panel is easier when it is in expanded view, so if you prefer, you can click the Files panel Expand/Collapse button shown in Figure A.6 to make the Files panel expand to fit the screen.

To connect to the server that will be hosting your site, click the Connects to remote host button shown in Figure A.6. A Status dialog box will appear to let you know the connection status. If you are not online when you click the Connects to remote host button, a message box will appear stating that an FTP error occurred

Figure A.6 • Site and Remote View Selected in Files Panel

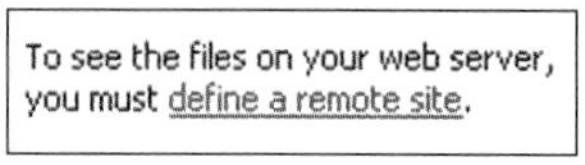

Figure A.7 • Remote Site Message

DREAMWEAVER MX 2004

and that the connection to the host cannot be made. Once the host server is found, the Connects to remote host button displays a green light to show that you are connected as shown in Figure A.8. Clicking the Put File(s) button shown in Figure A.9 opens a message box asking if you want to put your entire site on your remote site if no files are selected in the Files panel. Click the OK button to put the entire contents of your local site on your remote site. If you want to put individual files instead of the entire site, select the files before you click the Put Files(s) button. You can select more than one file at a time by holding down the Ctrl key when selecting files. After you have selected the files you want to put and clicked the Put File(s) button, a message appears asking if you want to put dependent files. An example of a dependent file is an image file called for in the code for an HTML page. Click the Yes button if you also want to put dependent files. After the files have been put on the remote site, you can see them in the *Remote Site* section of the Files panel on the left side of the expanded Files panel screen as shown in Figure A.10. View them by clicking the Expand/Collapse button or by clicking the unlabeled site view list box down-pointing arrow and then selecting *Remote view* from the list that appears as shown in Figure A.11.

Deleting or Removing Files from a Remote Site

After you have uploaded files to your remote site, you might want to remove files. Files can be deleted by selecting them and then pressing the Delete key. A message will appear asking if you really want to delete the files. Click the Yes button to proceed. If you want to download files from the remote site to your local site, select the files and then click the Get Files(s) button shown in Figure A.9 to get (download) the files. If the file or files you are getting have dependent files, you will see a message asking if you want to get dependent files.

Changing Files Panel Viewing Preferences

The contents of the remote site are displayed on the left side of the expanded Files panel screen, and the contents of the local site are displayed on the right

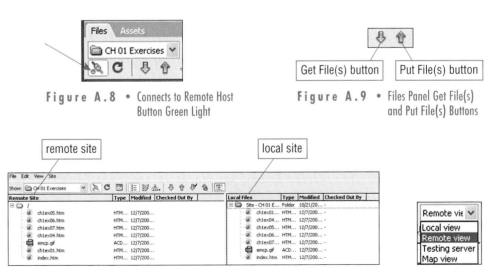

Figure A.8 • Connects to Remote Host Button Green Light

Figure A.9 • Files Panel Get File(s) and Put File(s) Buttons

Figure A.10 • Files Panel in Expanded View

Figure A.11 Files Panel Site View List Box

side of the screen as shown in Figure A.10. This is the opposite of most stand-alone FTP programs. If you want to switch the position of the two sites on the screen, you can exit the Files panel, click Edit on the Menu bar, and then click Preferences to open the Preferences dialog box. Click *Site* from the Preferences dialog box *Category* list box to display Site preferences. At the top of the Site Preferences page there is an *Always show* list box with a down-pointing arrow that can be used to select *Remote Files* or *Local Files* as shown in Figure A.12. Next to the *Always show* list box is the *on the* list box. Clicking the *on the* list box down-pointing arrow offers a choice of *Left* and *Right*. If you want the local files (local site) to be displayed on the left side of the Files panel, make sure *Local Files* is displayed in the *Always show* list box and then select *Left* from the *on the* list box.

Using the Files Panel Site Map

If you have defined a home page for your site, you can view all of the hyperlinks between pages in your local site by clicking the Files panel Site Map button as shown in Figure A.13. Orphaned (unlinked) documents in your site will not be displayed in the **site map**, a map showing hyperlinking between the files in a local site. Clicking the Site Files button restores the Files panel to the previous view of the remote and local sites.

If you have not defined a home page for your local site at the time you click the Site Map button, a message appears as shown in Figure A.14 advising that you need to define a home page first. You can click the Manage Sites button in the message box to open the Manage Sites dialog box. The current site is highlighted in the list box. You can click the Manage Sites dialog box Edit button and then click *Site Map Layout* from the Site Definition dialog box *Category* list box (Advanced mode). The Site Map Layout page contains a *Home page* text box as shown in

Figure A.12
Setting Remote and Local
Files Panel Viewing
Preferences

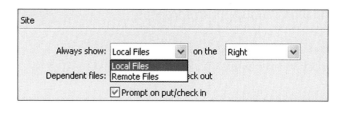

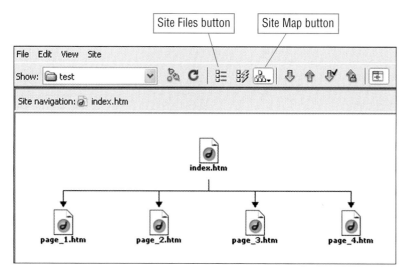

Figure A.13
Files Panel Site Map

DREAMWEAVER MX 2004

Figure A.15. Clicking the Browse for File button opens a Choose Home Page dialog box that can be used to browse for and select a file that will serve as the home page for your site as shown in Figure A.16. After the home page file has been selected, its name appears in the Choose Home Page dialog box *File name* text box, and you can click the Open button to close the dialog box. You also need to close the Site Definition dialog box by clicking the OK button at the bottom of the page and the Manage Sites dialog box Done button to complete this task.

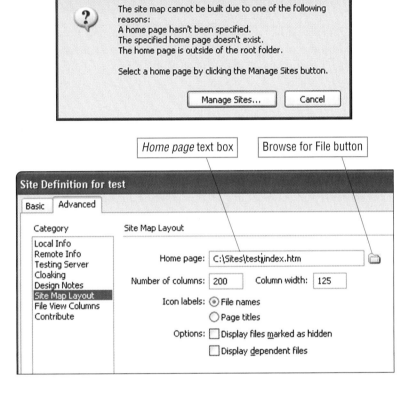

Figure A.14
Site Map Home Page Message

Home page text box   Browse for File button

Figure A.15
Files Panel Site Map Layout Page

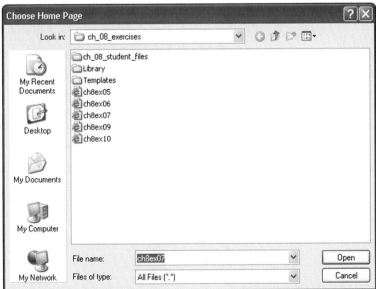

Figure A.16
Choose Home Page Dialog Box

Clicking a document displayed in the Site Map view causes a *Point to File* icon to appear. The *Point to File* icon can be dragged to another document to create a link. The new link is displayed in the site map as shown in Figure A.17. When a link has been created this way, a hyperlink is inserted in the document as shown in Figure A.18. Right-clicking a document displayed in the Site Map view brings up a context menu as shown in Figure A.19. The context menu contains a number of different options, including commands to create new links, to create links to existing files, to change links, and to remove links.

Cloaking Folders or File Types

At times, you might not want to put or get certain files or file types. For example, you might have a folder containing image files that you do not want to put every time you put a site. Dreamweaver MX 2004 offers a feature called **cloaking** that

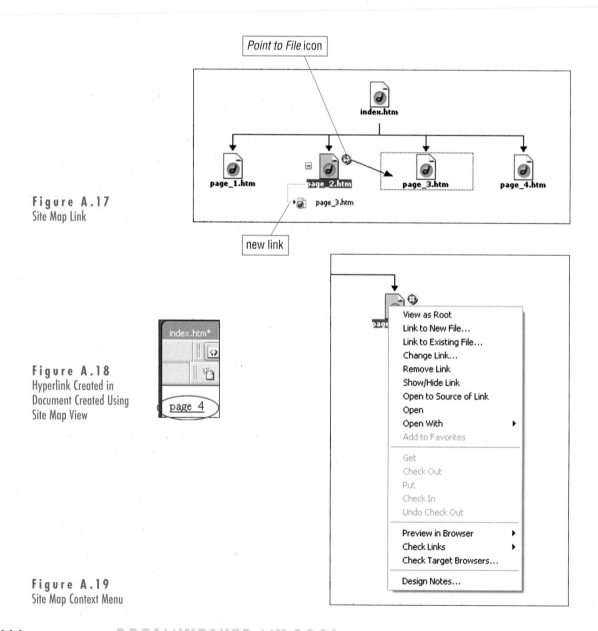

Figure A.17
Site Map Link

Figure A.18
Hyperlink Created in
Document Created Using
Site Map View

Figure A.19
Site Map Context Menu

DREAMWEAVER MX 2004

allows you to specify folders or file types that will be excluded from getting and putting. The Cloaking feature can be enabled for a site by right-clicking any folder or file in a site, pointing to Cloaking, and then clicking Enable Cloaking as shown in Figure A.20. After cloaking has been enabled for a site, individual folders can be cloaked by right-clicking them, pointing to Cloaking, and then clicking Cloak. All of the folders on a site cannot be cloaked, but more than one folder can be cloaked at a time. Once a folder has been cloaked, its cloaked status and the cloaked status of its contents are indicated with diagonal red slashes as shown in Figure A.21. The procedure for uncloaking a folder is the same as the cloaking procedure, except that you select Uncloak All from the context menu. This uncloaks all cloaked folders in a site, so you will have to recloak any folders that you want to remain cloaked if you choose this option. If the file cloaking option is disabled by removing the check mark next to Enable Cloaking, all folders and file types that were previously cloaked will be uncloaked. If the option is enabled again, previously cloaked folders and file types once again will be cloaked.

File types can be cloaked by right-clicking a file, pointing to Cloaking, and then clicking Settings. This displays the Cloaking page of the Site Definition dialog box as shown in Figure A.22. To specify the file types that will be cloaked, click the *Cloak files ending with* check box and then type the file extension(s) of the file type(s) you want to exclude in the text box. Extensions should be separated by a single space. File type cloaking can be undone by reopening the Cloaking page of the Site Definition dialog box and removing the check mark from the *Cloak files ending with* check box.

Figure A.20 • Enable Cloaking Command

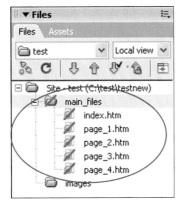

Figure A.21 • Cloaked Folder and Folder Contents

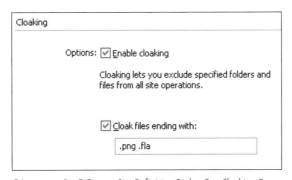

Figure A.22 • Site Definition Dialog Box Cloaking Page

KEY terms

cloaking A Dreamweaver MX 2004 feature that can be used to prevent specified folders or file types from being uploaded to, or downloaded from, a server.

File Transfer Protocol (FTP) A method used to upload files to a server (put), or download files from a server (get).

FTP host The address of the server that hosts a Web site, such as *ftp.angelfire.com*.

get To download files from a server.

host directory The folder on a Web server that contains a site's root directory.

put To upload files to a server.

remote site A site that resides on a server that will be used to publish the contents of a local site so that others can view it.

site map The Site Map view is a Files panel view that displays a site map showing hyperlinks between the files in a local site.

CONCEPTS check

Indicate the correct term or command for each item.

1. This is the name for a copy of a local site that resides on a server.
2. This is a method used to upload files to, or download files from, a server.
3. This is a Dreamweaver MX 2004 method of preventing specified folders or file types from being uploaded to or downloaded from a server.
4. This is the name for the directory on a server designated by the Web host to contain a root directory.
5. If you "put" a file, you are doing this.
6. If you "get" a file, you are doing this.
7. This Files panel view provides a map showing linked documents in a local site.
8. For security reasons, the confirmation for this vital piece of information needed to log on to an FTP server is usually sent by e-mail.
9. Files on a remote server can be removed by selecting them and then pressing this key.
10. The Files panel Site Map feature can be used to display all of the hyperlinked pages in a site if this has been done.

INDEX

  (nonbreaking space code), 114
../ in relative path, 78
/ in relative path, 78
{ } (curly braces), 262

A

absolute paths, 77–78
accessibility
  alternate text for images, 166,
    167–168, 174
  D links for images, 168–170
  fieldset tags for forms, 446–447
  for form fields, 428
  frame titles, 247–250
  long descriptions for images, 168
  noframes content, 248–250
  requirements for, 57
  for Shockwave movies, 395
  table summary text, 118
  turning on features, 58
action attribute, 421
active links, 88
ActiveX controls, 383, 384, 404–408
Adobe PDF files, 382
alignment
  of cell contents, 129
  of Flash text, 393
  of images, 176–177
  of layers, 310
  of tables, 128
a:link pseudo class, 278–279
alphanumeric data, 426
alternate text, 166, 167–168, 174
anchor links, 82–83
anchor tags, 77
animations
  Flash, 385–388
  Flash text, 392–395
  GIF images, 162
applets, 381, 399–402
Assets panel
  attaching templates to documents,
    345–351
  creating favorites, 75–76, 204, 206
  creating Favorites folders, 204–205,
    206–207
  creating library items, 364
  creating nested templates, 358–360
  creating templates with, 336
  managing images with, 203–207
  using, 74–75
audio files, 408–410

autostretch, 142
.avi extension, 381

B

background color
  of Flash buttons, 389
  of frames, 224
  of layers, 304
  of pages, 70–74
  of table cells, 127, 130
  of tables, 127, 128
background images
  of layers, 304, 314
  of pages, 190–192
  of table cells, 130, 192–193
  of tables, 128, 192–193
background music, 408–410
banner frames, 219
Basic page document type, 16
behaviors, 194–196, 317–319
blanks (spaces) in file names, 11
blockquote tags, 69
borders
  of cells, 130
  of forms, in Document window, 422
  of framesets, in Document window,
    231
  of frames, in browsers, 238
  of frames, in Document window, 220,
    232
  of images, 175
  of layers, in Document window, 305
  of tables, 112, 113, 128
break tag, 18
broken links, 86
browsers
  checking compatibility with, 54–56
  checking support for, 2
  and multimedia content, 380, 408
  and plugins, 382, 383
  preview preferences, 52–54
  primary and secondary, 52
  support for ActiveX controls, 384
  support for DHTML, 380
  support for frames, 217
  support for layers, 301
  window size and page layout, 115–116
bulleted (unordered) lists, 89–90

C

captions, 118
Cascading Style Sheets (CSS). *See also*

CSS styles
  advantages of, 259, 261
  creating external style sheets,
    263–266, 267–271
  creating internal style sheets, 283–285
  exporting internal style sheets,
    285–287
  predefined, 280–282
  removing, 291–293
Cascading Style Sheets-Positioning
  (CSS-P), 325, 380
cell padding, 112, 113, 127
cells
  alignment of content, 129
  backgrounds of, 130, 192–193
  borders of, 130
  defined, 112, 113
  drawing, in Layout mode, 141
  formatting, with Property inspector,
    129–131
  height of, 130
  moving, in Layout mode, 141
  resizing, in Layout mode, 141
  selecting, 123, 124
  splitting and merging, 130
  using grid with, 146–148
  width of, 129
cell spacing, 112, 113, 127
CGI (Common Gateway Interface)
  scripts, 420
check boxes, 432–433
Check Spelling dialog box, 93–95
Check Target Browsers tool, 54–56
child layer, 306–307
.class extension, 399
Class styles, 262, 275–278
Clean Up HTML command, 58–59
Clean Up Word HTML command,
  58–60
clip property, 315
cloaking folders or file types, 466–467
Close button, 10
Code and Design view, 22–23, 24
Coder Workspace
  choosing, 8
  features of, 6, 7
Code view, 22, 23
ColdFusion-style Workspace layout. See
  Coder Workspace
Color Picker, 68–69
colors. See also background color
  creating favorites, 74–76
  of Flash text, 392
  of frame borders, 239
  hexadecimal values for, 69
  of links, 78, 88
  pre-defined schemes, 71

  selecting from palettes, 68
  setting page defaults, 70–74
  of tables and cells, 127, 128
  using descriptive names for, 69
  Web-safe, 68
Color Wheel button, 68
column headers, in tables, 117–118
columns
  adding and deleting, 131–134
  enabling autostretch, 142
  selecting, 124
  sorting by contents of, 148–150
  specifying number of, 127
  width of, 113, 114, 129
commands
  creating, from recorded steps, 97
  Menu bar (See Menu bar
    commands)
comments in HTML code, 98–99
connection speed, 21
context-sensitive help, 41
context-sensitive menus
  benefits of, 3
  creating links, 80
contextual selectors, 262, 274–275
Copy command, 60–61
Copy HTML command, 60–61
Create Web Photo Album command,
  196–200
.css extension, 264
CSS Properties panel, 289
CSS rules. See CSS styles
CSS styles
  Class styles, 262, 275–278
  contextual selectors, 262, 274–275
  creating, 264–266
  declarations, 262
  editing, 287–290
  features of, 261–262
  grouped selectors, 262, 271–274
  inheritance, 263
  inline styles, 262–263
  internal styles, 263
  pseudo classes, 262, 278–280
  redefining HTML tags, 264–265
  removing, 291–293
  selectors, 262
CSS Style Sheet document type, 16
curly braces, 262
Customize Favorite Objects dialog box,
  25

D

.dcr extension, 381
declarations, 262
definition lists, 89–90
delimited text files, 65

description meta tags, 99–100
Designer Workspace, 6, 7, 9–11
design files
  benefits of, 2
  creating, 17
  opening and working with, 17–18
Design view, 22
dictionary, spell-checking, 94
division tags, 302
D links, 168–170
.doc extension, 381
docking panel groups, 29
document relative paths, 78
documents
  adding library items to, 364–365
  attaching external style sheets to, 267
  attaching templates to, 345–351
  checking browser compatibility, 54–56
  creating, 4–6, 14–16, 17
  detaching from templates, 361
  editing, 4–6
  frameset, 218, 220–223
  inserting comments in code, 98–99
  as instances of a template, 334–335
  links to, 77–78
  links to locations within, 82–83
  opening in Dreamweaver, 58
  opening in frames, 223–224
  opening in layers, 323–325
  previewing in a browser, 52
  saving, 15–16
  searching for code and text in, 91–93
  selecting views, 22–24
  showing recent, 9
  untitled, 18
  updating library items in, 366
Document Size/Estimated Download
    Time indicator, 21
document tabs, 10
Document toolbar, 21–24
document types, 16
Document window, 9, 10
domain names, 77
down image, 244
download time, estimating, 21
draggable layers, 318–319
Dreamweaver help, 34–41
Dreamweaver sites
  creating, 11–14
  editing, 12
  local *vs.* remote, 11
  naming, 12
  removing, 12
drop-down menus, 436–438
.dwt extension, 335
dynamic HTML (DHTML), 380
Dynamic page document type, 16

E

editable regions, 334, 338–341
editable tag attributes, 352–355
element display states, 243
e-mail links, 84–86, 247
embedded style sheets, 263, 283–287,
    291
embed tags, 383, 402–403
events. *See* behaviors
Excel documents
  copying content from, 63–65
  importing, 65
expander arrows, 29
extensions, file name, 16
external style sheets
  advantages of, 261
  attaching to documents, 267
  creating, 263–266, 267–271
  removing from documents, 291–293
Eyedropper, 68

F

favorites
  Asset favorites, 74–76, 204
  color favorites, 75–76
  help topics, 35
  Insert bar favorites, 25, 26–27
fields. *See* forms
fieldset tags, 446–447
file browser, 32–34
file checkin/checkout, 462
file extensions, 16, 381. *See also specific
    extensions*
file fields, 444–445
file name guidelines, 11
files. *See also* documents; media files
  checkin/checkout, 462
  cloaking, 466–467
  copying, 32
  creating, 32
  deleting, 32
  design, 17–18
  duplicating, 32
  form fields for uploading, 444–445
  moving, 32
  orphan, 86
  renaming, 32
  temporary, 53
  uploading, to remote site, 462–463
Files panel, 32–34, 463–464, 464–466
file uploads, 444–445
Find and Replace dialog box, 91–93
Fireworks MX 2004
  creating photo album images with, 196
  opening from Image Property inspec-
    tor, 171
  optimizing images in, 185–187

Flash buttons, 389–392
Flash movies and animations, 385–388
Flash MX 2004, 385
Flash text, 392–395
flexible tables, 115
floating panels, 29
font size and style
    CSS styles, 266–271
    in Property inspector, 66–68
font tags, 65
Format Table command, 137–139
forms
    check boxes in, 432–433
    controlling appearance with tables, 421, 424–425
    creating, 422–425
    creating buttons, 445–446
    file fields in, 444–445
    hidden fields in, 431–432
    image fields in, 442–443
    jump menus in, 440–442
    lists in, 436–437
    menus in, 436–438
    method for transmitting data, 424
    naming, 422–423
    password fields in, 427, 430
    planning and design of, 421–422
    radio buttons in, 434–436
    Reset button in, 420, 445–446
    Submit button in, 420, 442–443, 445–446
    text fields in, 426–429
    user testing of, 422
    validating input data in, 447–450
form tags, 420
forums, online, 37–41
frame move icon, 223
frames
    backgrounds of, 224
    borders of, 234, 238, 239
    changing height and width of, 234–236
    choosing documents to open in, 223–224
    defined, 218
    defining navigation bars in, 243–247
    deleting, 224
    disabling resize of, 239
    drawbacks of, 217
    enabling scroll bars in, 238
    frame titles, 247–250
    names of, 238
    saving, 224
    selecting, 232, 233–234
    setting margins of, 239
    splitting, 222–223
framesets
    changing frame size in, 234–236

creating, 220–223, 225–227
defined, 218
deleting, 224
Frameset document type, 16
nested, 218, 222–223
noframes content in, 248–250
predefined, 220, 227–230
saving, 224
selecting, 231–232, 233–234
frameset tags, 218
frame tags, 218
frame titles, 247–250
ftp (file transfer protocol), 3, 460, 461, 462–463

G
GET method, 424
GIF (Graphics Interchange Format) images, 162, 198
Go button, 440
grid
    changing settings, 147
    enabling snap-to feature, 147
    viewing, 146
grippers, 28, 29
grouped selectors, 262, 271–274
gutters, 116

H
headers, in tables, 117–118, 130
heading frames, 219
heading levels, 66
height
    of cells, 130
    of frames, 234–236
    of images, 173–174
    of layers, 314
    of tables, 127
helper applications, 381–382
help system, 34–41
hexadecimal color values, 69
hidden fields, 431–432
History panel
    changing maximum undo steps, 96
    creating commands, 97
    undo and redo, 95
home page, defining, 464–465
HomeSite-style Workspace layout. *See* Coder Workspace
horizontal alignment, 129
horizontal panels. *See* panels
horizontal space, 175
hotspots, 178–179
href attributes, 77–78
HTML documents. *See also* files
    cleaning up, 58–60
    creating, 4–6, 15–16

editing, 4–6
saving, 15–16
HTML tags
  anchor tags, 77
  comments, 98–99
  copying and pasting, 60–61, 62–63
  displaying, in Design view, 19–20
  division tags, 302
  document links, 77–78
  embed tags, 383
  fieldset tags, 446–447
  font tags *vs.* CSS, 259, 261
  form tags, 420
  frameset tags, 218
  frame tags, 218
  hexadecimal color values, 69
  href attributes, 77–78
  image tags, 162
  input tags, 420
  label tags, 426, 446
  meta tags, 99–101
  nonbreaking space character, 114
  object tags, 383, 393
  presentational, 260–261
  redefining, with CSS selectors,
    264–265
  script tags, 380
  searching for, in documents, 91–93
  structural, 260
  table data tags, 114
  for tables, 114
  working in Code and Design view, 22,
    24
  working in Code view, 22, 23
.htm *vs.* .html extension, 16
HTTP (Hypertext Transfer Protocol), 77
Hyperlink dialog box, 79
hyperlinks. *See* links
hypertext documents, 76–77

I

image fields, 442–443
image maps, 178–179, 182–183
image placeholders
  benefits of, 2
  changing properties of, 171
  inserting, 170, 172
image previews, 177
Image Property inspector, 170–171,
  172–185
images
  adding behaviors to, 194–196
  alignment of, 176–177, 180
  alternate text for, 166, 167–168, 174
  assigning names to, 179
  borders of, 175, 180
  brightness and contrast of, 188

cropping, 187
  CSS class style of, 174
  dimensions of, 173–174, 179
  D links for, 168–170
  editing, 183–184, 187–190
  file formats of, 162–163, 196
  height of, 173–174
  hotspots in, 178–179, 182–183
  inserting in documents, 164–166, 171
  as links, 175, 181
  long descriptions for, 168
  low resolution previews, 177
  managing, with Assets panel, 203–207
  as navigation bar elements, 243–244
  optimizing, in Fireworks, 185–187
  placeholders for, 170–172
  resampling, 188
  sharpening, 188
  source path of, 174
  space around, 175, 179–180
  as spacers in autostretch tables, 142
  as table backgrounds, 192–193
  target browser window for, 175
  thumbnails of, 165
  tracing, 200–203
  width of, 173–174
image tags, 162
indented text, 69
inheritance, 263
inline styles, 262–263, 291
input forms. *See* forms
input tags, 420
Insert bar
  adding behaviors to images, 194–196
  creating layers, 304–306
  creating lists, 90
  creating predefined framesets, 227
  creating tables, 117–121
  creating templates, 336
  Expanded Tables mode, 122
  Favorites, 25, 26–27
  inserting applet class files, 400–402
  inserting comments, 98–99
  inserting document links, 79
  inserting e-mail links, 84
  inserting Flash buttons, 389–392
  inserting Flash movies and animations,
    385–388
  inserting Flash text, 392–395
  inserting forms, 422
  inserting images, 164–165
  inserting media files, 384
  inserting meta tags, 100–101
  inserting parameters for media con-
    tent, 402–404
  inserting Shockwave movies, 395–398
  inserting text, 25–26
  using, 9, 24–25

Insert Rows or Columns dialog box, 132
instances, 334–335
integrated file browser, 3, 32–34
interlaced GIF images, 162
internal style sheets, 263, 283–287, 291

J

Java applets, 381, 399–402
JavaScript
  and dynamic content changes, 380
  and image behaviors, 194
  and layer behaviors, 317
JPEG (Joint Photographic Experts
    Group) images, 163, 198
jump menus, 440–442

K

Keyboard Shortcuts dialog box, 95
keyword meta tags, 99–100

L

label tags, 426, 446
layer-code markers, 305
layers
  adding behaviors to, 317–325
  adding content to, 312–313
  aligning, 310
  backgrounds of, 304, 314
  clipping in, 315
  content overflow in, 315
  converting to tables, 325–326
  coordinates of, 314
  creating, 304–306
  deleting, 306
  dimensions of, 314
  draggable, 318–319
  features of, 302–303
  layer coordinates, 302
  moving, 309
  naming, 309, 314
  nested, 304, 306–308
  Netscape 4 compatibility, 304
  pop-up message windows, 320
  positioning, 314
  resizing, 310
  scroll bars in, 315
  selecting, 308–309
  show/hide behavior, 321–323
  stacking order of, 303
  URL behavior, 323–325
  viewing, in Document window, 305,
    309
  z-index, 303, 309, 314
Layers panel, 308–309
Layout mode *vs.* Standard mode,
    139–140
.lbi extension, 363

library items
  adding to documents, 364–365
  benefits of, 363
  creating, 364, 367–369
  deleting, 366
  editing, 365–367
  updating, in documents, 366
Link Checker panel, 86–87
links
  active, 88
  automatic updating, 2, 34
  changing colors of, 78, 88
  changing frame content with, 241–242
  checking and repairing, 86–87
  to documents, 77–78
  editing, 88–89
  e-mail, 84–86
  images as, 175, 181
  inserting, into documents, 76–86
  to locations within documents, 82–83
  modifying appearance of, 278–280
  removing, 88–89
  rollover, 88
  in templates, 362
  underline style of, 88
  visited, 88
link target, 77
liquid tables, 115
lists
  creating, in documents, 89–91
  creating, in forms, 436–437, 439
local site, 11, 460
locked regions, 334
long descriptions for images, 168
low source images, 177

M

Macromedia Online Forums, 37–41
mailto links, 84–86, 247
Manage Sites dialog box, 11, 12
margins
  of frames, 239
  of pages, 116
Maximize button, 10
media files
  and ActiveX controls, 383, 384,
    404–408
  audio files, 408–410
  Flash buttons, 389–392
  Flash movies and animations, 385–388
  Flash text, 392–395
  and helper applications, 381–382
  and Java applets, 381
  and plugins, 382–383, 404, 409–410
  previewing in Dreamweaver, 384
  Shockwave movies, 395–398
Menu bar commands

Commands, 71, 137, 148
Edit, 60, 63, 91–92
File, 14, 16, 58, 65
Help, 34–38
Insert, 79, 84, 117, 164–165, 422
Modify, 131–132, 190, 200, 221, 244, 310
Site, 11–12
Text, 90, 93
View, 139, 201
menus
context-sensitive, 3, 80
Dreamweaver MX 2004 Menu bar, 9, 10
drop-down, in forms, 436–438
meta tags, 99–101
Microsoft Excel documents
copying content from, 63–65
importing, 65
Microsoft Windows, 3
Microsoft Word documents
copying content from, 63–64
importing, 65
.mid and .midi extensions, 381
MIME (Multipurpose Internet Mail Extension) types
defined, 381
for form data, 424
.mov extension, 381
movies
Flash, 385–388
Shockwave, 395–398
Windows Media Player, 405–408
.mp2 and .mp3 extensions, 381
.mpe, .mpeg and .mpg extensions, 381
multimedia, 379. See also media files
multiple selectors, 262, 271–274
music files, 408–410

N

named anchors, 82–83
navigation bars, 243–247
navigation frames, 219–220
nested layers, 304, 306–308
nested lists, 89–91
nested tables, 134–136
nested templates, 355–360
Netscape-style plugins, 382–383, 384, 404
New Document dialog box, 14
noframes content, 248–250
nonbreaking space, 114

O

object tags, 383, 393, 402–403
online forums, 37–41
optional regions, 338

Options menu (panel groups), 29
ordered lists, 89–90
orphan files, 86
Other document type, 16
outdent, 69
overflow property, 315
over image, 244
over while down image, 244

P

Page Designs document type, 16
page loading time, 21
pages. See Web pages
panel groups
benefits of, 3
working with, 28–31
panels
features of, 28
moving to another panel group, 29
paragraph tag, 18, 58
parameters for media content, 402–405
parent layer, 306–307
parent table, 134
parent template, 356–357
password fields, 427, 430
Paste command, 60–61, 63
Paste Formatted command, 63–65
Paste HTML command, 60–61
Paste Text command, 60–61
path (to link target), 77–78
personal dictionary, 94
photo albums, 196–200
placeholder content, 16
plugins, 382–383, 404, 409–410
PNG (Portable Network Graphics) images, 163
Point to File button, 78
pop-up message windows, 320
POST method, 424
predefined CSS style sheets, 280–282
predefined framesets, 220, 227–230
preferences. See also favorites
accessibility features, 58, 166, 247
automatic spacer image insertion, 143
browser preview, 52–54
comments visibility, 98
CSS instead of HTML tags, 65, 260
default connection speed, 21
Files panel viewing, 463–464
hidden form field visibility, 431
image editors, 184–185
layer properties, 303–304
named anchor visibility, 82
nesting option for layers, 307
number of history steps, 96
region highlighting, 363
spelling dictionary, 94

Start Page, 10
workspace layout, 8
preformatted text, 66
preload image behavior, 194
presentational tags, 260–261
Preview/Debug in browser button, 52–53
primary browser, 52
primary image, 194
privacy statements, 422
Property inspector
adding links to frames, 241–242
adding to available fonts list, 67
changing frame properties, 237–240
changing frameset properties, 234–236
changing layer properties, 314–316
changing text properties, 65–70
creating external style sheets, 264
creating internal style sheets, 283
creating lists, 90
editing links, 88–89
formatting tables and cells, 127–131
inserting document links, 78–79,
80–81
removing links, 88–89
removing table rows and columns, 132
setting background color, 70–74
setting default text color, 70–74
property, of CSS style, 262
proportional widths, 113–114
pseudo classes, 262, 278–280

Q

Quick Tag Editor
automatic update feature, 19
using, 19–20

R

radio buttons, 434–436
.ra, .rm and .ram extensions, 381
RDS (Remote Development Services),
461
recent documents, 9
redirect, 100–101
redo, 95–97
refresh meta tags, 100–101
regular expressions, 93
relative paths, 78
Relevant CSS panel, 287–290
remote site management
changing Files panel preferences,
463–464
cloaking folders or file types, 466–467
removing files from, 463
setting up, 459–462
site map, 464–466
uploading files to, 462–463
repeating regions, 342–343

repeating tables, 343–345
resampling images, 188
Reset button, 420
resize arrow, 10
Restore button, 10
rollover images, 194–196
rollover links, 88
root folders, 11, 13
row headers, in tables, 117–118
rows
adding and deleting, 131–134
defined, 112, 113
selecting, 124
sorting, 148–150
specifying number of, 127

S

scaling images in Web photo albums,
198
script tags, 380
scroll bars, in frames, 238
scroll bars, in layers, 315
secondary browser, 52
secondary image, 194
secure ftp, 3, 462
selectors, 262
server-side scripts, 420, 421
Set Color Scheme command, 71
sharpening images, 188
Shockwave movies, 395–398
Site Definition dialog box, 2, 11–12,
464–465
site map, 464–466
slash (/) in relative path, 78
Snap to Grid, 147
sorting table contents, 148–150
sound files, 408–410
source attribute, 162, 174, 238, 386
SourceSafe Database, 461
space characters
in file names, 11
nonbreaking, in HTML code, 114
spacer images
in autostretch tables, 142
creating, 143
inserting into tables, 143–144
spell-check tool, 93–95
splash pages, 101
Split Frame commands, 222
stacking order, 303, 309, 314
Standard mode *vs.* Layout mode,
139–140
Standard toolbar, 27
starting Dreamweaver MX 2004, 3
Start Page
benefits of, 2
disabling, 9

DREAMWEAVER MX 2004

features of, 9–10, 37
start-up document type, 16
Status bar, 18
Strikethrough button, 68
structural tags, 260
Submit button, 420, 442–443
summary text, 118
Support Center, 37
swap image behavior, 194
.swf extension, 381

T

table data tags, 114
table row tags, 124
tables
    adding/deleting rows and columns,
        131–134
    alignment of, 128
    assigning identification to, 127
    backgrounds of, 127, 128, 192–193
    borders of, 112, 113, 128
    column headers in, 117–118, 130
    components of, 112–113
    converting to layers, 325–326
    creating, in Layout mode, 139–146
    creating, in Standard mode, 117–121
    CSS class style of, 128
    dimensions of, 113–114, 127, 128
    enabling autostretch, 142
    fixed-width, 113, 115–116, 120–121
    formatting, with Format Table,
        137–139
    formatting, with Property inspector,
        127–129
    height of, 127
    HTML tags, 114
    inserting spacer images into, 143–144
    inside forms, 421, 424–425
    Make All Widths Consistent com-
        mand, 114
    navigating within, 125–126
    nested, 134–136
    as page layout tool, 112, 115–116
    proportional-width, 113, 115–116,
        118–120
    resizing by dragging handles, 114, 141
    row headers in, 117–118, 130
    selecting elements of, 122–125
    sorting contents, 148–150
    summary text for screen readers, 118
    title of, 118
    using grid with, 146–148
    width of, 113–114, 127
Tag selector, 19–20, 123, 134
target attribute, 421
target browser window, 175
target frame, 241

Template page document type, 16
templates
    attaching to documents, 345–351
    benefits of, 2, 333
    creating, 335–338
    creating links in, 362
    editable regions in, 334, 338–341
    editable tag attributes, 352–355
    instances of, 334–335
    locked regions in, 334
    nested, 355–360
    optional regions, 338
    region highlighting preferences, 363
    repeating regions, 342–343
    repeating tables, 343–345
    updating template-based documents,
        360–362
temporary files, 53
text. *See also* CSS styles
    alternate text for images, 166,
        167–168, 174
    changing alignment, 69
    changing colors, 68–69
    changing fonts, 66–67
    changing font size, 68
    in columns, using tables, 116–117
    copying, 60, 62
    entering, in a document, 58
    find and replace, 91–93
    Flash text, 392–395
    formatting, 25–26, 65–70
    indenting, 69
    in input forms, 426–430
    long description for images, 168
    paragraphs in, 18, 58
    pasting, 60, 62
    preformatted, 66
    setting default color, 70–74
    summary text for tables, 118
    wrapping, in form fields, 427
    wrapping, in table cells, 130
text documents
    delimited, 65
    opening, 58
text fields, 426–430
thumbnails, 165, 196, 198
tiling of images, 190
Title bar, 9, 18
toggle triangles, 9, 28, 29
tooltips, 9
tracing images, 200–203
transparent GIF images, 162
tutorials, 37
.txt extension, 58
typefaces
    changing, in Property inspector, 66–68
    changing, with CSS styles, 266–271

U

undo, 95–97
Uniform Resource Locator (URL),
77–78, 165
unordered lists, 89–90
up image, 244
uploading files
to remote site, 462–463
user form fields for, 444–445
user dictionary, 94
Using Dreamweaver dialog box, 35

V

validating input forms, 447–450
values, 262
vertical alignment, 129
vertical panels. *See* panels
vertical space, 175
visited links, 88

W

.wav extension, 381
Web Accessibility Initiative, 57
Web browsers. *See* browsers
WebDAV (Web-based Distributed
Authoring and Versioning), 461
Web pages. *See also* documents
backgrounds of, 70–74, 190–192
checking browser compatibility, 54–56
interactive, 194
layout of, using frames, 217–220
layout of, using layers, 301–303
layout of, using tables, 115–116,
139–146
layout of, using tracing images,

200–203
margins of, 116
pre-defined color schemes for, 71
previewing in a browser, 52
recommended maximum size in bytes,
162
setting default colors, 70–74
Web photo albums, 196–200
Web-safe colors, 68
width
of frames, 234–236
of images, 173–174
of layers, 314
of tables and cells, 113–114, 127, 129
windows
Close button, 10
Insert bar, 9
Maximize button, 10
Menu bar, 9, 10
Restore button, 10
size in pixels, 21
Status bar, 18
Title bar, 9, 18
Windows Color Selection palette, 68
Window Size indicator, 21
Windows Media Player movies, 405–408
Windows XP, 3
Word documents
copying content from, 63–64
importing, 65
opening, in browsers, 381–382
workspace layout options, 6–8
World Wide Web. *See* Web

Z

z-index, 303, 309, 314